An A–Z of English Grammar and Usage

An A–Z of English Grammar and Usage

Geoffrey Leech

Associate authors:
Benita Cruickshank
Roz Ivanič

Edward Arnold
A division of Hodder & Stoughton
LONDON MELBOURNE AUCKLAND

First published in Great Britain 1989

British Library Cataloguing in Publication Data

Leech, Geoffrey, *1936–*
An A–Z of English grammar and usage.
1. English language. Grammar
I. Title II. Ivanic, Roz III. Cruikshank, Benita
428.2

ISBN 0–7131–8472–8

Cartoons by Matthew Doyle

Typeset in 9/10½ Helios Compugraphic by
Colset Private Limited, Singapore
Printed and bound in Great Britain for Edward Arnold, the educational, academic and medical publishing division of Hodder and Stoughton Limited, 41 Bedford Square, London WC1B 3DQ by Richard Clay, Bungay, Suffolk

ACKNOWLEDGEMENTS

In its manuscript stage, this book benefited greatly from detailed critical comments made by teachers and English language specialists in various parts of the world. For this help, we are very grateful to Małgorzata Bonikowska, Tom Lavelle, Constant Leung, Juana Marín, Sophia Papaefthymiou-Lytra, Monica Poulter and Edward Woods.

Contents

Introduction

1. Who is this book for?

This book is a basic guide to the grammar and usage of English for anyone learning or teaching the language. If you are a learner, it is a reference book in which to look up problems you encounter in using the language, as well as a book to find out more about the way English works. If you are a teacher, it is a basic reference book to turn to when faced with something you are not sure of, as well as a source book to help you present grammar in class.

2. How is this book organised?

To make grammar as accessible as possible, *An A–Z of English Grammar and Usage* is arranged alphabetically, like a dictionary. There are plenty of cross references so that, to look things up, it is not necessary to know any grammatical terms. For example, to find information on "the articles", you could look up *a*, *the*, *zero article* or *articles*, or, for information on conditionals, you could look up *conditionals*, *if* or *unless*. You could even look up the ending *-ed* to find information on the past tense and the past participle. Because of this alphabetical arrangement, there is no need for an index.

3. What is in this book?

There are three kinds of entry in this book.

(i) There are ordinary words of the language, such as *if*, *when*, *should*, and parts of words, such as the verb ending *-ing*.

(ii) There are grammatical terms such as *conditional*, *present perfect*, *sentence*, *clause*.

(iii) There are entries which cover a variety of things not usually found in a book on grammar. Some, such as *invitations*, *thanking people*, *apologies*, *agreeing and disagreeing* give examples of how grammar is used to perform these functions. Others, such as *intonation*, *stress*, *spelling*, *paragraphs*, show how the language is written and spoken. And others, such as *letter-writing*, *formal and informal English*, *geographical names*, give information on a variety of topics.

At the end of the book, there is a list of irregular verbs.

4. What kind of grammar is in this book?

The grammar "rules" in this book are the rules of standard English. Incorrect English is shown by crossing out, e.g.: Adam is very ~~much~~ old. This is a descriptive grammar book and, where a form is considered right by some native speakers and wrong by others, we point this out without being prescriptive. Where American usage is different from British English, the difference is briefly described.

5. How to use this book.

An A–Z of English Grammar and Usage is a reference book. The complete list of entries will show at a glance which words appear in the book. But the book can also be read to find out about the forms and structures of grammar. In that case, we suggest you begin by reading the entries for *sentence* and *clause*, and the entries for word classes (parts of speech): *noun*, *verb*, *adjective*, *preposition*, *conjunction*, *pronoun*, *determiner*. From these, cross-references will lead you to other aspects of grammatical structure, such as *subject*, *object*, *phrase* and *adverbial clause*.

6. How does this book describe grammar?

The explanations in this book avoid difficult grammatical terms. However, it is not possible to write about grammar without using some grammatical terms. If you do not know the meanings of these, you can look them up in their alphabetical position.

All the explanations have carefully chosen examples, often with cartoon drawings to make the meaning absolutely clear. Many of the explanations use diagrams and tables, and there are structural patterns where helpful. In most cases, entries begin with "key points" indicated by a flag: ▶. The descriptions usually begin with an explanation of form followed by an explanation of use.

How to use this book

On these pages, pieces from different entries are shown to help you make full use of the features of the book. The numbers ①, ② etc. on the left hand pages refer to the explanations on each facing right hand page.

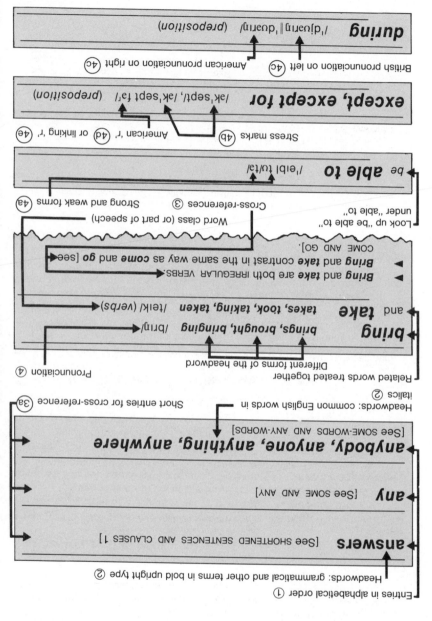

Entries in alphabetical order ①

Headwords: grammatical and other terms in bold upright type ②

answers [See SHORTENED SENTENCES AND CLAUSES 1]

any [See SOME AND ANY]

anybody, anyone, anything, anywhere
[See SOME-WORDS AND ANY-WORDS]

Headwords: common English words in italics ②

Short entries for cross-reference (3a)

Related words treated together

Different forms of the headword

Pronunciation ④

bring ***brings, brought, bringing*** /brɪŋ/
and ***take*** ***takes, took, taking, taken*** /teɪk/ (*verbs*)

► ***Bring*** and ***take*** are both IRREGULAR VERBS.
► ***Bring*** and ***take*** contrast in the same way as ***come*** and ***go*** [see COME AND GO].

Look up "be able to" under "able to"

Word class (or part of speech)

Cross-references ③

Strong and weak forms (4a)

be ***able to*** /ˈeɪbl tʊ/tə/

Stress marks (4b)

American 'r' (4d) or linking 'r' (4e)

except, except for /əkˈsept/, /əkˈsept fəʳ/ (*preposition*)

British pronunciation on left (4c)

American pronunciation on right (4c)

during /ˈdjʊərɪŋ‖ˈdʊərɪŋ/ (*preposition*)

Detailed explanations

The numbers below, (**1**), (**2**), etc., refer to numbers on the opposite page and give further help in explaining the features of this book.

1 Alphabetical arrangement
Entries are arranged alphabetically to help you find what you need easily. You can look up common English words like *the*, *can*, endings like *-ing*, grammatical terms like *noun*, *article*, or terms like *agreeing and disagreeing* which describe what you do with the language.

2 Headwords
Common English words or word-parts which are important in grammar are in bold italic type, e.g. ***the***, ***of***, ***-er***, ***-est***. Grammatical and other (non-grammatical) terms are in bold upright type, e.g. **noun**, **modal auxiliary**, **invitations**.

3 Cross-references
When you look something up, it will often help you to look up other related entries too. Most entries have cross-references to other entries. These cross-references are in small capital letters, e.g. SOME AND ANY. Sometimes the words are part of a sentence (e.g. "Bring and take are both IRREGULAR VERBS."), sometimes they are in square brackets, e.g. "[see WORD ORDER]", "[see QUANTITY WORD 2]". The number (or number and letter) tells you what section of the entry to read.

3a Short entries
Some entries act as cross-references to other entries, e.g. the entry ***any*** tells you to look up ***some and any*** for a full explanation.

4 Pronunciation
At the top of most entries for common words we give the pronunciation between slant lines / /, using phonetic symbols. [See CONSONANTS AND VOWELS for a list of symbols.]

4a Weak forms
Sometimes there are three slant lines, e.g. /ˈeɪbl tʊ/tə/ for *able to*. Here the symbols between the last two slant lines show the weak pronunciation of the last word or syllable, usually used in the middle of a phrase or sentence. [For more information on weak forms, see STRESS 4.]

4b Stress
The main stress in a word is shown by a mark in front of the stressed syllable, like this: ˈ
[For more information on stress, see STRESS 2.]

4c American pronunciation
For important differences between British English <G.B.> and American English <U.S.> we use a double line (‖) with the British pronunciation (/djʊərɪŋ/) on the left and the American pronunciation (/dʊərɪŋ/) on the right.

4d American r
Most <U.S.> speakers pronounce an /r/ after some vowels and diphthongs, where <G.B.> speakers usually do not. For example, *car* <G.B.> = /kaː/, <U.S.> = /kaːr/; *world* <G.B.> = /wɜːld/, <U.S.> = /wɜːrld/. We use a small raised ^{r} to show this difference, e.g. /kaː^{r}/.

4e Linking r
A raised ^{r} at the end of a word also shows a "linking" /r/ in <G.B.>, that is, an /r/ pronounced at the end of a word, when the next word begins with a vowel, e.g. /əkˈsəpt fə^{r}æn/ = *except for Ann*.

How to use this book — *continued*

Sections and sub-sections

Flags for key points ⑤

Repeat of headword or associated word in bold type

a bit, a bit of /əˈbɪt/, /əˈbɪtəv/

► ***A bit*** and ***a bit of*** behave like QUANTITY WORDS and ***a bit*** also behaves like an adverb of DEGREE.

► The meaning of ***a bit*** and ***a bit of*** is 'a small amount or piece (of)'.

► ***A bit*** and ***a bit of*** are generally used in the same way as ***a little*** [see LITTLE / A LITTLE], but are <more informal>.

1 ***A bit*** (***of*** X) is used only when X is uncountable.

E.g. ***a bit of*** *wood,* ***a bit of*** *cheese*

But where X is a drink we use another word such as ***drop***.

E.g. ***a drop of*** *water*

1a You can say just ***a bit*** (= 'a little') when the hearer knows what you are talking about.

E.g. '*Why don't you try* ***this cake?***' '*I've already had* ***a bit****, thank you.*'
Do you have ***any string****? I just need* ***a bit****.*

Examples in italic type

Pointed brackets for "style" or "variety of English" ⑧

Three dots for missing words ⑨

Structural patterns in capital letters

2 To use fractions in phrases and sentences, put:
FRACTION + OF + . . . NOUN

The noun following the fraction can be:
(i) countable (singular). E.g. *a quarter of the* ***cake***
(ii) countable (plural). E.g. *two thirds of the* ***children***
(iii) uncountable. E.g. *three quarters of the* ***money***
[See COUNTABLE AND UNCOUNTABLE NOUNS.]

NOTE: But before ***half*** we can omit ***a****, and after ***half*** we can omit ***of***. So we can say:

a half of *the* } *egg / eggs / water*
Or: ***half of*** *the*
Or: ***half*** *the*

*Except when ***half*** follows a whole number: ***two and a half***, not ~~***two and half***~~

Smaller type for notes ⑥ and asterisked notes ⑦

Crossing out for "incorrect" English ⑩

Detailed explanations

5 Flags
We signal important key points at the beginning of entries by flags: ► Make sure you always read these key points.

6 Notes
We put less important points in smaller type in Notes (marked NOTE, NOTE (i), NOTE (ii), etc.)

7 Asterisked notes
Other less important points refer to particular parts of an explanation. These are also in smaller type and are marked by asterisks (*,**, etc.)

8 Pointed brackets
A word in pointed brackets, e.g. <formal>, tells you what "style" a grammatical form or structure belongs to. E.g.: "*whom* <formal>" means that we use *whom* in formal kinds of English.
The labels we chiefly use are:

<formal> and <informal> English [look up FORMAL AND INFORMAL ENGLISH]
<written> and <spoken> English (or <writing> and <speech>)
<polite> and <not polite> English [look up POLITE AND NOT POLITE]
<G.B.> and <U.S.> English (i.e. British and American).

9 Three dots
We use three dots . . . to show that extra words can or should be added at this point.

10 Crossing out
When something is "incorrect" or "not English", we show this by crossing it out, using a diagonal line through one word or a horizontal line through a number of words.

How to use this book — *continued*

Forms of the verb with endings (11)

1a With the PRESENT PROGRESSIVE form (***be*** **+ always** + Verb-ing) ***always*** means 'continually'. We often use it to describe a habit we don't like.

E.g. *She****'s always smoking*** *and* ***coughing****. Ugh!*
I'm always losing my glasses.

4 We can link more than two items by coordination. (Note the use of INTONATION.)

E.g. *Which of these fruit juices do you want? The apple, the grapefruit,* ***or*** *the orange?*

Intonation marks (12)

Table which can be read horizontally and diagonally (13)

She *It* *My son*	***loves***	*ice-cream.*
I *We* *Italians*	***love***	*ice-cream.*
The bus *They*	***arrived***	*late.*

Table which can only be read horizontally (13)

subject	verb phrase	complement	. . .
Fresh bread	*is* ***becoming***	***expensive***	*(in this town).*
This chair	***looks***	***comfortable.***	
Our friends	***seem***	***ready*** *to help.*	
The weather	*will* ***stay***	***fine***	*(tomorrow).*

Brackets show words that can be omitted

Detailed explanations

11 Forms of the verb

In structural patterns we use Verb with a capital V as follows:

Verb	indicates the basic form of the verb, e.g. *want*
Verb-s	indicates the *-s* form of the verb, e.g. *wants*
Verb-ed	indicates the *-ed* form of the verb, e.g. *wanted*
Verb-ing	indicates the *-ing* form of the verb, e.g. *wanting*

12 Intonation

We mark intonation (↘ ↗↘↗) when it is important to show how the height or pitch of a voice changes during a sentence. For details of these symbols, look up INTONATION.

13 Tables

Most of the tables in this book can be read without any explanatory notes. But there are two kinds, illustrated opposite, which need some explanation.

The first table has vertical as well as horizontal lines. The vertical lines between different parts of a phrase or sentence show that you can read horizontally or diagonally. In the example opposite, you can make the correct sentences: *She loves ice-cream. It loves ice-cream. My son loves ice-cream.* However, you cannot cross a horizontal line. *My son love ice-cream* would be incorrect.

The second table has no vertical lines so the sentences can only be read horizontally, e.g. *Fresh bread is becoming expensive*. You cannot read diagonally; for example *Fresh bread looks ready to help* is obviously incorrect!

a or ***an*** **a** /eɪ/ (weak form /ə/ is usual)* **an** /æn/ (weak form /ən/ is usual) (*determiner*)

► ***A*** / ***an*** is called the 'indefinite article'.

* The letter '***a***' is always pronounced /eɪ/ (as in ***a***, ***b***, ***c***, . . .)

1 **When to use *a*; when to use *an***
Use ***a*** before a consonant sound.

E.g. *He's* ***a*** /ə/ *doctor.* *What* ***a*** /ə/ *nice picture!*

Use ***an*** before a vowel sound.

E.g. *He's* ***an*** /ən/ *actor.* *What* ***an*** /ən/ *ugly picture!*
Also: ***an*** *hour*, ***an*** *honest person*, etc. [See AN: Note (ii).]

[For more examples, see AN.]

2 ***A*** or ***an*** comes before a singular countable noun:

a / ***an*** } + singular countable noun

E.g. ***a*** *man*, ***a*** *union* /ju:nɪən/, ***an*** *idea*

a / ***an*** } + modifier(s) + singular countable noun

E.g. ***a*** *happy woman*, ***a*** *very famous author*, ***an*** *interesting new book*

2a ***A*** / ***an*** has no plural form. In the plural, instead of ***a***, we use either no word at all [see ZERO ARTICLE] or ***some***.

E.g. *This is* ***a cat***. *This is* ***a rabbit***. *And that is* ***a camel***.

a dog + ***a*** dog + ***a*** dog . . . = ***some*** /səm/ dogs
[To find out how to choose between zero article and ***some***, see ZERO ARTICLE 2.]

3 The meaning and use of *a* / *an*

A / ***an*** means any one of a kind or group. It contrasts with THE (the definite article) and with the zero article. [See THE 3 and ZERO ARTICLE to see how these are used.]

3a ***A*** / ***an*** is used especially after the verb BE, for example in naming a person's job.

E.g. *'What does your father do (for a living)?' 'He's **a** teacher.' 'Oh, really? Mine's **a** pilot.'*

3b ***A*** / ***an*** is used when something is mentioned for the first time. But when the same thing is mentioned again, use ***the***.

E.g. *My friends live in **a** very beautiful house. But **the** house has only a small kitchen.*
*Once we had **a** dog and **a** cat. But **the** dog was always eating **the** cat's dinner. In the end, we gave **the** cat to **a** friend.*

3c ***A*** / ***an*** means the same as ***one*** when it contrasts with ***two***, ***three***, etc.

E.g. *I'd like **two** cups of tea and **a** glass of milk, please.*
We stayed in Austria for { ***a** week.* / ***three** weeks.* / ***a** month and **a** half.* (= '1 ½ months') }

3d In NUMBERS, we generally use ***a*** instead of ***one*** in front of:

FRACTIONS	<informal> numbers	large numbers
***a** half* (½)	***a** couple* (= 2)	***a** hundred* (100)
***a** third* (⅓)	***a** dozen* (= 12)	***a** million* (1,000,000)

3e ***A*** / ***an*** also means 'per' or 'every' in phrases of MEASURING or FREQUENCY.

E.g. *once / twice / six times / . . . times* } { ***a** day* / ***a** week* / ***a** month* / ***a** year* }

HOUSE TO LET
How much is the rent ?
A thousand dollars a month.

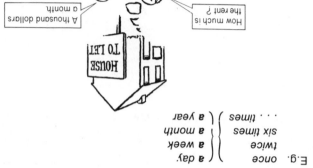

Some more examples:

***An** apple **a day** keeps the doctor away.* (a saying)
*My son goes to the dentist twice **a year**.*
*'How fast are we travelling?' 'Sixty miles **an hour.**' 'That's the same as **a** hundred kilometres **an hour**, isn't it?'*

3f ***A** / **an*** also has a general use, which describes 'all examples of the same kind', or 'any example of the same kind'.

E.g. *'What is **a** dictionary?' '**A** dictionary is **a** book which tells you about the meanings of words.'*
*If **a** man and **a** woman are in love, they will have **a** happy marriage.*
*There are many ways of learning **a** language.*
***A** teacher earns less than **a** lawyer.*

NOTE (i): ***A** / **an*** is not used for describing substances, masses or abstractions in general. [See ZERO ARTICLE 1-3 to find out about these.]

NOTE (ii): A special use of ***a*** is found before QUANTITY WORDS and ADVERBS OF DEGREE. For example:

***a** bit* (of)* <informal>	***a** (great) deal (of)*
***a** few* (of)*	***a** (good) many**
a little (of)*	***a** (large) number (of)*
	a lot (of)* <informal>

*[These words have separate entries in this book. Look them up for further details.]

E.g. ***A few** / **A lot of*** } parents attended the meeting.

In this example, ***parents*** is a plural noun, but ***a*** can still come before it because ***a few*** and ***a lot of*** are plural in meaning.

NOTE (iii): Often ***a*** also comes before 'part nouns' like ***piece***, 'unit nouns' like ***cup***, ***box***, and 'NOUNS OF KIND' like ***kind***, ***type***.
E.g. ***a piece** of cake*, ***a cup** of tea*, ***a type** of cup**
*After ***a kind of***, ***a sort of***, ***a type of***, we usually omit the second ***a*** which would come before a countable noun.
E.g. *He lived in **a kind of** tent.*
*A Jaguar is **a type of** car.*

NOTE (iv): When the determiners ***what***, ***such*** and ***many*** are used with a singular countable noun, ***a*** follows the determiner.
E.g. ***What a** noise!* [See WHAT 4.]
*She was **such a** kind person.* [See SUCH.]
***Many a** man died in that battle.* <formal and archaic> [See MANY.]
Also, ***a*** often follows the adverbs ***quite*** and ***rather*** [see QUITE AND RATHER].
E.g. *We had* { ***rather** / **quite*** } ***a** busy day.* (Also . . . ***a rather** busy day.)*

a- words

1 Some common English words begin with **a-** (pronounced /ə/) and have stress on the second syllable:

PREPOSITIONS		ADVERBS		ADJECTIVES
against	*aboard* ↔	*aboard*	*abroad*	*afraid* * * * *(of)*
amid * *	*about* * ↔	*about* *	*again*	*alike*
among * *	*above* * ↔	*above* *	*ago*	*alive*
	across * ↔	*across* *	*alone*	*alone*
	along * ↔	*along* *	*ahead*	*ashamed* * * * *(of)*
	around * ↔	*around* *	*aloud*	*asleep*
			apart	*awake*
			aside	*aware* * * * *(of)*

*[These words have separate entries in this book. Look them up for further details.]
* * ***Among*** and ***amid*** have <rarer> forms ***amongst*** and ***amidst***.
* * * ***Afraid***, ***ashamed*** and ***aware*** can be followed both by an ***of***-phrase and by a ***that***-clause [see THAT 1, ADJECTIVE PATTERNS 1, 2].
E.g. *I'm **afraid of mice.***
*I'm **afraid that I'll lose my job.***

2 As the arrows (↔) above show, some words can be both prepositions and adverbs [see PREPOSITIONAL ADVERB].

E.g. *The snail crept slowly* ***along***.
(***Along*** is an adverb)

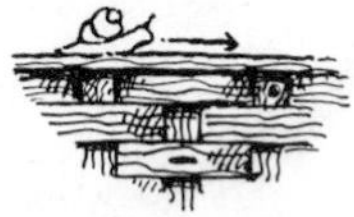

The snail crept slowly ***along*** *the fence.*
(***Along*** is a preposition)

3 The ***a- words*** which are adjectives usually follow the verb BE or another LINKING VERB.

E.g. (i) '***Are*** *the children* ***asleep?***' '*No, they'****re*** *still* ***awake***.'

(ii)

Are you afraid ?
No, nothing frightens me !

(iii)

Your children are very alike, aren't they ?

These adjectives usually cannot come before a noun [see ADJECTIVE 1a]. Instead, we have to use another adjective with the same meaning.

E.g. *two* {~~***afraid***~~ / ~~***asleep***~~ / ~~***alike***~~} *children* *two* {***frightened*** / ***sleeping*** / ***similar***} *children*

a bit, a bit of /əˈbɪt/, /əˈbɪtəv/

- ***A bit*** and ***a bit of*** behave like QUANTITY WORDS and ***a bit*** also behaves like an adverb of DEGREE.
- The meaning of ***a bit*** and ***a bit of*** is 'a small amount or piece (of)'.
- ***A bit*** and ***a bit of*** are generally used in the same way as ***a little*** [see LITTLE / A LITTLE], but are <more informal>.

1 ***A bit*** (***of*** X) is used only when X is uncountable.

E.g. ***a bit of*** *wood,* ***a bit of*** *cheese*

But where X is a drink we use another word such as ***drop***.

E.g. ***a drop of*** *water*

1a You can say just ***a bit*** (= 'a little') when the hearer knows what you are talking about.

E.g. '*Why don't you try* ***this cake?***' '*I've already had* ***a bit****, thank you.*'
Do you have ***any string****? I just need* ***a bit***.

1b You can also use ***a bit*** (***of***) with abstract nouns.

E.g. ***a bit of*** {*peace and quiet* / *news*} ***a bit of*** {*advice* / *fun*}

NOTE: Sometimes in <informal> English we put ***little*** in front of ***bit*** in order to be <polite>.
E.g. *Could I borrow* ***a little bit of*** *chalk?*
Have the rest of the meat. It's only ***a little bit***.

2 ***A bit*** (or ***a little bit***) as an adverb of degree (= 'a little') often goes with words which have a negative or unpleasant meaning.

E.g. *Janet felt* ***a bit annoyed*** *when Pete borrowed her bicycle.*
'How is your arm after the accident?' 'It still ***hurts a bit.***'

And we can use ***a bit of a*** with a noun implying degree.

E.g. *He's **a bit of a fool**.*
*We had **a bit of a shock**.*

A bit also goes with COMPARATIVE words (without a negative or unpleasant meaning).

E.g. *'How are you feeling?' 'Oh, I'm feeling **a (little) bit better** today, thanks.'*

3 After a negative, ***a bit*** adds negative emphasis (= 'at all').

E.g. *'Would you like something to eat?' 'No, thanks, I'm **not a bit** hungry.'*

*'It must be twenty years since we met'. 'Yes and you haven**'t** changed **a bit**.'*

---

be **able to** /ˈeɪbl tʊ/tə/

---

1 ***Be + able to*** + Verb is a VERB IDIOM. On the whole, it has the same meaning as CAN, but is < less common >.

E.g. *My father is over 90, but he **is** still **able to drive** a car.*
(= 'he can still drive . . .'; 'he is still capable of driving . . .')
***Are** you **able to see** the sea from where you live?*
(= 'Can you see the sea . . .?'; 'Is it possible to see the sea . . .?')

NOTE (i): There is also a negative form ***unable to***.
E.g. *If the bad weather continues, the climbers will be **unable to reach** the top of the mountain.*
*I was **unable to swim** under water for more than two minutes.* (= 'I couldn't swim')

NOTE (ii): Other LINKING VERBS as well as **be**, especially ***seem*** or ***feel***, are followed by ***able to***.
E.g. *No one seemed **able to** help.*

1a When ***can*** means 'know how to', we cannot easily replace it by ***be able to***.

E.g. ***Can** you* } ***speak** English?*
~~*Are you able to*~~ }

2 ***Can*** has no infinitive. Therefore ***be able to*** is used instead in places where the infinitive is needed.

E.g. *I would like **to be able to afford** a new car.*

2a MODAL AUXILIARIES like ***might*** [see COULD AND MIGHT] are followed by ***be able to***.

E.g. *Why don't you talk to the secretary? She **might be able to help** you.*

3 ***Can*** has no -ing form [see -ING / -ING FORM], so we use ***being able to*** instead.

E.g. *I enjoy **being able to take** a swim every morning.*

NOTE: But do not use the PROGRESSIVE form of ***be able to***. We cannot say ***I am*** ~~***being able to***~~ etc.

4 **Past**

Can has no regular past form, so we often use ***was*** / ***were able to*** instead.

E.g. *She was very ill, but the doctors **were able to save** her.* *

*Notice the difference between COULD and ***be able to***.

(i) *The clever young doctor **could cure** many illnesses.*

(ii) *The clever young doctor **was able to cure** the queen's illness.*

Example (i) means that he ***knew how to cure illnesses***, but maybe he didn't actually cure anyone.

Example (ii) means that he ***could*** and ***did*** cure the queen (on one occasion).

5 **Perfect**

Can has no perfect form, so we use ***has*** / ***have been able to*** instead.

E.g. *Unfortunately, he **hasn't been able to walk** since his accident.*

6 **FUTURE with WILL**

Can has no future form, so we use ***will be able to*** instead.

E.g. *When **will** you **be able to repay** me?*
*If I get a job in London, I **will be able to visit** you every week.*

---

about /əˈbaʊt/ and ***around*** /əˈraʊnd/

- ***About*** and ***around*** are both PREPOSITIONS and ADVERBS.
- Their meaning is sometimes the same and sometimes different.

1 ***About*** (preposition) means 'on the topic or subject of'.

E.g. '*What's the book **about?***' '*It's **about** the Second World War.*'

2 ***About*** and ***around*** are used to talk about place.

2a Prepositions and Adverbs:
About means 'scattered'.

Around* means 'round'. We also use ***around*** to mean 'scattered,' however.

E.g. (i) *The children ran* {**about** / **around**} *the park.*

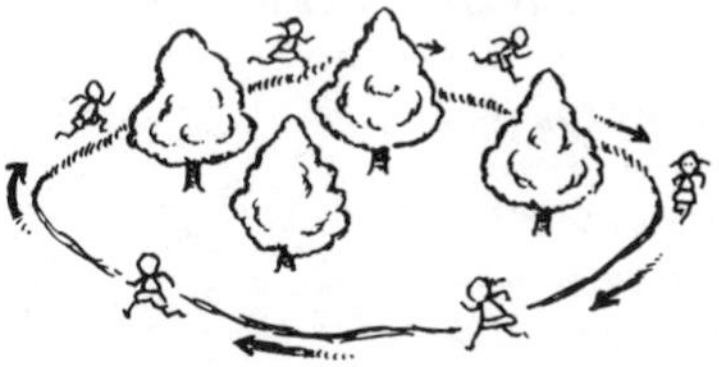

(ii) *The children ran* ***(a)round**** *the park.*
(iii) *Don't turn* ***(a)round****; *there's someone following us.*

****Around*** is preferred in <U.S.>; ***round*** is preferred in <G.B.>.

2b Adverbs:
When we add ***around*** and ***about*** to some verbs to make phrasal verbs, ***around*** means the same as ***about***.

E.g. *The guests were* ***standing*** {***about***. / ***around***.}

3 ***About*** and ***around*** both mean 'approximately' or 'not exactly', when we are talking about numbers, e.g. for distance or time or money. With this meaning, ***about*** and ***around*** are adverbs of degree.

E.g. *'What's the time please?' 'It's* {***about*** / ***around***} ***3***.*'*
'How old is your sister?' 'She's {***about*** / ***around***} ***40***.*'*

3a ***About*** (but not ***around***) can be followed by an adjective or a verb when it means 'approximately'.

E.g. *I think that's* ***about right***.
We've just ***about finished*** *the shopping.*

above and **below** /əˈbʌv/, /bəˈləʊ/ (*prepositions or adverbs*)

► ***Above*** and ***below*** have opposite meanings.

1 ***Above*** and ***below*** are prepositions of PLACE. ***Above x*** means 'higher than x', and ***below x*** means 'lower than x'.

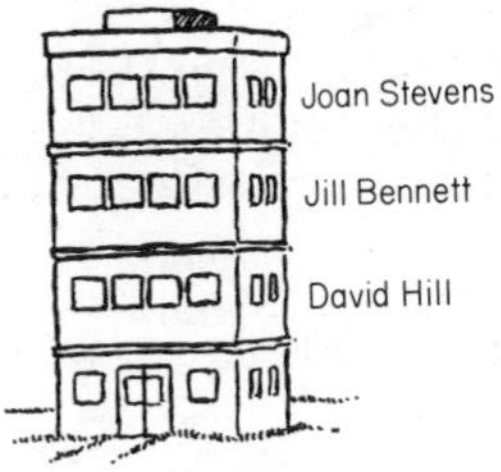

E.g. (i) *Jill Bennett lives* ***above David Hill*** *but* ***below* Joan Stevens****.*

* ***Beneath*** and ***underneath*** are less common words similar in meaning to ***below***.

(ii) *Astronauts work a long way* ***above the surface of the earth****.*
(iii) *Miners work a long way* ***below the surface of the earth****.*

2 ***Above*** can also mean 'higher in one's job or position', or 'higher on a scale of MEASURING', e.g. of price or speed. Again, ***below*** means the opposite.

E.g. *On a ship, the captain gives the orders. He is* ***above all the other officers and sailors****. The other members of the crew are* ***below him****, and take orders from him.*
It is extremely cold at the North Pole: the temperature can sink to 50 degrees ***below zero****.*
You were driving ***above the speed limit****.*

NOTE (i): When ***above*** and ***below*** are adverbs of place, they may follow a noun or a preposition.
E.g. (i) *From the ship, we could see nothing except* ***the sea below*** *and* ***the sky above****.*

(ii) *A shout* ***from above*** *warned the climbers of falling rocks.*

NOTE (ii): ***Above*** can also be an adjective meaning 'at an earlier point in the book'; ***below*** means 'at a later point in the book'.
E.g. *the example* ***above****, the explanation* ***below***

abstract noun

- An abstract noun is the opposite of a CONCRETE NOUN.
- An abstract noun refers to something which has no physical form, something which we cannot see or touch.

1 Abstract nouns stand for general feelings, ideas or concepts

1a Abstract nouns for feelings:
Love is the name of a feeling we have for certain people, things, ideas. We cannot touch ***love***, but we feel it. Each person has this feeling for different people and things, but everyone shares the general idea of what ***love*** is.

1b Abstract nouns for ideas:
In the same way, ***education*** is the general name for how our minds develop when we learn things.

2 Abstract nouns are often based on the meanings of adjectives and verbs

particular	general	abstract noun (very general indeed!)
*a **brave** child*	***brave** actions*	***bravery***
*I **know** you*	*people **know** lots of things*	***knowledge***

3 Types of abstract noun
Although we cannot see what an abstract noun describes, we can divide abstract nouns into different types or classes.

3a Nouns which describe qualities:

E.g. *ability, beauty, freedom, goodness, honesty, importance, length, strength, truth, wealth*

Most of these are related to adjectives. They can all be used as uncountable nouns. But some can be used as countable nouns too. [See COUNTABLE AND UNCOUNTABLE NOUNS.]

E.g. *able* → {*ability* / *abilities*} *free* → *freedom* *good* → *goodness*

3b Nouns which describe states (e.g. states of mind): [Compare STATE VERBS AND ACTION VERBS.]

E.g. *belief, hope, judgement, need, emotion, employment, knowledge, peace, permission, sleep, trust*

Most of these are related to verbs. They can be used as uncountable nouns, but some can be used as countable nouns, too.

E.g. *believe* → {*belief* / *beliefs*} *judge* → {*judgement* / *judgements*}
know → *knowledge* *permit* → *permission*

3c Nouns which describe events or actions:

E.g. *act, answer, attempt, change, cost, examination, fall, fight, laugh, reply, shout, start, victory, whisper*

These are generally countable nouns, and are usually related to verbs. In fact, most of them have the same form as the verb.

E.g. { *The two brothers were **fighting**.*
*What was the **fight** about?* }
{ *Emma wants to **change** her job.*
*A **change*** is as good as a rest. (a saying) }

4 **Endings of abstract nouns**
Many abstract nouns can be recognised by their endings. For example:

*quali**ty***	*tri**al***	*feel**ing***	*wid**th***	*happi**ness***
*uni**ty***	*refus**al***	*mean**ing***	*streng**th***	*weak**ness***
*ac**tion***	*judge**ment***	*differ**ence***	*difficul**ty***	*man**hood***
*invita**tion***	*treat**ment***	*appear**ance***	*hones**ty***	*child**hood***

5 **Countable and uncountable abstract nouns**
Some abstract nouns are countable. This means they have a SINGULAR and a PLURAL form: ***deed – deeds***; ***difficulty – difficulties***.*

* ***Difficulty*** can also be an uncountable noun.

E.g. *With great **difficulty**, the climbers reached the top of the mountain.*

5a Some examples of abstract countable nouns:

accident, example, fact, form, visit, cause, process, event, poem, month

5b Some examples of abstract uncountable nouns. They cannot have a plural or an indefinite article:

advice, help, information, music, news, homework, weather, anger, progress, research*

* Although ***news*** ends in **-s**, it is uncountable, and is always singular.

E.g. ***News*** { ***travels*** / ~~***travel***~~ } *quickly in the modern world.*
*No **news is** good **news**.* (a saying)

5c Many abstract nouns can be both countable and uncountable.

E.g. { *There was **a murder** last night.* (countable)
***Murder** is a terrible crime.* (uncountable) }
{ *The President has introduced many **changes**.* (countable)
*We live in a time of great **change**.* (uncountable) }
{ *How **many times** have you visited Italy?* (countable)
*How **much time** did you spend in Italy?* (uncountable) }

Sometimes, however, the meaning is different in the two uses. For example, ***work*** is normally an uncountable noun (meaning the opposite of 'play' or 'free time').

E.g. ***Work** is a necessary evil.*

But ***works*** (countable) means the '***works*** of art written or painted or made by an artist'.

accepting and refusing [See OFFERS, INVITATIONS]

accusative

In grammar, accusative is the term sometimes used for pronouns like ***me***, ***us***, ***him***, ***her***, ***them***, which can act as OBJECT of a clause. In this book, we use the term OBJECT PRONOUN instead.

across /əˈkrɒs/ (*preposition or adverb*)

1 ***Across*** is a PREPOSITION of PLACE.
Across = 'on the other side of'.

E.g.

Look! There's John
across the road.

Across = 'from one side to the other'.

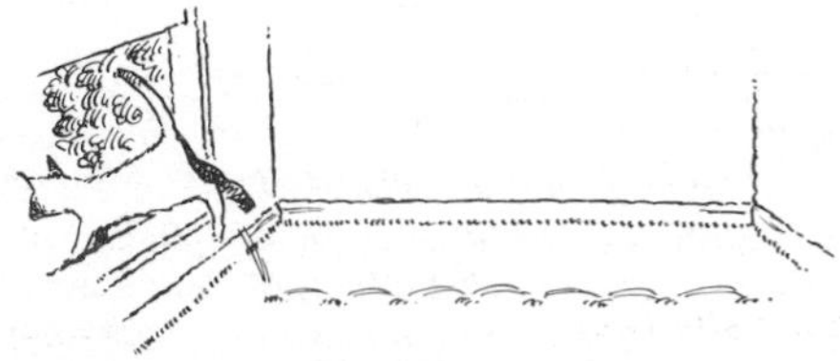

E.g. *The cat ran **across** the room and jumped out of the window.*

2 As an adverb [see PREPOSITIONAL ADVERB], ***across*** has the same meaning.

E.g. *There was no bridge* {***across*** / *over*} *the river, so we had to swim* ***across***.

NOTE: ***Across*** is also part of some PHRASAL VERBS and PREPOSITIONAL VERBS.
E.g. *come across, put (something) across.*

---

action verbs [See STATE VERBS AND ACTION VERBS]

---

active [See PASSIVE]

---

actually /ˈæktʃəlɪ/ (*adverb*)

- ***Actually*** means 'in fact' or 'in reality'.
- We use ***actually*** in two ways: (i) for emphasis, and (ii) to disagree with something.
- ***Actually*** does not mean 'now' or 'at present'.

1 ***Actually*** is used for emphasis (when you have something really surprising to say).

E.g. *She stole a gold ring. I* ***actually*** *saw her pick it up.*
There is a beautiful view from this window. You can ***actually*** *see the sea on a clear day.*

Actually for emphasis occurs in middle position [see ADVERB 3].

2 ***Actually*** for disagreeing:
If you think what someone has said or done is not correct, you can correct them by using ***actually*** in front or end position [see ADVERB 3].

E.g. *'Money is not important.' 'If you're running a business, it matters a great deal,* ***actually****'.*
'Here's the £50 I owe you.' 'Well, ***actually*** *you owe me £100!'*

---

adjective

- After nouns and verbs, adjectives are the largest WORD CLASS in English.
- Adjectives describe the qualities of people, things, places, etc.

E.g. A: *What's your sister like?*
B: *Well, she's* ***tall*** *and* ***slim****. She has* ***black*** *hair.*
A: *Is she* ***beautiful****?*

B: *No, but she's very* ***clever****.*
A: *How* ***old*** *is she?*
B: *She's quite* ***young****.*
A: *And is she* ***married****?*
B: *No, she's* ***single****.*
A: *Is she* ***rich****?*
B: *Don't be* ***nosy*** *– mind your own business!*

1 Positions of adjectives

Adjectives can be used in several different positions in a sentence. The most important positions are described below.

1a Position 1:

When an adjective comes before a noun, we say that it is a modifier of the noun [see MODIFIER AND HEADWORD]. (It is also called an 'attributive adjective'.)

	adjective	noun
a	***young***	*woman*
	tall	*trees*
this	***narrow***	*road*

	adjective	noun
an	***old***	*town*
the	***early***	*train*
our	***national***	*sport*

More than one adjective can modify the same noun:

	adjectives	noun
a	***tall young***	*woman*
a	***beautiful old***	*town*

NOTE: Some adjectives occur only in position 1.
E.g. *only, main, western, chief, fellow, mere, utter, upper*

1b Position 2:

Adjectives also come after the verb BE. In this position, the adjective is called the COMPLEMENT. (It is also called a 'predicative adjective'.) It describes a quality of the SUBJECT:

subject	verb phrase	complement	. . .
The road	***is***	***narrow***	*(here).*
The train	*will* ***be***	***late***	*(this evening).*
Your ideas	***are***	***interesting.***	
It	*has* ***been***	***sunny***	*(today).*

Instead of the verb ***be***, another LINKING VERB can be used before the adjective, e.g. ***become***, ***look***, ***seem***, ***stay***:

subject	verb phrase	complement	. . .
Fresh bread	*is* ***becoming***	***expensive***	*(in this town).*
This chair	***looks***	***comfortable*.**	
Our friends	***seem***	***ready** to help.*	
The weather	*will* ***stay***	***fine***	*(tomorrow).*

NOTE: Some adjectives are not usually used in position 1. They are often used in position 2.
E.g. *able* [see (BE) ABLE TO], *glad*, *ill*, *ready*, *sorry*, *well* ('in good health') [see WELL 3], *bound*.
*The children are **ready***. But not: *the **ready** children*

2 Order of adjectives

The order of adjectives before a noun is not always fixed. But this table shows some orderings we prefer:

	adjectives					noun
	describing or expressing feeling	size	age	colour	defining	
a				***green***	***Indian***	*mat*
an			***old***	***black***		*horse*
a		***tall***			***medical***	*worker*
the	***beautiful***	***little***				*flowers*

Of course, we can have more than two adjectives in a series.

E.g. *a **fine old Spanish** wine*
*a **tall Indian medical** worker*
*a **splendid white Arab** horse*

3 Comparative and superlative adjectives

3a Most adjectives also have comparative and superlative forms using ***-er***, ***-est*** or ***more***, ***most***.

E.g. *good ~ better ~ best*
large ~ larger ~ largest
famous ~ more famous ~ most famous
fortunate ~ more fortunate ~ most fortunate

[For the rules on how to form them, see COMPARATIVE and SUPERLATIVE, -ER / -EST, and MORE / (THE) MOST.]

3b Some adjectives do not normally have comparative and superlative forms.

E.g. *absent, equal, left, opposite, right, single*

4 Words which modify adjectives

Very or another adverb of degree can modify most adjectives:

modifier +	adjective
very	*good*
too	*cold*

modifier +	adjective
rather	*hungry*
utterly	*stupid*

modifier +	adjective
quite	*large*
more	*careful*

The adverb modifier + adjective can modify the noun [see 1a above] or act as complement [as 1b above].

E.g. *This book was written by a **very famous author**.*
= *The author of this book **is very famous**.*

NOTE: The only adverb of degree which follows its adjective is ENOUGH, e.g. ***good enough**, a **large enough** room.*

5 Forms of adjectives

5a Most common adjectives have no special ending. They can be paired with adjectives of opposite meaning.

E.g. *large ~ small, old ~ young, old ~ new, long ~ short, hard ~ soft, rich ~ poor, hot ~ cold, black ~ white, good ~ bad.*

5b But you can recognise many adjectives by their endings. They include:

-al: *actual, final, general, mental, physical, special*
-ent: *ancient, convenient, excellent, frequent, urgent*
-ous: *anxious, conscious, famous, serious, various*
-ic: *atomic, basic, electric, scientific, sympathetic*
-y: *angry, dirty, funny, guilty, healthy, hungry, icy*
-ive: *active, attractive, expensive, native, sensitive*
-ed*: *confused, excited, limited, related, surprised*
-ble: *enjoyable, fashionable, possible, probable, sensible*
-ful: *beautiful, careful, faithful, grateful, skilful*
-an: *American, Christian, German, human, Indian, Russian*
-ing*: *amusing, disappointing, surprising, willing*
-less: *blameless, careless, childless, harmless, senseless*
-ar: *familiar, particular, popular, regular, similar*

Less common endings:
*child**like**, dai**ly**, fool**ish**, sol**id**, wood**en**, ordin**ary***

* [These endings have separate entries in this book. Look them up for further details.]

6 Less common positions for adjectives

In addition to modifier (position 1) and complement (position 2), adjectives can have other, less common positions in a sentence.

6a Position 3:
An adjective can follow ***the***, and act as the main word of a noun phrase, i.e. no noun follows it.

E.g. ***The young*** *should look after* ***the old.***
There is a great division between ***the employed*** *and* ***the unemployed.***
The English *have a lot to learn from* ***the Japanese***. *

In these sentences, the adjectives refer to a class of people, so the phrase is plural. But unlike a noun, the adjective does not have an -s ending.

E.g. *the* ***young~~s~~*** *the* ***unemployed~~s~~*** *the* ***English~~es~~***

* Only some names of nations have an adjective like ***English*** and ***Japanese***. For other nations we use a Noun ending with -s e.g. *the Americans* [see COUNTRIES 2a].

6b Position 4:
After some verbs [see VERB PATTERNS 12], an adjective can follow the object:

subject +	verb phrase +	object +	adjective
I	*like*	*my **coffee***	***black.***
My sister	*keeps*	*her **room***	***very tidy.***

Here the adjective is called an OBJECT COMPLEMENT.

6c Position 5:
Occasionally, an adjective follows the noun which it modifies.

E.g. *The chairman asked the* ***people present*** *(at the meeting) to express their views.*
The ***boys involved*** *(in the fight) were sent away to another school.*

This position is used mainly where the adjective is followed by another structure [see ADJECTIVE PATTERNS] such as the prepositional phrases in brackets in the examples above.

NOTE: The adjective is in position 5 after pronouns ending with ***-body***, ***-one***, and ***-thing*** [see INDEFINITE PRONOUN 3].
E.g. *She hopes to marry* ***someone rich.***
Did you buy ***anything nice*** *at the store?*

6d Position 6:
Another rare position for adjectives is in a VERBLESS CLAUSE.

E.g. ***Sorry!*** *Very* ***good!*** ***Careful!***
Angry *and* ***disappointed***, *the crowd attacked the building.* <formal>

adjective patterns

► Some adjectives are followed by special patterns (compare VERB PATTERNS) which complete their meaning. Here are the most important patterns.

1 ADJECTIVE + PREPOSITIONAL PHRASE

1a

afraid of *full of*	*ashamed of* *proud of*	*aware of* *short of*	*fond of* *tired of*

E.g. *I'm **afraid of** heights.*

1b

angry with * *bored with*	*familiar with* *pleased with*	*delighted with* *satisfied with*

E.g. *I'm **delighted with** my new camera.*

1c

angry at * *sorry about* *different from* *close to*	*good at* *annoyed about* *distant from* *due to*	*hopeless at* *worried about* *free from* *similar to*

E.g. *I'm **hopeless at** sport.*
*I'm **worried about** the exams.*
*Jack is very **different from** his brother.*
*I live **close to** the station.*

* There is a difference between ***angry with*** and ***angry at*** or ***angry about***: you are ***angry with*** a person, but you are ***angry at*** or ***about*** an action or event.
E.g. *I'm angry **with Jim.*** But: *I'm angry **at what he said**.*

2 ADJECTIVE + THAT-CLAUSE [see THAT 1]

afraid that *sorry that*	*angry that* *surprised that*	*happy that* *pleased that*

E.g. *I'm **happy that** you have arrived safely.*

2a IT + BE + ADJECTIVE + THAT-CLAUSE
In this pattern, the adjective follows ***it*** [see IT-PATTERNS 1b]:

certain that *important * that* *necessary * that*	*clear that* *likely that* *possible that*	*essential * that* *obvious that* *true that*

E.g. ***It's certain that*** *the parcel arrived safely.*
It's essential that *the parcel (should) arrive safely.*
It's important that *we (should) be there on time.*

* With the adjectives marked *, we use the BASIC FORM of the verb, or ***should*** <mainly G.B.> [see SHOULD AND OUGHT TO 6] as in the second and third examples above.

3 ADJECTIVE + TO + VERB

able to *afraid to* *anxious to* *ashamed to* *careful to* *certain to*	*content to* *delighted to* *determined to* *due to* *eager to* *fit to*	*free to* *glad to* *keen to* *likely to* *nice to* *ready to*	*sure to* *surprised to* *thankful to* *willing to* *wise to* *worried to*

E.g. *We are* ***delighted to meet*** *you.*
The plane is ***due to take off*** *at 7 p.m.*
They are ***ready to sign*** *the agreement.*
You were ***wise to sell*** *that old car.*

3a { IT + BE + ADJECTIVE (FOR . . .) TO + VERB
ADJECTIVE + (FOR . . .) TO + VERB

difficult to *impossible to*	*easy to* *nice to* <informal>	*hard to* *pleasant to*

These adjectives can be used in two related patterns, the first with ***it*** [see IT-PATTERNS 1a] and the second without ***it***.

E.g. { ***It is difficult to park*** *these big cars.*
These big cars are ***difficult to park***.

Before the ***to***, we can place a ***for***-phrase, containing the subject of the TO–INFINITIVE verb (***thief*** in the example below).

E.g. { *It is easy* ***for a thief*** *to break into this house.*
This house is easy ***for a thief*** *to break into.*

NOTE: Some adjectives have the ***it***-pattern only:

essential to *sad to*	*strange to* *lovely to*	*important to* *annoying to*	*necessary to* *surprising to*

Again, a ***for***- phrase can be placed before the TO–INFINITIVE.
E.g. ***It would be lovely*** *(for my wife)* ***to meet*** *you again.*
It is important *(for a witness)* ***to speak*** *the truth.*

adverb

- Adverbs form a large and varied WORD CLASS.
- Adverbs add information to a clause (e.g. about the time or place of an action). Here the adverb is called an ADVERBIAL.
- Adverbs add information to another word, such as an adjective or another adverb. Here the adverb is called a modifier [see MODIFIER AND HEADWORD].

1 Adverbs have many different kinds of meaning. The most common are:

MANNER: e.g. well *, hard, how *, fast *, slowly, quickly
PLACE: e.g. above *, up *, here *, there *, upstairs
TIME: e.g. now *, then *, soon *, recently *, afterwards
DEGREE: e.g. very *, much *, really *, quite *, too *, so *
FREQUENCY (including number of times): e.g. always *, never *, often *, generally, sometimes

1a Other kinds of adverb:

linking: e.g. firstly, therefore *, however *, nevertheless [See LINKING ADVERBS AND CONJUNCTIONS.]
comment and attitude: e.g. actually *, perhaps, surely *, oddly, wisely
adding and limiting: e.g. also *, either *, else *, neither *, only *, too *
viewpoint: e.g. mentally, morally, officially, strictly
LENGTH OF TIME: e.g. long *, always *, never *, just *

* [These words have separate entries in this book. Look them up for further details. For **above** see ABOVE AND BELOW; for **up** see UP AND DOWN; for **long** see LONG/LONGER/LONGEST.]

1b Examples of adverbs:

Our new neighbour greeted us **politely**.	(**manner**) *
'How long have you lived **here**?' she asked.	(**place**) *
'We arrived only **yesterday**,' we replied.	(**time**) *
'Well, I hope you'll be **really** happy.'	(**degree**) *
After that we met her quite **frequently**.	(**frequency**) *
However, we learned very little about her.	(**linking**)
Strangely, she never talked about herself.	(**comment and attitude**)
She talked **only** about us and the weather.	(**adding and limiting**)
Personally, I found that annoying.	(**viewpoint**)
Have you **ever** met anyone like that?	(**length of time**) *

* [These types of adverb have separate entries in this book. Look them up for further details. For linking adverbs look up LINKING ADVERBS AND CONJUNCTIONS.]

2 Wh- adverbs belong to some of the types listed above:

MANNER	PLACE	TIME	DEGREE	(REASON AND CAUSE)
how *however*	*where* *wherever*	*when* *whenever*	*how* *however*	*(why)*

[These words have separate entries in this book. Look them up for further details. See also WH- WORDS, and WH- EVER WORDS.]

3 Positions of adverbs

3a There are three main positions for adverbs:

(i) FRONT POSITION – before the subject:

	ADVERB +	SUBJECT +	VERB PHRASE	(+ . . .)
E.g.	***Occasionally***	*John*	*missed*	*lessons*

(ii) MIDDLE POSITION

either: (a) after the first auxiliary:

	SUBJECT +	FIRST AUXILIARY +	ADVERB	+ REST OF VERB PHRASE	(+ . . .)
E.g.	*John*	*has*	***occasionally***	*missed*	*lessons*

or: (b) after ***be*** as a finite verb:

	SUBJECT +	BE +	ADVERB	(+ . . .)
E.g.	*John*	*is*	***occasionally***	*absent from lessons*

or: (c) if there is no auxiliary, before the finite verb (other than BE):

	SUBJECT +	ADVERB	+ FINITE VERB	(+ . . .)
E.g.	*John*	***occasionally***	*missed*	*lessons*

(iii) END POSITION – at the end of the clause:

	SUBJECT +	VERB PHRASE	(+ . . .) +	ADVERB
E.g.	*John*	*missed*	*lessons*	***occasionally***

But for each type of adverb, one position is the most common.

3b The most common positions for adverbs:

type of adverb	typical position	example
manner:	end	*She dances very* ***gracefully****.*
place:	end	*Shall I drive you* ***home****?*
time:	end	*I'll be seeing you* ***again tomorrow****.*
degree:	middle	*We are* ***thoroughly*** *enjoying the party.*
frequency:	middle	*Guy (has)* ***often*** *fished in that lake.*
linking:	front	*They arrived. . . .* ***So*** *we left.*
comment or attitude:	front	***Fortunately*** *no one noticed.*
adding or limiting:	middle	*Cora can* ***also*** *play the piano.*
viewpoint:	front	***Officially****, Ivan was the boss.*
length of time:	middle	*He hadn't* ***long*** *left school.*

3c Adverbs as modifiers almost always come before the word they modify (an exception is ENOUGH). Such adverbs are generally adverbs of degree [see DEGREE]:

adverb + adjective	
very	*broad*

adverb + adverb	
too	*soon*

adverb + preposition	
just	*after*

adverb + determiner	
too	*much*

adverb + pronoun	
so	*few*

adverb + conjunction	
right	*until*

4 Forms of adverbs

Adverbs are of three formal kinds:

(I) Most adverbs are formed by adding ***-ly*** to an adjective [see -LY].

E.g. *slow* ~ ***slowly****,* *thorough* ~ ***thoroughly****.*

(II) A number of adverbs have the same form as adjectives. The most important are:

hard, straight, far, near, early, late, fast, east, west, north, south, left, right, just, opposite, pretty, direct, little, backward, forward, well

(III) Many of the most common adverbs are not related to adjectives at all. They include PREPOSITIONAL ADVERBS such as ***in*** and ***about***, and also such words as:

so, too, there, here, as, quite, very, now

4a Many adverbs have COMPARATIVE and SUPERLATIVE forms [see MORE / (THE) MOST, -ER / -EST].

E.g. *early ~ earlier ~ earliest*
well ~ better ~ best
easily ~ more easily ~ most easily

adverbial

► An adverbial is a part of a CLAUSE which gives extra information about the time, place, manner, etc. of the event described by the rest of the clause.

1 **Some facts about adverbials**

1a An adverbial can usually be omitted; it adds information to a complete clause.

E.g. *Paul plays tennis.*
Paul plays tennis ***every week****.*

1b Most adverbials can change their position in the clause.

E.g. *Paul plays tennis* ***every week****.*
Every week*, Paul plays tennis.*

1c We can add more than one adverbial to a clause:

adverbial		adverbial(s)
Every week	*Paul plays tennis*	***with his friend Tim****.*
Every week	*Paul plays tennis*	***at the club with his friend Tim****.*

1d Adverbials answer such questions as 'How?', 'Where?', 'When?', 'Why?', 'How far?', 'How much?', 'How often?', 'How long?'.

2 **Meanings of adverbials**
[To find out about the most common meanings of adverbials, see: DEGREE, DISTANCE, FREQUENCY, INSTRUMENT, LENGTH OF TIME, MANNER, MEANS, MOTION, PLACE, PURPOSE, REASON AND CAUSE, TIME.]

2a [Some other meanings of adverbials are listed under ADVERB 1 and ADVERBIAL CLAUSE 2, 2a.]

3 Forms of adverbials

An adverbial can be:

(i) a single word.

E.g. *Ella visited us* ***yesterday***. [see ADVERB]

(ii) a phrase.

E.g. *Ella visited us* ***on Friday***. [see PREPOSITIONAL PHRASE]
Ella visited us ***very recently***. [see PHRASE]
Ella visited us ***last year***. [see NOUN PHRASE]

(iii) a clause.

E.g. *Ella visited us* ***before she flew to Japan***. [see ADVERBIAL CLAUSE]

4 Positions of adverbials

4a [For details of the positions of adverbs, see ADVERB 3.]

4b Adverbial phrases and clauses can go in the same positions as adverbs:

(i) FRONT POSITION

E.g. ***Because of the strike****, the teachers have stopped work.*

(ii) MIDDLE POSITION

E.g. (a) *The teachers have,* ***because of the strike****, stopped work.* * <rare>
(b) *The teachers are,* ***in spite of the strike****, working normally.* * <rare>
(c) *The teachers,* ***because of the strike****, stopped work.*

(iii) END POSITION.

E.g. *The teachers have stopped work* ***because of the strike***.

* Adverbial phrases and clauses do not usually go in middle position as in (ii)(a) or (b) above. But unlike most adverbs, they can go before the first auxiliary or ***be***. This is called ***middle position*** too.
E.g. *The teachers,* ***because of the strike****, have stopped work.*

4c Some adverbial phrases and clauses can go in all three positions, like ***because of the strike*** in the examples above. But some adverbials cannot be moved.

E.g. *She sings* ***very well***. (end position only)

4d [For more examples of the positions of adverbial clauses, see ADVERBIAL CLAUSE 3.]

4e As a general rule:

(I) By far the most common types of adverbial are adverbs and prepositional phrases.
(II) By far the most common position for adverbials is end position.
(III) When more than one adverbial is at end position, we prefer to place shorter adverbials (especially one-word adverbs) before longer adverbials.

E.g. *I phoned her* ***yesterday*** ***at half past two.***
adverb + prepositional phrase

Cora went ***to the store*** ***to buy some vegetables.***
prepositional phrase + clause

(IV) When more than one adverbial is at end position, place adverbials of manner or means before adverbials of place, and adverbials of place before adverbials of time, i.e. The preferred order of adverbials is 'M P T', with the letters in alphabetical order.
'M' stands for MANNER, and MOTION (OR MOVEMENT).
'P' stands for PLACE, and
'T' stands for TIME, including FREQUENCY and LENGTH OF TIME.

E.g. *Please sit* ***quietly*** ***on the floor.*** (M + P)
Did you meet anyone ***in town*** ***yesterday?*** (P + T)
They argued ***violently*** ***for forty minutes.*** (M + T)

(V) If you write an adverbial in front position, you can separate it from the rest of the clause by a comma.

E.g. ***To my knowledge,*** *no one has borrowed your pen.*

Always use the comma when the adverbial is a phrase or a clause.

(VI) An adverbial phrase or clause is rarely used in middle position. If it is, we separate it from the rest of the clause by two commas.

E.g. *Elephants,* ***on the whole,*** *are friendly animals.*
You can, ***if you prefer,*** *arrive a day later.*

4f These rules are only rough. We can change the order of the adverbials for special emphasis. On the whole, the adverbial with the most important information should be placed at the end.

adverbial clause

1 Adverbial clauses are SUBORDINATE CLAUSES which act as an ADVERBIAL part of another Clause (i.e. of a MAIN CLAUSE). They can answer such questions as 'When?', 'Why?', 'If what?', and 'What for?'.

2 **Conjunctions which begin adverbial clauses**
Most adverbial clauses begin with a CONJUNCTION such as IF, WHEN, and BECAUSE:

meaning	conjunctions which begin the clause
TIME:	*after, before, as, once, since, until, when, whenever, while*
condition [see CONDITIONAL CLAUSE]:	*if, unless*
CONTRAST:	*although, whereas, while*
REASON AND CAUSE:	*because, since, as*
PLACE:	*where, wherever*

[The conjunctions in the above table have separate entries in this book. Look them up for further details. For ***before*** see AFTER AND BEFORE.]

E.g. *Zoe and I once met* ***when we were at school***. (clause of TIME)
I won't know her ***if we meet again***. (CONDITIONAL CLAUSE)
Although Grandpa is over eighty, he is still very active. (clause of CONTRAST)
I bought a new typewriter ***because the old one was broken***. (clause of REASON AND CAUSE)
'Where shall we go for a walk?' 'We can go ***wherever you like***.' (clause of PLACE)

NOTE: Some conjunctions contain two or three words:

meaning	conjunctions which begin the clause
TIME:	*as soon as, immediately (that), now (that)*
condition [see CONDITIONAL CLAUSE]:	*so long as, provided (that), in case*
CONTRAST:	*even though*
REASON AND CAUSE:	*seeing (that)*

E.g. ***Now that*** / ***Now*** } ***you're here***, *we can enjoy ourselves.*

2a In addition, adverbial clauses express some less important meanings:

meaning	conjunctions which begin the clause
PURPOSE:	*in order to, in order that, so as to, so that* <all formal>
RESULT:	*so that, so . . . that, such . . . that*
comparison of manner [see AS]:	*as, as if, as though*
proportion:	*as . . . (so)* *, *the . . . the* *

E.g. *I left early* ***(so as) to catch the train***. (clause of PURPOSE)
They ignored the young prince, ***so that he became very angry***.
(clause of RESULT)
She treats him {***as if*** / ***as though***} ***he*** {***'s*** / ***were*****} ***a child.***
(clause of comparison of manner)
As time passed, so *our hopes grew stronger*. (clause of proportion)

* The conjunctions of proportion are DOUBLE CONJUNCTIONS [See ***as*** 2e].
** [On the choice of ***were***, see UNREAL MEANING.]

3 **Position of adverbial clauses** [see ADVERBIAL 4.]
Adverbial clauses usually go at the end of the main clause, like most examples in 2 above. Most types of adverbial clause (but *not* result clauses) can also be used in front position.

E.g. = {*The bus will be waiting at the airport* ***when you arrive.*** / ***When you arrive****, the bus will be waiting at the airport.*}
= {*They finished the game,* ***although the weather was wet.*** / ***Although the weather was wet****, they finished the game.*}

4 **Nonfinite adverbial clauses**
In addition to the FINITE clauses above, NONFINITE CLAUSES can also act as adverbials.

(i) TO-INFINITIVE clause: ***to*** + Verb . . .

E.g. *The country is working hard* ***to increase food production***.
(= '. . . in order to improve . . .') (clause of PURPOSE)

(ii) -ING CLAUSE: Verb-***ing*** . . .

E.g. ***Being a teacher****, I believe in higher standards of education.*
(= 'Because I am a teacher . . .') (clause of REASON AND CAUSE)

(iii) PAST PARTICIPLE clause: Verb-***ed*** . . .

E.g. ***Taught by Einstein****, he became one of the best scientists of his age.*
(= 'After he was taught . . .') <rather formal> (clause of TIME)

4a 'Reduced' clauses:
Some participle clauses are like finite clauses, except that the subject and finite verb are omitted. In these 'reduced clauses', the conjunction ***when*** or ***after*** etc., comes before a participle.

(i) -ING CLAUSE: conjunction + Verb-***ing*** . . .

E.g. ***After leaving school,*** *she worked in an insurance office.*
(= '. . . after she left . . .')

(ii) PAST PARTICIPLE clause: conjunction + (adverb) + Verb-***ed*** . . .

E.g. ***If (firmly) planted in a rich soil,*** *the tree will grow very quickly.*
(= 'If it is (firmly) planted . . .')

5 **Verbless adverbial clauses**
'Reduced clauses' can also have no verb [see VERBLESS CLAUSE].

E.g. *Old clocks are very valuable* ***when in good condition***.
(= '. . . when they are in good condition')

advising, advice

1 In giving advice, these patterns are useful:

If I were you, I'd + Verb . . .
Why { *don't you* + Verb . . .? / *not* + Verb . . .? }
I('d) advise you to + Verb . . . <most formal>
IMPERATIVE <most informal> (E.g. *Go! Come!*)

2 Examples:

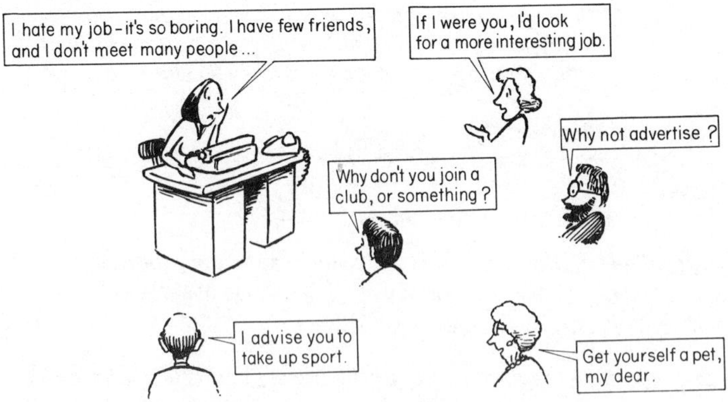
I hate my job - it's so boring. I have few friends, and I don't meet many people ...
If I were you, I'd look for a more interesting job.
Why not advertise ?
Why don't you join a club, or something ?
I advise you to take up sport.
Get yourself a pet, my dear.

NOTE: You can also use ***should*** and ***ought to*** for giving advice. [See SHOULD AND OUGHT TO 3a for further details.]

afraid /əˈfreɪd/ (*adjective*) [see A-WORDS, and ADJECTIVE PATTERNS 1, 2]

---

after and ***before*** /ˈɑːftəʳ‖ˈæftəʳ/, /bəˈfɔːʳ/ (*prepositions, conjunctions or adverbs*)

- ► ***After*** and ***before*** have opposite meanings.
- ► ***After*** means 'later than . . .'; ***before*** means 'earlier than . . .'.

1 ***After*** and ***before*** are prepositions of TIME.

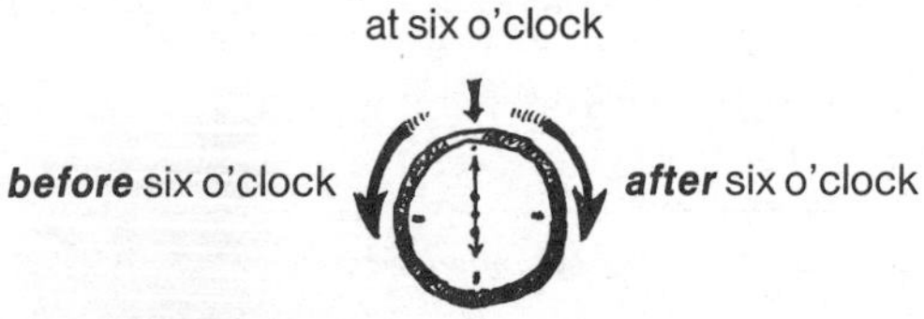

E.g. ***After the meal,*** *we felt sick.*
Before 1940, *few people owned a telephone.*

2 ***After*** and ***before*** can introduce CLAUSES. When they do this they are called subordinating conjunctions. [See CONJUNCTION 3.]

2a Position:
The ***after***-clause and the ***before***-clause can be at the end of the sentence or at the beginning of the sentence.

E.g. (i) *The airport police searched*[2] *all the passengers* ***after the plane landed***[1].
Or ***After the plane landed***[1], *the airport police searched*[2] *all the passengers.*
(ii) *We cleaned*[1] *the house* ***before our friends arrived***[2].
Or ***Before our friends arrived***[2], *we cleaned*[1] *the house.*

([1]=first action; [2]=second action)

2b Past time:
In the clauses which describe the first action ([1]), we can use the PAST PERFECT in place of the PAST SIMPLE.

E.g. (i) *The airport police searched*[2] *all the passengers* ***after the plane had landed***[1].
(ii) ***We had cleaned***[1] ***the house*** *before my friends arrived*[2].

NOTE: But the words ***before*** and ***after*** are enough to indicate which event happened first, whatever tense you use.

2c Future time:
We use the present form for future time in ***after-*** and ***before-*** clauses [see FUTURE 3b].

E.g. *The mother bird will continue to feed her children* ***after they leave the nest****.*
I'll see you again ***before you return home****.*

NOTE: In an ***after***-clause the Present Perfect can also be used for talking about the future.
E.g. *We will know the results of the election* ***after the votes have been counted****.*

3 ***After*** and ***before*** are used as ADVERBS of time. ***After**** means: 'after this, after that'. ***Before*** means: 'before this, before that, before now'. They go at the end of a phrase or sentence.

E.g. *At last the war was over, and not long* ***after*** *, the soldiers returned home.*
(***after*** = 'after the war was over')
Haven't I met you ***before****?*
(***before*** = 'before now')

* Social usage: ***after*** as an adverb is <informal>; ***afterwards*** is regarded as more <correct>.

---

ago /əˈgəʊ/ (*adverb*)

---

1 ***Ago*** is an adverb of TIME. It measures the time from 'now' back to a fixed point. For example:

1963 . . . 25 years . . . 1988
President Kennedy died NOW

President Kennedy died 25 years ***ago****.* (= 25 years before 'now')

subject	verb in the Past Tense	length of time phrase	**ago**
Kennedy	*died*	*25 years*	***ago.***

2 ***Ago*** can follow many different length of time phrases.

E.g. *I got married +* ***a long time***
I can't find my pen. I had it + ***a minute***
The builders started work + ***ages***
} ***ago****.*

NOTE (i): Question form: ***How long ago*** *did he leave the University?*

NOTE (ii): The time phrase + ***ago*** can come first.
E.g. ***A few weeks ago****, we were complaining about the rain.*

NOTE (iii): Do not use ***ago*** with the Present Perfect.
E.g. ~~*The doctor has examined her several weeks* ***ago****.*~~

agreeing and disagreeing

1

agreement	
with positive	**with negative**
(i) ***Yes*** + subject + auxiliary / BE. (ii) *Yes, (definitely).* (iii) *I quite agree.* (iv) *I couldn't agree more.*	(i) ***No*** + subject + auxiliary / BE + ***n't***. (ii) *No, (definitely not).* (iii) *I agree (that . . . not . . .).*

disagreement
(It is more <polite> to disagree partly than wholly.) (i) *Yes, but (on the other hand) . . .* (ii) *True, but (then) . . .* (iii) *I'm afraid I disagree (with you).*

2 Positive agreement:

She sings very well, don't you agree ?
Yes, (she does).
Yes, definitely.
I quite agree.
I couldn't agree more.

3 Agreement with a negative:

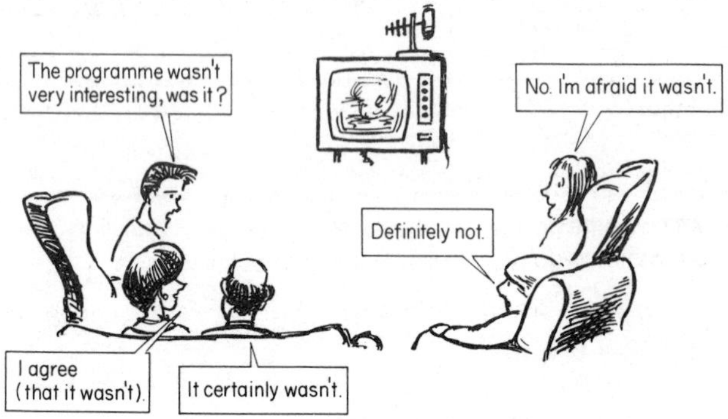
The programme wasn't very interesting, was it?
No. I'm afraid it wasn't.
Definitely not.
I agree (that it wasn't).
It certainly wasn't.

4 Disagreeing: (It is more < polite > to disagree partly than wholly.)

This tax is unfair, don't you think?
I'm afraid I disagree with you.

True, but then no tax is perfectly fair.
Well, it's unfair to some people perhaps.
Yes but (on the other hand) it hits the rich rather than the poor.

5 When we want people to agree with us, we often use TAG QUESTIONS like ***isn't she?*** and ***wasn't it?***

agreement

(Also called ***concord***) [See also AGREEING AND DISAGREEING]

► Agreement is a matching relation between SUBJECT and VERB (in FINITE clauses).

► The main rule of agreement is simple:

SINGULAR subjects go with SINGULAR verb phrases.
PLURAL subjects go with PLURAL verb phrases.

This rule applies to 3rd Person subjects. But there are some exceptions! [See 2 below.]

1 **The rule of agreement**

In the Present Tense (3rd Person):
– if the noun is singular, the verb must have an **-s**.
– if the noun is plural, the verb does not have an **-s**.

	noun	verb
singular	–	+-s
plural	+-s	–

E.g. *The **carpet needs** cleaning.*
*The **carpets need** cleaning.*

1a More examples:

subject (SINGULAR) +	verb phrase (. . .) (SINGULAR)
This **rose**	***looks*** *beautiful.*
She	***does*** *the cooking.*
One ***pear***	***has*** *been eaten.*

subject (PLURAL) +	verb phrase (. . .) (PLURAL)
These ***roses***	***look*** *beautiful.*
They	***do*** *the cooking.*
Two ***pears***	***have*** *been eaten.*

NOTE (i): The noun which marks plural in the subject is the headword of the phrase [see MODIFIER AND HEADWORD]. It is not always the noun next to the verb. In the examples below, ***laws*** and ***chair*** are the headwords.
E.g. *The **laws** of science **have** no exceptions.*
*That **chair** with the wooden arms **belongs** to us.*

NOTE (ii): Some nouns ending in **-s** are not plural, e.g. ***news***, ***measles***, ***mathematics***, ***billiards***.
E.g. ***Measles is*** *a disease.* ***Billiards is*** *a game.*
Also, some plural nouns do not end in **-s** [see IRREGULAR PLURALS]. E.g. ***men***, ***women***, ***children***.

NOTE (iii): The singular verb is the form we use when the subject is: (a) uncountable.
E.g. ***Milk keeps*** *children healthy.*
or (b) a clause.
E.g. ***That he returned the money proves*** *his honesty.*

1b Verbs have singular and plural forms only in the PRESENT TENSE: ***looks*** ~ ***look***, ***goes*** ~ ***go***, etc. In the PAST TENSE there is no agreement problem, because the verb does not change.

E.g. *The **rose looked** beautiful.* *The **roses looked** beautiful.*

1c But the verb ***be*** has singular and plural forms in both the Present Tense and the Past Tense. It must follow the rule of agreement in the Past Tense too.

	singular	plural	
E.g.	*The box **is** empty.* *The box **was** empty.*	*The boxes **are** empty.* *The boxes **were** empty.*	(PRESENT) (PAST)

1d MODAL AUXILIARIES like CAN, WILL, and WOULD do not have singular and plural forms. They are the same for all subjects.

E.g. *I **can** swim.* *She **can** swim.* *They **can** swim.*

2 Special problems of agreement

There are some exceptions to the rule of agreement, and sometimes we can choose whether to follow the rule of agreement or not.

2a Agreement with ***and*** and ***or***:

Where the subject consists of two or more items joined by AND, the subject itself is plural, and is followed by a plural verb.

E.g. *My husband **and** I both **have** a job.*

But two singular noun phrases joined by ***(either) . . . or*** [see EITHER and OR] are followed by a singular verb phrase. Compare, for example, the following:

*I think football **and** tennis **are** on the television tonight.*
*I don't know whether football **or** tennis **is** on the television tonight.*

NOTE: The rule for ***or*** is that the verb phrase matches the last of the items joined by ***or***.
E.g. *Either the judge **or the two witnesses were** wrong.*
*Either the two witnesses **or the judge was** wrong.*

2b Agreement with quantity words:

As subjects, the pronouns ***any***, [see SOME AND ANY], EITHER, NEITHER, and NONE sometimes take a singular verb, and sometimes take a plural verb.

E.g. *I don't think* {***any*** / ***either***} *of the winners* {***deserves*** / ***deserve***} *a prize.*

Her sons are grown up, but {***none*** / ***neither***} *(of them)* {***is*** / ***are***} *married.*

The singular verb is preferred in <formal, 'correct'> English. But often, we prefer the plural verb when a strong idea of 'plural' is present, e.g. when ***none***, for example, is followed by a phrase like ***of them***, containing a plural noun or pronoun.

2c We rarely use nouns such as ***number***, ***majority***, ***plenty***, with a singular verb, in spite of the rule of agreement.

E.g. *A (large)* ***number*** / *The* ***majority*** / ***Plenty*** } *of the miners* { ***was*** / ***were*** } *still on strike.*

2d Agreement with group nouns:
When singular GROUP NOUNS such as ***audience***, ***committee***, ***family***, ***government***, ***team***, act as subject, the verb is sometimes plural, especially in <G.B.>.

E.g. *The committee* { ***meets*** / ***meet*** } *every week.*

It is best to choose the singular verb, except where the idea of 'plural' is strongly suggested.

E.g. *The audience* ***were*** *clapping and waving* ***their arms*** *in excitement.*

Here ***was*** would be odd because of the 'plural idea' expressed by ***their arms***.

---

alike, alive [see A-WORDS]

---

all /ɔ:l/ (*determiner, pronoun, or adverb*)

- ***All*** (as a DETERMINER or INDEFINITE PRONOUN) is a QUANTITY WORD.
- ***All*** contrasts with ***some*** [see SOME AND ANY].
- ***All*** has similarities with EVERY and BOTH.

1 **Positions of *all***
All can appear in many different positions in a sentence.

1a Position 1: ***all*** + ***of*** + noun phrase or pronoun.
All of can be followed by:

(i) a singular countable noun. E.g. ***all of*** *the book* *
(ii) a plural countable noun. E.g. ***all of*** *the books*
(iii) an uncountable noun. E.g. ***all of*** *the oil*
(iv) a personal pronoun. E.g. ***all of*** *them*, ***all of*** *it*

Other determiners can replace ***the***: e.g. *all of* ***our*** *friends*, *all of* ***that*** *soup*.

* With a singular countable noun, ***all (of)*** is not common. We prefer ***the whole*** [see WHOLE].

1b Position 2: ***all*** + noun phrase.
We can omit ***of*** from Position 1 (i)–(iii). For example:

(i) singular countable noun: ***all*** *the book* * *, ***all*** *this tree* * *
(ii) plural countable noun: ***all*** *the books,* ***all*** *our friends*
(iii) uncountable noun: ***all*** *the oil,* ***all*** *that soup*

* * [See * above.]

But we cannot omit ***of*** before a personal pronoun: ~~***all them***~~.
Instead, we can place the pronoun before ***all***: ***them all***.
(This is 'position 3' below.)

NOTE: The ***of*** must be omitted if the noun has no determiner.
Instead of: ***All of roses*** *are beautiful.*
we must say: ***All roses*** *are beautiful.*

1c Position 3: personal pronoun + ***all***.
We place ***all*** after a personal pronoun whether the pronoun is subject, object, etc.

E.g. (i) ***We all*** *enjoyed the play.*
(ii) *A Happy Christmas to* ***you all***.
(iii)

Once you've seen one cowboy film, you've seen them all.

1d Position 4: noun phrase or pronoun + . . . ***all***.
When the noun phrase or pronoun is a SUBJECT, we can often separate ***all***, and place it after BE or the AUXILIARY VERB.

E.g. ***You*** *are* ***all*** *welcome.*
The children *are* ***all*** *playing in the garden.*
This snow *will* ***all*** *have melted soon.*

1e Position 5: pronoun.
As a pronoun, ***all*** can stand on its own. The ***of***-phrase is omitted if its meaning is known [see INDEFINITE PRONOUN].

E.g. *'Would you like to buy anything else?' 'No, thank you. That's* ***all***.*'*
(= 'That's all that I want')

NOTE (i): ***All*** is an adverb of DEGREE in the following examples.
Jim lives ***all alone***. (= 'completely')
They sell their goods ***all over the world.*** (= 'everywhere')
If you cut these plants down, they grow ***all the more***.

NOTE (ii): IDIOMS with ***all***
all but = 'almost'; ***all day***, etc. [see LENGTH OF TIME];
all over [see OVER AND UNDER]; ***all right*** – an adverb meaning 'O.K.';
all through [see THROUGH].

almost and ***nearly*** /ˈɔːlməʊst/, /ˈnɪəʳlɪ/ (*adverbs*)

► ***Almost*** and ***nearly*** are adverbs of DEGREE with the same meaning [see DEGREE].

► ***Almost*** is more <common> than ***nearly***.

E.g. *This bottle is* {***almost*** / ***nearly***} *full.*

(full)

This bottle is {***almost*** / ***nearly***} *empty.*

(empty)

1 ***Almost*** and ***nearly*** can go before adjectives, adverbs, and quantity words.

E.g. *My bicycle is **almost new**.*
*She plays the violin **almost perfectly**.*
*We got married **nearly forty** years ago.*

2 When ***almost*** and ***nearly*** modify a verb, we place them in middle position, before the main verb [see ADVERB 3c].

E.g. *We were late, and **nearly missed** the train.*
*She has a bad cold: she's **almost lost** her voice.*

NOTE (i): When there is a negative auxiliary, ***almost*** / ***nearly*** must go before it.
E.g. *When I heard the tickets were £25 each, I **almost didn't** go to the theatre.*

NOTE (ii): ***Almost*** and ***nearly*** cannot always be used in the same place. For example, we generally use ***almost***, not ***nearly***, in front of ***like***.
E.g. *It was* {***almost*** / ~~***nearly***~~} ***like*** *a dream.*

alone [See A-WORDS]

along /əˈlɒŋ/ (*preposition or adverb*)

1 ***Along*** is a PREPOSITION of MOTION (OR MOVEMENT) or PLACE meaning 'from one end towards the other end'. [Compare ACROSS.]

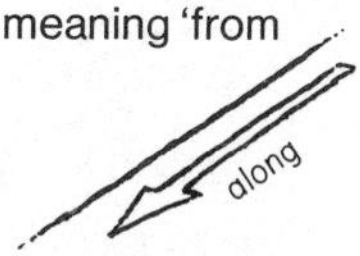

E.g. *Taxis often come **along** this street.*
*I love to see trees **along** the sides of the road.*

Along as a PREPOSITIONAL ADVERB has a meaning similar to 1 above, but the noun phrase after it is omitted.
E.g. *The soldiers marched **along**, singing noisily.*

Along is also used in the idiom ***along with*** ('in company with').
E.g. *We're going for a ride. Why don't you come **along with** us?*

We often omit the ***with*** + noun phrase.
E.g. *Why don't you come **along**?*

already, still, and ***yet*** /ɔ:lˈredɪ/, /stɪl/, /jet/ (*adverbs*)

► These three TIME adverbs all refer to time before 'now', up to 'now'.
► They are often used with the PERFECT or PRESENT form of the verb (simple or PROGRESSIVE).

1 Meanings

Already = 'sooner than expected'.
Yet = 'before now' (***yet*** is the form we usually use instead of ***already*** after negatives and in questions).
Still = 'continuing later than expected'.

All these adverbs express an element of surprise.

1a Examples:
(i)

(ii) *'I suppose you've **already** passed your driving test?' 'No, I haven't even learned to drive properly **yet**. I'm **still** having lessons.'*

2 *Already / yet / still* with the Present Perfect

2a ***Already / yet / still*** with the Present Perfect refers to a past action with a present result.

E.g. (i) *'Is Joy in her office?' 'No, she**'s already gone** home.'*
(ii)

2b ***Yet*** is used after a negative or in questions with the Present Perfect. [See SOME-WORDS AND ANY-WORDS 2b.]

E.g. (i)

Sorry, I haven't done it yet. I'll do it in a minute.

(ii) *'**Have you done** your homework **yet?**' 'No, I've started it, but I **haven't yet finished it.**'*

NOTE: If we expect a 'yes' answer to the question, we use ***already*** instead of ***yet***.
E.g. *'Have you done your homework **already**?'*

2c ***Still*** can be used before the negative auxiliary ***hasn't*** / ***haven't*** + past participle.

E.g.

He still hasn't mended that fence. He said he would mend it last week.

Notice that, in these two sentences, negative + ***yet*** and ***still*** + negative have almost the same meaning, but example (ii) emphasises the point and suggests that you are annoyed about it.

E.g. (i) *I have**n't** passed my driving test **yet**.*
(ii) *I **still** have**n't** passed by driving test.*

NOTE (i): In <U.S.>, the Past Simple is often preferred to the Present Perfect with ***already*** and ***yet***.
E.g. ***Have** you **already finished** those letters?* <G.B.>
***Did** you **already finish** those letters?* <U.S.>

NOTE (ii): ***Already*** / ***still*** / ***yet*** are also used with the Past Perfect.
E.g. *By the age of 19, Pat **had already taken part** in several national competitions. But she **hadn't yet won** any prizes.*

3 *Already* / *yet* / *still* with the Present Simple or Present Progressive

3a ***Already*** and ***yet*** can go with the Present Simple or Progressive with reference to a present state of affairs.

E.g. *'Would you like to meet my boss?' 'No thanks, I **already know** him.'*
***Are you going** to bed **already?** It's only nine o'clock.*

3b ***Yet*** is used after negatives and in questions.

E.g. ***Is the breakfast*** *ready* ***yet?***
'Is your son *working* ***yet?'*** *'No, he doesn**'t yet have** a job.'*

3c ***Still*** is also used with the Present Simple and Progressive referring to a continuing state of affairs.

E.g. (i) *My father* ***is still*** { ***working.*** / ***at work.*** } *He has**n't** retired* ***yet.***

(ii)

(iii) *Are you* ***still*** *here? I thought you had gone home a long time ago.*

If the clause is negative and the auxiliary or main verb is a part of BE, ***still*** can be placed before or after the negative word.

E.g. (i)

(ii)

NOTE (i): The usual negative form of sentences with ***still*** replaces ***still*** by ***not*** / ***n't*** + ***any more***.

E.g. *'Does Mr. Marin* ***still*** *live in that house?'*
{ *'Yes, he* ***still*** *lives there.'*
{ *'No, he does**n't** live there* ***any more.'***

NOTE (ii): ***still*** and ***yet*** can also be linking adverbs, and in this case they usually appear in front position. [See LINKING ADVERBS AND CONJUNCTIONS].

4 The basic sentence types with the Perfect form of the verb

	positive statement	negative statement	positive question	negative question
already	*I've* ***already*** *finished!*	* X	*Have you* ***already*** *finished?*	*Haven't you* ***already*** *finished?* <rare>
yet	X	*I haven't finished* ***yet****.*	*Have you finished* ***yet?***	*Haven't you finished* ***yet?***
still	* * X	***I still*** *haven't finished.*	* * X	*Have you* ***still*** *not finished?*

* A negative sentence '*You haven't finished* ***already!***' is possible, but it has the effect and intonation of a question [see YES-NO QUESTION 4].
E.g. *You haven't finished* ***already*** *(have you)?*
If you say this, it means that you can hardly believe that the statement is true!

* * A positive statement or question with ***still*** is possible, but not with the Perfect form of the verb [see 5c below].

5 Position (of *already*, *still* and *yet*)

5a ***already:***
– before the verb.

E.g. *I* ***already know*** *how to get there.*

– before the participle.

E.g. *I have* ***already seen*** *that film.*

– at the end of the sentence.

E.g. *I know how to get there* ***already****.*
I have seen that film ***already****.*

5b ***yet:***
– at the end of the sentence.

E.g. *Britain hasn't had a communist government* ***yet****.*

– in a negative statement, ***yet*** can go before the participle.

E.g. *Britain has****n't yet had*** *a communist government.*

5c ***still:***
– immediately after the subject.

E.g. ***We still*** *haven't done the shopping.*

– except when the auxiliary is part of the verb ***be***. In this case ***still*** follows it.

E.g. *We* ***were still*** *waiting for the plane three hours later.*

also /ˈɔːlsəʊ/ (*adverb*)

Also is an adverb meaning 'in addition', 'as well', 'too'.

E.g. *Eva is captain of the women's hockey team. She* ***also*** *plays tennis for her college.*
(***also*** = 'in addition to being captain of the women's hockey team.')

although /ɔːlˈðəʊ/ (*subordinating conjunction*)

Although introduces an ADVERBIAL CLAUSE expressing a CONTRAST with the idea in the main clause.

E.g. ***Although this computer is quite cheap****, it is one of the best machines on the market.*

[See ADVERBIAL CLAUSE, CONTRAST, LINKING ADVERBS AND CONJUNCTIONS.]

always /ˈɔːlweɪz/ (*adverb*)

► ***Always*** is an adverb of 1. FREQUENCY, and 2. LENGTH OF TIME.
► ***Always*** is generally used in middle position [see ADVERB 3] in the clause.

1 Frequency: ***always*** = 'on all occasions', 'at all times'.

E.g. *The bus is* ***always on time.***
Meg and Philip ***always visit*** *their parents on Sunday.*
(= 'They visit them every Sunday').

1a With the PRESENT PROGRESSIVE form (***be*** + **always** + Verb-ing) ***always*** means 'continually'. We often use it to describe a habit we don't like.

E.g. *She****'s always smoking*** *and* ***coughing****. Ugh!*
I'm always losing my glasses.

2 Length of time: ***always*** = 'for all time'.

E.g. *Have you* ***always lived*** *in the country?* (= 'all your life')
Marion and I will ***always be*** *close friends.*

am /æm/ (contraction: **'m** /m/) [See BE]

Am is the form of the verb ***be*** used after ***I***.

E.g. ***I am*** / ***I'm*** } *coming.*

Question: ***Where am I?***

NOTE: The negative question contraction (especially in <G.B.>) is ***aren't I?***.
E.g. *Why **aren't I** on the list?*

among, amongst [See BETWEEN AND AMONG]

amount [See QUANTITY WORDS, MEASURING]

an /æn/ (weak form /ən/ is usual) (*determiner*)

An is the form of ***a*** (the indefinite article) used before vowel sounds. [See CONSONANTS AND VOWELS.]

E.g. ***an*** /ən/ *apple*	***an*** *angry fairy*
an /ən/ *egg*	***an*** *excellent idea*
an /ən/ *idea*	***an*** *interesting book*
an /ən/ *orange*	***an*** *open door*
an /ən/ *uncle*	***an*** *ugly face*

NOTE (i): Words like ***European***, ***union***, ***university***, ***used***, ***useful*** are pronounced with a consonant sound at the beginning (/ju:/-), so the form ***a*** is used with them: ***a*** *used car* /ju:zd kɑ:^{r}/.

NOTE (ii): In words like ***hour***, ***honest***, ***honour***, ***honourable***, ***hourly***, on the other hand, the '***h***' is silent. They are pronounced with a vowel at the beginning, and so the form ***an*** is used with them.
E.g. ***an hour*** /ən ˈaʊə^{r}/; ***an honest*** *witness* /ən ˈɒnəst . . ./.

and /ænd/ (weak form /ənd/ or /ən/ or /n/ is usual) (*coordinating conjunction*) [See COORDINATION]

► The special symbol **&** is sometimes used for ***and***.
► ***And*** expresses the general idea of 'addition'.

1 An example of ***and*** used to express 'addition':

*Jane received two letters **and** a postcard.*

2 ***And*** can also have more particular meanings of:
(a) time ('and then').

E.g. *She washed **and** wiped the dishes.*
(= she washed the dishes ***and then*** wiped them.)
*He felt in his pocket **and** pulled out a key.*

(b) reason ('and so').

E.g. *It rained hard, **and** we all got wet.*
(= '. . . ***and so*** we all got wet')

(c) condition ('if').

E.g. *You scratch my back, **and** I'll scratch yours.*
(A saying which means 'If you help me, I'll help you'.)

NOTE (i): In <speech>, we sometimes use ***and*** in place of ***to*** (before an infinitive).
E.g. *I'll try **and** help you.* (= 'I'll try ***to*** help you')

NOTE (ii): ***And*** in expressions like ***up and down***, ***in and out***, ***round and round***, ***again and again***, ***on and on***, expresses the meaning of 'repeating' or 'continuing'.
E.g. *There are **thousands and thousands** of books in the library.*

NOTE (iii): [To find out about agreement when ***and*** is used in and between noun phrases see AGREEMENT 2a.]

---

animals

► Nouns describing animals have various plural forms.

1 Most nouns describing animals have regular plurals.

E.g. *a cow ~ two cows* *one snake ~ some snakes*
an ant ~ many ants *that fox ~ those foxes*

2 Some animal words have irregular plurals [see IRREGULAR PLURAL 1–4].

E.g. *a goose ~ two geese* /gi:s/ *one mouse ~ some mice* /maɪs/

3 Some animal words have no change in the plural ('zero plurals') [see IRREGULAR PLURAL 4a].

E.g. *a sheep ~ two sheep* *one deer ~ several deer*

---

another /əˈnʌðəʳ/ (*determiner or pronoun*)

► ***Another*** has two meanings: (i) 'one more / additional'.
(ii) 'a different one'.

1 ***Another*** (determiner) + noun or pronoun.

E.g. *They have two dogs, and now they want* ***another*** { ***dog***. / ***one***. }
(= 'one more / additional dog')

This hotel is too expensive. Let's find ***another place*** *to stay.*
(= 'a different one')

1a ***Another*** can come before a number or some other expression of quantity or measure.

E.g. *Can I have* ***another two*** *ice-creams, please?*
(= 'two more ice-creams')
In ***another 50*** *years, the world will be quite different.*
(= 'after 50 more years')

2 ***Another*** (pronoun) has no following noun or pronoun.

E.g. *You've finished your drink. Have* ***another***.
(= 'one more drink')

---

answers [See SHORTENED SENTENCES AND CLAUSES 1]

---

any [See SOME AND ANY]

---

anybody, anyone, anything, anywhere [See SOME-WORDS AND ANY-WORDS]

---

anyway /ˈenɪweɪ/ (*adverb*)

1 ***Anyway*** is an <informal> linking adverb [see LINKING ADVERBS AND CONJUNCTIONS] meaning 'in any case'.

E.g. *'Mummy, can I have that doll for my birthday?' 'No. It's too expensive.* ***Anyway***, *you have enough dolls already.'*

2 In end position, ***anyway*** can also mean 'in any case', but here it is not always a linking adverb.

E.g. *I don't care what you say, I'm going to do it* ***anyway***.

apart from /əˈpɑːʳt frəm/ (*preposition*)

Apart from is a preposition meaning 'except for'.

E.g. *No one knew that one of the aircraft's engines had failed,* ***apart from the pilot***.

apologies

1 When we apologise, we 'say sorry' for something we should not have done. Intonation is important when we apologise, as you will see in the examples below.

1a To apologise for something not very important, e.g., not having any change, say ***sorry***.

E.g.

1b To apologise for something more serious, you can say:

* As these examples show, we sometimes put stress on the auxiliary verb or the verb BE. This makes the apology more emphatic.

1c A <more formal> apology:

'I'd like to apologise for what I said last night.'
'That's O.K. Forget it.'
'I apologise for leaving school without your permission.'
'Well, don't let it happen again.'

1d A formal written apology:

We regret that*, because of a typing error, you were sent a supply of new* ***boots****, instead of new* ***books****. We sincerely apologise for any inconvenience this may have caused.*

2 Patterns:

I'm (really) { *(very)* / *(extremely)* / *(terribly)* / *(so)* } *sorry* { *(for+* { noun phrase / Verb-ing . . . }) / (*that*+clause) }

{ *I* / *We* } *('d like to) apologise (for+* { noun phrase / Verb-ing . . . })

{ *I* / *We* } *regret that*+clause

---

apposition

► Apposition is a relation between two NOUN PHRASES which describe the same thing, person, etc. One of the phrases is a modifier of the other [see MODIFER AND HEADWORD].

1 Examples of apposition:

Rosa is married to { ***Charles Bell, a teacher****.* / ***a teacher, Charles Bell****.* }

I live in ***Aswan, a town in the south of Egypt****.*

The next train, the 10.45 to Dover*, leaves from Platform 14.*

NOTE: Usually the phrases in apposition are joined by a comma (,).

---

are

is the 3rd person plural present form of BE.

---

aren't

is the negative form of ***are***. [See BE 1c]

---

around

[See ABOUT AND AROUND]

---

articles

[See also A OR AN, THE, ZERO ARTICLE]

► The articles are ***a*** /ə/, ***an*** /ən/ (indefinite article), and ***the*** /ðə/ /ðɪ/ (definite article).

► Articles are DETERMINERS.

1 Using the articles

The can be used before all COMMON NOUNS, i.e. SINGULAR and PLURAL, countable or uncountable [see COUNTABLE AND UNCOUNTABLE NOUNS]. ***A*** / ***an*** can be used only with singular countable nouns:

countable singular	countable plural	uncountable (singular)
the *girl* ***a*** *girl*	***the*** *girls* ~~***a***~~ *girls*	***the*** *milk* ~~***a***~~ *milk*

1a We do not put ***a*** / ***an*** in front of plural or uncountable nouns, because ***a*** means 'one'. When a noun has no article or determiner before it, we call this a ZERO ARTICLE.

1b NAMES (= proper nouns) do not usually have articles.

E.g. ~~***the***~~ *Paris,* ~~***a***~~ *Paris.*

2 Singular *a* / *an* and plural *some* / *any*

Some and ***any*** [see SOME AND ANY 1] are often used as the plural of ***a*** / ***an***.

E.g. *Would you like* ***a*** *banana?*
Would you like ***some*** /səm/ *bananas?*
Would you like ***any*** *bananas?*

NOTE (i): You can say ***some*** when you are offering. You can say ***any*** when you are asking a question for information [see YES-NO QUESTION].

NOTE (ii): [To find out how to choose between zero article and ***some***, see ZERO ARTICLE 2.]

3 Word order

The article is usually the first word in a NOUN PHRASE:

the / ***a*** / ***an*** } + number + adjective + noun

E.g. ***the*** *third floor,* ***the*** *three wise men*
a *beautiful picture,* ***a*** *fine old Dutch painting*

3a Only a few words go before ***a*** / ***an*** or ***the*** in a noun phrase. ALL, BOTH, and HALF go before ***the***; ***quite***, ***rather*** [see QUITE AND RATHER], SUCH, and WHAT go before ***a*** / ***an***:

all / ***both*** / ***half*** + ***the*** } + (other modifiers) + noun
quite / ***rather*** / ***such*** / ***what*** / ***half*** + ***a*** / ***an*** } + (other modifiers) + noun

E.g.	*all* ***the*** *men*	*half* ***the*** *loaf*	*such* ***a*** *pity*	*quite* ***a*** *risk*
	both ***the*** *men*	*half* ***a*** *loaf*	*what* ***a*** *pity*	*rather* ***a*** *risk*

4 Meanings of the articles

Notice that all the articles can have both particular meanings and general meanings.

4a Particular meanings:

The following examples refer to particular or specific dogs:

(i) *She keeps **dogs** for breeding.*
(ii) *I would like to have **a dog** as a pet.*
(iii) *Did you take **the dog** for a walk?*

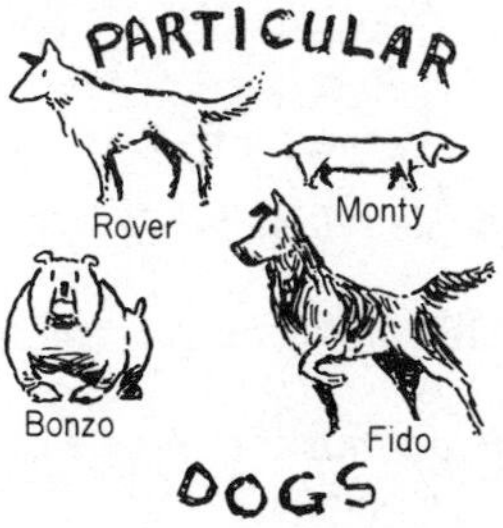

In examples (i)–(iii), ***dogs, a dog***, and ***the dog*** mean something different from one another.
A (indefinite article) means any one of a kind or group: ***a dog*** in (ii) means any dog – it is not possible to say which.
The (definite article) means one(s) which the speaker and hearer know about: ***the dog*** in (iii) means a dog which the speaker and hearer know about.
[For more details and examples of the particular meanings of the articles, see ZERO ARTICLE, A OR AN 3a–e and THE 3a–f.]

4b General meanings:

In contrast, the following refer to the whole class of dogs in general:

(iv) ***Dogs** are man's best friends.*
(v) ***A dog** is man's best friend.*
(vi) ***The dog** is man's best friend.*

[For details of how to use the articles to refer to things in general, see ZERO ARTICLE 3, A OR AN 3f, and THE 3g.]

as /æz/ (weak form: /əz/) (*adverb, conjunction, or preposition*)

► You can always use the weak form /əz/.

1 ***As . . . as* in comparisons** [see COMPARISON 3].

1a Forms:

as + { adjective / adverb + (. . .) / { ***many*** / ***much*** } } ***as*** + { noun phrase / clause / adjective e.g. ***necessary*** / ***possible*** / ***usual*** / adverb e.g. ***ever*** }

E.g. (i) *John is (almost)* ***as tall as his father****.* (***as*** + adjective + ***as*** + noun phrase)

(ii) *Please come* ***as quickly as you can****.* (***as*** + adverb + ***as*** + clause)

(iii) ***As many as five thousand people*** *attended the meeting.* (***as many as*** + noun phrase)

(iv) *I'll do* ***as much as possible****.* (***as much as*** + adjective).

NOTE: If there is an adjective between ***as*** and the noun, ***a*** / ***an*** must go after the adjective, i.e. ***as*** + adjective + ***a*** / ***an*** + noun. (Not: ***an*** + ***as*** + adjective + noun).

E.g. *The female lion is* { ***as good a*** / ~~***an as good***~~ } ***hunter*** *as the male lion.*

1b Quantity expressions before ***as . . . as*** [see FRACTIONS and NUMBERS]:

{ ***half*** / ***two-thirds*** / ***twice*** / ***ten times*** / ***fifty times*** } ***as*** { old / tall / long } ***as*** . . .

E.g. *This boy is* ***twice as tall as*** *that girl.*

This tree is ***half as tall as*** *that one.*

This tower is ***three times as tall as*** *that house.*

2 ***As* as a subordinating conjunction**
As introduces different kinds of subordinate clause.

2a ***As***-clauses of COMPARISON [See 1a(ii) above, and COMPARATIVE CLAUSE 2.]

2b There is another type of **as**-clause expressing similarity or comparison.
E.g. *He behaved badly, (just)* ***as I thought he would***.
This is an ADVERBIAL CLAUSE, not a comparative clause. ***Just*** can be added for emphasis. Some people use ***like*** here instead of **as** [See LIKE 3].

2c ***As***-clauses of TIME
E.g. ***As the police arrived***, *the crowd began to shout angrily.*
I saw the thief (just) ***as he was leaving the building***.
Here we use **as** to connect two events which happened at the same time.
As has a meaning similar to when.

2d ***As***-clauses of reason [See REASON AND CAUSE 2.]
E.g. ***As Linda is the eldest child***, *she has to look after the other children.*
As the weather was fine, *we held the party outside.*
As here is similar to BECAUSE or **since** [See SINCE 3].

2e ***As***-clauses of proportion
E.g. ***As prices rise***, *(so) the demand for higher wages will increase.*
As you get older, *(so) you become less willing to change your ideas.*
As here means 'over the same period of time that . . .'. The **so** which comes at the beginning of the main clause is <formal>, and can be omitted.

2f ***As***-clauses as comment clauses [See COMMENT CLAUSE].
E.g. ***As everyone knows***, *taxes are unpopular.*
Compare: *Everyone knows* **that** *taxes are unpopular.*
The meeting, ***as often happens***, *became very noisy.*
Compare: *It often happens* **that** *the meeting becomes very noisy.*

3 ***As* as a preposition**
The preposition **as** has two main uses [compare LIKE 2].

3a ***As*** expressing COMPARISON (See 1 above.)
E.g. *She sat there* ***as quiet as a mouse***.
Here, **as** comes before a noun phrase. There are many idiomatic comparisons ('similes') of this kind.
E.g. *as good* ***as gold***, *as white* ***as a sheet***, *as brave* ***as a lion***,
as black ***as pitch***, *as hard* ***as nails***, *as old* ***as the hills***,
as deaf ***as a post***, *as poor* ***as a church mouse***

NOTE: In these comparisons we sometimes omit the first **as**.
E.g. *She sat there quiet* ***as a mouse***.

3b ***As*** expressing the meaning of the verb ***be***:

E.g. ***As your father****, I have a duty to give you advice.*
(= Being your father . . .)
She worked ***as a model*** *before she got married.*
(i.e. 'She was a model.')

As can come before not only a noun phrase, but an adjective or a PARTICIPLE.

E.g. *The police described him* **as**
- ***a (dangerous) criminal***. (**as** + noun phrase)
- ***(very) dangerous***. (**as** + adjective phrase)
- ***having an ugly face***. (**as** + Verb-ing . . .)
- ***badly hurt***. (**as** + past participle)

Compare: *The police described him* ***to be*** *a dangerous criminal.*

4 Idioms

4a ***As if, as though*** (subordinating conjunctions):
As if and ***as though*** are used in the same way, to express a comparison with something that may be true or may be imaginary.

E.g. (i) *It looks* ***as though the weather is improving***.
(ii) *She treats me* ***as if she hated me***.
(iii) *She treats me* ***as if I were her servant***.

Example (i) contains the Present Tense form ***is*** (for something which may be true).
Example (ii) contains the Past Tense form for UNREAL MEANING.
Example (iii) contains the were-form for unreal meaning, [see WERE 2].

4b ***As well*** (adverb) means the same as ***too*** [See TOO 1] and ALSO.

E.g. *'The food is good at this restaurant'.*
'Yes, the prices are quite reasonable, ***as well***.*'*

As well is usually used in end position.

4c ***As well as*** (preposition) (= 'in addition to')

E.g. ***As well as*** *being an actor, Morley was a theatre manager, and even wrote his own plays.*

4d There are many other idioms containing ***as***. Look them up in a dictionary.

---

asleep, awake, aware [See A- WORDS]

---

aspect

Aspect is the grammatical term we use for the following structures in the VERB PHRASE:

(i) Perfect aspect: ***have*** + past participle.

E.g. *We **have had** dinner.*

(ii) Progressive aspect (also called 'continuous'): ***be*** + Verb-ing.

E.g. *We **are having** dinner.*

(iii) Perfect Progressive aspect: ***have*** + ***been*** + Verb-ing.

E.g. *We **have been having** dinner.*

Aspect describes the way we look at an action or state, in terms of the passing of time. [See PERFECT, PROGRESSIVE for further details.]

at /æt/ (weak form: /ət/ (*preposition*)

► ***At*** is a common preposition with two main meanings. ***At*** indicates a ***position in space*** [see 1 below]; and ***at*** indicates a ***point in time*** [see 2 below].

► Also, ***at*** occurs in many other uses and idioms, such as ***laugh at***, ***at last*** [see 4 below].

1 ***At*** **= 'at a position in space'**

[See PLACE 2a.]

At is used for place, when you cannot use ON or IN [see PLACE 2b], e.g. ***at*** = 'close to, with a purpose'.

E.g. (i) *The children were sitting **at the table**, doing their homework.*

(ii) *There's someone **at the front door**: I heard the bell ring.*

1a Notice the frequent use of ***at*** before the following nouns referring to place or position.

***at** the beginning,*	***at** the end,*	***at** the entrance*
***at** the front,*	***at** the back,*	***at** her side*
***at** the top,*	***at** the bottom,*	***at** the centre*

1b In some common phrases, ***the*** is omitted.

E.g. ***at** home,* ***at** school,* ***at** work*

1c Either ***at*** or ***in*** can be used before buildings or names of places.

E.g. ***in*** / ***at*** *the* *airport* / *post office* ***in*** / ***at*** *Tunis* / *Stratford-on-Avon*

2 ***At* = 'at a position or point in time'**

2a ***At*** is used with expressions of clock time [See (TELLING THE) TIME].

E.g. *The concert starts* ***at 7.30*** *on Saturday evening.*

2b ***At*** is also used for other points of time, or 'stages' of the day.

E.g. ***at*** *the moment,* ***at*** *lunch time,* ***at*** *midday*

NOTE: Exceptions are uses where ***at*** refers to a period of time. Here ***at*** is similar to DURING.
E.g. (i) ***at*** + ***time***: ***At that time****, we lived in Lagos.*
(ii) ***at*** + special times of the year: ***at*** *Christmas,* ***at*** *the New Year,* ***at*** *Easter.* (Here the period can be more than one day.)
(iii) ***at night: At night****, the noise of traffic kept us awake.*

3 ***At* with Numbers**
(i) age.

E.g. *Nowadays most people retire* ***at the age of 60****.*

(ii) price.

E.g. *You can buy eggs* ***at 80p a dozen****.*

(iii) speed.

E.g. *The police arrested him for driving a car* ***at 100 m.p.h.*** (= miles per hour)

4 ***At* = 'towards'**
At comes before a noun phrase describing the goal of the action: the thing towards which the action of the verb is directed [See PREPOSITIONAL VERB].

E.g. ***Smile at*** *the lion,* ***aim at*** *the lion,* ***point at*** *the lion,*
shout at *the lion,* ***throw a stone*** *at the lion.*

NOTE: This use of ***at***:
(a) often implies doing something unpleasant.
E.g. *It's rude to point* ***at*** *people, and it's very dangerous to shoot* ***at*** *them!*

(b) does not imply that the goal is reached.
E.g. *You can shoot* ***at*** *the lion, but you probably won't hit him!*

5 ***At*** occurs also in many idioms. Look up ***at*** in a dictionary.

auxiliary verb

- An auxiliary verb is usually before another verb [see MAIN VERB].
- Auxiliary verbs 'help' other verbs to form VERB PHRASES (e.g. ***is*** *leaving*, ***would*** *help*).

1 These are the auxiliary verbs in English:

primary auxiliary verbs	*be have do* (these can also be main verbs)
modal auxiliary verbs	{*will* *would*} {*can* *could*} {*may* *might*} {*shall* *should*} *must* *ought to* * *used to* *

[Look up each of these words for further details.]

* ***Ought*** and ***used*** are less common, and not quite like other MODAL AUXILIARIES, because they are followed by ***to***.

2 **The forms of auxiliary verbs**

2a The primary auxiliary verbs have irregular (i) -S FORMS, (ii) PAST TENSE forms, and (iii) PAST PARTICIPLE forms:

	-S FORM	PAST TENSE	PAST PARTICIPLE
BE:	*is*	*was / were*	*been*
HAVE:	*has*	*had*	*had*
DO:	*does*/dʌz/	*did*	*done*

2b The modal auxiliaries have no **-s** form at all, and they also have no PARTICIPLE forms and no INFINITIVE.

E.g. ***must*** ~ ~~***musts***~~ ~ ~~***musting***~~ ~ ~~***to must***~~

[For further details of modal auxiliaries, see MODAL AUXILIARY.]

3 **Position**
If the auxiliary is the first word of the verb phrase:
(i) To make a negative sentence [see NEGATIVE WORDS AND SENTENCES], add NOT after the auxiliary, or use a negative contraction [see CONTRACTIONS OF VERBS AND NEGATIVES].

E.g. She ***will*** *come* → *She* {***will not*** / ***won't***} *come.*

(ii) To make a question, put the auxiliary before the subject.

E.g. *She* ***will*** *come* → ***Will*** *she come?*

(iii) We can omit the main verb after an auxiliary if the meaning is clear from the situation.

E.g. *'Will she come tonight?' 'No, she* ***can't****.'*
'I've never been to China. ***Have*** *you?'*

This is the exception to the rule that an auxiliary verb requires a main verb. [See SHORTENED SENTENCES AND CLAUSES.]

3a The 'empty auxiliary' DO is used for negatives, questions, and to avoid repetition, if there is no other auxiliary.

E.g. *I love her.* → *I* ***don't*** *love her.*
→ ***Does*** *she love you?* → *Yes, she* ***does****.*

4 [For more details, look up each auxiliary. See also MODAL AUXILIARY, VERB IDIOMS and VERB PHRASE.]

---

away /ə'weɪ/ (*adverb of* PLACE *or* MOTION (OR MOVEMENT)) Also ***away from*** (*preposition*)

---

1 Place: ***away*** = 'not here or not there'.

E.g. (i)

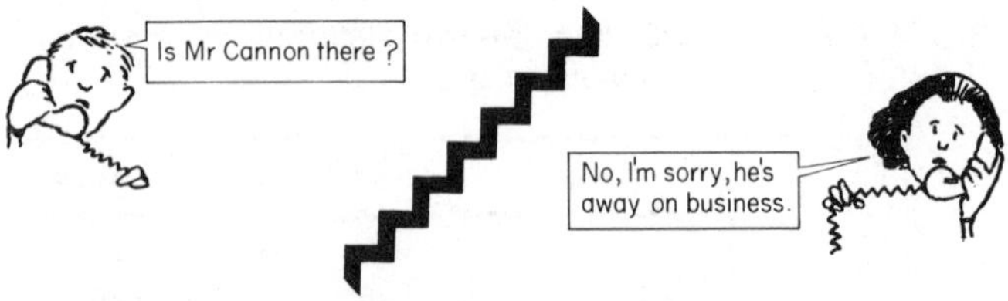

Is Mr Cannon there ?
No, I'm sorry, he's away on business.

(ii) *Keep* ***away****! This animal is dangerous.*
(iii) *I live thirty miles* ***away****.* [See DISTANCE]

2 Motion: ***away (from)*** = the opposite of 'towards here' or 'towards there'.

E.g. (i) *The dog was afraid, and ran **away**.*
(ii) *Please go **away**. I'm busy.*

3 ***Away from*** (preposition) means the opposite of **at** or **towards**.

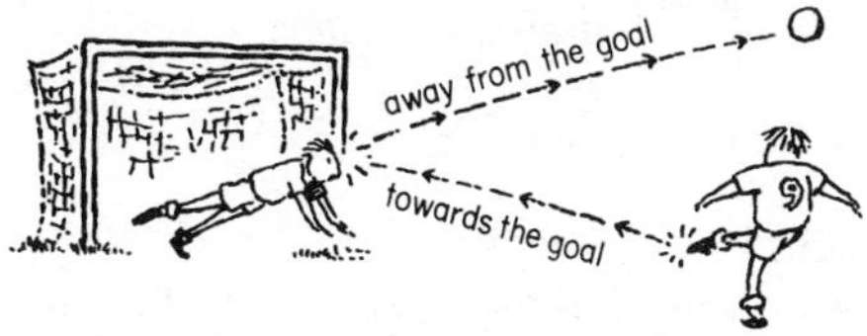

E.g. *He kicked the ball **towards** the goalkeeper, who fortunately headed it **away from** the goal.*

---

bad, **worse, worst** /bæd/ /wɜːʳs/ /wɜːʳst/ (*adjective*)
badly, **worse, worst** /ˈbædlɪ/ /wɜːʳs/ /wɜːʳst/ (*adverb*)

► ***Bad*** is an ADJECTIVE and ***badly*** is an ADVERB.
► ***Bad*** is the opposite of GOOD.
► ***Badly*** is the opposite of WELL.
► Both ***bad*** and ***badly*** have the irregular forms ***worse*** as COMPARATIVE and ***worst*** as SUPERLATIVE.

1 ***Bad* (adjective)**

E.g. *The **bad** weather stopped our football game.*
*Smoking is **bad** for your health.*
*'How was the game?' 'Not **bad**.'*

1a Comparative and superlative:

E.g. *The weather this winter is **worse** than it was last year.*
*Sugar is **the worst** food for your teeth.*

1b ***Bad at:***
Bad at means 'not able to do it well'. It is the opposite of ***good at***.

E.g. *I'm **bad at** tennis. I always lose.*

2 ***Badly* (adverb of MANNER)**

E.g. *I play football very **badly**, but I play tennis quite **well**.*

2a Comparative and superlative:

E.g. *I play football* ***worse*** *than I play tennis.*
In prison, it seemed that the ***worse*** *you behaved, the* ***worse*** *they treated you.*
In times of trouble, old people often suffer ***(the) worst***.

3 ***Bad*** and ***badly*** do not mean 'ill'. There's a difference between: *The child looks* ***ill*** (= 'in bad health') and *The future looks* ***bad*** (= 'unpleasant'). When ***well*** is an adjective, its opposite is ***ill*** (= 'in bad health').

E.g. *James is feeling* {***well*** / ***ill***} *after his operation.*

(We don't say: *'He is feeling* ~~***badly***~~.)

4 ***Badly*** **(adverb of DEGREE)**
As an adverb of degree, ***badly*** means 'very much', and it is used before certain verbs like ***want***, ***need***, and certain participles like ***hurt***, ***injured***, ***wounded***.

E.g. *Some of the soldiers were* ***badly*** *injured.*
This car is so dirty: it ***badly*** *needs a wash.*

NOTE: As a DEGREE adverb, ***badly*** does not have the comparative and superlative forms ***worse*** and ***worst***.

---

basic form [See VERB]

The basic form of the verb is sometimes called the 'base' form. It is the form of the verb which has no ending or change of vowel.

E.g. *take, bring, kill*

The basic form is the verb form you find in a dictionary.

---

be /bi:/ (weak form /bɪ/) (*verb*)

► The verb ***be*** is the most common and most IRREGULAR VERB in English.

1 **Forms of the verb *be***
Be has 8 different forms:

BASIC FORM	
be	used as the INFINITIVE, the IMPERATIVE and the SUBJUNCTIVE
PRESENT forms	
am /æm/, /m/*	with ***I*** as subject
are /ɑːʳ/, /əːʳ/*	with ***we***, ***you***, ***they***, or PLURAL noun phrase as subject
is /ɪz/	with ***he***, ***she***, ***it***, or SINGULAR noun phrase as subject
PAST forms	
was /wɒz/, /wəz/*	with ***I***, ***he***, ***she***, ***it***, or singular noun phrase as subject
were* /wɜːʳ/, /wəʳ/	with ***we***, ***you***, ***they***, or plural noun phrase as subject
PARTICIPLES	
being /biːɪŋ/	-ing participle [see -ING / -ING FORM]
been /biːn/, /bɪn/*	PAST PARTICIPLE

*The second pronunciation is a weak form.
** ***Were*** can be used with singular subject for 'unreal' meaning [see WERE 2].
E.g. *If Cleopatra **were** alive today . . .*

1a Examples:
Basic form.

E.g. *I will **be** here at ten.*
(IMPERATIVE:) *Please **be** quick.*
(SUBJUNCTIVE:) *God **be** with you.*

Present forms.

E.g. ***I am** ready to help you now.*
***It is** late. **She is** ready, but **he is** not.*
***You are** ready, **they are** ready, and **we are** too.*

Past forms.

E.g. ***It was** late. **I was** asleep, but **Ann was** still up.*
***We were** ready before **they were**. But where **were you**?*

-ing participle.

E.g. *The road **is being** widened.*

PAST PARTICIPLE.

E.g. *Where **have** you **been**? **I've been** looking for you.*

1b There are contractions of the Present Tense forms of ***be*** particularly in <speech>:

I am	→ ***I'm*** /aɪm/	E.g.	***I'm*** *sorry I'm late.*
you are	→ ***you're*** /jɔːʳ/	E.g.	*Thanks,* ***you're*** *very kind.*
they are	→ ***they're*** /ðeəʳ/	E.g.	***They're*** *changing the law.*
he is	→ ***he's*** /hiːz/	E.g.	*Where's Dan?* ***He's*** *in bed.*
she is	→ ***she's*** /ʃiːz/	E.g.	***She's*** *writing a letter.*
it is	→ ***it's*** /ɪts/	E.g.	*Look –* ***it's*** *snowing.*

NOTE (i): Contractions are not used at the end of a clause or sentence.
E.g. *I'm older than* ***she is***. not: *I'm older than* ~~*she's*~~.

NOTE (ii): The contraction ***'s*** for ***is*** is used with many different types of subject.
E.g. ***That's*** *my umbrella.* ***There's*** *the bus.* ***The school's*** *closed.*

1c All the present and past forms of ***be***, except ***am****, have negative contractions ending in ***-n't***:

E.g.	is not	→ ***isn't*** /ˈɪzn̩t/	E.g.	*This pen* ***isn't*** *mine.*
	are not	→ ***aren't*** /ɑːʳnt/	E.g.	***Aren't*** *you coming?*
	was not	→ ***wasn't*** /wɒzn̩t/	E.g.	*Jim* ***wasn't*** *at home.*
	were not	→ ***weren't*** /wɜːʳnt/	E.g.	*We* ***weren't*** *noticed.*

* In questions in <informal speech>, ***aren't*** <especially G.B.> is used as a contraction for ***am not***. E.g. ***Aren't I*** *lucky?*

2 Structures with *be*

2a Main verb ***be***:
Be is a MAIN VERB when it is followed by an adjective, a numeral, a noun phrase, or a prepositional phrase (its COMPLEMENT):

subject	+ be	+ complement	
I	***'m***	*hungry.*	(adjective)
My son	***is***	*eighteen.*	(numeral)
Mrs King	*has* ***been***	*a good friend.*	(noun phrase)
We	***'re***	*from Japan.*	(prepositional phrase)

Here ***be*** is called a LINKING VERB: it links the subject with a complement which describes it.

NOTE: Other structures with ***be*** as a main verb are those beginning with IT and THERE.
E.g. ***It's*** *Oscar that she likes best.*
There's *someone at the door.*
[See IT-PATTERNS 2 and THERE IS / THERE ARE.]

2b Auxiliary verb **be**:
Be is an AUXILIARY VERB when it is followed by a PARTICIPLE.
(i) ***be*** + -ing form = PROGRESSIVE:

subject	+ be	+ Verb -ing	. . .
Mr. Joyce	***is***	*waiting.*	
My sister	***'s***	*studying*	*physics.*
They	*will* ***be***	*leaving*	*tomorrow.*

This is the progressive pattern of the verb phrase, and indicates 'temporary' action, or action 'in progress'. [See –ING / –ING FORM.]

(ii) ***be*** + past participle = PASSIVE:

subject	+ be	+ past participle	. . .
The house	***is***	*surrounded*	*by trees.*
Two apples	*have* ***been***	*eaten.*	
He	***'s***	*considered*	*a great man.*

3 **Idioms**
Be to [see FUTURE 5b, WERE], BE ABLE TO, ***be about to*** [see FUTURE 5c], ***be bound to***, (BE) GOING TO [see FUTURE], ***be sure to***.

---

because /bɪˈkɒz/ (weak form /bɪˈkəz/) (*subordinating conjunction*)

because of /bɪˈkɒzəv/ (weak form /bɪˈkəzəv/) (*preposition*)

Because and ***because of*** introduce a reason for what is in the main part of the sentence. These are the two structures which occur with ***because***:
(i) BECAUSE + CLAUSE

E.g. *We couldn't play tennis* ***because it was raining.***

(ii) BECAUSE OF + NOUN PHRASE

E.g. *We couldn't play tennis* ***because of the rain***.

[See REASON AND CAUSE for further details and examples.]

become **becomes, became, becoming, become** /bɪˈkʌm/ (*verb*)

- ***Become*** is a LINKING VERB, like ***be*** and ***seem***.
- ***Become*** has the same forms as ***come*** (with ***be***- added).
- ***Become*** means that there is a change of state.
- ***Become*** can be followed by a NOUN PHRASE or by an ADJECTIVE (as COMPLEMENT).

E.g. *Before you **become a doctor**, you have to study for six years in a medical school.*
*He suddenly **became ill**, and died shortly afterwards.*
*Ruth and her new neighbour soon **became friends**.*

being, been

are the -ing participle (see -ING / -ING FORM] and the PAST PARTICIPLE forms of the verb ***be*** [See BE].

before

[See AFTER AND BEFORE]

behind

[See (IN) FRONT OF AND BEHIND]

below

[See ABOVE AND BELOW]

beside /bɪˈsaɪd/ (*preposition*)

1 ***Beside*** means 'by' or 'at the side of'. It is a preposition of PLACE.

E.g. (i) *Why don't you sit* {***beside*** / ***next to***} ***me****?*
(ii) *Lord and Lady Mildew stood **beside one another** as they shook hands with the guests.*

besides /bɪˈsaɪdz/ (*preposition or adverb*)

1 ***Besides*** (preposition) means 'in addition to', 'apart from'.

E.g. ***Besides the captain and the crew***, *there were fifty passengers on the ship.*
Olga is a wonderful woman: ***besides writing books***, *she runs a farm and looks after her six children.*

2 ***Besides*** is also a linking adverb in <spoken English>. In front position, ***besides*** means 'moreover, anyway'. It adds another point to an argument.

E.g. *Moya didn't want to go out for a walk. The weather was wet and miserable.* ***Besides***, *she had a headache.*

best, better are the SUPERLATIVE and COMPARATIVE forms of GOOD and WELL.

between and ***among*** /bɪˈtwiːn/, /əˈmʌŋ/ (*prepositions*)

1 ***Between* is a preposition of PLACE and TIME**

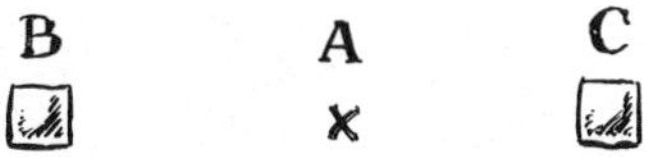

E.g. *A is* ***between*** *B and C.*

(i) Place

E.g. *The river flows* ***between*** *two mountains.*

(ii) Time

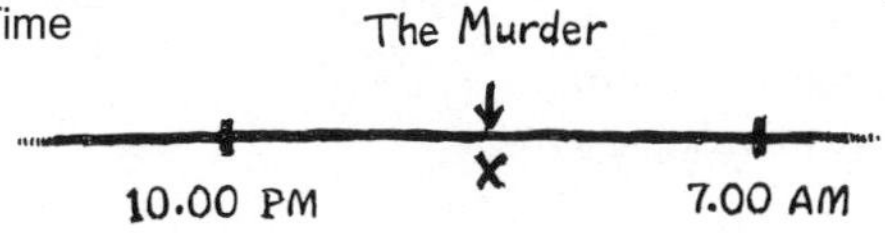

E.g. *The murder must have taken place* ***between*** *10 p.m. and 7 a.m., when everyone was asleep.*

1a In addition, ***between*** is used after words like ***difference***, ***divide***, ***choose*** which involve two people or things.

E.g.

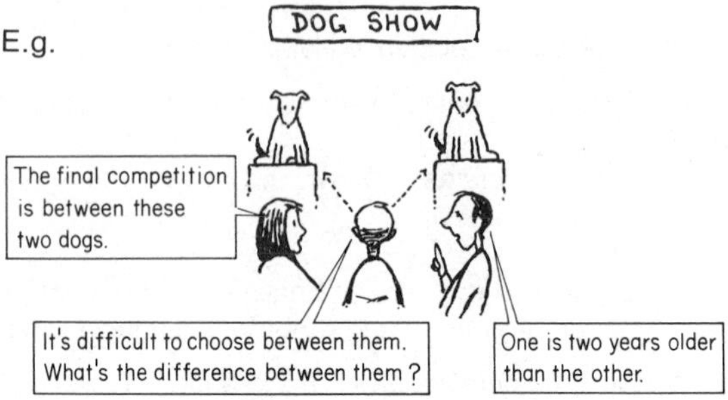

NOTE: Occasionally we use ***between*** (or ***in between***) as an adverb.
E.g. *Tall cliffs rose on both sides, with a narrow stretch of water (**in**) **between**.*

2 Choosing between *between* and *among*

2a ***Among*** is an adverb of PLACE like ***between***, but it always introduces more than two people, things, etc. For example:

*a village **between** two lakes*

means that there are two lakes only.

*a village **among** lakes*

means that there are more than two lakes.

NOTE (i): Some people consider it is not correct to use ***between*** for more than two people or things. So they will say:
E.g. *The King divided his kingdom **between** his two children.*
But: *The King divided his kingdom **among** his three children.*

NOTE (ii): ***Among*** also has a more abstract meaning, when we are talking about members of a group.
E.g. *When you are **among** friends, you can say what you like.*

NOTE (iii): ***Amongst*** is a <rarer> form of ***among***. <mainly G.B.>.

beyond /bɪˈjɒnd/ (*preposition or adverb*)

Beyond means 'on the other / far side (of something)'.

1 Preposition

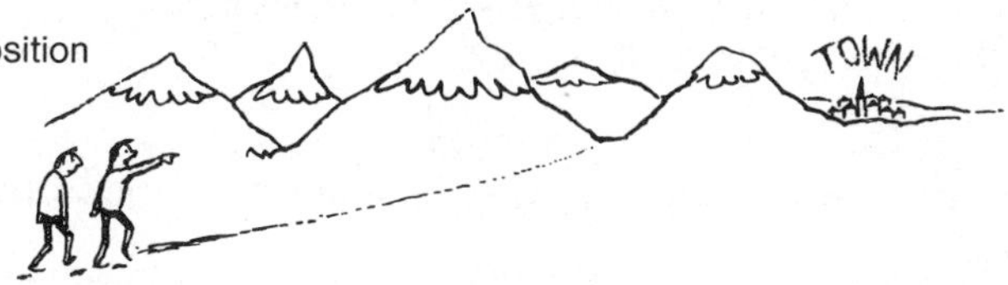

E.g. *The nearest town is **beyond** those mountains.*

NOTE: ***Beyond*** can be used in an abstract way.
E.g. *This poetry is very difficult: it is quite **beyond** me.* (= 'I can't understand it.')

2 Adverb <rare>
E.g. *The house has a beautiful view – with the fields and trees in front, and the sea **beyond**.*

a ***bit***, a ***little***, a ***lot***

[See separate entries. For ***a bit*** see A BIT / A BIT OF.
For ***a little*** see LITTLE / A LITTLE.
For ***a lot*** see (A) LOT (OF) / LOTS (OF)]

borrow ***borrows, borrowed, borrowing*** /ˈbɒrəʊ/
and **lend** ***lends, lent, lending*** /lend/ (*verbs*)

These verbs are sometimes confused. Remember: the person who has the money ***lends*** it; the person who doesn't have the money, but who wants it, ***borrows*** it.

E.g.

NOTE: ***Borrow*** and ***lend*** are used for other things, as well as money.
E.g. *Please can I **borrow** your ladder?*

both /bəʊθ/ (*determiner or pronoun*)

- ► ***Both*** always refers to two things, two people, etc.
- ► ***Both*** is very similar to ALL (which refers to more than two). Compare the positions of ***both*** (see 2 below) with the positions of ***all***.
- ► [For ***both . . . and***, see DOUBLE CONJUNCTION 1, 2.]

1 ***Both*** can be used with singular noun + ***and*** + singular noun; ***Both + of*** cannot.

E.g. ***Both*** *his* ***mother*** *and* ***father*** *. . .*
Both ~~***of***~~ *his* ***mother*** *and* ***father*** *. . .*

Both + of is followed by a plural noun phrase.

E.g. ***Both of*** *his* ***parents***.

2. Positions of *both*

2a Position 1: ***both*** + **of** + (plural) {NOUN PHRASE. / PRONOUN.}

E.g. ***both of*** *the players,* ***both of*** *these jobs*
both of *my parents,* ***both of*** *them*

2b Position 2: ***both*** + (plural) {NOUN PHRASE. / ~~PRONOUN~~.}
We can omit ***of*** before a noun phrase, but not before a personal pronoun.

E.g. ***both*** *the players,* ***both*** *these jobs*
both *my father and mother*
But not: ~~*both them*~~

Also we can omit ***the*** after ***both***.

E.g. ***both*** *(the) players,* ***both*** *(the) halves*
It will be a good match. ***Both*** {***players*** / ***sides***} *have been playing well recently.*

2c Position 3: (plural) PERSONAL PRONOUN + ***both***.
Both comes after, not before, the personal pronouns ***we***, ***us***, ***you***, ***they***, ***them***.

E.g. *Ann and Jim have similar tastes. For example,* ***they both*** *like music, poetry, and sport.*
I'd like to invite ***you both*** *to dinner next Saturday.*

2d Position 4: (plural) {NOUN PHRASE / PRONOUN} + ***both***.
When a noun phrase or pronoun referring to two people / things is SUBJECT, we can place ***both*** in middle position* [see ADVERB 3].

E.g. ***His father and mother*** *were **both** excellent cooks.*
The teams *have **both** scored one goal.*

* Middle position means that ***both*** comes after the auxiliary verb or BE as a main verb, but before other main verbs.

2e Position 5: ***both*** as PRONOUN alone.
As a pronoun, ***both*** can stand on its own. We can omit the ***of***- phrase if its meaning is known.

E.g. *This dress is cheaper, but that one is more attractive. I think I'll buy **both**.*
(= 'both of them')

---

bring and *take*

bring — ***brings, brought, bringing*** /brɪŋ/
and *take* — ***takes, took, taking, taken*** /teɪk/ (*verbs*)

► ***Bring*** and ***take*** are both IRREGULAR VERBS.
► ***Bring*** and ***take*** contrast in the same way as ***come*** and ***go*** [see COME AND GO].

1 ***Bring*** means 'make {someone / something} come' } e.g. by carrying or leading
Take means 'make {someone / something} go' }
(Come → 'towards the speaker / hearer')
(Go → 'not towards the speaker / hearer')

E.g.

Bring those books here.*
O.K. I'm coming.

Take that dog away.*
O.K. We're going.

* ***Bring*** is often followed by ***here***; ***take*** is often followed by ***away***.

2 ***Bring*** and ***take*** with two objects: [See VERB PATTERNS 11.]

E.g. *When Uncle Bill visits us at Christmas, he always* ***brings us presents*** *from the family.*
When Mrs White visits her husband in hospital, she always ***takes him*** *some fresh* ***fruit****.*

3 **Idioms**
Bring and ***take*** often occur in PHRASAL VERBS. Look these up in a dictionary: ***bring up***, ***bring about***, ***bring off***, ***bring out***, ***take up***, ***take over***, ***take off***, ***take in***.

---

but /bʌt/ (weak form /bət/) (*conjunction, preposition and adverb*)

- ***But*** is nearly always a coordinating conjunction [see COORDINATION]. (Its uses as a preposition and as an adverb are <not common>.)
- The conjunction ***but*** indicates a contrast [see CONTRAST 1] between two ideas (***but*** = 'and yet').
- [For the use of ***but*** after ***not*** (***only***), [see DOUBLE CONJUNCTION 4, 5].

1 In a sentence 'X ***but*** Y', the information in Y contrasts with the information in X.

E.g. X ⟵ Contrast ⟶ Y

Rob eats a lot,	**but**	*but never gets fat.*
We used to have a cat,	**but**	*now we have mice!*
She's still in hospital,	**but**	*she's making good progress.*

1a ***But*** can link two whole clauses, as in the examples above, but sometimes we omit the first part of the second clause.

E.g. *I like Paul,* ***but*** *(I) dislike his opinions.*
The house is old, ***but*** *(it is) very comfortable.*

1b Notice the use of ***but not*** and ***but also*** at the beginning of the second clause or clause part.

E.g. *I have been to Florence,* ***but not*** *to Rome.*
I enjoy reading novels, ***but not*** *history books.*
The government is increasing its chances of success, ***but also*** *(increasing) its chances of failure.*

1c ***But*** can come at the beginning of a sentence. In conversation, you can use it to show that what you have to say contrasts with or disagrees with what someone else has said [see AGREEING AND DISAGREEING].

E.g.

NOTE (i): ***But*** sometimes links contrasting adjectives [see CONTRAST] before a noun.
E.g. *He gave away all his money. It was a **generous but foolish** thing to do.*

NOTE (ii): ***But*** as a preposition means 'except, apart from'.
E.g. *We've looked everywhere **but** in the kitchen.*
*Eat snails? I'll do anything **but** that!*

NOTE (iii): ***But*** as an adverb is <rare>. It means 'just, only'.
E.g. *She was **but** a baby when she first appeared on the stage.*
*We can **but** try.* ('Things are not hopeless.')
*You can't **but** admire him.* ('You cannot help it.')

by /baɪ/ (*preposition or adverb*)

► There are four important uses of ***by***: PLACE; MEANS; after a PASSIVE; and TIME.

1 *By* as a word indicating place

By (preposition) referring to position means 'near' or 'beside' or 'next to'.

E.g.

1a With a verb of MOTION (OR MOVEMENT), ***by*** has the same meaning as ***past***.

E.g. (i) *We **drove by** your house.*
(ii) *The bus was **going by** the supermarket as I came out.*

1b ***By*** as an ADVERB also has the same meaning as ***past***. It usually follows the verb, and does not come before a noun phrase.

E.g. *Thousands of people were lining the street, hoping to see the royal visitors **go by**.*

2 ***By* as a PREPOSITION indicating *means*, *method* (= way of doing something)**

E.g. *The thief must have left the building **by the back door**.*
(= 'through', 'by way of')
*You start the car **by turning this key**.*
*This coal is mined **by a totally new method**.*

2a Notice that ***by*** can be followed by Verb-ing.

E.g.

2b In talking of means of transport in general, we use ***by*** + noun without ***a*** or ***the*** [see ZERO ARTICLE].

E.g. *Fred goes to work* { ***by bus.*** / ***by car.*** / ***by train.*** } *I came home* { ***by bicycle.*** / ***by air.*** / ***by boat.*** }

NOTE: But we say ***on foot*** and ***on horseback***. We can also say:
Fred goes to work { ***in his car***. (etc.) [See IN 1] / ***on the bus***. (etc.) [See (MEANS OF) TRANSPORT] }

3 ***By* following a PASSIVE verb**
In a passive clause, the doer of the action is not the subject, but can be added after ***by***.

E.g. *This city was built* ***by the Turks***. (i.e. 'The Turks built this city.')
The letter should be signed ***by the president***.

3a Past participle + ***by*** + noun phrase.

E.g. *a city* ***built by*** *the Turks* or:
a story ***written by*** *Tolstoy*

Notice that we can also say:

a story **by** *Tolstoy, a painting* **by** *Monet*
a play **by** *Shakespeare, a song* **by** *Schubert*

i.e. we can omit the verb ***written***, etc. [For further details, see PASSIVE 3.]

4 ***By* as a preposition indicating TIME**
By as a time preposition means 'on or before'.

E.g. *The photographs will be ready* ***by Friday***.
(= 'on or before Friday')
Please deliver the new motorcycle ***by next week***.
(= 'next week or before')
By the end of the second year*, the students have learned most of the basic grammar.*
By the end of the third year*, the students are using English quite well in conversation.*

5 **Idioms**
Look up these idioms in a dictionary: ***by hand***, ***by now***, ***by all means***, ***by any means***, ***by no means***, ***by day***, ***by night***.

NOTE: ***by oneself*** = 'alone'.

---

the **calendar** [See DATES, TIME]

---

can /kæn/ (weak form /kən/) is a MODAL AUXILIARY verb.

► **Can** has two negative forms:
cannot /ˈkænɒt/, /kæˈnɒt/, /kəˈnɒt/ <more formal>.
can't /kɑːnt ‖ kæːnt/ <normally used in speech>.

► **Can** goes before another verb in the BASIC FORM.

E.g. **can** *be*, **can** *have*, **can** *see*, etc.

► **Can** is never followed by ***to***.

► **Can** has three main uses:
– ability. [Compare (BE) ABLE TO.]
– possibility. [Compare MAY 2.]
– permission. [Compare MAY 3.]

1 Forms of *can*

positive statement

I		*be . . .*
you		*have . . .*
we	**can**	*see . . .*
she		*go . . .*
noun phrase		*find . . .*
etc.		etc.

negative statement

I		*be . . .*
you		*have . . .*
we	**can't**	*see . . .*
she	**cannot**	*go . . .*
noun phrase		*find . . .*
etc.		etc.

question

	I	*be . . .*	
	you	*have . . .*	
Can	*we*	*see . . .*	?
	she	*go . . .*	
	noun phrase	*find . . .*	
	etc.	etc.	

negative question

	I		*be . . .*	
	you		*have . . .*	
Can't	*we*		*see . . .*	?
Can	*she*	**not**	*go . . .*	
	noun phrase		*find . . .*	
	etc.		etc.	

NOTE: Since ***can*** has no INFINITIVE or PARTICIPLE forms, we often use (BE) ABLE TO instead of ***can*** when these forms are needed, e.g. to refer to a future possibility after WILL.
E.g. *We **can't** finish the job this week, but we will **be able to** finish it next week.*

2 *Can* = ability

2a ***Can*** means (a) 'be (physically) able to'.

E.g. *I **can** climb that mountain in five hours.*

(b) 'know how to'.

E.g. (i) ***Can*** *you ride a bicycle?*
(ii)

Young Jasmin is very clever. She can play the violin, she can speak three languages, and she can beat her father at chess.
Really! Is there anything she can't do?

2b ***Can't*** and ***cannot*** mean the opposite of ***can***, i.e. they indicate inability to do something.

E.g. *Grandpa is getting old: he* ***can't*** *hear very well, and he* ***can't*** *see without his glasses.*
Tim ***can't*** *spell very well yet.*

3 ***Can*** = **POSSIBILITY**

3a ***Can*** means 'it is possible'.

E.g. *The weather* ***can*** *be very hot in Delhi.*
(i.e. 'Very hot weather is possible . . .')
If it rains, we ***can*** *hold the party indoors.*
(i.e. 'it will be possible for us to hold the party indoors.')

3b ***Can't*** (or ***cannot***) means 'it is impossible'.

E.g. *People* ***can't*** *live on nothing.*
She lives in Paris but she speaks with a German accent. She ***can't*** *be French – she must be German.* *

*[For this meaning of ***can't***, compare MUST 2d, 2e.]
NOTE: ***Can't*** in questions often expresses annoyance. E.g. Someone might say ***Can't you*** *be quiet?* to a noisy person, or ***Can't you*** *drive straight?* to a bad driver.

3c After ***can*** (= 'possible') the PASSIVE is quite <common>.

E.g. *These days, goods* ***can be sent*** *all over the world by air.*
Many plants ***can be grown*** *easily indoors.*

3d Use the PERFECT and PROGRESSIVE forms after the negative ***can't*** (but not after ***can***).
(i) Perfect:
CAN'T + HAVE + PAST PARTICIPLE

E.g. *They* ***can't have eaten*** *all that food.*

(ii) Progressive:
CAN'T + BE + Verb-ing

E.g. *Surely he* ***can't be working*** *at this time of the night.*

4 ***Can*** = **PERMISSION**

4a ***Can*** means 'be {allowed / permitted} to'.

E.g. *You* **can** *borrow this radio until tomorrow.*
(= 'You are allowed to . . .')
The students **can** *live at the college during the vacation, if they wish.*
Can *I pay by* {*check* <U.S.> / *cheque* <G.B.>}, *please?*
When **can** *we start work?*
(***can*** *we* = 'are we allowed to')

It is possible for MAY to replace ***can*** in these sentences, but ***may*** is more <formal or polite>.

4b The negative forms ***can't*** and ***cannot*** mean the opposite of ***can***, i.e. that something is forbidden or not allowed.

E.g. (i) *I'm sorry, you* **can't** *smoke in the hospital.*

(ii) *Visitors* **cannot** *fish on this side of the river.*

(iii) *You* **can't** *go abroad without a passport.*

5 After some verbs, ***can*** is often used to refer to the immediate state of being able to do something. These verbs are:
(i) Verbs like ***see***, ***hear***, and ***smell*** [see PERCEPTION VERBS].

E.g. *I* ***can smell*** *something burning.*
Can *you* ***hear*** *what he's saying?*

(ii) Verbs of mental state like ***remember***, ***imagine***.

E.g. *I* ***can't imagine*** *what they're doing.*
I ***can remember*** *the first day I went to school.*

6 **Special uses of *can***
Can is used in REQUESTS [see also COULD AND MIGHT].

E.g. ***Can** you open the door, please?*

Can is also used in OFFERS.

E.g. ***Can** I help you?*

cardinal numbers [See NUMBERS]

case

Case is a grammatical term we use for the different forms a word takes according to its role or position in a sentence. For example, the PERSONAL PRONOUNS have case forms in English: ***he*** (= SUBJECT form), ***him*** (= OBJECT form), ***his*** (= POSSESSIVE form). In some grammar books these are called 'subjective case', 'objective case', and 'genitive (or possessive) case'. Case forms are not very important in English, so we avoid the word 'case' in this book.

cause [See REASON AND CAUSE]

certain /ˈsɜːʳtn̩/ (*adjective or determiner*)
and *sure* /ʃʊəʳ/ or /ʃɔːʳ/ (*adjective or adverb*)

1 ***Certain*** and ***sure*** (adjectives) both mean 'there is no doubt'.

E.g. (i) *The President feels {**certain** / **sure**} that he will win the next election.*
*But many people think he is {**certain** / **sure**} to lose.*
(ii) *'All the tickets have been sold.' 'Are you {**certain** / **sure**} (of that)?'*

[For sentence patterns with ***certain*** and ***sure***, see ADJECTIVE PATTERNS 2a, 3, and IT-PATTERNS 1.]

2 ***Certain*** (determiner) is used in these patterns:
{***A certain*** + singular countable noun.
{***Certain*** + plural noun.

A certain + singular = a stronger form of ***a*** or ***an*** [see A OR AN].
Certain + plural = a stronger form of ***some*** [see SOME AND ANY].

Certain = 'particular', or (roughly) 'known but not named'.

E.g. *If you want to be slim, you should try to lose* ***a certain amount*** *of weight every week.*
The club meets on ***certain days*** *every month.*

3 ***Sure*** (adverb), in <U.S. speech>, means 'certainly'. It is used in replies, and in adding emphasis to STATEMENTS.

E.g. *'Can you lend me a few dollars?'* ***'Sure.'***
'Jill sings well, doesn't she?' 'Yes, she ***sure*** *does.'*

---

certainly /ˈsɜːʳtn̩lɪ/ (*adverb of comment and attitude*)

Certainly means 'without doubt', 'of course'.

E.g. *She will* ***certainly*** *be on time: she's always punctual.*

Certainly appears on its own in replies; it is an emphatic form of ***yes***.

E.g. *'Will you help me move these bags?'* ***'Certainly.'***

The negative ***certainly not*** expresses strong disagreement or refusal.

E.g. *'Could I invite you and your wife to dinner?'* ***'Certainly not!*** *It's our turn to invite you!'*

[See AGREEING AND DISAGREEING, REPLIES.]

---

clause

► Clauses are the main structures of which SENTENCES are built.
► A sentence contains at least one MAIN CLAUSE. It may also contain SUBORDINATE CLAUSES.

1 **Clause structure**
A clause itself contains one or more clause elements:

element	examples	usual position and form
CONJUNCTION:	***and***, ***or***, ***if***, ***when***	a word which begins the clause (but conjunctions are not always needed)
SUBJECT:	***she***, ***it***, ***something***, ***the car***	a pronoun or noun phrase which comes before the verb phrase
VERB PHRASE:	***likes***, ***is living***, ***has gone***	the central part of the clause, containing one or more verbs
OBJECT: (direct or indirect)	***the glass***, ***Ann***, ***people***, ***him***	a pronoun or noun phrase which follows the verb phrase
COMPLEMENT:	***very cold***, ***bad***, ***a nurse***, ***this***	a pronoun, noun phrase, adjective, or adjective phrase which follows the verb phrase and sometimes follows an object
ADVERBIAL	***away***, ***well***, ***at home***, ***last night***	an adverb, adverb phrase, prepositional phrase, or noun phrase which often comes after the other elements in the clause

1a Examples of clauses with:–

(i) Two elements:

subject	verb phrase
Henry	*arrived.*

subject	verb phrase
The weather	*has changed.*

(ii) Three elements:

subject	verb phrase	object	complement	adverbial
My mother	*likes*	*dogs.*		
Sandra	*is*		*very angry.*	
They	*are living*			*not far from here.*

(iii) Four elements:

subject	verb phrase	indirect object	direct object	complement	adverbial
Mary	*gave*	*Sandra*	*a glass.*		
Money	*makes*		*people*	*greedy.*	
Peter	*sent*		*us all*		*home.*

NOTE: Clauses can have many different elements. For example, a clause can contain several adverbials [see ADVERBIAL 1c].

2 Main clauses and subordinate clauses

2a One clause may be part of another clause. For example, one clause may be an object or an adverbial in another clause:

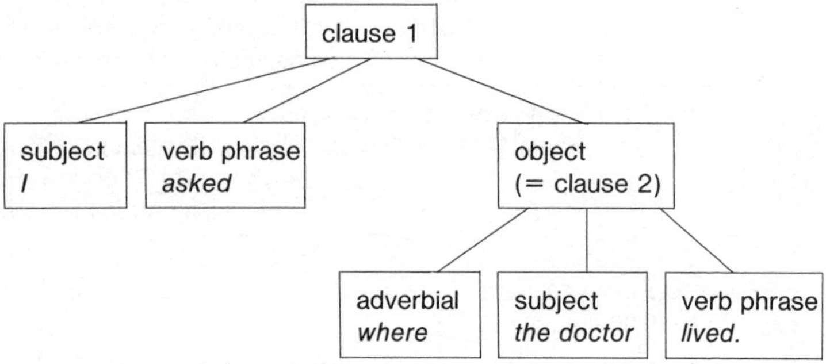

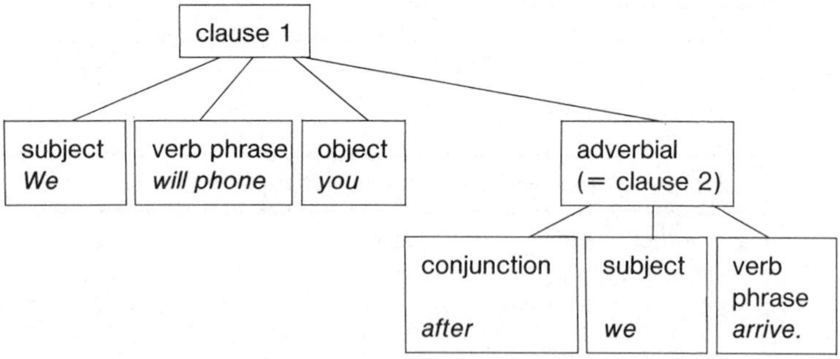

The clause (clause 1) which contains another clause is called a MAIN CLAUSE; the clause (clause 2) which is part of the main clause is called a SUBORDINATE CLAUSE.

3 Types of clause

3a Main clauses:
Main clauses are divided into these types:

types	examples	
STATEMENTS:	*We are lucky.*	*Eric's wife will be coming.*
QUESTIONS:	*How are you?*	*Will Eric's wife be coming?*
IMPERATIVES:	*Don't be silly.*	*Put your books away, please.*
EXCLAMATIONS:	*I'm so hungry!*	*What a surprise you gave me!*

3b Subordinate clauses:
Subordinate clauses are classified by the role they have in the main clause. [For further details, see ADVERBIAL CLAUSE, COMMENT CLAUSE, COMPARATIVE CLAUSE, NOUN CLAUSE, RELATIVE CLAUSE.]

3c But also, subordinate clauses are classified by the kind of verb phrase they contain. [For further details, see FINITE, INFINITIVE CLAUSE, PARTICIPLE CLAUSE, VERBLESS CLAUSE.]

collective noun

Collective nouns are called GROUP NOUNS in this book.

come and go

come /kʌm/ ***comes, came, coming, come***
and ***go*** /gəʊ/ ***goes, went, going,*** { ***gone*** /gɒn/ / ***been*** /bi:n/ } (*verbs*)

► ***Come*** and ***go*** are verbs of opposite meaning:

Come = move to the place where the speaker or hearer is.

Go = move to a place away from the speaker or hearer.

► ***Come*** and ***go*** do not have an OBJECT. But they are related to the TRANSITIVE VERBS ***bring*** and ***take*** [see BRING AND TAKE].

► ***Come*** and ***go*** are IRREGULAR VERBS. Notice that ***go*** has two different PAST PARTICIPLE forms, ***been*** and ***gone*** [see 3 below].

1 **_Come_** = 'to me, with me, or to where I'm imagining myself to be'.
_Go_ = 'away from me or from where I'm imagining myself to be'.
[See TO 1.]

E.g. (i) *'I'm **going** to the hospital this afternoon. Would you like to **come** with me?'*

(ii) *'Hello, Roy. Are you **coming** to the party tomorrow?'* (i.e. 'I'm going to be there')

(iii)

1a Look at the difference between these two newspaper reports:

The New York Times	**_The London Times_**
*This summer more American visitors **went** to Europe for a vacation than ever before.*	*This summer more American visitors **came** to Europe for a holiday than ever before.*

2 Notice that we use ***come*** for movement both towards the speaker (or writer) and towards the hearer (or reader).

E.g. *'Let's meet tomorrow.' 'Okay. Shall I **come** to your house, or will you **come** to mine?' 'I'll **come** to yours, if you prefer.'*

3 ***Gone* and *been***
Gone is the normal past participle of ***go***, in the sense 'go away', 'leave a place'.
Been is the past participle when it means 'gone away and returned'.

E.g. *'Where has your son **gone**?' 'He's **gone** to China, and he's coming back next month.'*
*'Where has your son **been**?' 'He's **been** to China. He came back last week.'*

4 ***Come*** and ***go*** are usually INTRANSITIVE VERBS – they have no object. But sometimes they are followed by an adjective [i.e. they are LINKING VERBS similar to ***become***].

E.g. *Unfortunately, fairy stories rarely **come true**.* *
*In hot weather, meat **goes bad** * and milk **goes sour** * quickly – so be careful.*

* Notice that ***come*** + adjective usually has a 'good' meaning, and that ***go*** + adjective usually has a 'bad' meaning.

5 ***Come*** and ***go*** can both be followed by ***and*** + Verb: this is a common pattern in <spoken> English.

E.g. *Why don't you **come and see** us next weekend?*
*I'll **go and fetch** the car.*

The meaning of this pattern is 'come to / go to + Verb'. For example, ***come and see*** means 'come to see'.

6 A similar pattern with both ***come*** and ***go*** is ***come*** / ***go*** + Verb-***ing***.

E.g. *My husband **goes fishing** every week.*
*Would you like to **come swimming** with us?*

In this pattern, Verb-ing describes some activity.

E.g. *Goodbye! I'm going shopping / swimming / dancing / climbing / etc.*

7 **Idioms**
Be going to refers to the future [see (BE) GOING TO].
Come from refers to a person's place of origin.

E.g. *'Where do you **come from**?' 'I **come from** Germany'.*
(= 'I am German')

Use ***come from*** to tell people about your home town, your home country, etc.

7a Many common PHRASAL VERBS and PREPOSITIONAL VERBS begin with ***come*** or ***go***. You can look these up in a dictionary: ***come along***, ***come off***, ***come on***, ***come up with***, ***go away***, ***go in for***, ***go on***, ***go through***, ***go without***.

---

comma (,) [See also PUNCTUATION]

► In writing, use a comma to divide a long sentence into smaller parts.
► Often you have a choice of using the comma or not. i.e., it is optional. If in doubt, leave it out! But if it helps to make your meaning clear, put it in.

1 **Coordination** [see COORDINATION]

$$\text{(A)}\quad Y\left\{\begin{matrix}\textbf{\textit{and}}\\ \textbf{\textit{or}}\\ \textbf{\textit{but}}\end{matrix}\right\}Z \qquad\qquad \text{(B)}\quad X,\ Y,\left\{\begin{matrix}\textbf{\textit{and}}\\ \textbf{\textit{or}}\\ \textbf{\textit{but}}\end{matrix}\right\}Z$$

1a The comma is optional before a CONJUNCTION (AND, OR, BUT). It is usual when Y and Z are clauses.

E.g. *Wendy works hard* **,** ***but*** *her sister is lazy.*

It is not usual when Y and Z are words or phrases.

E.g. *buses* ***and*** *trains*
by bus ***or*** *by train*

1b But when there is a list of three or more items, e.g. '(. . .) X , Y , or Z' we can put a comma between each pair of items.

E.g. *bananas* **,** *melons* **,** *grapes* **,** *apples* **,** *oranges* **,** *and pears* *
* [The comma between the last two items is optional. For further details, see COORDINATION 1.]

2 **Subordination** [See SUBORDINATE CLAUSE]
Place a comma between an ADVERBIAL CLAUSE and the MAIN CLAUSE, especially when the adverbial clause is at the beginning, or seems to be separated from the main clause in meaning.

E.g. *When the weather is hot* **,** *I like to sit in the sun.*
We can visit the museum **,** *if it's still open.*

2a If a subordinate (adverbial) clause is in the middle of the main clause, place a comma both before and after it.

E.g. *The date of Easter* **,** ***as is well known*** **,** *changes from year to year.*

2b But do not place a comma after a clause when it is subject, or before a clause as object or complement. Notice that both commas in the first example below would be wrong.

E.g. ***What he said ,*** *does not prove* ***, (that)*** *he's the murderer.* [Wrong]
The judge's opinion was ***that he was guilty***. [Right]

Do not use a comma after a clause which restricts or limits the subject (a RESTRICTIVE RELATIVE CLAUSE).

E.g. *The person* ***who stole the car ,*** *was never found.* [Wrong]

3 **Other adverbials**
Like adverbial clauses, adverbial words and phrases are separated by commas from the rest of the sentence if they seem to be separated in meaning. E.g. phrases like ***however***, ***nevertheless***, ***in my opinion***.

E.g. ***In my opinion ,*** *he was guilty.*
The judge's opinion , ***however ,*** *was that he was innocent.*

4 **In direct speech sentences.**
(a) Place a comma between ***He said*** *(etc.)* and the beginning of direct speech.

E.g. *She said (hastily) ,* *'That's none of your business.'*

(b) Place a comma between the end of direct speech and ***he said*** *(etc.)*.

E.g. *'Any progress is better than none ,' said Pete.*

provided there is no question mark (***?***) or exclamation mark (***!***) as in, for example:
'Any progress?' she asked.

(c) Place a comma before and after ***he said,*** etc, in the middle of direct speech.

E.g. *'In my view ,'* *said the judge ,* *'he is innocent.'*

---

command [See IMPERATIVE, INDIRECT COMMAND]

---

comment clause

A comment clause is a small CLAUSE which adds a comment to what is said in the MAIN CLAUSE or in the rest of the sentence.

E.g. *Jill's husband is a lawyer,* ***I believe.***
And the photograph, ***you see****, helped us to find the thief.*
As you know*, I've always wanted to visit Greece.*

The comment clause can occur in front, end, and middle positions in the main clause.

common noun

- ► Common nouns are the opposite of proper nouns [see NAMES].
- ► Common nouns are words for a kind of person, thing, substance, etc.

E.g. *friend, town, work, tiger*

Unlike proper nouns, common nouns generally begin with a small letter, and can have ***the*** in front of them.

E.g. *the friend, the town, the work, the tiger*

[Look up these classes of common noun for further information: COUNTABLE AND UNCOUNTABLE NOUNS, CONCRETE NOUN, ABSTRACT NOUN, GROUP NOUN.]

comparative

► The comparative of a word is the form we use when we compare two things (or groups of things). [For further details, see COMPARISON, -ER / -EST, MORE / (THE) MOST, SUPERLATIVE.]

1 The easiest rule for the comparative form is:
(I) Add the ending ***-er*** to one-syllable words and to two syllable words ending in ***-y***, e.g. *fast ~ fast**er**, early ~ earl**ier****.

*Words ending in ***-y*** change ***-y*** to ***-i-*** before adding ***-er***. With other words, other changes take place [see SPELLING 4].

(II) Put ***more*** (adverb of degree) in front of longer words, e.g. *difficult ~ **more** difficult*.

NOTE (i): Sometimes this general rule is broken: e.g., people will say ***more*** *tired* or *gent**le**r*. Exceptions like these are quite rare. [See -ER / -EST 1c.]

NOTE (ii): There are also some irregular comparative words.
E.g. *good ~ **better*** [See -ER / EST 2, 3c, 4.]

2 **Comparative of adjectives**
Comparisons involve (at least) two people or two things. We use ***than*** before the second part of the comparison:

X is adjective+***-er*** ***than*** Y

E.g. *Peter is tall**er than*** { *Jim.* / *the other boys in his class.* }

or
X is ***more*** + adjective ***than*** Y

E.g. *Mary is **more** beautiful **than** Sally.*

3 Short adjectives have other words as their opposites (contrast ***younger*** with ***older***).

E.g. *Mary looks **younger** than my sister. = My sister looks **older** than Mary.*

But especially with longer adjectives, we can use ***more*** and ***less*** to show the opposite.

E.g. *This bucket is **more** useful than that one. = That bucket is **less** useful than this one.*

4 **Comparative of adverbs**
The regular comparative form of adverbs is:
more + adjective + ***-ly*** or: ***less*** + adjective + ***-ly***:

E.g. *He drives* {***more** dangerous**ly*** / ***less** careful**ly***} *than a racing driver.*

4a But a few words, such as ***easy***, ***fast***, ***hard***, ***early***, ***late***, ***high***, ***low***, ***loud***, have the same comparative form for both adjective and adverb.

E.g. (i) *A racehorse can run **faster*** (adverb) *than a man.*
(ii) *This car is **faster*** (adjective) *than that one.*

NOTE: [See -ER / -EST 3c] for irregular comparative adverbs (e.g. ***well*** ~ ***better***) and for other kinds of comparative word.

5 **Leaving out *than***
Comparative words can be used without ***than . . .*** when we know what is being compared.

E.g. (i) *'Men have greater strength than women.' 'Yes, but women live **longer**.'* ('longer than men')
(ii) *'Air travel is becoming **more** popular.'* ('more popular than it used to be')
*'True, but I wish it was **cheaper**.'* ('cheaper than it is')

6 Repeating the comparative

To express the idea of continuing change we use these patterns:
X-***er*** and X-***er*** or: ***more*** and ***more*** X

E.g. (i)

Our sales figures are getting better and better.

(ii) *His visits are growing* ***more*** *and* ***more*** *frequent.* = *He visits us* ***more*** *and* ***more*** *often.*

7 Adverbs of degree such as MUCH, ***(a) little*** [see LITTLE / A LITTLE], ***any*** [see SOME AND ANY], NO, ***somewhat***, can make a comparative word stronger or weaker.

E.g. *This coat is* { ***much*** / ***a lot**** / ***somewhat*** / ***a little*** / ***no*** } ***cheaper*** *than that one.*

This coat isn't ***any cheaper*** *than that one.*

* ***A lot*** is <informal>.

---

comparative clause

- A comparative clause is a kind of SUBORDINATE CLAUSE.
- There are two kinds of comparative clause:
  (I) Clauses beginning with AS (= ***as***-clauses). These describe an equal comparison.
  (II) Clauses beginning with THAN (= ***than***-clauses). These describe an unequal comparison. [See COMPARISON.]

1 This example illustrates the general idea of equal and unequal comparison:

E.g. (I) *The TV set costs £100.*
The camera costs £100.
} *So, the camera costs* ***as much as the TV set does****.* (Equal comparison)

(II) *The TV set costs £100.*
The camera costs £120.
} *So, the camera costs* ***more than the TV set does****.* (Unequal comparison)

2 ***As*-clauses follow these patterns:**

2a AS + . . . + AS + CLAUSE [See AS 1]

E.g. *They brought* ***as*** *much food* ***as they could carry***.

2b NOT AS / SO + . . . + AS + CLAUSE [See AS 1, SO 1]

E.g. *The vegetables are* ***not as*** / ***so*** *cheap* ***as they were last week***.
(= 'they are more expensive')

2c THE SAME + (. . . +) AS + CLAUSE [See (THE) SAME 3]

E.g. *She's wearing* ***the same*** *dress* ***as her sister wore last year***.

2d SUCH + . . . + AS + CLAUSE [See SUCH 1b]

E.g. *I've never dreamed of* ***such*** *a wonderful job* ***as they offered me last week***.

3 ***Than*-clauses follow this pattern:**
COMPARATIVE WORD + (. . . +) THAN + CLAUSE
[For comparative words, see COMPARATIVE.]
The comparative word can be (i) a word ending in ***-er*** [see -ER / -EST];
(ii) ***more*** [see MORE / (THE) MOST]; (iii) ***less*** [see LESS / (THE) LEAST];
(iv) ***worse*** [see WORSE / (THE) WORST].

E.g. (i) *The concert lasted* ***longer than we expected***.
(ii) *The President is* ***more nervous than he looks***.

4 **Omission in comparative clauses**
(a) Omit parts of the comparative clause which repeat parts of the main clause, except for the auxiliary verb or BE.
(b) If there is no auxiliary verb or ***be***, add the 'empty auxiliary' ***do*** [see DO 2a, 2f].

E.g. (a) *John can run faster* ***than his brother can***.
(= than his brother can run)
(b) *Jane works harder* ***than her sister does***.
(= than her sister works)

comparison

► This entry is about COMPARATIVES and SUPERLATIVES.

1 To compare two things (two people, groups of people, etc.) we use the comparative form (with ***more*** or ***-er***), often followed by ***than***. When the comparison is between three things (three people, groups of people, etc.) we normally use the superlative form (with ***most*** or ***-est***) [see -ER / -EST, MORE / (THE) MOST].

1a In the following, notice the choice of ***warmer*** for comparing two countries, and ***warmest*** for comparing three.

E.g. *Which is the **warmer** of the two countries? Egypt or Nigeria?*
*Which is the **warmest** of the three countries? Egypt, Nigeria, or Indonesia?*

NOTE: The comparative is the <correct> form for comparing two things, but we sometimes use the superlative instead: before a boxing match, we can say to the two boxers: *May the **best** man win!*

2 **The opposites of *more* and *most* are *less* and *least***

E.g. *Guy drives **more** carefully than Hector.*
(= *Hector drives **less** carefully than Guy.*)
*But Roger is the **least** careful driver of all my friends.*

3 **Comparing height, size, age etc.**
The structure ***comparative + than*** and the structure ***as* + X + *as*** can be used to measure differences of height etc. [see MEASURING].

E.g. *The Eiffel Tower is 300 metres high, and Notre Dame is 150 metres high. So the Eiffel Tower is **150 metres higher than** Notre Dame.*

We can also say:

*The Eiffel Tower is **twice as high as** Notre Dame.*

Or we can say:

*Notre Dame is **half as high as** the Eiffel Tower.*

complement

- ► A complement normally follows the VERB PHRASE. (The main verb is usually BE.)
- ► A complement tells us something about the nature of the SUBJECT (or OBJECT).

1 A complement can be:–
(i) An ADJECTIVE (sometimes with modifiers like ***very***):

E.g.

subject	+ verb phrase	+ complement . . .
Her sister	*was*	***(very) famous.***
The bottle	*is*	***(nearly) empty.***
Those pears	*must be*	***ripe (enough to pick).***

(ii) A NOUN PHRASE:

subject	+ verb phrase	+ complement
Her sister	*was*	***a famous dancer.***
These	*are*	***my best shoes.***
You	*must be*	***Mrs Walker.***

E.g.

(iii) A PRONOUN or NUMBER:

subject	+ verb phrase	+ complement	
My advice	*is*	***this.***	
That cup	*was*	***mine.***	
My daughter	*will be*	***ten (years old)***	*on 20th April.*
This	*is*	***me.****	

E.g.

*[The choice of pronoun in ***'This is I'*** and ***'This is me'***, etc. is discussed under PERSONAL PRONOUN 2d.]

NOTE: Also some adverbs and prepositional phrases can be complements.
E.g. *The radio is* ***on.*** *My mother is* ***in good health.***

2 The complement can follow the verb BE, as in the examples above, or another LINKING VERB such as ***seem*** or BECOME:

subject	+ verb phrase	+ complement . . .
The judge	*seems*	***(extremely) annoyed.***
Vera and Ted	*became*	***our friends.***

3 A complement can also follow the OBJECT of the clause:

subject	+ verb phrase	+ object	+ complement . . .
This work	*is making*	*me*	***sleepy.***
Everyone	*thought*	*Joan*	***mad.***
He	*calls*	*his wife*	***'Rosie'.***

NOTE: In this case, the complement is called an OBJECT COMPLEMENT: it describes some quality of the object, not of the subject. In contrast, the complement we showed in 1 and 2 is called a subject complement.

4 [For details of verbs used with complements, see LINKING VERB, VERB PATTERNS 2, 12.]

complex sentence

[See SENTENCE 3]

compound sentence [See SENTENCE 3a]

compound word

1 A compound word is a word which is formed from two (or more) other words.

E.g. Compound noun: ***rainfall*** (= ***fall*** of the ***rain***)
Compound adjective: ***suntanned*** (= ***tanned*** by the ***sun***)
Compound verb: ***lipread*** (= to ***read lips*** e.g. this is what a deaf person does)

2 We sometimes write a compound word with a hyphen (-) between its parts. (Hyphens are not often used in <U.S.>.)

E.g. *birth-control, home-made, dry-clean*

and we sometimes write a compound word as two separate words.

E.g. *oil well, ash blonde, sleep walker*

3 There are no clear rules for writing compounds. You will find the same word written in different ways.

E.g. *oilwell, oil-well, oil well*

It is best to look up the compound in a dictionary if you are in doubt.

concord [See AGREEMENT]

concrete noun [See COUNTABLE AND UNCOUNTABLE NOUNS]

► A concrete noun is the opposite of an ABSTRACT NOUN.
► A concrete noun defines something which you can see or touch, and which has a position in time and space.

1 Many concrete nouns refer to:

(A) people. E.g. *baby, woman, doctor, cook*
(B) things. E.g. *wheel, knife, key, chair*
(C) animals. E.g. *horse, rabbit, snake, fish*
(D) places. E.g. *island, city, mountain, river*

These kinds of noun are countable: they can be counted and made PLURAL.

E.g. *two cooks, four wheels, thousands of rabbits* (etc.)

2 Other concrete nouns refer to:

(A) substances. E.g. *iron, flesh, skin, glass*
(B) liquids. E.g. *water, blood, rain, milk*
(C) gases, etc. E.g. *gas, air, steam, oxygen*

We call these mass nouns, or uncountable nouns. They describe masses which cannot easily be divided into individual items; hence we do not normally count these nouns or make them plural.
[For further details, see COUNTABLE AND UNCOUNTABLE NOUNS.]

conditional clause

1 A conditional clause is a type of ADVERBIAL CLAUSE. The event described in the MAIN CLAUSE depends on the condition described in the conditional clause.

E.g.

conditional clause	main clause
If it rains,	*we will get wet.*

main clause	conditional clause
The door opens	***if you press this button.***

2 By far the most common conditional CONJUNCTION is ***if*** [see IF]. Here we deal with conditional clauses in general, and with other conjunctions as well as ***if***. Conditional clauses begin with:
if*
unless* (= 'if . . . not', or more exactly 'except . . . if')
provided (that)* (= 'only if')
so long as or ***as long as***
on condition that <formal> (states a condition to which someone has to agree)

* [These words have separate entries in this book. Look them up for further details.]

E.g. ***If you feel ill,*** *take a couple of these pills.*
We will lose the game ***unless we try harder***. (= 'If we do not try harder, we will lose the game')
This climb is safe ***provided (that) you are careful.***
So long as the baby is fed, *he seems very happy.*
The loan is offered ***on condition that it is repaid within 12 months***. <formal>

3 [For real and unreal conditions, see UNREAL MEANING. For 1st, 2nd, and 3rd conditionals, see IF 1.]

congratulations

To express pleasure when something good happens to someone, we ***congratulate*** them.

E.g. (i) on passing an examination
(ii) on the birth of a baby
(iii) on an engagement or a wedding
(iv) on a wedding anniversary

} For all these, the word you use is ***congratulations***, and the reply is: ***Thank you (very much)***

E.g. (i) <spoken>
***Congratulations**, Keith! I understand you have passed your exam with excellent marks. Your family will be very proud of you. **Well done**!*

(ii) <written>
Dear John and Mary,
***Congratulations on** your engagement. I understand you are getting married quite soon. When will the happy day be? My very best wishes for your future happiness.*

[See also GOOD WISHES.]

conjunction [See COORDINATION, SUBORDINATE CLAUSE]

► A conjunction is a 'joining word'. Its main role is to link together two parts of a sentence. [To see how conjunctions compare with other 'linking words', see LINKING ADVERBS AND CONJUNCTIONS.]

► There are two types of conjunction: coordinating and subordinating conjunctions.

1 Coordinating conjunctions join equivalent parts of a sentence, e.g. two CLAUSES which make up a sentence. (This is called COORDINATION.)

	main clause		main clause
E.g.	*The sun shone*	***and***	*everyone felt happy*

2 Subordinating conjunctions join a SUBORDINATE CLAUSE to a MAIN CLAUSE. (This is called subordination.)

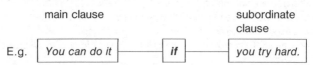

	main clause		subordinate clause
E.g.	*You can do it*	***if***	*you try hard.*

3 The following is a table of conjunctions, showing their meaning and function. Double conjunctions contain two words separated by one or more words.

Table of conjunctions

(A) ***Coordinating conjunctions***			
meaning or function	***simple conjunctions***	***2- or 3- word conjunctions***	***double conjunctions***
addition, listing:	*and**		*both . . . and,* *not only . . . but*
alternatives:	*or**		*either . . . or*
contrast*:	*but**		*not . . . but*
negative addition:	*nor*		*neither* . . . nor*
(B) ***Subordinating conjunctions***			
comparison*:	*as*, than*,* *like** <U.S.>	*as if, as though*	*as . . . so,* *as . . . as*
condition*:	*if*, unless**	*seeing (that),* *given (that),* *provided (that)*,* *as / so long as*	*if . . . then*
contrast*:	*(al)though*,* *while*,* *whereas**	*even though*	*although . . . yet*
degree* or extent:		*as far as*	*so . . . that*
exception:		*but (that),* *except (that)*	
place*:	*where*, wherever**		
preference:		*rather than, sooner than*	
proportion:			*as . . . so,* *the . . . the*
purpose*:		*so that,* *in order that*	
reason and cause*:	*because*,* *as*, since**		
respect:		*in that*	
result*:		*so that,* *such that*	
indirect question*:	*whether*, if**		*whether . . . or*
indirect statement*:	*(that)**		
time* (same time):	*when(ever)*,* *while*, as**	*now (that)*	
(earlier time):	*before*,* *until*, till*		
(later time):	*after*, since**		
(just after):	*once*, when*,* *whereupon*	*immediately (that)*	

*[These words have separate entries in this book. Look them up for further details. For ***condition*** see CONDITIONAL CLAUSE, for ***question*** see INDIRECT QUESTION, for ***because*** see BECAUSE, BECAUSE OF, for ***before*** see AFTER AND BEFORE.]

consonants and vowels [See also PRONUNCIATION OF ENDINGS]

1 The consonant sounds of English are:

/p/	as in ***part***	/f/	as in ***food***	/h/	as in ***has***
/b/	as in ***but***	/v/	as in ***voice***	/m/	as in ***mat***
/t/	as in ***too***	/θ/	as in ***thing***	/n/	as in ***not***
/d/	as in ***did***	/ð/	as in ***this***	/ŋ/	as in ***long***
/k/	as in ***kiss***	/s/	as in ***see***	/l/	as in ***let***
/g/	as in ***get***	/z/	as in ***zoo***	/r/	as in ***red***
/tʃ/	as in ***chin***	/ʃ/	as in ***she***	/j/	as in ***yes***
/dʒ/	as in ***joke***	/ʒ/	as in ***measure***	/w/	as in ***will***

2 The vowel sounds of English are:

(long vowels)		(short vowels)		(diphthongs*)	
/ɪː/	as in ***each***	/ɪ/	as in ***it***	/eɪ/	as in ***day***
/ɑː$^{(r)}$/	as in ***car***	/e/	as in ***then***	/aɪ/	as in ***by***
/ɔː$^{(r)}$/	as in ***more***	/æ/	as in ***back***	/ɔɪ/	as in ***boy***
/uː/	as in ***too***	/ʌ/	as in ***much***	/əʊ/	as in ***no***
/ɜː$^{(r)}$/	as in ***word***	/ɒ/	as in ***not***	/aʊ/	as in ***now***
		/ʊ/	as in ***put***	/ɪə$^{(r)}$/	as in ***near***
		/ə/	as in ***again***	/eə$^{(r)}$/	as in ***there***
				/ʊə$^{(r)}$/	as in ***truer***

* Diphthongs are composed of two vowel sounds in sequence.

NOTE (i): The symbol /^{r}/ indicates that the vowel is pronounced with an 'r' sound (i) in <U.S.>, and (ii) in standard <G.B.> when it is immediately followed by another vowel.
E.g. *car*:/kɑː/ <G.B.>; /kɑːr/ <U.S.>
But: *Take the **car out*** /ˈkɑːraʊt/ <G.B. and U.S.>

NOTE (ii): The two consonants /l/ and /n/ are sometimes pronounced as a separate syllable, i.e. as if they are vowels. In that case, we give them the symbols /l̩/ and /n̩/.
E.g. /ˈbɒtl̩/ *(bottle)*; /ˈwʊdn̩/ *(wooden)*.

NOTE (iii): The letter ***x*** normally stands for the two consonant sounds /ks/. E.g. /sɪks/ *(six)*. But at the beginning of a word, it is pronounced /z/: *xerox* /ˈziːrɒks/.

NOTE (iv): The letter ***-e*** is normally silent when it comes at the end of a word, after a consonent letter. E.g. /meɪk/ *(make)*, /haʊs/ *(house)*.

continuous [another term for the PROGRESSIVE]

contraction of verbs and negatives [See also AUXILIARY VERB, BE, NOT]

► A contraction is a short form of a word, used both in spelling and in pronouncing the word.

► Contractions are used in <speech and informal writing>. Do not use them in <formal writing>, e.g. business letters.

1 Contractions of verbs and how to pronounce them

The verbs which have contractions are some forms of ***be*** and ***have***, and also ***will*** and ***would***. The contractions are:

verb:	*am*	*is*	*are*	*have*	*has*	*had*	*would*	*will*
contraction:	***'m***	***'s***	***'re***	***'ve***	***'s***	***'d***	***'d***	***'ll***
pronunciation:	/m/	/z/ or /s/	*	/v/	/z/ or /s/	/d/	/d/ or /əd/	/l/ or /l̩/

*The contraction ***'re*** is pronounced in different ways:
you're /jɔːʳ/, ***we're*** /wɪəʳ/, ***they're*** /ðeəʳ/.

2 Where to put contractions of verbs

2a The contraction is added to the end of a word, and is marked in writing by an apostrophe ('). The word which comes before the contraction is usually a PERSONAL PRONOUN, as these tables show:

BE:	am	*I'**m***		
	are	*you'**re***	*we'**re***	*they'**re***
	is	*he'**s***	*she'**s***	*it'**s***

HAVE:	have	*I'**ve***	*you'**ve***	*we'**ve***	*they'**ve***
	has	*he'**s***	*she'**s***	*it'**s***	
	had	*he'**d*** *I'**d***	*she'**d*** *you'**d***	*it'**d**** *we'**d***	 *they'**d***

will	*he'**ll*** *I'**ll***	*she'**ll*** *you'**ll***	*it'**ll*** *we'**ll***	 *they'**ll***
would	*he'**d*** *I'**d***	*she'**d*** *you'**d***	*it'**d**** *we'**d***	 *they'**d***

* The contraction 'it'***d***' is <rare>.

2b Other words can take contractions: e.g. ***who*** [see WHO / WHOM / WHOSE], WHAT, THERE, HERE, and NOUNS (especially when the noun is a single word as subject).

E.g. ***Who's*** *there?* ***There's*** *someone at the door.* ***What's*** *the matter?* ***Here's*** *the bus.* ***Mary's*** *my friend.* *The* ***dinner's*** *ready.*

(***'s*** is a contraction of ***is*** in all these examples.)

NOTE: Contractions do not occur at the beginning or end of a sentence. They also do not occur before or after a major break, for example one marked by a comma.
E.g. {**'Is** / *''**s*** } *Diana ill?' 'Yes, she* { ***is,*** / ***'s,*** }*, I'm afraid.'*

3 Negative contractions and how to pronounce them

3a A negative contraction [see NEGATIVE WORDS AND SENTENCES] is a short form of NOT, and is spelled ***n't***. It is added to BE as a main verb, and to the auxiliaries ***be***, ***have***, ***do***, ***can***, ***could***, ***will***, ***would***, ***should***, ***must***, ***might***, ***ought*** and ***need***.

verb		negative contraction	pronunciation	
be:	*is*	~ *is**n't***	/ɪz/	/ˈɪzn̩t/
	are	~ *are**n't***	/ɑːʳ/	/ɑːʳnt/
	was	~ *was**n't***	/wɒz/	/ˈwɒzn̩t/
	were	~ *were**n't***	/wɜːʳ/	/wɜːʳnt/
have:	*have*	~ *have**n't***	/hæv/	/ˈhævn̩t/
	has	~ *has**n't***	/hæz/	/ˈhæzn̩t/
	had	~ *had**n't***	/hæd/	/ˈhædn̩t/
do:	*do*	~ *do**n't***	/duː/	/dəʊnt/
	does	~ *does**n't***	/dʌz/	/ˈdʌzn̩t/
	did	~ *did**n't***	/dɪd/	/ˈdɪdn̩t/
modal auxiliaries:	*will*	~ *wo**n't***	/wɪl/	/wəʊnt/*
	can	~ *ca**n't***	/kæn/	/kɑːnt/* <G.B.> /kæːnt/ <U.S.>
	would	~ *would**n't***	/wʊd/	/ˈwʊdn̩t/
	could	~ *could**n't***	/kʊd/	/ˈkʊdn̩t/
	should	~ *should**n't***	/ʃʊd/	/ˈʃʊdn̩t/
	might	~ *might**n't***	/maɪt/	/ˈmaɪtn̩t/
	must	~ *must**n't***	/ˈmʌst/	/ˈmʌsn̩t/*
	ought (to)	~ *ought**n't** (to)*	/ɔːt/	/ˈɔːtn̩t/
	need	~ *need**n't***	/ˈniːd/	/ˈniːdn̩t/

* ***Won't***, ***mustn't***, and <in G.B.> ***can't*** have irregular pronunciations.

NOTE (i): There are no negative contractions for ***am*** and ***may***. [But see BE 1c.]

NOTE (ii): Rare contractions: The negative contraction for ***shall*** is ***shan't*** (/ʃɑːnt ‖ ʃæːnt/), and the negative contraction for ***used to*** is ***usedn't to*** (/ˈjuːsn̩t/ or /ˈjuːzn̩t/).

NOTE (iii): As the table above shows, ***-n't*** after a consonant is pronounced as a syllable (-/n̩t/) and not (-/nt/).

4 **Verb contraction or negative contraction?**
In <informal> English, we often have a choice, in negative clauses, between contraction of the verb and contraction of ***not***; in other cases, only one contraction is possible:

	(A) verb contraction		(B) negative contraction
be:	***I'm*** *not an artist.* ***She's*** *not hungry.* –	or	— *She* ***isn't*** *hungry.* *They* ***weren't*** *at home.*
have:	***I've*** *not met him.*	or	*I* ***haven't*** *met him.*
do:	– –		*I* ***don't*** *eat meat.* *We* ***didn't*** *see anyone.*
modal auxiliaries:	– –		*He* ***couldn't*** *swim.* *You* ***mustn't*** *forget.*

contrast

► There are two types of contrast:
– where fact 2 is surprising in the light of fact 1.
– where fact 2 is the opposite of fact 1.

1 **Contrast of surprising facts**

Fact 1:  Fact 2: 

Ann's husband is an ugly, wicked devil. ◄—— ***CONTRAST*** ——► *She loves him.*

Fact 1 and fact 2 are in contrast: i.e., fact 2 is surprising or unexpected in the light of fact 1.
Ways of expressing this kind of contrast:

(A)	(B)	(C)	(D)	
but *yet*	*in spite of* *despite*	*although* *though* *even though*	*even so* *however* *nevertheless*	*none the less* *all the same* *still* *yet*

(A) = coordinating conjunctions [see CONJUNCTION, COORDINATION]
(B) = PREPOSITIONS
(C) = subordinating conjunctions [see CONJUNCTION]
(D) = linking adverbs and adverbials [see LINKING ADVERBS AND CONJUNCTIONS]

1a The most important word for expressing contrast of surprising facts in English is BUT, so we can join facts 1 and 2 together as follows, using ***but*** to link the two clauses.

E.g. *Ann's husband is an ugly, wicked devil,* ***but*** *she loves him.*

But is a coordinating conjunction ((A) above). ***But*** is also used for expressing contrast of opposite facts.

E.g. *This week the weather is good,* ***but*** *last week it was bad.*

[See 2 below for further details of expressing contrast of opposite facts.]

1b There are many other ways of expressing contrast of surprising facts in English.

(I) PREPOSITIONS: ***in spite of*** or ***despite*** <formal> ((B) above).

E.g. ***In spite of*** *his faults, she loves him.*
She loves him, ***in spite of*** *his faults.*
In spite of *knowing London, I got lost.*
Despite *the danger from the earthquake, the firemen continued to look for injured people among the ruins.* <rather formal>

(II) ADVERBIAL CLAUSES introduced by ALTHOUGH (or ***though***), ***even though***: ((C) above).

E.g. ***Although*** *I'm very fond of Joe, there are times when I could murder him.*
Tomorrow's weather will stay generally fine, ***(al)though*** *there will be occasional showers later in the day.*
I can still criticise her, ***even though*** *she's a friend of mine.*

(III) LINKING ADVERBS AND CONJUNCTIONS ((D) above):

	<rather formal>	**<formal>**	**<rather informal>**
yet	*however*	*nevertheless*	*all the same*
even so		*none the less*	*(but) still*

E.g. *Sam is not exactly the perfect husband: he is over forty, he is going bald, and he has little money.* {***Nevertheless*** / ***None the less***} *he and Sheila are going to get married.*
They haven't eaten for days, ***(and) yet**** *they look healthy.*
Stan was lazy, and failed his exam. His brother, ***however****, was successful, and later became a famous lawyer.*
The weather was miserable: it rained almost every day. ***All the same****, we all managed to enjoy our* {*holiday* <G.B.> / *vacation* <U.S.>}
We didn't win a single first prize at this year's flower show. ***Still****, our results were very good.*

* ***Yet*** is limited to front position, and ***and*** can be placed before it. In some ways, ***yet*** is more like a conjunction than an adverb. [See YET 2.]

2 Contrast of opposite facts

This is a less important kind of contrast:

Fact 1:		Fact 2:
In Britain the hottest month of the year is usually July.	◄ ***CONTRAST*** ►	*In Australia the coldest month of the year is usually July.*

Fact 1 and fact 2 are in contrast, i.e., they are directly opposite to each other. This type of contrast can be expressed by the coordinating conjunction ***but*** [see 1a above], and also by:

2a The subordinating conjunctions WHILE, WHEREAS.

E.g. *In Britain the hottest month of the year is usually July,* {***while*** / ***whereas***} *in Australia it is usually the coldest.*

2b The linking adverbials: ***on the other hand***, ***in*** / ***by contrast***, (especially <written English>).

E.g. *In Britain the hottest month of the year is usually July. In Australia,* ***on the other hand****, July is usually the coldest month.*
In Britain the hottest month of the year is usually July. ***By contrast,*** *July is usually the coldest month in Australia.*

---

coordination

► Coordination is a way of linking clauses, phrases and words. [See CONJUNCTION.]
► The main words which link by coordination are AND, OR, and BUT (also ***nor***).
► ***And***, ***or***, ***but*** and ***nor*** are called coordinating CONJUNCTIONS [see also DOUBLE CONJUNCTIONS].

1 Coordinating clauses

The conjunctions ***and***, ***or***, and ***but*** can join two clauses:

clause 1	link	clause 2
The police arrived (,)	***and***	*the thieves were arrested.*
Would you like tea (,)	***or***	*would you prefer coffee?*
We rang the bell (,)	***but***	*nothing happened.*

1a Using a comma in coordinating clauses:
In <writing> you should put a comma (,) at the end of the first clause unless

you have a good reason not to, for example, if the sentence is very short.

E.g. *The nation's industrial performance has improved greatly**, and** there is every reason to believe that it will continue to improve in the future.*

1b Omitting words in coordination:
We can often omit part of the second clause, and in this case we usually omit the comma, too:

(i) *The thief broke into the house **and** (he) stole the silver.*
(ii) *Many students can write English **but** (they) can't speak it very well.*
(iii) *Edna ordered an ice-cream, **and** Jill (ordered) a fruit juice.*
(iv) *If you are young **and** (if you) want adventure, this is the job for you.* [an advertisement]

The pattern of (i) and (ii) above is very common. We may call these 'forked clauses'.

E.g. *The thief broke into the house*
and
The thief stole the silver.
→ *The thief* ┬ *broke into the house*
├ ***and***
└ *stole the silver.*

Coordination can also join smaller units, such as PHRASES and words.

2 Coordination of phrases

E.g. ***Jill and my sister Ida** are friends.*
*I'd like a **cup of tea and a sandwich**, please.*
*You can pay **in cash or by credit card**.*
*The hotel is **small but very comfortable**.*

3 Coordination of words

E.g. *My favourite subjects are **history and literature**.*
*Do you like your coffee **with or without** milk?*
*No one has **seen or heard** anything of them for ages.*
*I have spoken to her only **once or twice**.*

NOTE (i): We usually do not repeat a DETERMINER (e.g. ***a***, ***the***, ***my***) after ***and***, ***or***, and ***but***:
E.g. *my father **and** mother* is more common than: *my father **and my** mother*

NOTE (ii): We usually do not coordinate possessives before a noun. So instead of ***our and your friends***, we prefer to say ***our friends and yours*** [see POSSESSIVE DETERMINER AND POSSESSIVE PRONOUN].

NOTE (iii): [See COMMA 1 for details of how to use a comma in coordinating words and phrases.]

4 We can link more than two items by coordination. (Note the use of INTONATION.)

E.g. *Which of these fruit juices do you want? The ápple, the grápefruit, **or** the òrange?*

As in the above example, in a coordinated list of three or more items, ***and*** or ***or*** is placed between the last two items in the list.

correlative (conjunction) [See DOUBLE CONJUNCTION]

could and *might* /kʊd/, /maɪt/ are MODAL AUXILIARIES.

- ► ***Could*** and ***might*** go with a main verb, e.g. ***could go***.
- ► They do not change their forms.
- ► They are the Past Tense forms of CAN and MAY – but their meaning is not usually past time.
- ► ***Could*** and ***might*** often have the same meaning.

1 Forms:

present simple

I *You* *We* *They* noun phrase etc.	***could*** ***might***	*be . . .* *have . . .* *feel . . .* *look . . .* etc.

negative

I *You* *We* *They* etc.	{***couldn't*** / ***could not***} {***mightn't*** / ***might not***}	*be . . .* *have . . .* *feel . . .* *look . . .* etc.

question

Could ***Might***	*I* *you* *we* *they* noun phrase etc.	*be . . .* *have . . .* *feel . . .* *look . . .* etc.	?

negative question

Couldn't	*I* *you* *we* *they* etc.		*be . . .* *have . . .* *feel . . .* *look . . .* etc.	?
Could . . .		**not**		
Mightn't				
Might . . .		**not**		

**couldn't* = /ˈkʊdn̩t/; *mightn't* = /ˈmaɪtn̩t/..

1a Perfect. E.g. *They* {***could*** / ***might***} *have arrived.*

Progressive. E.g. *They* {***could*** / ***might***} *be coming late.*

Passive. E.g. *They* {***could*** / ***might***} *be delayed.*

Perfect Passive. E.g. *You* {***could*** / ***might***} *have been killed.*

[See VERB PHRASE.]

2 **Meanings and uses** [Compare CAN, MAY 2, 3.]

2a ***Could* / *might*** means 'possible but unlikely'.

E.g. *Well! It* {***could*** / ***might***} *rain tomorrow, but there are no clouds in the sky today.*

One day I {***could*** / ***might***} *become a millionaire, but the chances are very small.*

*'You **might** be offered the job of manager.' 'Yes, and pigs **might** fly!'* *

* 'Pigs might fly' is a saying which means that everything is possible, even if it's very very unlikely!

NOTE: This meaning of ***could*** / ***might*** is used in WARNINGS.

E.g. *Don't cross the road here; you* {***could*** / ***might***} *be run over.*

2b ***Could*** (and rarely, ***might***) is used for asking PERMISSION.

E.g. *'**Could** I see you for a few minutes?' 'Yes, certainly.'* <polite>

{*Do you think* / *I wonder if*} ***I could*** *borrow* {*a pen?* / *some sugar?* / *your typewriter?*} <more polite>

Could and ***might*** are more polite than ***can*** and ***may***, because they are more tentative.

2c ***Could* / *might*** is used in making a SUGGESTION.

E.g. Student: *What shall I do to improve my English?*
Teacher: *Well, you **could** / **might** try some of these grammar exercises.*

2d ***Could* / *might*** is used in complaining about someone's behaviour. (This is *not* <polite>!)

E.g.

NOTE (i): Complaining often involves a COMPARATIVE form.
E.g. *You **could** try to talk **more** quietly!*

NOTE (ii): To complain about past behaviour, we use the Perfect Tense.
E.g. *You **could have told** me the boss was angry!*
*You **might have asked** me before you took the money!*

3 Differences between *could* and *might*

3a We use ***might*** more often for POSSIBILITY and ***could*** more often for PERMISSION.

3b ***Could*** can be used in REQUESTS.

E.g. ***Could*** *you wait over there, please?*
Could *you possibly lend me $10?*

3c ***Could*** can be used to mean 'was able to' or 'would be able to'.

E.g. *In those days, you* ***could*** *buy a coat for $20.*
If you were here, we ***could*** *play tennis together.*
[See IF 1c.]

3d The negative meanings of ***could*** and ***might*** are different:
In ***could not*** + Verb . . ., ***not*** applies to ***could***.
In ***might not*** + Verb . . ., ***not*** applies to the Verb and what follows it.

E.g. *You* ***couldn't*** *have met my grandmother: she died before you were born.*
(i.e. 'it is not possible that you met . . .')
You ***might not*** *have met my grandmother.*
('It is possible that you have not met her.')

3e There is also a slight difference in the use of ***could*** and ***might*** for UNREAL MEANING, e.g. in IF-clauses.

E.g. ***If it should rain****, the games* ***could*** *take place indoors.*
(= 'It would be possible to organise the games indoors'.)
If it should rain*, the games* ***might*** *take place indoors.*
(= 'It is possible that the games would take place indoors'.)

4 We express a possibility in the past by ***could*** / ***might have**** [see PERFECT].

E.g. A: *'Did you pass the exam?'*
B: *'No, I didn't.'*
A: *'Well, if you had worked harder, you* ***might have*** *passed it.*

****could have*** = /ˈkudəv/; ***might have*** = /ˈmaitəv/.

---

count noun

Another term for a countable noun [See COUNTABLE AND UNCOUNTABLE NOUNS]

---

countable and uncountable nouns

- In English, NOUNS can be divided into countable and uncountable nouns.
- Most COMMON NOUNS are countable: i.e. they have both SINGULAR and PLURAL forms: e.g. *hand – hands.*
- Other common nouns are uncountable: they have a singular, but no plural: e.g. *bread –* ~~*breads*~~.
[See UNCOUNTABLE NOUNS for more details, and for a list of such nouns.]

1 Examples of countable and uncountable nouns

1a Countable nouns can be both singular and plural:

singular	~ plural
the baby	~ *the babies*
a rose	~ *some roses*
that cup	~ *those cups*

singular	~ plural
the bird	~ *the birds*
a key	~ *some keys*
that shout	~ *those shouts*

[For details of how to form plurals, see PLURAL and IRREGULAR PLURAL. For types of countable noun, see COMMON NOUN.]

1b Uncountable nouns have no plural: they refer to things you cannot count. Here are examples of CONCRETE NOUNS (referring to the physical world) which are not countable.

E.g. substances: *bread* ~ ~~*breads*~~, *dust* ~ ~~*dusts*~~, *steel* ~ ~~*steels*~~
liquids: *blood* ~ ~~*bloods*~~, *milk* ~ ~~*milks*~~, *alcohol* ~ ~~*alcohols*~~
gases: *air* ~ ~~*airs*~~, *steam* ~ ~~*steams*~~, *oxygen* ~ ~~*oxygens*~~

Many ABSTRACT NOUNS are also uncountable.

E.g. *peace* ~ ~~*peaces*~~, *evidence* ~ ~~*evidences*~~, *information* ~ ~~*informations*~~, *history* ~ ~~*histories*~~, *work* (= job) ~ ~~*works*~~, *advice* ~ ~~*advices*~~, *gratitude* ~ ~~*gratitudes*~~

[For more examples, see UNCOUNTABLE NOUNS.]

2 How countables and uncountables behave

2a Countable nouns:
(i) can follow ***a***, ***an*** or ***one*** [see A OR AN, ONE].
(ii) can follow MANY, ***few*** [see (A) FEW], ***these*** [see THIS AND THESE], THOSE.
(iii) can follow a NUMBER such as ***two***, ***three***, ***four***, . . .

		(countable)	(uncountable)
E.g.	(i)	*Do you have **a** pleasant **job**?*	(But not: . . . ***a** pleasant ~~**work**~~*.)
	(ii)	***Those meals** you cooked were delicious.*	(But not: ***Those ~~foods~~*** . . .)
	(iii)	*I bought **two loaves**.*	(But not: . . . ***two ~~breads~~***.)

2b Uncountable nouns:
(i) can have no article and can follow ***some**** [see SOME AND ANY] (in the singular).
(ii) can follow MUCH or ***little*** [see LITTLE / A LITTLE].
(iii) can easily follow expressions like ***most of the***, ***all of the****, ***all the****, ***half the*** (in the singular).

		(uncountable)	(countable)
E.g.	(i)	*It's made of* ***wood***.	(But not: *made of* ***~~tree~~***.)
	(ii)	*There's too* ***much traffic***.	(But not: *too* ***much ~~vehicle~~***.)
	(iii)	*I sold* ***all the furniture***.	(But not: ***all the ~~table~~***.)

* ***Some*** and ***all the*** are occasionally followed by a singular countable noun. But this is exceptional.
E.g. *That was* ***some party***! (= 'a very special party'.)
I've eaten ***all the loaf***. (= 'the whole loaf'.)
[See ALL 1a, 1b, SOME AND ANY, WHOLE.]

3 Many nouns have both countable and uncountable uses. Some common examples:

(countable)	(uncountable)
A dozen *(= 12)* ***eggs****, please.*	*There's* ***some egg*** *on your chin.*
I've told him so ***many times***.	*We've wasted so* ***much time***.
The crowd threw ***rocks*** *at us.*	*a tunnel through hard* ***rock***.
a *strong* ***wind****; light* ***winds***.	*There's* ***a lot of wind*** *about.*
She gave ***a talk*** *on sailing.*	*That's foolish* ***talk***.
the *bright* ***lights*** *of the city.*	***Light*** *travels very fast.*

Some more examples:

a glass

a cake

two papers

(some) glass

(some) cake

(some) paper

3a For many nouns, the countable use is for separate items or things, but the uncountable use is for (an amount of) the material or substance. For example:

two onions

a (whole) cheese

a chicken

(some) onion

(some) cheese

(some) chicken

NOTE (i): Less commonly, a countable noun describes '***a kind*** or ***type*** of X', where X is the uncountable noun.

E.g. *Gold and silver are valuable* ***metals***. ('kinds of metal')
This store sells health ***foods*** *and baby* ***food(s)***.
Oak is a hard ***wood***.

NOTE (ii): We sometimes change an uncountable noun into a countable noun. E.g. nouns for liquids such as ***tea*** and ***coffee*** are normally uncountable, but we can use them as countable nouns meaning (a) '***a glass*** or ***cup*** of X' or (b) '***a type*** of X'.

E.g. (a) ***'A tea*** *and* ***two coffees*** *please.'*
'This is ***an*** *excellent* ***mineral water*** *from Belgium'.*

NOTE (iii): The meaning of a noun does not always help us to decide whether it is uncountable. For example, ***traffic***, ***furniture*** and ***baggage*** (<G.B.> ***luggage***) refer to a group of separate things. But English treats them as uncountable: we could say that English 'sees' these as a mass.

countries

1 With the name of a country, there is also an adjective describing the people, places, language, etc. which belong to that country. There is also a noun describing people of that country (the noun often has the same form as the adjective):

name of country	adjective	noun for people singular	 plural
China	*Chinese*	*a Chinese*	*Chinese* *
Brazil	*Brazilian*	*a Brazilian*	*Brazilians*
Pakistan	*Pakistani*	*a Pakistani*	*Pakistanis*

*Nouns ending **-ese** do not change in the plural: ***a Chinese*** ~ ***two Chinese***; ***a Japanese*** ~ ***many Japanese***.

NOTE: Notice that we spell the adjective, like the noun, with a capital letter: ***Brazilian***, not ***~~brazilian~~***.

1a Examples:

(i) A: *Where do you come from?*
B: *I'm from* ***Italy***.
A: *You must be* ***Italian****, then.*
B: *Yes, I'm* ***an Italian****, and my parents were* ***Italians****, too.*

(ii) A: *Where do you come from?*
B: *I'm from* ***Poland***.
A: *You must be* ***Polish****, then.*
B: *Yes, I'm* ***a Pole****, and my children are* ***Poles*** *too.*

2 In the following tables are examples of the main patterns in which the 'people noun' has the same form as the adjective.

2a Adjectives ending in ***-an***:

name of country	adjective († = also language name)	noun for people singular	plural
A'merica	*A'meric**an***	*an A'meric**an***	*A'meric**ans***
Aus'tralia	*Aus'trali**an***	*an Aus'trali**an***	*Aus'trali**ans***
'Belgium	*'Belgi**an***	*a 'Belgi**an***	*'Belgi**ans***
'Germany	*'Germ**an**†*	*a 'Germ**an***	*'Germ**ans***
'India	*'Indi**an***	*an 'Indi**an***	*'Indi**ans***
'Hungary	*Hun'gari**an**†*	*a Hun'gari**an***	*Hun'gari**ans***
'Norway	*Nor'wegi**an**†*	*a Nor'wegi**an***	*Nor'wegi**ans***
'Russia	*'Russi**an**†*	*a 'Russi**an***	*'Russi**ans***

2b Adjectives ending in ***-ese***:

'China	*Chin'**ese** *†*	*a Chin'**ese***	*Chin'**ese***
Ja'pan	*Japan'**ese** *†*	*a Japan'**ese***	*Japan'**ese***
'Portugal	*Portu'gu**ese** *†*	*a Portu'gu**ese***	*Portugu'**ese***
Viet'nam	*Vietnam'**ese** *†*	*a Vietnam'**ese***	*Vietnam'**ese***

* Adjectives ending in ***-ese*** move their stress to the first syllable when they precede a noun.
Compare: *This vase is **Chin'ese*** But: *a '**Chinese** vase*

2c Adjectives ending in ***-i***:

I'raq	*I'raq**i***	*an I'raq**i***	*I'raq**is***
'Israel	*Is'rael**i***	*an Is'rael**i***	*Is'rael**is***
Paki'stan	*Paki'stan**i***	*a Paki'stan**i***	*Paki'stan**is***

2d Exceptions:

Argent'ina	*'Argentine*	*an 'Argentine*	*'Argentines*
Greece	*Greek†*	*a Greek*	*Greeks*
'Switzerland	*Swiss*	*a Swiss*	*Swiss*

3 In the following tables are examples where the 'people noun' has a different form from the adjective.

3a Adjectives ending in ***-ish***:

name of country	adjective († = also language name)	noun for people singular	plural
(Great) 'Britain	*'Brit**ish***	*a 'Briton* *	*'Britons* *
'Denmark	*'Dan**ish***†	*a Dane*	*Danes*
'Finland	*'Finn**ish***†	*a Finn*	*Finns*
'Poland	*'Pol**ish***†	*a Pole*	*Poles*
'Scotland	*'Scott**ish***	*a Scot*	*Scots* * *
'Spain	*'Span**ish***†	*a 'Spaniard* *	*'Spaniards* *
'Sweden	*'Swed**ish***†	*a Swede*	*Swedes*
'Turkey	*'Turk**ish***†	*a Turk*	*Turks*

* ***Briton*** and ***Spaniard*** are not often used. We refer to the people in general as ***the British*** or ***the Spanish***. [See GENERIC (OR GENERAL) USE OF ARTICLES.]
* * For ***Scotland***, there is also an adjective ***Scots***, and a noun ***Scotsman***.

3b In the following group, the noun has ***-man*** or ***-woman***:

'England	*'English* *†	*an 'English**man*** *	*'English**men*** *
France	*French* *†	*a 'French**man*** *	*'French**men*** *
'Holland, the 'Netherlands	*Dutch* *†	*a 'Dutch**man*** *	*'Dutch**men*** *
'Ireland	*'Irish* *	*an 'Irish**man*** *	*'Irish**men*** *
Wales	*Welsh* *†	*a 'Welsh**man*** *	*'Welsh**men*** *

* The noun is ***-man*** in a male form, and the female form ends in ***-woman*** (plural ***-women***): ***Frenchman***, ***Frenchwoman***, etc. But often today we avoid these words, and use ***a French person***, etc., instead. In any case, to describe the people of a country in general we use ***the*** + adjective: ***the English***, ***the French***, ***the Dutch***, ***the Irish***, ***the Welsh*** [see THE 3g].

'd

is the contraction (or short form) of ***had*** and ***would*** [see CONTRACTION OF VERBS AND NEGATIVES 2].

---

dare /deəʳ/ (*verb*)

1 ***Dare*** is a regular verb (~ ***dares***, ***dared***, ***daring***), normally followed by a TO-INFINITIVE [see VERB PATTERNS 7].

E.g. *He **dared to criticize** the king.*

2 ***Dare*** also sometimes behaves like a MODAL AUXILIARY, e.g. in coming before NOT. (But ***doesn't*** / ***didn't dare to*** is more common.)

E.g. *The administration **dare not** increase the tax on cigarettes.*

dates – saying them and writing them.

1 The months of the year

January	***May***	***September***
February	***June***	***October***
March	***July***	***November***
April	***August***	***December***

NOTE (i): Always write the names of months and days with a capital letter: ***April***, ***Monday***, but not ~~*april*~~, ~~*monday*~~.

NOTE (ii): Write the four seasons without a capital: ***spring***, ***summer***, ***autumn*** <G.B.> / ***fall*** <U.S.>, ***winter***.

2 The days of the week

Monday	***Thursday***	***Saturday***
Tuesday	***Friday***	***Sunday***
Wednesday		

3 <speech>

Here are examples of how to talk about dates:

'What's the date today?' 'It's ***the twenty-fifth of May****'.*
'When were you born?' ***'On the ninth of July, 1956*** **.'*
'In what year was Beethoven born?' ***'In 1770*** **.'*

* [For details of how to pronounce these numbers see 3b below.]

[On the use of ***on*** and ***in***, see TIME 4.]

3a Notice you can use either of these patterns:

A:	(name of day)	***the***	number of day	***of***	name of month	(number of year)
	(Monday)	*the*	*first*	*of*	*June*	*(1927).*

or

B:	(name of day)	name of month	***the***	number of day	(number of year)
	(Tuesday)	*March*	*the*	*third*	*(1564).*

3b How to pronounce the numbers:

(I) Use ORDINAL numbers (as above) for the number of the day.

(II) For the year, read the date like this:

ten sixty-six (= 1066)	*nineteen hundred* (= 1900)*
fourteen ten (= 1410)	*ninteen two* (= 1902)**
eighteen fifty (= 1850)	*nineteen eighty-four* (= 1984)

*Notice that for dates ending in ***-00***, we use the word ***hundred***. We can also use ***hundred*** with ***and*** in other dates.
E.g. *Eighteen* ***hundred and*** *fifty* (= 1850).

We usually add ***hundred and* or the letter ***0*** /əʊ/ when the date ends in single figures: 1901, 1902, . . . 1909 etc. Thus for 1902, we say ***nineteen hundred and two*** or ***nineteen-O-two***.

4 < **writing** >

When writing a date, you can choose one of the following patterns. Do not use ***the*** or ***of***:

<G.B.>:	A:	*(Monday,) 1st June, 1927*	Or: *1 June, 1927*
<U.S.>:	B:	*(Thursday,) March 5th, 1564*	Or: *March 5, 1564*

As you can see from the above examples, you can also omit the letters ***-th*** etc. after the ordinal number [see NUMBERS 1, 2]. Pattern A is the usual <British> style, and pattern B is the usual <American> style.

decimal numbers – how to say and write them

We write decimals with a decimal point ***(.)***.

E.g. 5.2 In <speech>: *five* ***point*** *two*
18.5 In <speech>: *eighteen* ***point*** *five*
6.36 In <speech>: *six* ***point*** *three six*

defining and nondefining relative clauses

[See RELATIVE CLAUSE 4]

definite article [See THE, ARTICLES]

degree [See ADVERB]

► Degree words answer the questions ***'How?'*** ***'How far?'*** or ***'How much?'***

► Degree words are adverbs. They modify other words, especially adjectives, adverbs, and verbs.

► We use degree words to place ideas or qualities on a scale.

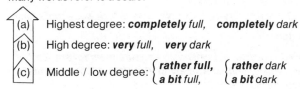

E.g.

GRAND THEATRE
What was the play like, mum?
Was it good?
Absolutely perfect! +++++++
Really excellent. ++++++
Very good indeed. +++++
Very good. ++++
Good. +++
Quite good. ++
Fairly good. +
Not very good. –
Rather poor. ––
Bad. –––
Very bad. ––––
Extremely bad. –––––
Utterly awful! ––––––

1 Scales of degree

Many words refer to a scale:

(a) Highest degree: ***completely*** *full,* ***completely*** *dark*

(b) High degree: ***very*** *full,* ***very*** *dark*

(c) Middle / low degree: { ***rather full,*** / ***a bit*** *full,* } { ***rather*** *dark* / ***a bit*** *dark* }

1a For some words, (b) and (c) are possible, but not (a).

E.g. *His hair is*
(a) ~~***completely***~~ *thin,* ~~***completely***~~ *long*
(b) ***very*** *thin,* ***very*** *long*
(c) { ***rather*** / ***a bit*** } *thin,* { ***rather*** / ***a bit*** } *long*

1b For other words, (a) is possible, but not (b) or (c).

E.g. *My job is* ***completely*** *finished.*
Your job is ***completely*** *impossible.*
Your views and mine are ***completely*** *opposed.*

Not: { ~~***very***~~ / ~~***rather***~~ / ~~***a bit***~~ } { *finished* / *impossible* / *opposed* }

NOTE: Many people dislike an expression such as ***very unique*** and ***rather perfect***, because 'unique' and 'perfect' are not qualities which allow different degrees.

2 Three kinds of degree word

The following are common adverbs in the three classes (a), (b), and (c) above:

(a) Highest degree:	*absolutely, altogether, completely, entirely, quite *, totally, utterly*
(b) High degree:	*very * *, very much * * *, much * * *, a lot * * *, a great deal * * *, considerably * * *, extremely * **
(c) Middle / Low degree:	*rather, quite *, fairly * *, pretty * ** <informal>, *somewhat, a bit* <informal>, *(a) little, a little bit* <informal>, *slightly.*

[The following words have separate entries in this book; look them up for further details: QUITE AND RATHER, VERY, MUCH, A LOT (OF) / LOTS(OF), A BIT / A BIT OF, LITTLE / A LITTLE. For the asterisked notes see 2a below.]

2a Examples:

(a) **Highest degree**

E.g. *I **agree** with you **completely**.*
*'What I said was **quite true**.' 'No, it wasn't – it was **utterly false**.'*

(b) **High degree**

E.g. *'How do you like his paintings?' 'I **admire** them **very much**.'*
*Thank you for your **extremely useful** advice. I'm **very grateful** for your help.*

(c) **Middle / Low degree**

E.g. *I was **slightly disappointed** with my results in the test: I found it **rather difficult**.*
*The climb was **somewhat easier** than I expected.*

* Notice that ***quite*** belongs to the two classes (a) and (c) [See QUITE AND RATHER 2].

* * ***Extremely***, ***very***, ***fairly***, and ***pretty*** go with ordinary adjectives and adverbs, but they do not go with:

(i) verbs.

E.g. You can say: *The party was **extremely enjoyable**.*
But not: *I **enjoyed** the party ~~**extremely**~~.*
Instead, say: *I **enjoyed** the party **very much**.*

(ii) comparative words:

You can say: *This party is **fairly good**.*
But not: *This party is ~~**fairly**~~ better than the last.*
Instead, say: *This party is **somewhat** better than the last.*

Other degree adverbs which behave like ***extremely*** and ***fairly*** (modifying adjectives and adverbs, but not verbs and comparatives) are ***as*** [see AS 1], ***so*** [see SO 1], and ***too*** [see TOO 2].

* * * ***Much***, ***very much***, ***a lot***, and other adverbs marked * * * do the opposite of those marked * *: they go with verbs or comparative words, but not with adjectives or adverbs.

E.g. You can say: *Adam is **very much older** than Eve.*
But not: *Adam is **very** ~~**much**~~ **old**.*
Instead, say: *Adam is **very old**.*

[On the choice of ***much*** and ***very much***, see MUCH 2c].

2b Other adverbs (particularly adverbs of high degree) go with particular verbs. For example, ***hard*** goes with ***work*** and ***try***.

E.g. *We are **working hard**, but the manager says we must **try harder**.*
*We **rely heavily** on our overseas market.*
*I **thoroughly approve** of your action.*

3 The positions of degree words

Degree words usually go before ADJECTIVES, ADVERBS and COMPARATIVE words.* For example:

adjectives	adverbs	comparative words
***quite** young* ***so** quiet*	***very** often* ***too** slowly*	***much** older* ***rather** more*

* ***Enough*** is a special exception to this rule: as a degree word, it follows the words it modifies, even when they are adjectives or adverbs, e.g. ***strong enough***, ***strangely enough***. [See ENOUGH.]

3a With verbs the position of the degree word varies:

(i) Some degree words go before the verb (***quite***, ***rather***). [See QUITE AND RATHER.]

E.g. *I **rather like** her.* *Have you **quite finished**?*

(ii) Some (those adverbs which begin with ***a***, such as ***a bit***, ***a lot***, ***a great deal***) go after the verb (and after the OBJECT, if there is one).

E.g. *I **like** her **a lot**.* *It doesn't **worry** me **a bit**.*

(iii) Most go both before and after the verb (+ object).

E.g. *We **completely failed.*** *We **failed completely.***

4 Three more kinds of degree word

These words are different from the three kinds (a–c) in 1 above, because they relate to the ***limits*** of a scale:

(d) **d** ***almost***, ***nearly*** and ***practically*** indicate something near the limit of the scale. [See ALMOST AND NEARLY.]

E.g. *I **almost won** the race.*
*My father is **nearly blind**.* (= 'He can hardly see at all.')

(e) ***(not) at all***, and ***(not) a bit*** refer to the negative end of a scale.

E.g. *That lecture was**n't at all useful**.* (= 'It was completely useless.')

e

(f) HARDLY, ***scarcely***, and ***barely*** indicate something near the negative end of the scale.

E.g. *Nora is **scarcely awake.*** (= 'almost asleep')
*You've changed so much – I **hardly recognized** you.*

f

5 Some degree words express attitudes (e.g. a 'good' or a 'bad' feeling about something). [For further examples, see ENOUGH 1, and TOO 2, QUITE AND RATHER, HOW 4, and SO 1.]

6 **What kinds of word can degree words go with?**
Apart from adjectives, adverbs, and verbs, degree words can go with some QUANTITY WORDS: MANY, MUCH, ***more***, ***most*** [see MORE / (THE) MOST]; (A) FEW, ***(a) little*** [see LITTLE / A LITTLE]; ***fewer***, ***fewest***; ***less***, ***least*** [see LESS / (THE) LEAST].

E.g.

demonstrative

1 The term demonstrative means 'showing' or 'pointing to' something. It refers to the four words ***this***, ***that***, ***these***, and ***those***, whose basic use is to point to something in the situation. [Look up THAT 3, THIS AND THESE, and THOSE for further details.]

	singular	plural
'near'	*this*	*these*
'far'	*that*	*those*

This and ***these*** are called 'near' because they indicate something near to the speaker.* ***That*** and ***those*** refer to something less near to the speaker.

* But there are other uses where ***this***, ***that***, ***these*** and ***those*** do not express the 'near' / 'far' difference. [See especially THAT 3, THOSE.]

2 All four demonstratives can act as (a) DETERMINER (usually with a following noun) or as (b) PRONOUN (without a following noun). For example:

determiner	pronoun
*'**That** man is my father.'* *'**This** room is where I work.'* *'Have one of **these** nuts.'* *'**Those** trees in the corner are oak trees,*	*'And who is **that**? Your mother?'* *'Oh, so **this** must be your desk.'* *'No, thanks, I'd prefer one of **these**.'* *and **those** over there are apple trees.'*

dependent clause

[Another term for SUBORDINATE CLAUSE, see CLAUSE 2]

determiner

- ► A noun usually has to have a determiner in front of it: ***the drum***, ***our children***. [See NOUN PHRASE.]
- ► The < most common > determiners in English are the definite article [see THE] and the indefinite article [see A OR AN].
- ► Determiners also precede other words which precede a noun; e.g. adjectives and numbers: ***the big drum***, ***our three children*** [see NOUN PHRASE].

1 The table below shows which determiners go with the different types of noun. [The determiners in this table have separate entries in this book; look them up for further details; See also POSSESSIVE DETERMINER AND POSSESSIVE PRONOUN.]

	kinds of determiner	with countable nouns		with uncountable nouns
		singular	plural	singular
definite	DEFINITE ARTICLE	***the*** *book*	***the*** *books*	***the*** *coffee*
	POSSESSIVES POSSESSIVE nouns	***my*** *book* ***Mary's*** *book*	***my*** *books* ***Mary's*** *books*	***my*** *coffee* ***Mary's*** *coffee*
	DEMONSTRATIVES	***this*** *book* ***that*** *book*	***these*** *books* ***those*** *books*	***this*** *coffee* ***that*** *coffee*
indefinite	INDEFINITE ARTICLE	***a*** *book*	*~ books* * *	*~ coffee* * *
	QUANTITY WORDS (general) (without comparison)	*(**all** the book* * * *)* *(**some** book* * * *)* *(**any** book* * * *)* ***no*** *book*	***all*** *books* ***some*** *books* ***any*** *books* ***no*** *books*	***all*** *coffee* ***some*** *coffee* ***any*** *coffee* ***no*** *coffee*
		every *book* ***each*** *book* ***either*** *book* ***neither*** *book* ***one*** *book* ***another*** *book*		
			both *books* ***several*** *books*	
			enough *books*	***enough*** *coffee*
	QUANTITY WORDS (with comparison)		***many*** *books* { ***more*** *books* { ***most*** *books* ***(a) few*** *books* { ***fewer*** * *books* { ***fewest*** * *books*	***much*** *coffee* { ***more*** *coffee* { ***most*** *coffee* ***(a) little*** *coffee* { ***less*** *coffee* { ***least*** *coffee*
wh-words	For expressing attitudes, etc	***such*** *(a) book!* ***what*** *(a) book!*	***such*** *books!* ***what*** *books!*	***such*** *coffee!* ***what*** *coffee!*
	For asking QUESTIONS (POSSESSIVE)	***what*** *book?* ***which*** *book?* ***whose*** *books?*	***what*** *books?* ***which*** *books?* ***whose*** *books?*	***what*** *coffee?* ***which*** *coffee?* ***whose*** *coffee?*
	WH-EVER WORDS	***whatever*** *book* ***whichever*** *book*	***whatever*** *books* ***whichever*** *books*	***whatever*** *coffee* ***whichever*** *coffee*

* We sometimes use ***less*** and ***least*** instead of ***fewer*** and ***fewest***.
** ~ signals that the indefinite article is absent before plural and uncountable nouns. [See ZERO ARTICLE.]
*** ***All***, ***some*** and ***any*** are less common with singular countable nouns. They have special uses in this position. [See ALL 1a, 1b, COUNTABLE AND UNCOUNTABLE NOUNS 2b*]

NOTE: the words within the heavy boxes in the table do not change their form; they stay the same whatever kind of noun they follow.

2 When there is more than one determiner follow these useful rules:

2a Place ***all*** and ***both*** in front of other determiners.

E.g. *We ate **all the** food.* ***Both my** sons are at college.*

2b Place ***what*** and ***such*** in front of ***a*** or ***an*** in exclamations.

E.g. ***What an** awful day!* *I've never seen **such a** crowd!*

2c Place ***many***, ***much***, ***more***, ***most***, ***few***, ***little*** after other determiners.

E.g. ***His many** successes made him famous.*
*They have **no more** food.*
***What little** money I have is yours.*

---

different /ˈdɪfrənt/ (*adjective*)

1 In <G.B.>, ***different from*** . . . is normally considered the <correct> construction.

E.g. *Maggie's views are **different from** mine.*
*Picasso's latest paintings are in a very **different** style **from** his early work.*

But many people use ***different to*** instead: ***different to mine***, etc.

2 In <U.S.> especially, ***than*** can be used instead of ***from***.

E.g. *Maggie's views are **different than** mine.*

<G.B.> speakers often consider this 'incorrect'.

---

direct object [See INDIRECT OBJECT, OBJECT]

direct speech [Compare INDIRECT SPEECH]

1 'Direct speech' means using the actual words spoken by someone.

E.g. (i) ***'There's our taxi,'** she said.*

The words ***There's our taxi*** are in direct speech. In English we normally use ' ' or " " (quotation marks or quotes) at the beginning and end of the words in direct speech.

2 The direct speech can be placed at the beginning (see example (i) above), at the end (see example (ii) below), or at the beginning and end of the sentence (see example (iii) below).

E.g. (ii) *She said, **'There's our taxi.'***
(iii) ***'There,'** she said, **'is our taxi.'***

NOTE (i): If the direct speech is an exclamation or a question, place the **!** or **?** before the closing 'quote', even if it is the middle of the sentence.
E.g. *'There's our taxi* **!***' shouted Max.*
'Where's our taxi **?***' asked Jill.*

directions

1 **Spoken directions**
Here is an example of how to give directions in <speech>.

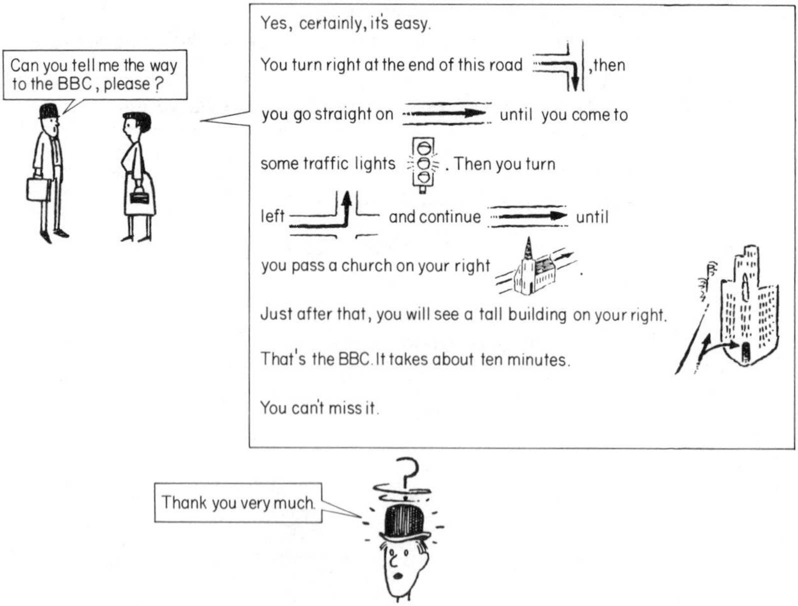

2 **Written directions** [See INSTRUCTIONS.]

disagreeing [See AGREEING AND DISAGREEING.]

distance [See also MEASURING]

1 **How to measure distances**

We measure distance in ***inches***, ***feet***, ***yards***, ***miles***, etc., or in ***centimetres***, ***metres***, ***kilometres*** <G.B.> (or ***centimeters***, ***meters***, ***kilometers*** <U.S.>). The 'old' system for measuring distances (widely used in English-speaking countries) is:

12 inches make ***one foot***, ***3 feet*** make ***one yard***
5280 feet make ***one mile*** (one mile is about 1.6 kilometres)

2 **Far and further**

Far and ***further*** are words expressing distance.

E.g. (i) *'**How far** is it (from here) to the nearest bank?'*

'It's (*(about / exactly / nearly)*) {***five miles.'*** / ***a hundred yards.'*** / ***a mile and a half.'***}

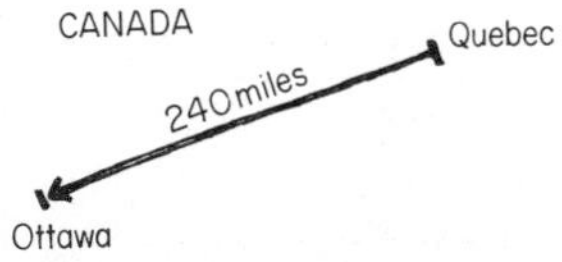

(ii) *'It's 240 miles from Quebec to Ottawa.'*
*'**How much further** is it to Toronto?'*
'It's (at least) {***200 miles (further).'*** / ***another 200 miles.'***}

3 **Some other expressions of distance**

*Yesterday I walked **30 kilometres**.*
*I have to travel **a long way** (to work).*
*Our grandson lives **several miles** away.*
*The post office is **only 100 yards** from here.*
*This book says it's **6790 miles** from Singapore to London.*

do /du:/ ***does***, ***did***, ***doing***, ***done*** (*verb*)

► ***Do*** is important both as an AUXILIARY VERB and as a MAIN VERB.
► The auxiliary ***do*** is important for forming negatives and questions.
► [For further information, look up AUXILIARY VERB, DO AND MAKE.]

1 **Forms of *do***
Do is an IRREGULAR VERB with 5 different forms:

do is the BASIC FORM, used as the INFINITIVE, the IMPERATIVE (and the SUBJUNCTIVE), (also as a Present Tense form – see below).

subject	forms	
	Present Tense	**participles (main verb only)**
he, ***she***, ***it***, or singular noun phrase	***does*** /dʌz/, /dəz/ *	**ing form** ***doing*** /du:ɪŋ/
I, ***we***, ***you***, ***they***, or plural noun phrase	***do*** /du:/, /dʊ/ *	
	Past Tense	**past participle:**
all kinds of subject	***did*** /dɪd/	***done*** /dʌn/

2 **Auxiliary *do***
As an auxiliary verb, ***do*** goes with the BASIC FORM of the main verb:

negative				
	auxiliary	*not**	main	
I	***do***	*-n't*	***play***	*golf.*

question			
auxiliary		main	
Do	*you*	***play***	*. . .?*

*In <spoken English> use the contraction ***-n't*** for ***not***. [See CONTRACTIONS OF VERBS AND NEGATIVES.]

2a As this example shows, auxiliary ***do*** is mainly used to form QUESTIONS and negative sentences [see NEGATIVE WORDS AND SENTENCES]. It has no meaning itself, but it is an 'empty helping verb', to help to form negatives, questions, etc. We also use ***do*** in forming tag questions, 'shortened answers', emphatic sentences, etc. [See also the use of ***do*** in INVERSION 4, QUESTIONS.]

NOTE: We do not use auxiliary ***do*** to form questions and negative sentences with ***be*** or with another auxiliary verb. [For further details, see BE, AUXILIARY VERB.]

2b Negatives: ***don't*** /dəʊnt/ (= do not)
doesn't /ˈdʌzn̩t/ (= does not)
didn't /ˈdɪdn̩t/ (= did not)

With the main verbs (except BE) we form a negative sentence like this:

DO + -N'T + MAIN VERB

E.g.	*I **enjoy** walking.*	→	*I **don't enjoy** walking.*
	*He **likes** cats.*	→	*He **doesn't like** cats.*
	*They **waited** for us.*	→	*They **didn't wait** for us.*
	*Please **go** away.*	→	*Please **don't go** away.*

Notice that the **-s** and **-d** move from the main verb to **do** in the negative. But with IRREGULAR VERBS, there may be no **-d** in the Past Tense:

Past Simple	→ negative	Past Simple	→ negative
took	→ ***didn't*** *take*	*saw*	→ ***didn't*** *see*
came	→ ***didn't*** *come*	*went*	→ ***didn't*** *go* etc.

* In ***doesn't*** and ***didn't***, **-*n't*** is pronounced as a separate syllable, rather like -/ənt/.

2c In <formal writing> and business letters, use:

DO / DOES / DID + NOT + MAIN VERB

E.g. *Dear Sir,*
I do not agree *with the view that violence is essential, as implied in yesterday's edition of your newspaper . . .*

2d Questions:
With main verbs (other than ***be***) we form a YES-NO QUESTION by placing the correct form of ***do*** in front of the subject. For example:

She *It* *My son*	***loves***	*ice-cream.*	→	***Does*** ***Doesn't***	*she* *it* *your son*	***love*** *ice-cream?*
I *We* *Italians*	***love***	*ice-cream.*	→	***Do*** ***Don't***	*you* *they* *Italians*	***love*** *ice-cream?*
The bus *They*	***arrived***	*late.*	→	***Did*** ***Didn't***	*the bus* *they*	***arrive*** *late?*

We also use ***do*** in some WH-QUESTIONS and in TAG QUESTIONS when the statement has just a main verb (other than ***be***).

E.g. *'What music **do** you **like** best?'* *'I **like** jazz best of all.'*

2e ***Do*** in tag questions:
When there is no auxiliary or ***be***, we can make a statement into a question by adding:

, + DO + PRONOUN + ?

E.g. *You speak Spanish,* ***don't you?***
She speaks Spanish, ***doesn't she?***

2f ***Do*** in SHORTENED SENTENCES AND CLAUSES:
We use ***do*** at the end of an answer, to avoid repeating the same words.

E.g. *'**Does** your husband smoke more than ten cigarettes a day?' 'Yes, I'm sorry to say he **does**'.*
('he does' = 'he does smoke more than ten cigarettes a day.')
*'You **don't** do enough exercise.' 'Perhaps I **don't**.'*
('I don't' = 'I don't do enough exercise')

The following are examples of shortened clauses [see SHORTENED SENTENCES AND CLAUSES 3] e.g. in COMPARATIVE CLAUSES:

*She speaks English much better **than he does**.*
(= 'than he speaks English.')
*The Chinese learned to make glass long **before the Western nations did.***
(= 'before the Western nations learned to make glass.')

NOTE: In the examples above, ***do*** comes at the end of the clause or sentence. Sometimes, however, it comes in the middle.
E.g. *Barry cooks dinner for his wife more frequently than she **does** for him.*
(= 'than she cooks dinner for him.')

2g ***Do*** for emphasis:
We use ***do*** in positive sentences, but only for special emphasis.

E.g. *I **did** enjoy that dinner! It was delicious.*
*We **don't** need advice, but we **do** need money.*
*'I wish I could lose weight.' 'Yes, well, you **do** eat a lot.'*

Here ***do*** always has stress, and emphasises positive meaning.
Do also comes at the beginning of an imperative sentence, for emphasis.

E.g. ***Do*** *write to us and tell us how you are.*
(Compare the negative: ***Don't*** forget to write . . .)

Sometimes ***do*** replaces the whole imperative.

E.g. *'May I have another cup of tea?' 'Yes, **do**.'* (= 'Yes, certainly.')

3 ***Do* as a main verb** [See also DO AND MAKE.]
Like the auxiliary ***do***, the main verb ***do*** is an 'empty' verb. It has little meaning itself, but can save us the trouble of repeating other words twice. You can often combine it with other words: ***do so, do it, do that*** etc.

3a ***What + do:***
What + do is a general way of getting information:

– asking about the present.

E.g.

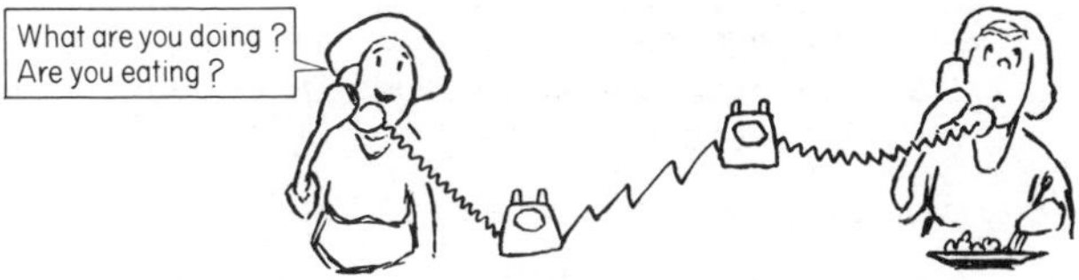

– asking about the future.

E.g.

– asking about someone's job.

E.g.

[See PRESENT TIME 2 for the difference between the Present Simple and the Present Progressive.]

*Notice that the auxiliary ***do*** and the main verb ***do*** can both be in the same clause, e.g. in a question.

3b ***Do so:***

We may use **do so** to refer to an action which we have already mentioned.

E.g. *If you have not posted the* { *cheque* <G.B.>, *check* <U.S.>, } *will you please* ***do so*** *immediately?* (***do so*** = 'post the cheque')

They intended to reach the top of the mountain, but no one knows if they ***did so***. (***did so*** = 'reached the top of the mountain')

'Are you taking your driving test?' 'No, I've already ***done so.****'* (= 'taken my driving test.')

NOTE: Rarely, ***do so*** precedes the words whose meaning it repeats.

E.g. *If you have not already* ***done so****, will you please post the* { *cheque* / *check* } *immediately?*

3c ***Do*** **with** IT and THAT:
Like ***do so***, ***do it*** refers to an action we have mentioned elsewhere.

E.g. *'Is Julia still writing her essay?'*
'Yes, she should have ***done it*** *ages ago.'*
(= 'written her essay')

Do that is similar, but is more emphatic.

E.g. *'I'm resigning from my job.'*
'Don't ***do that****! You'll never find a better one.'*
(= 'resign from your job')

4 ***Do*** **in greetings**
How are you doing? is a friendly question about a person's life (= 'How are you getting on?').
How do you do is a greeting we use when we meet someone for the first time.

---

do and *make* [See also DO and MAKE separately.]

1 Both these general verbs can be followed by a noun or noun phrase describing some object or action. We show the difference between them in the following table:

make means 'bring into existence', 'produce some result'	***do*** means 'perform an action'
For example:	For example:
make *a cake, a meal*	***do*** *a job*
make *bread, jam*	***do*** *something for a living*
make *a pot of tea, coffee*	***do*** *business (with someone)*
make *an appointment*	***do*** *one's homework*
make *war (on someone)*	***do*** *damage (to something)*
make *peace (with someone)*	***do*** *the housework, the dishes*
make *a good impression*	***do*** *the cooking, the shopping*
make *progress*	***do*** *one's hair, one's teeth*
make *a mistake*	***do*** *physical exercises*
make *a fuss, a noise*	***do*** *someone a favour, a good turn*
make *fun of someone, a fool of someone*	***do*** *well, better*
make *a phone call*	***do*** *something to someone*
make *a decision*	***do*** *something with something*
make *a fortune*	***do*** *anything, nothing*
	do *what you like*

double conjunction [See COORDINATION, CONJUNCTION]

1 The CONJUNCTIONS ***and***, ***or***, ***but***, and ***nor*** sometimes follow another word which emphasises their meaning:

both X ***and*** Y	***either*** X ***or*** Y	***not*** X ***but*** Y
neither X ***nor*** Y	***not only*** X ***but*** Y	***if*** X ***then*** Y

We call these pairs **double conjunctions**. [The above words all have separate entries in this book. Look them up for further details.]

2 ***both . . . and . . .*** **(Adding one item or idea to another)**

E.g. ***Both*** *my mother* ***and*** *her sister were born in Mexico.*
The cat family includes ***both*** *lions* ***and*** *tigers.*

3 ***either . . . or . . .*** **(Alternatives)**

E.g. *You can have* ***either*** *a dog* ***or*** *a cat. You can't have both.*
Either *you like boxing* ***or*** *you hate it.*

4 ***not . . . but . . .*** **(Replacing one idea by another)**

E.g. *We're leaving* ***not*** *next week,* ***but*** *the week after.*
It's ***not*** *the players,* ***but*** *the supporters, that cause trouble at football matches.* [See IT-PATTERNS.]

5 ***not only . . . but (also) . . .*** **(Adding one idea to another: emphatic)**

E.g. *She's* ***not only*** *beautiful,* ***but (also)*** *a great actress.*
Not only *is television boring,* ***but*** *it* ***(also)*** *wastes a lot of time.*
[On the WORD ORDER here, see NEGATIVE WORDS AND SENTENCES 6a]

This double conjunction has the same meaning of 'addition' as ***both . . . and***. But in ***not only*** X ***but*** Y, the X is something known or expected, and the Y is something unexpected, which receives emphasis. For extra emphasis, add ***also*** after ***but***.

6 ***neither . . . nor . . .*** **(Adding two negative ideas together)**

E.g. *She's* ***neither*** *beautiful* ***nor*** *clever, but everyone admires her.*
(= She is not beautiful and she is not clever.)
Neither *Otto* ***nor*** *his wife wanted children.*

NOTE: [On the similar use of ***neither*** as an adverb with INVERSION, see NEITHER 4.]

7 ***if . . . then . . .*** **(Logical Result)**
This is a different kind of double conjunction: the first word ***if*** is a subordinating CONJUNCTION, and the first part of the sentence is therefore a SUBORDINATE CLAUSE. We place ***then*** after the end of the if-clause, to emphasise the link between the condition (***if*** . . .) and its result (***then*** . . .).

E.g. ***If** you hate violence, **then** you must hate war films.*
***If** the law has been broken, **then** the police must take action.*

---

down [See UP AND DOWN]

---

due to /ˈdju:tu: ‖ ˈdu:tu:/ (weak form: /ˈdju:tə ‖ ˈdu:tə/ (*preposition*)

Due to expresses REASON AND CAUSE, and is similar in meaning to ***because of*** or ***owing to***.

E.g. (i) *His success was **due to** patience and hard work.*
(ii) ***Due to** bad weather, the farmers have lost much of their fruit crop.*

Some people dislike the use of ***due to*** in example (ii), because they consider that ***due*** is an adjective.

---

duration [See LENGTH OF TIME]

---

during /ˈdjʊərɪŋ ‖ ˈdʊərɪŋ/ (*preposition*)

1 We use ***during*** with periods of time.

E.g. (i) *We stayed at home **during last summer**.*
(ii) *I'll speak to him **during dinner**.*
(iii) *Jim fell off his chair **during our meeting**.*

2 ***During*** can describe:

(1) a state continuing throughout the period, as in example (i) above:

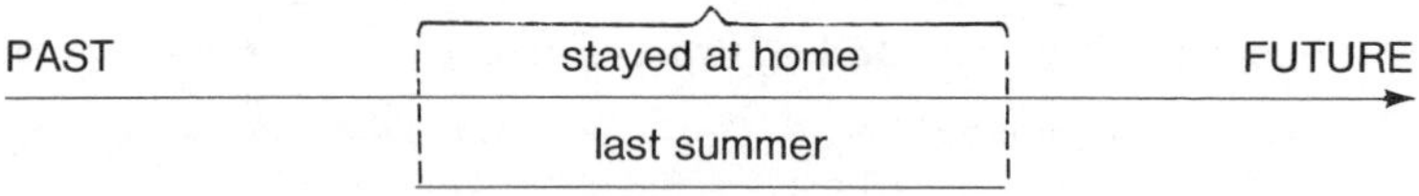

(2) a single happening in the period, as in example (iii) above:

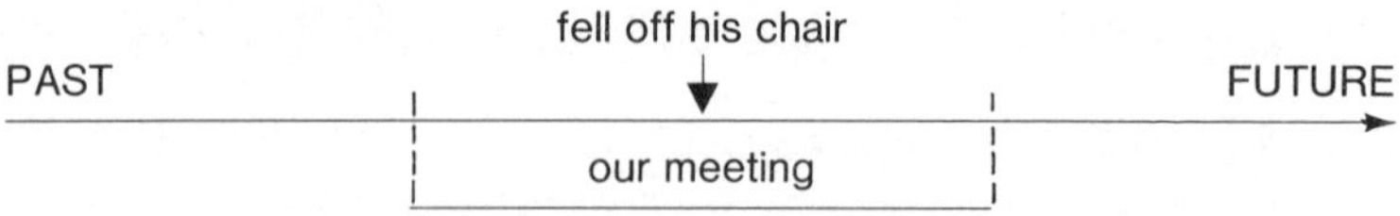

each /iːtʃ/ (*determiner or pronoun*)

► ***Each*** (like EVERY) refers to all members of a group.
► ***Each*** makes us think of the members of a group one by one.

1 ***Each* as DETERMINER**
Each is followed by a SINGULAR countable noun, or by ***one*** [see ONE 2].

E.g. ***each*** *girl,* ***each*** *ticket,* ***each*** *new performance,* ***each*** *one,*
each *taxi,* ***each*** *toy,* ***each*** *country in the world,* ***each*** *one of us*

Each girl *in the class has her own desk.*

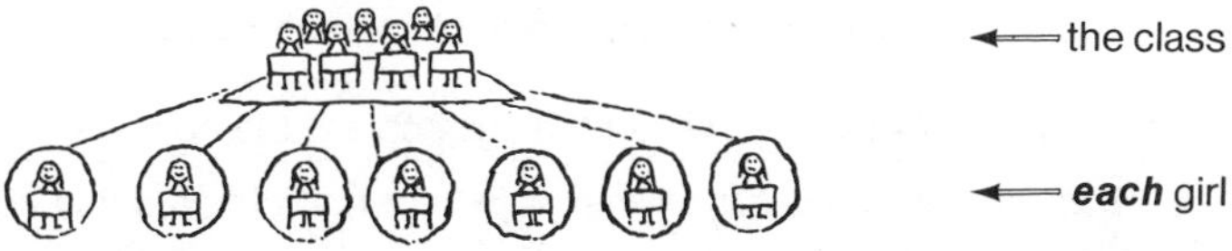

2 ***Each* as a PRONOUN**
Each as a pronoun has the above meaning, but is not followed by a noun.

E.g. ***Each*** *of the rooms has a telephone.* [See INDEFINITE PRONOUN 2.]
When the children entered, ***each*** *was given a present.*
('each of the children was given a present.')

2a There is a difference between ***all*** and ***each***. Compare (i) and (ii):

(i)

The teacher said 'hello' to ***each*** *of the new students.*

(ii)

The teacher said 'hello' to ***all*** *of the new students.*

Each means that the teacher repeated 'hello' many times; once for every student.
All probably means that the teacher said 'hello' just once for the whole class.

3 ***Each* following the noun or pronoun**
Each can follow the noun or pronoun it describes. You can use it in middle position [see ADVERB 3] after the subject or an auxiliary verb or ***are*** or ***were***.

E.g. (i) *The king divided his land equally between his three sons. So when he died, **they each** owned a third of his kingdom.* ('Each of them owned a third of his kingdom.')

(ii) ***The children** have **each** won a prize.* ('Each of the children has won a prize.')

(iii) ***These diamonds** are **each** worth £10,000.*

Notice that the verb in examples (ii) and (iii) above is plural, because the subject (*children, diamonds*) is also plural [see AGREEMENT].

3a Sometimes ***each*** follows not the subject, but the object.

E.g. (i) *We gave the children **a prize each**.* ('Each of the children got a prize.')

(ii) *They paid Tom and Tim **ten dollars each** for the work that they did.*

4 **Idioms**

Each other has the same meaning as ***one another*** [see ONE 4]. It behaves like a single pronoun, as object or after a preposition.

E.g. *'Do you and Joan know **each other**?'*
*'Yes, we talked to **each other** at the party last night.'*

-ed forms (written in this book as Verb-ed)

1 The ***-ed*** forms of the verb are the PAST TENSE form and the PAST PARTICIPLE form. REGULAR VERBS are spelled with ***-ed***, e.g. ***wanted***, ***wanted***. IRREGULAR VERBS do not end in ***-ed***: ***cut***, ***cut***. And with some irregular verbs the two forms are different: ***ate***, ***eaten***. But we will still call them '***-ed*** forms'.

E.g.	Past Tense form	past participle form
regular	*I **asked** for help*	*I have **asked** for help*
irregular	*I **cut** the cake* *I **ate** lunch*	*I have **cut** the cake* *I have **eaten** lunch.*

[On the spelling of the ***-ed*** forms, see SPELLING.]

2 **Rules for pronouncing *-ed* forms**
Pronounce ***-ed*** as /ɪd/ only after verbs ending /t/ or /d/.

E.g. *visit* → ***visited*** /ˈvɪzətɪd/ Compare: *name* → *named* /neɪmd/
land → ***landed*** /ˈlændɪd/ *look* → *looked* /lʊkt/

ed sounds like /d/ after verbs ending in other voiced consonants (/b/, /ð/, /g/, /l/, /m/, /n/, /ŋ/, /r/, /v/, /w/, /z/, /dʒ/, /ʒ/) and vowels.
-ed sounds like /t/ after verbs ending in other voiceless consonants: (/p/, /θ/, /k/, /f/, /s/, /tʃ/, /ʃ/).

e.g. /iːˈdʒiː/ (*adverb*) (abbreviation)

E.g. is a linking adverb, abbreviated from the Latin ***exempli gratia***. It stands for 'for example'. We can use it to link clauses or phrases in APPOSITION.

E.g. *The palace contains many famous works of art; **e.g.** paintings by Titian, Rembrandt, and Goya.*

E.g. is chiefly found in <written> English. Another abbreviation like this is ***i.e.*** [see I.E.].

either /ˈaɪðə^{r}/ or /ˈiːðə^{r}/ (*pronoun, determiner, or adverb*)

► ***Either*** is a word which we use chiefly in questions and after negatives, like ***any*** [see SOME-WORDS AND ANY-WORDS].
► Unlike ***any***, ***either*** involves a choice between two alternatives:

► [On ***either . . . or . . .***, see DOUBLE CONJUNCTION 3].

1 ***Either* as PRONOUN**
Either is a pronoun which describes a choice between two. It is often followed by ***of*** + NOUN PHRASE.

E.g. (i) *'Would you like **either** of these hats?' 'No, I don't want **either (of them)**, thanks.'*
(= 'I dislike both of them.')
(ii) *Noel is Rosa's boyfriend, but he hasn't met **either of her parents***, yet.
(= 'either her father or her mother.')

2 ***Either* as ADVERB**
Either can be a linking adverb at the end of a negative sentence.

E.g. (i) *'I didn't agree with John.' 'No, I didn't, **either**.'*
(ii) *John doesn't like Pam, and Pam doesn't like John, **either**.*

Either here is the opposite of the adverbs TOO or ALSO [see TOO 1]. It has heavy stress. The meaning of example (i) is similar to the following example:
*'I disagreed with John.' 'Yes, I did **too**.'*

2a ***Either*** as adverb always takes end position in the clause. But ***neither*** [see ADVERB 4] usually takes front position (with INVERSION).

E.g. *'I wasn't hungry.' 'No,* { *I wasn't, **either**.'* / ***neither** was I.'* }

'I've never met his wife,' 'No, { *I haven't, **either**.'* / ***neither** have I.'* }

'I can't swim very fast.' 'No, { *I can't, **either**.'* / ***neither** can I.'* }

3 ***Either* as DETERMINER**
The determiner ***either*** has a similar meaning to the pronoun, but it comes before a noun.

E.g. *As the President's car drove through the town, there were crowds on **either side** of the road.* (= 'on both sides of the road.')

---

else /els/ *(adverb)*

1 The adverb ***else*** is related in meaning to OTHER, and follows pronouns and adverbs ending in ***-one***, ***-body***, ***-thing***, and ***-where***.

E.g. *'Why did you sit there?' 'There was **nowhere else** to sit.'*
('no other place')
*I'm sorry, I'm too busy. Perhaps **someone else** will help you.*
('some other person').

1a ***Else*** can also follow ***what***, ***who***, etc. in questions or subordinate clauses [see WH-WORDS].

E.g. *I've invited Omar and Ella to the party.* ***Who else*** *shall we invite?* ('Which other people shall we invite?')

2 ***(Or) else*** is a linking adverb meaning 'if not' or 'otherwise' [see also OR 3].

E.g. *They should leave immediately,* ***or else*** *they will miss the train.*
The judge ordered him to pay the costs, ***or else*** *to go to prison.*

NOTE: ***Or else*** . . . is sometimes used as a threat.

end position

End position is the position of an adverbial (or other optional element) in the clause when it follows the verb (+ object or complement). [See ADVERB 3]

enough /ɪˈnʌf/ (*adverb, pronoun, or determiner*)

- ***Enough*** means 'sufficient' or 'sufficiently'.
- ***Not. . . enough*** means 'not sufficient(ly)', i.e. 'less than one would like'.
- ***Enough*** is the opposite of ***too (much)*** [see TOO 2].
- ***Enough*** is often followed by FOR or TO:

ENOUGH + FOR + NOUN PHRASE
E.g. *Is the water hot* ***enough for*** *a bath?*

or: ENOUGH + TO + INFINITIVE
He is old ***enough to*** *be her father.*

1 ***Enough* as an ADVERB of DEGREE**
Enough as an adverb of degree follows the word whose meaning it influences: adjective / adverb / verb + ***enough***.

adjective + ***enough***:

E.g. *This house is not* ***big enough*** *(for our family).*

adverb + ***enough***:

E.g. *Did you get up* ***early enough*** *(to eat a good breakfast)?*

verb + . . . ***enough***:

E.g. *She doesn't* ***love*** *her children* ***enough*** *(to look after them properly).*

2 ***Enough* as a PRONOUN**
Enough as a pronoun means the opposite of ***too much*** (i.e. the right amount).

E.g. *'Would you like some more bread?'*
'No, thank you – I've eaten (quite) ***enough****.'*
'How is your new job?'
'Fine, thank you – I will soon be earning ***enough*** *to buy a car.'*

3 ***Enough* as a DETERMINER**
Enough as a determiner precedes a singular uncountable noun or a plural noun, as in these patterns:

	enough + uncountable noun
Do they have	***enough*** *money?* ***enough*** *water?* ***enough*** *time?*

enough + plural noun	
enough	*people?*
enough	*jobs?*
enough	*cups?*

-er -/ər/ } endings for adjectives and adverbs
-est -/ɪst/ }

► ***-er*** is the ending of the COMPARATIVE form of most common adjectives: ***higher***, ***older***, ***taller***. [Compare ***more***: see MORE / (THE) MOST.]
► ***-est*** is the ending of the SUPERLATIVE form of the most common adjectives: ***(the) highest***, ***(the) oldest***, ***(the) tallest***. [Compare ***most***: see MORE / (THE) MOST.]
► Don't forget that ***the*** generally goes before the superlative ending in ***-est***.

E.g. *Jane is **tall** for a five-year-old.*
*Kate is **taller** than Jane, but **shorter** than Liz.*
*Liz is **taller** than Kate, and in fact she's **the tallest** of the three girls.*

1 There are a number of categories of adjective which can end with *-er* and *-est*

1a 'Short' adjectives of just one syllable. For example:

	comparative	superlative
high	*high**er***	*high**est***
old	*old**er***	*old**est***
hot *	*hot**ter***	*hot**test***
wet *	*wet**ter***	*wet**test***
nice * *	*nic**er***	*nic**est***
late * *	*lat**er***	*lat**est***

	comparative	superlative
low	*low**er***	*low**est***
young	*young**er***	*young**est***
cold	*cold**er***	*cold**est***
dry * * *	*dr**ier***	*dr**iest***
	etc.	

*Some adjectives double the last letter before adding ***-er*** or ***-est***. [See SPELLING 1]
* *Other adjectives lose their final ***-e*** before the endings are added, e.g. ***large***, ***larger***, ***largest***. [See SPELLING 2.]
* * *[See SPELLING 4.]

1b 'Longer' two-syllable adjectives which end with consonant +***-y***:*

busy	*bus**ier***	*bus**iest***
happy	*happ**ier***	*happ**iest***

early	*earl**ier***	*earl**iest*** *
heavy	*heav**ier***	*heav**iest***

*[See SPELLING 4b on changing ***-y*** to ***-i-***.]

1c Some other two-syllable words can take either ***-er*** and ***-est*** or ***more*** and ***most***.

E.g. *common* { *common**er*** / ***more** common* } { *common**est*** / ***most** common* }

Other examples are: ***able***, ***clever***, ***narrow***, ***noble***, ***simple***, ***shallow***, ***unkind***.

2 Irregular forms of adjectives

Three very common adjectives have irregular forms:

good ~ ***better*** ~ ***best***
bad ~ ***worse*** ~ ***worst***
far ~ ***further*** ~ ***furthest***

For example:

Exam results:	65%	75%	90%
In the exam,			
Sally was	*good,*		
John was		***better,***	
and Eva was			***the best!***

[See GOOD, BAD / BADLY and FAR 4 for examples.]

NOTE (i): ***Longer***, ***longest***, ***stronger***, and ***strongest*** have irregular pronunciation. They have a /g/ sound after the /ŋ/.
long /lɒŋ/ ~ ***longer*** /ˈlɒŋgəʳ/ ~ ***longest*** /ˈlɒŋgɪst/
strong /strɒŋ/ ~ ***stronger*** /ˈstrɒŋgəʳ ~ ***strongest*** /ˈstrɒŋgɪst/
young /jʌŋ/ ~ ***younger*** /ˈjʌŋgəʳ/ ~ ***youngest*** /ˈjʌŋgɪst/

NOTE (ii): ***Elder*** and ***eldest*** are old forms of ***older*** and ***oldest***. Nowadays they are used mainly in such phrases as ***elder brother***, ***elder sister***, ***elder son***, ***elder daughter***. We do not use them with *than*: *I am ~~elder~~ than my sister.*

3 Adverbs with *-er* / *-est*

3a ***-er*** and ***-est*** are added to adverbs which have the same form as adjectives, to make their comparative and superlative forms:

early	*earl**ier***	*earl**iest***	*late*	*lat**er***	*lat**est***
fast	*fast**er***	*fast**est***	*hard*	*hard**er***	*hard**est***

E.g. *Jim always goes to bed* ***earlier*** *than Mark, but Bill goes to bed* **(*the*)** ***latest***.

3b Other adverbs with ***-er*** comparison are:

*soon ~ **sooner** ~ **soonest*** *near ~ **nearer** ~ **nearest***

E.g. (i) *They arrived **sooner** than I expected.*

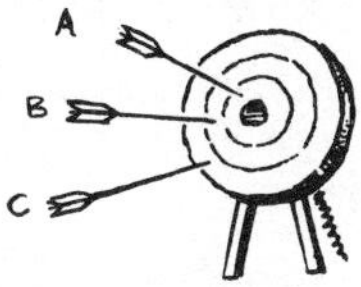

(ii) *'A' is **nearest** to the centre.*

3c Five common adverbs have irregular comparative and superlative forms:

*well ~ **better** ~ **best*** *badly ~ **worse** ~ **worst***
*far ~ **further** ~ **furthest*** *much ~ **more** ~ **most***
*little ~ **less** ~ **least***

[See WELL, BAD / BADLY, FAR / FURTHER, MUCH, MORE / (THE) MOST, LITTLE / A LITTLE, LESS / (THE) LEAST for further details.]

4 **Quantity words + *-er* / *-est***
The following QUANTITY WORDS (determiners and pronouns) also have special comparative and superlative forms:

*much ~ **more** ~ **most*** *little ~ **less** ~ **least***
*many ~ **more** ~ **most*** *few ~ **fewer** ~ **fewest***

[These words appear as separate entries in this book. Look them up for further details. For ***most*** see MORE / (THE) MOST, for ***least*** see LESS / (THE) LEAST, for ***fewer*** and ***fewest*** see (A) FEW.]

---

even /ˈi:vn̩/ (*adverb or adjective*)

- ***Even*** as an ADVERB goes before the word, phrase, or clause it qualifies.
- ***Even*** is also an ADJECTIVE, as in: '*2, 4, 6 and 8 are **even** numbers.*'

1 ***Even*** (adverb) means 'This is something more than you expected'.

E.g. *I liked her last book, but this one is **even better**.*
*'Can you stand on your head?' 'Yes, that's easy. **Even a fool** can do that.'*

After NOT or ***n't***, ***even*** means 'This is less than you expected'.

E.g. *'Have you finished your homework yet?' 'No. I have**n't even started** it.'*

2 Idioms

2a ***Even if*** and ***even though*** (subordinating conjunctions) mean: 'This is a condition that you would not expect'.

E.g. *He enjoys sailing* ***even if the weather is rough.***
I wouldn't sell that house ***even if you gave me a million pounds!***

Even if expresses a real or unreal condition. [See UNREAL MEANING.]

2b ***Even though*** is a stronger form of ***although***.

E.g. ***Even though the captain was badly injured****, he managed to save several of the crew from drowning.*

NOTE: Notice the difference between ***even if*** and ***even though***:
(i) ***'Even if*** / (ii) ***'Even though*** } ***he loves her****, he can't marry her.'*

(i) ***even if*** = 'I don't know whether he loves her . . .'
(ii) ***even though*** = 'I know he loves her, but in spite of this . . .'

2c ***Even so*** is a linking adverb expressing CONTRAST.

---

ever /ˈevəʳ/ *(adverb)*

- ***Ever*** means 'at any time' or 'at any time in your life'.
- ***Ever*** is the opposite of NEVER (***never*** = 'at no time').
- ***Ever*** is often used with the PRESENT PERFECT form of the verb.

1 ***Ever*** is an any-word [see SOME- WORDS AND ANY- WORDS]. It is generally used in questions and after negatives.

E.g. ***Have you ever*** *been to Paris?*
'Did you ever *see a snake dance when you lived in India?' 'No, never.'*
*I have****n't ever*** *seen such wonderful paintings.*
(= 'I have never seen such wonderful paintings.')

NOTE (i): ***Ever*** is used in the comparative expressions ***as ever*** and ***than ever***.
E.g. *She's over fifty, but she sings as beautifully* ***as ever*** (= 'as she has at any time in the past').
You'll have to try harder ***than ever****, if you want to win a prize* (= 'than you have at any time in the past').

NOTE (ii): We use ***ever*** to add emphasis to a WH- WORD.
E.g. *What* { ***ever*** / *on earth* } *are you doing?*
[Compare WH-EVER WORDS.]

every /ˈevrɪ/ (*determiner*)

- ***Every*** has roughly the same meaning as ALL.
- We use a singular countable noun after ***every***.

E.g. ***every*** *day*, ***every*** *house*, ***every*** *growing child*

- Compare ***every*** with EACH [See 4 below].

1 ***Every* + singular noun**

E.g. (i) ***Every house*** *in the street has a garden.*

(ii) *She gets up early* ***every day*** *of the week.* (= 'on Monday, Tuesday, Wednesday, Thursday, Friday, Saturday, and Sunday')

2 ***Every* + ONE**
Every has no PRONOUN form. [Contrast NO, which has the pronoun form NONE.] Instead, use ***every*** + ***one*** (and put a stress on ***one***).*

E.g. (i) *Our cat had five kittens, and* ***every one*** *of them was white.*

Last year, she had four and ***none*** *of them was white.*

(ii) *I like Iris Murdoch. I've read* ***every one*** *of her novels.*

*Notice the difference between ***every one*** (spelled as two separate words) and ***everyone*** (spelled as one word, with stress on the first syllable), which means 'everybody'.

3 ***Every* followed by a singular verb**
When ***every*** (. . .) + noun is the SUBJECT, use a singular verb (Verb + **-s**) [see AGREEMENT].

E.g. ***Every*** *growing* ***child needs*** *milk.*

The same applies to ***every one*** (. . .) as subject.

E.g. ***Every one*** *of the public telephones* ***is*** *broken.*

NOTE: [On ***every*** followed by ***he*** / ***she*** or ***they***, see HE AND SHE 2 and THEY 2a.]

4 ***Every* and *each***

Every (one) and ***each*** have generally the same meaning. But:

(a) You cannot use ***every*** in referring to ***two***:

> ***each*** *of my parents* but not: ~~***every***~~ ~~*one*~~ *of my parents*

(b) Use ***each*** when thinking of all members of a group one at a time. [See EACH 1, 2.]

---

everything /ˈevrɪθɪŋ/ everyone /ˈevrɪwʌn/ everybody /ˈevrɪbɒdɪ/ (*indefinite pronouns*), and everywhere /ˈevrɪweəʳ/ (*adverb of place*)

---

1 These '***every***-words' contain the meaning of ALL [compare EVERY].

Everything means 'all things'.

Everyone means 'all people'

> (***everybody*** has the same meaning as **everyone**, but is less common).

Everywhere means 'at / in all places'.

E.g. *The village store sells **everything** that you need.*
*The priest knows **everyone** in the village.*
*Have you seen my watch? I've looked **everywhere** for it.*

2 ***Everything*** and ***everyone***, if they are SUBJECT of a CLAUSE, take a SINGULAR verb.

E.g. ***Everything has*** *changed since I was last here.*
Everyone needs *friends.*

NOTE: [On ***he / she*** or ***they*** after ***every-*** words, see HE AND SHE 2, and THEY 2a.]

3 ***Everything*** + ADJECTIVE

Everything comes before, not after, an adjective.

E.g. *We'll do **everything possible** to support you.*

---

except, except for /əkˈsept/, /əkˈsept fəʳ/ (*preposition*)

► ***Except (for)*** is the opposite of ***in addition to*** or ***as well as***. It means '***apart from***'.

1 ***Except for*** introduces an adverbial, which can occur in front position.

E.g. ***Except for her awful hairstyle****, she's a good-looking woman.*
*The office was empty, **except for the secretary**.*

2 You can use ***except*** or ***except for*** before a phrase which modifies a noun.

E.g. *Everyone in the family is tall and dark,* ***except (for) my mother****: she's short and fair.*
None of the Common Market countries ***except (for) Belgium*** *has agreed to the proposal.*

except that /əkˈsept ðət/ (*subordinating conjunction*)

Except that introduces an ADVERBIAL CLAUSE. It expresses the same idea as ***except for***.

E.g. *We had a great time,* ***except that the weather was freezing***. (i.e. 'There was only one thing that was bad: the freezing weather.')

exclamations

► We use exclamations to express our feelings or emotions about something.

1 Here are some examples of exclamations in use:

1a

2 Some exclamations are special 'emotion words' (sometimes called 'interjections'). For example:

ah /ɑː/ satisfaction, recognition.
E.g. ***Ah**, there he is.*

hey /heɪ/ calling for attention.
E.g. ***Hey**! Just look at that!* <not polite>

oh /əʊ/ surprise, disappointment.
E.g. ***Oh**, I wasn't expecting you yet.*

ooh /uː/ pleasure.
E.g. ***Ooh**, how lovely!*

ow /aʊ/ pain.
E.g. ***Ow**, that really hurts!* (also ***ouch*** /aʊtʃ/.)

ugh /ʌh/ disgust.
E.g. ***Ugh**, this tastes awful.*

3 ***mm . . .*** (a continuous 'm' sound) has several different meanings.

E.g. ***mmmm****. That smells good!* (with long falling pitch.)
mm? (with high rising pitch) means 'Sorry, I didn't hear.'
mm . . . ***mm*** (with falling pitch) means 'Yes. (I agree).'

4 These exclamations are in order of greater and greater feeling:

Great!
Wonderful! } something good!
Fantastic!

Oh dear!
Damn! **!*** *Blast!* **!***
Oh hell! **!!*** *Oh God!* **!!*** } something bad!
Bloody hell! **!!!***

Oh! *Well!*
My goodness! *Good heavens!* } a surprise!
My God! **!*** *Good God!* **!***

*The words marked **!**, **!!**, **!!!** are taboo, i.e. are not in polite use. Don't use them unless you want to make a very strong impression (especially that marked **!!!**)!

NOTE: We usually use the exclamation mark **(!)** with exclamations, but this is not necessary [see PUNCTUATION 1d]. ***Good.*** and ***Good!*** are both correct, but ***Good!*** expresses a stronger feeling.

5 **What and How exclamations**

WHAT (A) + (ADJECTIVE) + NOUN

E.g. ***What*** *a surprise!* ***What a*** *shame!* ***What*** *fun!* ***What a*** *lovely day!*

HOW + ADJECTIVE / ADVERB

E.g. ***How*** *wonderful!* ***How*** *strange!* ***How*** *silly!* ***How*** *unfortunate!*

6 Exclamations are sometimes whole sentences. They contain one of these words: ***what*** [see WHAT 4], ***how*** [see HOW 4], ***such*** [see SUCH 1a], ***so*** [see SO 1].

6a Patterns:

WHAT (A) . . . SUCH (A)	+ (ADJECTIVE) + NOUN	***What*** *(a)* ***Such*** *(a)* } *(tasty) soup!*
HOW . . . SO	+ { ADJECTIVE ADVERB	***How*** ***So*** } { *quick!* *quickly!*

6b Exclamations with ***what*** and ***how*** have the ***what-*** or ***how-***phrase at the front. After the ***what-*** or ***how-***phrase the word order must be subject + verb.

E.g. (i) ***What terrible weather*** *we're having for the time of year!*
(ii) ***What an awful example*** *this is!*
(iii) ***How lovely*** *the garden looks today!*

6c The word order for exclamations with ***such*** and ***so*** is:

SUBJECT + VERB + { SUCH-PHRASE / SO-PHRASE }

Contrast examples (i)–(iii) above with:

E.g. (i) *We've been having **such terrible weather** for the time of year!*
(ii) *This is **such an awful example**!*
(iii) *The garden looks **so lovely** today!*

7 Questions as exclamations

Finally, we sometimes uses YES-NO QUESTIONS as exclamations.

E.g. (i) ***Isn't** it a pity!*
(ii) ***Aren't** you working hard!*
(iii) ***Didn't** Janet sing well!*

The exclamation begins with a negative and has a falling pitch. It is not really a question. Example (i) means 'What a pity it is!'.

---

excuse me [See PARDON, SORRY AND EXCUSE ME]

---

extent [See DEGREE]

---

far /fɑːʳ/ (*adverb or adjective*) Comparative: ***further**** /ˈfɜːʳðəʳ/ Superlative: ***furthest**** /ˈfɜːʳðɪst/

- The adverb and the adjective have the same form.
- ***Far*** refers basically to DISTANCE.
- ***Far*** means 'a long way (away)'.
- ***Far*** is the opposite of NEAR.
- [See the separate entry for FURTHER for more information.]

*There are two <less common> comparative and superlative forms ***farther*** and ***farthest***. But you can always use ***further*** and ***furthest*** instead.

1 The adverb *far*

Far expresses distance in questions and after negatives.

E.g. (i) *'**How far** is it from London Airport to central London?'*
*'**Not far**. It's about 15 miles.'*

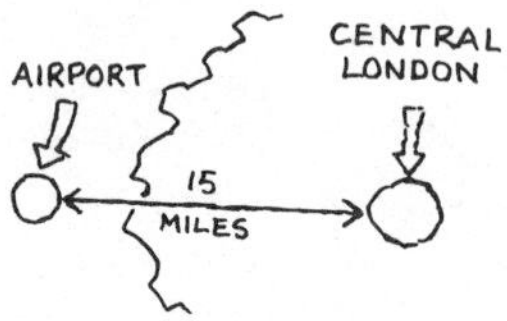

(ii) *'I'm going home now.' 'Do you have **far** to go?' 'No, I don't live (very) **far** from here.'*

A long way is used in positive statements.

E.g. *'Do you live **far (away)**?' 'Yes, I live **a long way** (away) from here.'* (Not: '~~I live far~~ . . .')

2 ***Far* as an adverb of DEGREE**

As an adverb of degree, ***far*** goes before ***too*** and comparative forms.

E.g. *'Grandfather used to be a **far better** golfer than I am.'*
*'Yes, but he's seventy. He's **far too old** to play golf now.'*

Here ***far*** means the same as MUCH.

3 ***Far* as an ADJECTIVE**

Far comes before a noun and is <quite rare>.

E.g. *I heard an explosion at the **far end** of the street, but I didn't see what happened.*
(*The **far end*** = 'the other end')

4 ***Further* and *furthest***

Further and ***furthest*** can be ADVERBS.

E.g. (i) *I've run ten miles – I can't possibly run any **further**!*
(ii) *'Who walked (the) **furthest**?' 'We did. We walked 20 miles.'*

Or, ***further*** and ***furthest*** can be adjectives.

E.g.

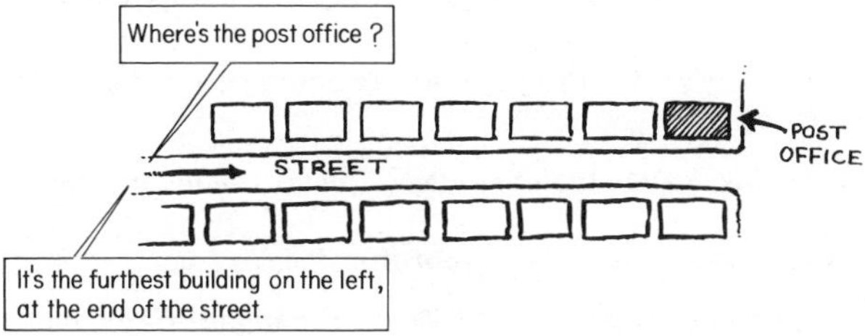

5 **Idioms:**

Far is often used with an abstract meaning.

E.g. *She really **went too far** when she called me an ugly old cow.* (= 'was too extreme')
*That child will **go far**: he's only 16, and he already has a place at Oxford University.* (= 'will be successful')

fast /fɑ:st‖fæ:st/ *(adverb or adjective)* Comparative: ***faster***
Superlative: ***fastest*** [See -ER / -EST 3; ADVERB 4.]

feel /fi:l/ (*irregular verb*) Past Tense and participle form: ***felt***

► ***Feel*** has several different uses. It means:
'think'.
'have the sensation of'. [See PERCEPTION VERB.]
'touch'. [See STATE VERBS AND ACTION VERBS.]

1 When ***feel*** means 'think' –
(a) it is followed by a ***that***-clause [see THAT 1].

E.g. ***I feel (that) you are right***.

(b) it is not used in the Progressive form.

E.g. *~~I am feeling~~ that you are right.*

2 When ***feel*** means 'have the sensation of being . . .' it is followed by a COMPLEMENT, or a LIKE-phrase, or an ***as if*** clause [see AS 4a].

E.g. ***I feel sick.***
I felt (like) an absolute fool.
*The water **feels warmer today**.*
*My arm **feels as if it may be broken**.* <formal> in <U.S.>.

2a It is not usually in the Progressive form, but if you are talking about a person's health, you can say:

*'How **are** you **feeling** today?' '**I'm** not **feeling** too good, actually.'*

2b Like other PERCEPTION VERBS, ***feel*** often follows CAN.

E.g. *'**Can** you **smell** the fire?' 'No, but I **can feel** the warmth.'*

This ***can feel*** describes a state, so the Progressive is not used. [For further details, see PERCEPTION VERB.]

3 When ***feel*** means 'touch', it is followed by an object.

E.g. (i) ***Feel this cloth** – it's like silk.*
(ii) *Why are you **feeling your head**? Did you bang it on the door?*

Here it is an action verb, not a state verb – so you can use the Progressive ***be feeling***. [See STATE VERBS AND ACTION VERBS.]

feminine [See SEX]

(a) few /(ə)ˈfju:/ (*determiner or pronoun*) Comparative: ***fewer*** /ˈfju:əʳ/ Superlative: ***fewest*** /ˈfju:ɪst/

► ***A few*** is a QUANTITY WORD meaning 'a small number (of)'.
► ***Few*** (without ***a***) has the negative meaning 'not many', 'only a small number'.
► ***(A) few*** goes in front of countable nouns. It is equivalent to the uncountable ***(a) little***: e.g. ***a few apples***, ***a little sugar***. [See LITTLE / (A) LITTLE.]

1 ***A few* as a DETERMINER**
A few as a determiner is followed by a PLURAL noun.

E.g. *'We're asking **a few friends** round* to dinner.'*
*'Would you mind waiting for **a few minutes**?'*

* <G.B.>: round || <U.S.>: around.

A few is often used in measurement of time, or distance: ***a few years***, ***a few miles***.

2 ***A few* as a PRONOUN**
A few as a pronoun is often followed by ***of*** + noun phrase.* [See INDEFINITE PRONOUN 2.]

E.g. *Would you like **a few of these flower pots**?*

A few contrasts with MANY or MOST.

E.g. *Only **a few** of the committee members went to the meeting.*
Most *of them stayed at home.*

You can omit the ***of***-phrase if the meaning is clear from the situation.

E.g. *'You should give up smoking cigarettes.'*
*'But I only smoke **a few** (of them) a day.'*

****A few*** must be followed by ***of*** if the noun phrase is a pronoun or a determiner + noun.
E.g. *a few **of us*** *a few **of my friends***.

3 ***Few*** (without ***a***) means 'not many'. It can be a DETERMINER or PRONOUN, and behaves like ***a few***, but the meaning is different. ***A few*** has a more positive meaning than ***few***.

E.g. *Unfortunately, the museum has **few visitors**.*
(= 'not many visitors', 'only a few visitors')
(Very) ***few of the climbers*** *reached the top of the mountain.*

NOTE (i): ***Few*** on its own is <rather formal> [compare MANY]. It is more common to say ***a few***, ***very few***, ***so few*** or ***only a few***.

NOTE (ii): [On ***fewer*** and ***less***, see LESS 2a.]

finite

1 All forms of the verb except INFINITIVES and PARTICIPLES (-ING FORM and -ED FORM), are called finite verbs.

2 MAIN CLAUSES contain finite VERB PHRASES. Non-finite verb phrases are generally found only in SUBORDINATE CLAUSES:

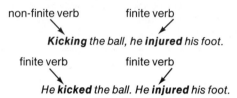

non-finite verb ↘ finite verb ↙

***Kicking** the ball, he **injured** his foot.*

finite verb ↘ finite verb ↙

*He **kicked** the ball. He **injured** his foot.*

3 Finite verbs can normally be changed from Present Tense to Past Tense, or from Past Tense to Present Tense.

E.g. *He **kicked** the ball.* ↔ *He **kicks** the ball.*

NOTE: In a finite verb phrase, the first verb is the only one which is finite. The other words cannot change. For example:

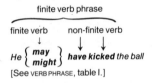

finite verb phrase

finite verb ↓ non-finite verb ↓ ↓

*He {**may** / **might**} **have kicked** the ball*

[See VERB PHRASE, table I.]

first person

1 The first person pronoun forms are:

singular:	*I*	*me*	*my*	*mine*	*myself*
plural:	*we*	*us*	*our*	*ours*	*ourselves*

[For further information, see PERSONAL PRONOUN, -SELF / -SELVES.]

2 ***I*** refers to the speaker.

E.g. *'Hello, can **I** help you?'*

We refers to the speaker and others.

E.g. (i) *In my family, **we** always eat a good breakfast.*
(ii) *'What shall **we** do?' 'Why don't **we** go for a swim.'*

Sometimes, as in example (i), ***we*** does not include the hearer. At other times, as in example (ii), the hearer is included.

3 For <politeness>, we put the first person after the second or third person (i.e. after other pronouns and noun phrases).

E.g. ***You** and **I** ought to work together.* (Not: ~~***I** and **you***~~)
Marilyn** and **I** are just good friends.* (Not: ~~I** and **Marilyn***~~)

4 With one verb, the verb BE, ***I*** has a special verb form: ***am*** or ***'m***. In all other examples of the Present Tense, first person subjects are followed by the BASIC FORM of the verb: ***I like***, ***we like***, etc.

---

for /fɔːʳ/ (weak form /fəʳ/) (*preposition or conjunction*)

- ***For*** is a PREPOSITION with two main uses: 'LENGTH OF TIME' and 'PURPOSE'.
- In <writing>, ***for*** is also a CONJUNCTION meaning 'because' [see BECAUSE / BECAUSE OF].

1 *For* (preposition) meaning 'length of time':

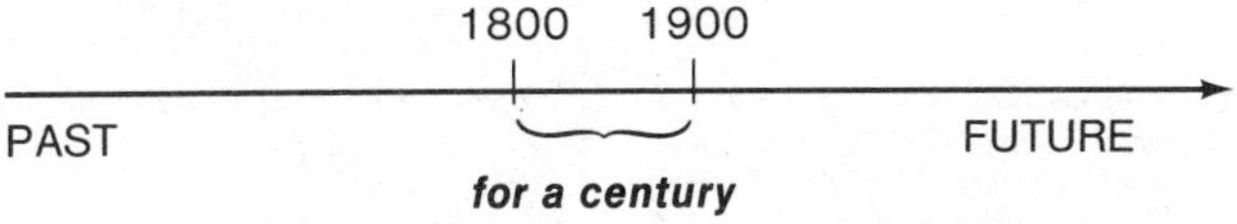

E.g. ***for*** *a second,* ***for*** *three hours,* ***for*** *weeks,* ***for*** *ever*
I've been studying English ***for five years****, but I've lived in England only* ***for a short time****.*
'Could you wait here ***for a minute*** *please?'*
'Darling, I will love you ***for ever****.'*

NOTE: We omit ***for*** in front of ***all***.
E.g. ***all*** *my life,* ***all*** *day,* ***all*** *night,* ***all*** *the time*
Hurry up! I'm not going to wait here ***all night****.* (Not: ~~*for*~~ *all night*)

1a ***For*** is used with the Perfect (or Perfect Progressive [see PRESENT PERFECT 3, 7]) when referring to a period of time which began in the past and continues up to the moment of speaking (or the moment we are thinking of).

E.g. *This farm* ***has belonged*** *to my family* ***for centuries****.*
(= we bought it in 1540 and we still own it now.)
The new political party ***has been developing*** *its policy* ***for only a year****.*
(= it began developing it last year and is still developing it.)

1b ***For*** can also be used with the PAST SIMPLE, in talking about a completed period of time.

E.g. *The course* ***lasted for a month****. It finished yesterday.*

1c ***For*** can also be used with the PAST PERFECT, in talking about a period in the past which lasted up to a specific point in the past.

E.g. *Jim* ***had been divorced for five months*** *when he met his second wife.*

1d ***For*** can be used with any other verb forms, e.g. to describe a period of time in the future.

E.g. *The Prime Minister* ***is likely to stay*** *in hospital* ***for two weeks***.

NOTE: Contrast ***for*** with SINCE.
E.g. *The police have been trying to find the stolen diamonds*
{ ***for*** *eighteen months.*
{ ***since*** *September 1984.* (It is now March 1986)

2 ***For*** **(preposition) meaning 'purpose'**
Examples:

These pills are ***for headaches***.
What *did you do that* ***for****?* (i.e.: '***Why*** did you do that?')
I'm working ***for*** *the United Nations.*

NOTE (i): There are other meanings of ***for***. For example, ***for*** means the opposite of ***against***.
E.g. *Did you vote* ***for*** *the President or* ***against*** *him?*
Also, ***for*** sometimes has the meaning of motion: 'to go to'.
E.g. *The children left home* ***for school*** *at 8.30 a.m.*
For also has the meaning of 'intended receiver'.
E.g. *I gave her a present* ***for the children***.

NOTE (ii): ***For*** also introduces a subject in INFINITIVE CLAUSES [see INFINITIVE CLAUSES 2a, 2b]:
E.g. *The best plan is* ***for Janet*** *to lend you her typewriter.*

4 ***For*** **(conjunction) meaning 'because'**
In <written> English ***for*** is sometimes a conjunction meaning the same as BECAUSE. [See REASON AND CAUSE.] You can use ***for*** instead of ***because*** only when ***for*** is:
(a) in the middle of the sentence (not at the beginning), and (b) before a clause.

E.g. *The village was full of crowds of people dressed in brightly-coloured shirts and summer dresses,* ***for*** *it was the middle of the tourist season.* <written only>

---

formal and informal English [See also POLITE AND NOT POLITE.]

► <Formal> English is the kind of English we use for serious public purposes, especially in print. E.g. official reports, business letters, serious books, public notices, important speeches, news broadcasts.

► <Informal> (or 'colloquial') English is the kind of English we use for private or personal reasons, especially in <speech>. E.g. conversations between friends, private letters, popular television programmes.

► An example:

► For most purposes, a neutral style (with not too many <formal> or <informal> features) is the best.

1 Some marks of <***formal***> style are:
—long, complex SENTENCES.
—ABSTRACT NOUNS (e.g. ***influence, establishment***).
—long, complex NOUN PHRASES.
—words with Latin or Greek roots such as ***ameliorate*** (= 'improve') and ***metamorphosis*** (= 'change of form').
—frequent use of the PASSIVE.
—frequent use of IT-PATTERNS (e.g. ***It seems that*** . . .)

2 Some marks of <***informal***> style are:
—contractions (e.g. ***I'm, didn't***). [See CONTRACTIONS OF VERBS AND NEGATIVES.]
—use of simpler words, especially PHRASAL VERBS (e.g. ***find out*** instead of ***discover***) and PHRASAL-PREPOSITIONAL VERBS (e.g. ***put up with*** instead of ***tolerate***).

E.g. *The wedding has been* ***postponed*** <rather ***formal***>
They've ***put off*** *the wedding.* <rather ***informal***>

forward, forwards /fɔ:ʳwəʳd/, /fɔ:ʳwəʳdz/ (*adverbs*)

1 The adverb ***forward*** refers to MOTION (OR MOVEMENT) towards the front. It is the opposite of ***back***:

forward → ***back*** →

E.g. *As one boxer moves* ***forward****, the other moves* ***back****.*

Forwards can sometimes be used instead of ***forward***, and ***backwards*** instead of ***back***.

2 **Idiom**
Look forward to + Verb-ing . . . means 'think about something nice in the future'. For example, at the end of a letter:

I ***look forward*** *to* ***hearing*** *from you.*

And at the end of a conversation:

I'm ***looking forward*** *to* ***seeing*** *you again.*

fractions How to write and speak them.

► A **fraction** is less than ***one***. [See DECIMAL NUMBERS, NUMBERS, HALF.]

1 $\frac{1}{2}$ = *a* ***half*** /ə/ ˈhɑ:f ‖ ˈhæ:f/ $\frac{2}{3}$ = ***two thirds***

$\frac{1}{4}$ = { *a* ***quarter*** /ˈkwɔ:ʳtəʳ/ ; *a* ***fourth*** /əˈfɔ:ʳθ/ <U.S.> } $\frac{3}{4}$ = { ***three quarters*** ; ***three fourths*** <U.S.> }

1a Except for ***half*** and ***quarter***, we use the ordinal number for the bottom part of a fraction:

$\frac{1}{5}$ = ***a fifth*** $\frac{1}{8}$ = ***an eighth*** $\frac{1}{15}$ = ***a fifteenth***

1b And we use the cardinal number [see NUMBERS 1] for the top part, except that we often use ***a*** / ***an*** instead of ***one***:

$\frac{1}{16}$ = ***a*** / ***one*** } ***sixteenth*** $\frac{3}{16}$ = ***three sixteenths***

1c If the fraction is used with a whole number, we add ***and*** after the whole number when we say the fraction:

$1\frac{1}{2}$ = ***one and a half*** $2\frac{3}{8}$ = ***two and three eighths***

2 To use fractions in phrases and sentences, put:
FRACTION + OF + . . . NOUN

The noun following the fraction can be:
(i) countable (singular). E.g. *a quarter of the* ***cake***
(ii) countable (plural). E.g. *two thirds of the* ***children***
(iii) uncountable. E.g. *three quarters of the* ***money***
[See COUNTABLE AND UNCOUNTABLE NOUNS.]

NOTE: But before ***half*** we can omit ***a****, and after ***half*** we can omit ***of***. So we can say:
a half of *the*
Or: ***half of*** *the* } *egg / eggs / water*
Or: ***half*** *the*
*Except when ***half*** follows a whole number: ***two and a half***, not ***two and half***.

2a Fractions (without ***of***) come before nouns and adjectives [See COMPARISON 3].
Examples:

This house is only ***half as big as*** *that one.*

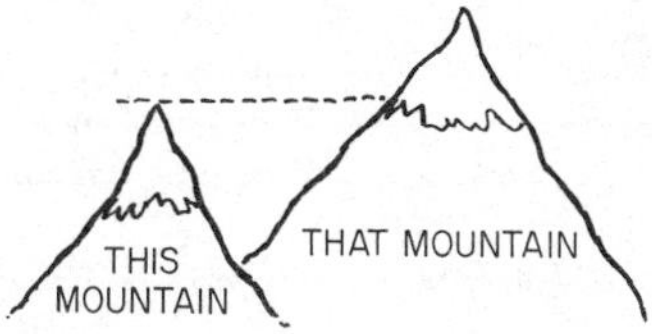

This mountain is (almost) ***three-quarters the height of*** *that one.*

The glass is (over) ***a third full***.

2b Fractions also come before TIME and DISTANCE words.

E.g. *We finished the run in less than* ***half the time*** *allowed.*
I couldn't finish the race: I ran only ***two-thirds of the distance****.*

2c [For ***half an hour***, ***a quarter of an hour***, etc. see TIME, (TELLING THE TIME).]

frequency

► ***Frequency*** words and phrases talk about 'number of times'. They answer the question 'how often?'

E.g. (i) *Ron goes running* ***once a day****, except at weekends, when he goes running* ***twice a day****.*

(ii)

Do you come here often?
Yes. About three times a week.

1 Adverbs of frequency form a scale:
always = 'every time'; ***ever*** = 'at any time'.
usually, ***generally*** = 'most times'.
often, ***frequently*** = 'lots of times'.
sometimes = 'some times'.
rarely, ***seldom*** = 'not many times'.
never = 'no times'.

↑ more often

[All the above adverbs except for ***generally*** and ***frequently*** have separate entries in this book. Look them up for further details. For ***seldom*** see RARELY AND SELDOM.]

1a These adverbs are often placed in middle position [see ADVERB 3]:

{noun phrase / pronoun}	(auxiliary)	adverb	main verb	. . .
The sun		***always***	*rises*	*in the east.*
We		***usually***	*have*	*rolls and coffee for breakfast.*
Presidents	*are**	***often***		*in danger of being killed.*
The trains		***sometimes***	*arrive*	*late.*
I	*have**	***rarely***	*met*	*a more charming person.*
You	*should**	***never***	*drink*	*before driving.*

*Notice the position of the adverb after the auxiliary or after BE.

1b But the adverbs can also appear in front or end position.

E.g. ***Sometimes*** *he's late, but* ***very often*** *he doesn't come at all.*
Why don't you come and visit us ***more often****?*

NOTE: [On ***never***, ***rarely***, and ***seldom*** in front position, see NEGATIVE WORDS AND SENTENCES 6a.]

2 Adverbs or adjectives of frequency in *-ly* [See -LY.]

daily = 'once a day' ***monthly*** = 'once a month'
hourly = 'once an hour' ***yearly*** = 'once a year'

For example:

ADJECTIVE		ADVERB
a ***daily*** *newspaper*	↔	*The newspaper appears* ***daily.***
a ***monthly*** *meeting*	↔	*The meeting takes place* ***monthly***.

Always put the ***-ly*** adverb in end position.

3 Frequency phrases

3a Pattern I:

EVERY + SINGULAR NOUN [See EVERY.]

E.g. ***Every day*** / ***Every morning*** } *he goes to the office.*

Our family visits the country { ***every weekend.*** / ***every month***.

Phrases of this pattern occur in front and end positions.

NOTE: These are some less common patterns with ***every***:
every two weeks (= 'once in two weeks')
every five years (= 'once in five years')
every other week (= 'every second week')
twice every winter ***every half hour*** ***three times every hundred years***.

3b Pattern II:

ONCE / TWICE, etc. + A + SINGULAR NOUN

Use ***a*** instead of ***every*** after words like ***once*** and ***twice***.

E.g. *We meet* ***once a month.***
Twice a year *they give us a medical examination.* (= twice every year)

from /frɒm/ (weak form: /frəm/) (*preposition*)

► ***From*** is a PREPOSITION of motion or movement [see MOTION (OR MOVEMENT) 5].
► ***From*** is the opposite of ***to*** [see TO 1].

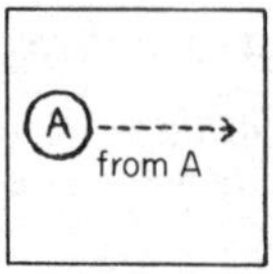

E.g. *I had an excellent flight* ***from Tokyo to Hong Kong****.*
The train ***from Philadelphia*** *is just arriving at Platform 4.*
'Where did you get this book?' 'I borrowed it ***from the library****.'*
Every year, I get a birthday present ***from Canada, from my grandmother****.*

NOTE (i): When you want to ask about someone's town or country, you can say: '*Where do you* ***come from****?*'
E.g. ***I come from Spain*** *– I was born in Madrid.*
But my wife is Russian – she ***comes from Leningrad****.*

NOTE (ii): ***From*** always indicates movement, but ***away from*** [see AWAY 3] often indicates position.
E.g. *Mr Webb, our boss, is ill: he has been* ***away from the office*** *all week.*

in ***front*** *(of)* and ***behind*** /ɪn ˈfrʌnt (əv)/, /bɪˈhaɪnd/ (*prepositions or adverbs*)

► ***In front of*** acts as a PREPOSITION (and is followed by a noun phrase or pronoun).
► ***In front*** acts as an ADVERB.
► ***Behind*** is the opposite of ***in front of*** and ***in front***.

1 Prepositions

E.g. *The car is* ***in front of*** *the bus.*

The bus is ***in front of*** *the cyclist.*
The cyclist is ***behind*** *the bus, which is* ***behind*** *the car.*

2 **Adverbs**

E.g.

front position

Front position is the position of an adverbial (or other optional element) when it comes at the beginning of a clause, before the subject. [See ADVERB 3.]

functions

► **Function** is a term used to describe the various things we can do with language.

1 If you speak you have a reason: the words have a function or purpose. For example, if you want to apologise, you say '***I'm sorry***'. The function of the words '***I'm sorry***' is ***apologising***.

1a To find the function of words, put the words into indirect speech [see INDIRECT SPEECH AND THOUGHT].

E.g. *'Stand up.'* → *He* ***ordered*** *them to stand up.*
'Please sit down.' → *She* ***asked*** *them to sit down.*
'Would you like to sit down?' → *She* ***invited*** *us to sit down.*

In some cases we cannot use the same words in indirect speech.

E.g. *'Hello, how lovely to see you!'* → *She* ***greeted*** *us enthusiastically.*

2 In this table of functions, we include the functions for which there are special entries in this book:

Table of *functions*

function	an example: direct speech		an example: indirect speech
advising [see ADVISING / ADVICE]	*'I think you'd better see a doctor.'*	→	*My friend* ***advised*** *me to see a doctor.*
AGREEING (AND DISAGREEING)	*'I agree. The price is too high.'*	→	*She* ***agreed*** *that the price was too high.*
apologising [see APOLOGIES]	*'I'm sorry (I spilt your coffee)'*	→	*I* ***apologised*** *(for spilling his coffee).*
condoling	*'I'm very sorry to hear of . . .'*	→	*I* ***offered*** *my condolences (or sympathy).*
congratulating [see CONGRATULATIONS]	*'Congratulations (on passing your exam).'*	→	*The teacher* ***congratulated*** *me (on . . .).*
GOOD WISHES	*'Good luck (with your interview)!'*	→	*He* ***wished me good luck*** *(with . . .).*
(SAYING) GOODBYE	*'Goodbye (See you next week!)'*	→	*We* ***said 'goodbye'*** *to them.* *
GREETINGS, saying 'hello'	*'Hello! (How nice to see you!)'*	→	*She* ***greeted*** *me. She said 'hello'.*
introducing [see INTRODUCTIONS]	*'Jane, this is my friend, Peter.'*	→	*She* ***introduced*** *Peter to Jane.*
inviting [see INVITATIONS]	*'Won't you stay for a meal?'*	→	*They* ***invited*** *me to stay for a meal.*
offering [see OFFERS / OFFERING]	*'Would you like an apple?'*	→	*She* ***offered*** *him an apple.*
giving opinions	*'In my view, Bob's lying.'*	→	*He* {***thought*** / ***expressed the opinion***} *that Bob was lying.*
giving PERMISSION	*'You can use my phone.'*	→	*He* ***gave*** *us* ***permission*** *to use the phone.*
prohibitions	*'Do not walk on the grass.'*	→	*Walking on the grass* ***is prohibited***.
promising [see PROMISES]	*'I will definitely pay the bill.'*	→	*John* ***promised*** *to pay the bill.*
giving REPLIES OR ANSWERS	*('How are you?') 'I'm fine.'*	→	*Pat* ***replied*** *that she was fine.*
requesting [see REQUESTS]	*'Would you please shut the door?'*	→	*She* ***asked*** (or *requested) me to shut the door.*
seasonal greetings	*'Happy New Year!'*	→	*They* ***wished*** *us a happy New Year.*
suggestions	*'Why don't we go by train?'*	→	*I* ***suggested*** *that we go by train.*
THANKING PEOPLE	*'Thank you (for being so kind.)'*	→	*They* ***thanked*** *her (for being so kind.)*
warning [see WARNINGS]	*'Drive carefully, now.'*	→	*She* ***warned*** *me to drive carefully.*

*There is no verb or noun for '***saying 'goodbye'*** ' in English. So we have to use direct speech even in reporting.

further /ˈfɜːʳðəʳ/ (*adjective, adverb or verb*) [See also FAR]

1 As an ADJECTIVE, ***further*** means 'extra', 'in addition', 'more'.

E.g. (i)

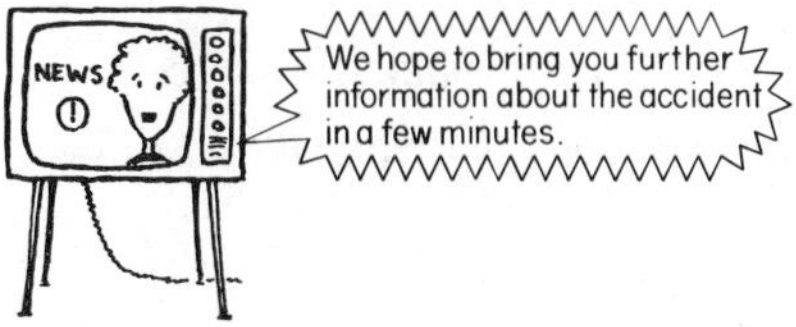
NEWS
We hope to bring you further information about the accident in a few minutes.

(ii) *The administration is having **further discussions** with the unions about pay and conditions.*

(iii) *I have nothing **further to say** at present.*

2 As an ADVERB, ***further*** has a meaning similar to ***further*** as an adjective.

E.g. *The administration wishes **to discuss** the matter **further**.*

It is also a linking adverb meaning 'moreover', 'in addition', 'furthermore' [see LINKING ADVERBS AND CONJUNCTIONS].

E.g. *Many people do not like the idea of performing experiments on animals. **Further(more)**, they disagree with those who kill animals for sport.* <rather formal>

3 Very occasionally, ***further*** is a verb.

E.g. *He married the boss's daughter to **further** his career.* (i.e. 'to be more successful in his job'.)

4 ***Further*** is also the COMPARATIVE form of ***far***;

future

► We use a number of different verb forms to refer to the ***future*** (= 'the time after now') in English:

1 ***will*** + Verb ↑ (most important)
2 ***be + going to*** + Verb
3 Present Simple
4 Present Progressive
5 ***will*** + ***be*** + Verb ***-ing*** (and other forms) ↓ (least important)

[See WILL, (BE) GOING TO, PRESENT SIMPLE, PRESENT PROGRESSIVE.]

► [On future in the past, see PAST TIME 4.]

1 **Will**

There is a future auxiliary WILL (or ***'ll***) + Verb which is used in the following ways:

1a Prediction (i.e. describing something we know or expect will happen).

E.g. *It'll **be** windy tomorrow. There **will be** rain in places.*
*My horoscope says that next year **will bring** me success and happiness.*

1b Expressing a decision about the immediate future.

E.g. *'Which handbag do you want?' '**I'll take** the brown one, please.'*

[See also SHALL.]

2 ***Be + going to* + Verb** [See (BE) GOING TO.]

2a This is very frequently used to talk about plans or intentions. The decision has been made before the moment of speaking.

E.g. (i) *'Do you remember that job I was talking about? **I'm going to** accept it.' 'Ah, good, you've made up your mind about it.'*

(ii)

What are you going to do when you grow up ?
I'm going to be a fireman.

2b ***Be + going to*** is also used for something in the future for which we have present evidence.

(i) *It**'s going to** rain.* ('I can see the clouds')
(ii) *Steve's running well. He**'s going to*** * *break a few records this afternoon.*

*Very often you can use either ***will*** or ***be going to*** for the same predictions. E.g., in (ii), you could say: *'He'**ll** break a few records this afternoon.'* But in the main clause of conditional sentences [see CONDITIONAL CLAUSE] you cannot usually replace ***will*** by ***be going to***.

E.g. *If you take this road you* { ***will*** / ~~***are going to***~~ } *get home quicker.*

[See IF 1b.]

2c How to choose between ***will*** and ***going to***:

3 The Present Simple

3a The Present Simple is used for ***future*** certainties.

E.g. *It's the 29th of May next Friday, isn't it?*
*My English language course **finishes** next week.*
*What time **does** your plane **take** off?*

3b The Present Simple is used for the future in some SUBORDINATE CLAUSES. We use the Present Simple instead of ***will*** mainly in clauses of TIME and in CONDITIONAL CLAUSES [see PRESENT SIMPLE 3a]. Examples of words which begin these clauses are:

if:	E.g. ***If** it **rains**, the match will be cancelled.*
as soon as:	E.g. *I'll call you **as soon as I'm** ready.*
before: ***after***: ***when***:	E.g. ***Before*** ***After*** ***When*** } *the princess **arrives**, the band will play some music.*
in case:	E.g. *I'll bring an umbrella, just **in case** it **rains**.*
unless:	E.g. ***Unless I find** the tickets, we won't be able to go to the theatre.*
until:	E.g. *Let's wait **until** it **stops** raining.*
while:	E.g. *I'll take a photo **while** you **are** on the dance floor.*

NOTE: There are also some ***that***-clauses [see THAT 1] and WH-CLAUSES which have a Present Simple verb for the future. E.g. after ***hope***, ***whatever*** or ***which***:
*I **hope** (that) you **have** a pleasant journey.*
*Don't get lost, **whatever** you **do**.*
*The team **which wins** tomorrow's match will be the best team in the world.*

4 The Present Progressive (*be* + Verb-ing)

This structure is used for talking about future plans or arrangements (but these plans are not so fixed as with the Present Simple).

E.g. (i)

Mr Black is working in Glasgow next Friday. But he'll be back in the office on Monday.
SECRETARY

(ii) ***I'm meeting** her next week.*
(iii) *Next winter, the rock group **is touring** the U.S.A.*
(iv) *Their friends **are driving** to Scotland at the weekend.*
(v) *'When **are** you **leaving**?' 'On Saturday.'*

5 Other ways of talking about the future

These are some other ways of talking about the future:

(a) WILL + BE + Verb-ing [See WILL.] ('future progressive')
E.g. *Next week **I'll be talking** about how to use a microscope.*

(b) IS + TO + Verb or: ARE + TO + Verb
E.g. *The West German President **is to visit** Russia.*

(c) BE + ABOUT + TO + Verb (= near future)
E.g. *The mayor **is about to announce** the result of the election.*

(d) BE + ON THE POINT OF + Verb-ing (= near future)
E.g. *The oil company **is on the point of making** an important decision.*

---

gender

is a grammatical term. It refers to the difference between male and female words such as HE AND SHE. (In grammar, the terms 'masculine' and 'feminine' are often used instead of 'male' and 'female'.) [See SEX.]

---

generic

(or general) use of articles [See ARTICLES 4, A / AN 3f, THE 3g, ZERO ARTICLE 3.]

---

genitive

[See POSSESSIVE.]

---

geographical names

(= names of places)

1 Like names of people [see NAMES], names of places generally have no ARTICLE in front of them.

E.g. *Asia,* *India,* *Bali,* *Lagos,* *Texas,* *Oxford Street,*
Central Park.

2 Some geographical names – especially names of mountain ranges and of islands – are plural. In this case, they usually have ***the***.

E.g. Mountains: ***the*** *Andes,* ***the*** *Rockies,* ***the*** *Himalayas.*
Islands: ***the*** *West Indies,* ***the*** *Canaries,* ***the*** *Bahamas.*
Others: ***the*** *Netherlands,* ***the*** *Midlands* (= part of England)

3 With two-word names for the following features, we normally use ***the***.
(a) Hill and mountain ranges.

E.g. ***the*** *Appalachian Mountains,* ***the*** *Black Hills.*

(b) 'Watery' places such as seas, canals, islands.

E.g. ***the*** *Indian Ocean,* ***the*** *Black Sea,* ***the*** *Suez Canal,* ***the*** *Canary Islands.*

(c) 'Manmade' places: buildings, etc.*

E.g. ***the*** *Globe Theatre,* ***the*** *Hilton Hotel,* ***the*** *British Museum,* ***the*** *National Gallery,* ***the*** *Albert Hall,* ***the*** *Eiffel Tower.*

* But no ***the*** is added if the first part of the name is POSSESSIVE.
E.g. *Brown's Hotel,* *Guy's Hospital,* *St. John's Church.*

4 The names of rivers, lakes, and mountains are often in the opposite order to the examples in 3: not 'name word' + 'general word', but 'general word' + 'name word'.

E.g. ***the*** *(River) Thames,* ***the*** *(River) Amazon,* ***the*** *(River) Seine.*
Lake Erie, *Lake Titicaca,* *Lake Baikal.*
(Mount) Vesuvius, *(Mount) Everest,* *Ben Nevis.*

NOTE: The word ***mount*** or ***river*** is often omitted.

---

gerund

[See -ING, -ING FORM, -ING CLAUSE.]
Some grammar books use the word 'gerund' for ***-ing*** participles which act like nouns.

---

get

/get/, ***gets, got, getting,*** { ***got*** <G.B.> / ***gotten*** <U.S.> } (*verb*)
[See also HAVE GOT, HAVE GOT TO.]

► ***Get*** is a very useful verb in <spoken> English.
► ***Get*** has many meanings: look them up in a dictionary.

► In <writing> it is better to avoid ***get*** (except in personal letters), because it belongs to <informal> style.

► Here are some patterns with ***get***:

1 GET + NOUN PHRASE (= 'receive, obtain') [See VERB PATTERN 1.]

E.g. *He **got this car** from a friend.*
*She's hoping **to get a job** as a nurse.*

NOTE: There are particular meanings in this pattern; e.g. ***get*** = 'fetch'.

E.g. *Would you **get** some stamps from the Post Office, please?*

2 GET + ADJECTIVE (PHRASE) (= 'become') [See VERB PATTERN 2.]

E.g. *Don't eat so much. You'll **get fat!***
*The weather's **getting colder** again.*
*They **got lost**.* (i.e. 'They lost their way')

3 GET + ADVERBIAL OF PLACE (= 'arrive') [See VERB PATTERN 3.]

E.g. *The family **gets home** at six.*
*When I **get to New York**, I'll phone you.*

4 GET + PAST PARTICIPLE (+ ***by*** . . .) [See VERB PATTERN 10.]
This pattern is like the PASSIVE.

*E.g. I {**don't get** / **'m not**} **paid** very much.*
*Nothing **gets done** around here unless I do it.*

5 GET + NOUN PHRASE + NOUN PHRASE (= 'fetch') [See VERB PATTERN 11.]

E.g. *Could I **get you something to eat**?*

6 GET + NOUN PHRASE + ADVERBIAL (= 'take', 'put', etc.) [See VERB PATTERN 13.]

E.g. *Wait a minute – I have to **get some money out of the bank**.*

7 GET + NOUN PHRASE + TO-INFINITIVE (= 'make someone do something') [See VERB PATTERN 17.]

E.g. *They tried to **get me to sign** an agreement, but I refused.*

8 GET + NOUN PHRASE + Verb ***-ing*** (= 'make someone / something start an activity') [See VERB PATTERN 19.]

E.g. *My car is stuck in the mud. Could you help me to **get it moving**?*

9 GET + NOUN PHRASE + PAST PARTICIPLE ('make something be done') [See VERB PATTERN 20.]

E.g. *I'm **getting my motorcycle repaired** tomorrow.*
*Jason is **getting his hair cut** at last.*

10 Idioms

There are many idioms with ***get***, so look in a dictionary for examples. They are all <informal>.

---

go /gəʊ/ ***goes, went,*** {***been*** / ***gone***}***, going***

Go is the most important verb of MOTION in English. [See COME AND GO for details.]
There is also a verb idiom ***be going to*** which refers to the FUTURE [See (BE) GOING TO].

(be) *going to* /'gəʊɪŋ tʊ/tə/ (*verb idiom*)

- ► This verb idiom is a common way of talking about the future. [See FUTURE 2 for a general comparison with ***will*** and other Future verb forms.]
- ► ***Be going to*** begins with a form of the verb BE, and is followed by an INFINITIVE (*to* + Verb).

1 Forms

*She **is** / We **are** / He **was*** } ***going to*** { *have a meal in town.* / *do the washing.* / *go * shopping.*

* Notice we do say ***going to go***.

2 Meanings

2a ***Be going to*** is used for talking about what we intend* to do (often in the near future).

E.g.

* This is after the decision is made: contrast ***will*** [see FUTURE 2c].

2b ***Be going to*** is also used for a future event or state for which there are signs or tendencies already in the present (i.e. 'future beginning in the present').

E.g.

Oh dear! I think
he's going to jump.

2c ***Be going to*** is often used as a general verb form for future, especially in <spoken English>. If in doubt about the future, use ***be going to*** and it will usually sound all right.

3 ***Be going to*** **can be used with any tense or verb form**

(A) PAST TENSE: [see PAST TIME 4, 7.]

E.g. *'Can I offer you a drink?' 'Oh, thanks. I **was** just **going to** offer one to you.'*

(B) MODAL AUXILIARIES: (e.g. where the future is not certain)

E.g. *'She looks happy.' 'Yes – I understand that she **may be going to** have a baby.'*

(C) PERFECT: (e.g. for an intention which has not been achieved.)

E.g. *For the past ten years they**'ve been going to** mend the bridge. Now at last they are doing the job.*

(D) PASSIVE:

E.g. *The whole house **is going to be** rebuilt.*

---

good /gʊd/ (*adjective* [*or noun*])

1 ***Good*** has the irregular COMPARATIVE ***better*** /ˈbetəʳ/ and SUPERLATIVE ***best*** /best/

1a ***Good*** as COMPLEMENT (predicative adjective).

E.g. *Jan is (very) **good** (at art). She is also **better** than her sister (at science). Her sister is the **best** in her class (at games).*

1b ***Good*** before a noun.

E.g. *Bob is a (very) **good swimmer**.* (= He swims well.) *He is also a **better student** than his brother. But his brother is the **best actor** in the school.*

2 ***Better*** and ***best*** are also the comparative and superlative of the adverb WELL, and of the adjective ***well*** [see WELL 3] meaning 'in good health'. Notice the difference between:

E.g. *'She looks really **good**. That new jacket suits her.' (**good** = 'handsome, good-looking') 'Yes, she looks **better** in that jacket than in her old one.'*
*'She looks really **well**. I'm so glad she's recovered from her illness.' (**well** = 'in good health') 'Yes, she says she feels much **better**.'*

3 **Idioms**

3a ***Good*** is sometimes a noun, especially in the phrases:

for X's ***good***, ***for*** the ***good of*** Y.

E.g. *Take this medicine – it's **for** your own **good**.*
*Parliament should make laws **for** the **good** of everyone – not just **for** the **good** of a few.*

3b ***Good*** is also a noun when it has a determiner (***no, any, much, some***) in front of it. Examples:

any good.

E.g. *'Will the exhibition be **any good?**'* (= 'at all good')
'Yes, the newspapers say it's excellent.'

no good.

E.g. *'This map may help you if you get lost.' 'That's **no good*** (= 'not useful at all'). *It's a map of Hong Kong, and we're going to Singapore.'*

good wishes

1 **What to say to people when you wish them luck.**

E.g. ***Good luck!*** ***Good luck with*** *your exam!*

I hope everything turns out all right for you.
Thanks. I hope so too. And the same to you. I wish you good luck with your new job.

2 Here are good wishes for special occasions

2a Birthday.

E.g. *Happy birthday.* *Many happy returns (of the day).*

2b Christmas and New Year.

E.g. *Happy* / *Merry* } *Christmas!* *Happy New Year!*
Best wishes for the New Year. <written>

2c Before a holiday, a vacation, a journey, a party, etc.

E.g. *Have a good time!* { *Enjoy yourself.* (one person)
Safe journey! { *Enjoy yourselves.* (more than one)

More <formal>.

E.g. *I (do) hope you have a wonderful time.*
I hope you enjoy your vacation. *I wish you a safe journey.*

---

saying **goodbye**

- ► There are a number of ways of saying '***goodbye***'.
- ► '***Goodbye***' is the most general and useful word.
- ► Always use rising (↗) or fall-rise (∨) INTONATION when saying '***goodbye***'.

1 An example

('***Bye***' is a shorter form of '***goodbye***' – it's more <informal> or <casual>).

2 Other <casual> forms of '*goodbye*'

2a Among younger people or close friends.

E.g. *'See you later.'*
'Yes, okay. ***Bye!****'*

2b One student might say to another.

E.g. *'Well, I'm off now.* ***I'll see you (around).****'*
'Yes, sure. Next week, possibly?'
'Okay, fine. ***Bye****.'*
*'****Cheers. Bye****.'*

3 Some more <formal> or <polite> forms of '*goodbye*'

3a To someone you know a little; for example, someone you have met in the street.

E.g. A: *'Well, I look forward to {meeting / seeing} you again.'*
B: *'Yes, that would be nice.'*
A: ***'Bye-bye.'*** (or '***Goodbye.***')
B: ***'Bye-bye.'*** (or '***Goodbye.***')

3b To someone you have just met for the first time.

E.g. *'Well, it's been really nice meeting you. I hope we meet again sometime.* ***Goodbye.****'*

4 [See LETTERS 4 for how to say '***goodbye***' in a letter.]

greetings

► A ***greeting*** is something you say when you meet someone.

Common ***greetings*** are:

Hello <informal>, (also spelt ***hullo*** in <G.B.>).
Hi! <very informal>.
Good morning, Good afternoon, Good evening <more formal>. (Use these at the time of day mentioned.)

group noun

► A ***group noun*** describes a set or group of people, animals, or things.
► A ***group noun***, like other nouns, can be SINGULAR or PLURAL.

1 Examples of *group nouns*

a ***flock*** (of sheep)

a ***team*** (of players)

2 Group nouns (especially general nouns such as ***group***, ***set***) are often followed by OF + PLURAL NOUN.

E.g. *a **committee of** scientists* — *a **family of** actors*
*a **team of** climbers* — *a **herd of** cattle*
*a **set of** books* — *a **class of** children*

3 Especially in <G.B.>, there is often a choice between SINGULAR and PLURAL verb, after a singular human group noun.

E.g. *The **crowd** {**was** / **were**} delighted by the actor's performance.*

[For further details, see AGREEMENT 2d.]

3a A list of some nouns like this is:

army,	*audience,*	*band,*	*class,*	*club,*
committee,	*council,*	*crowd,*	*department,*	*family,*
government,	*group,*	*nation,*	*navy,*	*the police* *,
population,	*the press* *,	*race,*	*team,*	*union* * *.

* ***The police*** and ***the press*** (= the group of people who work on newspapers) always follow ***the*** or some other definite determiner. They are rather like NAMES. Similar expressions are ***the working class*** and ***the middle class***.
* * ***Union*** in the sense of 'trade union'.

had better /hæd ˈbetəʳ/, or more usually 'd better /(d)ˈbetəʳ/ (*verb idiom*)

► ***Had better*** is similar to a MODAL AUXILIARY: it does not change its form for tense, person etc, and is followed by the BASIC FORM of the verb.
► ***Had better*** is used for recommending action or giving advice.

1 Structure

I / You / We / etc.	***'d*** / ***had***	***better*** Verb . . . (POSITIVE)
	'd / ***had***	***better not*** Verb . . . (NEGATIVE)

2 Use

E.g. *'I think **you'd better** type this letter again, before Mr Lawrence sees it.'*
'Oh dear! Is it as bad as that?'

3 People who say ***I'd better*** or ***We'd better*** are offering advice to themselves.

E.g. ***I'd better*** *go to bed early. I have to catch a train at 6 o'clock tomorrow morning.*

4 Note the use of the negative form.

E.g. *We**'d better not** make any mistakes.*

NOTE: In negative questions [see YES-NO QUESTION], we add ***n't*** to ***had***.
E.g. ***Hadn't*** *you* ***better*** *be more careful?* <rare>
We also add ***n't*** to ***had*** in negative tag questions.
E.g. *They**'d better** improve the standard of their work, **hadn't** they?*

---

half /hɑːf || hæːf/ (*determiner, pronoun, noun, or adverb*)

► ***Half*** represents the FRACTION $\frac{1}{2}$ or the DECIMAL 0.5:

half *a cake*

*a **whole** cake*

1 ***Half* as a determiner and pronoun**
Half is used a lot in expressions of MEASURING and QUANTITY, also in telling the TIME.

E.g. ***half*** a pint of milk ***half*** *an hour* = 30 minutes
half *a dozen* = 6 ***half*** *a dollar* = 50 cents
*It's **half past** three. (= 3.30)*

2 ***Half* as a noun**
When it is a noun, ***half*** has the plural form ***halves*** /hɑːvz || hæːvz/

E.g. *Two **halves** make a whole.*
*We bought the top **half** of the house, and my parents bought the other **half**.*

2a ***Half*** (noun) can also come before another noun.

E.g. *a **half** hour,* *a **half** pound,* *a **half** mile.*

3 ***Half* as an adverb**

As an adverb, ***half*** usually comes before the verb or adjective which it modifies.

E.g. *She **half promised** to lend us her house.*
*The poor animal looked **half dead** with fear.*

[For further details, see FRACTIONS, especially FRACTIONS 2 NOTE.]

---

hardly /ˈhɑːʳdlɪ/ (*adverb*)

- ***Hardly*** is an adverb of degree with a negative meaning (= 'scarcely', 'almost . . . not . . . at all'). E.g. *I **hardly** know her.*
- ***Hardly*** goes with verbs and adjectives, and also with any-words, such as *any*, *anyone*.
- Do not confuse ***hardly*** with *hard*, which is an adjective (as in *hard work*) or an adverb of degree (as in *He* {*works* / *tries*} *hard*).

1 ***Hardly* before an adjective**

E.g. *They made him start work, even though he was **hardly able** to walk.* (= 'almost unable')
*I read the newspapers. It's **hardly necessary** to listen to the news on the radio as well.* (= 'almost unnecessary')

2 ***Hardly* before a main verb**

E.g. *She was so ill that she could **hardly open** her eyes.* (= 'only with difficulty')
*Wendy has changed a lot: I **hardly recognized** her.* (= 'almost didn't recognize')

2a ***Had hardly*** + past participle in the main clause, followed by a *before*-clause [see AFTER AND BEFORE] or a *when*-clause [see WHEN 2], means 'only just':

E.g. ***I'd hardly finished*** *my breakfast* {***before*** / ***when***} *the doorbell rang.* (= 'only just finished')

You can reverse the order for more emphasis [see NEGATIVE WORDS AND SENTENCES 6a].

E.g. ***Hardly had I finished*** *my breakfast* ***when*** *the doorbell rang.* <formal written English>

3 ***Hardly + any-word***

3a ***Hardly any*** {***(one)*** / ***(thing)***} (= 'almost no {(-one) / (thing)}').

E.g. *We've **hardly** talked to **anyone*** / *We've talked to **hardly anyone*** } *about the accident.*
*They looked very thin. They had **hardly** had **anything** to eat for weeks.*

3b ***Hardly at all*** (= 'only a little bit', 'almost not at all').

E.g. *'Do you know Switzerland well?' 'Oh, no, **hardly at all**.'*

3c ***Hardly ever*** (= 'very infrequently', 'almost never').

E.g. *The old lady **hardly ever** goes out at night, because she's afraid someone will rob her.*

---

have /hæv/ (weak form /(h)əv/) (*verb*) [See also HAVE GOT, HAVE GOT TO, HAVE TO.]

► ***Have*** is both a MAIN VERB and an AUXILIARY VERB.
► ***Have*** as a main verb means 'possess', 'have got', etc.
► ***Have*** as an auxiliary verb is used to form the PERFECT.

1 **Forms of the verb *have***
Have has 4 different forms: ***have, has, had, having***.

have is the BASIC form, used as the INFINITIVE, the IMPERATIVE, and the SUBJUNCTIVE (as well as a present form – see below)	
present forms	
has /hæz/, /(h)əz/* contraction: ***'s*** /s/ or /z/**	with *he*, *she*, *it* or SINGULAR NOUN PHRASE as subject
have /hæv/, /(h)əv/* contraction: ***'ve*** /v/	with *I*, *we*, *you*, *they*, or PLURAL NOUN PHRASE as subject
past form	
had /hæd/, /(h)əd/* contraction: ***'d*** /d/	with all subjects
participles	(Main Verb only)
having /ˈhævɪŋ/ ***had*** /hæd/	-ING participle PAST PARTICIPLE

* The second pronunciation is the weak form.
** We pronounce ***'s*** as /s/ after voiceless consonants (e.g. ***Pat's*** /pæts/, and as /z/ after voiced consonants or vowels (e.g. ***Jim's*** /dʒimz/, ***he's*** /hi:z/). [See CONTRACTIONS.]

1a Negative forms: (auxiliary verb) [See CONTRACTIONS.]

have not → ***haven't*** /ˈhævn̩t/
has not → ***hasn't*** /ˈhæzn̩t/
had not → ***hadn't*** /ˈhædn̩t/

2 **The main verb *have*: questions and negatives**
To ask a question, use:

do / does / did + **have** +?

To make the negative, use:

don't / doesn't / didn't + ***have***

exactly as you do with all main verbs.

E.g. *She **has** a job.* ***Does** she **have** a job?* *She **doesn't have** a job.*

NOTE (i) In <G.B.> the auxiliary verb pattern [see 5 below] is sometimes used for a main verb ***have***.
E.g. *'**Have** you any stamps?' 'No, I'm sorry – I **haven't** a single one.'*

NOTE (ii) Instead of the main verb ***have***, in <speech> we often use the idiom HAVE GOT.
E.g. *'**Have** you **got** any stamps?' 'No, I'm sorry – I **haven't got** a single one.'*
Here ***have*** is an auxiliary verb.

3 **Using the main verb *have***
We can use ***have*** as main verb after all auxiliaries including the auxiliary ***have***!

SUBJECT + VERB HAVE + OBJECT

Present Simple:	*He **has** a large house in the country.*
Past Simple:	*We **had** lots of pets when we were children.*
Present Progressive:	*Are you **having** dinner at the Ritz?*
Past Progressive:	*Everyone **was having** a good time.*
Present Perfect:	*Have you **had** any news from your son?*
Past Perfect:	*After they **had had** breakfast, they went out.*
modal + ***have***	*Will you **have** some more to eat?*
modal + Perfect	*I'm feeling sick. I must **have had** too much to eat.* (= I no doubt ***had*** too much)

NOTE: ***Have*** with the passive is rare: ***you've been had*** (= 'you've been tricked').

3a As a main verb ***have*** means
(A) 'possess, have got' (which is a state meaning), or
(B) 'take, receive, eat, take part in' (which is an action meaning.)
[See STATE VERBS AND ACTION VERBS.]

3b For the state meaning:
We can use ***have got***.
We cannot use the Progressive (BE + Verb ***-ing***).

E.g. *Ella **has** a cold.* = { *Ella **has got** a cold.* / *Ella ~~**is having**~~ a cold.* }

Some examples of the state meaning.

E.g. (i) ***have*** {*an idea* / *an opinion*} (ii) ***have*** {*a headache* / *a toothache*}

(iii) ***have*** {*four legs* / *a gold watch*} (iv) ***have*** {*the measles* / *a cold*}

3c For the action meaning:
We cannot use ***have got***.
We can use the Progressive.

E.g.

Present Simple = habit	Present Progressive = activity now
*We **have** a good time (every Saturday night.)*	*We're **having** a good time at Monte Carlo.*
	But not: *We ~~**have got**~~ a good time.*

Some examples of the action meaning.

E.g. (i) ***have*** {*a bath, a shower** / *a haircut*} (ii) ***have*** {*drinks* / *tea or coffee*}

(iii) ***have*** {*breakfast* / *an evening meal*} (iv) ***have*** {*a good time* / *an argument, quarrel* / *(some) trouble (with . . .)*}

(v) ***have*** {*a baby* (i.e. give birth to . . .) / *an operation*} (vi) ***have*** {*a look* (= look) / *a rest*}

* In <U.S.> ***take a bath*** is more common than ***have a bath***.

3d Sometimes ***have*** + noun phrase can take both the ***have got*** and the ***be having*** constructions:

future meaning: We***'ve got***
future or present meaning: We***'re having*** } {a test / an exam / a lesson / a class} this morning.

4 Special verb patterns with *have*

HAVE + {PRONOUN / NOUN PHRASE} + Verb ***-ing*** . . .

E.g. *He **had** us work**ing** every night.* (= 'made us work')

HAVE + {PRONOUN / NOUN PHRASE} + PAST PARTICIPLE . . .

E.g. *John is hav**ing*** {*his car **repaired**.* / *his hair **cut**.* / *his temperature **taken**.*}

In these examples, ***have*** has the meaning of 'causing . . . to happen'.

4a Another pattern with the 'causing . . . to happen' meaning uses the basic form of the verb:

$$\text{HAVE} + \left\{\begin{array}{l}\text{PRONOUN}\\ \text{NOUN PHRASE}\end{array}\right\} + \text{Verb} \ldots$$

E.g. *You really ought to **have** the doctor take a look at that eye.* < especially U.S. >

4b With ***to*** before the basic form of the Verb, the meaning is not 'causing . . . to happen':

$$\text{HAVE} + \left\{\begin{array}{l}\text{PRONOUN}\\ \text{NOUN PHRASE}\end{array}\right\} + \text{TO Verb} \ldots$$

E.g. *Have you **had** something **to eat**?*
*Old Mr Bell **has** no one **to look after** him.*

5 **Auxiliary verb *have***
The auxiliary verb ***have*** is used to make the Perfect forms of all main verbs. Auxiliary ***have*** is normally pronounced as a weak form or contraction [see 1 above].

E.g.	Present Perfect:	*They **have lived** in Canada for years.*
	Past Perfect:	*The tourists said they **hadn't enjoyed** staying in the hotel.*
	Perfect Progressive:	*What **have** you **been doing** today?*
	Perfect Passive:	*Some of the furniture **has been damaged** in the fire.*

[For further details, see PERFECT.]

6 **Tag questions after *have***
Tag questions following the main verb ***have*** with state meaning are formed with ***have*** or ***do***.

E.g. *Cora **has** beautiful eyes,* { ***hasn't*** <G.B.> / ***doesn't*** } *she?*

But with action meaning they are formed only with ***do***.

E.g. *We **had** a marvellous time, **didn't** we?*

[See TAG QUESTIONS if you are not sure what they are.]

have got /(h)əv'gɒt/ (*verb idiom*)

► ***Have got*** is Present Perfect in form, but its meaning is the same as a Present Simple.

► [For more on ***have got***, see HAVE 2 NOTE, 3a, 3b, 3c, and HAVE GOT TO.]

1 **Forms of *have got*:**

basic form and **-s** form	short forms (contractions)	negative forms
have got /(h)əv gɒt/	***'ve got*** /v ˈgɒt/	***haven't got***
has got /(h)əz gɒt/	***'s got*** { /s ˈgɒt/ /z ˈgɒt/	***hasn't got***

The past forms ***had got, 'd got, hadn't got*** are <rare>. Use ***had*** (main verb) instead.

2 ***Have got*** means the same as the main verb HAVE (when HAVE has a state meaning). But it is more <informal>. Its meaning is 'possess', 'own', etc:

3 ***Have got* in different sentence types**

Question:

Negative:

Shortened sentence: In this case, we use ***have*** without ***got***.

E.g. *'**Has** your son **got** a bicycle?' 'Yes, he **has**.'*
*'Who **has got** a football?' 'I **have**.'*

4 ***Have got*** cannot follow an auxiliary verb. (In the idiom '***have got***', ***have*** is always a finite verb.) So we must use ***have***, not ***have got*** in:

E.g. *One day, we will **have** (~~got~~) our own home.*
*Sheila **has had** (~~got~~) many advantages in her life.*

NOTE (i) ***Have got*** is common in the U.K., but not so common in the U.S.A.
E.g. <G.B.> ***Have** you **got** the time?*
<U.S.> *Do you **have** the time?*

NOTE (ii) In <G.B.>, ***have got*** is also the PERFECT of the verb GET meaning 'become', 'obtain', etc.
E.g. *She'**s got** tired of this game.*
In <U.S.>, the form is ***have gotten***.
E.g. *She'**s gotten** tired of this game.*

---

have got to /(h)əv ˈgɒt tʊ/ (weak form: /vˈgɒt tʊ/, /v ˈgɒt tə/, /ˈgɒtə/) (*verb idiom*)

- ***Have got to*** is an <informal> idiom with a meaning very similar to HAVE TO. [Compare also MUST.]
- We usually use the short (contracted) forms ***'s got to*** (/zˈgɒttə/ or /sˈgɒttə/) and ***'ve got to*** (/vˈgɒttə/). We even omit ***have*** entirely in <speech>: /ˈgɒtə/.
- ***Have got to*** is followed by the BASIC FORM of the verb. It has three forms: ***have got to***, ***has got to***, ***had got to***.

1 ***Have got to*** + Verb means 'be obliged to' ('obligation by someone who is not the speaker').

E.g. *She'**s got to** take an English test tomorrow.*
*The cook says you'**ve got to** prepare the vegetables.*

2 ***Have got to*** + Verb means 'necessity'.

E.g. *You'**ve got to** work hard if you want to get rich.*

3 ***Have got to*** + Verb means 'It is necessary to conclude that . . .' ('deduction')

E.g. *'I have ten sons and ten daughters.' 'Twenty children? You'**ve got to** be joking!' 'No, it's a serious matter, believe me.'*

4 ***Have got to*** + Verb does not vary its form much. Also, it does not follow an auxiliary verb. In the following cases, use ***have to*** instead.

E.g. ***had*** (got) ***to*** ***is having*** (~~got~~) ***to*** ***will have*** (~~got~~) ***to*** ***has had*** (~~got~~) ***to***

5 [Compare ***have got to*** with MUST.]

have to /ˈhæv tʊ/, /ˈhæv tə/ (also pronounced /ˈhæf tə/) (*verb idiom*)

1 ***Have to*** is followed by the basic form of the verb: ***have to*** + Verb.
The meaning of ***have to*** is similar to ***must***: it means 'obligation', 'necessity', or 'deduction'.
[Compare MUST, HAVE GOT TO.]

2 **Forms of *have to***

have to, has to, had to, having to

Have to has all the forms of ***have*** as main verb. [See HAVE 1, 2.]

3 **Uses of *have to***

3a Obligation.

E.g. *This is a terrible job. We **have to** start work at 7 a.m.*
*In this country you **have to** be over 17 before you're allowed to drive.*

3b Necessity.

E.g. *Everyone **has to** eat to live.*

3c Deduction.

E.g. *You **have to** be joking!* (= 'you can't be serious.')
*There **has to** be some mistake.*

NOTE: ***Have to, have got to***, and ***must*** have similar meanings.
E.g. *You* {***must*** / ***have to***} *pass this test before you are allowed to join the course.*
But ***have (got) to*** can have a slightly different meaning from ***must***, because it usually describes 'obligation by someone else, not the speaker'. [See MUST 2c NOTE.]

4 **Sentence types with *have to***

E.g. Question: *Do I **have to** sign this form?*
Negative: *We didn't **have to** leave early.*
Shortened answers: *'I **have to** catch the 9 o'clock train.'*
*'Yes, I **do**, too.'*

5 ***Don't have to*** compared with ***mustn't***

Don't have to does not correspond to ***mustn't***.
Mustn't means 'it is essential that something does not happen'.
Don't have to means 'it is not necessary or essential'.

E.g. *Witnesses **mustn't** tell lies at a trial: they must tell the truth.*

But: *The defendant (the person accused) **does not have to** give evidence. He can remain silent if he chooses to.*

6 ***Have to*** can follow auxiliary verbs, e.g. ***will have to***, ***may have to***, ***has had to***, ***is having to***.

E.g. Future: *We **will have to** get up early to catch the bus.*
Perfect: *We **have had to** cut down the size of our work force.*
Progressive: *We've had no rain for months: people **are having to** save water.*

---

he and ***she*** /hi:/ (weak form /(h)ɪ/), /ʃi:/ (weak form /ʃɪ/) (*pronouns*)

► ***He*** and ***she*** are third person singular personal pronouns. [See PERSONAL PRONOUN 1, 3.]
► ***He*** refers to a male person, and ***she*** refers to a female person [but see 2 below].

1 **Forms**
He and ***she*** are forms used as SUBJECT of a clause or sentence. Their other forms are:

		object pronoun	possessive determiner	pronoun	reflexive
male:	***he***:	***him*** /hɪm/	***his*** /hɪz/	***his*** /hɪz/	***himself***
female:	***she***:	***her*** /hɜ:ʳ/	***her*** /hɜ:ʳ/	***hers*** /hɜ:ʳz/	***herself***

2 **Choosing *he* or *she***
There is a problem: what pronoun should we use when we don't know whether the person is male or female?

2a Many people (especially in <G.B.>) use ***he*** (***him, his, himself***).

E.g. (i) *Before starting the examination, every student should write* ***his*** *name on the paper.*
(ii) *A good teacher always makes sure that* ***he*** *is well prepared for the lesson.*

(This used to be generally considered 'correct'.)

2b Many other people use ***he or she*** (***him or her, his or her***, etc).

E.g. (i) *Before starting the examination, every student should write* ***his or her*** *name on the paper.*
(ii) *A good teacher always makes sure that* ***he or she*** *is well prepared for the lesson.*

(This is preferred because it does not favour males; but it can be awkward.)

2c In <informal English> we often use the third person plural pronoun THEY (***them***, ***their***, etc).

E.g. (i) *Before starting the examination, every student should write* ***their*** *name on the paper.*
(ii) *A good teacher always makes sure that* ***they*** *are well prepared for the lesson.*

(This form is popular, because ***they*** can refer to females and males. But ***they*** is plural, so many people think it is not 'correct' here. It is best to avoid ***they*** (meaning '***he or she***') in serious writing.)

2d Some people use a special written pronoun form ***s/he***, meaning '***she or he***'.

2e None of these choices is completely satisfactory. [For further discussion, see SEX.] But you can usually avoid the problem if you try. For example, you can change sentences (i) and (ii) into the plural.

E.g. (i) *. . . all* ***students*** *should write* ***their*** *names on the paper.*
(ii) *Good* ***teachers*** *. . . make sure that* ***they*** *are well prepared . . .*

3 ***He* and *she* in contrast to *it***
It is like ***he*** and ***she***, except that it refers to something which is not a person (or to a newborn baby whose sex we do not know). [See IT 2.]

headword (or head)

The main word of a phrase. For example, a noun is usually the ***headword*** of a noun phrase. [See MODIFIER, PHRASE 3a.]

hear /hɪəʳ/ ***hears, heard, hearing*** (*verb*) [See PERCEPTION VERB.]

her /hɜːʳ/ (weak form /(h)əʳ/). (*third person singular female personal pronoun or possessive determiner*)

Her is (a) the OBJECT PRONOUN form of ***she***,
and (b) the POSSESSIVE DETERMINER form of ***she***.

E.g. *'Do you know Joan?' 'Yes, I've met **her**, but I haven't met **her** husband.'*

[See PERSONAL PRONOUN, HE AND SHE.]

here /hɪəʳ/ (*adverb of place*)

► ***Here*** means '(at) this place': it is the opposite of THERE.

1 ***Here* can point to something near the speaker**

E.g. *'Where's the newspaper?' 'It's **here**, on this table.'*

or a place where the speaker is:

E.g. *This is a very good restaurant. I have eaten **here** lots of times.* (**here** = at this restaurant)

2 ***Here* can come after some prepositions of place**

in here, ***up here,*** ***down here,*** ***over here***

This is the highest mountain in the area. You get a wonderful view from up here.

3 ***Here* can announce something which the speaker is going to say**

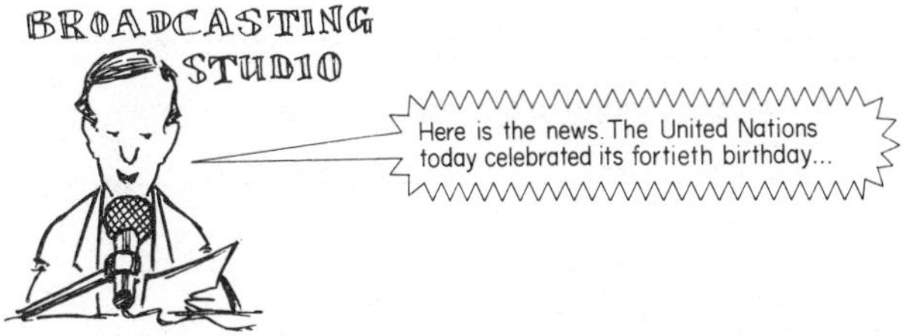
BROADCASTING STUDIO
Here is the news. The United Nations today celebrated its fortieth birthday...

4 Some sentences begin with ***Here is,*** ***Here are,*** ***Here come(s)***.

E.g. ***Here's*** *the money I owe you.* (We say this when we are giving the money.)
'Have you seen my glasses?' 'Yes, ***here*** *they are, on this shelf.'*
Here *comes the taxi you ordered.* (We say this when we can see the taxi coming.)

These sentences are emphatic, almost like exclamations.
We put the subject of the sentence at the end [see INVERSION 6, 6 NOTE] unless it is a personal pronoun. Contrast:

Here *are* ***the children***. but: ***Here they*** *are.* *

* No contraction is possible if the verb comes at the end: ***Here they~~'re~~***.

---

hers /hɜ:ʳz/ (*third person singular female possessive personal pronoun*)

Hers is the POSSESSIVE PRONOUN form of ***she*** [see HE AND SHE].

E.g. *'Whose is this car?' 'It's* ***hers.****'*
That smoker's cough of ***hers*** *will kill her one of these days.*
Ivan and Sonia are both good dancers, but his performance was better than ***hers***.

---

herself /həʳˈself/ (weak form /(h)əʳˌself/) (*third person singular female reflexive pronoun*) [see -SELF, -SELVES.]

Herself is the reflexive form of ***she*** [see HE AND SHE].

E.g. *That girl has hurt* ***herself****. Please help* ***her***.

him hɪm/ (weak form /(h)ɪm/) (*third person singular male personal pronoun*)

Him is the OBJECT PRONOUN form of ***he*** [see HE AND SHE].

E.g. *'I've just met Vera's brother.' 'Do you like **him**?'*

himself /hɪmˈself/ (weak form: /(h)ɪmˌself/) (*third person singular male reflexive pronoun*)

Himself is the reflexive form of ***he*** [see HE AND SHE].

E.g. *That boy has hurt **himself**. Please help **him**.*

[Compare HERSELF.]

his /hɪz/ (weak form /(h)ɪz/) (*third person singular male possessive determiner and pronoun*)

1 ***His*** is
(a) The possessive determiner form of ***he***.

E.g. *Sam loves **his** job.*

(b) The possessive pronoun form of ***he***.

E.g. *'Have you seen Andrew? This cassette is **his**.'*

[See HE AND SHE.]

2 Compare the different roles of ***his*** and HER / HERS:

		possessive	
	object pronoun	determiner	pronoun
male:	***him***	***his***	***his***
female:	***her***	***her***	***hers***

historic present [See PRESENT SIMPLE 3b]

This is the name usually given to the PRESENT TENSE describing the PAST.

home /həʊm/ (*noun*)

1 ***'Home'*** is the place where you live. ***Home*** normally has no ARTICLE (***a*** / ***an*** or ***the***) in front.

E.g. *I left **home** when I was 18.*
__Home__ is where I am happiest.
*His **home** is in Brussels, although he's Italian.*

2 Notice these common adverbial expressions:

at home E.g. *I'm **at home** if you need me.*

(*away*) ***from home*** E.g. *She's studying* {*away **from*** / *a long way **from***} ***home***.

home (adverbial of motion) E.g. *You're going **home** early. Are you bored?*

how /haʊ/ (wh- *adverb*)

► ***How*** is a WH- WORD, used in WH- QUESTIONS, EXCLAMATIONS, and for introducing SUBORDINATE CLAUSES.
► ***How*** is the only wh- word which is not spelled with a ***wh-*** (Compare ***who, what, when, why,*** etc.)
► ***How*** has many uses.

1 ***How* asks a question about means, manner, or instrument**
[See WH- QUESTION]. It means 'In what way?', 'By what means?'.

E.g. ***How*** *do you spell your name?*
*'**How** do you get from here to the City Hall?'* (asking for directions)
*'**How** are you travelling?' 'By plane, and then by boat.'*
*'**How** was he murdered?' 'With a knife, or with some other kind of sharp instrument.'*

2 ***How* also asks for your feeling or opinion about something**

2a It acts as an adverbial (= adverb of degree) with verbs such as ***like***.

E.g. *'**How** did you {like / enjoy} the party?' 'Very much.'*

2b It acts as COMPLEMENT with ***be, feel, look, seem, appear, sound, smell, taste***.

E.g. *'**How** is your leg? I hear you broke it when you went skiing.' 'Much better thank you.'*

How do I look? I've just had my hair done!
Er... wonderful!

3 ***How*** also comes before an adjective, an adverb, or a quantity word, in asking questions about DEGREE, DISTANCE, FREQUENCY, and LENGTH OF TIME:

3a Before adjectives (degree).

E.g. *'**How** old are you?' 'Nearly twenty.'*
*'**How** tall are you?' 'About six foot.'*

3b Before adverbs:
(I) degree

E.g. *'**How** soon does the next bus leave?' 'In 40 minutes.'*
*'**How** well can you speak Chinese?' 'Not at all well – I'm only a beginner.'*

3c (II) distance: ***how far?***

E.g. *'**How far** is it to the next garage?' 'Less than a mile'.*

3d (III) frequency: ***how often?***

E.g. *'**How often** do you visit the dentist?' 'I go for a check-up every six months.'*
*'**How often** is there a flight to Caracas?' 'Three times a week.'*

3e (IV) length of time: ***how long?***

E.g. *'**How long** are you going to stay in Bombay?' 'For two years.'*
*'**How long** will the meeting last?' 'About a couple of hours.'*
*'**How long** ago did all this happen?' 'More than three thousand years.'*

3f Before quantity words: ***how much? how many?***

E.g. *'**How much** does that jacket cost?' 'Ninety dollars'*

*'**How much** do you weigh?'* { *'About 140 pounds.'* <U.S.>. / *'About 10 stone.'* <G.B.>. }

*'**How much*** { gasoline <U.S.> / *petrol* <G.B.> } *did you put in the tank?'*
'Fifteen gallons'.

*'**How many** people voted for the motion?' '210'. 'And **how many** voted against?' 'Only 52.'*

4 ***How*** (as adverb of degree) also introduces exclamations [see EXCLAMATIONS 5, 6].

E.g. ***How** silly these latest fashions are!*
***How** I loved that little dog!* (= 'I loved him very much indeed')

5 ***How + about*** frequently introduces suggestions in conversation.

E.g. ***How about** going to the disco tonight?*
***How about** a cup of tea? Would you like one?*

6 We often say: *Hello, **how** are you?* when we greet somebody.

---

however /haʊˈevə^{r}/ (*adverb*)

► ***However*** is used to make contrasts [see CONTRAST]
(a) as a WH-EVER word (like WHOEVER, WHENEVER), and
(b) as a LINKING ADVERB, meaning 'yet' or 'nevertheless'.

1 As a wh-ever word, ***however*** has functions similar to HOW, especially as an adverb of degree.
However expresses a contrast between two ideas. (This type of clause is <rarer in U.S.>.)

E.g.
positive idea — ***However** rich he may be,* / negative idea — *he's still not marrying my daughter.*
negative idea — ***However** hard the work is,* / positive idea — *you can always succeed if you try.*

2 As a linking adverb, ***however*** also expresses a contrast, (like BUT). Its style is <rather formal>. ***However*** can be placed in the front, middle, or end position in the sentence.

E.g.
negative idea — *We've been advised by the government not to make any further offers to the unions.*
positive idea — *We have decided, **however**, to carry out a thorough re-examination of the pay and conditions of the work force.*

(a) hundred /ˈhʌndrəd/ (*number*) = 100 [See NUMBERS 5a, QUANTITY WORD.]

hypothetical meaning [See UNREAL MEANING.]

I /aɪ/ (*1st person singular personal pronoun*) [See PERSONAL PRONOUN.]

The forms of ***I*** are:

subject pronoun	object pronoun	possessive		reflexive pronoun
		determiner	pronoun	
I /aɪ/	***me*** /mi:/	***my*** /maɪ/	***mine*** /maɪn/	***myself***

I refers to the speaker or writer.

E.g. *'How are you?'* hearer → becomes → speaker *'**I'm** fine.'*

Notice that ***I*** is written with a capital letter, even when it is in the middle of a sentence.

E.g. *Can **I** help you?*

idiom

1 An ***idiom*** is a group of two or more words which we have to treat as a unit in learning a language. We cannot arrive at the meaning of the ***idiom*** just by adding together the meanings of the words inside it.

E.g. *John and Mary used to **be hard up**.* (= 'They had very little money'.)

2 PHRASAL VERBS and PHRASAL-PREPOSITIONAL VERBS are an important class of ***idioms***.

E.g. *I **get on with** my teacher very well.* (This is an ***idiom***: it's a phrasal-prepositional verb. It means, *'I have a friendly relationship with my teacher.'*)
*I saw him **get on** the bus*. (This is not an ***idiom***)

i.e. /aɪˈi:/ (*linking adverb*) (abbreviation) is short for Latin ***id est*** ('that is'). It links two clauses or ideas, where the second explains first.

E.g. *It's raining cats and dogs, **i.e.**, it's raining heavily.*

[Compare E.G., VIZ.]

if /ɪf/ (*subordinating conjunction*) [See CONDITIONAL CLAUSE.]

- ***If*** introduces a CONDITION (something which may or may not happen, depending on circumstances).
- The adverbial clause beginning with ***if*** usually comes before the main clause [see CONDITIONAL CLAUSE].
- The ***if***-clause does not contain WILL for future time.
- ***If*** also means 'whether', and introduces an indirect question [see INDIRECT QUESTION 1].

1 The four main kinds of condition

There are four main kinds of condition expressed by ***if***-clauses:

(A) The present condition (most common)
(B) The will-condition (often called the 'first conditional')
(C) The would-condition (the 'second conditional')
(D) The would-have-condition (the 'third conditional')

We give examples of these kinds, using this common pattern:

IF + CLAUSE , MAIN CLAUSE

NOTE (i): You can also place the ***if***-clause after the main clause, or <rarely> in the middle of it.
E.g. ***If you like,*** *you can borrow my bicycle.*
= *You can borrow my bicycle,* ***if you like.***
= *You can,* ***if you like,*** *borrow my bicycle.*

NOTE (ii): We can place ***then*** in front of the main clause to emphasise the preceding ***if***.
E.g. ***If*** *you are right,* ***then*** *everyone else is wrong.*
[For further examples, see DOUBLE CONJUNCTION 7.]

1a (A) Present condition

Form:
IF + . . . PRESENT SIMPLE . . . , . . . PRESENT SIMPLE . . .
Meaning: This has the present simple in both clauses, and means that the condition can be true at any time [see PRESENT SIMPLE 2a, 2b].

E.g. {***If*** / ***When***} ***I eat*** *too much,* ***I get*** *fat.* ('This always happens.')
{***If*** / ***When***} *somebody* ***waves*** *a red flag, it usually* ***means*** *danger.*
(A general rule)

In this type of condition, ***if*** means almost the same as WHEN or WHENEVER.

NOTE: But when ***if*** = ***'if*** *it is true that . . .'*, the present simple does not describe a general habit, and so ***when*** cannot replace ***if***.
E.g. ***If*** *you own a house in Hollywood, you are very lucky.* ('If it is true that . . .').

1b (B) The will-condition (the '1st conditional') [see WILL 2].

Form:
IF + . . . PRESENT SIMPLE . . . , . . . WILL / WON'T . . .
Meaning: Predicting a likely result in the future (if the condition is fulfilled).

E.g. *'The sky looks dark.* ***If*** *it* ***rains****, we'****ll*** *get wet.' 'OK. Let's go by car.'*

Other examples:

E.g. ***If*** *your boyfriend* ***phones****, I'****ll*** *tell him you've gone out with your mother.* (= It is possible or likely that he will phone.)
*'****If*** *we* ***leave*** *now, we'****ll*** *catch the 11.30 train.' 'Well, we* ***will if*** *we hurry.'*
If *you* ***take*** *this medicine, you* ***will*** *soon feel better.*

NOTE: ***When*** has a different meaning from ***if***: it claims that the event will definitely happen.
E.g. ***When*** *the Queen dies, her son will become king.* (i.e. 'This is a fact.')

1c (C) The would-condition (the '2nd conditional') [see WOULD 1, 2].

Form:
IF + . . . PAST SIMPLE . . . , { . . . 'D / . . . WOULD } . . .
Meaning: Imagining the present or future to be different

(ADVISING)
If I worked, I wouldn't be so poor.
If I were you, I'd get a job immediately.

Here, both speakers are talking about something unreal, unlikely or untrue. [See UNREAL MEANING.] They are talking about the situation now, and not in the past. Other examples:
*'****Would*** *you accept that job,* ***if*** *they offered it to you?' 'No, I* ***wouldn't*** *take it even* ***if*** *they gave me an extra £10,000 a year.'*

Imagining:
E.g. *'****If I were**** *a millionaire,* ***I'd*** *buy some land and a beautiful house.'*
'Would you? I wouldn't. ***If I had*** *a million pounds,* ***I'd*** *give it all away.'*

* You can use ***were*** for all forms of ***be*** in the ***if***-clause of would-condition sentences. [For further details, see WERE 2.]

NOTE: You can use ***were to*** + basic form of verb to express an imaginary condition in the future (not the present).
E.g. *'****If*** *you {* ***won*** */* ***were to win*** *} the first prize, what would you do with the money?' 'I* ***would*** *buy a new car.'*

1d (D) The would-have-condition (the '3rd conditional')

Form:
IF + . . . PAST PERFECT . . . , . . . 'D / WOULD HAVE . . . + PAST PARTICIPLE . . .
Meaning: Imagining the impossible, i.e. something which did not happen. The speaker is dreaming of or imagining a different past. But the past cannot be changed!

E.g. ***If*** *Christopher Columbus* ***hadn't discovered*** *America, the history of the world* ***would have been*** *quite different.*
Poor man! ***If*** *he had* ***driven*** *more carefully, he* ***wouldn't have been*** *injured.*
If *television* ***had not been*** *invented, what* ***would*** *we* ***have done*** *in the evenings?*

2 **Other forms of condition**
There are other forms of condition, apart from the four main types, so please don't think that (A)–(D) are the only possible forms. Here are a few others:

2a IF + PRESENT SIMPLE , . . . IMPERATIVE . . .

E.g. ***If*** *you* ***are*** *hungry, please* ***help*** *yourself.*

2b IF + $\left\{\begin{array}{l}\text{WILL}\\ \text{WON'T}\end{array}\right\}$ . . . , . . . $\left\{\begin{array}{l}\text{WILL}\\ \text{WON'T}\end{array}\right\}$ . . .
In this type ***will*** / ***won't*** in the ***if***-clause means want to / don't want to.
Promises or offers:
E.g. ***If*** *you'****ll*** *come this way, I'****ll*** *show you our latest fashions.*

Threat:
E.g. ***If*** *you* ***won't*** *agree, there'****ll*** *be trouble.*

2c IF + PAST SIMPLE , . . . PAST SIMPLE . . .

E.g. ***If*** *I* ***wanted*** *anything, I always* ***got*** *it.*

Here, ***when*** can replace ***if*** as in 1a.

2d IF + PAST SIMPLE , . . . PRESENT TENSE . . .
If + Past Simple = if it is true that . . .

E.g. ***If*** *she* ***went*** *to school in 1962 then she'****s*** *older than I thought.*

3 ***If*** **means the same as** ***whether*** **when it follows a verb like** ***ask*** **or** ***wonder***

E.g. 'Sally, what did your teacher say to you?' 'She asked me $\left\{\begin{array}{l}\textbf{\textit{if}}\\ \textbf{\textit{whether (or not*)}}\end{array}\right\}$ *I liked school.'*

This is an indirect question [see INDIRECT QUESTION 1].

* You cannot say ***if or not***, but you can say ***whether or not*** [see WHETHER 3].

4 **Idioms**
as if [see AS 4a], ***even if*** [see EVEN 2a], ***if I were you*** [see ADVISING].
[See also the separate entry for IF ONLY below.]

---

if only /ɪf ˈəʊnlɪ/ (*conjunction*)

1 ***If only*** is an idiom followed by a clause in the PAST TENSE. It begins an exclamation of regret or sadness about something which did(n't) or does(n't) happen. [See UNREAL MEANING, WISHES 1.] ***If only X*** means the same as ***I wish X***.

2a ***If only*** + . . . PAST SIMPLE (regret about the present):

IF ONLY + NOUN PHRASE or PRONOUN + PAST SIMPLE Verb . . .

E.g. ***If only we knew*** *where she was staying!* (= 'we regret that we don't know')
If only that piece of land belonged *to me!* (= 'It doesn't belong to me, but I wish it did.')

2b ***If only*** + . . . WOULD / COULD (regret about the present):

IF ONLY + NOUN PHRASE or PRONOUN + {WOULD / COULD} + Verb . . .

E.g. ***If only that boy would listen*** *to his parents.* (*But he never does.*)
If only I could *swim!* (*But I can't.*)

2c ***If only*** + . . . WERE (unreal) (regret about the present):

IF ONLY + NOUN PHRASE or PRONOUN + {WERE* / WEREN'T} . . .

E.g. ***If only the weather weren't*** * *so awful.*
If only I were * *still your age!*

* ***Were*** with unreal meaning: [See WERE 2.]

3 ***If only*** + . . . PAST PERFECT (regret about the past):

IF ONLY + NOUN PHRASE or PRONOUN + HAD + PAST PARTICIPLE . . .

E.g. ***If only you'd been*** *driving more carefully!*
If only my mother and father hadn't *quarrelled about me!*

imperative

► We use ***imperatives*** to make people do things.
► To form ***imperatives***, we use the basic form of the Verb.
► ***Imperatives*** can be impolite * .

* But they can be used, for example, if the other person is a close friend, or if you are telling the other person to do something pleasant or useful.

1 We use ***imperatives*** for giving orders or commands, and also for making offers, suggestions, invitations, giving directions, etc.
(a) Offers.

E.g. *'**Have** a cigarette.' 'No, **try** one of mine.'*

(b) Invitations.

E.g. ***Come** in and **sit** down.*

(c) Instructions.

E.g. ***Take** two tablets with a glass of water.*

(d) Suggestions.

E.g. ***Enjoy** yourself. **Relax**. **Have** fun.*

2 To make a request a little more <polite>, add ***please*** at the beginning or end of the sentence.

E.g. ***Please wait** a moment.*
***Turn** off the television, **please**.*

[See REQUESTS.]

3 To make an ***imperative*** negative, add ***don't*** before the verb.

E.g. ***Don't come*** *home too late!*
Don't make *such a noise!*
Don't worry*. Everything is fine.*
Please ***don't forget*** *to write a letter.*
Don't work *too hard.*

4 INTONATION is important for ***imperatives***. A falling tone (\ ) makes the ***imperative*** more <abrupt>, and perhaps <impolite>.

E.g. ***Come*** *over here.* ***Look*** *at this.*

A rising tone (/) makes the ***imperative*** more gentle: it is more like a suggestion.

E.g. ***Come*** *along.* ***Don't*** *cry.*

5 To give emphasis to an ***imperative***, put ***do*** before the verb. The emphasis can have a <friendly> effect.

E.g. ***Do have*** *another peach.*
Do sit *down, and make yourself at home.*

Or it can have an <unfriendly> effect.

E.g. ***Do be*** *quiet, please!*
Do sit *down, and get on with your homework.*

NOTE: (i) We sometimes add ***won't you*** after an ***imperative*** sentence. [See TAG QUESTION.]
E.g. ***Look*** *after your money,* ***won't you****.*
This makes the sentence sound more like a piece of advice. After a negative, ***will you*** has the same effect.
E.g. ***Don't miss*** *the bus,* ***will you****.*

NOTE: (ii) If we feel angry, we sometimes add ***will you*** after a positive ***imperative***.
E.g. ***Be*** *quiet,* ***will you****.*
This is <impolite>.

---

in /ɪn/ (*preposition or adverb*)

► ***In*** is a common preposition of PLACE and TIME.
► Be careful in choosing between AT, ON, and ***in***. [You will find rules for this under PLACE 2, TIME 4.]

E.g. *'Where is my coat?' 'It's* { ***at*** *the office.'* / ***on*** *the table.'* / ***in*** *the cupboard.'* }

► The opposite of ***in*** is ***out*** (adverb) and ***out of*** (preposition).
► The general meaning of ***in*** is 'inclusion'.

1 **Examples of *in* meaning 'inside an area or space'**: [see PLACE 2]

E.g. *The car isn't **in the garage**; I left it **in the street.***

Also: ***in the town***, ***in the country***, ***in the sky***, etc.
Also without ***the*** [see ZERO ARTICLE 4d]: ***in bed***, ***in church***, ***in town***, etc.

E.g. *I arrive **in** (or **at**) **Berlin** on Sunday.*

2 **Examples of *in* meaning 'inside a period of time'**: [see TIME 4]

E.g. *Beethoven was born **in 1770**.*
*I like going for a walk **in the afternoon**.*

Also: ***in (the) spring***, ***in the twentieth century***, etc.
(But: ***on Monday***, ***on Friday evening***, ***at Christmas***, etc.)

3 **Examples of *in* before ABSTRACT NOUNS**
in love (with): *Romeo was **in love (with** Juliet).*
in trouble: *This is an S.O.S. The ship is **in trouble** . . .*
in danger: *. . . and the passengers are **in danger**.*
in doubt: *If you are **in doubt** (about what to do), I will help you.*
in public: *I don't like arguing **in public**.*
in private: *Shall we talk **in private** in my room?*
Also: ***in debt***, ***in a hurry***, ***in time***, ***in tears***, ***in good condition***, ***in good health***, etc.

NOTE: ***In*** is also used for membership of groups, etc.
E.g. *My brother is **in the army**.*
*How many people are there **in this club?***

4 ***In* as adverb**
As a place adverb, ***in*** can replace ***in*** or ***into*** as preposition, if the 'place' is so obvious that we don't need to mention it.

E.g. *'Ms Cox is waiting at the door.'*
*'Well, why don't you invite her **in**?'* (i.e. 'into the room or house')

It's lovely in the water, mummy.
Yes, but it's rather cold, so don't stay in too long.

4a Some verbs followed by ***in***:

be in: *'**Is** your sister **in**?'* (= 'at home')
'No, but she'll be back later.'

come in: ***Come in**, please.* (= 'enter')

break in: *The thief **broke in** through an upstairs window.*

jump in: *'There's a boy in the river.'*
*'Did he **jump in**?'*
'No, someone pushed him in.'

4b Notice also these common PHRASAL VERBS:

fill in / out.

E.g. *Please* { ***fill in*** <G.B.> / ***fill out*** <U.S.> / *complete* } *this form.*

hand in.

E.g. *Will you please **hand in** your homework at the end of the class.* (= 'submit')

take in.

E.g. *I was **taken in** by his lies.* (= 'deceived')

5 **Some other idioms with *in***

in addition (to) (= as well (as), also) <formal>.

E.g. *The post requires someone who is hard-working and able. **In addition**, knowledge of foreign languages is an advantage.* <formal, written> (Linking adverbial)

in any case = anyway (making a stronger point).

E.g. *He can't come to the party this evening because his mother is ill. **In any case**, he doesn't enjoy parties very much.* (Linking adverbial)

in case (in preparation for something which might happen).

E.g. *Take an umbrella, **in case** it rains.*
***In case** the bomb exploded, people were told to leave their houses.* (Subordinating conjunction)

in fact ('I might go further, and say . . .').

E.g. *The Minister of Transport is the worst minister in the government. **In fact**, his policy has been a complete failure.* (Linking adverbial)

in front of [See *in* FRONT OF AND BEHIND.]

in order to, in order that (subordinating conjunctions) [see PURPOSE for examples.]

in other words ('expressing the same in different words').

E.g. *I sometimes find it difficult to believe what Hugh says. **In other words**, I think he's a liar.* (Linking adverbial)

in particular (making a more particular point).

E.g. *Most people don't like staying in a hospital.* ***In particular****, they are afraid of operations.* (Linking adverbial) <formal, written>

in short (or ***in brief***) (making a summary).

E.g. *'It's cold, cloudy, and wet, and the wind has been blowing hard since morning.* ***In short****, it's been a terrible day!* (Linking adverbial)

in that case ('if that is so').

E.g. *'She's not very clever: she got only 29% in the last test.'* ***'In that case****, she won't pass the exam.'* (Linking adverbial)

indeed /ɪnˈdiːd/ (*adverb*)

1 ***Indeed*** adds emphasis to VERY (as an adverb of degree):

E.g. *She is* ***very*** *clever* ***indeed***.(= 'very, very clever')

Notice that ***indeed*** follows the adjective (or other words) after ***very***.

2 When ***indeed*** is in middle position in the clause, it indicates emphatic agreement with what has been said.

E.g. *She is* ***indeed*** *a great artist.* (= 'I agree that she is.')

So here ***indeed*** is a linking adverb.

3 When ***indeed*** is in front position, it is also a linking adverb.

E.g. *Her paintings are well known all over the world.* ***Indeed****, she's a great artist.* (= 'In fact')

But here the meaning is that this sentence strengthens the force of what was said earlier.

indefinite article [See A or AN, ARTICLES.]

indefinite pronoun [See QUANTITY WORDS.]

- ► Some PRONOUNS have a definite meaning: PERSONAL, reflexive and DEMONSTRATIVE pronouns.
- ► Other pronouns, which do not have definite meaning, are called ***indefinite pronouns***.
- ► Here we deal with the two kinds of ***indefinite pronoun***: we call them ***of***-pronouns and compound pronouns.
- ► [See PRONOUN for various kinds of pronoun.]

1 ***Indefinite pronouns*** are like other pronouns. They can stand alone as SUBJECT, OBJECT, etc. of a sentence.

subject object

E.g. ***Everyone*** *has* **something** *to say.*

They can also be the head (or main word) of a NOUN PHRASE.

subject subject

E.g. ***Most*** *(of the boys) are camping, but* **some** *(of them) are staying in a hostel.*

2 ***Of*-pronouns**

Pronouns like MOST and SOME in the example above are called ***of***-pronouns because they can be followed by an ***of***-phrase, indicating quantity. [See also QUANTITY WORDS.]

2a If the ***of***-phrase is omitted, its information has to come from the situation.

E.g. *'Where are the boys staying?'* ***'Most*** *are camping, but* ***some*** *are staying in a hostel.'*

Here, ***most*** means 'most of the boys' and ***some*** means 'some of the boys'.

2b Opposite is a Table of ***of***-pronouns, showing how they combine with COUNTABLE and UNCOUNTABLE nouns in this pattern:

PRONOUN + OF + NOUN

2c Compare the Table opposite with the table of determiners [see DETERMINER 1]. You will notice that all (except one) of the words which are ***of***-pronouns are also determiners. The one exception is ***none***, for which there is a different determiner form, ***no***. Contrast:

E.g. ***No girls*** *took part.* But: ***None*** *(of the girls) took part.*

With other words there is no difference.

E.g. ***Some girls*** *took part.* And: ***Some*** *(of the girls) took part.*

The word is a determiner if a noun follows it without ***of*** between them.

Table of ***of***-pronouns

group	countable		uncountable
	singular	plural	singular
(I)			
ALL	***all*** (of the book)	***all*** (of the books)	***all*** (of the rice)
SOME	***some*** (of the book)	***some*** (of the books)	***some*** (of the rice)
ANY	***any*** (of the book)	***any*** (of the books)	***any*** (of the rice)
NONE	***none*** (of the book)	***none*** (of the books)	***none*** (of the rice)
HALF	***half*** (of the book)	***half*** (of the books)	***half*** (of the rice)
ENOUGH	***enough*** (of the book)	***enough*** (of the books)	***enough*** (of the rice)
(II)			
EACH	*	***each*** (of the books)	
EITHER	*	***either*** (of the books)	
NEITHER	*	***neither*** (of the books)	
ONE	*	***one*** (of the books)	
ANOTHER	*	***another*** (of the books)	
(III)			
BOTH		***both*** (of the books)	
SEVERAL		***several*** (of the books)	
(IV)			
MUCH	***much*** (of the book)	***many*** (of the books)	***much*** (of the rice)
MORE	***more*** (of the book)	***more*** (of the books)	***more*** (of the rice)
MOST	***most*** (of the book)	***most*** (of the books)	***most*** (of the rice)
(a) LITTLE	(a) ***little*** (of the book)	(a) ***few*** (of the books)	(a) ***little*** (of the coffee)
LESS	***less*** (of the book)	***fewer*** (of the books)	***less*** (of the coffee)
LEAST	***least*** (of the book)	***fewest*** (of the books)	***least*** (of the coffee)

* In Group II, the asterisk (*) indicates that these pronouns are normally considered singular, although they are followed by a plural noun. This means that they go with a singular verb. E.g. ***Each*** *of my friends* {***has*** / ~~***have***~~} *children.*

3 **Compound pronouns**
We call these 'compound pronouns' because they each contain two word-elements:

First element: ˈ***every-***, ˈ***some-***, ˈ***any-***, ˈ***no-***
Second element: ***-thing***, ***-one***, ***-body***

The first syllable has the stress. Here is a table of compound pronouns:

	Not referring to persons	Referring to persons*	
every-	ˈ***everything***	ˈ***everyone***	ˈ***everybody***
some-	ˈ***something***	ˈ***someone***	ˈ***somebody***
any-	ˈ***anything***	ˈ***anyone***	ˈ***anybody***
no-	ˈ***nothing***	ˈ***no one***	ˈ***nobody***

* The ***-one*** and ***-body*** pronouns have the same meaning, but the ***-body*** forms are less frequent.

[To find out more about these pronouns, look them up under their first element, e.g. EVERY- etc.]

3a After compound pronouns, ***of***-phrases rarely occur, but other types of MODIFIERS are possible.

E.g. *Everything* ***else*** ('all other things') [see ELSE]
Anything ***strange*** [see ADJECTIVE 6c NOTE]
Nobody ***in the office*** [see PREPOSITIONAL PHRASE]
Someone ***I know*** ('some person . . .') [RELATIVE CLAUSE]

4 Indefinite pronouns, unlike personal pronouns, do not vary their form. There is just one exception: pronouns ending in ***-one*** and ***-body*** can have the POSSESSIVE ending ***'s***.

E.g. *'Whose is this belt?'* ***'Nobody's.'***
'Everyone's *life was in danger.'*

independent clause [See MAIN CLAUSE]

indirect command (*or* IMPERATIVE) [see INDIRECT SPEECH AND THOUGHT]

1 When we put an IMPERATIVE sentence into INDIRECT SPEECH, we usually use a verb like ***tell***, followed by a *TO*-INFINITIVE CLAUSE.

E.g. (i)

(ii)

(i) *'Give me the money.'* → (ii) *He* {***told*** / ***ordered***} *me* ***to give him the money***.

'Come in, please.' → *The manager* ***asked*** *me* ***to come in***.

2 For a NEGATIVE IMPERATIVE, we put NOT before ***to***:

DON'T + Verb . . . → . . . NOT TO + Verb

E.g.

(i)

(ii)

(i) ***'Don't sit*** *there!'* → (ii) *I told you* ***not to sit*** *there!*

'Don't worry. *'* → I ***advised*** *her* ***not to*** *worry.*

NOTE: We also use the INFINITIVE for INDIRECT SPEECH with REQUESTS, INVITATIONS, etc. [See FUNCTIONS.]

---

indirect object [See OBJECT.]

1 **Some verbs can be followed by two objects** [see VERB PATTERN 11].
In many cases, the ***indirect object*** (or first object) names someone (e.g. 'Margaret') who receives something.

			Indirect Object (1)	Direct Object (2)
E.g.	(i)	*I* ***gave***	*Margaret*	*the flowers.*
			Indirect Object (1)	Direct Object (2)
	(ii)	*I* ***bought***	*Margaret*	*a new dress*

1a WORD ORDER:
The ***indirect object*** always goes before the direct object. The order shows which is indirect and which is direct.

1b Notice that we can change the ***indirect object*** into a phrase beginning ***to*** [see TO 3] or ***for*** [see FOR 2 NOTE(i)].

E.g. (i) *I gave the flowers* **to** Margaret.
(ii) *I bought a dress* **for** *Margaret.*

1c Like direct objects, ***indirect objects*** can become the SUBJECT of a PASSIVE.

E.g. (i) *Margaret **was given** the flowers.*
(ii) *Margaret **was bought** a new dress.*

2a Common verbs with an ***indirect object*** or TO-phrase:

bring	*hand*	*owe*	*send*	*tell*
give	*lend*	*promise*	*show*	*throw*
grant	*offer*	*read*	*teach*	*write*

E.g. *The dog **brought** his master the stick.*
= *The dog **brought** the stick **to** his master.*

2b Common verbs with an ***indirect object*** or FOR-phrase:

buy	*find*	*leave*	*order*	*reserve*	*spare*
cook	*get*	*make*	*peel*	*save*	

E.g. *She **made** her grandson a birthday cake.*
= *She **made** a birthday cake for **her** grandson.*

2c Common verbs which behave differently:

ask *allow* *charge* *cost* *refuse* *wish*

We cannot use ***to*** or ***for*** with these verbs.

E.g. *He **asked** me a lot of questions.*

But not:

*He **asked** a lot of questions* { ~~***of***~~ / ~~***to me****~~ }.

*The coat **cost** George £70.*

But not:

*The coat **cost** £70 ~~**for** George.~~*

* It is possible but <rare>, to say: *He asked a lot of questions of me.*

---

indirect question [See also INDIRECT SPEECH AND THOUGHT]

---

1 **YES-NO QUESTIONS**

YES-NO QUESTIONS begin with ***if*** in INDIRECT SPEECH. (These are questions which invite ***yes*** or ***no*** as an answer).

E.g. *'Is it raining?'* → *The old lady **asked if** it was raining.*
'Do you have any stamps?' → *I **asked** them **if** they had any stamps.*
'Can I borrow your dictionary?' → *He **asked** her **if** he could borrow her dictionary.*

Notice that in DIRECT SPEECH the questions have inversion, but that in INDIRECT SPEECH the word order is normal: IF + SUBJECT + VERB . . . [See IF 3.]

NOTE: (i) Instead of ***if***, we can use WHETHER or ***whether or not***.
E.g. *The old lady asked **whether** it was raining.*
*I asked them **whether or not** they had any stamps.*
(ii) ***Whether or not*** is more emphatic than ***if*** or ***whether***, because it means an answer is being demanded.

2 **WH-QUESTIONS**

WH-QUESTIONS begin with the WH-WORD (HOW, WHAT, WHEN, WHERE, WHICH, WHO, WHOM, WHOSE, WHY) in indirect speech, just as in direct speech.

E.g. *'**Where** are you going?'* → *He **asked** her **where** she was going.*
*'**When** do you get up in the morning?'* → *I **asked** him **when** he got up in the morning.*

Notice also that the word order in indirect speech is normal, i.e. SUBJECT + VERB.

2a Some examples:

indirect speech and thought [Compare DIRECT SPEECH.]

► When we report what someone else has said, we use the form of language called ***indirect speech***.

E.g.

1 Changing from direct to indirect speech

We usually change the forms of verbs when we report in ***indirect speech***:

1a Present forms —— change to ——► Past forms

	Present Simple		Past Simple
E.g.	*'I **love** you.'*	→	*He told* her that he **loved her**.*
	Present Progressive		Past Progressive
E.g.	*'Be quiet. **I'm talking** on the phone.'*	→	*She told us to be quiet while she **was talking** on the phone.*
	Present Perfect		Past Perfect
E.g.	*'The rain **has stopped**.'*	→	*He said* that the rain **had stopped**.*
	Present Perfect Progressive		Past Perfect Progressive
E.g.	*'She**'s been having** a wonderful time in Italy.'*	→	*Mary's mother said she **had been having** a wonderful time in Italy.*

IMPORTANT: We don't always have to change the verb from present to past. Look at this example:

E.g. *'I **love** Jane.'* → *Jim admitted that he {**loved** / **loves**} Jane.*

We can leave the verb in the present form here, because *'Jim'* probably still *'loves Jane'* at the time of the report.

* Notice that after ***tell*** we have to mention the person addressed: *He **told her** that . . .* But after ***say*** we do not: *He **said that** . . .*

1b Past Forms ——— change to ———→ Past Perfect Forms

	Past Simple	→	Past Perfect
E.g.	*'I **met** you when you were a student.'*	→	*She told me she **had met** me when I was ** a student.*
	Past Progressive		Past Perfect Progressive
E.g.	*'I **was driving** carefully when the accident happened.'*	→ →	*He told the police he **had been driving** carefully when the accident happened**.*

** The Past Simple form in a subordinate clause in DIRECT SPEECH doesn't usually change into Past Perfect in ***indirect speech***.
E.g. *She said she had been very unhappy after her mother **(had) died**.*

NOTE: If a Past Perfect form occurs in direct speech, it does not change in ***indirect speech***.
E.g. *'I phoned you yesterday to find out if my letter **had arrived**.'* → *He claimed that he had phoned them the previous day to find out if his letter **had arrived**.*

1c What happens to MODAL AUXILIARIES in ***indirect speech***?

{WILL, CAN, MAY, SHALL} ——— change to ———→ {WOULD, COULD, MIGHT, SHOULD}

E.g.	*'**I'll** meet you at 10.'*	→	*He promised that he **would** meet her at 10.*
	*'I **can** fly.'*	→	*He said he **could** fly.*
	*'What **shall** we give Bill?'*	→	*They asked what they **should** give Bill.*
	*'The train **may** be late.'*	→	*He agreed that the train **might** be late.*

NOTE: If the modal auxiliaries MUST, OUGHT TO, USED TO occur in direct speech, they do not change in ***indirect speech***.

E.g.	*'You **must** relax.'*	→	*The doctor said you **must** relax.*
	*'You **ought** to give up smoking.'*	→	*The doctor said I **ought to** give up smoking.*
	*'I **used to** smoke forty a day.'*	→	*I confessed to him that **I used to** smoke forty a day.*

There is also no change if the 'past' modal auxiliaries ***would, could, should*** and ***might*** occur in direct speech.
E.g. *'**Would** you mind lending me your typewriter?'* → *I asked Betty if she **would** mind lending me her typewriter.*

2 **Other changes in indirect speech**

As well as changes in verb form, some other changes are often* required in ***indirect speech***.

2a First and second person pronouns usually change to third person pronouns [see PERSONAL PRONOUNS].

E.g. *'**I** like ice cream.' → He said **he** liked ice cream.*
*'**We** enjoyed **your** singing.' → They said that **they** had enjoyed **his** singing.*

2b Other words which talk about 'here' and 'now' may change:

this → that	***today → that day***
these → those	***yesterday → the previous day***
here → there	***tomorrow → the next day***
now → then or ***at that moment***	

			They said that . . .
E.g.	*'**This** is our favourite walk.'*	→	*. . . **that** was their favourite walk.*
	*'We like it **here**.'*	→	*. . . they liked it **there**.*
	*'We are leaving **now**.'*	→	*. . . they were leaving **at that moment**.*
	*'We'll see you **tomorrow**.'*	→	*. . . they would see me **the next day**.*

* Whether these changes are really required depends on the point of view of the reporter. For example, if you are reporting your own words, you do not change ***I*** to ***he*** or ***she***.
E.g. *'**I** am sorry.' → I said **I** was sorry.*

3 **Different kinds of sentence in *indirect speech*.**

If the direct speech sentence is:	in indirect speech, use:
a STATEMENT	a THAT-clause (THAT can be omitted)
a QUESTION	a WH-CLAUSE (or IF-clause)
a command (IMPERATIVE)	an INFINITIVE CLAUSE

For further details, see INDIRECT STATEMENTS, INDIRECT QUESTIONS, INDIRECT COMMANDS, FUNCTIONS].

4 **Indirect thought**

Verbs which describe thinking, feeling, etc. can also introduce indirect statements and indirect questions.

E.g. *Many people* { ***believed*** / ***supposed*** / ***thought*** } *that the spy was lying.* (INDIRECT STATEMENT)

indirect statements [See also INDIRECT SPEECH AND THOUGHT.]

If you want to report a statement someone has made, use this pattern:

SUBJECT + VERB (. . .) + (THAT) + SUBJECT + VERB . . .

E.g. *'The bus will be late.'* → *He said* ***(that) the bus would be late****.*
'The snow has melted.' → *The radio reported* ***(that) the snow had melted****.*

You can omit ***that***, especially in <speech> [see THAT 1].

[See INDIRECT SPEECH AND THOUGHT 1 for further examples.]

NOTE: If you don't want to report exactly what was said, or if you don't know exactly what was said, you can use a WH-CLAUSE or an IF-clause, just like INDIRECT QUESTIONS.
E.g. *He explained* ***why*** *he was late.*
They didn't tell me ***how*** *they got home.*
Did Jan say ***if*** *she is coming to the party?*

infinitive [See VERB, VERB PHRASE, NONFINITE, TO-INFINITIVE]

► An infinitive often has ***to*** in front of it.

1 **The term infinitive refers to three different kinds of thing**:
(a) An infinitive is a word, that is, a form of the verb.
(b) An infinitive is a phrase, that is, a verb phrase which begins with an infinitive word.
(c) An infinitive is a clause, that is, a clause with an infinitive verb phrase.
This is how (a), (b), and (c) fit together in a sentence:

E.g. (a) infinitive word: ***have***
is part of
(b) infinitive phrase: ***to have met***
is part of
(c) infinitive clause: ***to have met your family***
is part of
whole sentence: *I'm pleased* ***to have met your family****.*

1a An infinitive word (see (a) above) is a BASIC FORM of the verb (without any ending).

E.g. *(to)* ***be****,* *(to)* ***have****,* *(to)* ***do****,* *(to)* ***say****,* *(to)* ***make****,* *(to)* ***want****.*

But a basic form is not always infinitive: it can be a present tense, imperative, or subjunctive form. It is called 'infinitive' only when it is a NONFINITE VERB form, especially when it follows ***to***.

1b An infinitive phrase (see (b) above) is a VERB PHRASE which contains an infinitive word as its first or only word.

E.g. *(to)* ***be,*** *(to)* ***know,*** *(to)* ***be done,*** *(to)* ***have said,*** *(to)* ***be helping,*** *(to)* ***have been wanted***.

1c An infinitive clause (see (c) above) is a CLAUSE which contains an infinitive phrase as its verb phrase.

E.g. ***(to) be*** *hungry.* ***(to) be*** *eaten by a tiger.*
(to) have *a headache.* ***(to) give*** *a child a toy.*

[See INFINITIVE CLAUSE.]

2 to-infinitives and bare infinitives

2a Most infinitive phrases begin with ***to***. We call such a phrase a TO-INFINITIVE, and represent it: to + Verb.

E.g. *They allowed the children* ***to leave*** *school early.*
(Not: *They allowed the children ~~leave~~*) [See VERB PATTERN 17.]

2b An Infinitive phrase without ***to*** is called a 'bare infinitive', and we simply represent it: Verb.

E.g. *They let the children* ***leave*** *school early.*
(Not: *They let the children ~~to~~ leave*) [See VERB PATTERN 18.]

2c In some sentences, both the ***to***-infinitive and the bare infinitive are possible.

E.g. { *What she did was* ***to give*** *all her money away.*
{ *What she did was* ***give*** *all her money away.*
{ *He prefers* ***to rent*** *a house, rather than* ***to buy*** *one.*
{ *He prefers* ***to rent*** *a house, rather than* ***buy*** *one.*

[See INFINITIVE CLAUSE 3 and 4 about when to use ***to***-infinitives, when to use bare infinitives, and when you can use both.]

3 In main clauses (which are FINITE clauses) after (a) MODAL AUXILIARIES, (b) auxiliary DO, the form of the verb is the bare infinitive.

E.g. *You should* ***know*** — modal + Verb
I don't ***understand*** — ***do*** + Verb

---

infinitive clause [See INFINITIVE, TO-INFINITIVE.]

---

1 There are two kinds of infinitive clause
(a) The to-infinitive clause, in which the verb follows ***to*** (***to*** + Verb), and
(b) The bare infinitive clause, in which the verb does not follow ***to*** (Verb).
[See INFINITIVE 2 for examples.]

2 The infinitive clause is called a 'clause' because it can have clause elements such as SUBJECT, OBJECT, COMPLEMENT, and ADVERBIAL, as well as an infinitive VERB PHRASE:

2a

		subject		verb phrase	object	complement	adverbial
It's best			**to**	*write*	*those letters*		*immediately.*
It's best	*for*	*us all*	**to**	*be*		*ready*	*by 5 o'clock.*
It's best			**to**	*clean*	*the windows*		*thoroughly.*
It's best	*for*	*the job*	**to**	*be done*			*by an electrician.*
It's best			**to**	*be finishing*	*the work*		*when the boss comes in.*

2b As you see in the Table in 2a, infinitive clauses usually have no subject. When they do have a subject, it usually comes after the word ***for***.

2c An infinitive clause is similar to a finite or subordinate clause [see FINITE and SUBORDINATE CLAUSE] – e.g. a THAT-clause – as this example shows.

E.g. *I'm sorry **to have spelt your name wrongly***.

means the same as:

*I'm sorry **that I spelt your name wrongly***.

Also:

*It's best **for us all to be ready by 5 o'clock***.

means the same as:

*It's best **if we are all ready by 5 o'clock***.

3 **to-infinitive clauses – how to use them**

To-infinitive clauses have many uses. Here are the main ones:

3a They follow some verbs (as object) [see VERB PATTERN 7], e.g. ***hope, like, want, begin, learn, expect***:

. . . VERB + TO + Verb (. . .)

E.g. *I **hope to see you soon***.

NOTE: They also follow some LINKING VERBS as complement, e.g. ***be***, ***seem***, ***appear***.
E.g. *This timetable **seems to be out of date***.

3b They follow the object after some verbs [see VERB PATTERN 17], e.g. ***ask, tell, expect, consider***:

. . . VERB + OBJECT + TO + Verb (. . .)

E.g. *The secretary **asked** us **to come back later***.

3c They follow some adjectives [see ADJECTIVE PATTERNS 3], e.g. ***easy, hard, difficult, ready***:

. . . ADJECTIVE + TO + Verb (. . .)

E.g. *Some of these questions are **difficult to answer**.*

3d They follow some ABSTRACT NOUNS:

NOUN + TO + Verb (. . .)

(a) Nouns which come from verbs or adjectives.

E.g. *I mentioned my* {***desire*** / ***wish***} ***to work overseas***.

(b) General nouns like ***time, way, place, reason***.

E.g. *It'll soon be **time to go home**.*

3e They follow some COMMON NOUNS, or PRONOUNS. The infinitive is similar in meaning to a RELATIVE CLAUSE. The meaning is one of PURPOSE:

NOUN / PRONOUN + TO + Verb (. . .)

E.g. *Can I borrow **something to read?***

NOTE: Sometimes there is a preposition at the end of the clause which links back to the noun / pronoun.
E.g. *Could I have **something to sit on?***

3f They can follow ***too*** [see TOO 2] or ENOUGH, usually with a word between:

{TOO . . . / ENOUGH (. . .)} + TO + Verb (. . .)

E.g. *They gave us **too** much **to eat**.*

3g They can act as SUBJECT. More usually, the ***to***-infinitive is a 'delayed subject' at the end of a clause beginning with ***it*** [see IT-PATTERNS 1]:

TO + Verb (. . .) + VERB (. . .)

Subject

E.g. ***To prove his guilt*** *would be very difficult.*

Also:

IT + VERB (. . .) + TO + Verb (. . .)

Delayed Subject

E.g. *It would be very difficult **to prove his guilt**.*

Delayed Subject

*It's a pity **to be so mean**.*

3h They can act as an ADVERBIAL, especially of PURPOSE (answering the question ***why?*** or ***what . . . for?***).

E.g. *'**Why** did you get up so early?' '**To meet my family** at the airport.'*

In <formal> style, we add ***in order*** or ***so as*** before ***to***:

CLAUSE + ({IN ORDER / SO AS}) + TO + Verb (. . .)

E.g. *They are introducing new labour laws, **(in order) to improve** the performance of industry.*
*The sea wall must be repaired, **(so as) to prevent** further flooding.*

4 Using bare infinitive clauses
Bare infinitive clauses are much less common than ***to***-infinitive clauses. Some examples of the use of bare infinitive clauses are:

4a After the verb ***help***, or after a verb idiom such as HAD BETTER, or ***would rather*** [see VERB PATTERN 8].

E.g. *This medicine **helps keep you healthy.*** *
*We'**d better be careful**.*

4b After the object after some verbs [see VERB PATTERN 18], e.g. ***make, sure, hear, let***.

E.g. *The book was so sad, it made me **cry**.*

4c After {***what*** / ***all***} [X] (. . .) DO + BE . . .

E.g. ***What** they've done is **mend the water pipe**.* *
***All** I did was **report the accident**.* *

4d After ***rather (. . .) than*** (expressing preference).

E.g. *I'd **rather** work at home **than travel thirty miles to work every day**.*
*I prefer to do my own repairs, **rather than take the car to a garage.*** *

* These sentences could also have a ***to***-infinitive, instead of a bare infinitive; e.g. ***to keep, to mend, to report, to take***.

informal English [See FORMAL AND INFORMAL ENGLISH.]

-ing, -ing form [See -ING CLAUSE, VERB PHRASE, NONFINITE VERB.]

► ***-ing*** (-/ɪŋ/) is a very important ending (= suffix) in English:
(a) For all VERBS, ***-ing*** is added to the basic form to make an ***-ing* form**: ***do*** → ***doing***, etc.*

(b) Also, many ADJECTIVES and NOUNS are formed by adding ***-ing*** to the verb: e.g. the adjective ***missing*** (*person*) or the noun ***feeling***. (We will call these '***-ing*** adjectives' and '***-ing*** nouns'.)

► The ***-ing* form** of the verb has two uses:
(I) With ***be***, it makes the PROGRESSIVE form of the verb phrase: ***were eating***, ***is playing***, etc.
(II) Without ***be***, it forms the ***-ing*** participle, which is the first verb of an -ING CLAUSE, e.g. *I like* ***reading***, *I like* ***reading novels***.

► We write the ***-ing* form** like this: Verb-ing.

► Some grammar books use the term 'gerund' for ***-ing*** participles which act like nouns (e.g. ***reading*** in (II) above).

* Except modal auxiliaries, which have no ***-ing form***.

1 Spelling changes happen to some verbs when we add ***-ing***.

E.g. *get*, ***getting*** *begin*, ***beginning*** *have*, ***having*** *love*, ***loving***.

[For examples and exceptions, see SPELLING.]

2 Do not confuse the ***-ing form*** of the verb with ***-ing*** nouns and ***-ing*** adjectives. Here are some ideas for recognizing the differences:

2a ***-ing*** nouns:
(I) ***-ing*** nouns often have a plural: ***feeling*** → ***feelings***
Also: ***wedding(s)*** ***meeting(s)*** ***warning(s)*** ***drawing(s)***
(These are COUNTABLE NOUNS.)

(II) ***-ing*** nouns can follow a determiner (e.g. ***the, a*** / ***an***) or an adjective or a noun.

E.g. ***the*** *meaning of life*, ***dirty*** *washing*, ***her beautiful*** *singing*, ***chemical*** *engineering*, ***oil*** *painting*.

NOTE: ***-ing*** nouns can also come before another noun.
E.g. *'**dining** ˌroom, '**closing** ˌtime, '**heating** ˌsystem.'*
In these cases the main stress is on the first word. Sometimes the two words are joined by a hyphen (-): ***dining-room***. It is best if we think of these two words as forming a single compound noun.

2b ***-ing*** adjectives:
(I) ***-ing*** adjectives can come before a noun.

E.g. *the following* ***night***, *a paying* ***guest***, *growing* ***children***.

(II) ***-ing*** adjectives can often come after adverbs of DEGREE, such as VERY, QUITE AND RATHER, SO, TOO, AS.

E.g. ***very*** *surprising*, ***quite*** *promising*, ***so*** *charming*.

2c ***-ing* forms** of the verb (Verb-***ing***):
***-ing* forms** are verbs when they go before
(a) an OBJECT.

E.g. *buy**ing a present**, driv**ing the bus***

(b) a COMPLEMENT.

E.g. *becom**ing old**, feel**ing tired**, be**ing a child***

(c) an ADVERBIAL (e.g. an adverb).

E.g. *sing**ing beautifully**, liv**ing alone***.

NOTE: Sometimes we cannot decide if a word is a Verb-***ing*** or an ***-ing*** Noun.
E.g. *I enjoy **dancing**.*
***Farming** is the world's biggest industry.*

-ing clause [See -ING FORM, NONFINITE.]

- ► You can usually recognize an ***-ing* clause** because it begins with Verb+***ing*** [See -ING FORM above.]
- ► An ***-ing* clause** is a SUBORDINATE CLAUSE with several different uses within the sentence.
- ► It is important to notice differences between the use of the ***-ing* clause** and the use of the INFINITIVE CLAUSE. [See 6 below.]
- ► Always use Verb-***ing*** when you need a verb after a preposition.

E.g. *The builder insists **on seeing** you now.*

NOTE: The use of terms: An ***-ing*** clause is sometimes called a gerund construction (when it behaves like a noun phrase) and is sometimes called a present participle construction (when it behaves more like an adjective phrase). You do not need to worry about this difference.

1 The form of *-ing* clauses
We call ***-ing* clauses** 'clauses' because they can have clause elements such as OBJECT, COMPLEMENT and ADVERBIAL after the Verb-***ing***. They do not usually have a SUBJECT before the Verb-***ing***, but it is possible. Compare:

	subject	Verb-ing	object	adverbial
(i) *He insists on*		*seeing*	*you*	*now.*
(ii) *He insists on*	*you(r)*	*seeing*	*him*	*now.*

[See 3 below.] If the Verb-***ing*** has a subject, as in (ii) above, the subject can be
either: a POSSESSIVE form (e.g. ***your***) <formal>
or: a non-possessive form (e.g. ***you***) <informal>.
In the case of a PERSONAL PRONOUN subject, we use the OBJECT pronoun (e.g. ***us***) rather than the SUBJECT pronoun (e.g. ***we***).

E.g. *He insists on* {***our*** / ***us***} ***seeing*** *him now.* {<formal> / <informal>}

NOTE: In a negative ***-ing*** clause, ***not*** goes before the Verb-***ing***.
E.g. *He insists on* ***not seeing*** *you until next week.*

2 How to use *-ing* clauses

2a They follow many verbs (as object) [see VERB PATTERN 9]:

MAIN VERB + Verb-***ing*** (. . .)

E.g. *I have enjoyed* ***meeting you.***
Do you mind ***being quiet****?*

NOTE: [See COME AND GO 6 for the use of Verb-***ing*** after these verbs: ***come*** *shopp**ing***, ***go*** *walk**ing***, etc.]

2b They follow the noun phrase after some verbs [see VERB PATTERN 19]:

VERB + NOUN PHRASE + Verb-***ing*** (. . .)

E.g. ***I don't mind*** *them* ***staying here.***
You could still ***feel*** *the animal's heart* ***beating***.

2c They come before the main verb as subject:

Verb-***ing*** (. . .) + VERB (. . .)

E.g. ***Reading (poetry)*** *improves the mind.*
Watching television *can be a waste of time.*

3 *-ing* clauses after a preposition

The next set of patterns show Verb-***ing*** after a PREPOSITION:

3a ABSTRACT NOUN + OF + Verb-***ing*** (. . .)

E.g. *The* ***possibility of travelling*** *to India is very exciting.*

Also: ***hope of*** Verb-***ing***, ***chance of*** Verb-***ing***, ***act of*** Verb-***ing***.

3b ADJECTIVE + PREPOSITION + Verb-***ing*** (. . .)

E.g. *The President is* ***used to being attacked*** *by the press.*

Also: ***good at*** Verb-***ing***, ***afraid of*** Verb-***ing***, ***tired of*** Verb-***ing***.

3c VERB + (ADVERBIAL / NOUN PHRASE) + PREPOSITION + Verb-***ing*** (. . .)

E.g. *They* ***accused*** *a friend of mine* ***of stealing food***.

Also in the passive.

E.g. *A friend of mine was* ***accused of stealing food***.

Also: ***prevent someone from*** Verb-***ing*** . . .
look forward to Verb-***ing***.

4 ***-ing* clauses after a noun or pronoun**

***-ing* clauses** after a noun or pronoun are similar to RELATIVE CLAUSES, but without WHO or WHICH + BE. They are more common in <writing>.

E.g. *All the* ***people eating in the restaurant*** *were tourists.*
(= . . . people ***who were*** eating in the restaurant . . .)
The waiter brought a ***dish containing a delicious soup***.
(= a dish ***which contained*** a delicious soup.)
The phone was answered by ***someone speaking with a Scottish accent***. (= some ***who spoke*** with a Scottish accent.)

5 ***-ing* clauses as adverbials**

***-ing* clauses** as adverbials can come before or after the main clause. These are also more common in <writing>, and are <formal> in style.

E.g. *The manager greeted us,* ***smiling politely***.
Being a friend of the President's, *she has considerable influence in the White House.* ('Since she is a friend . . .')

5a The ***-ing* clause** can also go in middle position in the main clause.

E.g. *The children,* ***having eaten a large supper,*** *were ready for bed.*
('. . . after eating . . .')

6 **Differences between *-ing* clauses and *to*-infinitive clauses**

It is difficult to give rules for the choice between the ***to***-infinitive clause [see INFINITIVE CLAUSE 3] and the ***-ing* clause**. But here are one or two helpful ideas:

6a Remember that a ***to***-infinitive never follows a preposition, but an ***-ing* clause** often does.

6b After a main verb (e.g. ***love, like***), *the* ***to***-infinitive often describes a possible action, while an ***-ing* clause** describes the actual performance of the action. [See VERB PATTERNS 7, 9, 17, 19.]

E.g. *I'd love* ***to visit*** *the country – but I've got to stay here in the city.*
*I love visit****ing*** *the country. It's so nice, walking and getting some fresh air.*

There are similar differences for other verbs of liking and disliking:
like, dislike, prefer, hate, etc.

6c For the verbs ***remember, forget, regret, to***-infinitives are used for future or present events.

E.g. *Don't* ***forget to lock*** *the door this evening.*

***-ing* clauses** are used to talk about past events.

E.g. *I'll never* ***forget getting lost*** *when we were climbing in the Alps last year.*

7 With the verbs ***begin, start, continue***, and ***cease***, there is often little or no difference between the two verb forms.

E.g. *Iris **started** {**to work** / **working**} at the post office last Monday.*

*Our business has **continued** {**to expand** / **expanding**} during the last two years.*

NOTE: But avoid using two ***to***-infinitives or two ***-ing*** forms one after the other.

*E.g. I'd like to begin {**studying** / ~~**to study**~~} as soon as possible.*

*They are beginning {**to improve** / ~~**improving**~~} the road.*

---

instead of /ɪn̪ˈstedəv/ (*preposition*)
instead /ɪn̪ˈsted/ (*adverb*)

1 ***Instead of* means 'in place of'**

E.g. *Could I have a glass of fresh orange juice, **instead of** this lemonade, please?*

***Instead of** sitting there, you could help me clean the kitchen.*

2 ***Instead* is the adverb, meaning 'in place of X'**

E.g. *I'm sorry I can't give you a cup of tea. Would you like a cup of coffee **instead**?* (***instead*** = 'in place of tea').

---

instructions [See also DIRECTIONS.]

1 In <written> instructions, e.g. in recipes, we often use the IMPERATIVE.

E.g. *First, **empty** the powder into a cup. **Add** $\frac{1}{2}$ pint of boiling water and **stir** well. Then **sit back** and enjoy the delicious flavour of Mangolade.*

2 We often omit words (little words like ***a*** and ***it***) in <written> instructions. For example, [ ] shows where a word is omitted:

Empty [ ] powder into [ ] water container.

instrument [See ADVERBIAL.]

Here are some examples of how to express the idea of **instrument**.

E.g. *'The burglar broke into the house.'*
*'**How** did he do it?'*
*'**With** an axe.'*

*'**How** do you play chess?'*
*'You play it **with** a board and some chessmen.'*

*'**What** did you mend the pocket of your dress **with**?'*
*'I **used** a needle and thread.'*

'I lost my key.'
*'So **how** did you get into the house **without** a key?'*
*'**With** a brick!'*

intensification of meaning [See DEGREE]

interjection

is the grammatical term for an 'exclamation word' such as ***oh***, ***ah***, and ***wow***. [See EXCLAMATIONS 2, 4.]

interrogative [See QUESTION, INDIRECT QUESTION, WH- WORD.]

into /ˈɪntʊ/ (weak form /ˈɪntə/) (*preposition*) [Compare IN]

1 ***Into*** is a preposition of motion, and is the opposite of ***out of***.

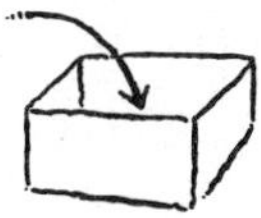
into

E.g. *He* {*entered* / *went **into*** / *walked **into*** / *came **into***} *the room and took off his jacket.*

*My wife's got to go **into** hospital.*

2 Note idiomatic abstract meanings.

E.g. **go into:** *They **went into** business together in 1972, and soon became rich and successful.*
come into: *Long hair and long dresses are **coming into*** fashion again.

intonation

Intonation (the way your voice moves up or down in speaking) can be important. So be careful!

1 **The three main patterns are**

Falling:	Really (*really*)	Thank you (*thank you*)
Rising:	Really (*really*)	*Thank you* (*thank you*)
Fall-rise:	Really (*really*)	Thank you (*thank you*)

2 If you use a falling tone too much, you may not sound <polite>.

3 **Asking a question**

3a If you use a falling tone when you are asking a question, you can sound as if you are making a statement. For example, a student asks a teacher this question:

student: *'The exam is very* ***difficult****.'*
teacher: *'****Is*** *it?'*
student: *'I don't* ***know****.* ***I'm*** *asking* ***you****.'*
teacher: *'Oh, you mean, "The exam is very* ***difficult?****"'*

Why did the teacher misunderstand? Because when the voice falls ↘ you are probably making a statement. You are certain about what you say – nothing needs to be added. When the voice rises ↗ you are probably asking a question [see YES-NO QUESTION 1].

E.g. *A: Can I ask you a question?*
B: Yes? What's the problem?
A: How do you spell machinery?

3b However, we usually use a falling tone if the question begins with a WH-WORD [see WH-QUESTION].

E.g. *'****What's*** *the problem?' '****How*** *do you spell machinery?'*

A rising tone on a WH-QUESTION sounds particularly interested and friendly.

4 **How to use the three patterns**

4a Falling ↘ :
This usually means something **certain** or **final** or **definite**. Especially a statement.

E.g. *It's five **o'clock**. Here is the **news**.*

or an <abrupt> ***order*** or ***instruction***.

E.g. *Go **away.*** *Please sit **down**.*

(More <polite> is: *Please sit **down**.*)

4b Rising:
This usually means something ***uncertain*** or where something needs to be added, for example in a YES-NO QUESTION.

E.g. *'Are you cold?' 'No, I feel quite **warm**.'*
*'Can I **help** you?' 'Oh, **yes**. Do you sell **T-shirts** please?' '**No**, I'm afraid we **don't**.*

4c Fall-rise
This means you feel certain, but something needs to be added. Perhaps there is a problem.

E.g. *'Would you like to go swimming this **weekend**?' '**Well**, I'd **like to**, but . . .*
*'This chicken is **delicious**.' '**Chicken**? We're not having **chicken**. It's **turkey**!'*

*'That's not **my signature**.'* (It must be someone else's.)

intransitive verb [See VERB PATTERN]

1 An **Intransitive verb** is a verb that is not followed by an object (or a complement).

E.g. *They **laughed.*** *We **paused**.*

2 Some verbs are both intransitive and TRANSITIVE, i.e. can be used with or without an object.

E.g. *Mary was **reading.*** *Mary was **reading** a novel.*

3 **Intransitive verbs** include 'verbs of position' (e.g. ***sit***, and ***lie***) and 'verbs of MOTION' (e.g. ***come, go, fall***). But these are often followed by phrases of place or motion.

E.g. *We were **sitting** by the fire.*
*I **went** to the theatre.*

introductions [See GREETINGS 4, THIS 4a]

inversion

► ***Inversion*** ⇄ means changing the word order in the sentence (especially changing the order of SUBJECT and VERB).

1 **Summary: kinds of inversion**

(A) subject-auxiliary inversion:

SUBJECT + AUX. (+ . . .) ⟶ AUX. + SUBJECT (+ . . .)

E.g. *You can . . .* ⟶ *Can you . . .?*

(B) subject-be inversion:

SUBJECT + BE (+ . . .) ⟶ BE + SUBJECT (+ . . .)

E.g. *You are . . .* ⟶ *Are you . . .?*

(C) 'inversion' pattern with auxiliary ***do***:

SUBJECT + MAIN VERB (not **be**) (+ . . .) ⟶ DO + SUBJECT + MAIN VERB (+ . . .)

E.g. *You know . . .* ⟶ *Do you know . . .?*

(D) subject-verb inversion:

SUBJECT + MAIN VERB + ADVERBIAL (. . .) ⟶ ADVERBIAL + MAIN VERB + SUBJECT (. . .)

E.g. *Anna is here* ⟶ *Here is Anna.*

NOTE: In some grammar books, all three patterns (A) (B) (C) are called 'subject-operator' ***inversion***.

2 **Subject-auxiliary inversion**

The usual order in STATEMENTS is:

	SUBJECT +	AUXILIARY +	REST OF VERB (+ . . .)
E.g.	*We*	*are*	*studying.*
	The cat	*has*	*been sleeping here all day.*
	The plane	*will*	*be two hours late.*

2a But to form a QUESTION*, we place the AUXILIARY VERB (which begins the verb phrase) in front of the subject:

	AUXILIARY +	SUBJECT +	REST OF VERB (+ . . .)
E.g.	*Are*	*you*	*studying?*
	Has	*the cat*	*been sleeping here all day?*
	Will	*the plane*	*be two hours late?*

[* See WH-QUESTION 9, YES-NO QUESTION 1, for details. Not all questions have ***inversion***.]

3 **Subject-be inversion**

Sometimes there is no auxiliary verb, but BE is the main verb:

	SUBJECT + BE + . . .		
E.g.	*Diana*	***is***	*older than me.*
	They	***are***	*art students.*

In this case, ***be*** behaves like an auxiliary, so place it in front of the subject:

	BE + SUBJECT + . . .		
E.g.	***Is***	*Diana*	*older than me?*
	Are	*they*	*art students?*

4 **Inversion pattern with auxiliary DO**

Sometimes there is no auxiliary, and the main verb is not ***be***:

SUBJECT + VERB (SIMPLE PRESENT / PAST TENSE) (+ . . .)

E.g. *I* ***play*** *football most weekends.*

In this case, use ***do*** as 'empty auxiliary' to form the question [see DO 2d]:

DO + SUBJECT + VERB (BASIC FORM) (+ . . .)

E.g. *Do* *you* ***play*** *football most weekends?*

5 **Inversion in statements**

Sometimes ***inversion*** occurs in statements, to give emphasis, especially when the statement begins with a negative word or idea, or with SO.

E.g. *She **at no time** admitted she was a murderer.*
→ ***At no time did** she admit she was a murderer.*

[For further examples, see NEGATIVE WORDS AND SENTENCES 6a, SO 4a.]

6 **Subject-verb inversion**

There is also a kind of ***inversion*** in which the main verb (not only ***be***) comes before the subject in statements:

	ADVERBIAL	+ VERB	+ SUBJECT (. . .)
E.g.	*Here*	*comes*	*the taxi.*
	In the town square	*stands*	*the market hall.*
	Now	*is*	*the best time to plant roses.*
	Up	*went*	*the prices again!*

This pattern is mainly limited to (a) adverbials of place, and (b) verbs such as BE, COME AND GO, *sit, lie, stand*. It is used to put the focus on the subject, which is the most important part of the sentence.

NOTE: Do not use subject-verb ***inversion*** if the subject is a pronoun. Compare:
There goes the bus. but: *There **it** goes.*
Down came the rain. but: *Down **it** came.*

invitations

1 Here are some examples of ***invitations*** in <informal speech>:

'***Would you like to*** *join me for* { *a cup of tea?'* / *something to eat?'* }

'***Thanks very much – it's very kind of you****. But I'm afraid I have to catch a train.'*

'***Are you doing anything*** *tomorrow evening?'*
'No.'
'Then ***why don't you*** *come and have a meal with me at the Copper Kettle? We can talk about old times.'*
'What a nice idea. ***Thanks. I'd love to*** *come.'*

'***I wonder if you'd like to come*** *and stay with us in the country some time.* ***You're very welcome*** *to come for a week or two this summer!'* '***How kind of you****. That's a great idea. Are you sure it wouldn't be too much trouble?'*

NOTE: If someone ***invites*** you to something, accept or refuse <politely> as shown in the examples. Do not just say ***Yes*** or ***No***. It is not very <polite>!

2 Here is a <very formal written> ***invitation***:

Mr and Mrs James Maxton
request the pleasure of your company
at Dinner
on Tuesday, 12 May
at 8.30 p.m.
*R.S.V.P. **
12, Rosemary St.,
Birmingham

* R.S.V.P. = *'Répondez s'il vous plaît.'* (French, = 'Please reply'.)

A <formal written> reply:

William Muffin thanks Mr & Mrs James Maxton for their kind invitation for Tuesday, 12 May, which he
{ *accepts with much pleasure.* / *very much regrets being unable to accept, because of absence abroad.* }

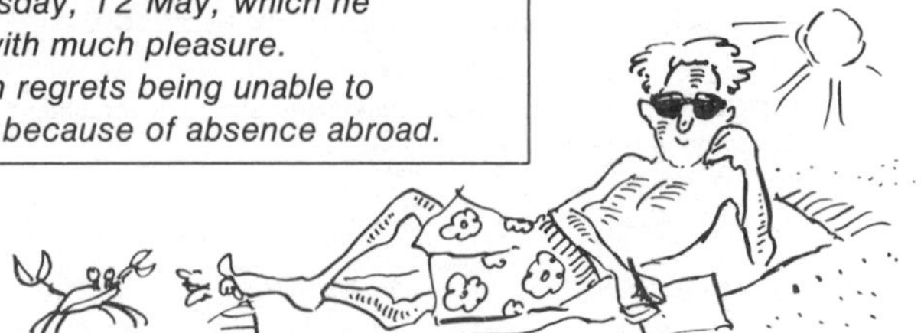

2a An <informal> written ***invitation***:

> *Dear Frederic,*
> *Jan and I are holding a party on Saturday, 6th June at 8.30 p.m. Please come if you can. We look forward to seeing you very much.*
>
> *{ Yours sincerely <G.B.> }*
> *{ Sincerely yours <U.S.> }*
> *Michael*

irregular plural

► We form the regular plural of English nouns by adding **-*s*** or **-*es*** [see PLURAL 2a]: ***day → days, box → boxes***.

► ***Irregular plurals*** are exceptions to this general rule. Below are the different types, with their most common examples.

1 **Changing the vowel**

singular	plural	singular	plural
man /mæn/	→ ***men*** /men/	***foot*** /fʊt/	→ ***feet*** /fi:t/
woman /ˈwʊmən/	→ ***women*** /ˈwɪmɪn/	***goose*** /gu:s/	→ ***geese*** /gi:s/
mouse /maʊs/	→ ***mice*** /maɪs/	***tooth*** /tu:θ/	→ ***teeth*** /ti:θ/

2 **Adding -*(r)en***:

child /tʃaɪld/ → ***children*** /ˈtʃɪldrən/   ***ox*** /ɒks/ → ***oxen*** /ˈɒksən/

3 **Changing the last consonant** (voicing /f/, /θ/, or /s/)

3a In most cases the change is from **-*f*** -/f/ to **-*ves*** -/vz/:

E.g. ***knife*** /naɪf/ → ***knives*** /naɪvz/.

calf → ***calves***	***leaf*** → ***leaves***	***shelf*** → ***shelves***
half → ***halves***	***life*** → ***lives***	***thief*** → ***thieves***
knife → ***knives***	***loaf*** → ***loaves***	***wife*** → ***wives***

NOTE: Here, the spelling and pronunciation change; in 3b and 3c the spelling stays the same and the pronunciation changes.

3b Change from **-*th*** -/θ/ to **-*ths*** -/ðz/:

E.g. ***mouth*** /maʊθ/ → ***mouths*** /maʊðz/
path /pɑ:θ‖pæ:θ/ → ***paths*** /pɑ:ðz‖pæ:ðz/

3c Change from **-se** -/s/ to **-ses** -/zɪz/:

E.g. ***house*** /haʊs/ → ***houses*** /ˈhaʊzɪz/

NOTE: For the following words, the change in the last consonant is possible, but the regular plural is also possible.
E.g. *truth(s), oath(s), sheath(s), wreath(s), youth(s), dwarf(s), hoof(s), scarf(s), wharf(s),* (also: *dwarves, hooves, scarves, wharves*).

4 With the following nouns, the plural is the same as the singular

4a Nouns for some animals, birds and fish.

E.g. *sheep* → *sheep*   *deer* → *deer*
grouse → *grouse*   *fish* → *fish* *

* Rarely: *fishes*.

4b Nouns for people ending in **-ese** or **-ss** [see COUNTRIES].

E.g. ***Chinese*** → ***Chinese***   ***Japanese*** → ***Japanese***
Swiss → ***Swiss***

Also: ***Portuguese, Lebanese, Vietnamese, Sinhalese***

E.g. *one* / *many* } ***Chinese***   *a* / *ten* } ***Japanese***   *this* / *these* } ***Swiss***

4c Some nouns referring to numbers [see NUMBERS 5] and measurement [see MEASURING], when they come after a number or a quantity word.

E.g. 'How many plants would you like?' { *'Three* ***dozen****.'** / *'A few* ***hundred****.'** }
'This engine has 15 ***horse power****.'*
'One pound is worth about 230 ***yen****.'* (yen = Japanese money).

* The nouns ***dozen*** (12), ***score*** (20), ***hundred*** (100), ***thousand*** (1,000) and ***million*** (1,000,000) normally have a regular plural.
E.g. ***hundreds*** *of people*. [See NUMBERS 5a.]

4d Nouns ending in **-ies** (-/ɪz/) in the singular:

series → ***series***   ***species*** → ***species***

E.g. *a new* ***species*** ~ *several new* ***species*** *of insects*

4e Some nouns ending in **-s** in the singular.

E.g. ***crossroads*** → ***crossroads***   ***barracks*** → ***barracks***
means → ***means***   ***headquarters*** → ***headquarters***

E.g. *a busy* ***crossroads*** ~ *several* ***crossroads***
every ***means*** ~ *all* ***means*** *of transport*

4f A mixed group of nouns:

offspring* → *offspring ***dice* → *dice***
data** → *data ***(air)craft* → *(air)craft***

* People disagree on the singular use of ***data***. The 'correct' Latin singular is ***datum.***

5 Foreign plurals

Some words from foreign languages keep their foreign plural in English. But they also usually allow a regular plural. The foreign plural tends to be more <formal>, and to be preferred in <scientific> English.

5a Latin nouns changing singular ***-us*** (-/əs/) to plural ***-i*** (-/aɪ/):
Latin plural only:

E.g. ***stimulus*** /ˈstɪmjʊləs/ → ***stimuli*** /ˈstɪmjʊlaɪ/

Other words allow both a regular and a Latin plural. The Latin plurals are as follows.

cactus* → *cacti ***crocus* → *croci*** ***focus* → *foci***
nucleus* → *nuclei ***octopus* → *octopi*** ***radius* → *radii***
syllabus* → *syllabi ***terminus* → *termini***

NOTE: ***Genus*** has the Latin Plural ***genera*** /ˈdʒenərə/ (and the regular plural).

5b Latin nouns changing singular ***-a*** (-/ə/ or -/ɑː/) to ***-ae*** (-/iː/):
Latin plural only:

E.g. ***larva* → *larvae*** ***alga* → *algae***

Usually with the foreign plural:

formula /ˈfɔːˈmjʊlə/ → ***formulae*** /ˈfɔːˈmjʊliː/

Other examples of nouns with both a regular and a Latin plural:

antenna* → *antennae ***nebula* → *nebulae***
vertebra* → *vertebrae

5c Latin nouns changing singular ***-um*** (-/əm/) to ***-a*** (-/ə/ or -/ɑː/):
Latin plural only:

E.g. ***curriculum*** /kəˈrɪkjʊləm/ ***curricula*** /kəˈrɪkjʊlə/

Other words allow both plurals.

E.g. ***medium* → *media**** ***aquarium* → *aquaria***
memorandum* → *memoranda
spectrum* → *spectra ***stratum* → *strata***
millenium* → *millenia

* The Latin plural ***media*** is used for means of communication, e.g. ***mass media***.

5d Latin nouns changing singular ***-ix*** or ***-ex*** (-/ɪks/ or -/eks/) to ***-ices*** (-/ɪsiːz/).

E.g. ***index*** /ˈɪndeks/ → ***ˈindices*** /ˈɪndɪsiːz/

Also: ***appendix*** → ***appendices*** ***apex*** → ***apices***

Nouns of this type allow both the Latin and the regular plural.

5e Greek nouns changing singular ***-is*** (-/ɪs/) to ***-es*** (-/iːz/): Nouns of this type have the Greek plural only.

E.g. ***analysis*** /əˈnæləsɪs/ → ***analyses*** /əˈnæləsiːz/

Other examples:

axis	→ ***axes***	***diagnosis***	→ ***diagnoses***
oasis	→ ***oases***	***crisis***	→ ***crises***
hypothesis	→ ***hypotheses***	***thesis***	→ ***theses***

5f Greek nouns changing singular ***-on*** (-/ɒn/) to ***-a*** (-/ə/ or -/ɑː/).

E.g. ***criterion*** /kraɪˈtiːrɪən/ → ***criteria*** /kraɪˈtiːrɪə/

Other examples:

phenomenon → ***phenomena*** ***automaton**** → ***automata***

* ***Automaton*** can also take a regular plural.

6 **Compound nouns** (i.e. nouns consisting of more than one word element – see COMPOUND WORD)
Some compound nouns have the plural ending on the first noun element, instead of on the whole compound. This is because the first noun is the head.

E.g. ***sister-in-law*** → ***sisters-in-law*** (Also: ***sons-in-law***, etc.)
court martial → ***courts martial***
commander-in-chief → ***commanders-in-chief***

irregular verb

1 Many of the most common main verbs in English are **irregular**. This means that they form their PAST TENSE form and their PAST PARTICIPLE form in a different way from the regular -ED ending.

2 At the back of the book there is a detailed list of **irregular verbs**.

3 [See also AUXILIARY VERB, BE, DO, HAVE, MODAL AUXILIARY.]

is the 3rd person singular present tense form of ***be*** [See BE.]

it /ɪt/ (3rd person singular personal pronoun), ***its*** /ɪts/, ***itself*** /ɪtˈself/.

► ***It*** refers to anything which is not a person. [See HE AND SHE on choosing between ***he***, ***she***, and ***it***.]

► ***It*** is also an 'empty' pronoun in such sentences as:

*'**It** is raining.'* *'**It**'s lucky that you came.'*

[See 3 below, and also IT-PATTERNS.]

1 The forms of ***it*** are:

subject / object pronoun	possessive determiner*	reflexive pronoun
it /ɪt/	***its*** * * /ɪts/	***itself*** /ɪtˈself/

* ***It*** has no possessive pronoun.
* * Note no apostrophe. (***It's*** = ***it is***.)

2 **Some uses of *it***

2a We use ***it*** in talking about a thing or (sometimes) an animal.

E.g. *Jill made **a cake** and gave **it** to the children.*

*'Why is **this cat** so fat?' '**It** eats too much.'*

NOTE: Sometimes we use ***she*** (instead of ***it***) to refer to vehicles or machines, and especially to boats.
E.g. *'What a lovely car!' 'Yes, isn't **she** a beauty?'*
*'What a lovely **boat**! Is she yours?' 'Yes, I bought **her** last month?'*

2b ***It*** introducing people.

E.g. on the phone: *'Hello; **it**'s Margaret.'*
in the street: *'Who's that over there?' '**It**'s the Queen!'*
at the door: *'Who was that?' '**It** was Dr Small.'*

3 **'Empty' *it***

3a We use ***it*** as an 'empty' SUBJECT in talking about the ***time***, the ***weather***, and other background conditions.

E.g. *'What time is **it**?' '**It**'s nearly eight o'clock.'*
*'**It**'s warm today, isn't it?' 'Yes, **it**'s been very fine just recently.'*
*'How far is **it** to Los Angeles?' '**It**'s over 3000 miles.'*

3b We use ***it*** in talking about 'life in general' <very informal>.

E.g. *'How's **it** going?' 'Not too bad, thanks.'*

NOTE: ***It*** can replace a COMPLEMENT; e.g. a NOUN PHRASE or an ADJECTIVE.
E.g. *She was **rich** – and she looked **it**.* ('looked rich')
*He was **an old man** – but he didn't seem **it**.*

it-patterns

► ***it*-patterns** are special clause patterns which occur when a clause begins with 'empty ***it***' [see IT 3]. E.g. ***It****'s a pity that she left*. The 'empty ***it***' has no meaning: its function is simply to fill the position of SUBJECT. So it may be called 'introductory ***it***'.

► There are two main types of ***it*-patterns**: we call them
(a) delayed subject patterns [see 1 below], and
(b) divided clause patterns [see 2 below].

[Other types of clause patterns or structures are illustrated in VERB PATTERNS and THERE IS / THERE ARE.]

1 Delayed subject patterns
A clause as a subject is rather awkward.

E.g. (i) ***That she left*** *is* { *a pity.* / *certain.* }

In (i) the subject is a THAT-clause. To avoid this, we replace the subject by introductory ***it***, and place the ***that***-clause at the end.

E.g. (ii) ***It*** *is* { *a pity* / *certain* } ***that*** *she left.*

1a Notice that the delayed subject may be (i) a THAT-clause, (ii) a WH-CLAUSE (= INDIRECT QUESTION), (iii) a TO-INFINITIVE clause, (iv) an -ING CLAUSE, (v) an IF-clause.

E.g. (i) ***It****'s odd **that** the bicycle has disappeared.*
(ii) ***It*** *doesn't matter **what** you say.*
(iii) ***It*** *is compulsory **to wear** a safety belt.*
(iv) ***It*** *was fun **looking after** the children.*
(v) ***It*** *would be a shame **if** they forgot their passports.*

1b Common delayed-subject patterns

(a) IT + BE + ADJECTIVE (PHRASE) + CLAUSE

E.g. ***It****'s strange that Janet is so late.*

(b) IT + BE + NOUN PHRASE + CLAUSE

E.g. ***It****'s no use getting angry with the waiter.*

(c) IT + VERB + CLAUSE

E.g. ***It*** *happened that the summer was particularly dry.*

(d) IT + PASSIVE VERB + CLAUSE

E.g. ***It****'s not known whether any lives were lost.*

1c Some other patterns.

E.g. ***It*** *shocked me that she couldn't even speak to her own sister.*
It *gives me great pleasure to announce the winner of the competition.*

2 **Divided clause patterns**
In these patterns we divide a clause into two parts, in order to place emphasis or **focus** on one element. The general pattern is:

it	*be*	**focus**	*that*	rest of clause

E.g. (i)

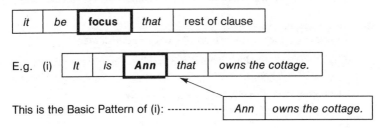

It	*is*	***Ann***	*that*	*owns the cottage.*

This is the Basic Pattern of (i): ---------------

Ann	*owns the cottage.*

2a In (i) the **focus** was the subject:

focus ↓

it	*be*	**subject**	*that*	rest of clause

E.g.

It	*'s*	***my father***	*that*	*was born in India.*

Other patterns have another element as ***focus***:

2b **focus** ↓

it	*be*	**object**	*that*	rest of clause

E.g.

It	*was*	***the last dance***	*that*	*I enjoyed most.*

2c **focus** ↓

it	*be*	**adverbial**	that	rest of clause

E.g.

It	*'s*	***in London***	*that*	*the traffic is noisiest.*

NOTE (i): If the ***focus*** refers to a person, we can replace ***that*** by ***who***.
E.g. *It's **my father who** was born in India.*
*It's **my father who(m)** I really miss.*

NOTE (ii): We can omit ***that*** entirely if the ***focus*** refers to something that is not a person, or else if it is an adverbial.
E.g. ***It was the last dance** I enjoyed most.*
***It's in London** the traffic is noisiest.*
These details show that the second part of a divided clause is very similar to a RELATIVE CLAUSE.

3 it-Patterns can be negatives, questions, or shortened answers

3a Examples of delayed subject sentences.

E.g. Negative: ***It's not** necessary to lock the window.*
Question: ***Is it** important to take your passport?*
Negative Question: ***Wasn't it** lucky that they caught the bus?*

3b Divided clause sentences:

Shortened answers contain only ***it*** + ***be*** + noun phrase.

E.g. *'Who cooked the dinner?' '**It was Rick**.' (= 'It was Rick who cooked the dinner.')*

Further examples of divided clause sentences:

* *'**It** was me . . .'* is an <informal> equivalent of *'**It** was I . . .'* in this example. [See PERSONAL PRONOUN 2d.]

just /dʒʌst/ (*adverb [or adjective]*)

► ***Just*** is an adverb with several meanings.
► ***Just*** goes before the word or phrase to which it applies.
► ***Just*** usually goes in middle position [see ADVERB 3].

1a ***just*** = 'very recently', 'a short time ago':

E.g. *'I saw her **just** now'* means *'I saw her a moment ago'.*

HAVE + JUST + PAST PARTICIPLE [See PRESENT PERFECT 5d.]

E.g.

Look, they've just got married.
JUST MARRIED

1b ***Just*** = 'immediate future':

BE + JUST { Verb-***ing*** / GOING TO Verb / ABOUT TO Verb } [See FUTURE 2, 4, 5c.]

E.g.

Look, he's just about to dive in. Watch!

2 Degree and emphasis

2a ***Just*** = 'exactly'.

E.g. *That house is **just** what I've always wanted.*
*My children are **just** as good at science as your children are!*

2b ***Just*** = 'only', 'not more than'

E.g. *'Would you like something to eat?' 'No, thank you, I'll **just** have a cup of tea.'*
*You can't blame him – he's **just** a silly little boy.*

*'**Just** a moment / minute!'* is a useful phrase meaning *'wait for a short time.'*

2c ***Just*** = emphasis

E.g. *'She's in a hurry.' 'Too bad. She'll **just** have to wait!'*
*'I **just** don't like it. That's all.'*

3 ***Just*** is an adjective meaning 'fair'.

E.g. *'The judge sent the thief to prison for twelve months. I thought it was a **just** decision.'*

(Compare the noun ***justice*** and the adverb ***justly***.)

---

kind (of), sort (of), and *type (of)* /ˈkaɪnd(əv)/, /ˈsɔːˈt(əv)/, /ˈtaɪp(əv)/ (*nouns*)

- ► These three nouns are interchangeable in 1 and 2 below.
- ► These three nouns are often followed by ***of***.
- ► They are nouns which 'classify' other nouns [see NOUN OF KIND].

1 **Examples**
Kinds *of vegetable*

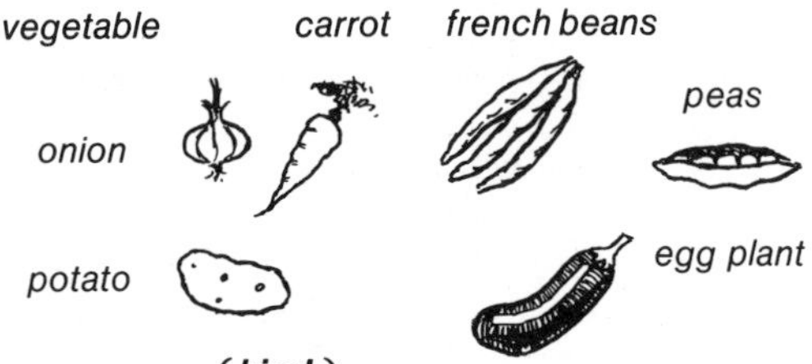

E.g. *An egg plant is a* {***kind*** / ***sort*** / ***type***} ***of*** *(a) vegetable.*
Coffee is a {***kind*** / ***sort*** / ***type***} ***of*** *drink.*

1a We can omit ***of*** + noun when the noun's meaning is obvious from the situation.

E.g. *Let me get you an ice-cream. What **kind** would you like? Chocolate, strawberry, or vanilla?*

2 Notice these patterns.

E.g. *I enjoy most **kinds of*** {*novel.* <more formal> / *novels.* <more informal>}
*A **new kind of** computer* / *An **odd kind of** (a) man* } (Place the adjective before ***kind (of)***)
This kind of lock *is very secure.* <more formal>
These kind of locks *are very secure.* <informal>

3 ***Kind of*** **and *sort of* meaning 'rather'** [see QUITE AND RATHER.]
In <informal> conversation, ***kind of*** and ***sort of*** can come before adjectives, verbs, and adverbs as adverbs of DEGREE.

E.g. *Some people are* {***kind of**** / ***sort of****} ***careless*** *about their appearance.*
(= 'rather careless', or 'careless, in a way')
I ***sort of respect*** *him for admitting his mistakes.* (= 'respect him, in a manner of speaking')

* ***Kind of*** and ***sort of*** are commonly used in this way, but many people feel them to be 'bad English'. ***Kind of*** is especially <U.S.>, and ***sort of*** especially <G.B.>.

---

kindly /ˈkaɪndlɪ/ (*adverb of manner / politeness*) (*or adjective*)

---

1 ***Kindly*** (a) can be <polite> (= 'please')
(b) is more often too polite! (i.e., the speaker is just pretending to be <polite>!)

E.g. (a) *'Would you* ***kindly*** *keep us informed?' 'Yes, certainly.'*
(b) Mother: *You never tidy up your room.*
Son: *But . . .*
Mother: *And could you* ***kindly*** *put away all these records and tapes.*
Son: *Okay, Mum.*

2 ***Kindly*** is also an adverb meaning 'in a kind manner'.

E.g. *The children like Dr Molloy. He always talks to them* ***kindly***.

---

last /lɑːst‖læːst/ (*ordinal or adverb*) [See ORDINALS 1]

► ***Last*** refers to anything / anyone that comes at the end of a series.

1 ***Last*** **is the opposite of *first***

Last is an ordinal in:

'The captain was the ***last*** *of the crew to leave the sinking ship.'* ('Everyone else left before the captain.')
Beethoven's Ninth Symphony was the ***last*** *one that he wrote.*

Last is an adverb in:

Because of engine trouble, Watson's car finished ***last***.

2 When ***last*** goes before nouns of time, it means 'the most recent', or 'the one before this'.

E.g. ***last*** *night,* ***last*** *Tuesday,* ***last*** *week,* ***last*** *year*

In the following example, ***last*** contrasts with ***this*** and ***next***.

E.g. ***Last*** *month was July,* ***this*** *month is August, and* ***next*** *month will be September.*

[See TIME 4c, 5.]

late /leɪt/ (*adjective or adverb*) Comparative: **later,** Superlative: **latest**

► ***Late*** usually means 'not in time; after the right time'.
► ***Late*** is the opposite of ***early***.
► The adjective ***late*** and the adverb ***late*** have the same forms. [See ADVERB 4(II).]

1a Adjective

E.g. *The train's* ***late****. It should have arrived at nine o'clock, and it's now half-past nine.*
We'll get there in the ***late*** *afternoon, if we leave now.*

NOTE: ***Late*** before a human noun can mean 'recently dead'. E.g. *your* ***late father*** <formal>.

1b Adverb

E.g. *I have to work* ***late*** *this evening, so don't wait for me.*

2a ***Later*** = '(further) in the future' (as well as being the comparative form of ***late***).

E.g. *Goodbye for now – I'll see you* ***later****.'*
The baby arrived ***later*** *than expected.*

2b ***Latest*** = 'most recent' (as well as being the superlative form of ***late***).

E.g. *The* ***latest*** *news is that the patient's health is improving.* (= 'most recent news')

least [See LESS, LEAST.]

length of time (or 'duration')

► Adverbials of ***length of time*** answer the question *How long?*

1 Patterns

for + NOUN PHRASE

from + NOUN PHRASE + { ***to**** / ***through**** } + NOUN PHRASE

MAIN CLAUSE + { ***since*** / ***until*** / ***till***** } + { NOUN PHRASE / CLAUSE }

{ ***all through*** / ***throughout*** } + NOUN PHRASE

up to + NOUN PHRASE

while + CLAUSE

during + NOUN PHRASE

[See FOR, FROM, SINCE, UNTIL, THROUGH, WHILE, DURING for further details.]

* In <U.S.> English, ***through*** means 'up to and including'.
* * ***Till*** is a <less common and less formal> form of ***until***.

2 An example

Here is a short story, as an example:

Linda's parents decided to sail around the world. They left home on 1st July, and returned on 30th September. ***During the same period,*** *Linda stayed at a summer camp for children.*

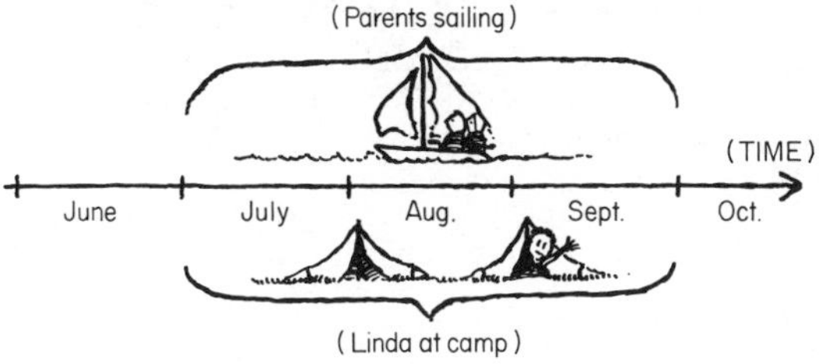

So, if someone asks:

How long *did Linda stay at the camp?*

we can answer in many different ways.

Compare these examples with the patterns at 1 above:

She stayed at the camp
- ***for*** *three months.*
- ***from*** *July* { ***to*** / ***through*** } *September.*
- ***since*** *the beginning of July.* *
- { ***until*** / ***till*** } { *the end of September.* / *her parents returned.* }
- { ***all through*** / ***throughout*** } *the summer.*
- ***up to*** *30th September.*
- ***while*** *her parents were away.*
- ***during*** *her parents' absence.*

* ***Since*** sometimes causes problems. See SINCE for more information.

3 **Other expressions**

These are some other expressions of ***length of time***:

My cousin is staying here ***over*** { *the weekend.* / *Christmas.* }

The mountain top is covered with snow ***all the year round***.

That boy's been watching TV ***all evening***.

(Also: ***all day (long),*** ***all night (long),*** ***all the summer***, etc.)

---

less, (the) least /les/, /(ðə)ˈliːst/ (*adverbs, determiners, or pronouns*), comparative and superlative forms of LITTLE. [See -ER / -EST 3c, 4]

---

1 **Adverbs**

2 **Determiners and pronouns**

E.g. *'The* ***least*** *amount of money I can live on is £100 per week.'*
'Well, I have to live on ***less*** *than that: I earn only £80 a week.'*

2a Use ***less*** and ***(the) least*** with uncountables, and ***fewer*** and ***fewest*** with countables.

E.g. *'This year we had **less** rain than last year.' 'Yes. We also had **fewer** thunderstorms.'*

NOTE: LITTLE as an adjective has no comparative or superlative. Instead of ~~*littler*~~, ~~*littlest*~~, people usually say ***smaller***, ***smallest***. However, ***least*** can be used with abstract ideas [see ABSTRACT NOUN] in the sense of ***'smallest'***.
E.g. *I don't feel the **least** bit hungry.* *That is the **least** of our problems.*

3 **Idioms**
at least = adverb of degree ('not less than').

E.g. *This temple is **at least** 3000 years old.*

at least = linking adverb ('if nothing else').

E.g. *The food at school isn't very good, but **at least** it's cheap.*

in the least (adverb of degree) means 'at all' after negatives.

E.g. *I'm not **in the least** upset that we lost.*

---

let /let/ ***lets, let, letting*** and ***make*** /meɪk/ ***makes, made, making*** (*verbs*)

- ***Let*** and ***make*** are verbs with similar meanings and related sentence patterns [see VERB PATTERN 18.]
- ***Let*** means 'allow / not prevent' and ***make*** means 'force / compel'.
- [On other uses of ***let***, see LET'S.]
- [On other uses of ***make***, see DO and MAKE.]

1 LET + OBJECT + VERB MAKE + OBJECT + VERB

Notice there is no ***to*** in these patterns.

E.g. *Some parents **let their children stay** up late. Other parents **make their children go** to bed early.*
*The police **let the thief escape**. But when they caught him, they **made him give back** the money.*

NOTE: With ***allow, force***, and ***compel, to*** would be used.
E.g. *They **allowed him to escape**.*
*They **forced him to give back** the money.*

let's /lets/

► ***let's*** = let us (plural)

1 ***Let's*** + Verb is a way of making a suggestion for the speaker and hearer(s) to do something.

E.g. ***Let's*** *play cards.*
Let's *have a meal at the new restaurant.*
*'**Let's** go swimming next Sunday (, shall we)?*' 'Yes, **let's**.'*

* In <G.B.> the TAG QUESTION ***shall we?*** can be added at the end of the sentence.

NOTE: Do not confuse ***let us*** (= let's) with the IMPERATIVE form of LET (= 'allow').
E.g. *Please* ***let*** {*me* / *us*} *help you.* (= 'allow me / us to help you')

2 **Negative of *let's***

E.g. ***Let's not*** *talk about it: it makes me feel ill even to think of it.*

<G.B.> speakers can also say ***don't let's*** <informal>.

E.g. ***Don't let's*** *invite George to the party: he's such a bore!*

letters, letter-writing

1 If you are writing a ***letter*** to a friend or relative, the language is friendly or <informal> as in example A below. If you are writing a business ***letter***, the language is <formal> as in example B below. [See FORMAL AND INFORMAL ENGLISH.]

2 Example A: **a letter** to a friend

(1) *51, Poplar Grove,*
London W6 7RE
(2) *29th December, 1988*

(3) *Dear Jenny,*
(4) *It was great to hear from you! I'm glad you're enjoying your life and your job in Angola.*
(5) *If you'd like to come and stay in July, you're welcome. I'd love to see you, though you know how busy I am!*
(6) *Everything is fine here. My new job is keeping me active, and I have plenty of friends. My new flat in London has given me a few problems, but I've stopped worrying about it.*
(7) *I'm really looking forward to seeing you again. Let me know your plans.*

(8) *Love,*
(9) Brenda

(10) *P.S. Do you know my phone number? It's 682-8117*

key
1. Your address (but not your name)
2. The date
3. Greeting (saying 'hello')
4. Why you are writing or replying
5. What you want to say (= 'the message')
6. . . . including news about yourself
7. Finishing remarks
8. 'Friendly' way to end the letter
9. Your (first) name
10. 'Postscript' or P.S.: for things you may want to add as an afterthought

3 Example B: **a business letter**

(1) *51, Poplar Grove,*
London W6 7RE
(2) *29 April 1986*

(3) *Stevens and Dickinson, Solicitors,*
203, Castle Street,
Farnham,
Surrey GU9 7HT
(4) { *For the attention of* / *Attention* } Mr R. Cox { <especially G.B.> / <especially U.S.> }

(5) *Dear Sir,*
(6) <u>*Re: The late Roland James, 26, Waveney Rd., Farnham*</u>
(7) *I am writing to you because I understand that you are my late uncle's solicitor.*
(8) *Since I have heard nothing from you regarding my uncle's will, I would be grateful for any information you may have.*
(9) *He died on Sunday, 6th April, 1986, and Mrs Vera Smith, my aunt, tells me that he left me a sum of money in his will.*
(10) *I look forward to hearing from you.*
(11) *Yours faithfully,*
BMG Kelly
(12) *Miss B.M.G. Kelly*

key
1. Your address (but not your name)
2. The date
3. The name and address you are writing to
4. <Not usual>: The person who should receive the letter (if not mentioned in 3.)
5. Greeting to a person you don't know
6. Heading: the subject of the letter

7., 8. Why you are writing

9. Any further information
10. Concluding the letter
11. Formal way to end a letter
12. Your name, under your signature

4 Saying 'hello' and 'goodbye' in *letters*

These examples show a range, from the most <formal> to the most <informal>:

4a

the situation	'hello'	'goodbye'
You haven't met, and it's a business matter:	*Dear Sir,* *Dear Madam,* *Dear Sirs,*	*Yours faithfully* *J. M. Wright*

4b

the situation	'hello'	'goodbye'
You have met in business or social life, but you are not great friends:	*Dear Mr Green,* *Dear Miss* Black,* *Dear Mrs* Brown,* *Dear Dr White,*	*Yours sincerely,* *John Wright*

4c

To good friends, relatives, etc.:	*Dear Jim,* *Dear Jenny,* *Dear Uncle Sam,*	*Best wishes,* *All the best,* *Kind regards,* *John*

4d

To very close friends or close relatives:	*Dear Tom,* *My dearest** Ann,* *Darling** Roy,*	*Love,*** *Lots of love,*** *Love** from* *Mum*

* [On the use of ***Miss***, ***Mrs***, and ***Ms***, see NAMES OF PEOPLE 1(B).]

** Generally used only in writing to people of the opposite sex, or by parents in writing to their children. Not generally used by men writing to men.

5 British and American styles

The **letters** in the examples above show British styles. In American **letters** there are one or two differences:

5a The opening 'Dear X' is followed by a colon.

E.g. *Dear Mr. Smith:* *Dear Sir:* etc.

5b In the date, change the order to month, day, year.

E.g. *April 29, 1986*

5c Before signing the *letter*, put ***sincerely yours*** or ***sincerely***, instead of <G.B.> ***yours sincerely***.

letters of the alphabet

1 How to pronounce their names

a /eɪ/	***b*** /bi:/	***c*** /si:/	***d*** /di:/	***e*** /i:/	***f*** /ef/	***g*** /dʒi:/
h /eɪtʃ/	***i*** /aɪ/	***j*** /dʒeɪ/	***k*** /keɪ/	***l*** /el/	***m*** /em/	***n*** /en/
o /əʊ/	***p*** /pi:/	***q*** /kju:/	***r*** /ɑ:^{r}/	***'s*** /es/	***t*** /ti:/	***u*** /ju:/
v /vi:/	***w*** /ˈdʌblju:/	***x*** /eks/	***y*** /waɪ/	***z*** /zed‖zi:/		

2 Consonant letters

b, c, d, f, g, h, j, k, l, m, n, p, q, r, s, t, v, x, z.

3 Vowel letters

a, e, i, o, u

4 Consonant-and-vowel letters

w and ***y*** are **consonant letters** when they come before a **vowel letter**: ***want, yet, backward, back-yard***. But they are **vowel letters** when they come after another **vowel letter***: ***cow, day, laws, boyhood***. Also, ***y*** is a vowel when it follows a **consonant letter**: ***cry, silly***.

* Between **vowel letters**, ***w*** and ***y*** are **consonant letters** when the following syllable is stressed: ***awake***, ***beyond***. But they are **vowel letters** when the syllable before them is stressed: ***showing, player***.

like /laɪk/ (*verb or preposition or conjunction*)

► Verb forms: ***like, likes, liked, liking***

► ***Like*** as a verb is for talking about people's preferences.

1 The verb *like*

1a ***Like*** is followed by different structures:—

(i) ***like*** + object (noun). E.g. ***I like ice-cream***.
(pronoun). E.g. *Mary* ***likes him***.

(ii) ***like*** + Verb-ing. E.g. *My father* ***likes working*** *for the BBC.*

NOTE: This pattern is often used for talking about hobbies in <G.B.>.
E.g. *We* ***like swimming.*** *Do you* ***like running****?*

(iii) ***like*** + object + Verb *-ing*. E.g. *We don't* ***like anyone interfering***. ('anyone' is the subject of 'interfering')

(iv) ***like*** + to + Verb means 'prefer' or 'choose' in <G.B.>. E.g. *'I* ***like to go*** *to bed early'.*

(v) ***like*** + object + to + Verb. E.g. *'The Prime Minister* ***likes reporters to get*** *their facts right.'*

1b ***Would like*** *(or* ***'d like****)* is a <polite> way of saying 'want'.

E.g.

Would like is followed by the same structures as ***like***:

E.g. ***Would*** *you* ***like an ice-cream****?*
Your father ***would like working*** *for the B.B.C.*
You ***wouldn't like anyone interfering*** *in your business, so don't interfere in mine.*
Would *you* ***like to go*** *to bed early?*
The Prime Minister ***would like reporters to get*** *their facts right.*

2 **The preposition *like***

The preposition ***like*** means 'similar to': it is used for comparison.

(i)

(ii)

E.g. (i) *Marilyn is* ***like*** *her mother.* (i.e. 'she resembles her.')
(ii) *Bill looks just* ***like*** *a sheepdog, with that beard!*
Like *Spain, Portugal has many sunny beaches.*

NOTE (i): ***like*** and ***as*** [see AS 3] have different meanings in:
E.g. *My mother works* ***like*** *a slave.* (i.e. 'she isn't a slave, but she works as hard as a slave.')
My mother works ***as*** *a teacher in the local school.* (i.e. 'she's a teacher: that's her job.')

NOTE (ii): ***what . . . like?*** is a question about the nature or manner of something.
E.g. *'**What** was the dinner **like**?' 'It was delicious!'*
*'**What** does she sing **like**?' 'Well, her voice is rather loud, but she sings quite well.'*

NOTE (iii): [On ***like this, like that***, *see* MANNER.]

3 ***Like* as a conjunction** <informal only>

3a Be careful about using ***like*** instead of ***as if*** [see AS 4a]. Some people say:

(i) *It looks* ***like*** *it's going to rain.* <informal, esp. U.S.>

But most people prefer:

(ii) *It looks* ***as if*** *it's going to rain.*

3b Be careful, too, about using ***like*** instead of ***as*** in sentences like this:

(iii) *Janice is a good cook,* ***like*** *her grandmother used to be.* <informal>

Some people, especially in <G.B.>, consider this 'bad English', and prefer ***as***.

E.g. (iv) *Janice is a good cook, (just)* ***as*** *her grandmother used to be.*

So the safest rule is:
Use ***like*** as a preposition (followed by a pronoun or noun phrase), but do not use ***like*** as a conjunction (followed by a clause).

I.e. Preposition ***like*** + pronoun / noun phrase.
Conjunction ***as*** + clause.

E.g. (v) *This curry tastes hot, (just)* { ***like*** *all good curries.* / ***as*** *it should.* }

linking adverbs and conjunctions

► **Linking words** link ideas together in a sentence or a text.

► There are three main kinds of **linking words**: (a) coordinating conjunctions, (b) subordinating conjunctions, (c) linking adverbs. [See CONJUNCTION, COORDINATION.]

1 The **linking words** on the next page are followed by:

(a) a coordinate clause
(b) a subordinate clause
(c) a sentence (in written English)

2 [To find examples of these linking words in use see the following words:]

2a Coordinating: [see AND, OR, BUT.]

2b Subordinating: [see AFTER AND BEFORE, ALTHOUGH, AS, BECAUSE, FOR 3, SINCE 3, THOUGH, WHEN, WHILE.]

They link:	(a) a coordinate clause	(b) a subordinate* clause	(c) a sentence (in written English or (a) or (b))
	conjunctions		
some meanings	coordinating	subordinating*	linking adverbs
adding ideas together:	*and*		*In addition,* *Also* *moreover* <formal> *Further(more),* <formal> *. . . too* *. . . as well*
showing alternatives:	*or*		*Alternatively,* *(or) else* *Otherwise,*
contrasting ideas: [See CONTRAST]	(a) *but* *yet* * *	*Although* *Even though* *Though*	*However,* <rather formal> *Yet* * *, Even so,* *(but) still,* *Still* *Nevertheless,* <formal> *Nonetheless,* <formal>
	(b)	*Whereas* *While*	*On the other hand*
showing cause reason or effect: [See REASON AND CAUSE]		*Because* *Since* *As* *for* *so* * *	*Therefore* <formal> *Consequently* <formal> *(and) so* * * *thus* <formal> *hence* <formal>
relating ideas in TIME (a) one idea following another: (b) one at the same time as another:		(a) *After* *Before* *When(ever)* *As soon as* (b) *While* *As* *When(ever)*	(a) *Then* *After(wards)* *Beforehand* *Soon* (b) *Meanwhile*

NOTE: All words in the above table which begin with capital letters can go first in a sentence. All words without capital letters must usually go in the middle.* * *

* A subordinate clause is 'dependent on' a main clause. [See CLAUSE 2.]

* * ***Yet*** and ***so*** are a mixture: sometimes they behave like conjunctions, and sometimes they behave like ***linking adverbs***.

* * * But in <informal written English>, we often begin a sentence with ***and***, ***or***, or ***but***.

2c Linking Adverbs: [see AFTER AND BEFORE, ALSO, ELSE 2, FURTHER 2, HOWEVER 2, OTHERWISE, TOO 1, YET 2.]

3 Here are some examples of ***linking adverbs***. They are all of the kind found in <formal written> English.

(i) *The government has serious problems because of the economic troubles, and the rise in the value of the dollar.* ***Moreover****, the nation's debt to the World Bank is worse than ever before.*
(ii) *The princess is very intelligent.* ***Nevertheless****, she has a lot to learn.*
(iii) *We agree that the weather is bad and not suitable for working in the open.* ***However****, we have the seeds, and they must be planted now.*
(iv) *The students haven't seen the play being performed on the stage.* ***Therefore*** *they can't discuss it on the basis of experience.*

NOTE: Most **linking adverbs** can go in middle position in the clause. For example, (ii) above could change to:
. . . *She* ***nevertheless*** *has a lot to learn.*

Some **linking adverbs** (***so, yet***) can go only at the front of the clause. Others (***too, as well***) cannot go at the front of the clause.

---

linking verb [See VERB PATTERNS 2, 3]

- Some verbs are called *linking* because they link the subject of a clause to another element, which describes something about the subject.
- The most important linking verb is BE (called the 'copula').
- Verbs which behave like ***be*** are also linking verbs. E.g.: BECOME, FEEL, LOOK, GET (= become), ***seem, appear***.

1 **The chief patterns for linking verbs are**

(A) SUBJECT + LINKING VERB + ADJECTIVE (PHRASE)

E.g. *The manager* ***is*** *(too) busy*

[See VERB PATTERN 2.]

(B) SUBJECT + LINKING VERB + NOUN PHRASE

E.g. *Football* ***is*** *my favourite sport.*

[See VERB PATTERN 2.]

(C) SUBJECT + LINKING VERB + ADVERBIAL

E.g. *This place* ***is*** *where Napoleon died.*

[See VERB PATTERN 3.]

2 Here is a list of the main *linking verbs* other than *be*

patterns

2a

(I) verbs of 'seeming' or 'perception'			(A)	(B)	(C)
The children	***appear***	*happy enough.*	✓		
This	***appeared*** *	*the only solution.*		✓	
The teachers	***are feeling***	*very annoyed.*	✓		
I	***felt*** *	*a complete idiot.*		✓	
The patient	*is* ***looking***	*much better.*	✓		
It	***looks***	*a fine day.*		✓	
The class	***seems***	*rather restless.*	✓		
The show	***seemed*** *	*a great success.*		✓	
This soup	***smells***	*delicious.*	✓		
The party	***sounded***	*very noisy.*	✓		
That	***sounds*** *	*a good idea.*		✓	
Our apples	***tasted***	*rather sour.*	✓		

* In <U.S.> English, this pattern is very rare. Pattern (D) or (E) [see 3 below] can be used instead.

2b

(II) verbs of 'becoming'			(A)	(B)	(C)
The hotel	*has* ***become***	*quite famous.*	✓		
Margaret	***became***	*a famous singer.*		✓	
The couple	***ended up***	*married.*	✓		
He	***ended up***	*chairman of the club.*		✓	
Many thieves	***end up***	*in prison.*			✓
We	*must* ***get***	*ready to go*	✓		
A large dog	***got***	*into the garden.*			✓
Children	*grow*	*tired (easily).*	✓		
Your lectures	*have* ***proved***	*very useful.*	✓		
Mr James	*has* ***proved***	*a good boss.*		✓	
The weather	*has* ***turned***	*very cold.*	✓		
The dinner	***turned out***	*delicious.*	✓		
Her illness	*may* ***turn out***	*a blessing.*		✓	

2c

(III) verbs of 'remaining'			(A)	(B)	(C)
The President	***remains***	*popular.*	✓		
Ann and Jim	***remain***	*good friends.*		✓	
You	*should* ***remain***	*in bed.*			✓
The witness	***kept***	*silent.*	✓		
The children	*must* ***keep***	*out of sight.*			✓
The soldiers	***stayed***	*perfectly still.*	✓		
You	*'d better* ***stay***	*at school.*			✓

3 **Other patterns typical of linking verbs**

(D) SUBJECT + VERB + TO BE + COMPLEMENT.

E.g. *Jacobs* ***seems to be*** *an excellent golfer.* [See VERB PATTERN 7.]

(E) SUBJECT + VERB + LIKE + NOUN PHRASE

E.g. *The object* ***looked like*** *a flying saucer.*

(F) SUBJECT + VERB + AS IF* + CLAUSE

E.g. *The milk* ***tastes as if*** *it has been boiled.*

* In pattern (F), ***seem*** and ***appear*** can follow an 'empty ***it***' as subject [see IT] before ***as if***.
E.g. ***It*** {***seems*** / ***appears***} ***as if*** *the earth is gradually moving nearer to the sun.*
[See LIKE 3a about the use of ***like*** in this pattern.]

little, a little /'lɪtl̩/, /ə'lɪtl̩/

► ***Little*** is (1) an adjective, or (2) a QUANTITY WORD, or (3) an adverb of DEGREE.
► ***A little*** is (1) a quantity expression, or (2) an adverb of degree.
► ***A little*** is the opposite of ***a lot***.
► ***(A) little*** is UNCOUNTABLE; ***(a) few*** is COUNTABLE. Compare:

E.g. ***a little*** *cheese* ('a small quantity of cheese')
a few *apples* ('a small quantity of apples')
We have ***little*** *time.* (= 'not much time')
We have ***few*** *friends.* (= 'not many friends')

1 **Little**

1a ***Little*** (adjective) means the opposite of ***big***.

E.g. *They have a beautiful* ***little*** *garden.*
Those ***big*** *tomatoes are not so cheap as these* ***little*** *ones.*

NOTE: Don't use the comparative and superlative forms ~~*littler*~~, ~~*littlest*~~. Use ***smaller***, ***smallest*** instead. [See also LESS, (LEAST).]

1b ***Little*** (quantity word) has a negative meaning (= 'not much').

E.g. *In those days there was very* ***little*** *food in the shops.* (determiner)
When you go away, you should lock all doors and windows: give thieves as ***little*** *help as possible.* (determiner)
I remember ***little*** *about my childhood.* (pronoun)

1c ***Little*** (adverb of degree) means 'not much'.

E.g. *'How is your mother?' 'Not very well: she eats and sleeps very* ***little****. But she talks quite a lot.'*

NOTE: Like MUCH, ***little*** is not often used alone. It is unusual to say *She eats* ***little***: it is better to say *She eats* ***very little***, or *She doesn****'t*** *eat* ***much***.

2 ***A little***

2a ***A little*** (quantity word) means 'a small amount'. Here it is a determiner:

There's only a little milk left.
Shall I buy some more ?

Here it is a pronoun:

'How much money do we have in the bank?' 'Only ***a little****, I'm afraid.'*
'What would you like to eat?' 'I'd like just ***a little*** *of that cheesecake, please.'*

2b ***A little*** (adverb) means 'a bit', 'to some extent'.

E.g. *'How is your grandmother?' 'She's getting* ***a little*** *better, thank you. She is sleeping* ***a little*** *in the afternoon, and she is eating and drinking* ***a little*** *at every mealtime.'*

3 [On ***a little bit***, see A BIT.]

'll [See WILL]

long, *longer, longest* /lɒŋ/ /ˈlɒŋgəʳ/ /ˈlɒŋgɪst/ (*adjective or adverb*)

- ► Both adjective and adverb have the same forms.
- ► The adjective has meanings of size, distance and time.
- ► The adverb has a meaning of time only.
- ► Remember to pronounce the /g/ in ***longer*** and ***longest*** [see -ER / -EST 2 Note (i)].

1 ***Long*** is an adjective in:

*Of the three swords, A is **long** and C is short, while B is shorter than A and **longer** than C.* (size)
*New York is a **long** way from Los Angeles.* (distance)
*'How **long** is the **longest** bridge in the world?' 'I think it's about four miles **long**.'* (size)
*It's a **long** time since we saw each other.* (length of time)

2 ***Long*** as an adverb means length of time only*.

E.g. *'How **long** have you been waiting?'*
{ *'Not **long** – about five minutes.'*
{ *'A **long** time – more than half an hour.'*

Notice that we prefer ***a long time*** (with the adjective ***long***) when the meaning is positive. But when we use a question or a negative, we can use ***long*** as an adverb.

E.g. *'How **long** will the meeting take?' 'It won't take **longer** than 2 hours.'*

* For distance, use FAR, not ***long***:
E.g. *'How **far** is your house from here?' 'Not very **far** – about half a mile'.*

look, ***looks, looked, looking*** /lʊk/ (*verb or noun*)

► ***Look*** is a REGULAR VERB, but it is an example of a verb with many idioms and structures, such as ***look at***, ***look like***.

1 ***Look*** is a LINKING VERB like BE, ***appear***, and ***seem*** in:
(i) LOOK + ADJECTIVE or NOUN PHRASE

E.g. *He **is** happy.*
*He **looks** tired.*
*She **seems** (to be) a good player.*

(ii) LOOK LIKE + NOUN PHRASE

E.g. *The children naturally **look like** their parents.*
*He **looks like** a boxer: strong but ugly.*
*It **looks like** rain. ('The weather looks as if it is going to rain.')*

(iii) LOOK AS IF + CLAUSE

E.g. *The children **look as if** they need a bath.*
*You **look as if** you've had a hard day.*
*It **looks as if** the weather is improving.*

2 **Some idioms with *look*:**

look after, ***look at***, ***look for***, ***look into*** – These are PREPOSITIONAL VERBS
look up – This is a PHRASAL VERB

E.g. *'Sally! Come here!' 'I can't come now. I'm **looking after** the children.'*
*If you don't know the meaning of a word, you should **look** it **up** in a dictionary.*

NOTE: ***Look*** is also a noun, as in:
*'Would you like to have **a look** at the photos we took in Greece?'*

3 **The difference between *look (at)*, *see* and *watch***
All these verbs are concerned with vision.

3a ***See*** is the most common verb: it is normally followed by an OBJECT.

E.g. *We **saw** some rare **animals** at the zoo.*

But ***see*** has no object here:

*I can't **see** very well: I need some glasses.*

3b ***Look (at)*** means 'using your eyes for a purpose'.

E.g. ***Look!*** *There's a strange bird in that tree.*

But ***look*** refers to appearance when the thing you see is the SUBJECT.

E.g. *Their* ***house looks*** *very modern and comfortable.*

3c ***Watch*** is used when people or animals look at something (happening) for a period of time.

E.g. *I always* ***watch*** *a film on Saturday afternoon.'*
'Do you? I prefer ***watching*** *sports.'*

3d ***See*** (meaning vision) usually cannot take the PROGRESSIVE form, but ***look (at)*** can.

E.g. *What are you* ***looking at****?*
But not: *What are you* ***~~seeing~~****?*

[For further examples and details, see PERCEPTION VERBS and STATE AND ACTION VERBS.]

---

a lot (of), lots (of) /əˈlɒt(əv)/, /ˈlɒts(əv)/ (*quantity words or adverbs of degree*)

► We use ***a lot (of)*** and ***lots (of)*** in <informal> English instead of MANY and MUCH.

► ***A lot (of)*** and ***lots (of)*** both mean 'a large quantity (of)'.

1

	Countable plural	Uncountable
<rather formal>	***many***	***much***
<informal>	***a lot (of)***	***a lot (of)***
<more informal>	***lots (of)***	***(lots) of***

E.g. *We've invited* {***a lot*** / ***lots***} *of guests to the party,*
so we'll need to buy {***a lot*** / ***lots***} *of food.*

1a Do not use ***many*** *guests* or ***much*** *food* in the above example [for explanation, see MANY 2 and MUCH 1]. But in the negative, it is better to use ***not (. . .) much*** or ***not (. . .) many*** rather than ***not a lot of*** / ***not lots of***.

E.g. *We haven't invited* ***many*** *guests, so we won't need to buy* ***much*** *food.*

2 Notice that both ***a lot of*** and ***lots of*** can be used with singular (uncountable) and plural nouns and verbs.

There was {***a lot of*** / ***lots of***} *traffic on the road.*
There were {***a lot of*** / ***lots of***} *cars on the road.*

3 ***A lot*** and ***lots*** can be used without ***of*** when we know what we are referring to.

E.g. *'Have the children eaten* ***any of*** *the* {*cake?'* / *sandwiches?'*}
'Yes, (they've eaten) {***a lot****.'* / ***lots****.'*}

4 The following table shows when you can use ***a lot (of)*** / ***lots (of)*** and when you should use ***much*** / ***many*** [see MUCH and MANY]:

Statement	*I've got* {***a lot*** / ***lots***} ***of*** *money / friends.* not: *I've got ~~**much**~~ money.* not: *I've got ~~**many**~~ friends.*
Question	*Have you got **much** money?* *Have you got **many** dollars?* *Have you got **a lot of** money / friends?*
Negative	*I haven't got **much** money.* *I haven't got **many** friends.* *I haven't got **a lot of** money / friends.*
<Formal> <Informal>	*I spend **much of** my time reading.* ***Many of** my friends also enjoy reading.* *I spend **a lot of** my time reading.* ***A lot of** my friends also enjoy reading.*

5 ***A lot*** and ***lots*** are adverbs of degree.

E.g. *'How is your mother?' 'She's feeling **lots** better, thank you. She sleeps **a lot** in the daytime, but she also reads **a lot** and listens to the radio.'*

-ly -/lɪ/

► Most ADVERBS end in **-ly**: e.g. ***quickly, usually, finally***.
► Some ADJECTIVES also end in **-ly**: e.g. ***likely, beastly, friendly***.

1 To make an **-ly** adverb, add **-ly** to an adjective*.

E.g.

adjective	+ ly	=	adverb
strange	+ ***ly***	=	***strangely***
particular	+ ***ly***	=	***particularly***

You sometimes have to change the spelling of the adjective [see SPELLING, e.g. ***happy*** → ***happily***.]

* Exceptions: adjectives ending **-ic** normally form their adverbs by adding **-ally**. (This does not change the pronunciation of the root e.g. ***basic***.)
E.g. ***basic*** -/ɪk/ ⟶ ***basically*** -/ɪklɪ/
One **-ic** adjective does not behave like this: ***public*** ⟶ ***publicly***.

2 Many **-ly** adverbs are adverbs of MANNER. Compare:

*a **slow** march* → *They marched **slowly**.*
*a **loud** shout* → *He shouted **loudly**.*
*her **gentle** speech* → *She spoke **gently**.*

3 But many **-ly** adverbs are of other kinds [see ADVERB].

E.g. degree:* *absolutely, completely, entirely, nearly* [see ALMOST].
time:* *immediately, lately, recently, suddenly.*
frequency** *frequently, rarely, usually, occasionally.*
linking:* *alternatively, consequently, firstly, lastly.*
attitude: *actually* [see ACTUALLY 2], *fortunately, personally, possibly.*

* These words have separate entries in this book. Look them up for further details. [For 'linking', see LINKING ADVERBS AND CONJUNCTIONS.]
** The frequency words ***daily, monthly, nightly, weekly, yearly*** can be both adjectives and adverbs [see FREQUENCY 2].

main clause

► A SENTENCE must have a main clause.
► A main clause is a clause which is not dependent on, or part of, another clause. [See CLAUSE 2.]

main verb

► Verbs are either main verbs or auxiliary verbs.

1 There are 14 auxiliary verbs in English:

be *	*will* *	*can* *	*may* *	*shall* *	*ought (to)* *	*must* *
have *	*would* *	*could* *	*might* *	*should* *	*used (to)* *	*do* *

* These words have separate entries in this book. Look them up for further details.

2 All other verbs (e.g. *make* *, *go* *, *take* *, *come* *, *see* *, *get* *, *look* *, *become* *) are main verbs.

* These words have separate entries in this book. Look them up for further details.

[For the forms of main verbs, see REGULAR VERBS and IRREGULAR VERBS. For the way main verbs pattern in phrases and clauses, see VERB PHRASE 2, 3, and VERB PATTERNS.]

3 ***Be, have***, and ***do*** can be main verbs as well as auxiliary verbs.

E.g. ***have***:
*We **have** finished our homework.* (auxiliary verb)
*We **have** three children.* (main verb)

make /meɪk/ ***makes, making, made*** /meɪd/ (*verb*)

► [See DO AND MAKE for the difference between these verbs. See also LET AND MAKE.]

1 ***Make*** is a transitive verb with a number of different uses and patterns. The most important uses are:
make = 'create'.

E.g. *'What are you **making**?' 'I'm **making** a summer dress, for my daughter.'* [See VERB PATTERN 1.]

make = 'prepare, produce'.

E.g. *Would you **make** me a cup of tea?* [See VERB PATTERN 11.]

make = 'force . . . to'.

E.g. *They **made** him pay his taxes.* [See VERB PATTERN 18.]

2 **Idioms**

Make sure and ***make certain*** have the same meaning, and are normally followed by a THAT-clause.

E.g. *Please* ***make sure*** *(that) you lock the door when you leave.*
(= Please be careful to . . .)
The crew ***made certain*** *(that) no one was left on the sinking ship.*

---

man /mæn/ has the irregular plural ***men*** /men/ (*noun*)

1 In a general sense, ***man*** refers not just to male people, but also to the whole human race (= 'mankind').

E.g. ***Man*** *is the only animal that uses language.*
Early {***man*** / ***men***} *learned how to use simple tools.*

With this meaning, ***man*** is often singular, and has no determiner such as ***the***. It is almost like a proper noun.

E.g. *Christians believe that God created* ***man***.

2 Nowadays, many people dislike this general use of ***man***, because it seems to give more importance to the male sex. We can instead use ***human being***, ***people***, ***the human race***, etc. [See SEX.]

---

manner

► Adverbials of manner answer the question HOW? or ***In what manner***?

1 E.g. '***How*** *did she greet him?*'

(i) *'She greeted him* ***warmly****.'*

(ii) *'She greeted him* ***coldly****.'*

2 We usually express the manner or way of doing something by using manner adverbs. These are formed with an adjective **+*ly*** (e.g. *badly, quickly, slowly*) or else have exactly the same form as adjectives (e.g. *well, better, worse, straight, hard*).

NOTE: But not all adjectives have a manner adverb. E.g. ***lively*** has no adverb ~~***livelily***~~, which would be difficult to pronounce.

3 To express manner, use these patterns:

main part of clause	+	(a) MANNER ADVERB (b) IN A(N) + ADJECTIVE + MANNER / WAY (c) WITH (. . .) + ABSTRACT NOUN

Patterns (b) and (c) are <less common> and <more formal> than (a).

E.g.

He faced his problems (a) ***bravely***. (b) ***in a** responsible **manner***. (c) ***with** great courage.*

She always dances (a) ***gracefully** and **skilfully***. (b) ***in a** lively **manner***. (c) ***with** grace and skill.*

4 Manner expressions usually go in end position in the clause [see ADVERB 4]. But you can also put manner adverbs in middle position, especially if there is another adverbial or clause in end position.

E.g. *Linda **politely** asked me to go away.*
*Mark **carefully** placed the bottle on the table.*

---

many /ˈmenɪ/ (*determiner or pronoun*) (The comparative and superlative forms of ***many*** are MORE and MOST.)

► ***Many*** is a QUANTITY WORD meaning 'a large number (of)'.
► ***Many*** can come before PLURAL nouns only: ***many** friends*, ***many** windows*. (Here it is a determiner.)
► ***Many*** is also an ***of***-pronoun [see INDEFINITE PRONOUN 2] (followed by OF or by nothing): *many of us*, *many of her friends.*

1 ***Many*** is similar to MUCH, except that ***much*** is uncountable. ***Many*** is <rather formal> in positive statements.

E.g. ***Many** of his friends lived in Hamburg.*

[See (a) LOT (OF), LOTS (OF) 1a, 4.]

2 With ***many*** there should be 'something special' about the sentence. For example, it should be either:

2a NEGATIVE.

E.g. *I have**n't** read **many** of Lawrence's novels.*

2b A YES-NO QUESTION.

E.g. *'I've been looking for wild flowers.' '**Did** you find **many**?'*

2c Or else ***many*** should follow a degree adverb such as AS, HOW, SO, TOO.

E.g. *'**How many** wine glasses did you bring?' '**As many** as I could.'*
*'I've never seen **so many** people in one car!' 'Yes, there are far **too many** for safety.'*

---

masculine is the word we often use in grammar for 'male' words such as ***man*** (noun) or ***he*** (pronoun). [See SEX.]

---

mass noun another word for UNCOUNTABLE NOUNS

---

matter /ˈmætəʳ/ (*noun or verb*)

1 Both the noun ***matter*** and the verb ***matter*** are used in idioms.

2 ***Matter*** is a noun in:

What's the matter ?
(= What's wrong ?)
I've lost my Mummy
and Daddy.

Also in:

E.g. *'Is anything the **matter**?' 'No, nothing's the **matter**.'*

3 ***Matter*** is a STATE verb.

E.g. *'I'm sorry I forgot to return the books I borrowed.' 'It doesn't **matter**!'* (= 'It's not important')
*'They're closing that soap factory.' 'Does it **matter**?' 'It **matters** to me – I have a job there.'*

4 { ***No matter wh-*** / ***It doesn't matter wh-*** } are idioms introducing a clause of CONTRAST.
You can use any ***wh***-word after ***matter***.

E.g. *French food is good,* ***no matter where*** *you eat.* (= 'wherever you eat')
It doesn't matter what *I say, she still takes no notice.* (= 'whatever I say')

---

may /meɪ/ (*modal auxiliary*) [Compare COULD AND MIGHT.]

- ► ***May*** goes before a main verb, e.g. ***may*** *lose*.
- ► ***May*** never changes its form.
- ► ***May*** is not followed by **to**.

1 Forms

1a present simple:

You *We* *They* etc.	***may***	*have . . .* *get . . .* *see . . .* etc.

negative:

You *We* *They* etc.	***may not***	*have . . .* *get . . .* *see . . .* etc.

question (used only for asking PERMISSION) + answer:

May	***I*** ***we***	*leave the room?* *see the photographs?* *offer her a drink?*

Yes,	*you*	***may****.*
No,	*you*	***may not****.*

1b Perfect: *They* ***may have*** *miss****ed*** *the bus.*
Progressive: *They* ***may be*** *arriv****ing*** *tomorrow.*
Passive: *The ladder* ***may be*** *need****ed*** *next week.*
Perfect Progressive: *We* ***may have been*** *mak****ing*** *mistakes.*
Perfect Passive: *The road* ***may have been*** *blocked.*
etc. [see VERB PHRASE.]

(NOTE: ***might*** is often preferred to ***may*** in <U.S.>)

2 *May* = POSSIBILITY

2a ***May*** means 'It is possible that something will happen or is happening'.

E.g.

The same meaning is expressed by ***perhaps*** or ***possibly***.

E.g. ***Perhaps*** *he's ill.*

2b ***May*** often refers to a future possibility.

E.g. *It* ***may*** *rain tomorrow, but I hope it will be sunny.*
'Will they reach the South Pole before winter sets in?' 'I don't know. They ***may possibly**** *succeed, but on the other hand they* ***may well**** *fail.'*

* After ***may***, ***possibly*** weakens the possibility, while ***well*** strengthens the possibility.

2c We can also use:
(I) ***may have*** + PAST PARTICIPLE (for a past possibility), or
(II) ***may be*** + Verb-***ing*** (for a continuing possibility).

E.g. *'Where's James?' 'I don't know, Mr. Baker. He* ***may have*** *miss****ed*** *the bus. He* ***may be*** *com****ing*** *to school on foot.'*

2d Negative of ***may*** = possibility.
May not means 'It is possible that something will not happen, or is not happening'.

E.g. *'How do you feel about the exam? Do you think you will pass it?'*
'It's difficult to say. I ***may*** *pass, but on the other hand I* ***may not****: I* ***may*** *fail.'*
'The weather is bad. We ***may not*** *be able to go swimming today. We* ***may*** *have to stay indoors.'*

NOTE: The difference between ***can't*** or ***cannot*** [see CAN 3b] and ***may not***. ***Cannot*** means 'It is not possible'. ***May not*** means 'It is possible that something does not happen.' Compare:
That { ***cannot*** / ***can't*** } *be true: it* ***must*** *be false.* ('I'm sure')
That ***may not*** *be true, but on the other hand, it* ***may*** *be (true).* ('I'm not sure')

2e Questions about possibility:
We cannot ask questions about possibility with ***may***. Instead, we use CAN (or could) [see COULD AND MIGHT]:

E.g. { ***Can*** / ~~***May***~~ } *they have lost their way?* ('Is it possible . . .?')

3 ***May*** **= permission**

E.g. *'****May*** *I use your telephone?' 'Yes, certainly you* ***may****. Help yourself!'*
*'****May*** *we leave now, Miss Black?' 'No, you* ***may not****. You haven't finished your work yet.'* (***May not*** means there is no permission!)

3a ***May*** (= 'permission') is <less common> than ***can***. You can always* use ***can*** (= 'permission') instead of ***may***, but many people think that ***may*** is more <polite> and 'correct' than ***can***.

* An exception is the phrase ***if I may***.
E.g. *'I'd like to make a phone call* ***if I may****.'*

me /miː/ (*personal pronoun*)

► ***Me*** is the 1st person singular object pronoun [see the subject pronoun, ***I***.]
► ***Me*** refers to the speaker or writer.
► ***Me*** comes after a verb or a preposition. (In <informal> style, this also means after BE, AS, LIKE, THAN). [See PERSONAL PRONOUN 2d.]

means [See BY 2.]

measuring – How to talk about measurements

[See also DISTANCE, MONEY, AGO.]

1 **Some units of measurement**

You will find a table of ***weights*** and ***measures*** in many dictionaries. These are a few examples:

		measurements		(abbreviations)		
		'old style'*	'new style' (metric)**	'o.s.'*	'n.s.'	adjective
1a	length width height depth [see DISTANCE]	*inch(es)* *foot / feet* *yard(s)* *mile(s)*	*centimetre(s)* *metre(s)* *kilometre(s)*	*in* *ft* *yd* *mi, m*	*cm* *m* *km*	*long* *wide / broad* *high* *deep*
1b	area	*square inch(es)* *square feet* *square mile(s)*	*square centimetre(s)* *hectare(s)*	*sq in* *sq ft* *sq mi*	*sq cm* *ha*	
1c	volume	*pint(s)* /paɪnt/ *gallon(s)*	*litre(s)* *decalitre(s)*	*pt* *gal*	*l* *dl*	
1d	weight	*ounce(s)* *pound(s)* *ton(s)*	*gram(s)* *kilo(gram)(s)*	*oz* *lb*	*g* *kg*	
1e	age length of time	*day(s)* *week(s)* *year(s)*				*old*

[See also separate entry LENGTH OF TIME]

* The 'old style' measures are still in common use in English-speaking countries. But the metric system ('new style') is used in science and technical writing and is becoming more general.

** ***Metre***, etc. are <G.B.> spellings. In <U.S.>, the words end in ***-ter***, e.g. ***meter***.

2 **Measure phrases are often used before adjectives and nouns such as *long* and *length***
Pattern:

(ADVERB OF DEGREE) + NUMBER + UNIT(S) + { ADJECTIVE / IN + NOUN }

E.g. . . . *about twenty miles* { *long* / *in length.* }

2a Length, height, depth, width:

E.g. (i) *The table is* ***(exactly) 8 feet long*** *and* ***3 feet wide***.
(ii) *At this point, the sea is* ***(over) a mile deep***.

(i)

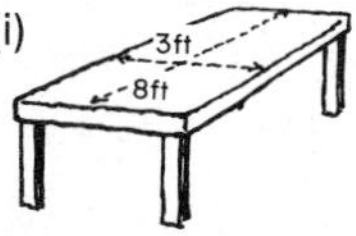

(ii)

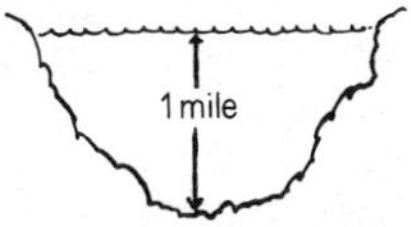

We can also say:

E.g. ***The depth*** *of the sea at this point is* ***(over) a mile***. etc.

2b Area:

E.g. *The average football pitch is* ***9600 square yards in area***.

(Or: *The* { ***area*** / ***size*** } *of the average football pitch is* ***9600 square yards***.)

2c For volume and weight we use a verb + measure phrase pattern.

E.g. (i) *This jug* ***holds (just) (under) four litres***.
(ii) *This can* ***holds (just) (over) a gallon of*** { *gasoline.* <U.S.> / *petrol.* <G.B.> }

(i)

(ii)

NOTE: A ***gallon*** is a smaller measure in <U.S.> than in <G.B.>.

3 Comparing measurements [see COMPARISON 3.]

---

middle position is the position of an adverb or other adverbial element when it is in the middle of the clause, especially after the auxiliary or the main verb BE. [See ADVERB 3.] We also use middle position in talking of other adverbials, e.g. prepositional phrases [see ADVERBIAL 4].

---

might /maɪt/ (*modal auxiliary*) [See COULD AND MIGHT.]

a million /ˈmɪljən/ (*number, noun*) = 1,000,000. [See NUMBERS 5a.]

mind /maɪnd/ **minds, minding, minded** (*verb or noun*)

1 ***Mind* as a verb means 'look after'**

E.g. *Will you please* ***mind*** (= 'look after') *the baby while I'm out?*

2 **Notice these special uses of *mind* (verb)**

2a Warning:

E.g. ***Mind!*** ('Be careful') <G.B.>
Mind *your head!* ('Be careful of . . .')

2b Request:

E.g. *'Do you* ***mind*** (= 'have any objection') *if I open the window?'*
'No, I don't – please open it.'

'Would you ***mind*** { *lending me this pen?'* / *if I borrowed this pen?'* }
'No – help yourself!' [See IF 1c.]

NOTE: In requests, ***mind*** means 'dislike', (i.e. *Would you* ***dislike*** *it if I borrowed your pen?*), so when we agree to these requests, we say ***no***!

2c Replying to an offer:

E.g. *'What would you like to drink?' 'I* ***wouldn't mind*** *a cup of tea.'*
(= 'I'd like . . .')
'What would you like to do?' 'I ***wouldn't mind*** *going for a walk.'*

mine /maɪn/ (*possessive pronoun*)

1 ***Mine*** is the 1st person singular possessive pronoun [see POSSESSIVE DETERMINER and POSSESSIVE PRONOUN], related to I.

E.g. *This new bicycle is* ***mine***. (= 'It belongs to *me*.')

modal auxiliary [See also AUXILIARY VERB, VERB PHRASE.]

1 **There are 11 modal auxiliary verbs in English**

1a Here is a diagram of the modal auxiliaries and their usual meanings. Look up each modal auxiliary for further details:

meanings	modal auxiliaries									
	can*	may*	might*	could*	would*	will*	shall*	must*	should*	ought to*	used to*
possibility	●	●	●	•							
ability	•			•							
permission	•	·	·	·							
habit					•						
volition (or wish)		·			•	•	•				
prediction (or future)					•	●	●				
unreal meaning			·	●	●				•		
'tentative' meaning									·		
strong obligation								•			
weak obligation									•	•	
strong deduction								•			
weak deduction		•	●	●							
past state or habit											•

● = Main use
• = Less important use
· = Uncommon use

* These words have separate entries in this book. Look them up for further details.

NOTE: Also, ***need*** and ***dare*** sometimes behave like modals.

2 **The modals are a special class of words which behave in a special way**

2a Modal auxiliaries have no -S FORM for the 3rd person singular. Compare:

*He **works** ~ They **work*** But: *He **will** ~ They **will***

Also, modal auxiliaries do not change their form in other ways: they have no ***-ing*** form or past participle form. We have:

works** ~ **working** ~ **worked But not: ~~***must***~~ ~ ~~***musting***~~ ~ ~~***musted***~~

2b Modal auxiliaries always take the first position in a verb phrase [see VERB PHRASE].

E.g.

	verb phrase		verb phrase
They	***must** win.*	*They*	***must** have been winning.*
They	***must** have won.*	*The cup*	***must** be won.*
They	***must** be winning.*	*The cup*	***must** have been won.*

2c Modal auxiliaries come before the NEGATIVE word ***not***.

E.g. *She **may** see the play.* → *She **may not** see the play.*

2d Modal auxiliaries (except MAY) have a negative contraction.

E.g. *She **could not** see the play.* → *She **couldn't** see the play.*

2e Modal auxiliaries go before the SUBJECT in YES-NO QUESTIONS.

E.g. *She **could** see the play.* → ***Could** she see the play?*

(Also in other cases of subject-auxiliary inversion) [see INVERSION 2.]

2f Modal auxiliaries carry the emphasis in emphatic sentences.

E.g. *'You should speak to Paul.'* → *'Yes, I **will** speak to him.'*

NOTE: In contrast, main verbs require ***do*** to carry the emphasis [see DO 2g].
E.g. *'Why didn't you win the game?'* → *'But I **did** win.'*

2g Modal auxiliaries are used in SHORTENED SENTENCES.

E.g. ***Will** you speak to him?* → { *Yes, I **will**.* / *No, I **won't**.* }
***I'll** speak to him.* → *Yes, so **will** I.* [See SO 4a.]

2h Modal auxiliaries come before adverbs like ALWAYS and words like ALL and BOTH, when they are in middle position [see ADVERB 3].

E.g. *I **always** enjoy acting.* → *I **will always** enjoy acting.*
***All** the girls **will** be here.* → *The girls **will all** be here.*

modifier and head-word

1 In English PHRASES, there is usually one word which is the main word in the phrase, and we can add one or more ***modifiers*** to this to specify its meaning more exactly. The main word is called a ***head-word***.

2 In a NOUN PHRASE, a noun is usually the head-word.

E.g.

	modifier(s)	head-word	modifier(s)	
I like	*popular*	*music*		*very much.*
	the	*wines*	*of France*	
	these new	*dresses*		
	a cooked	*breakfast*		
	most	*concerts*	*on the radio*	
	every	*hour*	*I spend here*	

Notice that we can usually omit the modifiers. E.g. *I like music / wines / dresses / breakfast.*

3 In an ADJECTIVE PHRASE [see PHRASE 3d], an adjective is the head-word.

E.g.

	modifier(s)	head-word	modifier(s)
This photograph is		*good*	*enough.*
	rather	*small.*	
	much	*better*	*than that one.*
	the very	*best*	*of them all.*

4 Modifiers which come before the head-word are 'premodifiers'. Those which come after the head-word are 'postmodifiers'.

5 [See PHRASE for examples of modifiers in different kinds of phrases.]

---

money (and how to talk about it)

1 **Sums of money**
Notice the difference between the way we write sums of money, and the way we talk about them:

[On pronouncing numbers, see NUMBERS.]

1a The dollar sign ($) and the pound sign (£) come before the numeral in writing, but after the numeral in speech.

E.g. *$420 = 'four hundred and twenty dollars'*
£5215 = 'five thousand two hundred and fifteen pounds'

1b But the signs for 'cent(s)' and 'penny / pence' come after the numeral.

E.g. *84¢ = 'eighty-four cents'*
15p = 'fifteen pence' (or *'fifteen p'* /pi:/*)

1c If the sum of money includes both $ and ¢ (or both £ and p) we write it and say it like this.

E.g. *$11.64 = 'eleven dollars (and) sixty-four cents'*
or *'eleven dollars sixty-four'*
or *'eleven sixty-four'* <informal>
*£3.99 = 'three pounds ninety-nine pence / p'**
or *'three pounds ninety-nine'*
or *'three ninety-nine'* <informal>

We can omit the words ***cent(s)*** etc., if we want to.

* We shorten ***pence*** to ***p*** in writing, and often pronounce it /pi:/, also, in <informal speech>.

2 Coins and notes <G.B.> / bills <U.S.>

2a U.S. coins and bills:

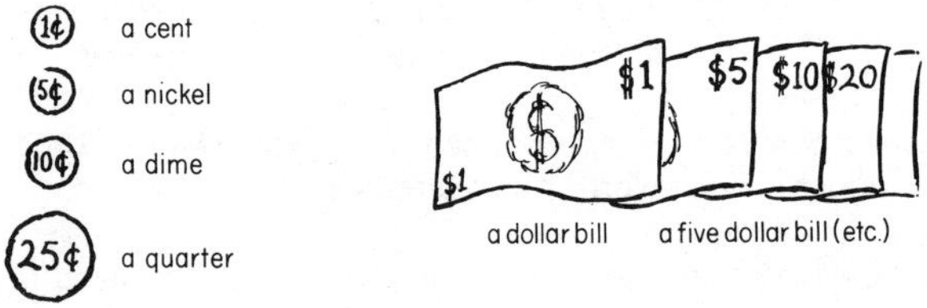

2b British coins and notes:

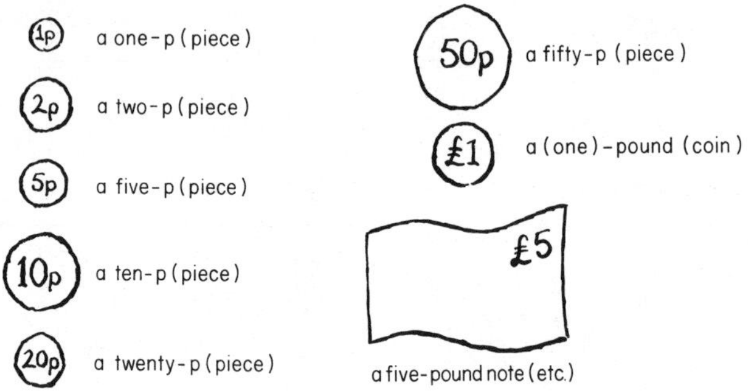

We sometimes omit the word ***piece***, so that a ***one-p*** /pi:/ and a ***two-p*** can refer to the 1p and 2p coins, etc. Note the plural ***p's*** /pi:z/.

E.g. *Can you change this pound coin for two 50**p's** /pi:z/ please?* <informal>

3 Notice that the nouns ***money*** and ***change*** are UNCOUNTABLE nouns. They go with a question *How much . . .?*, not *How many . . .?*.

E.g. *How much **money** did she give you?*
How many pounds did she give you?
*How much **change** do you have in your purse?*
How many coins do you have in your purse?

NOTE: ***Pence***, however, is a countable noun – the plural of ***penny***.
E.g. *How many **pence** are there in a pound?*
The shortened form of ***pence***, ***p***, is also a countable noun.
E.g. *How many **p** /pi:/ are there in a pound?*

---

mood is a grammatical term sometimes used for the IMPERATIVE, INFINITIVE, and SUBJUNCTIVE forms of the Verb. The usual finite verb form (*he / she likes, they like*), is called the 'indicative mood'. We do not use these words 'mood' or 'indicative' in this book.

---

more /mɔːʳ/ (*adverb, determiner, or pronoun*)
(the) most /məʊst/ (*adverb, determiner, or pronoun*)

---

1 ***More*** **and *most* as adverbs of degree**

1a ***More*** expresses a comparison between two people or two things (or between two groups of people or things) [see COMPARATIVE].

E.g. *Jill is **more** popular than her brother.*

The opposite of ***more*** is LESS. The example above means the same as:

*Jill's brother is **less** popular than Jill.*

1b ***Most*** means 'more than any other' [see SUPERLATIVE]. *

E.g. *She is the **most** beautiful girl in India.*

Most is the opposite of ***least***.

E.g.

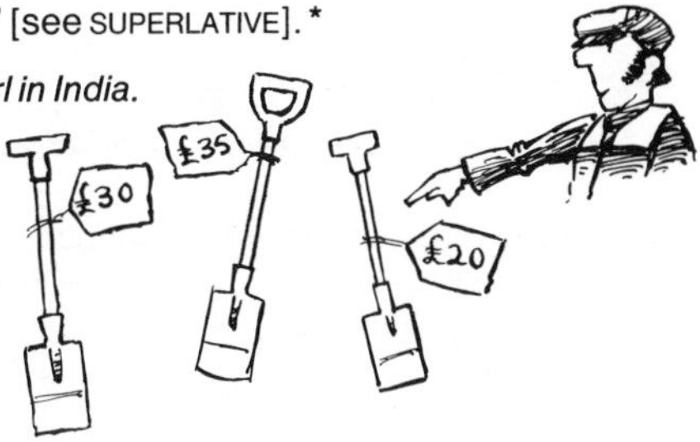

*I'll buy this shovel: it's the **least** expensive (of the three).* (***least*** *expensive* = cheapest)

* ***Most*** before an adjective or adverb can also mean 'very'.
E.g. *You have been **most** { kind. / helpful.*

2 ***More*** **and *most* before adjectives**

2a ***More*** (adverb of degree) is used for the comparative of 'long' adjectives; e.g. ***more*** *polite*. [See COMPARATIVE 1, 2.] (Adjectives of one syllable take -***er***.)

2b ***Most*** (adverb of degree) is used for the superlative of long adjectives; e.g.: ***the most** polite.* [See SUPERLATIVE 1, 2.] (Adjectives of one syllable take -***est***.)

3 *More* and *most* before adverbs

3a ***More*** (adverb of degree) is used for the comparative of adverbs ending in **-*ly***;* e.g. ***more** slowly.* [See COMPARATIVE 4.]

* Exceptions: the COMPARATIVE of badly is ***worse***; the SUPERLATIVE form is ***worst***.

3b ***Most*** is used for the superlative of adverbs ending in **-*ly***; e.g. *(the)* ***most** slowly.* [See SUPERLATIVE 1, 2.]

4 *More* and *most* (adverbs) as the comparative and superlative of *much*

More (adverb of degree) or ***most*** (adverb of degree) is used on its own after a verb or verb + object.

E.g. *'Which do you enjoy **more**? Swimming or walking?' 'Swimming. But I enjoy tennis (the) **most** of all sports.'*

5 *More* and *most* as quantity words (= comparative and superlative of *much* / *many*)

5a ***More*** (determiner) and ***most*** (determiner) go before a noun. Here ***more*** means 'a larger amount or number of' and ***most*** means 'the largest amount or number of'.

E.g. ***More** people live in cities than in the country.*
*I dislike **most** modern music.* (= I don't like much modern music.)

5b ***More*** (pronoun) and ***most*** (pronoun) often come before ***of***.

E.g. ***Most of** you are from other countries.*

5c ***More*** (as a determiner or pronoun) can have the meaning 'extra, additional, in addition'. With this meaning it often goes after ***some, any, no; one, two, three, . . .***; and quantity words like ***many, much, a few, several***.

E.g. *I would like* {***two*** / ***a few*** / ***several***} ***more** of those pears, please.*
*'Do you have **any more** milk?' 'Yes, how **much more** do you want?' 'Just **one more** pint, please.'*

5d ***More*** and ***most*** (pronouns) can also occur on their own without ***of*** or a noun.

E.g. *'This is good coffee.' 'You can have some **more** (of it) if you like.'*
*Ten dollars is the **most** I can afford.* ('The largest amount')

5e ***More*** and ***most*** (determiners or pronouns) with countable and uncountable nouns:

(I) ***More*** and (*the*) ***most*** are the comparative and superlative forms of ***many*** with countable nouns:

many ~ more ~ most

E.g. *'How* ***many*** *coins do you have for the telephone?' 'I don't have* ***many****. I did have* ***more****, but I have used* ***most*** *of them.'*

(II) ***More*** and (*the*) ***most*** are also the comparative and superlative forms of ***most*** with uncountable nouns:

much ~ more ~ most

E.g. *'How* ***much*** *money do you have?' 'I don't have* ***much****. Tom has (the)* ***most*** *money – he has* ***more*** *than either of us.'*

---

most [See MORE, (THE) MOST]

---

motion (or movement) [See also PLACE, COME AND GO.]

1 Many verbs describe motion or movement from one place to another

E.g. *come, go, enter* (= 'go in(to)'), *progress* (= 'go forward'),
climb (= 'go upward'), *fall* (= 'go downward'),
hurry (= 'go quickly'), *pass* (= 'go past'),
return (= 'go back').

2 In addition, verbs of motion are often followed by PREPOSITIONS or ADVERBS which describe the direction, goal, etc, of the movement:

3 The main prepositions of *motion* go in pairs, as in the table below

(The words in {brackets} are the equivalent prepositions of position.)

E.g. { *She went* ***to*** *school.*
She is ***at*** *school.* }

to {at}	*from {away from}*	*across*	*along*
into {in}	*out of*	*around <U.S.>*	*round <G.B.>* *
onto {on}	*off*	*over*	*under*
up	*down*	*through*	*past*
		toward <U.S.>	*towards <G.B.>* *

[You can look up each preposition or pair of prepositions for further details.]

* Here '<U.S.>' means '<u>mainly</u> in American English' and <G.B.> means '<u>mainly</u> in British English.'

4 The main adverbs of motion are the same as the prepositions, except that ***to, from, into*** and ***out of*** are not adverbs. (The adverbs equivalent to ***from, into***, and ***out of*** are ***away, in***, and ***out***.)

5 The most important prepositions of motion are TO and FROM:

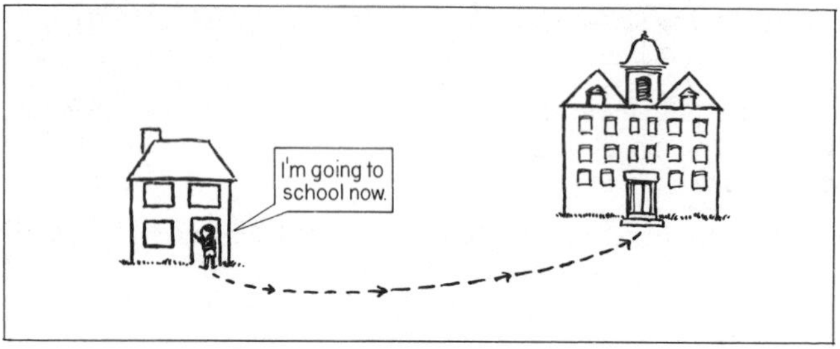

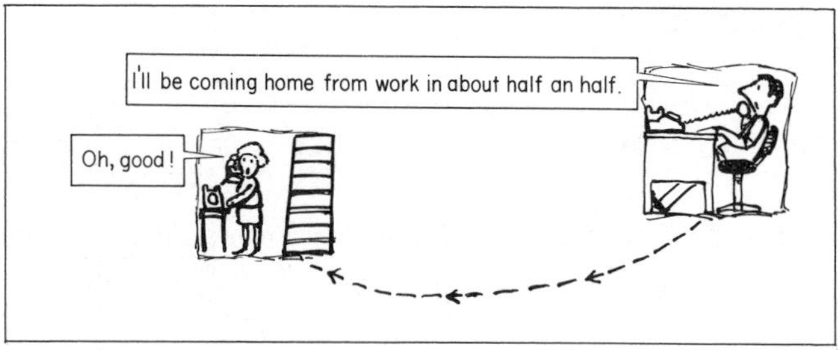

To names the endpoint of the journey, and ***from*** names the starting point.

5a If you want to, you can combine ***from*** and ***to*** in the same phrase.

E.g. *The train travels* **from** *Tokyo* **to** *Osaka in about three hours.*
How far is it **from** *Cairo* **to** *Aswan?*
The Orient Express runs **from** *Paris* **to** *Istanbul.*

NOTE: You can also use these prepositions after nouns like *bus* or *train*.
E.g. *the bus* **to** *London* *the train* **from** *Brussels*

5b Notice that these verbs do not go with ***from*** or ***to***:

The plane **left** *Hong Kong at 7.00, and* { ***reached*** / ***arrived** at* } *Karachi at 14.00.*

Arrive is followed by the 'position' prepositions AT, ON, and IN.

E.g. *We will arrive* { ***on** the island* / ***in** Japan* } *on Tuesday morning.*

[On the choice between ***at, on***, and ***in***, see PLACE.]

6 Here are some examples of pairs of opposites acting as prepositions and as adverbs of motion.

(i)

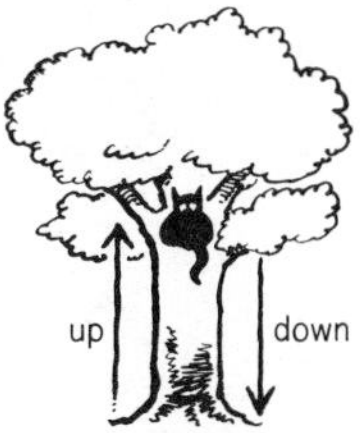

(ii)

E.g. (i) *The cat climbed **up** the tree, but then she couldn't get **down** again.*
(ii) *'Is it easier to climb **over** the fence or to crawl **under** it?'*
*'The fence is broken here, so it's easiest to crawl **through**.'*

When the word is not followed by a NOUN PHRASE (e.g. ***down*** in (i) and ***through*** in (ii)) it is an adverb. [See PREPOSITIONAL ADVERB.]

7 This picture shows other prepositions / adverbs of motion:

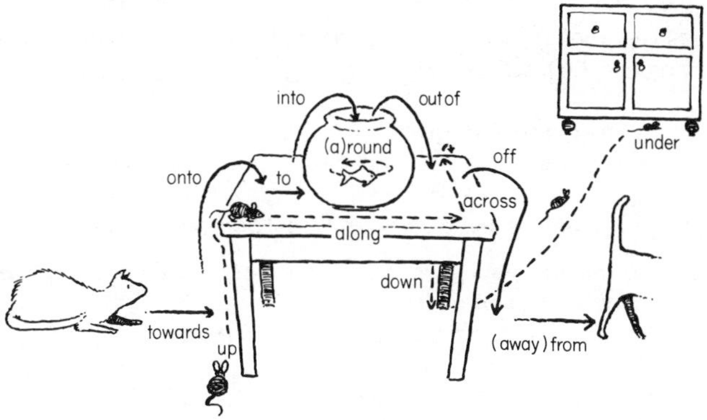

---

much /mʌtʃ/ (*determiner, pronoun*, or *adverb of degree*) The comparative and superlative forms of ***much*** are MORE and MOST.

► ***Much*** is a QUANTITY WORD meaning 'a large amount (of)'.

► ***Much*** (as a determiner) can go before UNCOUNTABLE nouns only: ***much water***, ***much food***, ***much time***.

► ***Much*** is also an ***of***-pronoun [see INDEFINITE PRONOUN 2], followed by OF or by nothing.

E.g. *They don't own **much of the land** / **much of it** / **much**.*

► As an adverb, ***much*** means 'a great deal', 'to a considerable extent'.

E.g. *I (very) **much** enjoyed the play.*

270 *much*

1 **_Much_ as a quantity word** [see also A LOT (OF), LOTS (OF).]
Much is used with uncountable nouns; MANY is used with countable nouns. With ***much***, as with ***many***, there should be 'something special' in the sentence. E.g. It should be either:

1a NEGATIVE:

E.g. *We have**n't** had **much** snow this winter.*

1b or a YES-NO QUESTION:

E.g. *'Are you doing **much** painting these days?' 'No, not **much**.'*

1c or it should follow a degree adverb such as AS, HOW, SO, TOO:

E.g. *'I've never seen **so much** traffic on this road.' 'I know. There's far **too much**. It's dangerous for children.'*

1d ***Much*** is <rather formal> in positive statements. [See A LOT (OF), LOTS (OF).]

E.g. ***Much** of his time was spent studying the Italian painters.*
***Much** art represents the personal vision of the artist.*

(These sentences are <rather formal>, but would be normal, for example, in a book on the history of art.)

2 **_Much_ as an adverb of degree**
Again, ***much*** requires 'something special' in the sentence.

2a ***Much*** can go before some verbs and most comparative forms.

E.g. *'I **much admire** the work of Michelangelo.' 'Do you really? I **much prefer** Leonardo da Vinci.'*
*This exam is **much more difficult** than the last one.*

2b ***Much*** can follow a negative or be in a yes-no question.

E.g. *'Our daughter is working overseas.' 'Really? Do you miss her **much**?'*
'Yes, we miss her { ***~~much~~***.'
a great deal.'
a lot.' }

2c Like the quantity word ***much***, the adverb ***much*** can go with adverbs of degree, especially VERY, AS, HOW, SO, TOO.

E.g. *'**How much** do you weigh?' 'I don't know exactly, but I weigh far **too much**.'*

NOTE: You can use ***very much*** in many places where you cannot use ***much***: especially at the end of the sentence. E.g., you can say:
*Thank you **very much**.* But not: *Thank you ~~much~~.*
If you are in doubt, it is safer to use ***very much***, rather than ***much***.

must /mʌst/ (weak form: /məst/, /məs/)

- ► ***Must*** is a MODAL AUXILIARY.
- ► ***Must*** goes before a main verb, e.g. ***must*** *go*.
- ► ***Must*** does not change its form.
- ► ***Must*** has a negative form ***mustn't*** (/ˈmʌsn̩t/).
- ► ***Must*** is not followed by ***to***.

1 Forms

1a Present Simple

E.g.

I *You* *We* *They* etc.	***must***	*be . . .* *have . . .* *go now.* *see . . .* *etc.*

negative

I *You* *We* *They* etc.	***mustn't*** ***must not***	*be . . .* *have . . .* *go yet.* *see . . .* etc.

question (use these for making protests!)

E.g.

must *(Why **must**)*	*you* *we* *they* etc.	*go now?* *leave before midnight?* *be so noisy?* *make such a noise?*

1b Perfect: *They **must have left** early.*
Progressive: *They **must be working** late.*
Passive: *The bag **must be** mended.*
Perfect Passive: *The bag **must have been** mended.*
etc. [See VERB PHRASE.]

1c ***Must*** has no past tense form. For the Past Simple, use ***had to*** [see HAVE TO]: (meaning 'was / were obliged to').

E.g. *'Where is the post office? I* { ***have to*** / ***must*** } *post this letter.'*

But: *'Where have you been?' 'I've been to the post office – I **had to** post a letter.'*

NOTE: In indirect speech we can use ***must*** for describing something in the past [see INDIRECT SPEECH 1c Note].
E.g. *I told her she **must** be more careful.*

2 Meanings of *must*

2a ***Must*** = obligation.
Must means 'It is important or essential to do something.'

E.g. *You **must** eat to live.* ('. . . if you don't, you will die.')
Teacher: *Sheila **must** work harder: if she doesn't, she'll fail her exams.*
Doctor: *You **must** give up smoking: it's bad for your health.*

2b ***Mustn't*** = negative obligation:
The negative ***mustn't*** means 'it is important or essential not to do something.'

E.g. *You **mustn't** drink water from the river.*

2c Absence / lack of obligation:
There is a different way to make ***must*** negative.

don't have to + Verb
don't need to + Verb
needn't + Verb <G.B.>
} All these mean 'It is not important to do something.'

E.g.:

Must = 'it's essential'

negative obligation

mustn't = 'it's essential not to'

absence of obligation

don't have to = it's not essential to

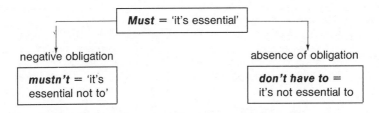

NOTE: ***I must(n't)*** and ***we must(n't)*** describe the speaker's own feeling about what is important.
E.g. ***I must*** *be more careful – I have lost my keys.*
We must *go home early – my mother is ill in bed.*
Compare ***have to*** [see HAVE TO 3], which often describes what other people – e.g. *the boss* or *the government* – require.
E.g. ***I have to*** *type these letters (for the boss).*
We have to *pay our taxes (to the government).*

2d ***Must*** = deduction.
Must means 'I feel certain that this is true'. We use it when we do not know, but we have plenty of evidence, that it is so. Compare:

That church is very old. ('I know.')
That church ***must*** *be very old. ('I don't know, but it certainly looks old.')*

A: *There's somebody knocking on the door.*
B: *Yes, it* ***must*** *be my son. He always gets home at this time.*
A: *Hasn't he got a key?*
B: *He* ***must*** *have left it at the office. He often does that.*

NOTE: This meaning of ***must*** can go with the Perfect form.
E.g. *James has a black eye. Someone* ***must*** *have hit him.*
And the Progressive form.
E.g. *What a wonderful present! It can't be real! I* ***must*** *be dreaming!*

2e Negative deduction
The negative of this meaning of ***must*** is ***cannot*** or ***can't*** (= 'it's impossible') [see CAN].

E.g. *She* ***can't*** *be happy with her husband in prison.* (= 'She must be unhappy . . .'.)
The thief ***can't*** *have escaped through this window. It's much too small.*

3 ***Must and should***
Must is stronger than SHOULD. Both have similar meanings of obligation and deduction, but ***should*** is weaker. (OUGHT TO has the same meaning as ***should***.)

3a	**Obligation** MUST + VERB = 'it's essential' i.e. If this isn't done, there will be a lot of trouble, or a big problem. E.g. *You **must lose** weight.* (You are dangerously overweight.)	SHOULD + VERB = 'it's important, but not essential' i.e. If this isn't done, it is likely there will be trouble, but it is not certain. E.g. *You **should lose** weight.* (You are slightly overweight.)
3b	**Deduction** MUST + VERB = 'This is a logical conclusion' *She was born in 1945. It's 1989 now, so she **must be*** 44.	SHOULD + VERB = 'This is a logical conclusion, but I may be wrong.' E.g. *She's famous. She's rich. She's beautiful. She **should be** happy, (but maybe she's not).*

my

/maɪ/ (*1st person singular possessive determiner*, related to ***I*** [see I]).

myself

/maɪˈself/ (*1st person singular reflexive pronoun*, related to I).

names

- Names begin with capital letters: *Eric, Diana, Smith, Mrs Williams, Chicago, Sri Lanka.*
- The most important names are:
  (I) Names of places [See the separate entries GEOGRAPHICAL NAMES and COUNTRIES.]
  (II) Names of people [For further details, see NAMES OF PEOPLE below.]
- A 'proper noun' is normally a single-word name. It usually refers to just one person (e.g. *Mary*), or just one place (e.g. *Rome*), or just one organization (e.g. *UNESCO*).

1 **Proper nouns in contrast to common nouns**
A proper noun normally has no determiner in front of it:* ~~*The*~~ *Chicago,* ~~*The*~~ *Napoleon,* ~~*The*~~ *Frederic.*
It also normally has no plural: *Chicago~~s~~, Frederic~~s~~.* *

* [See geographical names for exceptions, e.g. ***The** Hague* is the capital of ***The** Netherlands*.]

2 Proper nouns behaving like common nouns
But sometimes proper nouns behave like common nouns. In this case, they can have articles, adjectives, etc. before them.

E.g. *She's* ***a modern Cleopatra***.

2a Proper nouns behaving like common nouns can have a following PREPOSITIONAL PHRASE.

E.g. *She's written a new historical novel. It's about* ***the Paris of Louis XIV***.*

Or can have a following RELATIVE CLAUSE.

E.g. *'I'm staying with my friend Helen.' 'Is she* ***the Helen (that) I met last year?'***

* Read the names of kings, queens, etc. as follows:

<written>		<spoken>
George I	=	George the first
Queen Elizabeth II	=	Queen Elizabeth the second
Louis XIV	=	Louis the fourteenth
Pope John XXII	=	Pope John the twenty-second

2b They can also be used in the plural.

E.g. *Have you met our neighbours* ***the Carters****?* (= 'the family called Carter.')
There are ***three Susans*** *in my class.* (= 'people called Susan.')

NOTE: Notice that we can add adjectives like ***dear*** before a person's name to express our feelings about him/her.
E.g. ***dear*** *José,* ***poor*** *Mrs Miller,* ***old*** *Mr Bailey.*
We can also add adjectives before place names to describe the place.
E.g. ***beautiful*** *Greece,* ***historic*** *York,* ***ancient*** *Nara.*

names of people

► How to name people when you talk to them or about them.

1 Talking to people and about people
You can use:
(A) The first name (also called 'given name' or 'Christian name').

E.g. *Ann, Susan, Andrew, Frederic, James*

This is <friendly>.

or:
(B) The last name (also called 'family name' or 'surname') after:
Mr /ˈmɪstə^r/ e.g. *Mr White*
Mrs /ˈmɪsɪz/ (for married women) e.g. *Mrs Jones*
Miss /mɪs/ (for unmarried women) e.g. *Miss Williams*

Ms /mɪz/ (for both married and unmarried women – this is becoming popular) e.g. *Ms Jackson*
This form of address is <polite and respectful>.

NOTE (i): Don't use both first name and last name when you are speaking ***to*** people (e.g. *(Mr) Michael Long*). But you can use them when you are talking ***about*** people.

NOTE (ii): The last name alone, e.g. *Short, Kennedy, Mills* is <not friendly> and <not respectful>. So we do not use it very much, except for convenience, in talking or writing about well-known people. E.g.: *Mozart, Shakespeare, Gorbachov.*

or:
(C) The shortened first name, or 'pet' name, or nickname.

E.g. *Annie, Sue, Andy, Fred, Jim*

This is especially for people you know well: it is <casual and informal>.

1a You can add a title before the name in all three types:

(A) title + first name, e.g.: *Uncle James*.
(B) title + last name, e.g.: *Dr Fraser* (= Doctor).
(C) title + 'pet' name, e.g.: *Auntie Sue*.

2 **Position**
The name of the person you are talking to usually goes in the front or end position* in a sentence [see ADVERB 3].

E.g. ***Mrs Smith**, would you come this way, please?*
*Would you please come this way, **Mrs Smith**?*

* Middle position is possible, but <rare>.
E.g. *Would you, **Mrs Smith**, come this way, please?*
Here, middle position puts emphasis on the word ***you***.

3 **Different ways of addressing someone**

3a <friendly and casual> (first name)

E.g. *Good luck, **Bill**.*
***Moira**, what are you doing this evening?*

3b <very friendly and casual>

E.g. *Lovely to see you, **my dear**.*
*How about a game of cards, **you guys***. <U.S.>
***Darling**, you're looking wonderful.*

3c <distant and showing respect> (second name)

E.g. ***Ms Carter**, I believe you wanted to see me.*

3d <very respectful>

E.g. *Can I help you, **madam**?* (talking to a female customer)
*Would you like a menu, **sir**?* (talking to a male customer)

3e <impolite>

E.g. (i) *Don't make such a noise,* ***you fool****.*

(ii)

Where's my hat ?
It's on your own head, stupid !

3f Here are five methods of addressing the same person:

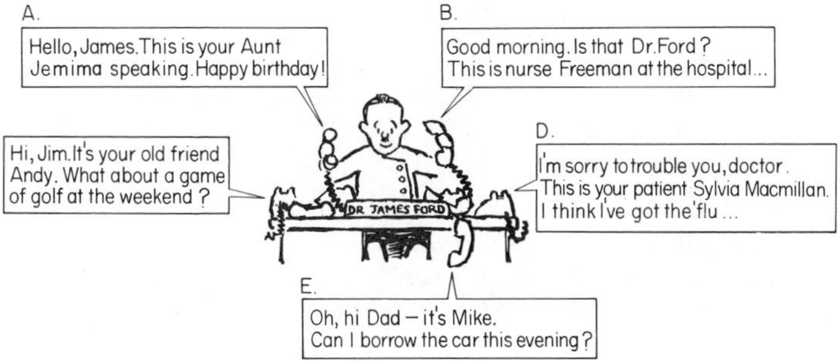
A.
Hello, James. This is your Aunt Jemima speaking. Happy birthday!
B.
Good morning. Is that Dr. Ford ? This is nurse Freeman at the hospital...
C.
Hi, Jim. It's your old friend Andy. What about a game of golf at the weekend ?
D.
I'm sorry to trouble you, doctor. This is your patient Sylvia Macmillan. I think I've got the 'flu ...
DR JAMES FORD
E.
Oh, hi Dad – it's Mike. Can I borrow the car this evening ?

nationality words [See COUNTRIES.]

near /nɪəʳ/ (*preposition or adverb or adjective*)

1 ***Near*** has the comparative and superlative forms ***nearer*** /ˈnɪərəʳ/ and ***nearest*** /ˈnɪərɪst/:

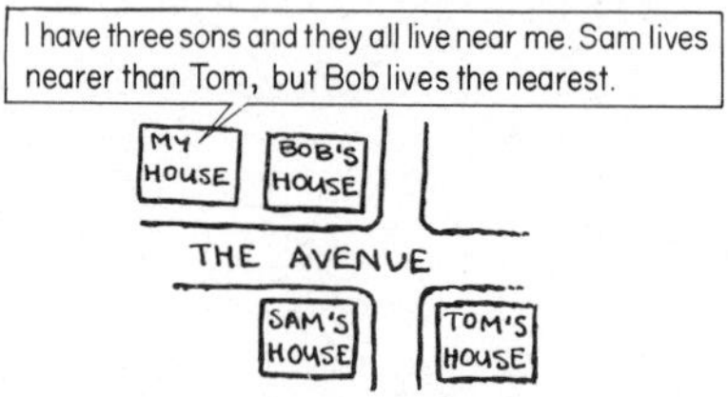
I have three sons and they all live near me. Sam lives nearer than Tom, but Bob lives the nearest.
MY HOUSE
BOB'S HOUSE
THE AVENUE
SAM'S HOUSE
TOM'S HOUSE

2 ***Near*** can be a
PREPOSITION ~ *We sat **near** the door.*
ADVERB ~ *Don't go too **near**.*
ADJECTIVE ~ *There will be another meeting in the **near** future.*

3 Instead of the preposition, we can use ***near to***, ***nearer to***, and ***nearest to***.

E.g. *She runs a dress shop **near (to)** the station.*
*I would like to live **nearer (to)** my job.*
*The longest arrow came **nearest (to)** the centre.*

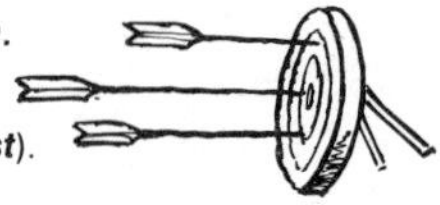

NOTE: ***Near*** (***nearer***, ***nearest***) is the opposite of FAR (***further***, ***furthest***).

nearly /ˈnɪəʳlɪ/ (*adverb of degree*) [See ALMOST AND NEARLY.]

need /ni:d/ (*verb or noun*)

► ***Need*** is a regular main verb ***need, needs, needing, needed***.
► ***Need*** is a modal auxiliary verb ***need, needn't*** (/ˈni:dn̩t/).
► ***Need*** has only one main meaning, whatever the form.

1 **The main verb *need***
Like many other verbs (e.g. *want, like*) [see VERB PATTERNS 1, 7], ***need*** can go with a noun phrase or with a ***to*** + infinitive. For example:

1a NOUN PHRASE + NEED + NOUN PHRASE

E.g. *All animals* ***need*** *food.*

1b NOUN PHRASE + NEED + TO + INFINITIVE . . .

E.g. *All animals* ***need*** *to eat.*

1c Other examples:

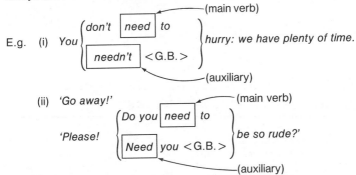

* Notice that the negative of ***need*** as a main verb is ***don't + need to*** + Verb. Compare the negative of the modal auxiliary, ***needn't*** + Verb [see 2 below].

NOTE: Instead of the passive infinitive, i.e. ***to be washed*** (e.g. *my hair needs* ***to be washed***), we can use the ***-ing*** form: *My hair* ***needs*** *wash****ing***; *my car* ***needs*** *mend****ing***; *it* ***needs*** *clean****ing*** etc.

2 **The modal auxiliary *need***

The modal auxiliary ***need*** is found mainly in <G.B.>, and is quite rare these days.

Auxiliary ***need*** has no past tense form, and in general occurs only in negatives (see (i) below) or in questions (see (ii) below).* To be safe, always use the main verb ***need***.

E.g. (i) *You* { *don't* [*need*] *to* (main verb) / [*needn't*] <G.B.> (auxiliary) } *hurry: we have plenty of time.*

(ii) *'Go away!'*

'Please! { *Do you* [*need*] *to* (main verb) / [*Need*] *you* <G.B.> (auxiliary) } *be so rude?'*

* ***Need*** as an auxiliary can occur in other contexts, where the meaning is 'negative' or 'questioning'.

E.g. *I don't think she* ***need*** *be informed.*
I doubt whether anyone ***need*** *know.*

NOTE (i): ***Needn't*** is one of the negative equivalents of ***must*** [see MUST 2c].

E.g. *You* ***must*** *wear your uniform every day except Sunday. But on Sunday you* ***needn't*** *wear it.* (= 'you don't have to wear it') (*Mustn't* would mean: 'you are forbidden to wear it')

NOTE (ii): There is a small difference between ***didn't need to*** (past form of main verb) and ***needn't have*** (Perfect form of auxiliary).

E.g. (a) *You **needn't have** cooked for us.*

(b) *You **didn't need to** cook for us.*

Both (a) and (b) mean 'It wasn't necessary to cook for us', but (a) also implies that 'you did cook for us'. Note this contrast:

3 The noun ***need*** is both (a) COUNTABLE and (b) UNCOUNTABLE.

E.g. (a) *Young babies have many **needs**.*

(b) *The poorer nations are in great **need**.*

negative words and sentences

1 **Negative and positive**

Negative STATEMENTS have the opposite meaning to positive statements.

E.g. (i) positive: *I am fond of Maria.*
(ii) negative: *I am **not** fond of Maria.*
positive: *Joe **sometimes** makes mistakes.*
negative: *Joe **never** makes mistakes.*

[On negative questions, see YES-NO QUESTION 2.]

2 **The most important negative word: *not***

Not makes a whole clause negative. [See NOT, DO 2.] ***Not*** is often contracted to ***-n't***.

E.g. ***was not → wasn't*** ***do not → don't***
have not → haven't ***would not → wouldn't***

[See CONTRACTION OF VERBS AND NEGATIVES 3, 4.]

3 **Other negative words**
Other negative words are in the following table.

neither*	determiner,* pronoun,* adverb*
neither . . . nor	double conjunction*
never*	adverb* (of time or frequency)
no*	determiner,* 'response word'
nobody*	pronoun (referring to people)
no one*	pronoun (referring to people)
none*	pronoun*
nor	adverb (linking),* conjunction*
nothing*	pronoun (not referring to people)
nowhere*	adverb (of place)

* These words have separate entries in this book. Look them up for further details.

4 **Words with negative meaning**
In addition to the words in the above table, there are several words which are negative in meaning, but which do not begin with ***n(o)-***:

*few**, *little**	determiners*, pronouns*
rarely, seldom	adverbs of frequency*
*hardly**, *scarcely, barely*	adverbs of degree*

* These words have separate entries in this book. Look them up for further details.

5 **Negative and positive clauses behave differently**
All the words above give a clause negative meaning. Notice the difference between a negative and a positive clause:

(a) After negative words, we normally use ANY, ANYONE etc.

E.g. *He sometimes says something interesting.*
*He **never** says **anything** interesting.*

[See SOME-WORDS and ANY-WORDS.]

(b) After a negative clause, we normally add a positive TAG QUESTION.

E.g. *She often makes mistakes, doesn't she?*
*She **rarely** makes mistakes, **does** she?*

6 **Negative words and phrases which require a change of word order**
To emphasise a negative, we can place it at the front of the clause.

E.g. *She* ***at no time*** *mentioned her earlier marriage.*
↓
At no time *did she mention her earlier marriage.*

6a In the example above notice that there is inversion [see INVERSION 2–4]. This means the order of the new sentence is:

NEGATIVE PART + AUXILIARY / BE + SUBJECT + (VERB) (. . .)

E.g. *I **not only** heard the car, I actually saw it crash.*
→ ***Not only** did I hear the car, I actually saw it crash.*
*He **hasn't once** offered to help.*
→ ***Not once** has he offered to help.*
*You must **under no circumstances** make jokes about religion.*
→ ***Under no circumstances** must you make jokes about religion.*
***No sooner** was I in bed, than the phone started to ring.*
***Hardly** * had we arrived at the camp site, when it began to rain cats and dogs.* * *
***Seldom** * have I been to a more terrible concert.*

* ***Hardly*** and ***seldom*** are negative in meaning.
* * ***Rain cats and dogs*** is an idiom meaning 'rain very heavily.'

7 'Negative transfer'
To make the THAT-clause in example (i) below negative, we can say either (ii) or (iii).

E.g. (i) *I think (that) Mary takes sugar.*
(ii) *I think (that) Mary **doesn't take** sugar.*
(iii) *I **don't think** (that) Mary takes sugar.*

Sentences (ii) and (iii) have the same meaning, but (iii) 'transfers' the negative to the main clause. We call this 'negative transfer', and we prefer it to the ordinary negative in (ii). Negative transfer takes place with verbs like ***think***, ***believe***, and ***expect***. Some more examples:

Jan believes (that) Harry is honest. → *Jan **doesn't believe** that Harry is honest.*
I expect (that) we will win the match. → *I **don't expect** (that) we will win the match.*

---

neither /ˈnaɪðəʳ/ or /ˈniːðəʳ/ (*conjunction, pronoun, determiner or adverb*)

- ***Neither*** is a word with 'double negative' meaning. It always means: 'not one and not the other.'
- ***Neither*** is always negative, so the verb following it is always positive: ***Neither can I*** but not: ***Neither ~~can't~~ I***.
- As a conjunction, ***neither*** is part of the double conjunction ***neither . . . nor***. [See DOUBLE CONJUNCTION 6.]
- ***Neither*** can also be an indefinite pronoun, normally in the pattern:

NEITHER + OF + PLURAL NOUN PHRASE

E.g. ***neither** of the boys*

► ***Neither*** can also be a DETERMINER, normally in the pattern:

NEITHER + SINGULAR NOUN

E.g. ***neither** boy*

► ***Neither*** can be a LINKING ADVERB, normally in the pattern:

$$\text{NEITHER} + \left\{\begin{array}{l}\text{AUXILIARY VERB}\\ \text{THE VERB BE}\end{array}\right\} + \text{NOUN PHRASE} (\ldots)$$

E.g. ***neither** are they*

Examples:

1 *Neither . . . nor* as conjunction

E.g. ***Neither** Emma **nor** Laura like Susan.*
(= 'Both Emma and Laura dislike Susan.')
(= 'Emma and Laura don't like Susan.')

2 *Neither* as pronoun

3 *Neither* as determiner

E.g. *The game was very even: **neither** player was able to beat the other.*

4 *Neither* as linking adverb
If someone says something negative, and you agree with them, you can use ***neither***.

E.g.

*Her family couldn't help her, and **neither** could her friends.*

Note different ways of saying the same thing.

E.g. *'I don't like mathematics.' '**Neither** do I.'*
*'I dislike mathematics.' '**So** do I.'* [See SO 3.]
*'I don't like mathematics.' 'I do**n't, either**.'* [See EITHER.]

never /ˈnevəʳ/ (*adverb* of FREQUENCY or LENGTH OF TIME)

1 ***Never*** is a negative word meaning '0 times' or 'at no time'.

E.g. *'I'm terribly sorry. I'll **never** tell you (any) lies again.'*

[Compare ALWAYS.]

next /nekst/ (*ordinal or adverb*) [See ORDINALS.]

1 **Ordinal**
In any sequence, *first, second, third . . .*, ***next*** means 'the one after this one':

1a Time:

E.g. (i) ***Next*** *Thursday* (= 'the Thursday after this') *I'm working late, but I'm free the Thursday after that.* [See TIME 4c, 5.]

(ii)

1b Place:

E.g. *Our house is the second one in the street. The **next** house belongs to the Barnabys. They're our **next**-door neighbours.*

2 **Adverb of time**
Next means 'after this / that.'

E.g. ***First*** *fry the onions.* ***Then*** *add the tomatoes.* ***Next*** *add the meat.*

3 **Linking adverb**
Next means 'after this.'
Next belongs to the list of introductory words ***first, second, next, . . . last***.

E.g. . . . ***Next**, I would like to introduce the Minister of Education, Mr. Geoffrey Smith; and **last**, but not least, here is the Prime Minister.*

---

no /nəʊ/ (*determiner, response word or adverb*)

► ***No*** is always a NEGATIVE WORD.

1 *No* as a response word

No as a response word [see REPLIES (OR ANSWERS)] gives a negative answer to YES-NO QUESTIONS, IMPERATIVES, REQUESTS, etc.

E.g. *'Did he pass the driving test?' '**No**, he failed it.'*
*'Have a chocolate cake.' '**No**, thank you.'*

NOTE: If you want to agree with a negative statement, you use ***no***.
E.g. *'I don't enjoy boxing.'*
'No, I don't, either.' [See EITHER]
Also use ***no*** if you want to agree with a negative question.
E.g. *'Didn't you go?' '**No**, I didn't.'*
*'You didn't go, did you?' '**No**, I didn't.'*

2 *No* as a determiner

No as a determiner (= 'not (. . .) any', 'not . . . a') can go before:

singular countable nouns	plural nouns	uncountable nouns
no pilot *no recent photograph*	*no passengers* *no clean cups*	*no meat* *no heavy rain*

E.g. ***No** trained **pilot** would make a mistake like that.*
*I have **no cigarettes** left.* (= 'I haven't any . . .')

After ***no*** we can use ***any***-words [see SOME-WORDS AND ANY-WORDS].

E.g. *We received **no** help from **any** of the politicians.*

3 *No* as an adverb of degree

No as an adverb of degree (= 'not (. . .) any') goes before comparative words.

E.g. *The team played badly last week, and I'm sorry to say that they were **no better** this week.*
*The painting fetched **no less** than £5 million.* (= 'as much as £5 million')

4 Idioms

4a ***No longer*** means 'not any longer', 'not after this'.

E.g. *I **no longer** live in that house.*

4b ***No sooner*** *X than Y* means 'As soon as X, Y'.

E.g. ***No sooner had the keeper opened*** *the cage door,* ***than the lion attacked*** *and injured him.* <formal, written>

[See NEGATIVE WORDS AND SENTENCES 6a.]

4c ***No one*** [See the separate entry below.]

4d ***No matter wh-*** [See MATTER 4.]

---

no one, nobody /ˈnəʊwʌn/, /ˈnəʊbədɪ/ (*indefinite pronouns*)

- ***No one*** is a negative pronoun [see NEGATIVE WORDS AND SENTENCES] meaning 'no person'.
- ***No one*** is normally spelled as two words: ***no one***.
- ***Nobody*** can be used wherever ***no one*** is used, but ***nobody*** is less common.

1 Example

'Where's Alice?' ***'No one*** *knows where she is.'*
No one *understands me – not even my psychiatrist.*

2 *No one* can be followed by an any-word

E.g. ***No one*** *saw* ***anyone*** *leave the building after the murder.*
No one *has* ***ever*** *climbed this mountain.*

3 *No one* can be followed by *his, he, him, her, she, their, them, they*

E.g. ***No one*** *had finished*
- ***his*** *homework* * <formal, written>
- ***her*** *homework* * <formal, written>
- ***their*** *homework.* <informal, spoken>

* [On the choice of these forms, see HE AND SHE.]

---

nominative

In grammar, the term 'nominative' is sometimes used for the form which a word has when it is SUBJECT of a clause. E.g. ***he*** (nominative) contrasts with ***him*** (accusative). We do not use the term 'nominative' in this book. We call words like ***he*** subject pronouns instead. [See PERSONAL PRONOUN.]

nominal clause is another term for NOUN CLAUSE.

noncount noun the same as UNCOUNTABLE NOUN.

nondefining relative clause [See RELATIVE CLAUSE 4.]

none /nʌn/ (*indefinite pronoun*)

► ***None*** means: (i) *'not one'* (countable)
(II) *'not any'* (uncountable)

1 ***None*** is a negative **of**-pronoun [see INDEFINITE PRONOUN 2].
It can be:
(i) followed by an ***of***-phrase.

E.g. ***None of us speaks*** *Italian. One of us speaks German, and the others all speak Japanese.*

(ii) followed by ***at all***.

E.g. *'Have you got any money?' 'No,* ***none at all****. Sorry!'*

(iii) at the end of a phrase or sentence.

E.g. *'How many fish did you catch?'*
'None.'

2 **Form of verb after *none***

2a When ***none*** means *'not any of it'* (uncountable) it takes an **-s** form of the verb.

E.g. ***None*** *(of this bread)* ***looks*** *fresh.*

2b **When *none*** means *'not one of them'* (countable) we often use a plural form of the verb in <informal English>.

E.g. ***None*** *(of these apples)* ***are*** *ripe.*
None *(of the guests)* ***have*** *arrived yet.*

In <formal written> English, however, people consider the **-s** form more <'correct'>.

E.g. ***None*** *(of these apples)* ***is*** *ripe.*
None *(of the guests)* ***has*** *arrived yet.*

[See AGREEMENT 2b.]

nonfinite clause [See also CLAUSE, INFINITIVE CLAUSE, -ING CLAUSE, PARTICIPLE CLAUSE, TO-INFINITIVE.]

► A **nonfinite clause** is a clause without a finite verb.

► It will be helpful, before you read this entry, to read the next entry, NONFINITE VERB.

► In a **nonfinite clause**, the first verb form is either:
(a) an infinitive form with ***to*** (***to*** + Verb) [see 1 below]
or (b) an -ing form (Verb + ***ing***) [see 2 below]
or (c) a past participle form (Verb + ***ed***) [see 3 below]
or (d) an infinitive without ***to*** (Verb) (less common) [see INFINITIVE CLAUSE and 4 below]
These verb forms are all called nonfinite verbs.

1 To + infinitive clauses

1a These clauses usually have no subject.

E.g. *The best thing is **to leave your family at home**.*

1b If there is a subject, it is usually introduced by ***for***.

E.g. *The best thing is **for you to leave your family at home**.*

1c A ***to***-infinitive clause can replace a finite clause.

E.g. *I hope **to be present**.*

Instead of: *I hope **that I will be present**.*

NOTE: This depends on the verb, however. For example you can say:
*I want **to be happy***. But not: ~~*I want that I will be happy*~~. [See VERB PATTERNS 4 and 7.]

2 -ing clauses

2a There is usually no subject in the ***-ing*** clause, but the ***-ing*** verb uses the subject of the main clause as its own subject.

E.g. ***Entering the room**, I fell over the cat.* (i.e. 'I entered the room')

2b In <more formal>, written English, ***-ing*** clauses sometimes do have a subject.

E.g. ***The two sides having reached agreement**, we shook hands and went home.*

2c An ***-ing*** clause can take the place of a finite clause.

E.g. ***Living in the country**, we had few visitors.*

Compare: ***When we lived in the country**, we had few visitors.*

2d An ***-ing*** clause can be like a finite clause with the subject and the verb ***be*** omitted.

E.g. *He wrote his greatest novel **while working as an ordinary seaman.***

Compare: *He wrote his greatest novel **while he was working as an ordinary seaman**.*

3 **Past participle clauses**
These are more common in <written> than in <spoken> English. They have a PASSIVE meaning.

3a Usually they have no subject.

E.g. *The woman lay on the ground, **ignored by the people around her**.* (i.e. '. . . she was ignored . . .')

3b But a past participle clause can have a subject different from the subject of the main clause.

E.g. *Both sides signed the agreement. **That done**, the chairman brought the meeting to an end.* (***That done*** = 'After that was done.')

3c A past participle clause can take the place of a finite clause.

E.g. *The boy **who was injured by a bullet** was taken to hospital.* [See FINITE (Relative Clause).]
→ *The boy **injured by a bullet** was taken to hospital.*

These sentences mean the same.
Here, as in 2d, the participle clause omits the subject and the verb ***be*** of the finite clause.

4 Nonfinite clauses are useful, especially in <formal, written> English, because they do not require so many words as finite clauses.

E.g. Finite clauses:
***Since we had arrived** late and **were exhausted** by the journey, we decided **that we should go** to bed immediately.*
Nonfinite clauses:
***Arriving** late and **exhausted** by the journey, we decided **to go** to bed immediately.*

nonfinite verb, nonfinite verb phrase

1 There are two kinds of verb forms: FINITE and nonfinite:

finite verb forms		nonfinite verb forms	
-s form:	*likes, takes*	**-*ing*** form:	*liking, taking*
basic form: (when used for the present tense)	*like, take*	basic form: (when used for the infinitive)	*(to) like, (to) take*
past tense form:	*liked, took*	past participle form:	*liked, taken*

The finite forms are normally required for the main clause of a sentence, i.e. every sentence normally has a finite verb.

2 We also use the words 'finite' and 'non-finite' for VERB PHRASES:

2a A finite verb phrase is a verb phrase which contains a finite verb form.

E.g. *She* { ***studies / studied*** / ***is / was studying*** } *English.*

(It may also contain nonfinite verbs after the finite verb form, e.g. ***studying*** in this example.)

2b A nonfinite verb phrase is a verb phrase which contains one or more nonfinite verb forms (but no finite verb forms).

E.g. ***Studying*** *English is useful.*
It is useful ***to have studied*** *English.*

3 Compare:

finite verb phrases	non-finite verb phrases
John ***smokes*** *heavily.*	***To smoke*** *like that must be dangerous.*
Mary ***is working*** *hard*	*I found her* ***working*** *hard.*
When he ***had left*** *the office, he went home by taxi.*	***Having left*** *the office, he went home by taxi.*
*The message which they (**had**)* ***sent*** *from Berlin never reached me.*	*The message* ***sent*** *from Berlin never reached me.*

4 [For further information, see VERB, PARTICIPLE, INFINITIVE, -ING FORM.]

nonrestrictive relative clause is another term for nondefining relative clause. [See RELATIVE CLAUSE 4.]

not /nɒt/ (*negative word*), *-n't* /n̩t/, /nt/ (contraction)

- ► ***Not*** is the main NEGATIVE word in English.
- ► To make a clause negative, place ***not*** after the AUXILIARY VERB or the verb BE.
- ► When there is no other auxiliary, use ***do*** (***does, did***) before ***not*** [see DO 2].
- ► In <speech>, we usually use the negative contraction or 'short form' ***-n't*** /nt/ instead of ***not*** [see CONTRACTION OF VERBS AND NEGATIVES 3]. E.g. **didn't** /dɪdn̩t/.

1 **This is how to form a negative clause (or sentence) using *not*** (notice that all these examples are more natural with contractions)

1a If the clause has a form of ***be***, simply put ***-n't*** or ***not*** after ***be***.

E.g. *My parents **are** at home.* → *My parents* { ***aren't*** / ***are not*** } *at home.*

*Margaret **was** angry.* → *Margaret* { ***wasn't*** / ***was not*** } *angry.*

1b If the clause has an auxiliary verb, simply put ***not*** after the auxiliary (or 1st auxiliary, if there is more than one).

E.g. *Max **has** left home.* → *Max* { ***hasn't*** / ***has not*** } *left home.*

*We **will** win a prize.* → *We* { ***won't*** / ***will not*** } *win a prize.*

*Eva **would** have liked that.* → *Eva* { ***wouldn't*** / ***would not*** } *have liked that.*

1c If the clause does not have a form of ***be*** or an auxiliary verb, add a form of the 'empty' auxiliary ***do*** before ***not***.

(A) . . .	main Verb	. . .	→	. . .	*do*	+ { ***-n't*** / ***not*** } + main Verb . . .
(B) . . .	main Verb **-s**	. . .	→	. . .	*does*	
(C) . . .	main Verb ***-ed***	. . .	→	. . .	*did*	

E.g. (A) *I **feel** tired.* → *I* { ***don't*** / ***do not*** } ***feel*** *tired.*

(B) *Paul **enjoys** poetry.* → *Paul* { ***doesn't*** / ***does not*** } ***enjoy*** *poetry.*

(C) *It **rained** last night.* → *It* { ***didn't*** / ***did not*** } ***rain*** *last night.*

2 ***Not* can be followed by *any* or *any*-words** [see NEGATIVE WORDS AND SENTENCES 5.]

E.g. *They have* ***some*** *fruit.* → *They do* ***not*** *have* ***any*** *fruit.*
I want ***something*** *to eat.* → *I do**n't*** *want* ***anything*** *to eat.*
The pears are ***already*** *ripe.* → *The pears are* ***not yet*** *ripe.*

3 **In questions with inversion** [see YES-NO QUESTION]
Mostly speakers use the contraction ***-n't***, which goes before the subject.

E.g. *Have you been to Rome?* → ***Haven't*** *you been to Rome?*
Can I help you? → ***Can't*** *I help you?*

If you don't use the contraction (***-n't***), then ***not*** must follow the subject.

E.g. ***Have*** *you* ***not*** *been to Rome?* ***Can I not*** *help you?* <rare>

[On negative questions, see YES-NO QUESTION 2.]

4 **In** IMPERATIVE **sentences, *not* goes after *do***

E.g. ***Don't* waste time.** Or: ***Do not*** *waste time.*

5 **In** NONFINITE CLAUSES, ***not*** **goes before the main verb, normally at the beginning of the clause**

E.g. *They told me* ***not to say*** *anything.* (***not*** + to + Verb)
They accused him of ***not reporting*** *a crime.* (***not*** + Verb ***-ing***)

[See INDIRECT COMMAND.]
No contraction is possible here, or in 6–7 below.

6 ***Not* acts as a replacement for a negative *that*-clause** [see THAT 1]

E.g. *'Are the tickets ready?' 'I'm afraid* ***not****.'* (= 'I'm afraid that they are not ready.')
They told me that the flight would arrive late, but I hope ***not***. (. . . 'that it won't arrive late.')

Not here is the opposite of ***so*** [see SO 3].

7 ***Not* is not always linked with the verb**
It can go before phrases of various kinds, especially of QUANTITY or DEGREE. In this case, it often begins the sentence.

7a ***Not many, not much, not all***:

E.g. ***Not many*** *tourists visit this part of the coast.*
Not much *attention has been given to the country's labour troubles.*
Not all *(of) our students live on the campus.*

7b In replies:

E.g. *'I'm afraid I have been troubling you.' '**Not** at all.'*
*'Have you finished your homework?' '**Not** yet. I'm still working on it.'*

8 Idioms
not . . . but . . ., not only . . . but . . . [See DOUBLE CONJUNCTION 1, 4, 5.]
not at all, not a bit, not in the least. These are emphatic negatives.

E.g. *I'm **not at all** busy at the moment, so I have plenty of time to talk to you.*
*I'm **not a bit** surprised that they refused the offer. I would have done the same.*
*'I hope you didn't find my speech too boring.' '**Not in the least**: it was very interesting.'*

9 ***Not at all*** is also a <polite> reply to an apology. [See APOLOGIES.]

nothing /ˈnʌθɪŋ/ (*indefinite pronoun*)

Nothing is the negative pronoun which applies to things or to anything that is 'not a person.' (For a person, use ***no one*** or ***nobody***.)

E.g. *'Did you buy **anything** at the market?' 'No. I bought **nothing** at all.'*
*There's **nothing** in the room: it's completely empty.*

(You can also say: *'I **didn't** buy **anything** at all'* and *'There **isn't anything** in the room'*.)

noun

- ► Nouns are the largest class of words.
- ► Nouns are the main words of NOUN PHRASES.
- ► Most nouns have a PLURAL form in ***-(e)s***: *ear ~ ears, wish ~ wishes* [but see IRREGULAR PLURAL.]

1 This table shows the main kinds of noun.
Those on the left contrast with those on the right.

countable nouns *(a ball ~ balls)*	uncountable nouns *(food)*

concrete nouns* *(a ball ~ balls) (food)*	abstract nouns* *(a dream ~ dreams) (love)*

common nouns* (a ball ~ balls) (food) (a dream ~ dreams) (love)	proper nouns (names*) (James) (Madrid) (Andes)

* These words have separate entries in this book. Look them up for further details. [See also COUNTABLE AND UNCOUNTABLE NOUNS.]

2 In addition, there are some small but useful classes of noun (often followed by OF) which you can look up under their own entries.

GROUP NOUNS: e.g. *a crowd ~ crowds; the press.*
NOUNS OF KIND: e.g. *kind ~ kinds; type ~ types.*

noun clause

1 Noun clauses are SUBORDINATE CLAUSES which can fill the position of NOUN PHRASES. That is, they take the position of SUBJECT, OBJECT, COMPLEMENT, etc. in a clause.

2 There are four main kinds of noun clause in English:

that-clause:	*No one believes* ***that the earth is flat***. [See THAT 1.]
wh-clause:*	***What I believe*** *is no business of yours.*
infinitive clause:*	*Our plan is* ***to catch the early train***.
-ing clause:*	*You are in danger of* ***making a bad mistake***.

* [Look up each of these clause types for further information.]

noun of kind

► Nouns of kind are nouns such as *kind, type, sort, species, class, variety, make, brand.*

1 These words divide a mass or a set of objects into 'kinds' or 'species'.

E.g. *Pine is a* ***type*** *of wood.*
A Cadillac is a ***make*** *of car.*
Players is a ***brand*** *of cigarette.*
A bee is a ***species*** *of insect.*
'A tomato is a ***kind*** *of vegetable.' 'No, it isn't – it's a* ***kind*** *of fruit.'*

2 ***Kind***, ***sort*** and ***type*** are the most general and useful of these nouns. [See KIND (OF), SORT (OF) AND TYPE (OF).]

noun phrase [See PHRASE]

- ► A noun phrase usually begins with a DETERMINER.
- ► It normally has a NOUN as its most important word, or head-word. (But often the head-word is a pronoun.)
- ► A noun phrase can act as SUBJECT, OBJECT, or COMPLEMENT in the clause. It can also follow a PREPOSITION [see PREPOSITIONAL PHRASE].

1 Examples of noun phrases. The determiner is in bold; the head is marked like this: *head*:

the *future*	***a*** *young woman*	***all the*** *schools in the country*
this *problem*	***an*** *old man*	***the*** *people at the meeting yesterday*

The other parts of the noun phrase (not marked) are MODIFIERS. They include adjectives (before the noun) and prepositional phrases (after the noun).

2 Notice that some noun phrases contain one word only. We still call them noun phrases, because they can act as subject, object, etc. in a clause.

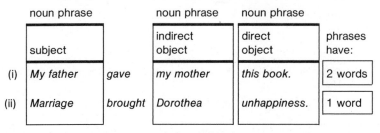

	noun phrase		noun phrase	noun phrase	
	subject		indirect object	direct object	phrases have:
(i)	*My father*	*gave*	*my mother*	*this book.*	2 words
(ii)	*Marriage*	*brought*	*Dorothea*	*unhappiness.*	1 word

3 Noun phrases like those in example (i) and (ii) above can be replaced by PRONOUNS. (The noun phrases in the following example are in ***bold*** print.):

E.g. ***My father*** *gave* ***this book*** *to* ***my mother***.

→ ***He*** *gave* ***it*** *to* ***her***. [See PERSONAL PRONOUN.]

3a A pronoun is (usually) the only word of its noun phrase. It is still called the head-word.

4 In the following, noun phrases are in ***bold***.

E.g. ***The boy*** *went out.* ***They*** *had eaten with* ***no light*** *on* ***the table*** *and* ***the old man*** *took off* ***his trousers*** *and went to* ***bed*** *in* ***the dark***. ***He*** *rolled* ***his trousers*** *up to make* ***a pillow***, *putting* ***the newspaper*** *inside* ***them***.

(Ernest Hemingway, *The Old Man and the Sea*)

now /naʊ/ (*adverb*)

1 **Adverb of time**

Now means (a) *'at this time', 'at the present time'.*
(b) *'very soon'.*

E.g. (a) *He used to be a miner.* ***Now*** *he's retired.*
(b) *We'd better eat* ***now****: it's eight o'clock.*

NOTE: When ***now*** refers to a long(ish) period of time, as in (a), you can replace it by ***nowadays***.
E.g. *In the old days, people used to go out to enjoy themselves.* ***Now(adays)*** *they stay at home and watch television.*

2 **Linking adverb**
As a linking word in spoken English, ***now*** means 'I am changing the subject, and returning to something I was thinking about before'.

E.g. (i) ***Now*** *where did we put those maps?*
(ii) *Let's see,* ***now****. You must be older than me.*
(iii) ***Now****, I have one more point to make . . .*

With this meaning, ***now*** is either unstressed, as in (i), or heavily stressed, as in (iii).

3 **Idioms**
By now

E.g. *The train's late. They should be here* ***by now****.* (= 'before now')

Now (that) is a subordinating conjunction mixing the meanings of time and reason.

E.g. *Let's have a drink,* ***now (that)*** *you're here.* (= 'because you are now here')
Now (that) *I've learned to drive, I will be able to go to work by car.*

nowadays /ˈnaʊədeɪz/ (*adverb of time*) [See NOW 1 note.]

nowhere /ˈnəʊweəʳ/ (*adverb of place*)

Nowhere (or *no place* <informal U.S.>) is negative, in contrast to ***somewhere***, ***anywhere***, and ***everywhere***.

E.g. *'Where did you go last night?'*
*'****Nowhere****. I stayed at home.'*

-n't (= not) [See NOT, CONTRACTION OF VERBS AND NEGATIVES 3.]

number

In English grammar, the term ‘number’ refers to the difference between singular and plural. [See PLURAL.]

a number of /əˈnʌmbərəv/ (*quantity term*)

A number of + plural noun means ‘several’, ‘a few’.
[See AGREEMENT 2c.]

numbers

[See also ORDINALS, FRACTIONS, DATES, DECIMALS, MONEY, MEASURING.]

► There are two kinds of number words in English:
(A) Cardinal numbers (for counting): *one, two, three, . . .* etc.
(B) Ordinal numbers (for putting things in a sequence or order): *first, second, third, . . .* etc.

1 **Note the spellings and pronunciations in this table**

cardinal	ordinal (Add *-th* (-/θ/) to the cardinal)
0 zero* /ˈzɪərəʊ/	
1 *one* /wʌn/	1st *first*** /fɜːʳst/**
2 *two* /tuː/	2nd *second*** /ˈsekənd/**
3 *three* /θriː/	3rd *third*** /θɜːʳd/**
4 *four* /fɔːʳ/	4th *fourth* /fɔːʳθ/
5 *five* /faɪv/	5th *fifth*** /fɪfθ/**
6 *six* /sɪks/	6th *sixth* /sɪksθ/
7 *seven* /ˈsevən/	7th *seventh* /ˈsevənθ/
8 *eight* /eɪt/	8th *eighth*** /eɪtθ/
9 *nine* /naɪn/	9th *ninth*** /naɪnθ/
10 *ten* /ten/	10th *tenth* /tenθ/
11 *eleven* /əˈlevən/	11th *eleventh* /əˈlevənθ/
12 *twelve* /twelv/	12th *twelfth*** /twelfθ/**
13 *thirteen* /θɜːʳˈtiːn/***	13th *thirteenth* /θɜʳˈtiːnθ/***
14 *fourteen* /fɔːʳˈtiːn/***	14th *fourteenth* /fɔːʳˈtiːnθ/***
15 *fifteen* /fɪfˈtiːn/***	15th *fifteenth* /fɪfˈtiːnθ/***
16 *sixteen* /sɪksˈtiːn/***	16th *sixteenth* /sɪksˈtiːnθ/***
17 *seventeen* /sevənˈtiːn/***	17th *seventeenth* /sevənˈtiːnθ/***
18 *eighteen* /eɪˈtiːn/***	18th *eighteenth* /eɪˈtiːnθ/***
19 *nineteen* /naɪnˈtiːn/***	19th *nineteenth* /naɪnˈtiːnθ/***
20 *twenty* /ˈtwentɪ/***	20th *twentieth* /ˈtwentɪəθ/***

* **O** has three pronunciations:
/ˈzɪərəʊ/ ***zero*** especially in mathematics and for temperature.
/nɔ:t/ ***nought*** <G.B.>.
/əʊ/ especially when reading out long numbers, e.g. telephone numbers like ***01-643*** etc.
** Notice that these are exceptions in the spelling or pronunciation of ordinals.
*** Notice that the stress is on ***-teen*** -/ˈti:n/, while for ***thirty, sixty***, etc the stress is not on -/tɪ/. Contrast.

E.g. ***13*** /θɜ:ʳˈti:n/ and ***30*** /ˈθɜ:ʳtɪ/
16 /sɪksˈti:n/ and ***60*** /ˈsɪkstɪ/ (etc).

But the stress moves from ***-teen*** in the middle of a phrase, or in counting.

E.g. *We had* ***15*** /ˈfɪfti:n/ *guests.*
. . . ***16*** /ˈsɪksti:n/, ***17*** /ˈsevənti:n/, ***18*** /ˈeɪti:n/ . . .

2 Numbers from 20 to 100

cardinal	ordinal	cardinal	ordinal
21 *twenty-one*	21st *-first*	40 *forty*	40th *-tieth*
22 *twenty-two*	22nd *-second*	50 *fifty*	50th *-tieth*
23 *twenty-three*	23rd *-third*	60 *sixty*	60th *-tieth*
24 *twenty-four*	24th *-fourth*	70 *seventy*	70th *-tieth*
. . .	. . .	80 *eighty*	80th *-tieth*
30 *thirty*	30th *thirtieth*	90 *ninety*	90th *-tieth*
. . .	. . .	99 *ninety-nine*	99th *-ninth*
35 *thirty-five*	35th *-fifth*	100 *a hundred* *	100th *-edth*

* It is possible, but not usual, to say ***one hundred***. Similarly: ***a / one thousand***, ***a / one million***.

3 Larger numbers

(Note that the ordinal numbers are formed regularly, using the forms from 1–100. Note the use of **and**.)

E.g.
101 *a hundred* **and** *one*
203 *two hundred* **and** *three*
310 *three hundred* **and** *ten*
421 *four hundred* **and** *twenty-one*
1538 *a/one thousand five hundred* **and** *thirty-eight*
11,649 *eleven thousand six hundred* **and** *forty-nine*
50,000 *fifty thousand*
600,000 *six hundred thousand*
1,000,000 *a million*

NOTE (i): 250,000 = *a quarter of a million*; 500,000 = *half a million*; 750,000 = *three-quarters of a million*.

NOTE (ii): Very large numbers include: *billion* = (in <U.S.>) 1,000,000,000 or (in <G.B.>) 1,000,000,000,000.

4 How number words behave in grammar

Number words have varied roles in the sentence: they can behave like:
(A) Determiners before nouns, etc.

E.g. *The zoo contains* **3** *elephants and* **7** *lions.*
I've got **five** *elder sisters, and* **one** *younger one.*

(B) Pronouns at the end of a phrase or sentence or followed by *of*.

E.g. *'How many people were competing in the race?' 'About* ***two hundred and fifty****.* (250) *Only* ***five*** *of them finished the race, though.'*

(C) Nouns: As a noun, a number word can be plural, can have determiners, etc.

E.g. ***Seven*** *is a lucky number.*
He's in his ***thirties****.* ('His age is between 30 and 40.')
Nine *times* ***eight*** *is 72.* / ***Nine eights*** *are 72.* } (9 × 8 = 72)

5 Number nouns

hundred	= 100	*couple*	= 2	rather <informal>
thousand	= 1000	*dozen*	= 12	
million	= 1,000,000	*score*	= 20	

Although these nouns have an exact meaning, they can also be used in an inexact way. For example, ***a couple of days*** often means 'a few days', and ***hundreds of people*** often means simply 'a large number of people'.

5a *Hundred*, *thousand*, and *million* are basically nouns. They can be used: (I) with determiners.

E.g. ***several hundred*** *men,* ***a thousand*** *copies, half* ***a million****.*

(II) with a plural **-s** and an *of*-phrase.

E.g. ***hundreds of*** *people, many* ***thousands of*** *tourists,* ***millions*** *and* ***millions of*** *ants.*

But: Do not add **-s** when using them as exact numbers.

E.g. *two* ***hundred*** (= 200), *not two* ~~***hundreds***~~.

6 Approximate numbers

6a ***About*** (or ***around***) means 'approximately' or 'roughly', i.e. 'not exactly'.

E.g. *There are* ***about*** *400 children in the school.*

[See ABOUT AND AROUND 3.]

6b Another way of expressing the same meaning is to add ***or so***.

E.g. *There are 400* ***or so*** *children in the school.*

NOTE: Compare ***or more***.
E.g. *There are 400* ***or more*** *children in the school.*
This means that there are ***about*** 400 children, or perhaps ***more*** than that.

object

- The ***object*** is the grammatical term for one of the parts of a clause or sentence.
- The ***object*** is usually a NOUN PHRASE.
- The ***object*** normally follows the VERB PHRASE.
- The ***object*** usually describes someone or something {to / for} {which / whom} the action of the verb 'is done'.
- The ***object*** can usually change into the SUBJECT of a matching PASSIVE clause or sentence.

1 In these patterns, the verb phrase + object are marked:

E.g.	subject noun phrase	verb phrase	object noun phrase	
(i)	*My mother*	*keeps*	*two dogs.*	
(ii)	*Sheila*	*has lost*	*a blue scarf.*	
(iii)	*I*	*am painting*	*this door*	(*white*).
(iv)	*Too much money*	*makes*	*some people*	*rather greedy*.
(v)	*Peter*	*sent*	*my brother*	*home*.
(vi)	*You*	*must put*	*these books*	*away*.

1a We can make these examples passive without mentioning the subject. The object of the active sentence becomes the subject of the passive sentence. Examples (ii) and (iii) become:

(ii) *A blue scarf has been lost.*
(iii) *This door is being painted (white).*

Because we can do this, we know that *a blue scarf* and *this door* are objects in 1 (ii) and (iii).

1b Another way of telling if a word is an object is to ask yourself the following question:
Does it answer a question with this pattern?

{***what*** / ***which*** / ***who(m)***} + auxiliary + subject + main verb?

E.g. Question: '***What** would you like?*'
Answer: '*I'd like **an omelette**.*'

We know ***an omelette*** is an object because it is answering the question: ***What** would you like?*

2 Some clauses have two objects.
The first object is called an INDIRECT OBJECT, and the second object is called a direct object.

E.g.	verb phrase	indirect object	direct object
Mary	*gave*	*Sandra*	*a glass.*
He	*has been showing*	*the family*	*his pictures of China.*

[See INDIRECT OBJECT for further details.] If a clause has only one object, it is usually a direct object.

3 Different types of object
These are exceptions to the rules (marked ►) at the top of this entry:

3a Some objects are not noun phrases, but clauses. Compare:

		object
	(i) *The captain has admitted*	***his mistakes.***
with	(ii) *The captain has admitted*	***that he was wrong.***

In (i), the object is a noun phrase, but in (ii) it is a *that*-clause. Similarly,

E.g. *I asked her* { *a question about money.* / ***how much they earned***. (object = WH-CLAUSE) }

Joe likes { *the study of architecture.* / ***studying architecture***. (object = -ING CLAUSE) }

3b Some objects do not follow the verb phrase. For example, if the object is a WH-WORD, or a relative pronoun, it takes first position in the clause.

E.g. '***What** would you like?*' '*I'd like an **omelette**.*'

↑ Object in first position. Normal position of ↑ Object

*The city **which** I like best is Monte Carlo.* (***which*** is object of *like*)

4 [For further examples of objects, see VERB PATTERNS 1, 4–7, 9, 11–20. All these patterns contain at least one object.]

object complement

- An object complement is a 'complement after the OBJECT' of a clause.
- An object complement contrasts with a subject complement, which is a 'complement after the SUBJECT'.
- [See COMPLEMENT, VERB PATTERN 12 for further information and examples.]

1 Here are some examples of sentences with an object complement (the object is marked like this: *object*).

E.g. (i) *The minister considers himself* ***a supporter of free speech***.
(ii) *I have often wished myself* ***a millionaire***.
(iii) *The long walk made us all* ***hungry***.
(iv) *They keep the streets* ***nice and clean***.

In (i) and (ii) the object complement is a noun phrase. In (iii) and (iv) the object complement is an adjective phrase.

2 The relation between the object and object complement can be represented by the verb BE. (i) and (ii) above mean the same as:

(i) *The minister considers that he is* ***a supporter of free speech.***
(ii) *I have often wished I was* ***a millionaire***.

object pronoun [See PERSONAL PRONOUN 2.]

1 The object pronouns in English are ***me***, ***her***, ***him***, ***us***, and ***them***. They are special forms of the personal pronouns used, among other things, in the position of OBJECT in the sentence.

2 Other terms for object pronouns are 'objective pronouns' or 'accusative pronouns'.

objective case

Objective case is a grammatical term sometimes used for the OBJECT PRONOUN form of personal pronouns.

obligation

To express obligation we can use ***must***,* ***have got to***,* or ***have to***.*

* These words have separate entries in this book. Look them up for further details. [See also SHOULD AND OUGHT TO.]

o'clock /əˈklɒk/ (*adverb*) [See TIME, (TELLING THE) TIME.]

of /ɒv/ (use the weak form: /əv/) (*preposition*)

- ► ***Of*** is the most common preposition in English.
- ► ***Of*** usually makes a link of meaning between two nouns or noun phrases: we will call them N_1 and N_2.
- ► ***Of*** has many different meanings: see 2–12 below for eleven different uses of ***of***.

1 Forms of nouns which follow ***of***

N_1	***of***	N_2

(a) If N_2 is a pronoun, it must normally be a possessive pronoun*.
(b) If N_2 refers to a particular person, it is usually a possessive noun, i.e. *noun + 's*.
(c) If N_2 refers to an unspecified person – or is not a person – it cannot be a possessive noun, i.e. it cannot have *'s*:

	N_1	***of***	N_2
(a)	*a book*	***of***	*mine* *
(b)	*a friend*	***of***	*Mozart('s)*
	a {movie / film}	***of***	*Paul McCartney('s)* *
	a guest	***of***	*my father('s)*
	the owner	***of***	*a Rolls-Royce*
(c)	*the Queen*	***of***	*Spain*
	the income	***of***	*an average teacher*
	the heart	***of***	*a lion*
	the colour	***of***	*a rose*

* See 13 below about exceptions to (a), and about the change of meaning if you omit the ***'s*** of *McCartney****'s***.

2 ***Of*** often means 'having', 'owning', possession

E.g.

N_1 ***of*** N_2		N_2 ***has*** N_1
the owner ***of*** *the car*	↔	*the car* ***has*** *an owner*
a friend ***of*** *Mozart's*	↔	Mozart ***has*** *a friend*

Here ***of*** is an alternative form for the possessive ***'s***:
N_1 ***of*** N_2 ↔ N_2 ***'s*** N_1

E.g. *the uniform* ***of*** a policeman ↔ *a policeman****'s*** *uniform*

[For further information, see POSSESSIVE 4.]

3 ***Of*** is used to link ***part*** to ***whole*** in:

N_1 ***of*** N_2
part

the top ***of*** *the hill*   *the roof* ***of*** *the house*   *the handle* ***of*** *a knife*
the end ***of*** *the week*   *the front page* ***of*** *a popular newspaper*

4 ***Of*** is used to link a ***member*** to its group in:

N_1 ***of*** N_2
member

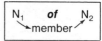

a Member ***of*** *Parliament*   *the last month* ***of*** *the year*
the youngest ***of*** *the three girls*

5 ***Of*** is very common in expressions of ***amount*** [see QUANTITY WORDS]:

N_1 ***of*** N_2
amount of

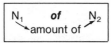

a lot of *noise / noises*   ***a large number of*** *people*   ***a pair of*** *trousers*   ***a litre of*** *oil*   ***thousands of*** *babies*   ***two tons of*** *coal*

5a N_1 is often a pronoun such as ***all, some, much*** [see INDEFINITE PRONOUN 2].

all of *the women*   ***a few of*** *those nuts*
much of *his advice*   ***none of*** *these animals*

6 ***Of*** is used after GROUP NOUNS like ***crowd, group, bunch***:

N_1 ***of*** N_2
(group)

a group of *students*   ***a range of*** *mountains*   ***a bunch of*** *flowers*
a flock of *sheep*

Here N_2 describes **members of the group**.

7 ***Of*** follows nouns referring to ***containers*** or ***units*** of something [See UNIT NOUN]:

N_1 ***of*** N_2
contains

a ***bowl of*** fruit   a ***bag of*** nails   a ***bottle of*** milk
a ***handful of*** coins

8 The relation between N_1 and N_2 can be like the relation between verb and object:

	N_1 ***of***	N_2
X . . .	*studies . . .* →	*history*
	verb	object

~ *the election* ***of*** *the President*
the study ***of*** *history*
the invention ***of*** *radio*
your kind offer ***of*** *help*

9 The relation between N_1 and N_2 can be like the relation between verb and subject:

N_1	***of***	N_2
roars ← . . .		*lion*
verb		subject

~ *the death* ***of*** *Alexander**
the roar ***of*** *a lion*
the growth ***of*** *industry*

* This is an exception to Rule 1(b) above.

10 The link between N_1 and N_2 can be like the link of the verb *be* [see LINKING VERB]:

N_1	***of***	N_2
exciting ←	***is*** ←	*The game*

~ *the weakness* ***of*** *the pound*
the excitement ***of*** *the game*
the difficulty ***of*** *learning English*

10a In the following examples, N_1 and N_2 refer to the same person or thing:

N_1	***of***	N_2
a city ←	***is*** ←	*Athens*

~ *the art* ***of*** *painting*
the city ***of*** *Athens*
the job ***of*** *being President*
the problem ***of*** *how to improve education*

11 ***Of*** can link N_1 to a quality expressed by N_2 <formal, written>:

N_1	***of***	N_2
woman →	*has* →	*charm*

~ *a man* ***of*** *courage*
a woman ***of*** *charm*
a building ***of*** *great beauty*

12 There are many other ways in which ***of*** can link two nouns.

E.g. *a game* ***of*** *football*
a difference ***of*** *age*
the people ***of*** *ancient China*
a ring ***of*** *pure gold*

13 After nouns such as *picture*, *drawing*, *film*, *movie*, ***of*** can be followed by ordinary personal pronouns like *him* and *me*.

E.g. *This is an old* ***photograph of me****.*
Joan does not like this ***painting of her****.* (= 'this painting representing her')

NOTE (i): *A painting* ***of*** *her* has a different meaning from *her painting*, or *a painting* ***of*** *hers*, which would usually mean 'The / a painting that belongs to her'.

NOTE (ii): Also, *a film / movie* ***of*** *Paul McCartney* (= 'about Paul McCartney') is different from *a film / movie* ***of*** *Paul McCartney****'s*** (= 'one made by him').

14 ***Of*** does not always come between two nouns. It also follows some adjectives and verbs.

E.g. *I am* ***afraid of*** *snakes.*
You must be ***tired of*** *watching television.*
The explorers ***died of*** *hunger and cold.* (***of*** = 'because of')

of-pronoun [See INDEFINITE PRONOUN 2.]

off /ɒf ‖ ɔf/ (*preposition or adverb*)

► As a word meaning place or movement, usually ***off*** means the opposite of ***on***:

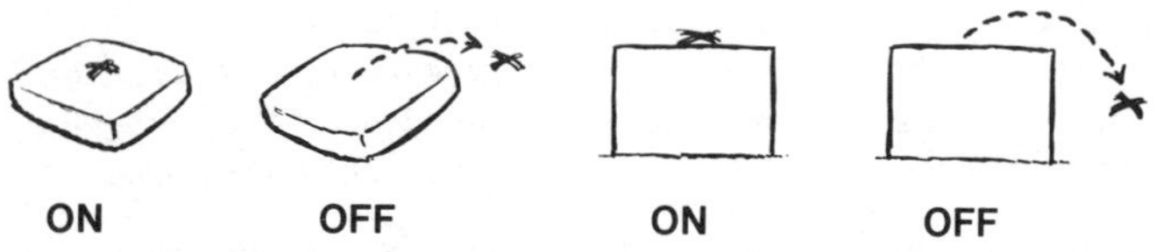

1 *He fell* ***off*** ** the stage.* (preposition)
He fell ***off***. (adverb)
I watched the airplane taking ***off***. *One minute it was taxiing* ***on*** *the runway. The next minute it was* ***off*** *the ground.*

* <U.S.> speakers sometimes use ***off of*** as a preposition, instead of ***off***.

2 ***Off*** is also the opposite of ***on*** in other meanings.

E.g.	***put on*** *your coat*	***take*** *it* ***off*** *again*
	switch on *the light*	***switch off*** *the light*

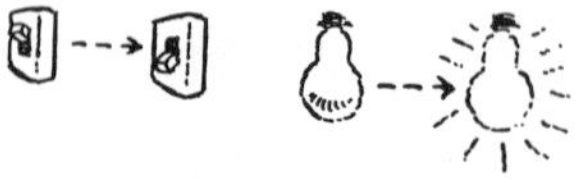

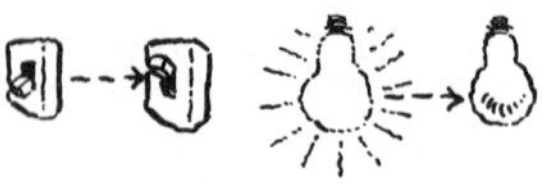

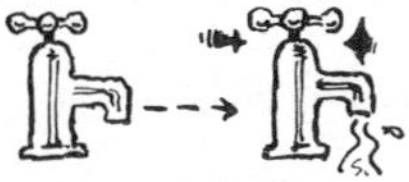

***turn on** the water*

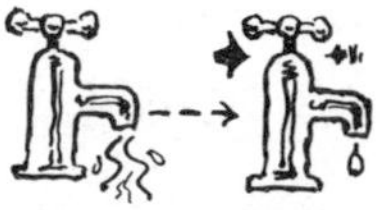

***turn off** the water*

[See PHRASAL VERB.]

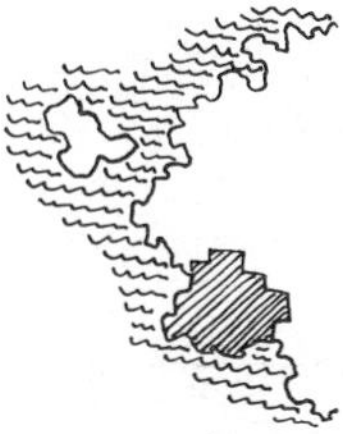

*The town is **on** the coast.*
*The island is (just) **off** the coast.*

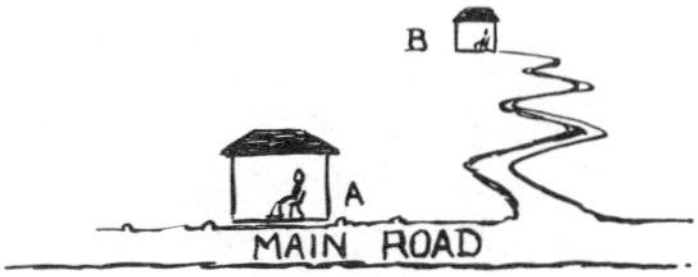

*A lives **on** the main road.*
*B lives (a mile) **off** the main road.*

*There's a 15% tax **on** furs.*
*But there's 20% **off** in the sale.*

*I'm taking a day **off*** (= away from work) *next week, so I'm staying **on** late* (= continuing work) *this week.*

3 ***Off*** can mean 'leaving a place' or 'starting a journey, a race,' etc.

E.g. *We're going* { ***off*** / *away* } *to the seaside for the summer.*

4 **Idioms**
There are some common PHRASAL VERBS with ***off***, such as *put **off*** ('postpone'), *lay **off**, come **off***.

offers, offering

► Some ways of making an ***offer*** are:

Type A. { *Shall I* / *Do you want me to* / *Would you like me to* } + Verb (. . .)?

Type B. { *Would you like* / *Do you want* } + Noun Phrase?

1 Type A

E.g. *Shall I. . .?* (***offering*** to do something – <mainly G.B.>)

E.g.

It's too heavy. I can't carry it.
Shall I carry it for you?

*Do you **want** me to buy the tickets?*
*Would you **like** me to phone the doctor?* <a little more polite and more formal>

2 Type B

These structures are used in ***offering*** a drink, etc.

E.g. <more polite> *Would you **like*** / *Do you **want*** } *a coffee?* { *Yes, please.* * / *No, thank you.* *

* This is how you should accept or refuse an ***offer***. If you say only 'Yes' or 'No', it's not very <polite>!

2a These structures are also used in ***offering*** a choice between two (or more) things [see OR 6b]:

{ *Would you like tea or coffee?* / *Tea or coffee?* } { *I'd like some coffee, please.* / *Coffee, please* }

3 Reporting *offers*

E.g. *He **offered** to help me.* [See VERB PATTERN 7.]
*She **offered** the visitor a cup of coffee.* [See VERB PATTERN 11.]
*She **offered** a meal to all the visitors.* [See VERB PATTERN 13.]

---

often /ˈɒf(t)ən/ (*adverb of* FREQUENCY)

Often means 'many times'. It usually goes in middle position [see ADVERB 3].

E.g. *'Do you **often** play football?'*
*'Yes, quite **often** – about once every two weeks.'*

[See FREQUENCY for details of word order.]

NOTE: The usual COMPARATIVE and SUPERLATIVE forms are ***more often*** and ***most often***. But ***oftener*** and ***oftenest*** are also occasionally used.

on /ɒn/ (*preposition or adverb*)

► ***On*** concerns PLACE, movement, means of travel, or TIME.

1 *On* for 'place'

1a ***On*** means 'in contact with a surface' or 'touching'.

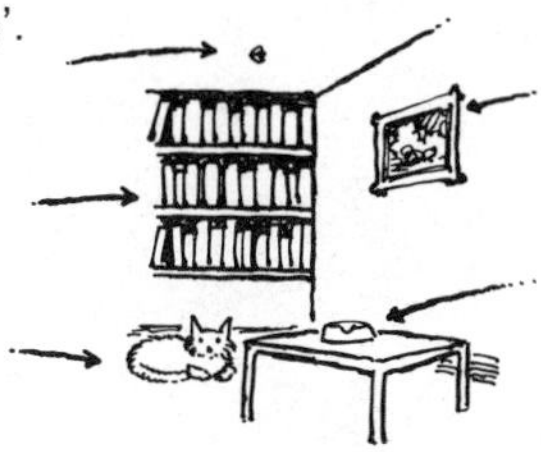

E.g. *There's a fly* ***on*** *the ceiling.*
The books are ***on*** *the shelves.*
The cat is sitting ***on*** *the floor.*
The picture is hanging ***on*** *the wall.*
The ashtray is ***on*** *the table.*

Notice that ***on*** frequently means 'on top of':

E.g. ***on*** *the table* ***on*** *the chair* etc.

Also: ***on*** *the sea,* ***on*** *land,* ***on*** *a ship,* ***on*** *my head, etc.*

1b ***On*** and ***onto*** are used for movement to a place (surface):

Where has the cat gone ?
First she jumped on(to) the table, then she jumped on(to) the window sill, and from there she landed on the grass.

NOTE: ***On*** is the opposite of ***off*** when used for movement [see OFF].

1c We also use ***on*** for a line.

E.g. (i) *A is **on** the line B–C*

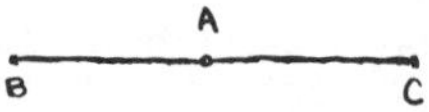

(ii) *Ecuador is **on** the equator.*

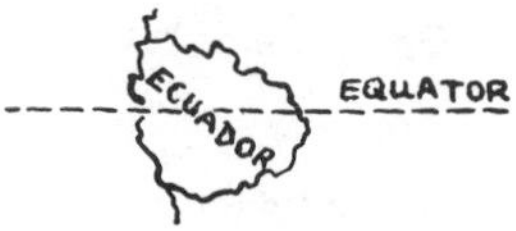

(iii) *Cairo is **on** the River Nile.*

(iv) *Lagos is **on** the coast.*

1d When giving directions, we say ***on*** *this side,* ***on*** *that side,* ***on*** *the left,* ***on*** *the right*, etc.

2 ***On*** **for 'means of travel'**
We use ***on*** for means of travel [see TRANSPORT, MEANS OF].

E.g. *I go to work **on** the bus*.

3 ***On*** **for 'time'**
We use ***on*** for referring to days [see TIME 4].

E.g. ***On*** *Sunday we stayed at home.*

4 **Other meanings of *on***

4a *What's **on**?* <informal> This question asks 'What's happening?' 'What interesting things are going on?' (Here, ***on*** is an adverb.)

E.g. ***What's on*** *at the movies?* <U.S.> / *cinema?* <G.B.>
What's on *at the theatre?*

4b In phrases like ***on*** *(the) television* and ***on*** *the radio*, ***on*** means 'through the medium of'.

E.g. *I heard it **on the radio**.*
*Be quiet! I'm (talking) **on the phone***.
*Would you mind putting **a tape on**?*
*'Are you going to watch anything on T.V.?' 'No, there's **nothing on**.'*
(But *'The T.V. is **on**'* means *'The T.V. is **switched on**'* [see OFF 2].)

4c ***On*** means 'about', 'on the subject of':

E.g. *The teacher gave us a* {*talk* / *lesson* / *test* / *a lecture*} **on** {*French.* / *history.* / *biology.* / *keeping fit.*}

I've been {*writing* / *reading*} {*a book* / *an essay*} **on** {*Indian cookery.* / *Greek architecture.*}

4d In <rather formal> English, ***on*** + Verb-***ing*** means 'when or as soon as something happens / happened'.

E.g. ***On reaching*** *the end of negotiations, the ministers agreed to send more aid.*

On can also precede a NOUN PHRASE with this meaning.

E.g. ***On his retirement****, my father went to live in the country.*
The wounded soldier was dead ***on arrival at the hospital****.*

5 **Idioms**

5a ***On*** is the first word of many idioms. Some, like ***on*** *business* are prepositional phrases. Some, like ***on*** *behalf of*, are complex prepositions [see PREPOSITION 2a]. Some, like ***on*** *condition that*, are conjunctions.

E.g. ***on holiday / vacation / business:*** *'Did you go to Italy* ***on*** {***vacation*** <U.S.>?' / ***holiday*** <G.B.>?'} *'No, I went* ***on business****.'*
on account of: [see REASON AND CAUSE]
on behalf of: *I am writing this letter* ***on behalf of*** *my husband, who is very ill.*
on condition that: [see CONDITIONAL CAUSE]
on earth: *What* ***on earth*** *are you doing?* [see WH-WORDS 2b Note.]
on purpose: *Did they hurt you accidentally or* ***on purpose****?*
on sale: *The new model of our sports car will be* ***on sale*** *next week.*
on to, onto: [see ON 1b]
on top of: (= 'on the top of') *Don't leave your coffee* ***on top of*** *the television set!*

5b ***On*** also follows some verbs:

{***depend on*** / ***rely on***} are PREPOSITIONAL VERBS.

E.g. *You can* {***depend*** / ***rely***} ***on*** *him: he's very honest.*

Carry on, come on, go on are PHRASAL VERBS.

E.g. *Please* ***carry on*** (= 'continue') *with your work.*

once /wʌns/ (*adverb*)

► ***Once*** has two uses:
1 as an adverb of frequency (= 'on one occasion')
2 as an adverb of time (= 'at some time in the past')

1 ***Once* = 'on one occasion'** is generally in end position

E.g. *'How many times have you visited Cairo?'*
'I've been there { ***(only) once****.'* / *twice.'* / *three times.'* }

Other expressions of frequency containing ***once***:

once *a day,* ***once*** *a week,* ***once*** *a month,* ***once*** *a year.*

2 ***Once* = 'at some time in the past'** is generally in front or middle position. It goes before a PAST TENSE verb.

E.g. ***Once we stayed*** *in a little cottage by the sea.*
I once saw *a girl save a man from drowning.*

3 **Idioms**
Look up the following adverbial idioms in a dictionary:

at ***once*** *for* ***once*** ***once*** *again* ***once*** *more* ***once*** *or twice*
once *upon a time*

one There are three different words spelled ***one***:

► 1 ***one*** /wʌn/ is the cardinal NUMBER '1'.
► 2 ***one*** /wʌn/, ***ones*** /wʌnz/ is an INDEFINITE PRONOUN.
► 3 ***one*** /wʌn/, ***one's*** /wʌnz/, ***oneself*** /wʌnˈself/ is a PERSONAL PRONOUN.

1 **The number *one***

1a Like other numbers, ***one*** can occur (i) in front of a noun or (ii) alone, as a subject, object, etc.

E.g. *'Would you like* ***one lump*** *of sugar or* ***two*** *in your coffee?'* ***'One*** *is enough, thanks.'*

1b ***One*** as a number often contrasts with ANOTHER or the OTHER [see the idiom ***one another*** in 4 below].

E.g. *A king had two sons:* ***one*** *(son) was thin, and the* ***other*** *(son) was fat.*

2 The indefinite pronoun *one*

2a This pronoun has a plural: ***ones***.

E.g.

Notice that ***one*** 'replaces' a singular countable noun that has been mentioned, and ***ones*** 'replaces' a plural noun.

E.g. *'I'm having a drink. Would you like* ***one****?'* 'Yes, just a small* ***one****, please.' 'I thought you preferred large* ***ones****!'*

* Notice we don't use ***a*** directly in front of ***one***.

E.g. *We need a taxi. Would you please order* {*a taxi* / ~~*a*~~ ***one***} *for us?*

3 The personal pronoun *one* <rather formal>

Here ***one*** is a pronoun of general meaning ('people in general'). In <less formal> English, we use ***you*** [see YOU 2] instead.

The personal pronoun ***one*** has the possessive form ***one's*** and the reflexive form ***oneself*** [see SELF / SELVES].

E.g. *These days,* ***one*** *has to be careful with* ***one's*** *money.* *
How does ***one*** *unlock this door?*
It's sometimes a good idea to see ***oneself*** *through the eyes of* ***one's*** *worst enemy!*

* Sometimes in <U.S.> ***one*** / ***one's*** / ***oneself*** is replaced by ***he*** / ***him*** / ***his*** / ***himself*** to avoid repetition.
E.g. *These days,* ***one*** *has to be careful with* ***his*** *money.*

4 Idiom

One another is a double pronoun, with the same meaning as ***each other*** [see EACH 4].

E.g. *'I didn't know that Max, Richard and Jan were friends.' 'Oh, yes, they've known* ***one another*** *for years'.*

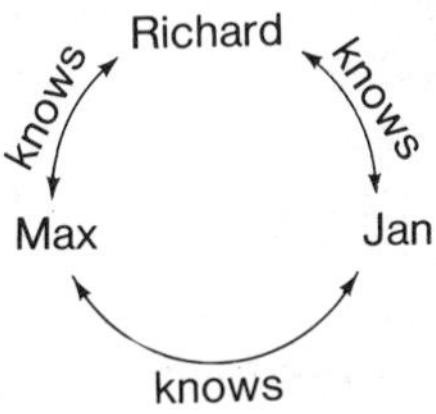

ones, oneself [See ONE 2, 3.]

only /ˈəʊnlɪ/ (*adverb, conjunction or adjective*)

► ***Only*** is a common adverb, and can appear in many different positions in a sentence.

► As an adjective, ***only*** usually goes after ***the*** or a possessive: *the only person, his only close friend*.

1 *Only* as a 'limiting' adverb means 'no $\left\{\begin{matrix}\text{more}\\\text{other}\end{matrix}\right\}$ than'

1a In <speech>, ***only*** frequently goes in middle position [see ADVERB 3].

E.g. *I've **only** visited France once.* ('no more than once')
*We've **only** spoken to the secretary.* ('to no one other than the secretary')

1b But in <writing> it is best to put ***only*** just before the phrase it applies to. Instead of the examples above, we prefer:

*I have visited France **only** once.*
*We have spoken **only** to the secretary.*

This is because in <writing> we cannot use main stress. In <speech> we can give a sentence with ***only*** a different meaning if we move the main stress from one place to another. This is an example of a sentence with 2 different meanings of ***only***:

*Maurice **only** ˈpeeled the potatoes.* (= 'He didn't do anything else to the potatoes, e.g. cook them.')
*Maurice **only** peeled the ˈpotatoes.* (= 'He didn't peel the carrots, onions, etc.') (Or: 'He didn't do anything else, e.g. cook the dinner.')

1c ***Only*** often goes before a noun phrase, especially a noun phrase beginning with a QUANTITY word or a NUMBER.

E.g. (i) *'They pay him **only £100** per month.' 'Yes, but he works **only a few** hours a week.'*

The meaning of ***only*** in (i) above is 'no more than . . .'. In example (ii) the meaning is 'no one other than . . .':

(ii) *'**Only** the manager is allowed to sign this agreement.' 'Yes, and **only** a lawyer can understand it!'*

1d Since ***only*** is a negative adverb, it can cause inversion [see INVERSION 5] when it is placed before an adverbial at the front of the sentence [see NEGATIVE WORDS AND SENTENCES 6]:

E.g. ***Only*** *in a few Western countries* ***does*** *religion* ***remain*** *an important power in politics.* <formal>
Only *recently* ***has*** *it* ***become*** *clear that both sides are ready for peace.* <formal>

2 ***Only*** **as a conjunction means 'but', 'except that'**
It is <informal> and expresses a CONTRAST between what has been said and what is going to be said.

E.g. *I'd like to stay and help you,* ***only*** *I've promised to be home at 5 o'clock.* (= 'but, except that')

3 ***Only*** **as an adjective means 'there is no other'**, and normally comes between *the* or a possessive and a noun.

E.g. (i) ***The only work*** *I can offer you is looking after the pigs.* (only = 'sole'; i.e. 'I can't offer you any other kind of work'.)
(ii) ***Her only mistake*** *was being too generous.*

4 **Idiom**
[See the separate entry for IF ONLY.]

---

onto (*preposition*) (Also spelt ***on to***) [See ON 1b.]

---

operator

- The first AUXILIARY VERB in a finite verb phrase is called the ***operator***. [See FINITE, VERB PHRASE.]
- Also, the finite verb BE is an ***operator***, even when it is a MAIN VERB.
- The ***operator*** is a helpful idea for explaining how we form negatives, questions, and other patterns in English.

opposite /ˈɒpəzɪt/ (*preposition or adjective or noun*)

► ***Opposite*** means 'facing', 'on the other side of'.

1 **Preposition**

E.g. *My house is **opposite** the post office.* (= 'on the other side of the street')

2 **Adjective**

E.g. *At the dinner table, Cathy sat next to John, and talked to Mary, (who sat) **opposite**.*
*My wife and I have **opposite** views on divorce.* (i.e. she agrees with divorce, but I don't)

3 **Noun**

E.g. *We asked Pamela to arrive early, but she did just the **opposite**.* (i.e. 'She arrived late'.)

or /ɔːʳ/ (weak form: /əʳ/) (*coordinating conjunction*)

► ***Or*** expresses a choice between alternatives.
When we say *X* **or** *Y*, we mean *one of X and Y, but not both*.

E.g. *You can sit in this chair **or** in that chair. Which would you prefer?*

1 **We can link, (i) words, (ii) phrases, or (iii) clauses with *or*.**

E.g. (i) *'When is Emma's birthday?' 'It's in **July or August** – I'm not sure which.'*
(ii) *Why don't we **go swimming or sit on the beach**? It's a very nice day.*
(iii) Travel Agent: *We could arrange a whole tour, **or** we could book the flight and the hotel for you, **or** we could just book the flight. The choice is yours.*

2 ***Or* linking more than two elements**
Notice from example (iii) above that we can link three or more elements with ***or***. We usually omit ***or***, except between the last two elements.

E.g. *'You can buy one of these handbags in **black, brown, blue, or dark green**.' 'I'll take the blue one, please.'*

3 ***Or (else)* = 'otherwise'** [see ELSE 2]
In <informal> style, we can even use ***or*** to link two sentences.

E.g. *We must act quickly and prevent violence on the streets.* ***Or (else)*** *the situation will become very dangerous.*

Or (+ else) here means 'otherwise'. It means we should choose the first alternative rather than the other!

4 ***Not . . . or* instead of *and***
We often use ***or*** instead of AND after a negative.

E.g. *I don't want anything to eat* ***or*** *drink.* (= I don't want anything to eat, and I don't want anything to drink.)

5 ***Or* in threats**
When ***or*** goes after an IMPERATIVE clause, it has a conditional meaning [see CONDITIONAL CLAUSE].

E.g. *Don't telephone me again –* ***or*** *I'll report you to the police.* (. . . if you telephone, I'll . . .)
Don't make a move, ***or*** *I'll shoot.* (If you move, I'll shoot.)

6 ***Or* in questions**
In QUESTIONS, ***or*** has two meanings:

6a ***Or*** in yes-no questions is like ***or*** in statements (e.g. as in 1–2 above).

E.g. *'Would you like something to eat* **or** *drink?' 'Yes – thanks, I'd like a glass of milk.'*

This is a YES-NO QUESTION with a rising tone [see INTONATION].

6b ***Or*** in alternative questions has a falling tone at the end.

E.g. *'Would you like coffee* **or** *tea?' 'Coffee, please.'*

This type of question invites you to choose one of two alternatives. There may also be three or more alternatives, with a rising tone on all alternatives except the last, which has a falling tone.

E.g. *'Is she married, single,* **or** *divorced?' 'Married.'*
'How will you get home? By bus, by bicycle, **or** *on foot?' 'On foot.'*

6c There is a kind of alternative question which has nearly the same meaning as a yes-no question. It offers a second, negative alternative ***or not***.

E.g. (I) *Are you going to resign* ***or not****?*
(II) *Are you* ***or*** *are you* ***not*** *going to resign?*
(I) *Should I lock the door* ***or not****?*
(II) *Should I* ***or*** *should I* ***not*** *lock the door?*

These questions (especially type (I)) can be <impolite> because they insist on an answer.

7 **Indirect alternative questions: *whether . . . or***
Like yes-no questions, these are introduced by ***whether***, but they also have ***or***.

E.g. *I don't know **whether** it's made of gold **or** of silver.*

[See WHETHER for further examples and discussion.]

8 ***Or* sometimes joins two equivalent names for the same thing**

E.g. *The **Soviet Union (or the U.S.S.R.**, as it is often called) is the largest country in the world.*

9 ***Either . . . or . . .* are sometimes used to emphasise the two alternatives.**
[See DOUBLE CONJUNCTION 3.]

10 **You can use *or* when you are not interested in exact numbers**

E.g. *He's **thirty or forty** years old.* (= 'Somewhere around 30–40')
*I'm asking **one or two** people to dinner.* (= 'a few')

11 **Idioms**
Special idioms are ***or more*** and ***or so***.

E.g. *a hundred **or more*** = 'about a hundred or more than a hundred'
*a hundred **or so*** = 'about a hundred'.

[See ELSE, OR 3 for ***or else***; see DOUBLE CONJUNCTION for ***either . . . or***.]

---

giving **orders** [See IMPERATIVE, INDIRECT COMMAND, REQUESTS, SUGGESTIONS]

---

ordinals (including NEXT and LAST)

- ***Ordinals*** are the numbers we use when we put things in order, e.g. *1st, 5th, 10th,* etc.
- How to form ***ordinals***: this is explained (with exceptions) in NUMBERS 1 and 2.

1 ***Next* and *last* as ordinals**
We call ***next*** and ***last*** ordinals because they refer to position in a sequence, and because they are just like ordinals in grammar.

2 How ordinals function in sentences

2a They are like adjectives after ***the***, ***my***, etc.

E.g. *her* {***first*** / ***next*** / ***last***} *novel* *the* {***second*** / ***next*** / ***last***} *town we visited*

Or after the verb ***be***.

E.g. *The guests have all arrived. Mr and Mrs Green were (the)* ***first*** *to arrive, and Dr Brown was (the)* ***last***.

(We can omit ***the*** before the ordinal word.)

2b They behave like pronouns (*of*-pronouns) when followed by *of*.

E.g. *Mr. and Mrs. Garrido were the* ***first of*** *the guests to arrive. And they were the* ***last (of*** *the guests) to leave.*

2c They behave like adverbs of time.

E.g. *'Who won the race?' 'Tim came* ***first***, *John came* ***second***, *and Bill came* ***third***. *I finished next to* ***last***.*'*

(Notice we cannot use *the* here.)

2d They also behave like linking adverbs. We use them when we want to present a list of points, or a series of events.

E.g. *'Why did the President's party lose the election?'* '***First****(ly), they had led the country into a financial crisis.* ***Second****(ly), they had caused a shortage of food and other consumer goods.* ***Third****(ly), their leaders were unpopular.* ***Fourth****(ly), their TV broadcasts were not successful.* ***Last****(ly), * the weather was so bad that their supporters stayed at home!*

We often prefer to use an adverb ending in ***-ly*** as a linking adverb, as the above example shows.

* It is better to use ***lastly*** or ***finally*** as linking adverbs, rather than ***last***.

NOTE: We also use ***last*** and ***next*** in referring to periods of time, meaning 'the one before now' and 'the one after now'. [See TIME 4c, 5.]

---

other

/ˈʌðə^{r}/ (*adjective or indefinite pronoun*) (The pronoun has the plural form ***others***.)

► ***Other*** means '(one(s)) apart from the one(s) already mentioned.'

1 *Other* as adjective

1a ***Other*** as an adjective goes before a noun.

E.g. *Peter Smith is younger than the **other** teachers in his school.* (i.e. Peter is the school's youngest teacher.)
*My sister Lucy is very generous: she's always giving her things away to **other** people.*

1b ***Other*** as an adjective also goes before numbers and the pronoun *one*:

Maybe he's a good horse,
but I like the other one better.
He's hurt his right foreleg, but the other three legs are fine.

2 ***Other, others* as a pronoun**
As a pronoun ***other*** is always singular, and ***others*** is always plural.

E.g. *She carried a case in one hand and an umbrella in the **other**.*
*I enjoyed her first novel so much, that I'm going to read all the **others**.* (= 'other novels')

3 **Idioms**
Each other [See EACH 4], ***(the) one . . . the other*** [See ONE 1b].
On the one hand . . . on the other (hand) are linking adverbs presenting opposite points of view.

E.g. ***On the one hand**, the law must be obeyed. **On the other (hand)**, we must show sympathy for those whose sufferings have caused them to break the law.*

The other end (of), the other side (of): In these phrases **other** means 'opposite'.

E.g. *I saw him on the **other** side of the road.*

Other than (preposition) means 'except, apart from':

E.g. *I like all dairy products **other than** yoghurt.*

otherwise /ˈʌðəʳwaɪz/ (*linking adverb*)

1 ***Otherwise*** = 'apart from this', 'if we disregard this'.

E.g. *The weather was terrible, but {**otherwise** / apart from that} we had a good time.*

2 ***Otherwise*** = 'if this does not happen'.

E.g. *I should wear an overcoat if I were you, {**otherwise** / if you don't} you'll catch a cold.*

ought to /ˈɔːt tuː/ (weak form /ˈɔːtə/) (*modal auxiliary*)

- ***Ought to*** is a modal auxiliary with the same meanings as ***should***. [For more information on *ought to*, see SHOULD AND OUGHT TO 1, 2 below.]
- ***Ought to*** is <not common> and is especially rare in <U.S.>. We can always use ***should*** instead of ***ought to***.
- ***Ought to*** has a negative form ***ought not to*** or ***oughtn't to*** /ˈɔːtnt tuː/ (weak form /ˈɔːtntə/).
- ***Ought to*** never changes its form or adds an -***s***.
- Unlike most other modal auxiliaries, ***ought to*** has an infinitive marker ***to***.

1 **Meanings of *ought to*** [see SHOULD AND OUGHT TO 3]

E.g. *You **ought to** clean your teeth before you go to bed.* (= It's a good thing to do this.)
*It's June: the roses **ought to** be in flower by now.* (= It's reasonable to assume this.)

2 Negative: *You **oughtn't to** smoke so much!*
Question: <not common> ***Ought (n't)** we **to go** home soon?*

NOTE (i): In 'shortened' sentences, people sometimes omit ***to***.
E.g. *He doesn't pay his staff as much as he **ought** (to).*
('. . . as much as he ought to pay them.')
They also omit the ***to*** in TAG QUESTIONS.
E.g. *She **ought to** see a doctor, oughtn't she?*

NOTE (ii): The only past time form is {***ought to*** / ***oughtn't to***} + *have* + past participle.
E.g. *You **ought to** have gone to the dentist earlier.*

---

our, ours /aʊə^{r}/, /aʊə^{r}z/ (*1st person plural possessives*). They are related to ***we*** and ***us***. [See POSSESSIVE DETERMINER AND POSSESSIVE PRONOUN.]

---

ourselves /aʊə^{r}ˈselvz/ (*1st person plural reflexive pronoun*). [See -SELF, -SELVES.]

---

out /aʊt/ (*adverb of place or motion*) [see also OUT OF]

1 ***Out*** is the opposite of ***in*** (adverb), especially expressing motion or (sometimes) position. [See IN, MOTION, PLACE 3a Note (i).]

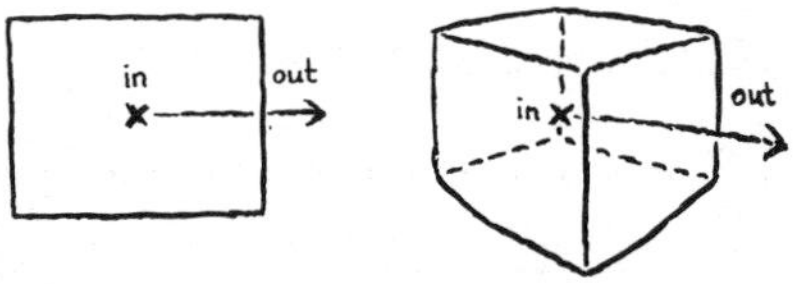

E.g. *He put his hand in(to) his pocket, and pulled **out** a sharp knife.*
*This room contains radioactive material. Keep **out**!*
*'Is Jill at home?' 'No, sorry, she's **out**.'*

2 ***Out*** has many abstract meanings. E.g. *to be **out*** means 'to be no longer taking part in a game'.

E.g. *The first player **to go out** loses the game.*

3 ***Out*** appears in many PHRASAL VERBS:

E.g. *look **out*** ('be careful')
*try (something) **out*** ('test')
*find (something) **out*** ('discover')

---

out of /ˈaʊtəv/ (*preposition*) [see MOTION, PLACE 2 Note (ii).]

Out of is the preposition matching OUT. It is always followed by a NOUN PHRASE.

E.g. *She took some money **out of** her purse.*
*John's mother missed him when he was **out of** the country.*

[Compare INTO.]

---

over and **under** /ˈəʊvə^{r}/, /ˈʌndə^{r}/ (*prepositions or adverbs*)

► ***Over*** and ***under*** are opposites. (***Underneath*** is sometimes used instead of ***under***.)

1 *Over* and *under* are prepositions connected with MOTION **and** PLACE.

1a ***Over*** and ***under*** with verbs of motion:

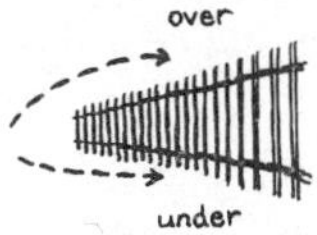

E.g. (i) *The dog **jumped over** the fence. The dog **crawled under** the fence.*

(ii) *I **ran over** a bridge. The boat was **going under** the bridge.*

1b ***Over*** and ***under*** when there is no movement:
(These sentences usually have the verb ***be*** in them.)

E.g. (i) *There **is** a picture of my mother **over** my bed. **Under** my bed **is** a pot.*

(ii) *You can see the moon **over** the trees. There **are** some children **under** the trees.*

1c ***Over*** means 'across' in some cases:

E.g. *We often walk **over** the fields.*
*My neighbour **over** the road has a large house.*

1d ***Over*** sometimes means 'covering', 'everywhere on/in', especially in the phrase ***all over***: *

E.g. This town is so busy: there are people and cars ***all over** the place.*

*That child is always running **over** the floor with muddy feet.*

* ***All over the world*** and ***all over the country*** are common phrases.

1e Other meanings of ***over*** and ***under*** as prepositions:
(I) ***Over*** in time phrases means 'during'.

E.g. { *We stayed with my aunt* / *I'll be seeing you again* } { ***over** the weekend.* / ***over** the New Year.* }

There have been a lot of industrial problems
{ ***over** the years.*
***over** the last century.* }

(II) When we talk of the status or position of people, ***over*** and ***under*** mean 'superior' and 'inferior'.

E.g. *This ship is **under** the command of Captain Peabody.*
*I don't like working with a younger man **over** me.* (i.e. a younger boss)

2 *Over* and *under* as adverbs of degree

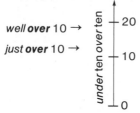

*well **over*** 10 →

*just **over*** 10 →

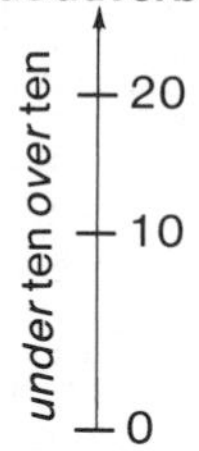

Over and ***under*** are adverbs of DEGREE meaning 'more than' and 'less than' on a scale.

E.g. *He weighs **over** 200 pounds.*
*I paid **under** £10 for this camera.*
*We were driving at a speed of **over** a hundred kilometres per hour.*

She was {***just*** / ***well***} {***over*** / ***under***} *twenty when she became world champion.*
(*just* = 'a little'; *well* = 'a lot')

3 *Over* is a prepositional adverb with various uses

3a Movement:

E.g. *I hurt my knee when I fell **over**.*

{ *This poor old lady has been knocked **over** by a cyclist.*
{ *The cyclist knocked **over** this poor old lady.*

3b Place:
Over means 'a small distance away' in phrases like ***over here*** and ***over there***.

E.g.

3c Time:
Over means 'past' or 'finished' after the verb *be*.

E.g. *It's Monday: the weekend* ***is over****.*
That bell means that the class ***is over****.*
When the war ***was over****, Floyd returned to his job as an electrician.*

NOTE: ***Under*** is occasionally a prepositional adverb.
E.g. *I'm a very poor swimmer. I can keep my head above water for a while, but I soon go* ***under****.*

4 **Idioms**
Over is common in phrasal and prepositional verbs.

E.g. *run* ***over****: The car* ***ran over*** *a rabbit.*
get ***over****:* = 'recover from': *It took her a long time to* ***get over*** *her illness.*

---

owing to /ˈəʊɪŋ tʊ/tə/ (*preposition*) [See REASON AND CAUSE 2.]

---

paragraphs

- ► A piece of writing is usually divided into ***paragraphs***.
- ► Each ***paragraph*** contains one or more sentences.
- ► The ***paragraph*** is about a topic.
- ► Anything in writing has a theme. Each ***paragraph*** should be about a topic related to the theme.

1 **Example**
Look at the description (on the left below) of the three ***paragraphs*** (on the right below). (The arrows show connections between sentences in a ***paragraph***.)

[Theme: ***communications satellites***]

paragraph 1 Topic: *Satellites*

1st sentence: *defines satellites.*	1. ***Satellites*** *are spacecraft that circle the earth in a carefully chosen orbit.*
2nd sentence: *communications satellites.*	2. ***Communications satellites*** *are equipped to receive signals from one ground station and then relay them to another.*
3rd sentence: *added information about communication satellites.*	3. *They can relay many television programmes and telephone calls at once.*

paragraph 2 Topic: *Advantages of satellites*

1st sentence: *advantage of satellites over aerials.*	1. *The great advantage of a satellite over an ordinary transmitting aerial (antenna) is that it can reach a very much wider area.*
2nd sentence: *added information about aerials.*	2. *An aerial is only a few hundred metres tall.*
3rd sentence: *added information about satellites.*	3. *But a satellite can be positioned thousands of kilometres up.*
4th sentence: *the same*	4. *A satellite above the Atlantic can carry signals from Europe to the Americas.*

paragraph 3 Topic: *Orbits*

1st sentence: *orbit of satellites.*	1. *The largest satellites are placed in an orbit at about 35,900 kilometres above the earth.*
2nd sentence: *added information about orbit.*	2. *At this height they orbit in the same time that the earth takes to rotate.*
3rd sentence: *satellite's appearance.*	3. *In other words, they appear to be stationary in the sky.*

[Source: Leonard Sealey (ed.) *Children's Encyclopaedia*. Macmillan (2nd ed.) Vol. II, p. 575.]

2 **How to write *paragraphs***

If you are beginning to write ***paragraphs***, this will help you:

1st sentence:	*Introduce the topic.*
Middle sentences:	*Explain, add supporting information, give examples, etc.*
Last sentence:	*Try to make a summary or some other kind of conclusion, and point the way to the next paragraph.*

---

pardon, sorry and excuse me

/ˈpɑːʳdən/, /ˈsɒrɪ/, /əkˈskjuːz mɪ/ are <polite> expressions we use in various situations.

---

1 When you do something wrong or impolite, e.g. pushing in front of someone, treading on someone's toe, you say ***sorry***.

[See also APOLOGIES.]

2 When you have to do something slightly impolite, e.g. interrupting a talk, sneezing, passing through a group of people, you can say ***excuse me***.

E.g.

(a)

(b)

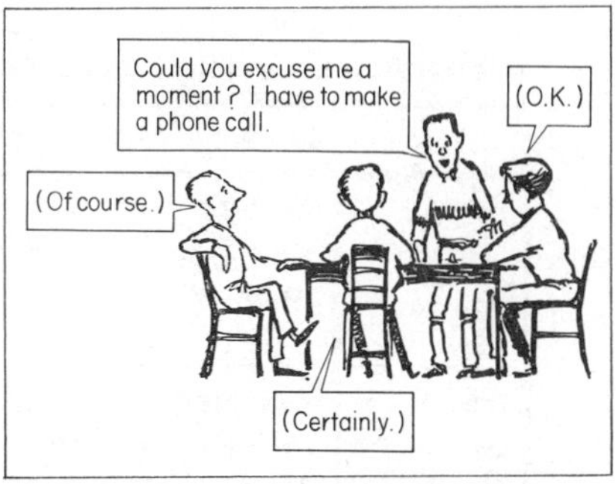

3 When you can't hear what someone is saying, and you want them to repeat it, you can say ***Sorry? / Excuse me?*** <U.S.>, or ***(I beg your) pardon? / Pardon me?*** <U.S.>.

participle [See also PARTICIPLE CLAUSE]

1 This is the term we often use for two forms of the English verb:

(A) The ***-ing*** participle (or ***-ing*** form) e.g. *work**ing***, *los**ing*** (sometimes called a 'present participle')
(B) The PAST PARTICIPLE e.g. ***worked***, ***lost****

* (Note irregular forms in the list of IRREGULAR VERBS at the back of the book.)

These are nonfinite forms of the verb [see REGULAR VERB, NONFINITE VERB].

2 Many adjectives have the same form as participles. Compare:

	Participle	Adjective
-ing form	*His mother is **working** in a factory.*	*a **working** * mother* *a **boring** * lecture*
past participle	*I have **lost** my purse.* *I was **bored** by the lecture.*	*a **lost** ** purse* *the **bored** ** students*

[For further discussion see -ING FORM, PAST PARTICIPLE.]

* The ***-ing*** form is an active adjective: it says what the noun 'is doing' or 'is feeling'.
** The ***-ed*** form is a passive adjective: it says what 'happens to' the noun.

participle clause [See -ING CLAUSE, PAST PARTICIPLE.]

1 A participle clause is a subordinate clause in which the ***-ing*** participle or the past participle is the main word. Such clauses are found particularly in <written> English [see NONFINITE CLAUSE 4].

2 **The participle normally begins the clause.**

	adverbial participle clause	relative participle clause
-ing clause	***Being*** *a woman of firm views, Margaret decided to resign.*	*The train* ***arriving*** *at Platform 3 is the 14.30 for Glasgow Central.*
past participle clause	***Accused*** *of dishonesty by the media, the Minister decided to resign.*	*The police are looking for a man* ***known*** *as 'The Grey Wolf.'*

2a Adverbial participle clauses:
Adverbial participle clauses are similar to clauses of TIME or REASON. Compare the {bracketed} clauses in each of the following examples.

E.g. {***Being*** *a woman of firm views,* / *Since she was a woman of firm views,*} *Margaret decided to resign.*

{***Accused*** *of dishonesty by the media,* / *After he had been accused of dishonesty by the media,*} *the Minister decided to resign.*

2b Clauses beginning with these following conjunctions can be formed with participles and without a subject:

E.g. ***if, unless*** [see CONDITIONAL CLAUSE]
(al)though, while, [see CONTRAST]
where, wherever, [see PLACE]
whether [see CONDITIONAL CLAUSE + CONTRAST]
when, whenever, before, after, while, once, until [see TIME]

The pattern is:

Conjunction +	Participle +	Rest of Clause
After	***being***	*accused of dishonesty . . .*
Before	***meeting***	*the President . . .*
While	***working***	*in a factory . . .*
If	***bought***	*from a recognized dealer . . .*
Once	***taken***	

E.g. ***After being** accused of dishonesty, he resigned.*
***Before meeting** the President, the press were warned not to ask awkward questions.*
***Once taken**, the drug has a deadly effect.*

2c Relative participle clauses:
Relative participle clauses give more information about a noun. The relative pronoun + *be* are omitted.

E.g. ***the train** (~~which is~~) **arriving at** Platform 3 . . .*
***a man** (~~who is~~) **known as** 'The Grey Wolf' . . .*

2d On the whole, it is better not to use participle clauses in <speech>: they are too <formal>. But in <writing> they can be useful, because they allow us to say the same thing as a finite subordinate clause, but with fewer words.

2e Sometimes a participle clause has an expressed subject:

E.g. *Our company's performance this year has been slightly disappointing. **That said**, we can look forward to improved results next summer.* (= 'Once that has been said, . . .')

parts and wholes [See WHOLE, FRACTIONS.]

passive [See VERB PHRASE]

► The ***passive*** form of the verb phrase contains this pattern:

be + past participle, e.g. { ***is used*** / ***was wanted*** / ***can be seen*** }

[See the list of IRREGULAR VERBS at the end of the book for irregular past participle forms.]

► The opposite of ***passive*** is ***active***.

1 **What is the passive?**
In most clauses, the subject refers to the 'doer', or 'actor' of the action of the verb.

E.g. ***Active***:

Subject

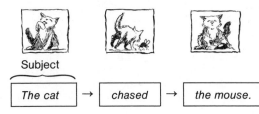

The cat → *chased* → *the mouse.*

But the passive form allows us to put someone or something that is not the actor first, in the position of subject.

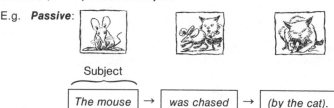

E.g. ***Passive***:

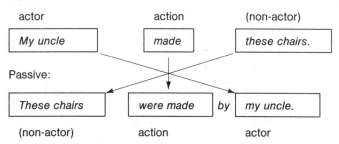

Subject: *The mouse* → *was chased* → *(by the cat).*

1a Active:

actor	action	(non-actor)
My uncle	*made*	*these chairs.*

Passive:

(non-actor)	action		actor
These chairs	*were made*	by	*my uncle.*

2 **Main forms of the passive verb phrase**
(Verb patterns show ***ask*** (regular verb) and ***eat*** (irregular verb).)

2a Present Simple:

	Active		Passive
E.g.	*asks* *eat*	→	*is asked* *are eaten*

E.g. (active) *My wife* ***calls me*** *'darling'.*
(passive) ***I am called*** *'darling' (by my wife).*

2b Past Simple:

asked *ate*	→	*was asked* *were eaten*

E.g. (active) *The police* ***brought*** *the child home.*
(passive) *The child* ***was brought*** *home (by the police).*

2c Modal pattern:

will ask *could eat*	→	*will be asked* *could be eaten*

E.g. (active) *Everyone* ***can enjoy*** *this type of music.*
(passive) *This type of music* ***can be enjoyed*** *(by everyone).*

2d Present Progressive:

is asking / *are eating*	→	*is being asked* / *are being eaten*

E.g. (active) *The Council* ***is rebuilding*** *the city hall.*
(passive) *The city hall* ***is being rebuilt*** *(by the Council).*

2e Past Progressive:

was asking / *were eating*	→	*was being asked* / *were being eaten*

E.g. (active) *My parents* ***were discussing*** *my future.*
(passive) *My future* ***was being discussed*** *(by my parents).*

2f Present Perfect:

has asked / *have eaten*	→	*has been asked* / *have been eaten*

E.g. (active) *The students* ***have invited*** *us to a dance.*
(passive) *We* ***have been invited*** *to a dance (by the students).*

2g Past Perfect:

had asked / *had eaten*	→	*had been asked* / *had been eaten*

E.g. (active) *He claimed that the club* ***had wasted*** *a lot of money.*
(passive) *He claimed that a lot of money* ***had been wasted*** *(by the club).*

2h Modal Perfect:

could have asked / *could have eaten*	→	*could have been asked* / *could have been eaten*

E.g. (active) *A bomb* ***might have destroyed*** *the building.*
(passive) *The building* ***might have been destroyed*** *(by a bomb).*

3 ***by*** **+ agent** [see BY 3.]

If you want to say who does the action of a passive verb, add ***by*** + noun phrase after the verb phrase. But we can omit this if we want. (The noun phrase following ***by*** is called the **agent**.)

Passive with agent:

I have been offered a new job ***by the manager***.

Passive without agent:

I have been offered a new job.

4 Why do we use the passive?

4a The passive without agent allows us to omit the 'actor' if we want to – e.g. if the 'actor' is not important or is not known:

In fact, most passives have no agent phrase.

4b The passive with agent allows us to save the 'actor' to the end of the clause. This is useful:

(I) if the 'actor' is the most important piece of new information.

E.g. *'This painting is very valuable. It was painted* ***by Van Gogh****.'* (Here the most important information is the name of the painter – ***Van Gogh***.)

(II) if the 'actor' is described by a long phrase which could not easily be the subject.

E.g. *The school will always be remembered and supported by* ***the boys and girls who received their education here***. (Here the agent is a long noun phrase (in bold letters), and would be awkward as subject.)

5 Which verbs allow the passive?

The passive normally requires a verb which takes an object (i.e. a 'TRANSITIVE VERB'). The object of the active sentence can become the subject of the passive.

E.g.

subject	verb	object
		↓
The president	*welcomed*	*the visitors.*

subject	passive verb	agent
↓		
The visitors	*were welcomed*	*by the president.*

5a Most verbs with an object [see VERB PATTERNS 1, and 11–19] allow the passive. 5b–5d show examples of the different patterns:

5b The simple subject + verb + object pattern [see VERB PATTERN 1], (e.g. with ***believe, do, keep, enjoy, meet, bring***):

E.g. *The show **was enjoyed** by everyone.*

5c The pattern with indirect object [see VERB PATTERN 11], (e.g. with ***give, bring, promise, tell, teach***):

E.g. *My father **was given** a gold watch (by . . .).*

With this verb pattern, it is normally the first object (or INDIRECT OBJECT) which becomes the subject of the passive.

E.g. *John sent me a card.* → *I **was sent** a card (by . . .).*

5d The other patterns are shown in these examples:

E.g. *The wine **must be kept** cool.* [See VERB PATTERN 12.]
*The lamp **was placed** in the corner of the room.* [See VERB PATTERN 13.]
*I **was told** that my mother was ill.* [See VERB PATTERN 14.]
*The secretary **was asked** how long the meeting would last.* [See VERB PATTERN 15.]
*We **were taught** how to drive a truck.* [See VERB PATTERN 16.]
*Helen **was advised** to take a long rest.* [See VERB PATTERN 17.]
*He **has been known** to object to the smallest change in the script.* [See VERB PATTERN 18.]
*The spy **was seen** leaving the building.* [See VERB PATTERN 19.]

6 **'Prepositional passives'**
The passive is not limited to cases where the object of an active becomes subject. There are some unusual passives, where the noun phrase following a preposition becomes the subject:

6a *be* + past participle + preposition:
This pattern can only be used if the verb and the preposition form a unit (e.g. if they form a PREPOSITIONAL VERB).

E.g.	*be called for*	*be hoped for*	*be looked after*
	be called upon	*be shouted at*	*be talked about*

(Active): *People talked about the wedding feast for many years.* →

(Passive): *The wedding feast **was talked about** for many years.*

Other examples:

*The President **was called upon** to make a speech.*
*Some improvement in the weather **can be hoped for** later next week.*
*I'm not going to stand here and **be shouted at by** a crowd of ignorant fools!*

6b *be* + past participle + adverb + preposition:
(This pattern is sometimes used with PHRASAL PREPOSITIONAL VERBS.)

E.g. *They have recently done away with the tax on cars.* →
The tax on cars has recently ***been done away with***. (***do away with*** = 'abolish')

Another example is ***put up with***.

---

past /pɑ:st ‖ pæ:st/ (*preposition or adverb*)

► ***Past*** has two main uses: (a) MOTION (OR MOVEMENT) and (b) TIME

1 ***Past*** **= motion**

1a The preposition ***past*** is followed by a pronoun or noun phrase.

E.g. *The taxi-driver drove* ***past*** *us without stopping.*

1b The adverb ***past*** is followed by nothing.

E.g. *The customs-officer was watching the passengers as they walked* ***past***.

2 ***Past*** **= time** means 'after', and is used especially in telling the time.

E.g. *'What's the time?' 'It's ten* ***past*** *three.'* (= '3.10')

3 ***Past*** is also a noun or an adjective: e.g. *in the* ***past****, in* ***past*** *years.*

---

past continuous [See PAST PROGRESSIVE.]

---

past participle [See PARTICIPLE.]

► Every verb in English (except MODAL AUXILIARIES) has a past participle form.

1 The form of the past participle

1a With regular verbs, we form the past participle by adding ***-ed*** [see -ED] to the basic form of the verb.

E.g. *walk* → ***walked*** *play* → ***played*** *wait* → ***waited***

[See SPELLING for the rules for adding the ***-ed*** ending.]

1b With irregular verbs, we form the past participle in different ways.

E.g. *know* → ***known*** *come* → ***come*** *drink* → ***drunk***

[See the list of IRREGULAR VERBS at the end of the book.]

2 The uses of the past participle

2a The past participle follows the auxiliary verb in a:

perfect verb phrase
has ***walked*** *have* ***waited*** *had* ***come***

passive verb phrase	
am ***known*** *is* ***played*** *are* ***drunk***	*was* ***eaten*** *were* ***found***

2b The past participle is also the verb of a past participle clause [see PARTICIPLE CLAUSE].

past perfect [See PERFECT.]

► The ***Past Perfect*** form of the verb phrase contains ***had*** (the past form of *have*) and a past participle:

had + past participle

1 Forms

Examples of forms:

positive and negative			
I, you *we, he,* *she, it,* etc	***had*** ***'d***	*been* *used* *done* *not / n't eaten*	. . .

question			
Had ***Hadn't***	*I, you,* *we, he,* *she, it,* etc	*been* *used* *done* *eaten*	*. . .?*

2 Uses

(A) 'Past in the past':

We use this form to show that one thing in the past (marked ① below) (expressed by the Past Perfect) happened before another thing in the past (marked ② below) (expressed by the Past Simple).

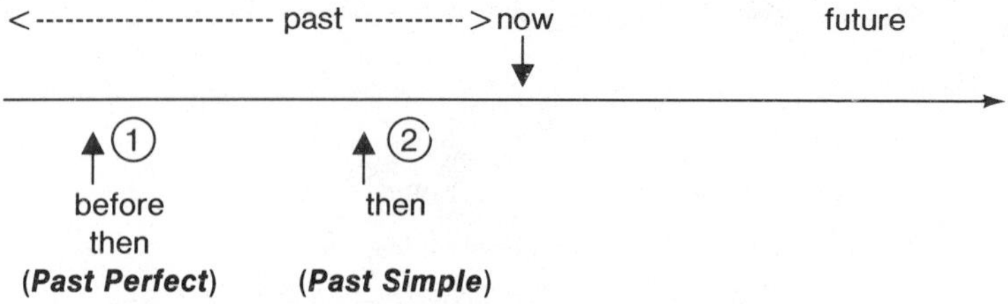

E.g. (i) *The army **had won**①* an important battle before they *__crossed__② the border.*

(ii) *The prisoner **was released**② after he **had been**① in prison for several years.*

(iii) *When the play **had finished**①, the audience **left**② quietly.*

(iv) *It **was**② the first time **he'd ever visited**① a night club.* (= 'He'd never visited a night club before that.')

2a If it is clear that one action happened before another action, you don't have to use the Past Perfect: you can use the Past Simple instead. In examples (i) and (iii) above you can change the Past Perfect to the Past Simple.

E.g. (i) *The army **won** an important victory **before** they **crossed** the border.*

(iii) ***When** the play **finished**, the audience **left** quietly.*

In example (i), ***before*** shows the relation between the two actions without the help of the verb. In example (iii), ***when*** means the play finished 'just before', so again you don't need the ***Past Perfect***.

3 **Uses**

(B) Unreal Past Perfect:

The Past Perfect is also used for unreal past states and actions [see UNREAL MEANING 2b]. E.g., in the *if*-clause of the *would-have* condition [see IF 1d]:

E.g. ***If you had been born** in Finland, **you would have been** Finnish.* (impossible)

(*But actually, you were born in Sweden, so you're Swedish!*) (true)

4 **More complex forms of the Past Perfect form of the verb phrase**

4a Past Perfect Progressive:

Form: *I / we / you / he /* etc. + { ***had*** / ***'d*** } + ***been*** + Verb-***ing*** . . .

E.g. (i) *It **had been raining** all night, and the streets were still wet in the morning.*

Question: ***Had*** + *I / we / you / he* / etc. + **been** + Verb ***-ing*** . . .?

E.g. (ii) ***Had*** *it* ***been raining*** *before he crashed his car?*

Negative answer:

E.g. *No, it* ***hadn't been raining*** *at all.*

The meaning of the Past Perfect Progressive form of the verb phrase is that something happened for a period of time before the past time you are thinking about. This is a picture of example (i) above:

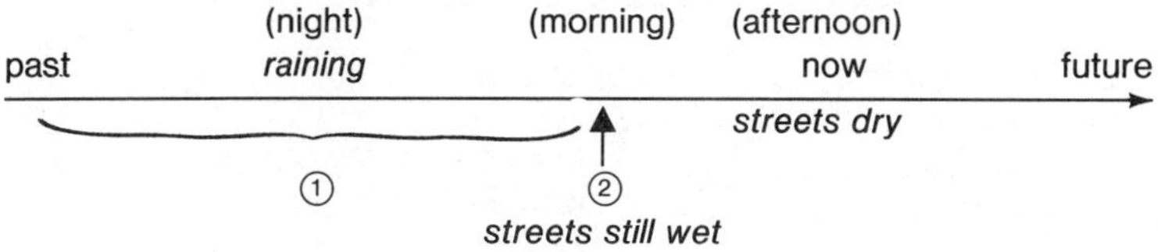

4b Past Perfect Passive:

Form: *I / we / you / they* / etc. + {***had*** / ***'d***} + **been** + past participle . . .

E.g. *When we arrived at the party, all the food* ***had been eaten***.

Question: ***Had*** + *I / we / you / they* / etc. + **been** + past participle . . .?

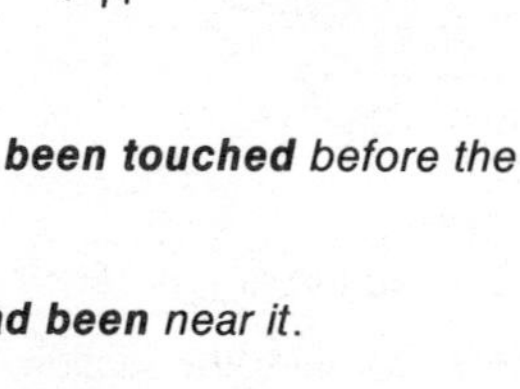

E.g. ***Had*** *the body* ***been touched*** *before the police arrived?*

Negative answer:

E.g. *No, no one* ***had been*** *near it.*

5 **The Past Perfect in indirect speech**
[See INDIRECT SPEECH AND THOUGHT 1b.]

past progressive (or 'past continuous')

► The ***Past Progressive*** form of the verb phrase contains ***was*** or ***were*** followed by the ***-ing*** form of the verb [see PAST, PROGRESSIVE]:

was / ***were*** + Verb ***-ing***

1 Forms

I, she, he, etc.	***was*** ***wasn't***	***having*** *a good time.* ***staying*** *at a hotel.* ***fishing***. etc.
you, we they, etc.	***were*** ***weren't***	

question forms:

Was ***Wasn't***	*I, he, she*, etc.	***having*** *a good time?* ***waiting*** *for the bus?* ***eating*** *?* etc.
Were ***Weren't***	*you, we, they*, etc.	

2 Meaning
We use the Past Progressive to show that a state or action was in progress in the past, i.e. it continued for a temporary period, but not up to the present. Often, this also means that the action was not complete at the time we are thinking about.

2a When one action (marked ① below) continued over a period, and a second action (marked ② below) happened in the middle of that period, we use the Past Progressive for ① and the Past Simple for ②:

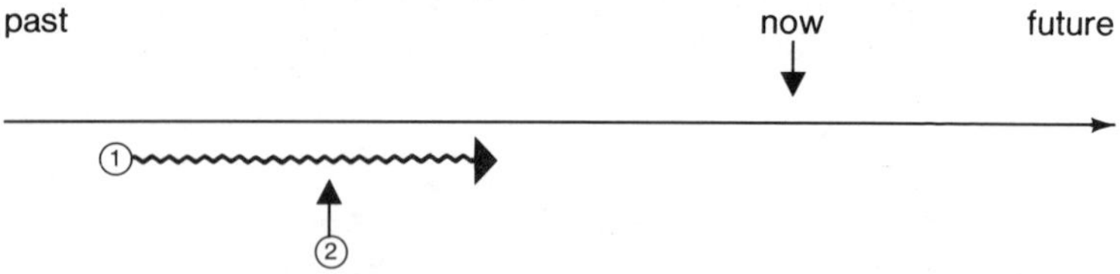

E.g. *It* ***was raining***① *when the doctor* ***left***② *his house this morning.*

One action (②) may interrupt the other action (①).

E.g. *The phone* ***rang***② *when you* ***were watching*** *T.V.*①.

While I ***was driving***① *from Rome to Naples, my car* ***broke down***②.

2b We use the Past Progressive for both actions ① and ② if both were continuing at the same time.

E.g. *I **was mending** the TV while my wife **was reading**.*
*As I **was driving** to Rome, I **was listening** to music on the car radio.*

2c We use the Past Progressive as the only verb in a sentence to talk about a continuing action at a point (①) or during a period of time (②):

E.g. *'**What were you doing** {at 8 o'clock / between 8 and 9} last Sunday morning?*
*'**I was eating** breakfast.'*

NOTE: If the past time or period you are thinking of is clear, you do not need to mention it.
E.g. *Harry got up early to feed the animals. It was a beautiful day, and **the birds were singing**.* (i.e. . . . 'when he got up'.)

3 The Past Progressive can refer not only to past time, but to the unreal present. It can be used in an *if*-clause with a *would*-condition [see IF 1c].

E.g. *'You're not gaining weight.' 'No, but I'd be happier **if I were losing** weight.'* [On the use of ***were*** here, see WERE 2]

4 Also, the Past Progressive can refer to future in the past [see PROGRESSIVE 2c], especially in indirect speech.

E.g. *When I told Pam that **I was getting married** (next month), she wouldn't believe me.*

past simple

► When we use a PAST TENSE main verb and no auxiliary verb, the form of the verb is called ***Past Simple***.*

► Most verbs form their Past Tense with ***-ed***. [See PAST TENSE for details of regular and irregular Past Tense forms.]

► The ***Past Simple*** has two main uses:
  (I) to describe something which happened at a definite time in the past [see 2a below].
  (II) to describe something which could not happen (or would be unlikely) in the present or future [see 2b below]. [See also UNREAL MEANING.]

* We do, however, make the negative or question form of the Past Simple with the auxiliary ***did(n't)*** + Verb [see DO 2].

1 Forms

I, we,	***played***	*football*	*(recently)*
you, he	***heard***	*about the exam*	*(last week)*
she, etc.	***gave***	*Jason a present*	*(ages ago)* etc.

question:

Did	*(n't)*	*we, I, you, he, she,* etc.	***play*** / ***hear*** / ***give***	. . .?

negative:

I, We, You, She, They, etc.	***didn't*** / ***did not***	***play*** / ***hear*** / ***give***	. . .

2 Meanings of the Past Simple

2a Past time:
The Past Simple places an action or state at a definite time in the past.

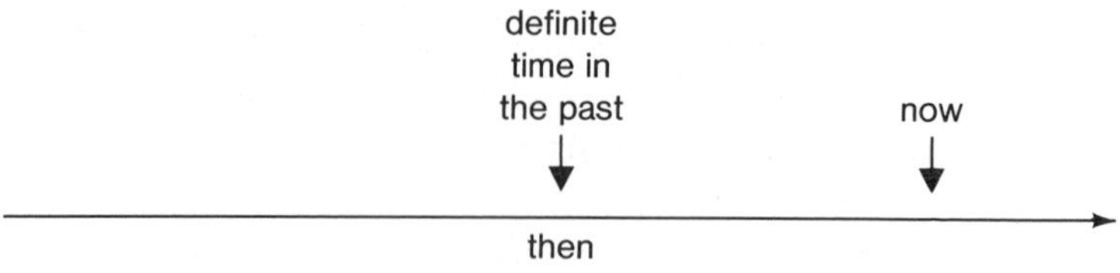

E.g. (i) *'When did you first meet your husband?'*
*'I met him **in 1954**, but we didn't marry until **quite recently**.'*
(ii) ***For many centuries*** *the Greeks were the rulers of the Mediterranean.*
(iii) ***Before their first child was two years old,*** *Maurice and Vera moved to a cottage in the country.*

Each of (i), (ii), and (iii) mention a period or point of time (marked by ***bold italics***) in the past, although the exact time may be unclear. Other examples do not mention a time, but it is clear that the speaker is still thinking of a particular time.

E.g. (iv) *'Where **did** you **get** that dress?' 'I **bought** it in a sale, at Harrods.'*
(v) *'**Did** you **see** that marvellous TV programme on tortoises?' 'No, I **was** busy upstairs.'*

2b Unreal present or future time:
(I) We use the Past Simple in the *if*-clause of a *would*-condition to show that this is not true.

E.g. *If I **owned** a house, I would look after it properly.* (I do not own a house).

(II) We use the Past Simple in some polite requests.

E.g. *Would you mind if I **borrowed** your lamp?*

[For further details, see UNREAL MEANING, also IF 1c, 1d.]

3 Other uses of the Past Simple

3a In addition to 'completed action', the Past Simple is used with state verbs to describe a state of affairs in the past [see STATE AND ACTION verbs].

E.g. *Once there **was** a fisherman, who **lived** in a little house by the sea.*

3b Also it is used with action verbs to describe a habit – i.e. a set of repeated actions.

E.g. *Every morning the two men **got up** and **ate** breakfast before they **went** fishing.*

The habit meaning *usually* requires a phrase of FREQUENCY (like ***every morning*** in the example above); or a phrase of LENGTH OF TIME.

E.g. ***All the summer** they **went** out in their tiny boat to catch fish.*

NOTE (i): Instead of the Past Simple, it is often clearer to use the *used to* + Verb form for state and habit in the past.
E.g. *They **used to go** fishing every morning.*

4 The difference between Past Simple and Past Progressive
The Past Progressive describes a state or action 'in progress', i.e. continuing, not completed.

4a Look at the difference between these examples

(i) *When we arrived*①, *the judge **made** a speech*②.
(ii) *When we arrived*①, *the judge **was making** a speech*②.

The Past Simple in example (i) sees the action of 'making a speech' as a whole, as a complete event in the past. The Past Progressive in example (ii) sees it as a continuing action, i.e. in progress, and incomplete:

Past Simple: 

Past Progressive: 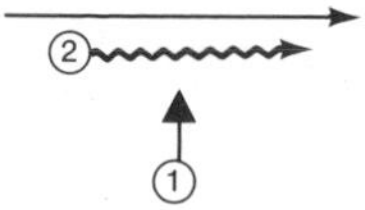

The judge in example (i) began his speech after we arrived. In example (ii), he began his speech before we arrived, and finished it after we arrived.

4b Now look at these examples:

(i) *The boy* ~~***drowned***~~*,*
(ii) *The boy* ***was drowning****,* } *but I dived into the water and saved him.*

We cannot use the Past Simple in example (i), because it says that the drowning was 'complete', i.e. *the boy died*. But the Past Progressive in example (ii) says that the drowning was incomplete – it could be interrupted.

E.g. *I* ***was walking*** *along last night,* ←continuing action

when I ***heard*** *a scream –*

←sudden event

so I ***went*** *back home and* ***phoned*** *the police.* ←completed action

past tense [See PRESENT TENSE, PAST SIMPLE, PAST PERFECT, PAST TIME]

1 If a word is a finite verb it normally has a difference of form between the Present Tense form and the Past Tense form. Both main verbs and auxiliary verbs BE, HAVE, and DO change their form for Past Tense:

	regular		irregular		
Present Tense:	***use(s)***	***look(s)***	***make(s)***	***come(s)***	***go(es)***
Past Tense:	***used***	***looked***	***made***	***came***	***went***

2 The Past Tense contrasts with the Present Tense, and indicates either (a) past time (excluding the present moment) or (b) unreal meaning.

E.g. (a) *In those days I **looked** young and handsome.* (i.e. 'then')
(b) *I wish I still **looked** young and handsome.* (i.e. 'now')

[See PAST TIME for the contrast between Past Simple and Present Perfect in describing past events.]

3 The regular Past Tense is formed by adding ***-ed*** [see -ED FORM]:
wait → ***waited***, ***ask*** → ***asked***, etc.
[See SPELLING for details of the spelling changes, and see PRONUNCIATION OF ENDINGS for how to pronounce the ***-ed***.]

4 Many common verbs have irregular Past Tense forms. E.g. *see* /siː/ → ***saw*** /sɔː/, ***bring*** /brɪŋ/ → ***brought*** /brɔːt/, etc. In one case (***go*** → ***went***) the form changes completely. [For details, see the list of IRREGULAR VERBS in the back of this book.]

5 The Past Tense forms of ***be***, ***have***, and ***do*** as auxiliaries are used at the front of larger verb phrases:

	be	have	do
Past Tense:	{ ***was*** (singular) / ***were*** (plural) }	***had***	***did***

E.g. Past Progressive: *was / were reading*
Past Perfect: *had eaten*
negative Past Simple: *did not leave*

5a BE is the only verb with a difference between singular and plural forms of the Past Tense: *it **was***, *they **were***.

6 **How to use the Past Tense**
[See PAST SIMPLE and PAST TIME. Also UNREAL MEANING]

past time

1 **There are several different ways of using a verb to refer to the past**
Look up each of these for further details:

PRESENT PERFECT — PRESENT PERFECT PROGRESSIVE
PAST SIMPLE — PAST PROGRESSIVE
PAST PERFECT — PAST PERFECT PROGRESSIVE

(Also, for past habit, we can use USED TO or would [see WOULD 3b].)

2 The difference between the Present Perfect and the Past Simple

The most important forms for expressing past time are the Present Perfect and the Past Simple.

2a In general, the Present Perfect relates a happening in the past to the present: the Past Simple relates a happening in the past to a past time:

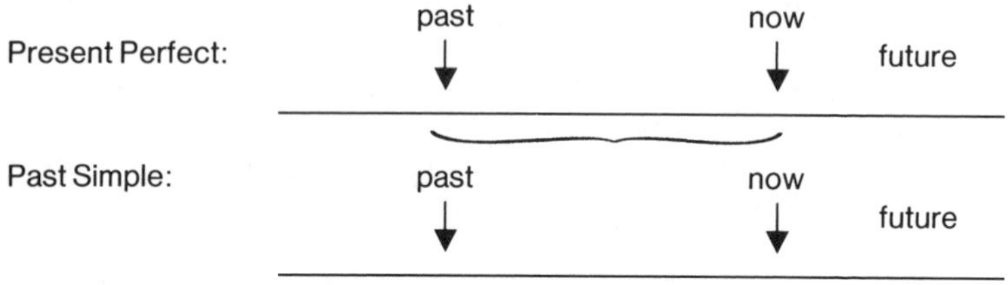

2b The Present Perfect sometimes means that a period of time continues up to the present (and will perhaps continue beyond the present into the future).

E.g. (i) *Mr Bird* ***has lived*** *in this street all his life.*
(ii) *Mr Bird* ***lived*** *in this street all his life.*

Example (i) suggests that Mr Bird is still alive and still lives in this street. Example (ii) suggests that he is dead.

2c The Present Perfect often implies that the result of the action continues up to the present.

E.g. (i) *Joan* ***has broken*** *the teapot*. (and it is still broken)
(ii) *Joan* ***broke*** *the teapot*. (but now it may have been mended)

2d The Present Perfect often implies that the action happened recently.

E.g. (i) ***Have*** *you* ***had*** *breakfast?* (= 'recently?')
(ii) ***Did*** *you* ***have*** *breakfast this morning?*

In example (i) no time is mentioned, so we assume a recent time.

2e The Present Perfect is the form we can use when we have no definite time in mind.

E.g. (i) A: *'**Have** you (ever) **visited** a mosque?'*
(ii) B: *'Yes, I **visited** one when I was in Cairo, two years ago.'*

Speaker A does not have a definite time in mind, so he uses the Present Perfect. But speaker B is thinking of a particular visit, so he uses the Past Simple.

NOTE: In <U.S.> the Past Simple is used more often than in <G.B.>. It can be used in examples (i), especially in 2c, 2d, and 2e, instead of the Present Perfect.

2f Choosing verb forms with adverbials [see ADVERBIAL, TIME.]

(I) The Present Perfect goes with adverbials describing a period up to the present.

E.g. *Mike and I* ***have been*** *good friends* { ***so far.*** / ***up to now.*** / ***since 1984.*** / ***since we met.*** }

(II) The Past Simple goes with adverbials naming a time in the past.

E.g. *I met his wife* { ***last night.*** / ***at 8 o'clock.*** / ***in 1984.*** / ***three months ago.*** }

(III) Other adverbials of time or length of time can occur with both the Present Perfect and the Past Simple. But the meaning may be different.

E.g. (i) *She* ***has already had*** *the baby.*
(ii) *She* ***already had*** *the baby.*

In example (i) ***already*** means 'by now'. In (ii) ***already*** means 'by that time' (in the past) [see ALREADY, STILL AND YET].

2g But finally remember that there is sometimes little difference between the Present Perfect and the Past Simple! You can sometimes use both forms for the same situation.

3 Past in the past

To describe an event or state which is past from the viewpoint of 'another' past time, we can use the PAST PERFECT.

E.g. *When we arrived at the bus station, our bus* ***had*** *already* ***left****.*

4 Future in the past

There are several verb forms we can use if we particularly want to describe a past event as seen in the future from a point further in the past:

(I) ***was / were to***. [See FUTURE 5b.]

E.g. *Henry, who* ***joined*** *the navy in 1798,* ***was to*** *become a captain in 1808.*

Other verb forms expressing future in the past:

(II) ***was / were going to***. [See GOING TO.]

E.g. *Everyone* ***was*** *excited because the new theatre* ***was going to*** *be opened the next evening.*

(III) ***would***.

E.g. *The building of the bridge* ***was*** *an important event which* ***would be*** *remembered for many years to come.* <written>

(IV) ***was / were*** + Verb ***-ing***. [See PROGRESSIVE 2c, PAST PROGRESSIVE 4.]

E.g. *Julia left the meeting early, because she* ***was flying*** *to Montreal the next morning.*

5 Here is a diagram of the Past Simple①, the past in the past②, and the future in the past③:

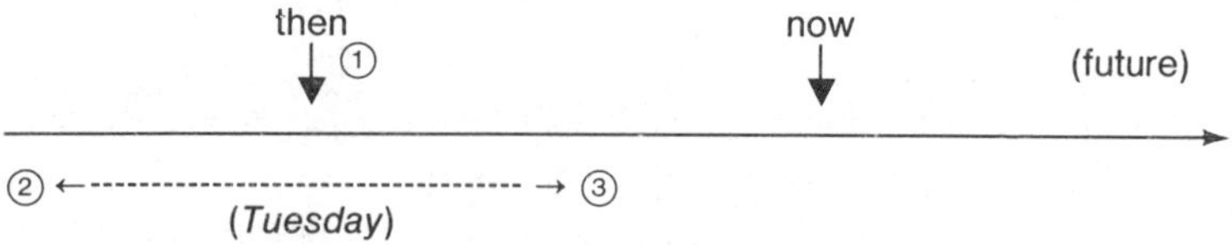

E.g. *Julia **visited**① us briefly on Tuesday: she **had flown**② home from Spain the previous evening, and **was going to**③ fly on to Montreal the next day.*

6 But note that you can repeat the Past Simple for a series of actions in the past. You do not have to use the Past Perfect, or a Future in the Past form.

E.g. *Julia **flew** home on Monday, **visited** us on Tuesday, and **flew** on to Montreal on Wednesday.*
*The building of the bridge **was** an important event which **was remembered** for many years.*

7 The Future in the Past is particularly common in INDIRECT SPEECH AND THOUGHT.

E.g. *She asked the nurse if her father **would** soon **be** better.*
*The passengers were afraid that the plane **was going to** crash.*

---

people /ˈpi:pl̩/ (*plural or singular noun*)

1 ***People*** is the irregular plural form of *person*.

E.g. *Several **people** agree with me.*
*Only one **person** disagrees with me.*

NOTE: There is also a regular plural of ***person***, ***persons***, which is <more formal> and less common.
E.g. *This law does not apply to young **persons** under the age of eighteen.*

2 ***People*** can also be a singular countable noun, meaning 'a race or nation'.

E.g. *The Chinese are a **people** with a long and splendid history.*

This use of ***people*** has a plural.

E.g. *The **peoples** of Africa speak many different languages.*

perception verbs (or *verbs* of 'sensation')

1 Perception verbs include ***see***, ***hear***, ***feel***, ***smell***, ***taste***, ***look***, ***sound***, ***listen***, ***watch***. These verbs describe the 5 senses: *sight*, *sound*, *feeling*, *smell*, *taste*.

In addition, the verbs ***seem*** and ***appear*** describe what we may call 'general perception' – not particular to one sense or another.

2 Perception verbs take several different verb patterns depending on the meaning you want to express. Notice that patterns (I)–(V) below start with the person who perceives something; the other patterns start with the thing / person which is perceived.

2a Patterns showing the most important perception verbs.

(I) NOUN + VERB + NOUN (event)

E.g. *I **heard** a noise (upstairs).* *I **felt** a stone in my shoe.*
*I **smelled** the fresh bread.* *I **tasted** it too.*

[See VERB PATTERN 1.]

(II) NOUN + VERB + NOUN (state)*

E.g. *You **can see** the stars.* *I **can feel** the wind.*
*I **can smell** onions.* *I **could taste** the salt in the soup.*

[See VERB PATTERN 1.]

* With ***can*** or ***could*** this verb pattern suggests a continuing state of affairs.

(III) NOUN + VERB + NOUN (activity)*

E.g. *I am **looking at** some photographs.* *I am **listening to** the radio.*
*I am **feeling** the thickness of the paper.* *I am **smelling** these roses.*

[See VERB PATTERN 1.]

* The activity meaning is clearest when we use the PROGRESSIVE form *be* + Verb *-ing*. This suggests that the person is consciously doing something. The Progressive is not generally used with other patterns.

(IV) NOUN + VERB + NOUN + Verb (event)

E.g. *I **saw** him break his leg.* *I **heard** the bomb explode.*
*We **felt** the earth shake.*

[See VERB PATTERN 18.]

(V) NOUN + VERB + NOUN + Verb ***-ing*** (activity)

E.g. *I **saw** her talking to Ann.* *I **heard** the train leaving the station.*
*I **could feel** the airplane losing height.* *I **could smell** the wood burning.*

[See VERB PATTERN 19.]

(VI) NOUN + VERB + ADJECTIVE (state)*

E.g. *That church **looks** old.* *His voice **sounded** thin.*
*This room **smells** damp.* *John **seems** unhappy.*
*The plan **appears** successful.*

[See VERB PATTERN 2.]

* [See * under (VII)].

(VII) NOUN + VERB + LIKE + NOUN (state)*

E.g. *He **looks like** a farmer.* *She **sounds like** an actress.*
*This cloth **feels like** silk.* *Her death **seemed like** an accident.*

* We can, if we want, add a *to*-phrase, to indicate who is the perceiving person.
E.g. *He **looks like** a farmer **to me**. The Church **looks** old **to me**.*

(VIII) NOUN + VERB + AS IF / AS THOUGH* + CLAUSE (state)

E.g. *Your hair **looks as if** it needs cutting.*
It * * ***sounds as if** you made a mistake.*
***I felt as if** I was dying.*
It * * {***seemed*** / ***appeared***} ***as if** the plan would fail.*

* ***As if*** and ***as though*** have the same meaning of comparison here. Particularly in <U.S.>, ***like*** can be used instead of as ***if*** [see LIKE 3a].
E.g. *The water **feels like** it's almost freezing.* <informal>
* * As these examples show, 'empty' *it* can occur with pattern (VIII) [see IT 3, IT-PATTERNS].

NOTE (i): ***Seem*** and ***appear*** also take the following pattern [see VERB PATTERN 7]:
NOUN + {SEEM / APPEAR} + TO + Verb . . .
E.g. *The guests **appeared to** enjoy the dinner.*
*Marcia **seems to** have a bad cold.*

NOTE (ii): [On patterns (IV) and (V) above, see VERB PHRASE, table III, *.]

perfect

► The Perfect form of the VERB PHRASE contains ***have*** + past participle: e.g. ***has eaten***, ***have worked***, ***had eaten***, ***'s eaten***, ***'ve worked***, ***'d eaten***. [See PRESENT PERFECT and PAST PERFECT for further details.]

1 **The Perfect refers to something which happened before or leading up to another time or event**

1a

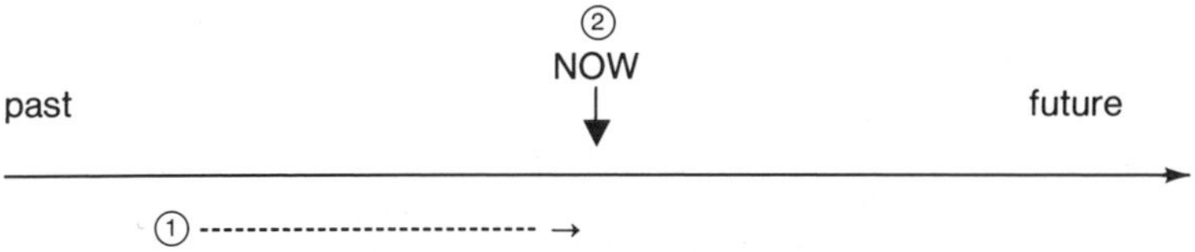

① Present Perfect ------ leads to -----→ ② present

E.g. *'I**'ve been** here since yesterday.'* ---- therefore ----→ *'I'm here now.'*

1b

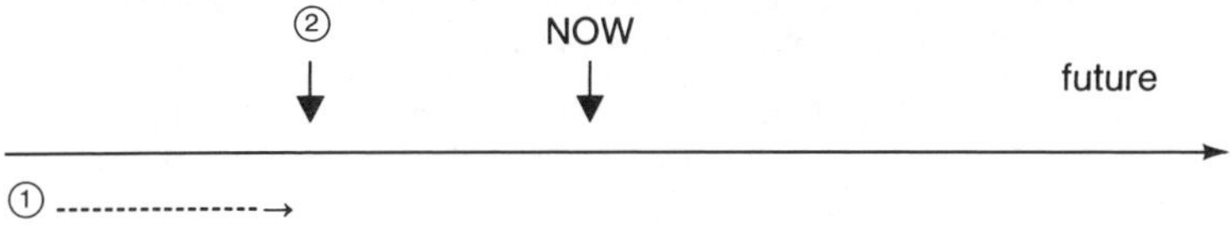

① Past Perfect ----- leads to ----→ ② past

E.g. *He**'d been** elected.* ----- therefore ----→ *He became president (in 1968).*

[See PRESENT PERFECT, PAST PERFECT, and PAST TIME for further details.]

2 **Other forms of the Perfect**

2a Perfect PROGRESSIVE forms

E.g. ***I've been reading***. ***I'd been reading***.

[See PRESENT PERFECT 3, 7, 8 and PAST PERFECT 4a.]

2b Perfect passive forms:

E.g. *Kim **has been arrested**.* *Kim **had been arrested**.*

[See PRESENT PERFECT 4, PAST PERFECT 4b, PASSIVE.]

2c The Perfect after a MODAL AUXILIARY:

MODAL + HAVE + PAST PARTICIPLE

E.g. ***Must have gone***, ***couldn't have left***, *will **have arrived***, ***might have been eaten***

[See also COULD AND MIGHT.]

These people are talking about something in the past; but they are uncertain about it:

NOTE: Unlike the Present Perfect [see PRESENT PERFECT 5a Note], the Perfect after a modal auxiliary can go with an expression of PAST TIME, such as ***yesterday***, ***last week***, ***a year ago***.
E.g. *Joe is twenty years old tomorrow. So he **must have been** born **in 1966.***
*You **ought to have locked** the door **last night**.*

3 ***Will / shall*** **+ Perfect**

Will + Perfect (or *shall* + Perfect) has the meaning of 'past in the future'. I.e., it refers to something which is in the past from a viewpoint in the future.

E.g. *I am sure that the parcel **will have arrived** by Tom's birthday.*
*Next year is our silver wedding: that means we**'ll have been** married for 25 years.*

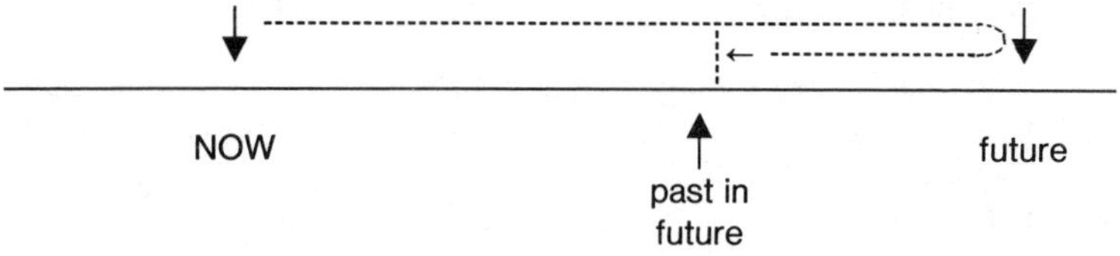

4 We can use the perfect in TO-INFINITIVE and -ING CLAUSES [see NONFINITE CLAUSE]:

TO HAVE + PAST PARTICIPLE or HAVING + PAST PARTICIPLE

E.g. *I'm sorry **to have caused** so much trouble.*
***Having seen** all your films, I have been longing to meet you.*

NOTE: Like the Perfect with modal auxiliaries, these infinitive and participle Perfects can go with an expression of past time [see 2: Note above].
E.g. *I'm delighted **to have met** your wife **yesterday**.*
***Having left** her native country **25 years ago**, she can no longer remember the language of her parents.*

perfect continuous

This form of the verb is called Perfect Progressive in this book. [See PRESENT PERFECT 3, 7 and 8.]

permission

asking and giving it

1 **To ask and give permission, you can use one of these patterns**

E.g.

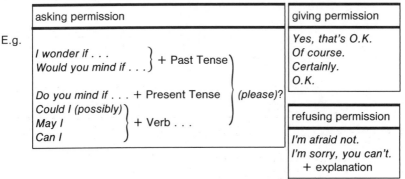

asking permission	giving permission
I wonder if . . . *Would you mind if . . .* } + Past Tense *Do you mind if . . .* + Present Tense *Could I (possibly)* *May I* *Can I* } + Verb . . . } *(please)?*	*Yes, that's O.K.* *Of course.* *Certainly.* *O.K.*
	refusing permission
	I'm afraid not. *I'm sorry, you can't.* + explanation

2 **Asking and giving** permission is a matter of politeness [see POLITE AND NOT POLITE], so the forms we use vary in different situations. The following illustrations give a rough idea of how forms vary.

2a <Very polite; talking to your manager!>
Employee: *'**I wonder if you would mind if** I took tomorrow morning off to go to the dentist's?'*
Employer: *'No, I don't mind at all. **That's quite all right**.'*

2b <Still polite; not such a big request>
Employee: *'**Do you mind if** I leave half an hour early? I need to meet my mother from hospital.'*
Employer: *'**Of course not**, Emily.'*

2c <Polite but more direct>

2d <Manager talks to employee>
Manager: *'**Can I** see you for a moment, please?'*
Assistant: *'Yes, **of course**.'*

2e <More casual>
Son: { ***'Can*** / ***'Could*** } *I borrow your car, Dad?'*
Father: ***'No, you can't.** I'm going to use it myself.'*

NOTE: MAY is less common and more formal than CAN.

E.g.

3 **Reporting** permission.

E.g. *Stephen **asked permission to** go to the dentist. The manager* { ***gave*** / ***refused*** } *(him) **permission**.*

*Emily **asked** (the manager) **if** she **could** leave early. The manager said she **could**.*

Laura { ***was*** / ***was not*** } ***allowed to** interrupt the meeting.*

---

person

is a grammatical term. We talk of '*1st* ***person***', '*2nd* ***person***', and '*3rd* ***person***'.

1 Personal pronouns change according to ***person*** [see PERSONAL PRONOUN 1, 5].

2 Nouns and noun phrases are always 3rd ***person***.

3 Verbs are affected by the ***person*** of the subject. [See -S FORM.]

---

personal pronoun

► ***Personal pronouns*** are used when it is clear who or what is being talked about. For example, *He* is a personal pronoun in:

***John** is my best friend. **He**'s a student.*

► ***Personal pronouns*** are very important: you cannot omit them.
► All ***personal pronouns***, except IT, can refer to people. (THEY can refer to both people and things.)
► [See HE AND SHE, IT, THEY, and ONE for further details of these pronouns.]

1 Subject pronouns

We use subject pronouns as the subject of the clause:

singular	plural	(person)
I* /aɪ/	***we*** /wi:/ (/wɪ/)**	1st
you /ju:/ (/jʊ/, /jə/)**	***you***	2nd
he /hi:/ (/hɪ/, /ɪ/)**		
she /ʃi:/ (/ʃɪ/)**	***they*** /ðeɪ/	3rd
it /ɪt/***		
one /wʌn/ <rather rare and formal>	–	3rd

* We always write ***I*** as a capital letter, even when it is in the middle of a sentence.
E.g. *Am **I** right?*
** The weak forms of pronouns are in brackets ( ). For ***he***, ***him***, etc. the form with no /h/ is usual when the pronoun is unstressed, except at the beginning of the sentence.
E.g. *'What's **he** /zɪ/ doing?' '**He's** /hɪz/ working.'*
*** Note ***it*** is pronounced /ɪt/, not /i:t/.

1a People

I = speaker. E.g.

I'm Jim.
This is my family...

She = female. E.g.

She's my mother.

He = male. E.g.

And he's my father.

They = male or female. E.g.

We = includes ***I*** and sometimes ***you***. E.g.

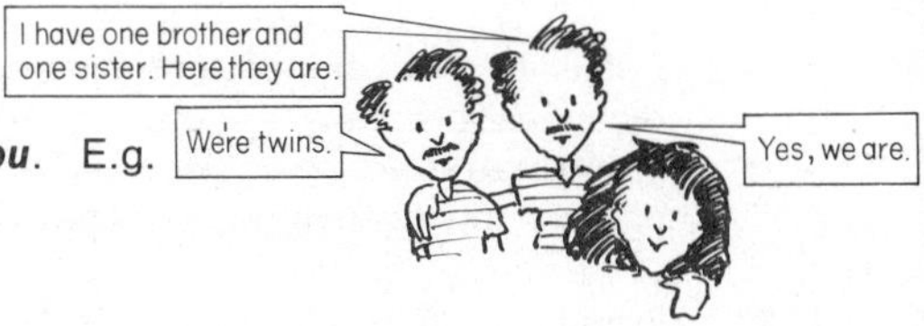
I have one brother and one sister. Here they are.
We're twins.
Yes, we are.

1b Things

It = anything that is not a person. E.g.

They = plural of ***it***. E.g.

NOTE: ***One*** = people in general. E.g.

2 **Object pronouns**

We use the object pronouns in all positions apart from subject. E.g. after the verb, or after a preposition.

subject	→ object etc.	
I	→ ***me*** /mi:/ (/mɪ/)*	E.g. *Help **me**, please.*
we	→ ***us*** /ʌs/ (/əs/)*	E.g. *Visit **us**, soon.*
you	→ ***you***** /ju:/ (/jʊ/)*	E.g. *I'll drive **you** home.*
he	→ ***him*** /hɪm/ (/ɪm/)*	E.g. *Don't send **him** away.*
she	→ ***her*** /hɜ:ʳ/ (/əʳ/)*	E.g. *They welcomed **her**.*
it	→ ***it***** /ɪt/	E.g. *Can I read **it**, please?*
they	→ ***them*** /ðem/ (/ðəm/)*	E.g. *I'll phone **them** tonight.*
one	→ ***one***** /wʌn/	E.g. *It makes **one** angry.*

* The weak forms again are in brackets ( ).
** ***You***, ***it***, and ***one*** are unchanged as object pronouns.

2a Remember: we call these pronouns object pronouns, but we use them in other positions, as well as object. A fairly safe rule is: use the subject pronoun as subject (i.e., generally, before the verb), and use the object pronoun elsewhere [but see 2d below].

2b In all the examples above the object pronoun acts as direct object. Now here is an example where the object pronoun follows a preposition:

*The examiners were annoyed **with*** { ***me*** / ***us*** / ***him*** / ***her*** / ***them***.

2c And here is an example where the pronoun is an INDIRECT OBJECT:

Mark sent {***me / us / him / her / them***} *a Christmas card.*
↑ (indirect object) ↑ (direct object)

NOTE: You can also say:
Mark sent a Christmas card to ***me****.*

2d There are three situations where the object pronoun is sometimes used (especially in <informal> English) although it is the subject in terms of meaning:

(A) After THAN or AS in COMPARISONS.

E.g. *Her sister can sing better than* {***she****.* / ***her****.*}

(B) In replies without a verb.

E.g. *'I am feeling very tired.'* ***'Me*** *too.'*

(C) After the verb BE (as COMPLEMENT).

E.g. *'Is that the Prime Minister, in the middle of the photograph?'*
'Yes, {*that is* ***he****.* / *that's* ***him****.*}

In all three cases, the subject pronoun is <uncommon and formal>, although some people think it is 'correct'. The object pronoun is much more common.
To be safe, use the subject pronoun + auxiliary; everyone is happy with this!

E.g. *Her sister can sing better than* ***she can****.*
'I am feeling very tired.' ***'I am****, too.'*

3 HE AND SHE, IT, and THEY are 3rd person pronouns. This means we can use these words to refer to people and things already mentioned.

E.g. *We asked the* {***girl*** *how old* ***she*** *was.* / ***boy*** *how old* ***he*** *was.* / ***students*** *how old* ***they*** *were.*}

We can also use these pronouns to refer to people or things in another sentence.

E.g. ***The guests*** *have arrived. Shall I show* ***them*** *in?*
Can you mend ***this chair****? I broke* ***it*** *yesterday.*
'Bella and Jenny *are here.' 'What do* ***they*** *want?'*

NOTE: Usually the pronoun (as above) follows the noun phrase (etc.) it refers to. But occasionally the noun phrase follows the pronoun. This happens when, for example, the pronoun is in a subordinate clause, and the noun phrase is in the main clause.
E.g. *When* ***she*** *became Queen,* ***Elizabeth*** *already had two children.*

4 Personal pronouns with AND

4a It is <polite> to put ***I*** and ***we*** after other noun phrases or pronouns.

E.g. *my husband and **I*** (not: *~~I~~ and my husband*)
*you and **I*** (not: *~~I~~ and you*)
*them and **us*** (not: *~~us~~ and them*)

Also, it is <polite> to put ***you*** before other noun phrases and pronouns.

E.g. ***you** and your family* (not: *your family and **~~you~~***)
you** and her* (not: *her and **~~you~~)

4b When you need to refer to a phrase with *and*, such as ***my husband and I***, follow these rules:
(I) If the phrase contains a 1st person pronoun, refer to it by ***we*** / ***us***.

E.g. ***You and I** have met before, haven't **we**?*

(II) Otherwise, if the phrase contains ***you*** (a 2nd person pronoun), refer to it by ***you***.

E.g. *If **you and your daughter** meet me tomorrow, I'll show **you** the sights of the city.*

(III) Otherwise, refer to it by ***they*** / ***them***.

E.g. ***Marlene and Peter** live in Berlin: **they** know the city very well.*

5 Personal, possessive, and reflexive pronouns

Here, to finish, is a table of personal pronouns and their matching possessive and reflexive pronouns [see POSSESSIVE DETERMINER AND POSSESSIVE PRONOUN; -SELF, -SELVES for further details of reflexive pronouns]:

			subject pronoun	object pronoun	possessive		reflexive pronoun
					determiner	pronoun	
singular	1st person		***I***	***me***	***my***	***mine***	***myself***
	2nd person		***you***	***you***	***your***	***yours***	***yourself***
	3rd person	male	***he***	***him***	***his***	***his***	***himself***
		female	***she***	***her***	***her***	***hers***	***herself***
		neither	***it***	***it***	***its***	*	***itself***
plural	1st person		***we***	***us***	***our***	***ours***	***ourselves***
	2nd person		***you***	***you***	***your***	***yours***	***yourselves***
(general)	3rd person		***they***	***them***	***their***	***theirs***	***themselves***
	3rd person (singular) <rather rare and formal>		***one***	***one***	***one's***	*	***oneself***

* There is normally no possessive pronoun for ***it*** or for ***one***.

phrasal-prepositional verb

► ***Phrasal-prepositional verbs*** are quite common in <informal, spoken English>.

► They are idioms with the form:

VERB + ADVERB + PREPOSITION

E.g. ***put up with*** (= 'tolerate')

► They are partly PHRASAL VERBS and partly PREPOSITIONAL VERBS.

► ***Phrasal-prepositional verbs*** can often be replaced by a single-word verb in <more formal> English. In this, they are like phrasal verbs.

1 Here are some examples.

E.g. *I have to* ***catch up on*** *my reading.*
I've got a bad cold. You'd better ***keep away from*** *me.* ('avoid')
We've got to ***face up to*** *our problems.* ('confront')
Children ought to ***look up to*** *their teachers.* ('respect')
We're ***looking forward to*** *meeting you again.*

Also:

catch up with = 'overtake'	***keep up with***
cut down on = 'reduce'	***run away with***
stand up for = 'defend'	***get away with***

phrasal verb

► A ***phrasal verb*** consists of verb + adverb (e.g. ***give up***). The two words form an idiom: it is called a ***phrasal verb*** only if the adverb changes the meaning of the verb.

► English has many ***phrasal verbs***: you will find their meanings in a dictionary.

► There are two kinds of ***phrasal verb***: Group A has no OBJECT, and Group B has an object [see 4, 5 below].

1 **Phrasal verbs and prepositional verbs**
You can add prepositions and adverbs to verbs in three different ways:

(I) prepositional verb:

VERB + PREPOSITION + NOUN PHRASE

E.g. *Listen to the radio.*

The purpose of the preposition is to link the noun phrase to the verb.

(II) phrasal verb:

VERB + ADVERB

E.g. *Carry on.*

The purpose of the adverb is to change the meaning of the verb [see 2 below].

(III) PHRASAL-PREPOSITIONAL VERB:

VERB + ADVERB + PREPOSITION + NOUN PHRASE

E.g. *Put up with the noise.*

The purpose of the adverb is to change the meaning of the verb and the purpose of the preposition is to link the noun phrase to the verb (+ adverb). (***Put up with*** means 'tolerate'.)

2 Phrasal verbs are common in <informal> English
We can often replace them with one word, which is more <formal>.

E.g. *The oil tank* ***blew up****.* (= 'exploded')
We decided to ***carry on****.* (= 'continue')
The two girls ***fell out****.* (= { 'quarreled' <U.S.> / 'quarrelled' <G.B.> })
Don't ***give away*** *any information.* (= 'reveal')
Don't ***leave out*** *anything important.* (= 'omit')
He's ***turned down*** *an excellent job.* (= 'refused')

3 What words can be used in phrasal verbs?
The verb is usually a common English verb.

E.g.	***ask***	***come***	***get***	***keep***	***make***	***set***
	be	***fall***	***give***	***let***	***put***	***take***
	break	***find***	***go***	***look***	***run***	***turn***

The adverb is usually an adverb of place.

E.g.	***about****	***around****	***by****	***in****	***out***	***under****
	across*	***away***	***down****	***off****	***over****	***up****
	along*	***back***	***forward***	***on****	***through****	

* These words can also be prepositions, so it is possible to confuse them with the second word of a prepositional verb [see 5b below].

4 Group A: phrasal verbs without an object
These are easy: they are like intransitive verbs [see VERB PATTERN 0]. Some examples are,

E.g. *My car has* ***broken ˈdown****.*** (= 'stopped working')
Lydia ***turned ˈup*** *at the last moment.* (= 'arrived')
The children are ***growing ˈup*** *fast.* (= 'becoming adults')
Look ˈout! *There's someone coming.* (a warning)
Go ˈon! *We're all listening.* (= 'continue what you were saying')

** Unlike prepositions, adverbs are usually stressed. This is why they have a stress mark in the examples. [See STRESS.]

NOTE: Many IMPERATIVES have the pattern of Group A.
E.g. ***Wake up, Get up, Come in, Sit down, Stand up, Shut up, Go away, Come on, Watch out,*** etc.

5 Group B: phrasal verbs with an object

E.g. *She's **bringing up** three children.* (= 'rearing')
*Try to **find out** whether he's coming.* (= 'discover')
*I'll **fix up** the meeting (tomorrow).* (= 'arrange')
*Don't **give away** all my secrets.* (= 'reveal')
*You should **give up** smoking cigarettes.* (= 'stop')
*Can you **fill** {**in** / **out**} this form, please.* (= 'complete')

5a If the object is a noun phrase, you can move the adverb after it.

E.g. *She brought* [***up***] *the children* [ ]

If the object is a personal pronoun, it **must** come before the adverb.

E.g. *She **brought** them **up**.*

This means that the phrasal verb is separated into two parts. Compare the following patterns.

(i) VERB + ADVERB + OBJECT

E.g. *Please **put on** {the light. / it.}*

(ii) VERB + OBJECT + ADVERB

E.g. *Please **put** {the light / it} **on**.*

Compare the order of words:

*'Have you **looked up** those words in the dictionary?'*
*'Yes, I **looked** them **up** last night.'*
*'Have they **put off** the meeting?'* (= 'postponed')
*'Yes, they've **put** it **off** until next month.'*
*'Has the army **taken over** the airport?'*
*'No, they haven't **taken** it **over** yet.'*

5b Group B **phrasal verbs** often look like prepositional verbs, i.e. verb + preposition. But we can see they are different when we use a pronoun as an object.

E.g. phrasal verb:
*I **looked up** the word.*
→ *I **looked** {the word / it} **up**.*

LOOK IT UP

E.g. prepositional verb:
*I **looked at** the painting.*
→ {*I **looked** ~~it at~~.* / *I **looked at** it.*}

LOOK AT IT

Sometimes, also, a **phrasal verb** uses the same words as a verb + preposition.

phrasal verb (idiom):

E.g. *He **ran down** his own wife.* (= 'criticised her')
→ *He **ran** her **down**.*

but:

prepositional verb (not an idiom):

E.g. *He **ran down** the hill.*
→ *He **ran down** it.*

NOTE: There is sometimes also a difference between a literal meaning and an idiomatic meaning.
E.g.

***bring up** a piano* (= 'carry it up')
***bring up** a problem* (= 'introduce it, as a topic for discussion')

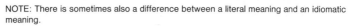

(i) *Bill and Jean **fell out**.*

(ii) *Bill and Jean **fell out**.* (= 'quarrelled')

phrase

► A ***phrase*** is a unit of grammar.
► We build clauses and sentences out of ***phrases***.
► A ***phrase*** may consist of one word or more than one word.

1 There are 5 kinds of phrase in English.

(A) A ***noun phrase*** generally has a noun (or pronoun) as its main word.
(B) A ***verb phrase*** generally has a main verb as its main word.
(C) A ***prepositional phrase*** has a preposition as its first word.
(D) An ***adjective phrase*** has an adjective as its main word.
(E) An ***adverb phrase*** has an adverb as its main word.

1a [See separate entries for NOUN PHRASE, VERB PHRASE, and PREPOSITIONAL PHRASE for the details of these kinds of phrase. Here we give just a general idea of how phrases are built.]

2 It is useful to call the main word (which normally has to be there) the *headword*, and the words which can be added to it *modifers* [see MODIFIER AND HEADWORD]. Modifiers give more information about a headword.

3 The structure of phrase types: some examples

3a Noun phrases:

noun phrase			
determiner(s)	modifier(s)	headword	modifier(s)
		him	
		Paula	
Alice's		*wedding*	
that		*boy*	*with the long hair*
all the	*nice warm*	*days*	*we had last summer*
	expensive	*clothes*	
		milk	*in bottles*
my	*favourite TV*	*programme*	

3b Verb phrases:

	verb phrase	
	auxiliary / auxiliaries	main verb
The door		*opened*
The door	*was*	*opening*
The door	*has been*	*opened*
The door	*must have been*	*opened*

3c Prepositional phrases:

	prepositional phrase	
	preposition	noun phrase
I called her	*on*	*the telephone*
	at	*six o'clock*
	from	*a town in northern France*
	for	*dinner*

3d Adjective phrases:

	adjective phrase		
	modifier(s)	adjective	modifier(s)
It is		*sad*	
		full	*of holes*
	almost	*impossible*	
	too	*easy*	
	much	*colder*	*than last winter*

3e Adverb phrases:

	adverb phrase		
	modifier(s)	adverb	modifier(s)
He comes here		*regularly*	
	quite	*often*	
	much	*later*	
	less	*willingly*	*than he used to*
	as	*quickly*	*as possible*

place [See also MOTION and DISTANCE]

1 Prepositions of place

E.g. **1.** *The clouds are* ***above*** *the plane.* **2.** *The plane is* ***in*** *the sky.* **3.** *There is snow* ***on top of*** *the mountain.* **4.** *There is a waterfall* ***beyond*** *the bridge.* **5.** *Trees grow* ***below*** *the snowline.* **6.** *The train is* ***on*** *the bridge.* **7.** *There is a hut* ***among*** *the trees.* **8.** *Two people are climbing* ***up*** *the mountain.* **9.** *One person is coming* ***down*** *the path.* **10.** *The valley lies* ***between*** *two mountains.* **11.** *The bridge stretches* ***across*** *the valley.* **12.** *The tunnel goes* ***through*** *the mountain.* **13.** *The river flows* ***under*** *the bridge.* **14.** *Here it runs* ***beside*** *the road.* **15.** *A fisherman is sitting* ***by*** *the* *river.* **16.** *There are a lot of fish* **in** *the river.* **17.** *There's a telephone* **at** *the crossroads.* **18.** *There is a line of people* **outside** *the phone box.* **19.** *The traffic is going* **along** *the road.* **20.** *The motorbike is going* **(a)round** *the corner.* **21.** *The cow is* **opposite** *the phone box.* **22.** *The van is driving* **past** *the cow.* **23.** *The car is* **behind** *the bus and* **in front of** *the van.* **24.** *There are lots of people* **inside** *the bus.* **25.** *The cyclist is* **in front of** *the bus.* **26.** *The car is parked* **off** *the road.*

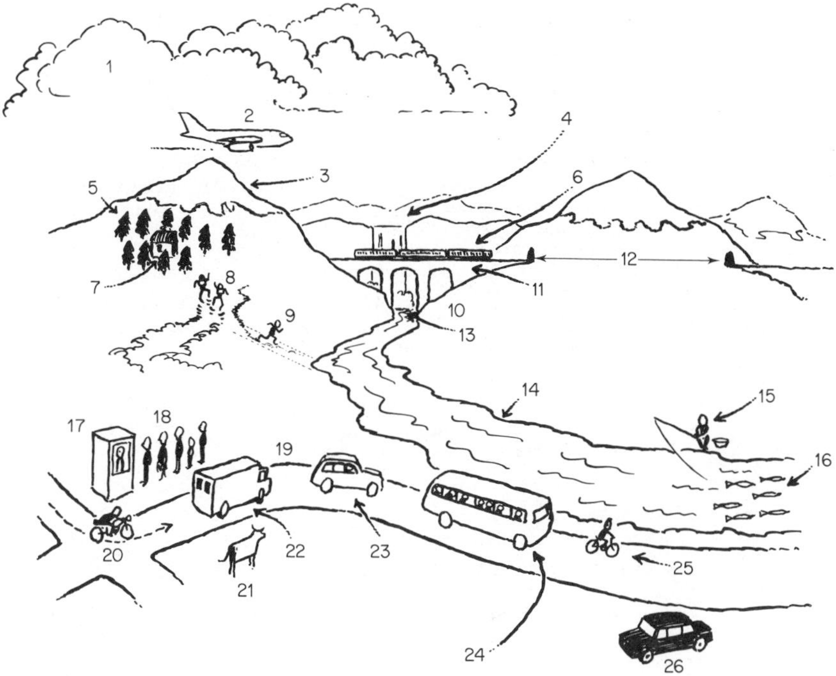

Place expressions answer the question: *Where?*

2 *At*, *on*, and *in* are three important prepositions of place

E.g. ***'Where*** *were you last night?'* ***'At*** *home* ***in*** *bed.'*
'Where*'s Mary?' 'She's over there* ***on*** *the other side of the street.'*
'Where*'s your bicycle?' 'It's* ***in*** *the street outside the house.'*

2a When do you use ***at***?:

With places, when you are not interested in exact position, but in general location.
at *home,* ***at*** *school,* ***at*** *the airport,*
at *the shops,* ***at*** *the door,* ***at*** *the station,*
at *the bus stop,* ***at*** *a hotel.*

2b When do you use ***on***?:

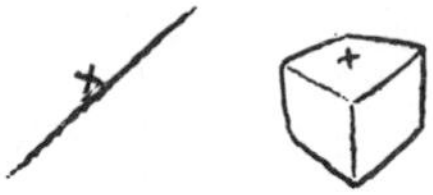

When you are talking about 'on top of', 'on a surface', 'on a line'.
on *a mountain,* ***on*** *the roof,* ***on*** *the bus,*
on *the table,* ***on*** *the wall,* ***on*** *the coast.*

2c When do you use ***in***?:

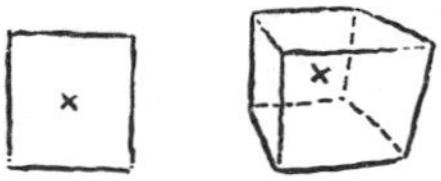

When you mean 'within' or 'enclosed by' an area of a space.
in *this box,* ***in*** *the water,* ***in*** *the town,*
in *the garden,* ***in*** *the sky,* ***in*** *that drawer,*
in *the kitchen.*

NOTE (i): Different prepositions with the same noun suggest different 'viewpoints'.
E.g. { ***at the hotel*** (= 'the hotel as a general location')
{ ***in the hotel*** (= 'inside the hotel as a building')
{ ***on the ground*** (= 'on the surface of the ground')
{ ***in the ground*** (= 'under the surface')
{ ***at the door*** (= 'general location')
{ ***on the door*** (= 'on the surface of the door')

NOTE (ii): The opposite of ***at*** is ***away from***.
The opposite of ***on*** is ***off***.
The opposite of ***in*** is ***out of***.
E.g. *Jim has been* ***away from*** *school for several days.* ('not at')
The island is a mile ***off*** *the coast.* ('not on')
I have been ***out of*** *hospital for a week.* ('not in')

3 **Place adverbs**

There are quite a few place adverbs. The following words and parts of words in ***bold*** have separate entries; look them up for further details:

here, ***there,*** ***some****where,* ***any****where,* ***every****where,* ***no****where,* *upstairs.*

3a In addition, place prepositions (except for AT, BETWEEN AND AMONG) become place adverbs when no noun phrase follows them.

E.g. (i) *He got* ***off*** *the bus.* → *He got* ***off***.
(ii) *She climbed* ***up*** *the hill.* → *She climbed* ***up***.
(iii) *They swam* ***across*** *the water.* → *They swam* ***across***.

We use the adverb when it is clear what noun phrase ought to follow.

E.g. *They came to a river. There was no boat, so they swam* ***across***.
(= 'across the river')

NOTE (i): Complex prepositions like ***away from***, ***on top of***, and ***out of*** have similar adverbs:
away from → ***away*** ***on top of*** → ***on top*** ***out of*** → ***out***
E.g. *He ran* ***away from*** *home.* ~ *He ran* ***away***.

NOTE (ii): Prepositional phrases of place are used as:
(A) ADVERBIALS.
E.g. *She works **in our office**. (**In our office** tells you more about where she works.)*
(B) MODIFIERS.
E.g. *The girl **in our office** likes her new computer.* (***In our office*** tells you more about the ***girl*** (noun).)

please /pli:z/ (*adverb or verb*)

The adverb ***please*** is used to make a <polite> request. [See POLITE AND NOT POLITE 2b.]

pluperfect

This is another term for the Past Perfect form of the verb.

plural

- ***Plural*** is the grammatical term for describing *more than one person or thing*. It is the opposite of SINGULAR.
- Most nouns, pronouns, and verbs have ***plural*** forms.

1

singular	plural	
one spoon 	***two spoons*** 	***three spoons*** 

2 **Nouns**
The nouns which have a plural form are called COUNTABLE NOUNS. Most nouns are countable.

2a The regular plural form of a noun adds **-s** (or **-es**) to the singular.

E.g. ***week → weeks*** ***cup → cups*** ***plan → plans***
law → laws ***uncle → uncles*** ***toy → toys***

Most nouns add **-s**, but if the noun already ends in **-s** or ***-z***, ***-x***, ***-ch***, ***-sh***, it adds ***-es***.

E.g. ***bus → buses*** ***buzz → buzzes*** ***box → boxes***
peach → peaches ***bush → bushes***

NOTE (i): [On other spelling changes in forming the plural, see SPELLING.]

NOTE (ii): [On how to pronounce the ***-(e)s*** ending, see PRONUNCIATION OF ENDINGS 2.]

2b Most nouns form their plural with ***-(e)s***. But a small number of nouns have a special plural form.

E.g. ***man*** → ***men*** ***child*** → ***children*** ***foot*** → ***feet***

[See IRREGULAR PLURAL for details of these special plural forms.]

3 **Pronouns and verbs**
[On the plural pronoun forms, see PERSONAL PRONOUNS. On the plural verb form, see AGREEMENT 1.]

---

polite and not polite

[See also APOLOGIES, PARDON, SORRY AND EXCUSE ME, PERMISSION, REQUESTS, THANKING]

- ► Being ***polite*** means showing consideration for the feelings or wishes of others.
- ► Sometimes we have to be more ***polite*** than at other times.
- ► In general, the people we wish to be more ***polite*** to are 'important' people or strangers. [See 2c below.]
- ► The usual rule is: 'The more words you use, the more ***polite*** you are!'

1 This is how the sentence gets more polite, the more words you use.

E.g. Order:	*The door!*
Imperative:	*Close the door.*
Imperative + *please*:	***Please*** *close the door.*
Question:	***Can you (please)*** *close the door?*
Question + Explanation:	***Can you*** *close the door,* ***please****? It's rather cold.*
Unreal past forms:	***Could you*** *close the door* ***please****?*
Or:	***Would you mind*** *closing the door,* ***please****?*
Extra polite:	***I wonder if you'd mind*** *closing the door,* ***please****?*

1a The above gives a general guide to how to be polite. But remember that being polite is different in different countries. E.g. the '*super* polite' request forms you hear in Britain are often felt to be too polite in the U.S.A. and in other countries. One country tends to use politeness in one way, and another in another.

2 You decide how polite you are going to be, according to how close you are to the person you are talking to.

2a It isn't necessary to be so very polite to friends, equals, or members of your family, unless they are old. (If you are too polite to them, they will think you are joking, or worse!)

Here is an example: you want someone to close the door. If it's a very good friend or member of the family you will probably use the IMPERATIVE.

E.g. *Close the door.*

(A rising tone at the end makes it less like a command [see INTONATION].)

2b To make it a little more polite, you can add ***please***.

E.g. *'Close the door,* ***please****.' 'Okay.'*

As well as saying ***please***, you can offer an explanation of your request.

E.g. *'It's a bit cold in here. {Can / Could / Would} you close the door?'*
'All right.'

2c Usually you will want to be polite to people such as your boss, your bank manager, your teacher. Also, to people you don't know well, to old people, etc.

2d If you want to be very polite, e.g. in talking to a stranger, you can say.

E.g. *{'Would you mind closing / 'Could you possibly close} the door, please?' 'Yes, certainly.'*

2e Another way to be polite is to give a hint, so that the other person can guess what you want!

E.g. *'It's rather cold in here, isn't it?' 'Oh, sorry! Do you want me to close the door?' 'Yes, please.'*

3 In English, it is polite to:

(a) Greet people when you see them, e.g. *Good morning* [see GREETINGS]
(b) Talk about *them* first. E.g. *How are you?*
(c) Use ***please*** and ***thank you***.
(d) Say ***sorry*** if you do anything wrong, however small.
(e) Say ***excuse me*** if you want to ask someone a question in the street.

4 In this book, we mark politeness wherever we can by signs like this: <polite>, <more polite>, <rather polite>, etc.

---

positive

This is a grammatical term for 'the opposite of negative.'

E.g. Question: *'Do you like dogs?'*
Answer: {Positive Statement: *'Yes, I like dogs.'* / Negative Statement: *'No, I don't like dogs.'*}

[See NEGATIVE WORDS AND SENTENCES, and NOT for fuller details.]

possessive [See also POSSESSIVE DETERMINER AND POSSESSIVE PRONOUN]

► Nouns have a ***possessive*** form, for which we add **-'s** (singular) or **-'** (plural) to the regular form of the noun.

E.g. *girl → girl'**s**,* *girls → girls**'***

► The ***possessive*** form usually precedes another noun.

E.g. *the **girl's** toys,* *the **girls'** teacher*

► The meaning of the ***possessive*** pattern ***X's Y*** is

typically: { *'the Y belonging to X'* / *'the Y of X'* / *'the Y which has some special relation to X'*. }

1 An example of the possessive

*the **girl's** teacher* (= 'the teacher { of / who teaches } the girl')
*the **girls'** teacher* (= 'the teacher who teaches the girls')

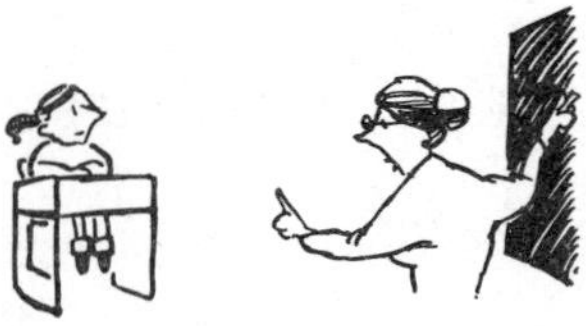

the girl —('s)— teacher

the girls —(')— teacher

2 How to write and pronounce the possessive

2a The possessive form of regular nouns:

	<written>		<spoken>	
	singular	plural	singular	plural
ordinary noun:	***boy***	***boys***	/bɔɪ/	/bɔɪz/
possessive noun:	***boy's***	***boys'***	/bɔɪz/	

Note that we write the plural and possessive forms differently, but we pronounce them the same. The possessive, like the plural, is pronounced with -/s/, -/z/, or -/ɪz/, according to the normal rule for pronunciation of endings. [See PRONUNCIATION OF ENDINGS 2].

2b The possessive form of plural nouns which do not have **-s** added:

[See IRREGULAR PLURAL.]	<written>		<spoken>	
	singular	plural	singular	plural
ordinary noun	***child***	***children***	/tʃaɪld/	/ˈtʃɪldrən/
possessive noun	***child's***	***children's***	/tʃaɪldz/	/ˈtʃldrənz/

In the plural, we add **'s** to the noun, just as in the singular.

E.g. ***men*** → ***men's*** *clothing,* ***women*** → ***women's*** *rights,*
people → *some* ***people's*** *opinions.*

NOTE: Occasionally the possessive just spelled **'** can be added to a singular noun ending in *-s*. This can happen with classical or religious names.
E.g. *Socrates**'** death* *St (= saint) James**'** church.*
But with other names, it is usual to add **'s** (-/ɪz/) after *-s*.
E.g. *Mrs Jones**'s** house* *Dennis**'s** girlfriend.*

3 How possessives occur with phrases and clauses

3a Possessives are basically like determiners. Compare:

{ ***John's*** / *this* }	*book*	{ ***women's*** / *some* }	*political views*
{ ***man's*** / *the* }	*future*	{ ***China's*** / *a* }	*new economic policy*

3b The possessive noun can itself become the main word (headword) of a phrase. Then it can have determiners and modifiers before it:

	X's	Y	
(i)	*My friend**'s***	*new bicycle*	*cost $150.*
(ii)	*Many people**'s***	*happiness*	*depends on your decision.*
(iii)	*The youngest girls**'***	*teachers*	*have not been invited.*
(iv)	*Every actor**'s***	*job*	*is to please the audience.*
(v)	*The French team**'s***	*recent successes*	*have been widely reported.*

Also: *this country**'s** economy,* *our plane**'s** crew.*

NOTE: We see above that ***X's*** in the possessive pattern can be several words. One result of this is that the **'s** can be added to a word which is not the main noun describing the 'possessor'.
E.g. *The President of **Mexico's** arrival* (= 'the Mexican President's arrival')
In some cases, the word ending **'s** is not even a noun.
E.g. *someone **else's** ticket* (= 'the ticket belonging to someone else')
*in an hour or **so's** time* (= 'in about an hour's time')

4 **Possessives compared with *of*-phrases**

The possessive pattern ***X's Y*** often has the same meaning as the of pattern ***the Y of X*** [see OF 2]. For example, (ii), (iii) and (iv) in 3b can be replaced by

E.g. (ii) *the happiness **of** many people*
(iii) *the teachers **of** the youngest girls*
(iv) *the job **of** every actor*

The rule is:

X's Y = the **Y** of **X**

E.g. *the ship's side = the side of the ship*

But this rule does not always work, because we prefer the possessive pattern or the ***of*** pattern in different conditions. So when do we choose the possessive?

In general, it is useful to follow this advice: prefer the possessive pattern ***X's Y*** in the following conditions. (If one or more of conditions I–IV do not apply, preference for ***'s*** will be weaker.)

(I) when **X** describes a person rather than a thing*.

E.g. ***Laura's** face,* *my **uncle's** return,* ***Jim's** boss*

* We can, if we like, allow 'people' (rather than 'things') to include not only humans, but (a) animals, and (b) groups of humans (e.g. *government*, *committee*, *audience*): *a **bird's** tail, the **government's** policy*.

(II) when ***X's Y*** describes a relation of possession (i.e. **X** has or possesses **Y**).

E.g. *my **aunt's** furniture,* *a **monkey's** brain*
*the **doctor's** house,* *the **club's** members*

(III) when ***X's Y*** describes the relation of a subject to a verb.

E.g. *the **train's** arrival* (↔ 'the train arrived')
*the **company's** development* (↔ 'the company developed')

NOTE: Notice that in the longer pattern ***X's Y of Z***, ***X*** is the subject of the 'verb' expressed in ***Y***, and ***Z*** is its object.
E.g. ***Newton's discovery** of the laws of motion* (= 'Newton discovered the laws of motion')
***Liverpool's defeat** of Manchester United* (= 'Liverpool defeated Manchester United')

(IV) when, in ***X's Y, X*** is much shorter than ***Y*** (i.e. contains many fewer words than ***Y***).

E.g. *the town's* *increasing problems of crime and violence.*
X ***Y***

5 **The possessive with place and time nouns**

For the possessive with place and time nouns there is no corresponding ***of***-phrase.

5a Place noun + **'s** + superlative or ordinal.

E.g. *The world**'s** tallest building* (= 'the tallest building ***in*** the world.')
*Africa**'s** first railway* (= 'the first railway ***in*** Africa.')

5b Time noun + **'s**.

E.g. *Next Friday**'s** meeting*, (= 'the meeting next Friday')
*this year**'s** fruit crop*.

6 Two special patterns with the possessive

6a Sometimes we use both the possessive and the ***of*** pattern to express possession. Thus we have a 'mixed' pattern ***Y of X's***.

E.g. *a friend **of** my mother's*   *some books **of** James's*

We use this mixed pattern particularly when **X** is a person, when **Y** has an indefinite meaning, and when **Y** is something belonging to **X**.

6b Sometimes we omit altogether the noun that would follow the possessive.

E.g. *My house is older than **Chris's***. (= 'Chris's house')
*'Whose are these **books**?'*
*'They're my **sister's**.'* ('my sister's books')

This is possible when the meaning of **Y** in **X's Y** is obvious from the situation.

NOTE: The possessive without a following noun can also describe (i) someone's home, or (ii) someone's place of work.

E.g. (i) *We're spending a few days at* { ***Peter's***. / ***the Smiths'***. }
(i.e. 'at his / their house')
(ii) *I have to go to the* { ***baker's***. (= 'baker's shop') / ***dentist's*** (= 'dentist's surgery') }

possessive determiner and possessive pronoun

1 The possessive forms of personal pronouns

	(I)	*(you)*	*(he)*	*(she)*	*(it)*	*(we)*	*(they)*
determiner:	***my***	***your***	***his***	***her***	***its***	***our***	***their***
pronoun:	***mine***	***yours***	***his***	***hers***	–	***ours***	***theirs***

[See PERSONAL PRONOUN.]
Personal pronouns have two possessive forms.

1a We call the first possessive form a possessive determiner, because it occurs before a noun, in the position of a word such as ***the*** or ***a(n)***.

E.g. ***my** cup*   (Compare: ***John's** cup* [see POSSESSIVE 3.])

1b We call the second possessive form a possessive pronoun, because it can stand alone as subject, object, etc, as pronouns can.

E.g. *This cup is* ***mine***.
(Compare: *This cup is* ***John's***. [See POSSESSIVE 6.])

2 What is the difference between determiners and pronouns?

2a Notice the different positions of the determiner and pronoun forms in the following.

E.g. *'Have you seen* ***my*** *tennis racket?'* (determiner)
'No. This one is ***mine.****'* (pronoun)
'You should improve ***your*** *handwriting.'* (determiner)
'Well, it's better than ***yours****!'* (pronoun)

The possessive determiner is usually not stressed, and the possessive pronoun is always stressed.

2b Add ***own*** to a possessive determiner to give it emphasis.

E.g. *Malcolm always cooks* ***his own*** *dinner.*

(Compare -SELF pronouns: = *'cooks dinner for* ***himself****.'*)

E.g. *'Do you buy your vegetables at the market?' 'No, we grow them in* ***our own*** *garden.'*

We can also omit the noun after ***own***.

E.g. *'Do you want to borrow my typewriter?' 'No, thanks. I'll use* ***my own****.'* (= 'my own typewriter.')

Notice the pattern with ***of*** + possessive + ***own***.

E.g. *She keeps wanting to use my telephone. I wish she would get* { *a telephone* / *one* } ***of her own***.

3 The possessive forms can either refer back to the subject, or to someone / something else. The situation makes it clear.

E.g. *'Myra lent Peter* ***her*** *watch.' 'Why did Peter want to borrow* ***her*** *watch?' 'Because someone else had borrowed* ***his****.'*

3a Notice that when a person is the subject, we use ***his***, ***her***, etc. in referring to parts of that person's body.

E.g. (i) ***My brother*** *broke* ***his leg*** *skiing*.
(ii) ***Maria*** *is drying* ***her hair***.

3b But when the person is the object, and the part of the body follows the object, we use ***the***.

E.g. *She kissed* ***her mother*** *on* ***the cheek.***
William banged ***himself*** *on* ***the head.***
We all gave ***the winners*** *a pat on* ***the back***.

possibility

1 Different ways of expressing possibility.

E.g. ***can*** ***could*** ***may*** ***perhaps*** ***possibly***
can't ***couldn't*** ***may not*** ***maybe*** ***It's (just) possible that . . .***

[See CAN, COULD AND MIGHT, MAY.]
For example:

The people in the above example could also have said:

E.g. ***Could*** *they have had an accident, do you think?*
They ***couldn't (possibly)*** * *have forgotten about us, surely?*
They {***may*** / ***might***} ***(well)*** * * *have decided to catch the next plane.*
Maybe *their car broke down.* <especially U.S.>

Can, ***can't*** and ***could*** (past time) also indicate general possibility.

E.g. *Odd things* ***can*** *happen at airports,* ***can't*** *they?*
In the old days, you ***could*** *depend on trains. But these days you* ***can't*** *rely on air travel,* ***can*** *you?*

* ***Possibly*** and ***just*** <G.B.> make the possibility weaker.
* * ***Well*** makes the possibility stronger.

prefixes

► A ***prefix*** is an element which we place at the front of a word.
► In English, ***prefixes*** add something to the meaning of a word, but they do not usually change its word class. [Contrast SUFFIXES.]

Common prefixes are.

E.g.	***a-***	***a****head*, ***a****float*	[see A-WORDS]
	anti-	***anti****social*, ***anti****-war*	= 'against'
	arch-	***arch****enemy*, ***arch****duke*	= 'supreme, highest'
	bi-	***bi****cycle*, ***bi****plane*	= 'two'
	co-	***co****operate*, ***co****pilot*	= 'with'
	de-	***de****crease*, ***de****scend*	= 'down' or 'negative'
	dis-	***dis****connect*, ***dis****own*	= 'do the opposite of'
	ex-	***ex****port*[1], ***ex****-president*[2]	= [1]'out of', [2]'former'
	fore-	***fore****ground*[1], ***fore****tell*[2]	= [1]'in front of', [2]'before'
	in-	***in****come*[1], ***in****complete*[2]	= [1]'in', [2]'not'
	inter-	***inter****national*	= 'between or among'
	mal-	***mal****formed*, ***mal****treat*	= 'badly'
	mis-	***mis****hear*, ***mis****lead*	= 'wrongly'
	mono-	***mono****rail*, ***mono****syllabic*	= 'one'
	multi-	***multi****-purpose*, ***multi****racial*	= 'many'
	non-	***non****sense*, ***non****-smoker*	= 'not'
	out-	***out****cast*[1], ***out****number*[2]	= [1]'out', [2]'more than'
	over-	***over****eat*, ***over****work*	= 'too much'
	post-	***post****pone*, ***post****-war*	= 'after'
	pre-	***pre****face*, ***pre****-war*	= 'before'
	pro-	***pro****vide*, ***pro****-communist*	= 'for, on behalf of'
	re-	***re****turn*, ***re****-use*, ***re****pay*	= 'back, again'
	sub-	***sub****conscious*, ***sub****divide*	= 'under, below'
	super-	***super****market*, ***super****man*	= 'higher, superior'
	trans-	***trans****atlantic*, ***trans****act*	= 'across'
	un-	***un****fair*[1], ***un****tie*[2]	= [1]'negative', [2]'opposite to'
	under-	***under****cooked*, ***under****paid*	= 'too little, not enough'

preposition [See also PREPOSITIONAL PHRASE]

1 A preposition is a word which typically goes before a NOUN PHRASE or PRONOUN.

E.g. ***of*** *the world,* ***with*** *my best friend,* ***by*** *us,* ***at*** *a hotel*

2 **Common prepositions**

about	***at***	***down***	***near***	***past***	***to***
above	***before***	***for***	***of***	***per***	***under***
across	***below***	***from***	***off***	***since***	***until***
after	***beside***	***in***	***on***	***till***	***up***
along	***between***	***into***	***onto***	***than***	***with***
around	***but***	***like***	***over***	***through***	***without***
as	***by***				

[Look these words up under their own entries.]

2a Many less common prepositions are written as two or three words. We call these complex prepositions.

E.g. *because of, instead of, other than, out of, up to,*
in accordance with, on top of, with reference to.

[Look these up under their first word: we treat them as IDIOMS.]

3 **Position**
As its name tells us, a preposition is normally 'placed before' a noun phrase or some other element. The preposition + noun phrase together form a PREPOSITIONAL PHRASE.

3a Sometimes the preposition goes at the end of a clause or sentence.

Social usage: The preposition at the end is common in <speech> and <informal writing>. But some people regard it as 'more correct' to put the preposition at the front of the clause. This is possible for (I) and (II) in 3b below.

E.g. (I) ***For whom** is she working?* <formal>
(II) *The town **in which** he was born.* <rather formal>

But the preposition at the front is common only in <formal writing>. In general, do not be afraid to put the preposition at the end.

3b Position of prepositions in different kinds of sentence:
In (I)–(VIII) below, the first example in each section shows the preposition at the end of the sentence, and the second example shows the preposition in its usual position, at the front of its noun phrase.

(I) QUESTION: ***Who** is she working **for**? She's working **for a friend**.*
(II) RELATIVE CLAUSE: *the town (**that**) he was born **in**. He was born **in the town of Omsk**.*
(III) INDIRECT QUESTION: *I wonder **which team** he plays **for**. He plays **for the home team**.*
(IV) EXCLAMATION: ***What** a terrible situation she's **in**! She's **in a terrible situation**.*
(V) PASSIVE: *He's being well **looked after**. They're looking **after him** well.*
(VI) COMPARATIVE: *She's been to more countries **than** I've been **to**. I've been **to fewer countries**.*
(VII) INFINITIVE: *This pen is difficult to write **with**. It's difficult to write **with this pen**.*
(VIII) Emphatic WORD ORDER: ***Some games** I'm quite good **at** . . .*
*. . . but I'm hopeless **at golf**.*

prepositional adverb

► Many word forms which are prepositions are also adverbs. We call them ***prepositional adverbs***. Most of them are adverbs of place.

1 A list of common prepositional adverbs.

about	***around***	***beyond***	***near***	***past***	***under***
above	***before***	***by***	***on***	***round***	***up***
across	***behind***	***down***	***opposite***	***since***	***within***
after	***below***	***in***	***outside***	***through***	***without***
along	***between***	***inside***	***over***	***throughout***	

[Look up these words (except for *beyond, inside*, and *outside*) in their separate entries.]

2 Prepositions are usually in front of a noun phrase, whereas prepositional adverbs usually stand alone, without a following noun phrase. Compare.

E.g. (i) preposition: *He stayed* ***in the house***.
adverb: *He stayed* ***in***.
(ii) preposition: *The guests were standing* ***around the room***.
adverb: *The guests were standing* ***around***.

2a Prepositional adverbs are always stressed. Prepositions are frequently unstressed.

prepositional phrase [See also PREPOSITION, PHRASE.]

► A ***prepositional phrase*** is a group of words composed of a preposition and the word(s) which follow(s) it (normally a noun phrase).

► Like ADVERBS, ***prepositional phrases*** express many different meanings, such as PLACE, TIME, REASON.

E.g. *We must discuss the matter* { ***in private***. (prepositional phrase) / ***privately***. (adverb) }

► Like adverbs, ***prepositional phrases*** are often optional parts of a sentence: we can omit them if we like.

1 **Forms of prepositional phrases**

most common:

PREPOSITION + { (i) NOUN PHRASE / (ii) PRONOUN }

less common:

PREPOSITION + { (iii) -ING CLAUSE / (iv) WH- CLAUSE / (v) ADVERB }

1a Examples:

(i) *Here's a letter* ***from my son Philip****.*
(ii) *Come* ***with me****, please.*
(iii) *This is an oven* ***for baking bread****.*
(iv) *I was surprised* ***at what they said****.*
(v) ***From here****, the road is very rough.*

2 **Positions of prepositional phrases in the sentence**
Prepositional phrases have two main roles in sentences:

(I) They can be ADVERBIALS.

E.g. ***On Friday****, the Prime Minister will make a press statement.* (Front position)
The castle is closed ***for urgent repairs****.* (End position)
This year's figures, ***to everyone's surprise****, showed a loss of $500 million.* (Middle position)

(II) They can be MODIFIERS after a noun.

E.g. *a loss* ***of $500 million****,* *the meeting* ***on Friday****,*
the smile ***on her face****,* *his marriage* ***to a princess***

2a One prepositional phrase can contain other prepositional phrases.

(i)
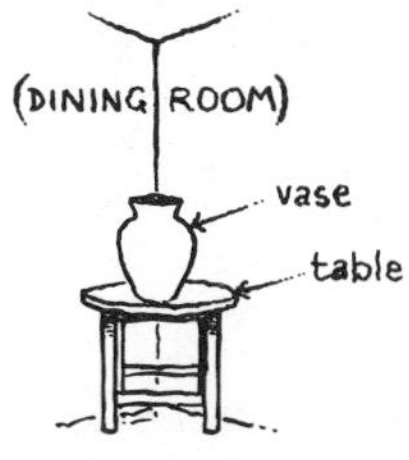

(ii)

E.g. (i) *'Where did you get that vase (****on*** *the table (****in*** *the corner (****of*** *the dining room)))?*
(ii) *'I bought it (****at*** *a little shop (****near*** *the post office (****in*** *Middle Street))).'*

3 A preposition sometimes follows a verb or an adjective, and forms an IDIOM with it.

(I) VERB + PREPOSITION

E.g. ***Look at*** *that picture.*
I ***approve of*** *what he said.*

[See PREPOSITIONAL VERB.]

(II) ADJECTIVE + PREPOSITION

E.g. *I'm not **fond of** tennis.*
*She's **afraid of** losing money.*

[See ADJECTIVE PATTERNS.]

prepositional verb

1 We use the term prepositional verb for an IDIOM made up of verb + preposition.

E.g.

add to	*believe in*	*insist on*	*pay for*
agree with	*belong to*	*listen to*	*pray for*
aim at / for	*call for / on*	*live on*	*refer to*
allow for	*care for*	*long for*	*rely on*
apply for	*consent to*	*look after*	*run for*
approve of	*deal with*	*look at*	*stand for*
ask for	*decide on*	*look for*	*take after / to*
attend to	*hope for*	*object to*	*wish for*

2 The verb and preposition express a single idea.

E.g. *She **takes after** her grandmother.* (= 'resembles')
*We've **asked for** help.* (= 'requested')
*I have to **look after** the house.* (= 'take care of')
*I'm **looking for** my keys. Have you seen them?* (= 'seeking')

3 The verb and prepositon are often together at the end of a sentence [see PREPOSITION 3].

E.g. *'What are you **listening to**?' 'I'm **listening to** the news.'*
*I don't know who this book **belongs to**.*
*We scarcely have enough to **live on**.*
*Have the new chairs been **paid for**?*

It is sometimes awkward or impossible to separate the prepositon from the verb.

E.g. *~~To~~ what are you **listening**?*
*I don't know ~~to~~ whom this book **belongs**.*

4 It is important to distinguish prepositional verbs and phrasal verbs such as ***look up***. [See PHRASAL VERB 1, 5b.]

present participle

This term is used in some grammars for the ***-ing*** participle, or ***-ing*** form.

E.g. *'What are you do**ing**?' 'I'm mak**ing** tea.'*

[See PARTICIPLE, -ING FORM.]

present perfect

► The ***Present Perfect*** form of the verb phrase contains ***has*** or ***have*** + past participle.

► See PAST TIME for the choice between the Past Simple form and the ***Present Perfect***.

► The ***Present Perfect*** describes a past happening which is related in some way to the present time.

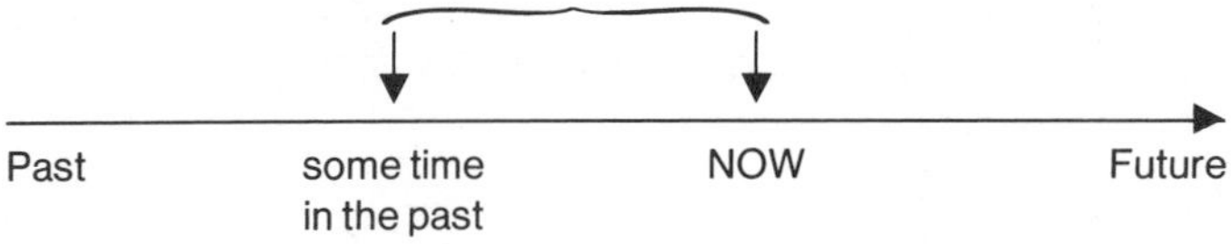

1 Here is a summary of the main uses of the Present Perfect, as shown below:
(i) Talking about something which began in the past and hasn't changed. (especially with FOR, SINCE) [see 5a below].
(ii) Talking about general experience; e.g. what you have done in your life up to now (especially with EVER or NEVER) [see 5b below].
(iii) Talking about recent events or states (especially with ALREADY, STILL AND YET) [see 5c below].
(iv) Talking about very recent events (with JUST) [see 5d below].
(v) Talking about events whose results are still noticeable (especially with the Present Perfect Progressive) [see 5e, 7d below].

NOTE: In <U.S.> the Past Simple is often used instead of the Present Perfect, especially with meanings (ii), (iii), and (iv).
E.g. ***Did** your friend **arrive** yet?*

2 **Present Perfect forms**

2a STATEMENT:

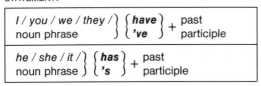

I / you / we / they / noun phrase	***have*** / ***'ve***	+	past participle
he / she / it / noun phrase	***has*** / ***'s***	+	past participle

E.g. ***I've been*** * *to Africa and Europe. My husband* ***has promised*** *to take me to the United States next year.* <mainly G.B.>

* [For the use of ***been*** see 5e: NOTE below.]

2b QUESTION form:

Have	*I / you / we / they / etc.*	+	past participle

Has	*he / she / it / etc.*	+	past participle

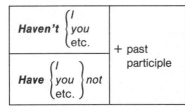

E.g. ***Have*** *you* ***had*** *breakfast?* ***Has*** *the bank* ***opened*** *yet?*

2c NEGATIVE form:

I / you / we / They / etc.	***haven't*** / ***have not***	+ past participle
He / she / It / etc.	***hasn't*** / ***has not***	+ past participle

E.g. *I* ***haven't paid*** *the bill, and they****'ve cut*** *off my phone.*
It ***hasn't rained*** *for months.*

2d Negative question form:

Haven't *I / you / etc.*	+ past participle
Have *I / you / etc.* *not*	

Hasn't *he / she / etc.*	+ past participle
Has *he / she / etc.* *not*	

E.g. ***Haven't*** *you* ***tasted*** *Chinese tea before?* <mainly G.B.>
Has *it not* ***arrived*** *yet?* <more formal>

3 Present Perfect Progressive forms

HAS / HAVE + BEEN + Verb ***-ing***

3a Statement:
E.g. *I* ***have been reading*** *all afternoon.* *It* ***has been raining*** *again.*

3b Question form:
E.g. ***Has*** *anyone* ***been working*** *today?* *What* ***have*** *you* ***been doing****?*

3c Negative form:
E.g. *I* ***haven't been getting*** *much exercise recently.*
My watch ***hasn't been keeping*** *time since I wore it in the bath!*

3d Negative question form:
E.g. ***Hasn't*** *anyone* ***been doing*** *the housework?*
Why ***haven't*** *you* ***been sleeping*** *properly?*

4 Passive forms

HAS / HAVE + BEEN + PAST PARTICIPLE

4a Statement:
E.g. *My car* ***has been stolen****. The police* ***have been informed****.*

4b Question form:
E.g. ***Has*** *the house* ***been sold*** *yet?*
Have *you* ***been given*** *any information?*

4c Negative form:
E.g. *The bill* ***hasn't*** *been* ***paid*** *yet. But fortunately the gas and electricity* ***have not yet been cut off****.*

4d Negative question form:
E.g. ***Haven't*** *you* ***been told*** *what to do?* ***Hasn't*** *the plan* ***been decided*** *yet?*

5 How to use the Present Perfect

5a When talking about something which began in the past, and has continued up to the present we use the Present Perfect:

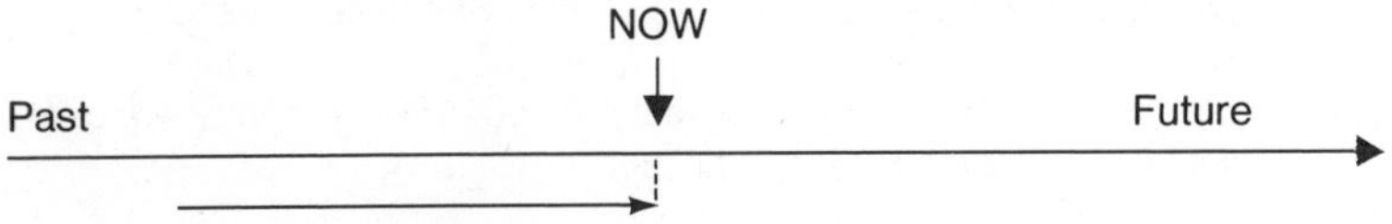

We always need to mention a period of time, e.g. a FOR-phrase, a SINCE-phrase, or a SINCE-clause.

E.g. *I* ***have studied*** *English* ***since*** *I started secondary school.*

The question ***how long?*** asks for a LENGTH OF TIME expression in reply.

E.g.

NOTE: The Present Perfect cannot go with an expression of PAST TIME.
E.g. *I have studied English for a long time ~~last year~~.*

5b We use the Present Perfect when talking about our experience up to now in life:

E.g. *I **have visited** Rio, but I **have** never **been** to Buenos Aires.*
(***never*** = at no time up to now)
*'**Has** anyone ever **climbed** that mountain?' 'Yes, several times.'*
(***ever*** = at any time up to now)

5c We use the Present Perfect when talking about something in the more recent past:

E.g. (i)

(ii) *'Do you want to see the new* {*movie* <U.S.> / *film* <G.B.>} "Flood and Fire"?' 'I've ***already*** *seen it. Have you seen "Zero"?'*

[See ALREADY, STILL, AND YET for further details. ***Already*** occurs mainly in statements, and ***yet*** occurs in questions or with negatives.]

5d When talking about something that happened very recently, we can use *has* or *have* + *just* + past participle:

E.g. ***I've just had*** *a delicious meal.*

5e When talking of an event or action which happened very recently, we often use the Present Perfect (especially the Present Perfect Progressive) without any adverbial. The meaning in this case is usually that the results are still there in the present.

E.g. (i) *Somebody**'s been washing** the floor.* ('It's still wet')
(ii) *Somebody**'s borrowed** my pen.* ('I can't find it')
(iii) ***Haven't*** *you* ***heard*** *the news? The President* ***has been shot!***
(iv) *Pam isn't here. She**'s gone** shopping.*

NOTE: The verb ***go*** has two past participles, ***gone*** and ***been***. [See COME AND GO for further details.]

6 **Present Perfect referring to the future**
After WHEN, AFTER, *as soon as*, or UNTIL we use the Present Perfect (instead of *will be* + Past Participle) in talking about the future [Compare PRESENT SIMPLE 3a].

E.g. *You can leave* ***as soon as*** *your passport* ***has been*** *checked.*
'Can I borrow your ladder for a moment?'
'No, I'm using it. You'll have to wait ***until I've finished****.'*

7 How to use the Present Perfect Progressive
[For the forms, see **3** above.]

7a We use the Present Perfect Progressive in talking about an activity in the recent past:

E.g. *'Where have you been?'* ***'I've been returning*** *a library book.'*
'What have you been doing?' ***'I've been*** { ***reading****.'* / ***washing*** *the car.'* / ***cooking*** *lunch.'* }

7b We can use this form to talk about a job or activity which is not finished:

E.g. (i) *He****'s been writing*** *the story of his life. It will take him years to finish.*

Contrast the ordinary Present Perfect:

E.g. (ii) *He****'s written*** *the story of his life.* (i.e. 'He's finished the whole job.')

7c We generally use the Present Perfect Progressive with a FOR- or SINCE-expression in talking about an action or activity which began in the past and has continued up to the present. This is similar to the ordinary Present Perfect in 5 above.

E.g. *They****'ve been building*** *that bridge for ages.*
*She****'s been working*** *at the factory since she left school.*
*We****'ve been living*** *in this* { *flat* <mainly G.B.> / *apartment* <U.S.> } *since 1980.*

NOTE (i): The Present Perfect Progressive is not used with a STATE VERB e.g. *know*, *understand*, *seem*.
E.g. *I've* { ***known*** / ~~***been knowing***~~ } *the Browns for about a year.*

NOTE (ii): In this use, the Progressive can refer to something continuing over quite a long period.
E.g. ***'How long*** *have you been learning English?' 'Oh,* ***for over ten years*** *now.'*

7d When the Present Perfect Progressive has no adverbial, this often means that the results of the activity can still be seen:

E.g. *Look! It**'s been raining**.* (i.e. 'The streets are wet')
*You**'ve been cooking** onions!* ('I can smell it')

NOTE: The Present Perfect Progressive can occur with the Passive, but it is <very rare>.
E.g. *That bridge **has been being built** for ages.*

8 Here are some examples showing the difference between:

	Present Perfect	Present Perfect Progressive

(i)	*'Who**'s eaten** my sandwich?'* (The plate is empty.)	*'Who**'s been eating** my sandwich?'* (some is left.)
(ii)	*'It **has snowed** every winter for years.'* (A repeated occurrence)	*'It **has been snowing** all day.'* (A continuing activity)
(iii)	*'I**'ve read** your book.'* (I've finished it.)	*'I**'ve been reading** your book.'* (I haven't finished it.)

---

present progressive (Also called 'Present Continuous')

This is the form of the Verb with ***am***, ***is***, or ***are*** followed by the -ING FORM.

E.g. *'What **are** you **doing** this evening?' 'Richard **is going** to the football match, but I**'m staying** at home.'*
*'Do you want to come for a walk now?' 'No, I**'m working**.'*

[See PROGRESSIVE for details of the Progressive form and its meaning. See PRESENT TIME and FUTURE to find out how to use the Present Progressive.]

---

present simple [See VERB PHRASE]

► When we use a Present Tense main verb and no auxiliary verb, the form of the verb is called ***Present Simple**** [contrast PRESENT PROGRESSIVE, PRESENT PERFECT]. E.g. ***come***, ***comes***.

► The ***Present Simple*** is the most common way of expressing PRESENT TIME.
► The ***Present Simple*** has three major meanings [see 2 below] and two 'special meanings' [see 3 below].

* In questions and negatives, however, the ***Present Simple*** is formed with ***do*** + main verb. [See DO 2.]

1 Forms of the Present Simple

1a 3rd person singular subjects:
He ***works***
Jane (= she) ***works***
The boss (= he or she) ***works***
The telephone (= it) ***works***
Her best friend ***works***

All other subjects:
I ***work***
You ***work***
We ***work***
They ***work***
Her best friends ***work***

NOTE (i): [On how to pronounce and spell the **-s** form, see PRONUNCIATION OF ENDINGS, SPELLING.]

NOTE (ii): Note the following irregularities:

	be	have	do	say
I	*am*			
we / you / they	*are*			
he / she / it	*is* /ɪz/	*has* /hæz/	*does* /dʌz/	*says* *

* The irregularity here is in the pronunciation: /sez/.

1b In questions, use ***do*** or ***does*** [see DO 2] before the subject:

DO + SUBJECT + Verb
E.g. *What* ***do*** *you mean?*

DOES + SUBJECT + Verb
Does *Mr Jones smoke?*

1c In negative sentences / clauses use ***do*** or ***does*** followed by ***not*** or ***-n't***:

E.g. *Cats* ***don't*** *like ice-cream.* *This lamp* ***doesn't*** *work.*

2 Three important meanings of the Present Simple

2a A present state:
The Present Simple often indicates a state which exists now. For example, it refers to a fact which is always or generally true.

E.g. *The sun* ***rises*** *in the east.*
Some teachers ***have*** *a difficult job.*
*'****Are*** *you from Singapore?' 'No, I* ***am*** *Japanese.'*

The Present Simple can also refer to states which could change.

E.g. *'Where **does** Mr Barr **live**?' 'I'm sorry, I **don't know**. I **think** he **lives** in the next street.'* [See STATE VERBS.]

NOTE: [On the difference between ***lives*** and ***is living*** see PRESENT TIME.]

2b A present habit:
The Present Simple can also refer to 'an action we repeat regularly', i.e. a habit or custom.

E.g. (i) *'What **do** you **do** on weekdays?' 'Well, I **get up** at seven, **have** breakfast, **walk** to the station, and **catch** the train to work. I **arrive** home from work at about six o'clock.'*

(ii) A: *I'd like to buy a present for my husband.*
B: ***Does** he **smoke**?*
A: *No, he **doesn't**.*
B: ***Does** he **play** any sport?*
A: *Yes, he sometimes **plays** tennis.*

The Present Simple can be used with FREQUENCY adverbs like *always*, *never*, *sometimes*, *ever*, *usually*, *often*.

E.g. *'What **do** you **do** at weekends?' 'Well, I **don't work** at weekends, so I **usually go** shopping on Saturday. In summer I **sometimes go** fishing and in winter, I **often play** football. I **never go** swimming. I **hate** it.'*

2c A present event:
This meaning of the Present Simple is less common; it refers to an event which happens at the very moment of speaking, for example when we describe what we are saying as 'offering', 'accepting', 'begging'.

Form: *I / we* + Verb + . . .

E.g. *I **regret** that I made a mistake.*
*We **accept** your kind offer.*
*I **beg** you to be more careful.*
<rather formal>

NOTE: The 'event' meaning of the Present Simple is found also (i) in newspaper headlines.
E.g. *Italy **wins** World Cup.* *Monkeys **escape** from London Zoo.*
(ii) in sports commentaries [e.g. football). E.g. *Gardiner **passes** the ball to Jones.*

3 **Two special meanings of the Present Simple**
These meanings are called 'special' because in them the Present Simple describes not present time, but future or past time.

3a Referring to future time:
The Present Simple can refer to the future [see FUTURE 3] in the following cases:
(i) in describing fixed or planned events.

E.g. *Tomorrow **is** Bella's birthday.*
*My plane **leaves** at 7 o'clock this evening.*

(ii) in IF-clauses, WHEN-clauses, etc.

E.g. *If it **rains**, we'll get wet.*
*They will phone us when they **arrive**.*

3b Referring to past time:
The Present Simple sometimes refers to events in the past. This is called the 'Historic Present' and is used in telling stories, but it is not common. The Present Simple makes a story more exciting and like real life.

E.g. *So she **comes** through the door, and he **says** 'Where were you at 9 o'clock?' She **replies** 'With Jack.' His face **goes** white with anger . . .*

Generally, however, we prefer the Past Simple.

E.g. *So she **came** through the door, and he **said** . . .*

present tense

1 If an English word is a FINITE verb, it normally has a difference of form between Present Tense forms (e.g. *look, looks*) and a Past Tense form (e.g. *looked*).

2 **Forms**
Most verbs form their Present Tense form like this:

singular	
I, you	***like, know***
he, she, it	***likes, knows***

plural	
we *you* *they*	***like, know***

When the subject is 3rd person singular, we use the -S FORM of the verb. Otherwise, we use the BASIC FORM of the verb (without any ending) [see AGREEMENT 1].

E.g. ***take** → **takes*** ***eat** → **eats*** ***go** → **goes***

[On how to spell and pronounce the **-s** form of the verb, see SPELLING, PRONUNCIATION OF ENDINGS.]

2a The verb BE is an exception; it has three Present Tense forms:

singular	
I	***am***
you	***are***
he, she, it	***is***

plural	
we *you* *they*	***are***

2b MODAL AUXILIARIES are also exceptions; they have no **-s** form, and so do not change their form at all:

E.g. *it* {***will*** / ~~***wills***~~} ~ *they* ***will***.

2c [See VERB PHRASE on how to combine Present Tense verbs with other verbs, to form the Present Progressive, Present Perfect, and Present Passive.]

3 **Meanings and uses**
[See PRESENT PERFECT, PRESENT SIMPLE and PRESENT TIME for further information.]

present time

► There are two main ways of using a verb to refer to the ***present time***: the Present Simple and the Present Progressive. Here we show how to choose between them. [For further details, see the separate entries for PRESENT SIMPLE and PROGRESSIVE.]

1 **Present Simple** (e.g. ***comes***)
Choose this if the time you are thinking of includes the present moment and is unlimited in length (i.e. it is always true):

1a General facts:

E.g. *Ice **melts** in a warm climate.*

1b Habits, i.e. happenings which are repeated:

E.g. *My brother **smokes** twenty cigarettes a day.*
*The doctor **gets up** at 6.30 every morning.*
*In Britain we **have** turkey for Christmas dinner.*

1c States, [See STATE VERBS AND ACTION VERBS]:

E.g. *She **looks** like her mother.*
*This building **is** very old.*
*I **don't know** his name.*

2 **Present Progressive** (e.g. ***is coming***)
Choose this if the time you are thinking of includes the present moment and is limited (i.e. temporary):

2a The Present Progressive is used for actions over a temporary period (short or long). This period includes the time leading up to and following the present moment:

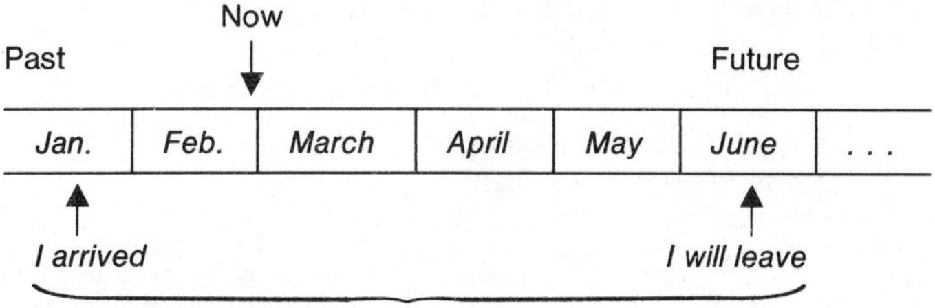

I ***am living*** *in Paris at the moment.*
I ***am staying*** *here for six months.*

Other examples:

NOTE: The temporary period can be as long as a few years, e.g. *Industry* ***is growing*** *in South America.* or as short as a few seconds, e.g. *Listen, it****'s thundering****.*

2b Also, choose the Present Progressive for a habit (or set of repeated events) which is temporary (i.e. lasts for a limited period).

E.g. *Gomez* ***is scoring*** *a lot of goals this season.*

3 **Note the contrast**

(i) *I* ***don't*** *usually* ***eat*** *sweet things.*	*But I****'m eating*** *some birthday cake today because it's Alan's birthday.*
(ii) *This watch generally* ***keeps*** *perfect time.*	*But these days it****'s not working*** *properly.*
(iii) *Normally I* ***smoke*** *twenty cigarettes a day.*	*But now* ***I'm smoking*** *only five a day, because I'm saving up for a new motorcycle.*

4 Other uses of the Present Simple

4a The Present Simple is used to refer to what is truly now.

E.g. *I **beg** your pardon. I **apologise**.*
*I **pronounce** you man and wife.*
*Gilbert **passes** the ball to Jones . . .*

These are examples of the 'event present' [see PRESENT SIMPLE 2c]. Here the present is truly now, i.e. an event at this moment.

4b With some verbs called 'state verbs' [see PROGRESSIVE] we use the Present Simple for a temporary situation.

E.g. *I **have** a headache.* *It **is** windy today.*
*You **seem** hungry.* *She **thinks** we are wrong.*

This is because these verbs cannot normally combine with the Progressive form.

E.g. *It **is** ~~**being**~~ windy today.*

5 Other uses of the Present Progressive

5a The Present Progressive is used in the following examples even though they refer to an unlimited period.

E.g. *You**'re always biting** your nails. Stop it!*
*Accidents **are always happening** on this terrible road.*
*Politicians aren't honest. They**'re always telling** lies.*

These are examples of the Progressive with ***always***: we use this IDIOM when we are annoyed about something which keeps on happening.

---

progressive (also called 'Continuous')

► The ***Progressive*** form of the verb phrase contains a form of the verb BE + the -ING FORM:

BE + Verb-***ing*** E.g. $\left\{\begin{matrix}\textbf{\textit{is}} \\ \textbf{\textit{was}}\end{matrix}\right\} \left\{\begin{matrix}\textbf{\textit{coming}} \\ \textbf{\textit{looking}}\end{matrix}\right.$

► The ***Progressive*** form usually describes a temporary happening, i.e. something which happens during a limited period.

► [See PRESENT TIME, PAST PROGRESSIVE, and PRESENT PERFECT 3, 7, 8 for further details of how we use the ***Progressive***.]

1 **Forms**

(A) Present & Past: ***be*** + Verb-***ing***

I	**{*'m* / *am*}** ***was***	***coming***
you *we* *they* (plural)	**{*'re* / *are*}** ***were***	***doing*** ***talking*** ***singing*** etc

he		***coming***
she *it* noun phrase (singular)	**{*'s* / *is*}** ***was***	***doing*** ***talking*** ***singing***

(B) Perfect: ***have*** + ***been*** + Verb-***ing***

I *you*	**{*'ve* / *have*}**	***been***	***coming*** ***doing***
we *they* noun phrase (plural)	**{*'d* / *had*}**	***been***	***talking*** ***singing*** etc.

he *she*	**{*'s* / *has*}**	***been***	***coming*** ***doing***
it noun phrase (sing.)	**{*'d* / *had*}**	***been***	***talking*** ***singing*** etc.

1a Other forms include:

(C) Modal ***Progressive***: Modal + ***be*** + Verb-***ing***

E.g. *She* ***should be working.***
You ***must be joking***.

[See MODAL AUXILIARY.]

(D) ***Progressive*** Passive: ***be*** + ***being*** + Past Participle

E.g. *Our team* ***was being*** *beaten.*
We ***are being*** *followed.*

(E) Infinitive:

E.g. ***to be playing*** ***to be lying***

NOTE: There are also <rare> forms which combine Modal, Perfect, and ***Progressive***.
E.g. *They **may have been going** to the theatre.*
And there are <very rare> forms which combine Modal and / or Perfect with the ***Progressive*** Passive.
E.g. *The cake **must be being cooked**.*
*The cake **has been being cooked** for an hour.*
*The cake **must have been being cooked**.*
[See VERB PHRASE, table II.]

1b To form the negative:
Add *-n't* or *not* after the auxiliary verb. (In <speech> we usually use a contraction [see CONTRACTION OF VERBS AND NEGATIVES 3.]
E.g. *isn't, aren't, wasn't*.)

E.g. *Lukas* {***isn't*** / ***is not***} *playing very well: he has scored only two goals this season.*

'Did you see that strange bird?' 'No, I {***wasn't*** / ***was not***} *looking.'*

1c To form a question:
Put the auxiliary verb (*am, is, was*, etc.) in front of the subject.

E.g. (i) ***'Are you getting*** *on all right?' 'Yes, I'm getting on fine.'*

(ii)

2 Uses of the Progressive

2a We usually use the Progressive to describe something that is temporary: i.e. it doesn't last long.

(i)

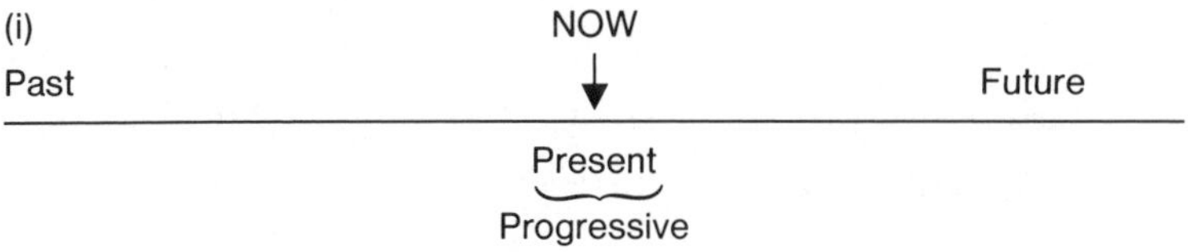

E.g. ***It is raining.***

(ii)

E.g. *It **was raining** at this time yesterday afternoon.*

(iii)

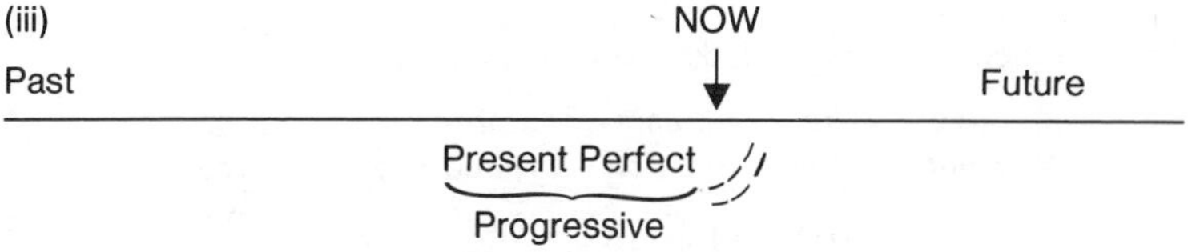

E.g. *It **has been raining** since yesterday afternoon.*

2b Normally, if something continues for a long time, it is no longer temporary: it is a state or a habit, and we use the Present Simple [see PRESENT SIMPLE 2a, 2b].

Compare: *We'**re living** in a small* {*apartment* <U.S.> / flat <mainly G.B.>} *(at present).*

*We (normally) **live** in a village near Rome.*

However, we can use the Progressive for a habit if it is temporary.

E.g. *She'**s travelling** to work by bicycle while the bus strike is on.*
*Margot **was working** in a night club when she was noticed by the manager of a West End theatre. Soon after that, she **was appearing** regularly on the West End stage.*

We can also use the Progressive for annoying habits [see PRESENT TIME 5a] with ***always***.

E.g. *You**'re always interrupting** when I talk.*
*She **was always running** away from home and **being brought** home by the police.*

Here the habit is not temporary: it goes on and on!

2c The Progressive for future actions:
The Progressive describes an action planned in the future. [See FUTURE 4.]

E.g. *'When **are** you **meeting** Bob?'*
*'**I'm meeting** him at 12 o'clock tomorrow.'*

2d *Will* + Progressive for future happenings:
Also *will* + Progressive has a special meaning in describing future happenings.

E.g. *'When **will** you **be meeting** Bob?' '**I'll be meeting** him at 12 o'clock tomorrow.'*

Unlike the example in 2c above, this example suggests that the meeting has not been specially planned.

3 Verbs not normally taking the Progressive
Be careful with verbs of the kinds outlined in 3a–3f below. They usually do not have a Progressive form, because they describe a state [see STATE VERBS AND ACTION VERBS].

3a Perception verbs (including 'seeming' verbs):

E.g.	***see***	***hear***	***taste***	***sound***	***seem***
	look	***feel***	***smell***	***recognize***	***appear***

[See PERCEPTION VERBS.]
See, ***hear***, ***feel***, ***taste***, and ***smell*** occur with CAN or COULD to express a continuing state.

E.g. ***Can*** *you **hear** the wind?*
*We **can see** the mountains from our bedroom window.*
*'That was delicious onion soup.' 'Onion soup? I **couldn't taste** any onion!'*

3b Emotion verbs and wishing verbs:

E.g.	***want (to)***	***refuse (to)***	***wish (to)***	***like***	***love***
	prefer (to)	***forgive***	***care (for)***	***dislike***	***hate***
	intend (to)	***hope (to)***	***can't stand***	***can't bear (to)***	
	don't mind				

NOTE (i): Emotion and wishing verbs can sometimes occur quite easily with the Progressive. The Progressive can have a <polite> and <tentative> meaning.
E.g. ***I am hoping*** *that you will take the part of Hamlet.*
In this situation, ***I am hoping*** is <more polite> than ***I hope***. The Past Progressive makes the sentence even <more polite>: ***I was hoping***. But in this case the Past form ***would*** has to be used, too.
E.g. ***I was hoping*** *that you* ***would*** *take the part of the Hamlet.*

NOTE (ii): Enjoy is an emotion verb, but it can occur easily with the Progressive: ***I am enjoying*** *this game.*

3c Verbs of thinking:

E.g.

think	***know***	***understand***	***realize***	***forget***
feel (= think)	***mean***	***believe***	***consider***	***remember***
imagine	***suppose***	***expect***	***doubt***	***guess***
	suspect	***wonder***	***agree***	***note***

These verbs cannot take the Progressive especially when they are followed by a THAT-clause or WH-clause.

E.g. *'**Do** you **know** whether the castle is open to visitors?'*
*'No. I **think** it is open on weekdays, but today is Sunday, so I **imagine** it is closed.'*

NOTE: But thinking verbs sometimes take the Progressive when thinking is an activity, not a passive state of mind.

(i)

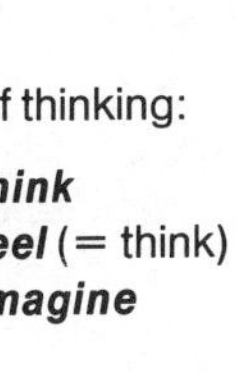

E.g. (i) *Be quiet! **I'm thinking**.*
(ii) *The police **are expecting** trouble.*

3d BE and HAVE as main verbs:
These are the most common state verbs.

E.g. *The children **have been** upstairs since 8 o'clock.*
*They **were** very tired, so I expect they **are** already asleep.*
(Not: ***are*** *already* ~~***being***~~ *asleep*)

*I **have** a headache. **Do** you **have** any sleeping pills?* (Not: ~~*are*~~ *you* ~~***having***~~. . .?)

NOTE (i): ***Have*** is also an action verb in expressions such as ***having dinner***, ***having a bath***, ***having a baby***, ***having fun***. [See HAVE 3c]

E.g.

Hello. We're at David's. He's having a party.
Oh, really ? I hope you're having a good time.

NOTE (ii): ***Be*** can also occur with the Progressive in expressions like ***being awkward***, ***being kind***, ***being a fool***, ***being a nuisance***, when these refer to actions or activities.

E.g. *You are stupid.* (A state that you can't change!)
but: *You are deliberately being stupid.* (An activity).

3e Other state verbs:

E.g.			
belong to	***contain***	***deserve***	***owe***
concern	***cost***	***keep on***	***own***
consist of	***depend (on)***	***matter***	***resemble***

*How much **does** this dictionary **cost**?*
*It **doesn't matter** if you arrive late.*
*This bottle **contains** a litre of milk.*

[See STATE VERBS.]

NOTE: Again there are exceptions where the Progressive is used, e.g. to emphasise temporary meaning.
E.g. *God knows what this meal **is costing** me!*

3f Some verbs, although they are state verbs, can occur easily with the Progressive. Here there is little difference of meaning between the Simple and the Progressive forms.

(I) ***live***, ***sit***, ***lie***, ***stand***, ***surround***

E.g. *We* { ***were sitting*** / ***sat*** } *underneath the trees.*

These verbs refer to position.

(II) ***hurt***, ***feel***, ***ache***

E.g. *I* { ***feel*** / ***am feeling*** } *ill, doctor. My back* { ***hurts*** / ***is hurting*** } *and my head* { ***aches***. / ***is aching***. }

These verbs refer to feelings inside the body.

promises

1 Forms of promise

I promise (that) { *I'll* + Verb . . . / *you will* + Verb . . . / *you can* + Verb . . . }

Or

I promise (not) to + Verb . . .

Or

{ *I'll* + Verb . . . / *You will* + Verb . . . / *You can* + Verb . . . }

2 Examples

OR

3 How to report a promise

{ *I* / *She* / *They* } ***promised*** { *(that)* { *she* / *they* } *would* + Verb . . . / *(not) to* + Verb . . . }

E.g. DIRECT SPEECH: *'I'll help you.'*

INDIRECT SPEECH: *She* ***promised*** { *that she would help me.* / *to help me.* }

---

pronoun

- A ***pronoun*** is a grammatical word which we use instead of a NOUN or NOUN PHRASE.
- ***Pronouns*** can be SUBJECT, OBJECT, or COMPLEMENT in a sentence. They can also follow a preposition.
- ***Pronouns*** have a very general meaning (either definite or indefinite – see Table below).

There are the following kinds of pronoun in English [look up each of them for further information]:

(definite pronouns)	personal pronouns:	e.g. ***I***, ***you***, ***he***, ***her***, ***we***, ***they***, ***them*** (including POSSESSIVE PRONOUNS, e.g. ***hers***, ***ours***)
	reflexive pronouns: [see -SELF, -SELVES]	e.g. ***myself***, ***herself***, ***yourself***, ***themselves***
	demonstrative pronouns: [see DEMONSTRATIVES]	***this***, ***that***, ***these***, ***those***
indefinite pronouns:		e.g. ***all***, ***any***, ***none***, ***some***, ***each***, ***everyone***, ***anyone***, ***nobody***, ***something***
relative pronouns: [see RELATIVE CLAUSE]		***who (whom***, ***whose)***, ***which***, ***that***
wh-pronouns: [see WH-WORDS]		***who (whom***, ***whose)***, ***what***, ***which*** (including also WH-EVER pronouns)

pronunciation of endings

1 The two most regular endings in English are the **-s** ending and the ***-ed*** ending. The rules for their pronunciation do not change. They are the same for different types of word. [See SPELLING for how to spell these endings.]

2 The **-s** ending has four different uses:

-s is used to form:	pronunciation add -/ɪz/	add -/z/	add -/s/
PLURAL nouns	*voice* → ***voices*** /vɔɪs/ → /vɔɪsɪz/	*day* → ***days*** /deɪ/ → /deɪz/	*act* → ***acts*** /ækt/ → /ækts/
POSSESSIVE nouns	*James* → ***James's*** /dʒeɪmz/ → /dʒeɪmzɪz/	*Ann* → ***Ann's*** /æn/ → /ænz/	*Mark* → ***Mark's*** /mɑːʳk/ → /mɑːʳks/
3rd PERSON singular verbs (-S FORM)	*teach* → ***teaches*** /tiːtʃ/ → /tiːtʃɪz/	*lead* → ***leads*** /liːd/ → /liːdz/	*like* → ***likes*** /laɪk/ → /laɪks/
CONTRACTIONS of ***is*** and ***has***	(no contraction)	*she is* → ***she's*** /ʃiː/ → /ʃiːz/	*it is* → ***it's*** /ɪt/ → /ɪts/

2a How to choose between the three pronunciations -/ɪz/, -/z/, and -/s/: Add -/ɪz/ after consonants which have a 'hissing' or 'buzzing' sound, i.e. after /z/, /s/, /dʒ/, /tʃ/, /ʒ/, /ʃ/.

E.g. *refuses, passes, judges, watches, garages, wishes.*

Add -/z/ after any other voiced sound: i.e. after a vowel, or after the voiced consonants /b/, /d/, /g/, /v/, /ð/, /m/, /n/ /ŋ/, /l/, /r/.

E.g. *boys, lies, ways, pubs, words, pigs, loves, bathes, rooms, turns, things, walls, cars.*

Add -/s/ after any other voiceless sound: i.e. after the consonants /p/, /t/, /k/, /f/, /θ/.

E.g. *cups, cats, walks, laughs, tenths.*

NOTE: [See IRREGULAR PLURAL for nouns which do not form their plural in this way. See -S FORM for irregular 3rd person singular verbs.]

3 The ***-ed*** ending is used for the Past Tense and Past Participle of regular verbs:

-ed is used to form:	pronunciation		
	add -/ɪd/	add -/d/	add -/t/
past forms of the verb	*need* → ***needed*** /ni:d/ → /ni:dɪd/	*fill* → ***filled*** /fɪl/ → /fɪld/	*work* → ***worked*** /wɜ:ʳk/ /wɜ:ʳkt/
	want → ***wanted*** /wɒnt/ → /wɒntɪd/	*try* → ***tried*** /traɪ/ → /traɪd/	*help* → ***helped*** /help/ → /helpt/

3a How to choose between the three pronunciations -/ɪd/, -/d/, and -/t/: Add -/ɪd/ after a /d/ or a /t/.

E.g. *add**ed**, land**ed**, arrest**ed**, start**ed**, visit**ed**, demand**ed***

Add -/d/ after any other voiced sound: i.e. after a vowel, or after the voiced consonants /b/, /g/, /v/, /ð/, /z/, /ʒ/, /dʒ/, /m/, /n/, /ŋ/, /l/, /r/.

E.g. *stay**ed**, ti**ed**, pai**d**, robb**ed**, liv**ed**, us**ed**, judg**ed**, seem**ed**, turn**ed**, long**ed**, fail**ed**, car**ed**.*

Add -/t/ after any other voiceless sound, i.e. the consonants /p/, /k/, /f/, /θ/, /s/, /ʃ/, /tʃ/.

E.g. *develop**ed**, look**ed**, laugh**ed**, berth**ed**, miss**ed**, wish**ed**, watch**ed***

NOTE (i): [See the list of IRREGULAR VERBS at the back of the book for verbs which have irregular Past forms.]

NOTE (ii): [On how to pronounce the endings ***-er*** and ***-est*** (comparative and superlative), see -ER / -EST (especially 2 Note (i), on exceptions).]

proper noun [See NAMES.]

provided (that), providing (that) /prəˈvaɪdɪd (ðət)/, /prəˈvaɪdɪŋ (ðət)/

These are conditional conjunctions with the same meaning. They mean 'if and *only* if', 'on condition that', and they introduce a SUBORDINATE CLAUSE.

E.g. ***Provided* / *Providing*** ***(that)*** *you leave now, you'll reach the library before it closes.*

punctuation

1 The main punctuation marks of English are:

1a [.] A full-stop <G.B.> (or period <U.S.>) marks the end of a sentence.
It also sometimes marks an abbreviation, as in:

m.p.h. = miles per hour
etc. = et cetera
in. = inch

1b [,] A comma helps us to divide a sentence into smaller units of meaning (e.g. clauses), so that it is easier to make sense of it when reading. [See the separate entry COMMA.]

1c [?] The question mark goes at the end of a sentence which is a question.

E.g. *Is that your answer?* *Why don't you listen?*

1d [!] An exclamation {mark <G.B.> / point <U.S.>} goes at the end of a sentence to express emotional emphasis, e.g. in an exclamation [see EXCLAMATION 4: Note]. But we do not use it too often. Compare:

What a nuisance! / *What a nuisance.* } *We've run out of fuel.*

NOTE: If a sentence has direct speech in it, question marks and exclamation marks can be used at the end of the direct speech within that sentence.
E.g. *'What a mess!'* / *'What a mess,'* } *she said.* *'Where to?' asked the taxi-driver.*

1e [;] The semi-colon is used in <rather formal> writing. It is 'heavier' than a comma. Use it especially to separate two sentences which are closely linked in meaning.

E.g. *Many people dislike using semi-colons; personally, I find the semi-colon a very useful punctuation mark.*

1f [:] The colon is similar to the semi-colon. But it implies that what follows it is an explanation of what goes before it.

E.g. *They ordered a huge four-course lunch: first they had soup, then a chicken curry; this was followed by ice-cream, and finally cheese and biscuits.*

1g [–] The dash <informal>.
[( )] Brackets* <more formal>. } These are useful for separating a part of a sentence which adds subordinate information, and could be omitted.

E.g. *The second of the two wanted men* {*– George Matthews –* / *(George Matthews)*} *has not been seen for several years.*

* Called 'parentheses' in <U.S.>.

1h [“ ”] or [‘ ’] Quotation marks or 'quotes' are used to enclose direct speech or other quoted material. [See DIRECT SPEECH for further details.]

---

purpose

► ***Purpose*** expressions answer the question WHY?

1 Ways of expressing purpose

1a Prepositional phrase beginning with FOR {+ noun (phrase). / + Verb-*ing*}

E.g. *'What is this £5* ***for****?' 'It's* ***for food****.'*
'What is this hole ***for****?'* ***'For*** *measur****ing*** *rainfall.'*

1b Clauses beginning with TO; or ***in order to*** <formal>; or ***so as to*** <formal>.

E.g. *'Why did you phone your wife?'* ***'To*** *tell her I would be late.'*
(In order) to *improve safety on the roads, the Ministry of Transport has begun a big new advertising programme.* <rather formal>

The negatives are: ***not to***, ***in order not to***, ***so as not to***.

E.g. {***In order*** / ***So as***} ***not to*** *disappoint the miners, the minister has offered them better pay and conditions.*

1c Clauses beginning with ***in order that*** <formal> or ***so that**** <not so formal>.

E.g. *We are advertising the course* {***in order that*** / ***so that****} *everyone will know about it.*

* [***So that*** can also mean RESULT.]

---

quantity words

► To express ***quantity***, we use DETERMINERS, PRONOUNS, NUMBERS, and NOUNS.

1 **Patterns**

These are the different patterns for expressing quantity:

(I) QUANTITY WORD alone

E.g. *'How many apples did you buy?'* ***'Five.'***

(II) QUANTITY WORD + OF + NOUN PHRASE

E.g. *I ate **five of the apples**.*

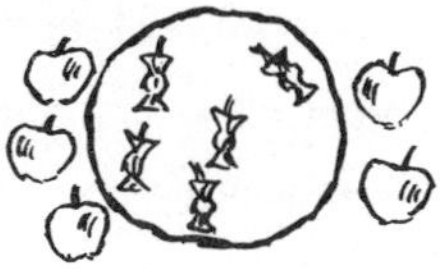

(III) QUANTITY WORD + (MODIFIER(S)) + NOUN

E.g. *I ate **five apples**.*

1a These quantity words can be used in all three patterns:

all, half, each, either, neither, some and any, enough, both, several, many, few, a few / fewer / fewest, more / most, less / least, much, little, a little, one, the whole

NOTE: These words have separate entries. Look them up for further details.

Also cardinal NUMBERS: ***two, three, . . . ten, . . . twenty, . . . forty-five, . . . a hundred, . . . a thousand, . . . a million, . . .*** etc. [see NUMBERS 5]

1b These quantity words can be used in patterns I and II only:

(pronoun): ***none***

(nouns): ***a lot lots*** [see LOTS OF, A LOT OF]

a bit a / the majority [see A BIT, A BIT OF]

a number numbers

a quantity quantities

a mass masses

a quarter, two-thirds, 2.3, etc. [see FRACTIONS, DECIMALS]

a couple, a dozen

dozens, hundreds, thousands, millions, etc.

1c These quantity words can be used in pattern III only:

(determiners): ***every, no***

NOTE: In pattern I or II, the ***quantity word*** is a noun or a pronoun. In pattern III, the ***quantity word*** is a determiner.

2 The noun phrase that goes with the quantity word
Different quantity words go with different types of noun phrase. For example, ***every*** can be followed only by a singular countable noun phrase.

E.g. *We study English* ***every*** *day.*

[To find out what type of noun phrase to use with a quantity word, look up the entry for the word.]

3 Meaning
There is an important difference of meaning between these two patterns:

QUANTITY DETERMINER + NOUN PHRASE	and	QUANTITY PRONOUN + ***of*** + NOUN PHRASE (Here ***of*** means '***part***', '***not all***')
E.g. *He gave me* ***a few*** *books.*	and	*He gave me* ***a few of*** *the books.*

(= 'about 3 or 4 books')

(= 'He had lots of books (e.g. 20), and he only gave me some of them (say, 3 or 4).')

This applies to all the words in 1a above.

4 *Whole* and *half*
WHOLE and HALF are rather different from other quantity words. [Look them up for details.]

(a) quarter /ə'kwɔ:^{r}tə^{r}/ (*noun*)

A ***quarter*** = $\frac{1}{4}$. [See FRACTIONS.] (also called ***a fourth*** <U.S.>)
A ***quarter*** *past eight* = 8.15.
A ***quarter*** *to seven* = 6.45. [See TIME (telling the)]
A ***quarter*** is also the name of a U.S. coin (= 25 cents) [see MONEY].

question

1 On how to ask a question, please see the following: YES-NO QUESTION; WH-QUESTION; TAG QUESTION; INDIRECT QUESTION.]

2 [On questions about alternatives, see OR.]

3 [On the way the voice rises or falls at the end of a question, see INTONATION 3.]

question word [See WH-WORD]

quite and *rather* /kwaɪt/, /ˈrɑːðəʳ‖ ˈræðəʳ/ (*adverbs of degree*)

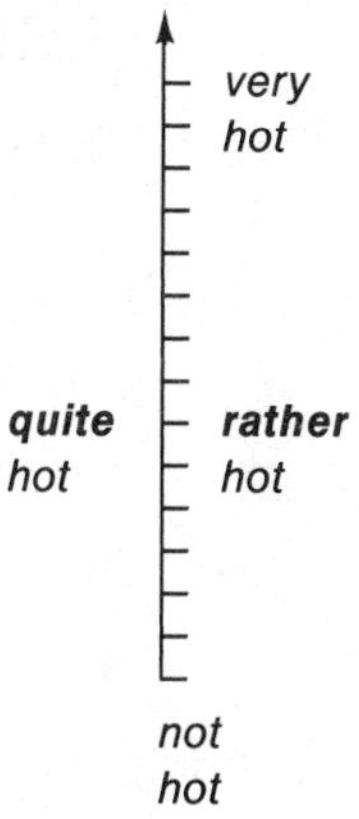

- **Quite** and **rather** are similar adverbs: they indicate a medium point on a scale [see DEGREE 2].
- But **quite** and **rather** sometimes suggest different attitudes [see 2 below].
- Also, **quite** has a special meaning of 'completely', 'entirely'. E.g. ***quite** impossible.*
- **Rather** is less used in <U.S.>.

1 Positions of *quite* and *rather*

QUITE / RATHER } + { ADJECTIVE (a) / ADVERB (b) / MAIN VERB (c) }

QUITE A / RATHER A } + SINGULAR NOUN (PHRASE) (d)

E.g. (a) adjectives:
***quite** old*, ***quite** tall*
***rather** old*, ***rather** tall*

(b) adverbs:
***quite** easily*, ***quite** often*
***rather** easily*, ***rather** often*

(c) main verbs:
*She **quite** likes him.*
*We **rather** enjoyed it.*

(c) noun phrases:
*There's **quite** a large crowd*
*I felt **rather** a fool.*

NOTE: Notice the word order in:

*This coat is **quite*** [*nice*] → *It's **quite*** [*a nice coat.*]
*My boss is **rather*** [*strict*] → *He's **rather*** [*a strict boss.*]
(adjective) (noun phrase)

2 Uses of *quite* and *rather*

2a ***Quite*** and ***rather*** have a similar meaning of medium degree.

E.g. *My neighbour is **quite** old: he must be nearly 60.*
*This house is **rather** old: it was built in 1880.*

But we prefer to use:

quite for a positive attitude: 'something good'.
rather for a negative attitude: 'something bad'.

E.g.

So we choose ***quite*** especially for words of 'good' meaning.

E.g. ***quite** bright,* ***quite** exciting,* ***quite** nicely,* ***quite** a good player*

We choose ***rather*** especially for words of 'bad' meaning.

E.g. ***rather** dull,* ***rather** boring,* ***rather** badly,* ***rather** an idiot*

NOTE (i): But we sometimes use these words in the opposite way.
E.g. *I'm **rather** fond of tennis.* *That play was **quite** dull.*
The difference between ***quite*** and ***rather*** is a matter of preference, not of strict rule.

NOTE (ii): Especially in <U.S.>, ***kind of*** can be used instead of ***rather***.

2b ***Quite*** also has the meaning 'completely' or 'entirely' with some words (for example, some verbs and adjectives).

E.g. *I **quite** agree with you.* (= I completely agree.')
*The statement in the newspaper was **quite** false. It was also **quite** unfair.*

Or ***quite*** has the meaning 'very much' with words which have an extreme meaning.

E.g. *His was **quite** the best performance of Macbeth I have ever seen. It was **quite** magnificent.*

NOTE (i): The meaning of ***quite*** when it follows ***not*** is 'completely' (i.e. ***not quite*** = not completely).
E.g. *I'm **not quite** ready to go. The garage has**n't quite** finished mending my car.*

NOTE (ii): The two different meanings of ***quite*** have different intonation especially when ***quite*** occurs at the end of a sentence or alone.

E.g. *'Did you enjoy the party?' 'Yes, **quite**.'* (= 'but not too much'.)

*'They must keep their promises.' 'Yes, **quite**.'* (<G.B.> only = 'I entirely agree with you.')

rarely and ***seldom*** /ˈreəʳlɪ/, /ˈseldəm/ (*adverbs of frequency*)

► ***Rarely*** and ***seldom*** have the same meaning (= 'infrequently' or 'not often') [see FREQUENCY 1].

E.g. *I've* {***rarely*** / ***seldom***} *seen a better game.*

NOTE: Word order: if ***rarely*** or ***seldom*** goes at the beginning of the sentence, the auxiliary follows [see INVERSION 5, NEGATIVE WORDS AND SENTENCES 6a].

E.g. {***Rarely*** / ***Seldom***} *have the media been so mistaken about the result of an election.* <formal>

rather [See QUITE AND RATHER]

► [For examples of ***rather than***, see THAN 3.]

► [For examples of ***would rather***, see VERB IDIOM.]

're (= are) [See BE]

really /ˈrɪəlɪ/ (*adverb*)

1 ***Really*** adds emphasis to the meaning of a sentence.

E.g. *'I'm **really** sorry that I forgot to return your umbrella.'*
(***really*** = 'very')
*'There's **really** no need to apologise. I didn't need it.'*
(***really*** = 'absolutely')

2 Often ***really*** goes in front of the auxiliary or BE. (This is not the usual middle position for adverbs: [compare ADVERB 3]).

E.g. *I **really** can't believe she's serious.*
*You **really** should be more careful.*

3 At the front of a sentence, ***really*** often indicates that the speaker is shocked, or disapproves of something.

E.g. ***Really**, I'm terribly disappointed by your behaviour.*

4 In a reply to a statement, ***really*** expresses surprise or polite interest.

E.g. *'Is that* ***really*** *true?'*
'Boris is giving up his job and becoming a priest.' ***'Really****? I didn't know he was a religious person.'*

NOTE: ***Really*** is an adverb of degree when it is used before an adjective or adverb.
E.g. *It was a* ***really*** *exciting race.* *She cares* ***really*** *deeply about her work.*

---

reason and cause

1 Phrases and clauses of reason or cause answer the question ***'Why?'***.

E.g. *'****Why*** *did Ted give up his job in the city?'*
reasons {
*'****(Because)*** *he wanted to live in the country.'*
*'****(Because)*** *he was too old to continue.'*
*'****(Because)*** *they didn't pay him enough.'* }

2 **Patterns**

2a The reason usually comes last:

MAIN CLAUSE + CONJUNCTION (***because, as, since, for***) + CLAUSE
MAIN CLAUSE + PREPOSITION (***because of, on account of, owing to***) + NOUN PHRASE

E.g. *The car crashed* ***because*** *the driver was careless.*
I can't give you this dictionary {***as*** / ***since***} *it's the only one I've got.*
My father never left his native country, ***for*** *in those days only rich people travelled abroad.* <rather formal, written>
He gave up his job ***because of*** *his age.*
The rice crop failed ***on account of*** *bad weather.* <rather formal>
The game was cancelled ***owing to*** *bad weather.* <rather formal>

NOTE: Compare also ***due to***: NOUN PHRASE + BE + DUE TO + NOUN PHRASE
E.g. *The failure of the rice crop was* ***due to*** *bad weather.* [See DUE TO.]

2b The reason can also come first:

CONJUNCTION (***Because, As, Since***) + CLAUSE, + MAIN CLAUSE
PREPOSITION (***Because of, On account of, Owing to***) + NOUN PHRASE + MAIN CLAUSE

This is a much less usual order, but is quite common with ***as*** and ***since***.

E.g. ***As*** *this is the beginning of the football season, there are bound to be large crowds at the match.*
Since *Britain is in the Northern Hemisphere, it has its summer in June, July, and August.*
Because of *the drought, all the plants had turned brown.*

3 In <written English>, there are other ways of expressing reason and cause in linking sentences.

E.g. *Luckily, none of the passengers were killed in the fire.* ***The*** {***reason*** / ***explanation***} ***for this was*** *that the seats were not flammable, and everyone had time to escape through the emergency doors.*

NOTE: It is not considered correct to write ***The reason . . . because***. This would use two 'reason' words when you need only one.

E.g. ***The reason (why)*** *he lost the court case was* {***that*** / ~~***because***~~} *he didn't have a witness.*

recently /ˈriːsəntlɪ/ (*adverb of time*)

Recently means 'not long ago'. It is used with a PAST TENSE or with a PERFECT form. It can go in front, middle or end position. [See ADVERB 3]

E.g. Past Simple: / Present Perfect: / Past Perfect: } *Three prisoners* {***recently escaped*** / ***have recently escaped*** / ***had recently escaped***}

reflexive pronoun [See -SELF / -SELVES]

regret, expressing [See APOLOGIES, IF ONLY, WISHES 1]

regular verb

1 Most English verbs are regular. They have four different forms:

BASIC FORM: (This is the form you will find in a dictionary).
-S FORM: Used in the 3rd person PRESENT TENSE.
-ED FORM: Used for the PAST TENSE and PAST PARTICIPLE.
-ING FORM: Used for the ***-ing*** (or 'present') participle.

2 In this book we write the above forms as follows:

BASIC FORM: Verb
-S FORM: Verb-***s***
-ED FORM: Verb-***ed***
-ING FORM: Verb-***ing***

3 Examples:

Verb	Verb-**s**	Verb-***ed***	Verb-***ing***
look	*looks*	*looked*	*looking*
call	*calls*	*called*	*calling*
seem	*seems*	*seemed*	*seeming*
want	*wants*	*wanted*	*wanting*

4 [See SPELLING for details of how to spell regular verb forms.]

5 [See IRREGULAR VERBS and the A–Z list of IRREGULAR VERBS at the back of this book.]

relative clause

- ► A ***relative clause*** adds extra information about one of the nouns in the main clause.
- ► The ***relative clause*** goes immediately after the noun it relates to.
- ► The relative pronoun goes at the beginning of the ***relative clause***.
- ► The relative pronouns are WHO (WHOM, WHOSE), WHICH and THAT.
- ► The relative pronoun can be omitted unless it is the subject of the ***relative clause***. [See 2b below.]

1 **The relative pronoun as subject of a relative clause.**

1a Relative clauses about people:
WHO (or THAT*) links two separate ideas about the same person or people. We join these two ideas by using ***who*** instead of the personal pronoun HE, SHE or THEY in the second clause.

E.g. *There's **the doctor.*** ***She** used to live next door.*

→ *There's **the doctor*** { ***who**** / ***that*** } *used to live next door.*
(main clause) (relative clause)

* Some people think ***who*** is more correct. You can use ***that***, but not to refer to a name (and not in non-defining clauses [see 4b below, and THAT 2]).

E.g. *I spoke to Mrs Pearson,* { ***who*** / ~~***that***~~ } *owns the bookstore.*

1b Relative clauses about things:
WHICH (or THAT*) links two separate ideas about the same thing or things. We join these two ideas by using ***which*** or ***that*** instead of ***it*** or ***they***.

E.g. *I'm writing about **a camera**.* ***It** doesn't work properly.*

→ *I'm writing about **a camera*** ***which** doesn't work properly.*
(main clause) (relative clause)

* We use ***that*** commonly instead of ***which***, especially in <speech>. But ***which*** is used in non-defining clauses [see 4b below].

2 **The relative pronoun as object of a relative clause.**

2a The relative pronoun goes at the beginning of the relative clause, even when it is the OBJECT of the clause.

E.g. (i) *There's* ***the doctor****.* *I met* ***him*** *yesterday.*

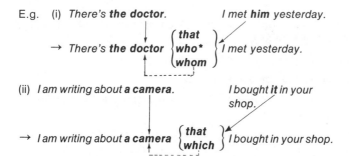

→ *There's* ***the doctor*** {***that*** / ***who**** / ***whom***} *I met yesterday.*

(ii) *I am writing about* ***a camera****.* *I bought* ***it*** *in your shop.*

→ *I am writing about* ***a camera*** {***that*** / ***which***} *I bought in your shop.*

* ***Who, whom***, or ***that*** can all be used as a relative object pronoun referring to a person. ***Whom*** is <rare>, but is more <'correct'> than ***who*** in <written English>.

2b Omitting the relative pronoun:
We often omit the relative pronoun when it is the OBJECT of the relative clause. (But don't omit it when it is the SUBJECT.) In these examples, the brackets (#) show where the pronoun is omitted.

E.g. (i) *There's the doctor (   ) I met yesterday.* (Compare 2a (i))
(ii) *I am writing about a camera (   ) I bought in your shop.* (Compare 2a (ii))

NOTE: This is sometimes called a ZERO RELATIVE PRONOUN. The CLAUSE is called a zero relative clause.

3 **The position of the relative clause**
A relative clause follows the NOUN it relates to, wherever the noun is in the SENTENCE. Here the relative clause is in the SUBJECT:

The new cars *have all been sold.* ***They*** *were made in Ireland.*
→ ***The new cars which*** *were made in Ireland have all been sold.*

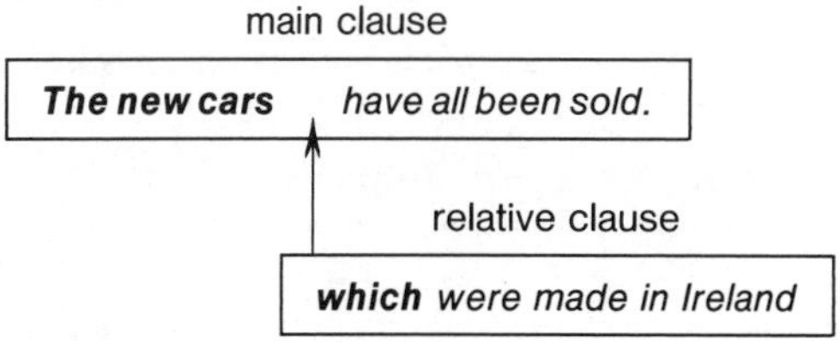
main clause
The new cars have all been sold.
relative clause
which were made in Ireland

4 **The functions of relative clauses**
Defining and non-defining* relative clauses have two functions:

4a Defining – to give essential information in order to identify what / who you are talking about.

E.g. *'The house has just been sold.' 'Which house are you talking about?'*
'The house ***(which) I showed you last week*** *(has just been sold).'*

4b Non-defining – to give extra information, not essential for identifying what you are talking about.

E.g. *'Mrs Porter's house has just been sold.'*

Adding another piece of information:

'Mrs Porter's house, ***which has been for sale for two years****, has just been sold.'*

We usually separate non-defining clauses from the rest of the SENTENCE. We do this by COMMAS in <writing> and by separate INTONATION in <speech>.

NOTE: Don't use ***that*** at the beginning of a non-defining clause. Use ***who*** (***whom, whose***) or ***which*** instead.

* Defining clauses are sometimes called 'restrictive', and non-defining clauses are sometimes called 'non-restrictive'.

5 ***Whose*** **+ clause**
Whose is the POSSESSIVE DETERMINER form of ***who***. It usually refers to a person or people. It replaces ***his***, ***her***, or ***their***.

E.g. ***That woman*** *is a well-known actress.* *You met* ***her*** *son.*

That woman whose *son you met is a well-known actress.*

NOTE: If you add commas here, they show that the relative clause is non-defining [see 4a above].
E.g. *That woman, whose son you met, is a well-known actress.*

6 **Prepositions in relative clauses**
We can place the preposition in front of the relative pronoun. But more often we place the preposition at the end [see PREPOSITION].

E.g. *This is the knife* ***with which*** *he was killed.*
*This is the knife (****which****) he was killed* ***with***. <more informal>

When the preposition is at the end, we can use ***that*** instead of ***which***, or we can omit the relative pronoun.

E.g. ***Sam is a student that**** *I once shared a room with.*
The bus ***we were waiting for*** *never arrived.*

* Do not use ***that*** after a preposition:
This is the school ***that my children go to***.
But not:
This is the school ~~***to that my children go***~~.

7 **Sentence relative clauses**

Sentence relative clauses refer back to the whole clause or sentence, not just to one noun. They always go at the end of the clause or sentence.

E.g. *Tina admires the Prime Minister,* ***which surprises me***. (= 'and this surprises me.')
He never admits his mistakes, ***which is extremely annoying***. (= 'and this is extremely annoying.')

8 **Relative adverbs**

WHEN and WHERE can be 'relative adverbs': they link a relative clause to the main clause by a connection of TIME or PLACE.

E.g. *Do you remember the day* ***(when)*** *we first met?'* (defines which day)
One day I'm going back to the town ***where*** *I spent my childhood.* (defines which town)

NOTE: After the noun such as ***time*** or ***place***, we can use ***that*** or ZERO THAT-CLAUSE, as well as ***when*** or ***where***.

E.g. *She felt ill all the time* {***(that)*** / ***(when)***} *we were living in that cottage.*
I've lost my purse. I'm going back to look for it in the place {***(that)*** / ***(where)***} *I was sitting.*

---

reported speech

is another name for INDIRECT SPEECH

---

requests

► If you want somebody to do something for you, you can use one of the forms in 1 below.

► Intonation is important when making ***requests*** and when replying to them.

1 **Forms**

Requests		Replies
(I) ***(Please**)*** {{***will*** / ***can***} you + Verb ... / {***would*** / ***could***} you + Verb ...}	(please**)?	*Okay.* / *Certainly.* / *Of course.* / *All right.* / *Yes, . . .*
(II) ***I wonder if*** *you* {***would*** / ***could***} + Verb . . .?		
(III) {***Can*** / ***Could***} *you* ***(possibly)*** + Verb . . .?		
(IV) {***Do*** / ***Would***} *you* ***mind**** + Verb-*ing* . . .?		*No.* / *Not at all.*

2 Examples

* [See MIND 2b.]
** ***Please*** can go at the beginning or at the end of a request.

2a On how to make a request <more polite> or <more direct>, see POLITE AND NOT POLITE. Remember these four MODAL AUXILIARIES:

<more direct> <more polite>

WILL CAN WOULD COULD

+ ***you***

3 Requests for information

---

restrictive relative clause is another name for defining relative clause [See RELATIVE CLAUSE 4]

---

result

The following are useful patterns introducing result clauses. Patterns (b) and (c) are a mixture of DEGREE and result.

(a) MAIN CLAUSE + { ***so that*** + RESULT CLAUSE / ***with the result that*** + RESULT CLAUSE }

E.g. *The prisoners had a secret radio,* ***so that*** *they could receive messages from the outside world.*
There had been no rain for six months, ***with the result that*** *the ground was as hard as iron.*

(b) . . . ***so*** + { adjective / adverb / ***much*** (. . .) / ***many*** (. . .) } + ***that*** + RESULT CLAUSE

(. . . ***so*** + { … } = MAIN CLAUSE)

E.g. *I feel* ***so*** *hungry* ***that*** *I could eat anything!*
Martin worked ***so*** *hard* ***that*** *he fell ill.*
We have had ***so*** *much rain* ***that*** *most of our land is flooded.*
They had ***so*** *many children* ***that*** *they couldn't remember their names.*

(c) . . . ***such*** (+(***a***) NOUN PHRASE) + ***that*** + RESULT CLAUSE

(. . . ***such*** (+(***a***) NOUN PHRASE) = MAIN CLAUSE)

E.g. *The factory has been* ***such*** *a success* ***that*** *we are employing an extra 500 workers.*

---

round /raʊnd/ (*preposition, adverb, adjective, or noun*)

- ***Round*** is a word with many different uses.
- Most of the uses of ***round*** are connected with circular motion or circular shape.

1 *Round* (preposition or adverb)

Round is used to express the idea of circular motion or position [see ABOUT AND AROUND.]

E.g. (i) *Don't look* ***round****! There's someone following us.*

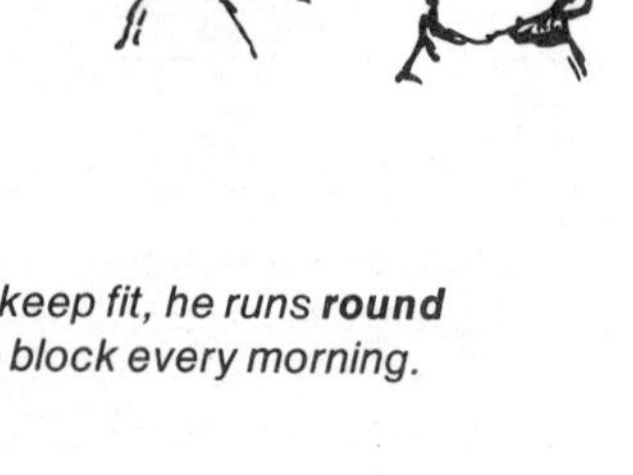

(ii) *To keep fit, he runs* ***round*** *the block every morning.*

(iii) *It was a cold evening, so we all sat* ***round*** *the camp fire, to keep warm.*

NOTE: In <U.S.>, ***around*** is preferred to ***round*** here.

2 ***Round*** **(= adjective)**
Round means 'of circular shape'.

E.g. *The child looked up with big,* **round** *eyes.*

-'s

1 (a) **'s** is the ending for the singular possessive form of nouns [see POSSESSIVE for further information].

E.g. *Mary* → *Mary***'s** *friend.*

(b) **'s** is also the contraction (or 'short form') of ***is*** and ***has***.

E.g. *Mary***'s** *coming.* (= Mary **is** coming.)
*Mary***'s** *gone home.* (= Mary **has** gone home.)

[See CONTRACTION OF VERBS AND NEGATIVES 2.]

2 [On how to pronounce **'s**, see PRONUNCIATION OF ENDINGS 2.]

-s'

This is the regular ending of the possessive form of plural nouns [see POSSESSIVE 2 for further information].

E.g. *the girl***s'** *faces.*

-s form

► We add **-s** (or **-es**) to a regular noun to make it PLURAL.

E.g. *day* → *day**s**,* *cat* → *cat**s**,* *bus* → *bus**es***

► We add **-s** (or **-es**) to a verb to make it 3rd person singular Present Tense.

E.g. *take* → *take**s**,* *need* → *need**s**,* *wish* → *wish**es***

1 **Nouns**
Many nouns have an irregular plural which does not end in **-s**.

E.g. *man* → ***men**,* *sheep* → ***sheep***

[See IRREGULAR PLURAL.] Some other nouns have an irregular **-s** plural.

E.g. *leaf* → *leave**s**,* *house* /haʊs/ → *house**s*** /haʊzɪz/.

2 **Verbs**
The **-s** form of the verb is used only in the PRESENT TENSE, with 3rd person PRONOUNS or NOUN PHRASES which are SINGULAR:

singular Present Tense
He / She / It / } Verb + **-s** . . .
The world etc. }

E.g. *The world long**s** for peace.*

[For details of when to use the **-s** in the Present Tense, look up AGREEMENT.]

NOTE: Modals such as CAN and WILL have no **-s** form. [See MODAL AUXILIARY 2a.]

3 **Pronunciation**
The **-s** form is pronounced /s/, /z/, or /ɪz/. [See PRONUNCIATION OF ENDINGS 2 for details.]

(the) same /ðəˈseɪm/ (*determiner or pronoun*)

► ***The same*** means 'identical'. It is the opposite of ANOTHER or (*a*) DIFFERENT.

1 DETERMINER: ***the same*** + NOUN = NOUN PHRASE.

E.g. (i) *My son and yours go to **the same** school.*
(ii) *Charles and I have **the same** tastes: we like **the same** music, we read **the same** books, and we watch **the same** TV programmes. No wonder we find one another so boring!*

2 PRONOUN: ***the same*** = NOUN PHRASE.

E.g. (i)

Could I have a chocolate-flavoured ice-cream ?
And I'll have the same please.

(ii) *'I'm sorry I got angry with your father.' 'Don't worry – I would have done **the same.**'*

3 ***The same*** is often followed by an AS-phrase, or AS-clause of comparison [see COMPARATIVE CLAUSE 2].

E.g. *My son goes to **the same** school **as yours.***

(Compare 1 (i) above.)

*She looks just **the same as she did five years ago**: she hasn't changed a bit.*

4 **Idiom**

All the same is a linking adverb (see LINKING ADVERBS AND CONJUNCTIONS) which starts a new sentence, expressing contrast. It is like YET, *nevertheless*; but not so <formal>.

E.g. *This year our team has lost some of its best players. **All the same,** we have won more games than we have lost.*

---

scarcely

/ˈskeəʳslɪ/ is a negative adverb of DEGREE meaning 'almost not at all'. It has the same meaning as HARDLY, but is less common.

---

second person

[See YOU]

---

see

[For the difference between ***look, look at, see*** and ***watch***, look up LOOK 3.]

seem (*verb*) [See PERCEPTION VERB]

E.g. *She **seems** rather worried about something.*

seldom

/ˈseldəm/ is a negative adverb of frequency, meaning 'infrequently', 'hardly ever'. It means the same as *rarely*. [See RARELY AND SELDOM.]

-self, -selves /ˈself/, -/ˈselvz/

- Words ending in ***-self*** or ***-selves*** are called 'reflexive pronouns': ***myself, ourselves***, etc.
- Reflexive pronouns usually refer back to the SUBJECT of the clause or sentence.

E.g. *I admire **myself**. But: James hates **himself***

- They can also be used for emphasis.

E.g. *The manager **himself** telephoned me.*

1 The following shows how ***-self*** pronouns can occur after subject pronouns [see PERSONAL PRONOUNS 5]:

singular (***-self***)	plural (***-selves***)
*I helped **myself***	*We helped **ourselves***
*You helped **yourself***	*You helped **yourselves***
*He helped **himself***	*They helped **themselves***
*She helped **herself***	
*It helped **itself***	
*(One helped **oneself** *)* [see ONE 3]	

* ***Oneself*** is rare in <G.B.> and very rare in <U.S.>.

1a If a singular noun phrase is subject, the ***-self*** pronoun is ***himself*** (male), ***herself*** (female), or ***itself*** (not a person). [See HE AND SHE, SEX on the problem of choice between male and female pronouns.]

E.g. (i) ***My brother** has hurt **himself**.* (male)
(ii) ***My aunt** lives by **herself**.* * (female)
(iii) ***A young bird** soon finds **itself** a new nest.*
(iv) ***My neighbour's** not feeling **herself*** * * *today.*
(v) *I hope that **the children** are enjoying **themselves**.*

If a plural noun phrase is subject, the ***-self*** pronoun is ***themselves***.

E.g. (vi) *I hope that **Sue and Stanley** are enjoying **themselves**.* * *

* ***By -self*** is an idiom meaning 'alone'.
* * ***Feel -self*** is an idiom meaning 'feel well'. A few verbs, such as ***behave -self*** and ***enjoy -self***, have a ***-self*** pronoun which forms an idiom with the verb.
E.g. ***Enjoy -self** means 'have a good time'.*
***Behave -self** means 'behave well'.*

NOTE: If the clause does not have a subject, the ***-self*** pronoun agrees with the implied subject.
E.g. *Behave **yourself**, John.*
*Help **yourselves** to food, everybody.*
*We invited them all to make **themselves** at home.*

2 The *-self* pronoun can appear in the following positions:

(i) DIRECT OBJECT, as in (i) above.
(ii) After a PREPOSITION, as in (ii) above.
(iii) INDIRECT OBJECT, as in (iii) above.
(iv) COMPLEMENT, as in (iv) above.

3 The *-self* pronoun and the object pronoun
There is a difference of meaning between the object pronoun and the ***-self*** pronoun in sentences like these:

E.g. *Mary poured **herself** a drink.* (**herself** = 'Mary')
*Mary poured **her** a drink.* (**her** = 'someone else')

4 *-self* pronouns for emphasis
The ***-self*** pronoun gives emphasis to the noun phrase or pronoun in front of it.

E.g. (i) *The great man **himself** visited us. We felt very proud.*

(ii) *We **ourselves** cooked the dinner.* (= and nobody else)

(iii) *They were introduced to the princess **herself**.*

(iv) *The garden's very untidy, but the house **itself** is beautiful.*

The pronoun has strong stress, as shown above.

4a If the ***-self*** pronoun follows the subject, the pronoun can be moved to the end. So instead of (i) and (ii) above we can say:

E.g. (i) *The great man visited us **himself**.*

(ii) *We cooked the dinner* ***ourselves****.*

5 Note the difference between the ***-self*** pronouns and ***each other*** (or ***one another***).

E.g. (i) *They saw* ***each other*** *at the airport.*

(ii) *They saw* ***themselves*** *in the mirror.*

sentence

► A ***sentence*** is the major unit of grammar.

► In <writing>, we begin a ***sentence*** with a capital letter and end it with a full-stop [.].

1 A simple sentence consists of one clause, and a complex sentence consists of more than one clause. [See CLAUSE for details of the structure of clauses, and their regular word order. See also WORD ORDER.]

2 **Sentence types**
We divide sentences into four sentence types:

(I) a STATEMENT.

E.g. *I like ice-cream.* *Michael doesn't like sweet things.*

(II) a QUESTION.

E.g. *Do you like ice-cream?* [see YES-NO QUESTION]
Who likes ice-cream? [see WH-QUESTION]
You like ice-cream? [see INTONATION 3]

(III) an IMPERATIVE.

E.g. *Come here.* *Don't sit there, please.*

(IV) an EXCLAMATION.

E.g. *What a terrible noise!* *How wonderful!*

NOTE: A simple sentence generally has a SUBJECT and VERB. We usually omit the subject in imperatives. We also often omit the subject and verb in exclamations.
E.g. *How wonderful it is!* → *How wonderful!*

3 **Complex sentences**
We make a complex sentence by joining clauses together by either subordination or coordination or both. [See CLAUSE for further details.]

3a A sentence which consists of clauses linked by coordination is often called a 'compound sentence'.

E.g. *I like ice-cream,* ***but*** *Michael doesn't like sweet things.*

NOTE: You can make a sentence as long as you like, by adding more clauses. But remember that the average length of a sentence in <written> English is about 17 words. If you make your sentences much longer than this, they may be difficult to understand.

3b [For further information, see CONJUNCTION, COORDINATION, SUBORDINATE CLAUSE.]

---

sentence adverb [See ADVERB, LINKING ADVERBS AND CONJUNCTIONS.]

---

sentence relative clause [See RELATIVE CLAUSE 7.]

---

several /ˈsev(ə)rəl/ (*determiner or pronoun*)

1 ***Several*** means 'a small number (of)', usually between 3 and 9. ***Several*** is similar to (A) FEW, but has a more 'positive' meaning.

2 **Patterns**

2a ***Several*** + plural noun:

E.g. *There was a bad accident in the street outside our house:* ***several*** *people were injured.*

2b ***Several*** + (*of . . .*):

E.g. *I know Hamburg very well.* ***Several*** *of my friends live there.*
'Can I borrow a pen?' 'Yes – help yourself. There are ***several*** *on my desk.'*

3 [See QUANTITY WORDS to compare ***several*** with other words which tell 'how many'.]

sex how to refer to male and female

1 Pronouns

In English, the difference of sex between male and female is shown only in the singular pronouns ***he*** and ***she*** [see HE AND SHE]. The plural pronoun ***they*** can refer to both sexes:

	singular	plural
male	***he***	***they***
female	***she***	

2 Nouns

Sometimes, the choice of different nouns shows the difference of sex:

(I) ***male***		***female***	
man	*uncle*	*woman*	*aunt*
boy	*nephew*	*girl*	*niece*
father	*brother*	*mother*	*sister*
son	*king*	*daughter*	*queen*

(II) ***male***		***female***	
*police**man***	*priest*	*police**woman***	*priest**ess***
*French**man***	*prince*	*French**woman***	*princ**ess***
actor	*duke*	*actr**ess***	*duch**ess***
manager	*host*	*manager**ess***	*host**ess***

In List (II), the female word has a special ending ***-woman***, ***-ess***. However, these endings are becoming rarer nowadays, especially ***-ess***.

2a Many other nouns are neutral: they are used for both males and females.

E.g. ***student, teacher, doctor, secretary, scientiest, nurse***.

If necessary, we can add a word in front of these to indicate sex.

E.g. ***female** student*, ***woman** doctor* (Plural: ***women** doctors*), ***male** nurse*.

3 So what is the problem?

3a There is no problem where English has a neutral word for male or female, as well as the male and female words.

E.g. *boy / girl = child*
mother / father = parent
brother / sister = sibling <rare>

3b But there is a problem where English has no neutral word.

E.g. *he / she* = ? *chairman / chairwoman* = ?

3c In the past, English has used the male pronoun to refer to both sexes.

E.g. ***Everyone** thinks **he** is right, so no one will admit that **he** is wrong.*
(***he*** = 'he or she')
***Men** have lived on earth for more than a million years.*
(***men*** = 'men and women')

3d But nowadays, many people (especially women) dislike this. They prefer:

(a) to use ***or*** (i.e. ***he or she*** instead of ***he***).
(b) to use a new word (i.e. a new pronoun ***s/he***, for ***he*** / ***she***; or ***chairperson***, for ***chairman***).
(c) to use the plural ***they*** for the singular <in speech> [see HE AND SHE].

[See HE AND SHE 2, and MAN 2, for further examples and discussion.]

3e The problem is: (a) ***he or she*** is sometimes awkward, and (b) not everyone likes new words! (c) In exams, using the plural instead of the singular is considered <incorrect>.

4 Is there an answer to the problem?
There is no 'correct' choice. So we suggest that you:

(A) Avoid the problem where you can, i.e. by using neutral words like ***they***, ***person***, and ***human being***.
(B) Otherwise, choose the form that you like best!

---

shall /ʃæl/, (weak form: /ʃəl/) (negative: *shan't* /ʃɑ:nt‖ʃæ:nt/ <rare>) (*modal auxiliary*)

► ***Shall*** is used mainly in questions with ***shall*** *I . . .?* or ***shall*** *we . . .?*
► ***Shall*** is rather rare in <G.B.> and very rare in <U.S.>.

1 ***Shall*** {***I*** / ***we***} . . .*?* is used in making an offer.

E.g. (i) ***Shall I** open the door?* (= 'Do you want me to . . .?')
(ii) ***Shall we** carry those bags for you?*

2 ***Shall we** . . .?* is a way of making a suggestion about the future in <G.B.> (***we*** here usually means 'you and I').

E.g. *'**Shall we** go abroad?' 'Yes, let's go to Morocco, **shall we**?'**

* Note that ***shall we*** can be used as a TAG QUESTION following LET'S.

3 ***Shall*** {***I*** / ***we***} . . .*?* is a way of asking for ADVICE or a SUGGESTION.

E.g. (i)

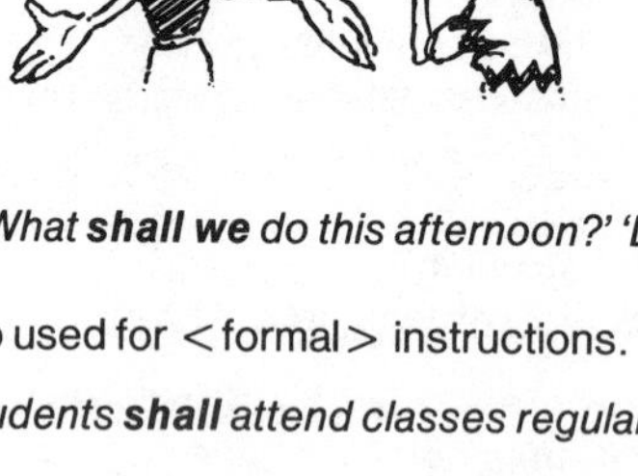

(ii) *'What **shall we** do this afternoon?' 'Let's go for a walk in the park.'*

4 ***Shall*** is also used for <formal> instructions.

E.g. *All students **shall** attend classes regularly.*

5 In an older or <more formal> kind of English, ***shall*** is sometimes used instead of WILL in STATEMENTS. Some people feel that it is <not correct> to use ***will*** after ***I*** or ***we*** in statements about the future, especially in writing. So they use ***I shall*** or ***we shall*** instead. You will often find ***shall*** used in this way in English literature written before c. 1950.

E.g. ***I shall** arrive next Monday.*
*We **shall** never forget you.*

6 ***Shan't*** (/ʃɑːnt ‖ ʃæːnt/), the NEGATIVE form of ***shall***, is <rare>, especially in <U.S.>.

E.g. *I **shan't** be here tomorrow, I'm afraid.* <G.B.>
*I **won't** be here tomorrow, I'm afraid.* <G.B.> and <U.S.>

she /ʃiː/ (weak form /ʃɪ/) *her, hers, herself*

► ***She*** is the 3rd person singular female personal pronoun. [See HE AND SHE for details of the use of ***she***.]
► ***She*** is the form of the pronoun used as SUBJECT of a clause.

E.g. *'Where's your mother?' '**She**'s gone to the bank.'*

[See PERSONAL PRONOUN.]

shortened sentences and clauses

► ***Shortened sentences*** are often used to answer questions.
► ***Shortened sentences*** consist of SUBJECT and AUXILIARY or BE (+ NOT) with the rest of the sentence omitted.

E.g. *'**Are** you enjoying the play?' 'Yes, **I am** (*enjoying the play*).'*

► ***Shortened sentences*** are useful, because they save words. The omitted words are not needed, because they repeat what has been said before.
► Notice that INTONATION is important in ***shortened sentences***.

1 We often use ***shortened sentences*** in reply to other sentences.

1a Shortened sentences to answer questions
Use the same choice of auxiliary or BE as in the question.

E.g. *'**Have** you ever been to Istanbul?' 'No, **I haven't**.'*
*'I **can't** speak Portuguese. **Can** you?' 'Well, **I can**, but only a little.'*

1b Shortened sentences to answer statements, requests, etc.

E.g. *'The bus must be late.' 'Yes, it always is (late).'*
'Please sit down.' 'Thanks, I will (sit down).'

2 There are also shortened clauses
They may be coordinated clauses [see COORDINATION].

E.g. *Ann said she would win the game, and **she has** (won the game).*

or SUBORDINATE CLAUSES.

E.g. *I would pay the whole fare, if **I could** (pay the whole fare).*

3 Notice we use ***do*** as an 'empty' auxiliary [see DO 2f].

E.g. *Ann plays chess, and **Betty does**, too.* (= 'plays chess, too')

4 Shortened clauses and sentences are used in many different sentence patterns. [See EITHER; NEITHER; SO; TAG QUESTION; COMPARATIVE CLAUSE 4 for further details].

should and ***ought to*** /ʃʊd/ (weak form: /ʃəd/), /ˈɔːt tuː/ (weak form: /ˈɔːtə/) (*modal auxiliaries*)

- ***Should*** and ***ought to*** are MODAL AUXILIARIES with similar meanings.
- You can always use ***should*** instead of ***ought to***.
- ***Should*** and ***ought to*** have negative forms ***shouldn't*** /ˈʃʊdn̩t/ and ***oughtn't to*** /ɔːtn̩t tuː/.
- ***Should*** was once the Past form of ***shall***. But now there is little connection between these two auxiliaries. [See 8 below.]

1 Forms

		main verb	
I		*be*	*grateful.*
You		*have*	*sent them a card.*
We	{***should*** / ***ought to***}	*go*	*to bed early.*
He, She		*feed*	*the animals regularly.*
They		etc.	etc.
etc.			

negative:

		main verb	
I		*be*	*so noisy.*
You		*have*	*forgotten her name.*
We	{***shouldn't*** / ***oughtn't to***}	*leave*	*the children at home.*
He, She		*tell*	*lies.*
They		etc.	etc.
etc.			

question:

		main verb	
Should* / **Shouldn't**	*I*	*be*	*working now?*
	you	*have*	*sent her a present?*
	we	*do*	*the washing?*
	he, she		
	they	*phone*	*the police immediately?*
	etc.	etc.	etc.

* ***Ought to*** is <rare> in QUESTIONS. The ***to*** follows the SUBJECT.
E.g. ***Ought(n't) we to*** post these letters? (***we*** = subject).

2 **Past time**
Should and ***ought to*** have no PAST forms. To express past time, use ***should*** or ***ought to*** + PERFECT:

SHOULD / OUGHT TO + HAVE + PAST PARTICIPLE

E.g. *You **should** write to her.* (present)
*You **should have*** written to her yesterday.* (past)

* Note that ***should have*** is pronounced /ˈʃʊdəv/.

3 **Meanings of *should* and *ought to***

3a ***Should*** / ***ought to*** + Verb means that Verb-*ing* is a good thing to do: something that is right or desirable (but is probably not done at the moment).

E.g. *The government **should** lower taxes.*
*You **ought to** phone your mother every week.* (but you don't!)

3b ***Should*** and ***ought to*** are sometimes used for rules and instructions.

E.g. *Children **should** be seen and not heard.* (an old saying)

3c The negative ***shouldn't*** / ***oughtn't to*** + Verb means that something isn't right – and probably no one will put it right!

E.g. *I **shouldn't** smoke so much.* (but I do!)

3d ***Should / ought to*** + Verb also means that something is probable, i.e. is likely to happen.

E.g. *The plane* ***should*** *be landing at Copenhagen right now.* ('It is 7 o'clock, and the plane is due to land at 7.')
You ***should*** *be able to see the Alps from here: they're only a few miles away.*

3e ***Shouldn't / oughtn't to*** + Verb has the opposite meaning – that something is improbable.

E.g. *There* ***shouldn't*** *be any problems at the airport. I've checked everything – tickets, passport, baggage . . .*

4 ***Should have*** **and** ***shouldn't have***

4a With past events, ***should have*** or ***ought to have*** implies that the event did not happen.

E.g. *You* ***should have*** *posted those letters. Why didn't you?*
He ***should have*** *been home long ago. Where is he?*

4b ***Shouldn't have*** or ***oughtn't to have*** implies that the past event did. happen.

E.g. *You* ***shouldn't have*** *lent him so much money.* ('but you did')

5 **The difference in meaning between *must* and *should / ought to***
The meanings of ***should / ought to*** above (3a–3e) are less strong than the meanings of ***must*** [see MUST 2]. [See MUST 3 for a comparison of ***must*** and ***should***.]

5a ***Must*** is useful for giving orders.

E.g. *You* ***must*** *clean your teeth after meals.*

But ***should*** or ***ought to***, being weaker, is useful for giving advice.

E.g. *You* ***should*** *take more exercise: it would do you good.*

5b ***Must*** + Verb implies that the 'verb' definitely happens.
Should / ought to + Verb implies that it may not happen.

E.g. *The boys* ***must*** *be working.* ('I feel certain')
The boys ***should*** *be working.* ('But they may not be working.')

6 ***Should*** **has a special 'tentative' use**
This is a use of ***should***, but not of ***ought to***. It is used mainly in <G.B.>.

6a ***Should*** in a conditional clause [see IF, CONDITIONAL CLAUSE] means that the condition is doubtful and unlikely to happen.

E.g. (i)

If anyone should phone,
tell them I'm very busy.
SECRETARY

(ii) ***Should*** *there be a problem, I hope you will call me immediately.* (= 'If there's a problem')

6b Some adjectives, verbs, and nouns can be followed by a THAT-clause [see THAT 1] containing ***should***. When we use ***should*** in these patterns, it means we are interested in the idea in the THAT-clause, not in the fact that something happened. [See ADJECTIVE PATTERNS 2, VERB PATTERNS 4.]

E.g. (i) *It's* {***odd*** / ***a pity*** / ***annoying***} ***that*** *the neighbours* ***should*** *object.*

(ii) *I was* ***anxious that*** *the game* ***should*** *be a draw.*

(iii) *I was* {***sorry*** / ***pleased***} ***that*** *they* ***should*** *think that.*

(iv) *The bank* ***insisted that*** *he* ***should*** *resign.*

6c You can always use another form instead of 'tentative ***should***'. Instead of 6a (i) above you can say:

E.g. *If anyone* ***phones****, tell them I'm very busy.*

Instead of 6b (iv) you can say:

E.g. *The bank insisted that he* {***resign.*** <more formal> / ***resigned.*** <less formal>}

7 ***Should*** **in WH- QUESTIONS**

Should expresses a feeling of surprise, protest, or disbelief.

E.g. ***How should*** *I know?* ***Why should*** *Philip resign?*

This is common in both <G.B.> and <U.S.>.

8 ***Should*** is occasionally the past form of SHALL in unreal conditions [see IF 1c].

E.g. ***I should*** *be grateful if you could help me.*

Here ***should*** is <polite and formal>, and it can be replaced by ***would*** [see WOULD 1].

9 [On ***should*** and ***ought to*** in indirect speech, see INDIRECT SPEECH 1c: Note.]

simple sentence [See SENTENCE 1, 2]

since /sɪns/ (*preposition, conjunction or adverb*)

► ***Since*** is a preposition, subordinating conjunction, and adverb of LENGTH OF TIME.

► ***Since*** is also a subordinating conjunction of REASON OR CAUSE [see 3 below].

1 *Since* meaning 'time up to now'

When referring to time, ***since*** measures time from a point in the past up to now:

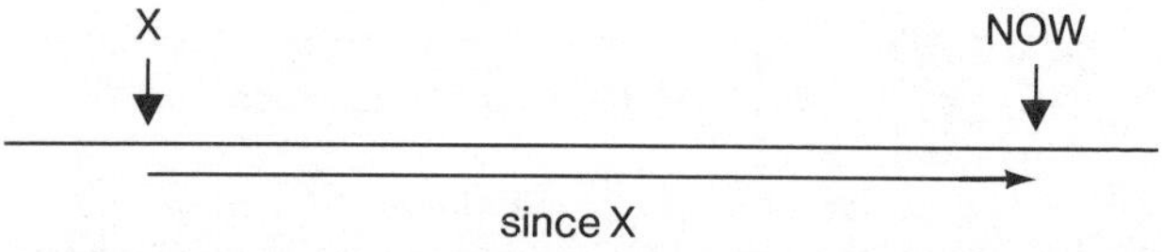

preposition + noun phrase
since *1973* [= from 1973 to now]
since *Christmas*
since *the Vietnam war*
since *last week*

conjunction + clause
since *I was born*
since *we moved here*
since *her aunt died*
since *the world began*

1a ***Since*** answers the question ***How long***? + PERFECT.

E.g.

How long have you two known each other?
Since we met at a party last year.

1b Other uses of ***since*** referring to time:

(A) ***since*** + -ING CLAUSE.

E.g. ***Since losing his wife*** *he has been very unhappy.*

(B) ***since*** + ADVERB.

E.g. *I first met Adam 10 years ago.* ***Since then*** *we have been great friends.*

(C) ***Since*** meaning 'a time from one point in the past up to another point in the past'. (The main clause contains a PAST PERFECT verb phrase.)

E.g. *Sam met his future wife in Nigeria in 1950. She* ***had*** *lived there* ***since*** *1939.*

1c ***Since*** as an adverb means the same as ***since then***; but it cannot go at the front of the clause.

E.g. *Sam wrote to me last winter, and I have had no news from him* ***since***. (= 'since last winter')

2 **The verb with *since***

Don't forget: ***since*** has to have a Perfect* verb phrase in the main clause [see PRESENT PERFECT 5].

E.g. *'How long has the President been in power?' 'Oh, he****'s been*** *in power* ***since 1985.'*** * *

I arrived at 10 o'clock, but the meeting ***had been*** *in progress* ***since 9 o'clock.***

Our neighbours ***have lived*** *next door* ***ever since*** * * * *I was a child.*

* A 'Perfect' verb phrase means either Present Perfect, Past Perfect, or modal + Perfect.
E.g. *They* ***must have known*** *each other* ***since*** *childhood.*
* * Notice we do not say *'He ~~is~~ in power* ***since*** *. . .'.*
* * * ***Ever*** adds emphasis to ***since***.

3 ***Since*** (subordinating conjunction) also means 'because'; it is <rather formal>.

E.g. *These plants should not be planted in the shade,* ***since*** *they require sunlight for healthy growth.*

[See REASON AND CAUSE.]

---

singular [See PLURAL]

'Singular' means 'one; not more than one'.
In English grammar, we use singular to describe:

(A) pronouns. 1st person singular = ***I***
2nd person singular = ***you*** (***you*** can also be plural)
3rd person singular = ***he, she, it***

(b) nouns. A singular noun has no ending added to it.
A regular plural noun (i.e. 'more than one') ends with **-s**.

E.g. *One* ***boy****, two* ***boys***

(C) verbs. A regular verb has **-s** in the 3rd person singular of the PRESENT TENSE. In the plural, the verb has no ending added to it.

E.g. *A dog* ***barks****. Dogs* ***bark***.

[See also PERSONAL PRONOUN, REGULAR VERB, AGREEMENT, -S FORM.]

SO /səʊ/ (*adverb, conjunction, linking adverb or pronoun*)

1 ***So* as an adverb of degree** [Compare SUCH.]

1a SO + ADJECTIVE / ADVERB / MUCH / MANY
In this pattern, ***so*** means 'very', but it doesn't express exactly how much. ***So*** shows that the speaker feels strongly about something.

E.g.

Why are you so late? Why did it take you so long to do the shopping?
We had to buy so many things.
We had so much to carry, we couldn't get on the bus.

[See also EXCLAMATIONS 6.]

NOTE: ***So*** is common in negative IMPERATIVES and EXCLAMATIONS.
E.g. *Don't be **so** silly!* *I've never been **so** angry in my life.*

1b SO + ADJECTIVE / ADVERB / MUCH / MANY + THAT + CLAUSE
In this pattern, ***so*** expresses result.

E.g. (i) *The teacher speaks **so** clearly that everyone can understand her.*
(ii) *The wind was **so** strong that it blew the roof off the house.*

[See RESULT for further examples. See also COMPARATIVE CLAUSE 2c.]

2 ***So* as a linking word** *
So links two clauses or sentences:

Fact 1, → (***and***) ***so*** → Fact 2
where { (i) Fact 1 is a reason for Fact 2. [See REASON AND CLAUSE.]
(ii) Fact 2 is a result of Fact 1. [See RESULT.]

E.g. (i) *We all felt tired, and **so** we went to bed.*
(ii) *Ben had lost his money, **so** he had to borrow some from me.*

* ***So*** in this pattern is either a conjunction or a linking adverb. Its word class is unclear.

2a In <spoken> English, we often begin a sentence with **so**, making a link with what has been said before.

E.g.

We'd been for a long walk and when we got home, we found that we had lost the key and couldn't open the door.
So what did you do ?

2b ***So*** is also a shortened form of ***so that***, expressing PURPOSE:

E.g. *You'd better get up early,* **so (that)** *you don't miss the train.* <informal>

3 ***So* as a pronoun in replies etc.**

3a ***So*** replaces a *that*-clause [see THAT 1] after some verbs [see VERB PATTERN 4, 14]:

E.g. *'Will you be able to help us?' 'I* {***hope*** / ***expect*** / ***believe***} ***so.***' (= '. . . that I will be able to help you.')

3b You can use **so** after some negative verbs, or you can use ***not*** instead [see NOT 6]:

E.g. *'Has the new carpet arrived?' 'I don't think* ***so.***' (= *I think* ***not.*** <rare>)

3c **So** also replaces a ***that***-clause after ***afraid***:

E.g. *'Have they cancelled the match?' 'I'm* ***afraid so.***'

3d ***So*** replaces a CONDITIONAL CLAUSE in ***if so**** [see IF]:

E.g. *They say the potato crop will be the best ever this year.* ***If so**** *, the price of potatoes will go down steeply.* (= 'If the potato crop is the best ever')

* The opposite of ***if so*** is ***if not***.

3e ***So*** is more or less equivalent to ***true***:

E.g. *'I understand that you are the wife of Robert Owen, who disappeared last week. Is that* ***so***?' *'Yes, that's* ***so.***' <formal>

4 **So at the front of a clause**

If ***so*** is used at the front of a clause, the word order is changed [see INVERSION 2–4]. (But see the Note below for an exception.)

4a SO + AUXILIARY / BE + SUBJECT

In this pattern, ***so*** is an adverb meaning '***too***'.

E.g. (i)

I've got a football.
So have I!
(I have, too.)

(ii) *'We often go to the theatre.'* ***'So do* we.'*** (= 'We often go to the theatre, ***too***.')

The negative of ***so*** in this pattern is ***neither*** [see NEITHER 4].

E.g. *'We don't often go to the theatre.'* ***'Neither do* we.'*** (= 'We don't often go to the theatre, ***either***.')

* Here we use ***do*** as an 'empty' auxiliary [see DO 2].

NOTE: SO + SUBJECT + AUXILIARY / BE

This pattern is a shortened clause like pattern 4a [see SHORTENED SENTENCES AND CLAUSES], but there is no inversion. It expresses surprise and agreement with what has just been said.

E.g. *'It's starting to snow.'* ***'So it is!'***

'You've spilled some coffee on your dress.' 'Oh dear, ***so I have****.'*

4b Moving SO + ADJECTIVE / ADVERB to the front of a clause also requires inversion [see INVERSION 2–4]. In this pattern ***so*** expresses result, as in 1b above, but the meaning is more emphatic than in 1b.

E.g. { *The concert was* ***so terrible*** *that half the audience left.*
So terrible *was the concert that half the audience left.* }

5 **Idioms**

There are many idioms with ***so***. If you wish, look up the following in a dictionary, and also look up the sections of this book as shown: ***do so*** [see DO 3b]; ***even so*** [see CONTRAST 1]; *. . .* ***or so*** [see NUMBERS 6b]; ***so as to*** [see PURPOSE]; ***so (that)*** [see PURPOSE, RESULT].

some and **any** /sʌm/ (weak form: /səm/), ˈenɪ/ (*determiners, pronouns or adverbs*)

► ***Some*** and ***any*** are QUANTITY WORDS.

1 When to use *some* and *any*

A / AN means 'one', but ***some*** replaces *a* / *an* when we are talking either about more than one or about something which we cannot count [see COUNTABLE AND UNCOUNTABLE NOUNS]. ***Some*** = 'an amount / number of'.

E.g.

an *egg*

some *eggs* (***any*** *eggs*)

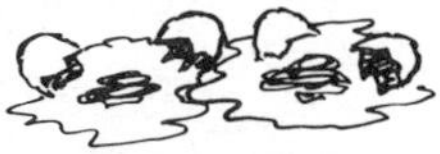

some *egg* (***any*** *egg*)

1a **Any** usually replaces ***some*** in questions and after negatives.

E.g. (i) *I want **some** eggs.*
(ii) *Do you want **any** eggs?*
(iii) *No, I don't want **any** eggs, thanks.*

1b Examples: ([✓] = positive; [?] = question; [X] = negative)

plural countable

[✓] *There are **some boys** in the swimming pool.*

[?] *Are there **any girls** in the pool?*

[X] *No, there aren't **any girls** * in the pool, because they're all playing tennis.*

uncountable

[✓] *There is **some salt** on the table.*

[?] *Is there **any pepper** on the table?*

[X] *No, I'm afraid there isn't **any pepper**. **

* We can also say *there are **no** girls* or *there is **no** pepper* [see NO].

NOTE (i): With UNCOUNTABLE NOUNS such as *pepper* the verb is singular [see AGREEMENT 1a: Note (iii)].

NOTE (ii): [See SOME-WORDS AND ANY-WORDS 2b: Note for some other situations in which we can use ***any***.]

2 ***Some* /səm/* and *any* as** DETERMINERS
Determiners come before a noun:

(I) plural noun.

E.g. ✓ *We have invited **some students** to the party.*
? *Have you invited **any students** to the party?*
✗ *We haven't invited **any students** to the party.*

(II) uncountable noun.

E.g. ✓ *They gave us **some advice** about the exam.*
? *Did they give you **any advice** about the exam?*
✗ *They didn't give us **any advice** about the exam.*

* When **some** is a determiner, we usually use the weak form /səm/. [But see 5 below.]

3 ***Some* /ˈsʌm/ and *any* as** PRONOUNS
As pronouns, ***some*** and ***any*** are followed by ***of***, or they stand alone as subject, object, etc:

plural:

E.g. ✓ ***Some of** the guests are married, and **some** (of them) are single.*

uncountable:

E.g. ✓ ***Some of** the tea in Chinese, and **some** (of it) is Indian.*

plural:

E.g. ? *'Have you met **any of** the passengers?'*
✗ *'No, I haven't even seen **any** (of them) yet.'*

uncountable:

E.g. ? *'Have you tried **any of** this delicious apple juice?'*
✗ *'No, and I don't want **any** (of it). I'm not thirsty, you see.'*

4 ***Some* in** requests **and** offers
(A) You can use ***some*** in requests (even when they have the form of questions).

E.g. *Can I have **some** milk, please?*
*Could you lend me **some** money?*

(B) You can also use ***some*** in OFFERS.

E.g. *Will you have **some** cake?*
*I've just picked these apples. Would you like **some**?*

Some makes the request or offer more positive. It means that you want the answer *'yes'*.

NOTE: You can also use ***some*** in any question when you expect the answer *'yes'*.
E.g. *'I've just been shopping.' 'Oh. Did you buy {**any** / **some**} rice?*

5 **The 'strong' use of *some* and *any***
As determiners (as well as pronouns) ***some*** and ***any*** can be (strongly) stressed.

5a The 'strong' use of ***some*** pronounced /sʌm/:
In example (i) below, ***some*** is an important word because it implies a contrast between two people.

E.g. (i) *ˈ**Some** people like red wine, and ˈ**some** people prefer white.*
(ii) *There has to be **some** reason for the murder.*

5b The 'strong' use of ***any***:
The 'strong' use of ***any*** can occur in positive statements, often with a singular countable noun.
'Strong' ***any*** generally goes with words like CAN, COULD, and WILL, and means that there is a choice from every possibility.

E.g. *You **can** paint the house ˈ**any** colour you like.*
*ˈ**Any** good guide **will** tell you the best places to visit.*
*ˈ**Any** dictionary is better than none.*

6 ***Some*** **and** ***any*** **as** ADVERBS OF DEGREE
Less commonly, ***some*** (/svm/) and ***any*** (/ˈenɪ/) are adverbs of degree.

E.g. (i) ***Some** two million tourists visit our country every summer.* (***some*** = 'about')
(ii) *Was the play **any** good?* (***any*** = 'at all')
(iii)

some- words and *any-* words

► ***Some-*** words and ***any-*** words are DETERMINERS, INDEFINITE PRONOUNS and ADVERBS.

► [For further details of ***some-*** words and ***any-*** words as pronouns, see INDEFINITE PRONOUN 3.]

1 **List of *some-* words and *any-* words**

Not all the words in this list begin with ***some-*** or ***any-***. But they all behave in the same way.

(I)

pronouns	(not person)	(person)*	(person)*
some- words	***something*** /ˈsʌmθɪŋ/	***someone*** /ˈsʌmwʌn/	***somebody*** /ˈsʌmbɒdɪ/
any- words	***anything*** /ˈenɪˌθɪŋ/	***anyone*** /ˈenɪˌwʌn/	***anybody*** /ˈenɪˌbɒdɪ/

(II)

adverbs	(place)**	(frequency)	(degree)
some- words	***somewhere*** /ˈsʌmweəʳ/	***sometimes*** /ˈsʌmtaɪmz/	***somewhat*** /ˈsʌmwɒt/
any- words	***anywhere*** /ˈenɪˌweəʳ/	***ever*** /ˈevəʳ/	***at all*** /ətˈɔːl/

* There is no difference of meaning between the words ending ***-one*** and ***-body***, except that those ending ***-one*** are more common.

** In <U.S.> ***someplace*** and ***anyplace*** are often used, instead of ***somewhere*** and ***anywhere***.

2 **How *some-* words and *any-* words behave** [See SOME AND ANY]

Use ***some-*** words in positive STATEMENTS.

Use ***any-*** words instead of ***some-*** words in QUESTIONS and after negatives [see NEGATIVE WORDS AND SENTENCES].

2a Examples:

(I) Pronouns. (E.g. *something, anything*):

✓ positive statement:

I want to tell you something.
?

? question:

Did you catch anything ?

[X] negative:

You don't know anything about the accident. You weren't there.

(II) Adverbs. (E.g. *sometimes, ever*):

[✓] *Margaret **sometimes** visits her grandmother.*

[?] *Does she **ever** telephone her parents?*

[X] *No, I don't think she **ever** writes to them, either.*

2b There are some other pairs of adverbs which correspond in this same way:

some- words:	***already****	***still****	***too****
any- words:	***yet****	***any more***	***either****

* [These words have separate entries in this book. Look them up for further details. See also TOO 1 and EITHER 2.]

NOTE: In addition to questions and negatives, there are some other places where you can use an ***any-*** word:

(A) In an INDIRECT QUESTION:

E.g. *We asked the doctor **whether anything** was wrong.*

(B) In an ***if-*** clause [see IF].

E.g. ***If anyone** calls, please tell them I'm out.*

(C) In a COMPARATIVE CLAUSE.

E.g. *We get more rain here **than anywhere else** in the country.*

(D) After a word with negative meaning.

E.g. *It was {**impossible** / **difficult**} for **anyone** to escape from the castle.*

3 ***Some-* words in OFFERS and REQUESTS**

Some- words can be used in special questions, particularly when they are offers or requests [compare SOME AND ANY 4].

E.g. *Would you like **something** to eat?*
*Could **someone** open this door, please?*

4 ***Any-*** words are used in positive statements when they mean there is a choice from every possibility [compare SOME AND ANY 5b].

E.g. ***Anyone** can make a mistake like that.* (**anyone** = 'everyone')
*Help yourselves to **anything** you want.* (**anything** = 'everything')

somebody, someone, something, sometimes, somewhat, somewhere [See SOME- WORDS AND ANY- WORDS]

sometimes /ˈsʌmtaɪmz/ and **sometime** /ˈsʌmtaɪm/ (*adverbs*)

1 ***Sometimes*** (= 'on some occasions') is an adverb of frequency. ***Sometimes*** generally goes in front position or in middle position in the sentence [see ADVERB 3].

E.g. ***Sometimes*** *I cook my own dinner, but often I prefer to eat at a cafe.*
The trains from London to Liverpool ***sometimes*** *arrive late, but they are usually on time.*

2 ***Sometime*** is an adverb of time meaning 'at some time in the future'. ***Sometime*** generally goes in end position. It is much less common than ***sometimes***. We can also write it as two words: ***some time***.

E.g. *Why don't you come and stay with us* ***sometime****?*

soon /su:n/, **sooner** /ˈsu:nəʳ/, ***(the)* soonest** /ˈsu:nɪst/ (*adverb of time*)

► ***Soon*** means 'in the near future, within a short time'. ***Sooner*** means 'nearer to now'. ***The soonest*** means 'nearest to now'.

E.g. (i)

It's five to nine. The train will arrive soon.
PLATFORM
4
How soon?
In five minutes.
The sooner the better. I'm cold.

(ii) *'How* ***soon*** *can you mend this watch?' 'The* ***soonest*** *we can do it is next Saturday.'*

sorry [See PARDON, SORRY AND EXCUSE ME]

sort (of) (*noun of kind*) [See KIND (OF), SORT (OF), AND TYPE (OF)]

spelling [See CONSONANTS AND VOWELS]

► When we add an ending to a word, we sometimes have to change the word's ***spelling***. There are four rules:

1 Double the consonant. E.g. *get* ~ *ge**tt**ing.*
2 Drop the silent ***-e***. E.g. *love* ~ *loving.*
3 Add ***-e*** before ***-s***. E.g. *pass* ~ *pass**es**.*
4 Change ***-y*** to ***-i(e)-*** (or ***-ie*** to ***-y-***). E.g. *fly* ~ *fl**ies**, d**ie*** ~ *d**y**ing.*

These changes of spelling do not alter the way we pronounce the word itself. [But see 3 on ***-es***.] [For words with changes of pronunciation see IRREGULAR VERB and IRREGULAR PLURAL.]

1 **Double the final consonant** when the last two letters of a word are a single vowel letter followed by a consonant letter (e.g. *stop*) and when the ending begins with a vowel (e.g. *-ed, -ing, -er*). The rule is: (C) + V + C + C + V . . . E.g. *sto**p**, sto**pp**ed, sto**pp**ing, sto**pp**er.*

1a Examples:

VERB	+*-ing*	+*-ed**	+*-er* (= noun)
get	***getting***		***go-getter***
rub	***rubbing***	***rubbed***	***rubber***
sit	***sitting***		***baby-sitter***
plan	***planning***	***planned***	***planner***
run	***running***		***runner***
swim	***swimming***		***swimmer***

* This column shows regular verb forms only.

1b Examples:

ADJECTIVE	+*-er*	+*-est*	*-en* (verb)
big	***bigger***	***biggest***	
sad	***sadder***	***saddest***	***sadden***
hot	***hotter***	***hottest***	

NOTE (i): Do not double the consonant if the vowel is written with two letters
E.g. ***great, greater, greatest***
look, looking, looked

NOTE (ii): The letters **w** and **y** count as vowels when they come after a vowel. So there is no doubling in these cases.
E.g. ***play, playing, played, player***
row, rowing, rowed, rower

NOTE (iii): Never double an ***X***.
E.g. *box* → *boxing* *tax* → *taxing*

1c In two- or three- syllable words, the rule for doubling is changed as follows:
Double the final consonant as described in 1, if the last vowel in the word is stressed (as in (A) below), but not if it is unstressed (as in (B) below):

Examples:

(A)	*beˈgin*	*beˈginning*		*beˈginner*
	ocˈcur	*ocˈcurring*	*ocˈcurred*	*ocˈcurrence*
	adˈmit	*adˈmitting*	*adˈmitted*	*adˈmittance*
	preˈfer	*preˈferring*	*preˈferred*	*[ˈpreference]*
(B)	*ˈenter*	*ˈentering*	*ˈentered*	
	ˈvisit	*ˈvisiting*	*ˈvisited*	
	deˈvelop	*deˈveloping*	*deˈveloped*	

NOTE: An exception to (B) in <G.B.> is that doubling does take place in words ending with an unstressed vowel +***l*** or (sometimes) ***s***, ***p***, or ***g***.

E.g.	*<U.S.>:*	*ˈtravel*	*ˈtraveling*	*ˈtraveled*
	<G.B.>:	*ˈtravel*	*ˈtrave**ll**ing*	*ˈtrave**ll**ed*
	<U.S. or G.B.>:	*ˈworship*	*ˈworshiping*	*ˈworshiped*
	<G.B.>:	*ˈworship*	*ˈworshi**pp**ing*	*ˈworshi**pp**ed*

2 **Drop the silent -*e*** when you add an ending beginning with a vowel. (E.g. *-ed*, *-er* and *-est*, *-ing**).

2a Examples:

VERB	+*-ing*	+*-ed*	+*-er* (= noun)
use	***using***	***used***	***user***
love	***loving***	***loved***	***lover***
come	***coming***	***came***	***newcomer***
write	***writing***	***wrote***	***writer***
change	***changing***	***changed***	–
suppose	***supposing***	***supposed***	–
argue	***arguing***	***argued***	–

2b Examples:

ADJECTIVE	+*-er*	+*-est*
pale	***paler***	***palest***
large	***larger***	***largest***
white	***whiter***	***whitest***
blue	***bluer***	***bluest***

* [See -ED FORM, -ER / -EST, and -ING FORM to find out how these endings are used in grammar.]

NOTE (i): If the word ends in ***-ee***, ***-oe***, ***-ye***, or (sometimes) ***-ge***, it drops the ***-e*** before ***-ed***, ***-er***, ***-est***, but not before ***-ing***.

E.g.	verbs:	*agree*	*agreeing*	*agreed*
		hoe	*hoeing*	*hoed*
		dye	*dyeing*	*dyed*
		singe	*singeing*	*singed*
	adjectives:	*free*	*freer* /ˈfriːəʳ/	*freest* /ˈfriːɪst/
		strange	*stranger*	*strangest*

NOTE (ii): If the word ends in ***-ie***, it drops the ***-e*** before ***-ed***, ***-er***, ***-est***, and also before ***-ing***, where the ***-i-*** changes to ***-y-***: e.g. ***die*** ~ ***dying*** ~ ***died***.

3 **Add *-e-* before *-s*** where the ***-s*** ending comes after a 'hissing' sound (sibilant) spelled ***-s***, ***-ss***, ***-sh***, ***-ch***, ***-tch***, ***-x***, ***-z***, ***-zz***.

E.g. verbs: *they* ***pass*** ~ *it* ***passes*** /ˈpɑːsɪz ‖ ˈpæːsɪz/
they ***watch*** ~ *she* ***watches*** /ˈwɒtʃɪz/
they ***wish*** ~ *he* ***wishes*** /ˈwɪʃɪz/
they ***teach*** ~ *he* ***teaches*** /ˈtiːtʃɪz/

nouns: ***box*** ~ ***boxes*** ***church*** ~ ***churches***
bus ~ ***buses*** ***quiz*** ~ ***quizzes***

Notice that this added ***-e-*** is never silent. It always represents the vowel of the ending -/ɪz/, spelled ***-es***.

NOTE: Also, add an ***-e-*** before the ***-s*** after these words ending in ***-o***:
verbs: ***I do*** /duː/ ~ *he* ***does*** /dʌz/. ***I go*** ~ *she* ***goes*** /gəʊz/.
nouns: ***potato*** ~ *three* ***potatoes****, please.*
tomato ~ *ripe* ***tomatoes****, please.*
hero ~ *a place fit for* ***heroes****.*
cargo ~ ***cargoes*** *of bananas.*
But most nouns ending in ***-o*** do not add the ***-e-***.
E.g. *radio* ~ *radios;* *zoo* ~ *zoos;* *video* ~ *videos;* *kilo* ~ *kilos.*
Never end a noun with ***-oes*** if:
(A) the ***-o*** follows another vowel (e.g. *radios*), or
(B) the noun is a shortened word such as *kilos* (= kilograms).

4 **How to deal with *y* and *i* after a consonant**

4a Change a final ***-y*** to ***-ie-*** before you add ***-s***:

E.g. verbs: ***fly*** ~ *The pilot* ***flies*** *regularly.*
cry ~ *The baby rarely* ***cries****.*
envy ~ *He* ***envies*** *her because she's rich.*

(Also: ***try*** ~ ***tries;*** ***carry*** ~ ***carries;*** ***copy*** ~ ***copies****, etc.*)

nouns: *a* ***baby*** ~ *two* ***babies;*** *a* ***city*** ~ *many* ***cities***
this ***body*** ~ *these* ***bodies;*** *my* ***family*** ~ ***families***

4b Change a final ***-y*** to ***-i-*** before you add ***-ed***, ***-er***, ***-est***, ***-ly***:

Examples:

VERB	+*-ed*	+*-er* (= noun)
cry	***cried***	***crier***
copy	***copied***	***copier***
carry	***carried***	***carrier***
worry	***worried***	***worrier***

ADJECTIVE	+-*er*	+-*est*	[+-*ly*]
happy ***funny***	***happier*** ***funnier***	***happiest*** ***funniest***	[***happily***] [***funnily***]

ADVERB	+-*er*	+-*est*
early	***earlier***	***earliest***

NOTE (i): Do not change **-y** to **-i-** or **-ie-** when **-y** follows another vowel: e.g. ***-ay, -ey, -oy, -uy***.
E.g. verbs: *play ~ plays ~ played ~ player*
nouns: *boy ~ boys; key ~ keys*

NOTE (ii): But there are three verbs which are exceptions to Note (i): ***lay***, ***pay***, and ***say***. These all have a past form spelled ***-aid***.
E.g. *'Did you* ***lay*** *this carpet on the floor?' 'Yes, I* ***laid*** *it there a few minutes ago.'*
'Did you ***pay*** *the bill?' 'Yes, I* ***paid*** *it last month.'*
'Did the witness ***say*** *anything?' 'Yes, she* ***said*** /sed/ *a great deal.'*
Also, ***-ay*** changes to ***-ai-*** in ***daily***.

4c Change ***-ie*** to ***-y-*** before ***-ing*** in these verbs:

die ~ dying; lie ~ lying; tie ~ tying

statement

1 If a SENTENCE or MAIN CLAUSE offers you information, it is a statement. A statement can be positive or negative.

(i) Positive statement. E.g. *The sun is shining.*
(ii) Negative statement. E.g. *I didn't play football yesterday.*

2 The statement is the commonest kind of sentence or main clause, contrasting with QUESTIONS and IMPERATIVES.

3 Most statements contain a SUBJECT followed by a VERB element:

E.g.

(. . .)	subject	verb (. . .)
	The manager	***has resigned.***
Now	*we*	***live*** *in Kowloon.*
	Jill and Mary	***played*** *tennis last night.*

NOTE: But in some statements the verb element comes before the subject.
E.g. ***'I enjoyed*** *the game.'* *'So* ***did I****.'*
subject verb verb subject
[See WORD ORDER for further examples.]

state verbs and action verbs

- ► State verbs describe states which continue over a period.
  E.g. ***be***, ***know***.
- ► Action verbs (also called 'event verbs') describe something which happens in a limited time, and has a definite beginning and end.

  E.g. ***come***, ***get***, ***learn***.

1 State verbs cannot usually have a Progressive form* [see PROGRESSIVE 3].

E.g. *I am learning Arabic* is a good English sentence, but:
I ~~am knowing~~ Arabic is not.

Instead, the Present Simple of ***know*** describes a continuing state.

E.g. *I* ***know*** *Arabic.*

1a Here is a list of state verbs which do not usually have a Progressive form:

appear (= 'seem')	*expect*	*know*	*own*	*seem*
	feel (= 'think')	*like*	*possess*	*smell*
be	*forget*	*love*	*prefer*	*suppose*
believe	*forgive*	*matter*	*realise*	*think*
(not) care	*hate*	*mean*	*recognise*	*trust*
concern	*have* (= 'possess')	*(not) mind*	*refuse*	*understand*
consist (of)	*keep (on)* (= 'continue')	*notice*	*remember*	*want*
dislike		*owe*	*see*	*wish*

But these verbs can be in the Progressive when they describe an action or process. Compare.

E.g. *I* ***see*** *what you mean.* (***see*** = 'understand') (Not *I ~~am seeing~~* . . .)

But: *I* ***am seeing*** *the manager tomorrow.* (= 'meeting')

* Note that these state verbs can be in the Progressive:
stand, sit, lie, live.

2 The state verbs (in 1 a) use the simple verb form, even when they describe something which lasts for a limited period.

	temporary state	temporary action
E.g.	*The teacher* ***thinks***	*that my work* ***is improving***.
	Malcolm ***is*** *tired.*	*That's why he****'s yawning***.

still /stɪl/ (*adverb*) [See ALREADY, STILL AND YET]

stress [See also INTONATION]

1 We pronounce some syllables with more force than others. These are stressed syllables. They sound louder than other syllables.

2 Stress in words

2a A stressed syllable is marked with ˈ in front of it in many dictionaries and grammar books.

2b Every English word of two or more syllables has one stressed syllable.

E.g. ***ˈhappen*** (= hap+pen), ***beˈcome*** (= be+come), ***reˈmember*** (= re+mem+ber).

3 Stress in sentences
To mark the strongest stresses in sentences we use these marks in this book:

↘ falling ↗ rising ↘↗ fall-rise

E.g. *'Where have you ˈbeen?' 'I've ˈbeen to the Uniˈversity.'*

[For further details, see INTONATION 4.]

4 Weak forms
About 50 short grammatical words in English have weak forms.

			(weak)			(weak)			(weak)
E.g.	*a*	/eɪ/	∿ /ə/	*at*	/æt/	∿ /ət/	*she*	/ʃiː/	∿ /ʃɪ/
	and	/ænd/	∿ /ən(d)/	*can*	/kæn/	∿ /kən/	*the*	/ðiː/	∿ /ðɪ, ðə/
	are	/ɑː^r/	∿ /ə^r/	*does*	/dʌz/	∿ /dəz/	*you*	/juː/	∿ /jʊ/

4a We normally use the weak form in sentences, when the word is not stressed. For example, in 3 above:

'Where have /əv/ *you* /jʊ/ *ˈbeen?'*
'I've /v/ *ˈbeen to* /tə/ *the* /ðə/ *ˌuniˈversity.'*

NOTE (i): We use the 'strong form' when we are talking about the word itself.
E.g. ***The*** /ðiː/ *is the most common word in English.*
or when we want to stress the word for special emphasis: for example, at the end of a sentence.
E.g. *He ˈ**can**/kæn/ work ˈhard, but he ˈrarely ˈ**does**/dʌz/.*

NOTE (ii): If a word has a weak form, the weak form is given at the beginning of its entry in this book.

5 Change of word stress

Look at the word ***present*** in this example:

May I pre'sent (= give) this picture to you, in the name of your home town?
LOCAL BOY MAKES GOOD
Thank you! It's a beautiful 'present (= gift)

pre'sent /pre'zent/ (with stress on the 2nd syllable) is a verb.
'present /'prezent/ (with stress on the 1st syllable) is a noun.

5a There are about 50 words like ***present*** in English. The most important are:

noun	verb	noun	verb
'conduct	*con'duct*	*'present*	*pre'sent*
'conflict	*con'flict*	*'progress*	*pro'gress*
'decrease	*de'crease*	*'protest*	*pro'test*
'export	*ex'port*	*'record*	*re'cord*
'import	*im'port*	*'suspect*	*sus'pect*
'increase	*in'crease*	*'transfer*	*trans'fer*
'insult	*in'sult*	*'transport*	*trans'port*
'permit	*per'mit*	*'upset*	*up'set*

5b Some other common two-syllable words with different stress for noun and verb are:

construct contest contrast convert convict
digest discount escort extract pervert produce
rebel refill refund reject resit survey
torment transplant

NOTE: Many words of two syllables which act as noun or verb do not change their stress.
E.g. ***'comfort*** is both noun and verb; ***sur'prise*** is both noun and verb.

subject

► The ***subject*** is a grammatical term for the part of a clause or sentence which generally goes before the VERB PHRASE (in STATEMENTS).

1 Some examples

subject	verb phrase (. . .)
Jane	*worked there.*
My sister and her husband	*are coming to stay.*
We	*sang and danced all night.*

2 Some facts about the subject

(A) The subject usually begins a statement.*

(B) The subject is normally a NOUN PHRASE or PRONOUN.**

(C) The verb agrees with the subject in choosing between singular and plural [see AGREEMENT].

(D) The subject normally describes the 'doer' of an action.***

* But in questions the subject often comes after the FINITE VERB, and in imperatives there is usually no subject. [See YES-NO QUESTION, WH- QUESTION 9, IMPERATIVE.] In statements, an adverb may go first [see ADVERB 3].

** The subject may also sometimes be a clause.

E.g. ***What we need** is a sharp knife.*

*** The subject is not the 'doer' of an action if the verb is a state verb [see STATE VERBS AND ACTION VERBS].

E.g. ***Pat** resembles her **mother**.*
*This **bottle** contains **acid**.*

Also, the subject is not the 'doer' in passive sentences [see PASSIVE].

E.g. ***The boys** were punished by **their mother.***
subject 'doer'

3 Subject pronouns

Subject pronouns [see PERSONAL PRONOUN] are pronouns which are used in the position of subject: I / YOU / HE / SHE / IT / WE / THEY / WHO.
Subject pronouns are sometimes called 'nominative' or 'subjective' pronouns. They contrast with OBJECT pronouns such as ***me, her, us***.

4 The subject is usually the topic of the sentence – i.e. it refers to what is in the front of your mind, the first thing that you want to talk about.

E.g. (i) ***This violin** is difficult to play.* (topic = ***this violin***)
(ii) ***I** find it difficult to play this violin.* (topic = ***I***)

But sometimes in <speech> the topic and subject are different.

E.g. (iii) *You know **this essay** I'm writing? Can you help me with **it** this evening?* { (topic = ***essay***) (subject = ***you***) }
(iv) ***That man** – I can't stand him.* { (topic = ***that man***) (subject = ***I***) }

In <writing> we do not separate topic and subject as in (iii) and (iv). We organize the sentence in a different way. Compare,

E.g. *Alan – I trust him completely.* <speech>
and
Alan is a person that I trust completely. <speech or writing>

subject pronoun [See SUBJECT 3, PERSONAL PRONOUN]

subjective case is a grammatical term sometimes used for the SUBJECT pronoun form of personal pronouns.

subjunctive

- ***Subjunctive*** is a term used for the verb in some situations where we use the BASIC FORM (or plural form) instead of an -S FORM.
- The ***subjunctive*** belongs mainly to <formal> or <written> English. It is not common.
- There are three kinds of ***subjunctive***.

1 **Subjunctive in *that*-clauses**
We use the subjunctive in *that*-clauses [see THAT 1] after some verbs and adjectives [see VERB PATTERNS 4, ADJECTIVE PATTERNS 2]. This subjunctive expresses an intention or proposal about the future.

E.g. (i) *The Minister **insisted** that he **leave** the country immediately.*
(ii) *I **propose** that Ms. Bond **be** elected secretary.*
(iii) *It is **essential** that the committee **resign**.*

You can use either the subjunctive or the S-FORM:

subjunctive: E.g. *he leave* *Ms Bond **be** elected*
-*s* form: E.g. *he leaves* *Ms Bond **is** elected*

This subjunctive is more common in <U.S.>. <G.B.> prefers ***should*** + Verb [see SHOULD AND OUGHT TO 6b].

E.g. (i) *The Minister insist**ed** that he **should leave** the country immediately.*

2 **Subjunctive in main clauses**
We use this in a few <formal> idioms expressing a strong wish.

E.g. *God **save** the Queen.* (= 'May God save . . .')
*Heaven **forbid** that you should suffer.*
***Bless** you!* (= 'May God bless you.')

3 ***Were*** is a subjunctive which we can use instead of ***was*** in expressing UNREAL MEANING. [See WERE 2.]

E.g. *I wish the meeting* {***were*** / ***was***} *over.*
If I {***were*** / ***was***} *still at school, I would work harder for my exams.*

subordinate clause

► A ***subordinate clause*** is one which is part of another clause, i.e. is dependent on a main clause. [See CLAUSE.]
► A ***subordinate clause*** cannot stand alone as a sentence. [See SENTENCE.]

1 Main types of subordinate clause

1a NOUN CLAUSE:

E.g. ***What this country needs*** *is a period of peace.*

1b ADVERBIAL CLAUSE:

E.g. ***If you follow my instructions****, nobody will be hurt.*

1c RELATIVE CLAUSE:

E.g. *The man* ***who owes me money*** *lives in Australia.*

1d COMPARATIVE CLAUSE:

E.g. *Malcolm spends money faster* ***than he earns it****.*

2 [For more information about different kinds of subordinate clause, see: ADVERBIAL CLAUSE; COMMENT CLAUSE; COMPARATIVE CLAUSE; FINITE CLAUSE; INFINITIVE CLAUSE; -ING CLAUSE; NONFINITE CLAUSE; NOUN CLAUSE; PAST PARTICIPLE CLAUSE; RELATIVE CLAUSE; TO-INFINITIVE; VERBLESS CLAUSE.]

such /sʌtʃ/ (*determiner or pronoun*)

► ***Such*** means { 'this or that kind (of)' / 'of this or that kind' }
► ***Such*** is used in patterns similar to those of the adverb of degree ***so*** [see SO 1].

1 ***Such*** **as a determiner**

1a ***Such*** is used to express strong feelings about something:

E.g. *I'm sorry you had* ***such*** *terrible weather!*
I'm glad we went to the dance. It was ***such*** *fun!*

Note the pattern: SUCH A / AN (+ ADJECTIVE) + COUNTABLE NOUN

E.g. *Don't be* **such an** *idiot!*
We haven't had **such a** *good time for ages.*

[See also EXCLAMATIONS 6c.]

1b Another pattern with ***such*** is:

SUCH (A / AN) (. . .) + NOUN + AS + { NOUN PHRASE / CLAUSE }

E.g. *I've never lived in* **such a** *large house* **as** *this before.*
These days, inflation isn't **such a** *(big) problem* **as** *it used to be.*

NOTE: ***Such*** usually follows a negative in this pattern.

1c ***Such*** comes before a clause of RESULT in the pattern:

SUCH (A / AN) + (. . .) + NOUN + (. . .) + THAT + CLAUSE

E.g. (i) *There were* **such** *a lot of people in the room* **that** *you could scarcely breathe!*

(ii)

We will create jobs...we will lower taxes...we will...
They're such liars that they're not worth watching.

2 ***Such*** **as a pronoun** is <less common> than ***such*** as a determiner.

E.g. *'My boyfriend doesn't want to see me any more!'* *'Oh dear!* ***Such*** *is life!'* (= 'Life is like that.')

3 ***Such*** **compared with** ***so*** [see SO 1]
Notice the different patterns for ***such*** and ***so*** in exclamations [see 1a above]:

SUCH + (A) + (ADJECTIVE) + NOUN

E.g. *We've had* { ***such*** *a (wonderful) day!* / ***such*** *(wonderful) weather!* }

SO + ADJECTIVE / ADVERB / DETERMINER

E.g. *The weather was* **so** *wonderful!*
The time went **so** *quickly!*
We've had **so** *much fun!*

[See EXCLAMATIONS 6c.]

suffixes [See also PREFIXES]

- A ***suffix*** is a word's grammatical ending.
- If you recognize ***suffixes***, it will help you with grammar and meaning.
- Many English words have no ***suffixes***.

1 There are two types of suffix:

(I) 'derivational'.
The 'derivational' suffix tells you what type of word it is (e.g. noun or adjective). For example, ***-or*** (in *act**or***) indicates a noun (= someone who does the verb's action).

(II) 'inflectional'.
The 'inflectional' suffix tells you something about the word's grammatical behaviour. For example **-s** indicates that a noun is plural.
'Derivational' suffixes go before 'inflectional' suffixes.

E.g. ***actor* + s**.

2 [For 'inflectional' suffixes, look up these endings in this book: -ED FORM; -ER / -EST; -ING FORM; -S FORM. For **-'s**, look up POSSESSIVE.]

3 It is best to look up 'derviational' suffixes in a dictionary. Here is a list of some of the most important ones:

3a Nouns (people):

-er, -or:	*writ**er**, driv**er**, act**or***
-ee:	*employ**ee**, pay**ee**, train**ee***
-ess [see SEX]:	*actr**ess**, waitr**ess**, princ**ess***

3b Nouns (abstract):

-ness:	*good**ness**, great**ness**, happi**ness***
-ity:	*qual**ity**, san**ity**, electric**ity***
-al:	*arriv**al**, approv**al**, refus**al***
-((a)t)ion:	*inten**tion**, invit**ation**, persuas**ion***
-ment:	*judge**ment**, advertise**ment**, improve**ment***
-hood:	*boy**hood**, child**hood**, sister**hood***

3c Nouns or adjecitves:

-ist:	*Buddh**ist**, typ**ist**, pian**ist***
-(i)an: } [See COUNTRIES.]	*hum**an**, Ind**ian**, Victor**ian***
-ese: }	*Chin**ese**, Japan**ese**, Portugu**ese***

3d Adjectives [See also ADJECTIVE 5b]:

-al:	*person**al**, natur**al**, post**al***
-ous:	*humor**ous**, fam**ous**, gener**ous***
-ic:	*histor**ic**, poet**ic**, electr**ic***
-ful:	*beauti**ful**, help**ful**, use**ful***
-less:	*child**less**, help**less**, use**less***

3e Verbs:

-ize, -ise*:	*modern**ize**, emphas**ize**, real**ise***
-ify:	*beaut**ify**, terr**ify**, simpl**ify***
-en:	*wid**en**, soft**en**, dead**en***

* In general, the spelling ***-ise*** is <G.B.>. But note that a few verbs are spelled ***-ise*** only, in both <G.B.> and <U.S.>.
E.g. *advert**ise**, adv**ise**, surpr**ise**.*

3f Adverbs [See -LY.] *quick**ly**, happi**ly**, natural**ly***

suggestions

To ***suggest*** what to do, you can use one of these patterns:

1 ***Why don't*** {***you*** / ***we***} +Verb . . .?

2 ***Shall*** {***I*** / ***we***} +Verb . . .?

3 {***How*** / ***What***} about+Verb-***ing*** . . .?

4 ***I suggest (that)*** . . .

5 ***Let's (not)***+Verb . . .?

6 {***You'd*** / ***We'd***} ***better (not)***+Verb . . .

7 ***I (don't) think we should*** + Verb . . .

E.g.

Help! Help! What shall I do ?
Hurry up and do something!
Why don't you try to move back ?
We'd better pull the car back onto the road.
I don't think we should touch the car.
What about fetching the police ?
Yes, let's do that. Shall I look for a phone box ?

superlative [see -ER/-EST, MORE/(THE) MOST]

1 **The use of the superlative**
The superlative of a word is the form we use to compare three* or more things and to pick out one thing as more 'X' than all the others.

E.g. *Everest is the high**est** mountain in the world. It is also the **most** famous mountain in the world.*

In Britain we have six coins. The 1p (/wʌn pi:/) *coin is the small**est** and it is also worth the **least**.* ** *The 50p coin is the **largest**, but the £1 coin is worth the **most**.*

* To compare two things, use the COMPARATIVE form.
E.g. *Which is the **older** of the two children?*
** [See LESS / (THE) LEAST to see how ***(the) least*** works.]

2 **The form of the superlative**
To form a superlative, we use the ending ***-est*** or the adverb ***most***. [See -ER / -EST 1 for details of when to use the ending ***-est*** and when to use ***most***]:

THE { ADJECTIVE / ADVERB + -EST / MOST + ADJECTIVE / ADVERB } { (IN . . .) / (OF . . .) }

E.g. *The small**est*** *the **most** quickly*

NOTE: There are also irregular superlatives ***best, worst, most, least, furthest***. [For irregular spellings and pronunciations, see -ER / -EST 2, 3c.]

3 Structures with the superlative

3a After a superlative we can use ***in*** or ***of*** + NOUN PHRASE to say what is being compared. Usually ***of*** is followed by a PLURAL noun, while ***in*** is followed by a SINGULAR noun.

E.g. *Ida is the **oldest of** the three girls.*
*Paul is the **tallest in** the room.*

NOTE: When a superlative adjective comes before a noun, the ***in***- or ***of***-phrase follows the noun.
E.g. *In Moscow you can see the **largest bell in the world**.*

3b We can also use a possessive noun or a possessive determiner before the superlative [see POSSESSIVE DETERMINER AND POSSESSIVE PRONOUN].

E.g. *The **world's largest** ocean is the Pacific.*
***His greatest** success was in the World Cup.*

NOTE: The words ***first, last***, and ***next*** behave like superlatives. [See ORDINALS, LAST, NEXT.]

---

suppose /sə'pəʊz/ (*regular verb*)

- ► ***Suppose*** means 'take it to be true', 'assume', 'imagine', 'think'.
- ► ***Suppose*** does not normally have a progressive form [see STATE VERBS and ACTION VERBS]

E.g. *I **suppose** he's late because of the heavy traffic.*

1 **Pattern:** . . . SUPPOSE (THAT) + CLAUSE [See VERB PATTERN 4]

E.g. *I **suppose** (that) it will rain this evening. Look at the clouds.*
*I **suppose** (that) it's a good idea – but I'm doubtful.*
*Just **suppose** (that) there were no doctors, dentists or hospitals! Life would be unpleasant and short.* [See UNREAL MEANING 2.]
*Do you **suppose** (that) the children would like an ice-cream?*

2 **Idioms:**
I suppose so (doubtful reply).

E.g. *'Are we meeting tomorrow as usual?' '**I suppose so**.'*

I suppose (= 'I think') (COMMENT CLAUSE).

E.g. *'What time is the meeting?' 'At nine, **I suppose**.'*

be supposed to /s'pəʊstə/ + Verb (VERB IDIOM).

E.g. *We**'re supposed to** feed the animals twice a day.* (= 'This is what we should do')
*Our airplane **is supposed to** take off at 10 a.m.* (= 'This is what should happen.')

sure /ʃʊəʳ/ or /ʃɔːʳ/ (*adjective* [*also adverb*]) [See CERTAIN AND SURE]

Sure (adjective) means 'certain'.

E.g. *'Are you **sure** that our team will win?' 'No – I'm not **sure**, but I think it very likely.'*
*'I'm very worried about my driving test. I feel **sure** I'll make mistakes.' 'Don't say that. You're **sure** to do well.'*

NOTE: ***Sure*** generally occurs in the same position as *certain* (adjective), but ***sure*** cannot replace *certain* in the pattern ***It's certain (that)*** . . .

surely /ˈʃʊəʳlɪ/ or /ˈʃɔːʳlɪ/ (*adverb*)

Surely has a different meaning from CERTAINLY. We use ***surely*** especially when we cannot believe what another person has said or implied. Notice that INTONATION is important in expressing surprise.

E.g. *A: 'Have we met before?'*

*B: 'Yes – **surely** you remember me? We went to school together.'*

(= B cannot believe that A does not recognize him.)

tag question

► A ***tag question*** is a little QUESTION we add to the end of a STATEMENT:

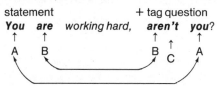

statement + tag question
You are *working hard,* ***aren't you***?

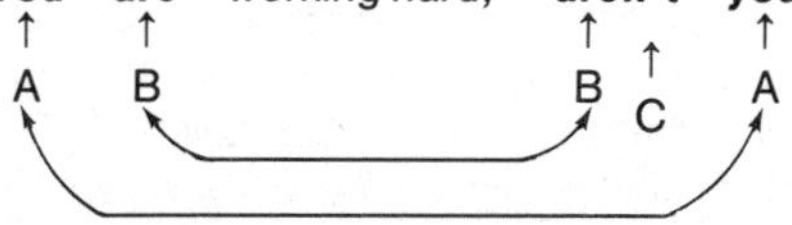

1 **Rules for forming tag questions**
(The letters A, B and C within these rules refer to the diagram above.)
(I) The tag question contains two words: (A) a subject pronoun after (B) an AUXILIARY or a form of BE (compare INVERSION in YES-NO QUESTIONS).
(II) Its subject matches the subject of the statement (A) [See 2 below].
(III) Its auxiliary (or *be*) matches the auxiliary (or *be*) in the statement (B), except that:
(i) If the statement is positive, the tag is negative (C). If the statement is negative, the tag is positive.
(ii) If there is no auxiliary or *be* in the statement, we use *do* [see DO 2e]* as the auxiliary in the tag question.

E.g. *Your sister **plays** tennis very well, **doesn't she**?*

* The main verb HAVE <in G.B.> sometimes behaves as an auxiliary.

E.g. *They **have** a large family,* { *don't they?* / ***haven't** they?* <G.B.> }

2 Look at these examples, and notice that the auxiliary or the main verb *be* is the same in the statement and the question (except where the auxiliary in the tag question is DO.) Notice that if the subject of the statement is a pronoun, the subject of the question is the same pronoun: i.e. *They . . ., . . . they?* If the subject of the statement is a noun phrase, the subject of the question is a pronoun which agrees with that noun phrase: i.e. *The students . . ., . . . they?*

E.g. ***It's** a beautiful garden, **isn't it?***
They can't** be serious, **can they?
You haven't** seen my cigarettes, **have you?
The students will** be arriving soon, **won't they?
The unions accepted** the offer, **didn't they?
I couldn't** borrow this table lamp, **could I?
The application was** refused, **wasn't it?
Someone's** got to do the job, **haven't they?*
There's** nothing** wrong, **is there?***
We ought** to be more careful, **oughtn't we?****

* Notice that INDEFINITE PRONOUNS like ***somebody*** tend to agree with the PLURAL pronoun ***they***.
** ***Nothing*** makes the statement negative, so the tag question has to be positive: . . ., ***is** there*?
*** ***There*** counts as a pronoun [see THERE IS / THERE ARE], so we repeat it in the question: ***There's** . . . **is there**?*.
**** ***Ought to*** loses its ***to*** in tag questions.

3 INTONATION is important in tag questions. We can have four kinds of tag question:

(I) A negative tag question with a rising tone. E.g. . . ., ***isn't it?***

(II) A negative tag question with a falling tone. E.g. . . ., ***isn't it?***

(III) A positive tag question with a rising tone. E.g. . . ., ***is it?***

(IV) A positive tag question with a falling tone. E.g. . . ., ***is it?***

3a The meaning of tag questions:
The tag question invites the hearer to respond to a STATEMENT. Negative tags expect a ***'Yes'*** answer, positive tags expect a ***'No'*** answer! For example:

(I) *'We've met before, **haven't we?**'*
(II) *'We've met before, **haven't we?**'* } ***'Yes.'***

(III) *'We haven't met before, **have we?**'*
(IV) *'We haven't met before, **have we?**'* } ***'No.'***

If the tag has a rising tone, it means '*I'm not sure, so please confirm that what I said is true*'.

E.g.

If the tag has a falling tone, it means '*I know that what I said is true, so please agree with me!*'

E.g.

NOTE (i): In talking about today's weather, you can use a falling tone, because you know about the weather.

E.g. *'It's a lovely day, **isn't it?**' 'Yes, it's absolutely wonderful.'*

NOTE (ii): Some less important kinds of tag question:
(a) a positive tag sometimes follows a positive statement. It expresses surprise or interest (in <G.B.>).

E.g. *'I shall be staying in an excellent hotel.' 'Oh, so you've stayed there before, **have you**?'*

*'Jenny wouldn't do a thing like that.' 'Oh, you know her, **do you**?'*

(b) after an IMPERATIVE, we can add a tag such as: ***will you*** or ***won't you***.

E.g. *Be careful, **won't you?** Don't be long, **will you**?*

(c) After LET'S, we can add ***shall we.***

E.g. ***Let's** go for a walk, **shall we?***

---

take (*irregular verb*) [See BRING AND TAKE]

tense

1 ***Tense*** is the name we give to two different forms of the verb: PRESENT TENSE and PAST TENSE.

E.g. Present Tense: ***works***, ***work***
Past Tense: ***worked***

2 ***Tense*** expresses:
(a) the difference between present and PAST TIME, and
(b) the difference between real and UNREAL MEANING.

3 Present and Past Tense can combine with Perfect and Progressive forms of the Verb. [See VERB PHRASE for further details.]

than /ðæn/ (weak form /ðən/) (*conjunction or preposition*) [See COMPARATIVE CLAUSE]

► If you want to compare two things which are different in size or degree, use ***-er*** or ***more . . . than***. [See DEGREE, -ER / -EST, MORE / (THE) MOST.]
► ***Than*** is used for comparisons with both adjectives and adverbs.

1 ***Than* as a subordinating conjunction**
Than introduces a COMPARATIVE CLAUSE:
(i) with an adjective.

E.g. *She is more* ***intelligent than (she is) beautiful***.

(ii) with an adverb.

E.g. *She drives more* ***quickly than she should***.

2 ***Than* as a preposition**

E.g. (i) *We're not allowed to drive at* ***more than 70 miles per hour.***
(ii) *Rosalind is older* ***than me***.*

* We can choose between ***me*** and ***I*** in (ii) [see PERSONAL PRONOUN 2d].

3 **Special idiomatic patterns with *than***

I'd rather + Verb + . . . ***than*** . . . (VERBAL IDIOM)

E.g. ***I'd rather play*** *football* ***than*** *go swimming.*

rather than + Verb (conjunction)

E.g. *I'd prefer to play football,* ***rather than go*** *swimming.*

different than [see DIFFERENT 2]; ***other than*** [see OTHER 3].

thanking people

1 When thanking someone who has been kind to you, say:

E.g. *'Thanks.'* <informal>
'Thank you.'
'Thank you very much.'
'That's really very kind of you. Thank you so much! I'm very grateful.'

The longer forms are (a) for more valuable things, and (b) to be more <polite>.

2 Replying to thanks:

Thank you for the lovely presents and cards. It's very kind of you.
Oh, it's nothing. I'm glad you like them.
That's OK. You're welcome. Once again, happy birthday.

3 In <formal> letters, i.e. to strangers, you can write:

E.g. ***I am*** {*very* / *extremely*} ***grateful*** *to you* ***for (kindly)*** *sending me the book . . .*
We *(very much)* ***appreciate*** *your help . . .*

Or you can thank someone for what you hope they will do!

E.g. ***I should be*** *(most)* ***grateful*** *if you would reply as soon as possible to this request.* <formal>

that /ðæt/ (weak form /ðət/*) (*conjunction, relative pronoun, demonstrative pronoun or determiner*)

- ***That*** is a very common word with various uses.
- We can often omit ***that*** (= conjunction, relative pronoun) at the front of a clause.
- ***That*** as a demonstrative pronoun [see 3, below] has the PLURAL form ***those***.

► You will find a lot about ***that*** under other headings.
[E.g. See INDIRECT SPEECH; INDIRECT STATEMENT; RELATIVE CLAUSE; IT-PATTERNS; DEMONSTRATIVES; THIS AND THESE 2; THOSE.]

* The weak form is used only for ***that*** as a conjunction or relative pronoun [see 1, 2 below].

1 That /ðət/ is a conjunction which introduces *that*-clauses

1a The positions of ***that***-clauses:
That-clauses are noun clauses; they can, for example, be subject (see example (i) below) or object (see example (ii) below) of a clause.

E.g. (i) *'**That the murdered man had my address in his note book** does not prove anything.'*
(ii) *'Yes, it does – it proves **(that) you were a friend of his.**'*

Most frequently of all, ***that***-clauses follow a verb in reporting statements in INDIRECT SPEECH AND THOUGHT [see VERB PATTERNS 4 and 14].

E.g. (iii) *They have told us **(that) our flight will be delayed**.*
(iv) *I believe **(that) he's quite a good painter**.*

That-clauses can follow a preposition only if we add *the fact* in front of them.

E.g. (v) *I was encouraged* { ~~*by*~~ / ***by the fact*** } ***that*** *so many people came to the meeting.*

But often we can simply omit *by the fact*. For example, we can omit *by the fact* after a PASSIVE.

E.g. (vi) *I was encouraged **(that) so many people came to the meeting**.*

That-clauses also go after certain adjectives [see ADJECTIVE PATTERNS 2].

E.g. (vii) *We're **afraid (that) the parcel must be lost**.*

Also as a 'delayed subject' in IT-patterns [see IT-PATTERNS 1].

E.g. (viii) *It's a pity **(that) we played so badly.***

Also after some ABSTRACT NOUNS (like *fact, belief, news*) (as MODIFIER in a NOUN PHRASE).

E.g. (ix) *The news **that he was resigning from his job** shocked us.*

1b Omitting ***that***:
We can omit ***that*** in all positions, except when the ***that*** goes at the beginning of the sentence (as in (i) above), or when the ***that***-clause is after an abstract noun, (as in (ix) above).

NOTE: When the ***that***-clause contains *should* [see SHOULD AND OUGHT TO 6b] or a subjunctive verb [see SUBJUNCTIVE 1], it expresses some kind of wish or intention.
E.g. *The committee has decided that our city hall **(should) be** rebuilt.* [See VERB PATTERN 4.]

2 ***That*** **/ðət/ is a relative pronoun which introduces a defining relative clause** (i.e. ***that*** = *who* or *which*).

E.g. (i) *The painting* ***(that) I bought*** *is on the table.*
(ii) *The man* ***that sold it to me*** *said it was painted by a famous artist.*

2a A defining relative clause is a clause which gives information necessary to identify the person or thing being discussed [see RELATIVE CLAUSE]. So if we omit the relative clause in example (ii) above, we don't know which man is being discussed.

E.g.

2b Omitting ***that***:
We cannot omit ***that*** if it is the subject of the relative clause as in example (ii) above. Otherwise, we usually omit ***that*** [see RELATIVE CLAUSE].

E.g. *The painting* ***I bought*** *is on the table.*
The school Ann ***went to*** *is in the centre of the city.*

3 ***That*** **is a singular demonstrative pronoun or determiner (*****those*** is its plural form).

3a [For the difference between ***this*** and ***that***, see DEMONSTRATIVE 1, and THIS AND THESE 2.]

3b ***That*** is a 'pointing' word. It indicates something which is not near to the speaker.

E.g.

3c ***That*** refers to something which has been mentioned.

E.g. *'I'm going to* ***Majorca*** *for two weeks.' 'Where's* ***that****?'* (= 'Where's Majorca?')
'It says here that ***tomatoes are fruit****.' '****That*** *can't be right. They're vegetables.'*

3d ***That*** refers to something which both the speaker and the hearer know about.

E.g. *'You remember* ***that*** *box of chocolates I bought for my mother?' 'Yes.' 'Well – I can't find it.'*

---

the /ði:/ (weak form /ðə/, /ðɪ/*) (*determiner or conjunction*)

- ***The*** is called 'the definite article'. It is the most common word in English.
- ***The*** contrasts with the 'indefinite article' A or AN, or with ZERO ARTICLE.
- You will find a lot about ***the*** under the heading ARTICLES.

* Use /ðə/ before consonant sounds: ***the cat*** /ðə ˈkæt/.
Use /ðɪ/ before vowel sounds: ***the eggs*** /ðɪ ˈegz/.
[See CONSONANTS AND VOWELS].

1 **The form of *the***
The always has the same form before singular and plural nouns, or before countable and uncountable nouns. Contrast ***the*** and ***a***:

	countable: singular	plural	uncountable
Definite	***the*** *town*	***the*** *towns*	***the*** *dust*
Indefinite	***a*** *town*	*towns*	*dust*

2 **The position of *the***
The goes before a noun*, and also before any adjectives or other words which describe the noun.

	the+noun	***the***+adjective+noun	***the***+number+noun
E.g.	***the*** *horses*	***the*** *young horses*	***the*** *five horses*

* ***The*** also sometimes goes before adjectives or pronouns without a noun [see ARTICLES].
E.g. ***the others, the old:***
These apples are unripe. Where are ***the others?***
The young *should help to care for* ***the old***.

2a ***All***, ***both*** and ***half*** go before ***the*** in the noun phrase:

E.g. ***all the food*** ***half the cake***

3 The meaning and use of *the*

We place ***the*** before a noun phrase to show that it has definite meaning. This means that the speaker and the hearer share knowledge about exactly what the speaker is talking about.

singular: ***the*** *X* implies 'You know which *X* I mean'
plural: ***the*** *Xs* implies 'You know which *Xs* I mean'

There are several reasons for using ***the***:

3a We use ***the*** when the situation tells us which *X* / *Xs*.

E.g. (i)

(There is only one cat and one kitchen table in the house, so you know which one!)

(ii) *Have you visited* ***the castle****?* (in a particular town)
(iii) *Don't* ***the roses*** *look lovely?* (in a particular garden)

3b We use ***the*** when general knowledge tells us which *X* / *Xs*.

E.g. ***The earth*** *moves round* ***the sun***.

(There is only one earth and one sun, so we know which one!) Here are other examples where we use ***the*** because there is only one *X* or group of *Xs*.

E.g. ***the North Pole*** ***the Pope*** ***the United Nations***
the sea ***the stars*** ***the sky***
the middle class ***the future***

NOTE: Similar to this:
<In the U.K.> ***the Queen*** = *'the Queen of the U.K.'*
<In the U.S.A.> ***the President*** = *'the President of the U.S.A.'*

3c We use ***the*** when the words after the noun tell us which *X* / *Xs*.

E.g. ***The*** *President* ***of Peru*** *is visiting Europe.*
The *girls* ***sitting over there*** *are my sisters.*
The *bicycle* ***John bought*** *has been stolen.*
I'm studying ***the*** *history* ***of Japan***.

3d We use ***the*** when what has been said before tells us which *X / Xs*.

E.g. (i) *They have **a son** and **two daughters**. **The son** is working as an engineer, but **the daughters** are still at high school.*

(Here, after the son and daughters have been mentioned once, we can use ***the***.)

(ii) *It's a beautiful bicycle, but **the brakes** don't work.*

(Here, we haven't mentioned which *brakes*, but we have mentioned ***the*** *bicycle* they belong to, so you know which *brakes* they are.)

3e We use ***the*** before some words which imply that the *X* is unique: SUPERLATIVE, ORDINALS, (THE) SAME, ONLY.

E.g. *They're all good players, but Jane is **the best**.*
*When is **the first** bus to Birmingham tomorrow?*
*Jim is **the same** age as Mary: they're twins.*
*This is **the only** pair of glasses I have.*

3f We use ***the*** in referring to media generally.

E.g. *We go to **the theatre** * every month.*
*The freedom of **the press** is very important.*
*What's on **the radio** this evening?*

* Note that ***the theatre*** does not have to mean 'a particular theatre'. When referring to television we sometimes omit the article.
E.g. *On **(the)** television.* [See ZERO ARTICLE.]

3g We also sometimes use ***the*** in talking about people / animals / things in general.

E.g. people: ***The Italians** are very keen on football.* [See COUNTRIES]
*We reported the theft to **the police**.*
***The rich** should pay higher taxes, but not **the poor**.*
animals: ***The elephant** is the largest animal on land.*
inventions: *Modern society has to learn to live with **the computer**.*
musical instruments: *I'm learning to play **the violin**.*

NOTE (i): We do not use ***the*** when describing substances or masses in general.
E.g. ***Water** contains **oxygen**. (~~the~~ water, ~~the~~ oxygen)*

NOTE (ii): We do not use ***the*** when describing abstractions in general.
E.g. *Which do you like best, **music** or **mathematics**? (~~the~~ music, ~~the~~ mathematics)*

NOTE (iii): We do not use ***the*** when referring in general to a whole class of things or people (except with nationality words like ***the Italians, the Chinese***).
E.g. ***Children** enjoy **games**. (~~the~~ children, ~~the~~ games)*

4 THE + COMPARATIVE (. . .) THE + COMPARATIVE (. . .)
In this pattern, ***the*** is like a conjunction, rather than an article.

E.g. ***The harder*** *you work,* ***the more*** *successful you will be.* (= 'As you work harder, you will become more successful.')
The more *she thought about it,* ***the less*** *she liked it.*

Sometimes we omit all words except ***the*** + comparative.

E.g. (i) *'Can I bring my friends to the party?' 'Yes,* ***the more, the merrier.****'* (This is a saying which means 'the more people there are, the better it is').

(ii)

5 [See NAMES and GEOGRAPHICAL NAMES for the use of ***the*** with names.]

---

their /ðeəʳ/, **theirs** /ðeəʳz/, **them** /ðem/ (weak form /ðəm/) and **themselves** /ðəmˈselvz/ are forms of the 3rd person plural pronoun THEY.

► [For details of how to use each form, see PERSONAL PRONOUN, POSSESSIVE DETERMINER AND POSSESSIVE PRONOUN and -SELF / -SELVES.]

1 ***Their*** = possessive determiner.

E.g. ***Martin and Sally*** *are our neighbours:* ***their*** *house is next to ours.*

2 ***Theirs*** = possessive pronoun.

E.g. ***This*** *house is* ***theirs***. *They own it.*

3 ***Them*** = object pronoun.

E.g. *Have you seen* ***my boots****? I can't find* ***them***.

4 ***Themselves*** = reflexive pronoun.

E.g. *We're leaving **the children** at home. They will have to look after **themselves**.*

then /ðen/ (*adverb*)

► ***Then*** has no weak form.

1 **Adverb of time**
Then means 'at that time' or 'after that'.

1a **Then** meaning 'at that time' usually refers to the past.

E.g. *'We met **in 1971**? I was still at school **then**.'*

Then can also refer to the future.

E.g. *We'll meet again **on Friday**, and **then** we'll decide what to do.*

1b ***Then*** meaning 'after that' in a series of points or events, ***first*** . . . ***then*** . . . ***then***, for example, in INSTRUCTIONS.

E.g. ***First** (of all) you take the wheel off the bicycle. **Then** you remove the tyre. **Then** you find the hole.*

Then meaning '*after that*' can refer to the past or the future.

E.g. Past: *We **went** to the zoo, and **then** we had lunch.*
Future: *We**'ll go** to the zoo, and **then** we'll have lunch.*

2 **Linking adverb**

2a ***Then*** can mean 'in that case' (mainly <spoken English>).

E.g. *'They've just telephoned to say John's in hospital.'*
{ *'**Then** we'd better go immediately.'*
{ *'We'd better go immediately, **then**.'*

2b ***Then*** can follow and strengthen the meaning of an ***if***-clause [see IF, DOUBLE CONJUNCTION].

E.g. *If you were born in 1962, **then** you were 24 in 1986.*

there /ðeəʳ/ (*adverb*) [See also THERE IS / THERE ARE]

► ***There*** is an adverb of place, meaning '(at) that place'.
► ***There*** is the opposite of HERE.

1 ***There*** can point to something in the situation you are in.

E.g.

2 ***There*** can refer to some place already mentioned.

E.g. *The '**Alpine Palace**' is a very good **hotel**. We stayed **there** in 1980.*

3 ***There*** can come after some prepositions of place.

E.g. ***in** there,* ***up** there,* ***down** there,* ***over** there*

*'What are you doing **up there**?' 'I'm trying to mend the roof.'*

4 Some exclamations begin with ***there*** [see INVERSION 6].

E.g. ***There's** an old friend of mine!* ***There** goes my train!* ***There** you are!*

there is, there are

► When you want to say that something exists, begin the sentence with ***there*** + ***be*** + noun phrase:

► In the ***there + be*** pattern, ***there*** is an 'empty' grammatical word (not an adverb of place).

► ***There*** is not stressed in the ***there + be*** pattern.

1 **Examples**

There's* *someone at the front door.*
There aren't *enough knives in the kitchen.*
Are there *any oranges?*
There will *now* ***be*** *a short break.*
There may have been *something wrong.*
There was *nothing to do.*

* ***There's*** is pronounced /ðeəʳz/.

2 **Why do we use *there is, there are*?**

English sentences do not usually begin with an indefinite noun phrase.

E.g. ~~*A knife*~~ *is on the table.*

This is 'good grammar' but we do not say it. Instead, we prefer to begin the sentence with ***there + be***, then place the indefinite SUBJECT after ***be***.

2a The rule for forming ***there + be*** sentences is:

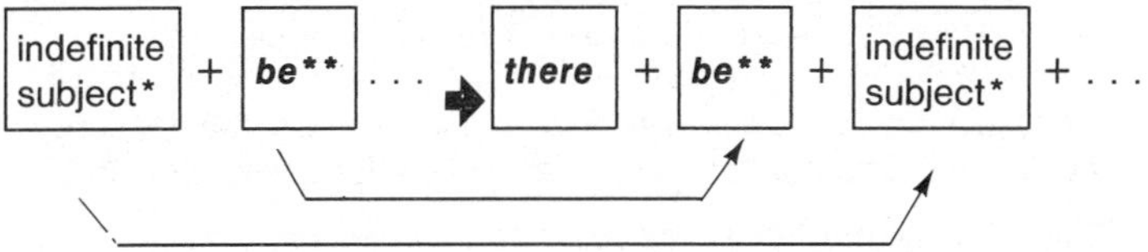

E.g.

A knife 1	***is*** 2	*on the table* 3	➡	***There*** 0	***is*** 2	*a knife* 1	*on the table* 3

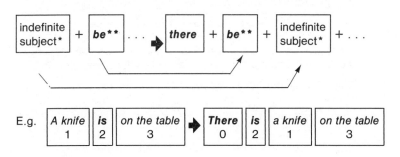

* An indefinite subject cannot normally be:
(a) a personal pronoun
(b) a phrase beginning with ***the***
(c) a phrase beginning ***this, that, these, those***
(d) a name

** ***Be*** means any verb phrase ending with ***be***. For example: ***is***, ***are***, ***was***, ***will be***, ***may have been***, ***seems to be*** (see examples in 1 above).

3 ***There*** **behaves like a subject in:**

(i) QUESTIONS.

E.g. ***Is there*** *anything else to eat?*

(ii) TO-INFINITIVE clauses.

E.g. *I don't want* ***there to be*** *any mistakes.*

(iii) -ING CLAUSES.

E.g. ***There being no further business****, the meeting was concluded.*
<rather formal>

therefore /ˈðeəʳfɔːʳ/ (*linking adverb*)

► ***Therefore*** means 'as a result', or 'that's why'. It introduces the sentence which explains the result of what was said in the previous sentence(s).

E.g. *When children reach the age of 11 or 12, they start growing fast.* ***Therefore*** *they need more protein.*

[See LINKING ADVERBS AND CONJUNCTIONS 3(iv), REASON AND CAUSE.]

these /ðiːz/ (*plural determiner or pronoun*)

[See DEMONSTRATIVE, THIS AND THESE; compare THOSE]

they /ðeɪ/, ***them, their, theirs, themselves*** is the 3rd person plural PERSONAL PRONOUN.

1 ***They*** can refer to people (male or female or both [see SEX]).

E.g. ***Teachers*** *don't earn very much, but* ***they*** *work hard.*

They can also refer to things.

E.g. *'How much are* ***these eggs****?' '****They****'re one pound a dozen.'*

2 ***They*** can also refer back to singular GROUP NOUNS like *team, family, audience, government* <especially G.B.> [see AGREEMENT 2d].

E.g. ***The committee*** *have admitted that* ***they*** *made a mistake.*

2a In <informal English> we also often use ***they*** to refer back to INDEFINITE PRONOUNS such as *everyone, someone, anyone, no one, none.*

E.g. *We told* ***everyone*** *to bring* ***their*** *passports with them.*

3 Also in <informal English> we use ***they*** to refer to 'people in general'.

E.g. { ***They*** *say* / ***People*** *say* } *that sugar is bad for your health.*

3a ***They, one*** [see ONE 3], ***we*** [see WE 2] and ***you*** [see YOU 2] can all refer to people in general. But ***they*** is different because it refers to people apart from the speaker and the hearer, especially unknown people who influence our lives.

E.g. *I see* ***they****'re putting up the train fares again.*

third person = 3rd person.

[See PERSON, PERSONAL PRONOUN, -S FORM, AGREEMENT]

this and ***these*** /ðɪs/, /ði:z/ (*determiners and pronouns*)

1 ***This* is *singular*, and *these* is *plural.***

E.g. ***this*** *book* (one only)
these *books* (more than one)
this *bread* (uncountable) [see UNCOUNTABLE NOUN.]

2 **The use of *this* and *these***
This and ***these*** describe things near the speaker. They contrast with THAT and THOSE, which describe things less near.

E.g.

2a ***This***, ***these***, ***that*** and ***those*** are called DEMONSTRATIVES: they are words which 'point' to things, people, etc. near to or far from the speaker.

3 ***This* and *these* as determiners**
This and ***these*** can be determiners (followed by a noun or by ***one*** [see ONE 2].

E.g. ***That*** *car is faster than* ***this one.*** *

This rice *isn't cooked yet.*
Try one of ***these nice ripe apples***.

* We use ***this one*** only for countables.

4 *This* and *these* as pronouns

This and ***these*** can also be pronouns (i.e. they can stand alone as SUBJECT, OBJECT, etc).

E.g. *Come and take a look at **this**.* * *

*Whose clothes are **these**?* * *

* * ***This*** and ***these*** as pronouns are usually stressed. This is why the intonation falls on ***this*** and ***these*** here.

4a As subject, ***this*** can refer to a person as well as a thing. For example, we use ***this*** when we answer the phone.

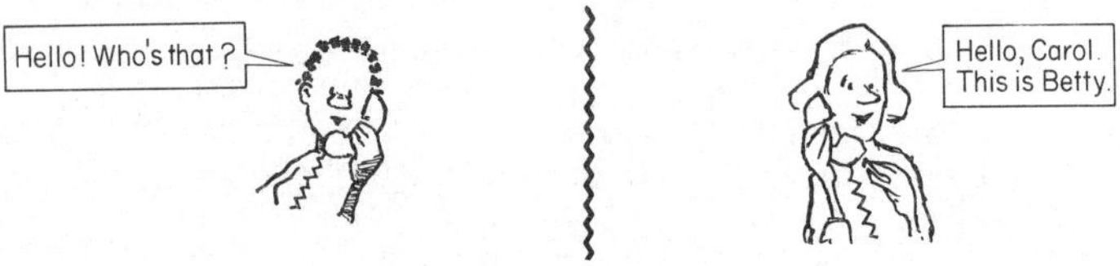

We also use ***this*** in introducing people [see GREETINGS].

E.g.

5 *This* in time phrases

[See TIME 5.]

E.g. *I will be visiting the hospital **this Thursday**.* (= the Thursday after today, i.e. the Thursday of this week)

NOTE: In contrast to ***this***, ***that*** points to a particular time in the past.
E.g. ***That** year the wheat crop was very poor.*

6 *This* and *these* pointing to earlier or later words in the text

This and ***these*** can point to an earlier part of the same sentence.

E.g. *There can be* {(a) *bad weather* / (b) *severe storms*} *in the summer, but fortunately* {(a) ***this** is* / (b) ***these** are*} *rare.*

6a ***This*** and ***these*** can also point to (a part of) an earlier sentence.

E.g. *They offered him a coconut. He didn't know what to do with it, as* ***this*** (coconut) *was the first he had ever seen.*
She took the part of Cleopatra in the play Antony and Cleopatra. ***This*** (part) *was her greatest performance as a stage actress.*

6b ***This*** and ***these*** can also occasionally point to a later part of the sentence, or to a later sentence.

E.g. ***This*** *is how you cook rice: Allow 1 cup of rice for 2 people and 2 cups of water. Bring to the boil, and cook for 15 minutes.*
These *languages can be studied by our students: Arabic, Chinese, French, German, and Spanish.* (these = 'the following')

7 In <informal> speech (especially in talking about what happened or in telling jokes), we use ***this*** or ***these*** in introducing a person for the first time.

E.g. *I was walking home, when* ***this*** *stranger came up to me and asked to borrow some money.* (***this*** *stranger* = 'a stranger I am going to say more about')

---

those /ðəʊz/ (*determiner or pronoun*)

► ***Those*** is the plural of the demonstrative ***that*** [see THAT 3, DEMONSTRATIVE].
► ***Those*** is the opposite of ***these*** [see THIS AND THESE 2].

1 ***Those*** points to things or people that are not near (in contrast to ***these***):

1a Determiner: ***those*** + plural noun.

E.g. *Who are* ***those people*** talking on the other side of the room?

Those flowers are much better than these roses that we planted last year.

1b Pronoun: ***those*** (without a noun).

E.g. *'**These** books are about office management.'*
*'What about **those** (over there)?'*

NOTE (i): ***Those*** can mean 'not near' both in a physical sense and in an emotional sense. For example, ***those*** expresses a negative feeling.
E.g. *I really hate **those** new supermarkets, don't you?*

NOTE (ii): ***Those*** in <writing> can mean 'the people . . .'
E.g. *James admires **those** who succeed.* ('the people who succeed')

NOTE (iii): ***Those*** in <writing> can also be a replacement for an earlier phrase. It means 'the ones . . .'.
E.g. *Clothes which are made by hand last much longer than **those*** (= 'the ones') *made in a factory.*

---

though /ðəʊ/ (*conjunction or linking adverb*)

► ***Though*** expresses contrast between two ideas. [See CONTRAST 3b, 3c.]

1 The conjunction ***though*** is a shorter form of ALTHOUGH.

E.g. ***Though*** / ***Although*** } *the weather is bad, we are enjoying ourselves.*

2 The linking adverb ***though*** is <informal>. It often goes in end position. It cannot be replaced by ***although***. [See LINKING ADVERBS AND CONJUNCTIONS.]

E.g. *I quite like studying Law. It's hard work, **though**.*

3 [Look up the conjunctions ***as though*** under AS and ***even though*** under EVEN. ***Even though*** is more emphatic than ***though***.]

(a) thousand /ˈθaʊzənd/ (*number*) = 1,000

[See NUMBERS 5, QUANTITY WORDS]

---

through /θruː/ (*preposition or adverb*)

1 ***Through*** is a preposition of MOTION (OR MOVEMENT):

E.g. *The train sped* ***through*** *the tunnel.*

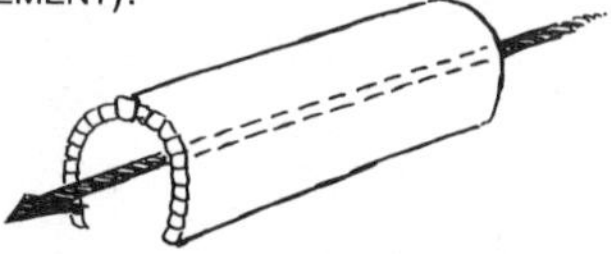

Or PLACE:

E.g. *I can't see* ***through*** *the window – it's so dirty.*

NOTE: The adverb ***through*** is similar to the preposition, but does not have a following noun phrase.
E.g. *The guards had locked the gate, so we couldn't get* ***through***. ('through the gate')

2 ***Through*** also refers to length of time.

E.g. *The fireman fought the flames all* ***through*** *the night.*
(*all through* = 'throughout')
The strike continued ***through*** *the summer.*

3 **Idioms**
Through is used in some PHRASAL VERBS. Look these up in a dictionary: ***get through*** ***be through (with)*** ***come through*** ***see (something) through***.

till /tɪl/ (*subordinating conjunction*) is an <informal> and less common form of UNTIL.

time [See also (TELLING THE) TIME; LENGTH OF TIME; FREQUENCY; DATES; AGO]

1 **How we deal with different ways of answering the question *'When?'***

E.g. ***'When*** *are you going to learn to drive?'*

Answers:
(A) *'(Very)* ***soon.'*** (ADVERB (phrase))
(B) ***'In*** *the spring.'* (PREPOSITIONAL PHRASE)
(C) ***'Next*** *year.'* (NOUN PHRASE)
(D) ***'As soon as*** *I reach the age of 17.'* (ADVERBIAL PHRASE)

2 The main structures for answering the question '*When?*' are:

adverbs:	***afterwards, before, immediately, never,* now,* once,* recently, sometime,* soon,* then,* today,* tomorrow, tonight, yesterday***. [See also ALREADY, STILL, YET].
prepositional phrases beginning with:	***after**** and ***before, between,* by,* from**** . . . ***to,* at,*, in,* on,* through*(out), till, until,* up to*** [see UP AND DOWN].
noun phrases beginning with:	***next,* last,* this,* that,* (every,* some)*** [See SOME AND ANY].
adverbial clauses beginning with:	***after**** and ***before, as,* once,* since,* till, until,*, when,* whenever,* while,* now*(that), as* soon as, immediately (that).***

* You can look up details and examples under the headings of separate words, i.e. the words marked * in the table above.

3 Positions of time adverbials

Most of the adverbials of time can be placed either in front or end position [see ADVERBIAL 4].

E.g. *We complained to the manager* { ***yesterday***. / ***on the following day***. / ***last week***. / ***as soon as we could***. }

{ ***Yesterday,*** / ***On the following day,*** / ***Last week,*** / ***As soon as we could,*** } *we complained to the manager.*

3a In addition, adverbs of one syllable (i.e. ***now***, ***then***, ***just***, ***soon***) can easily be placed in middle position.

E.g. *The meal will* ***soon*** *be ready.*
We were ***then*** *living in Bangladesh.*

3b Time adverbials sometimes follow the noun within a NOUN PHRASE.

E.g. *The meeting* ***next month*** *will discuss international trade.*
The situation ***at present*** *is one of uneasy peace.*

3c Or we can sometimes use the time adverbial as a POSSESSIVE or an adjective in front of the noun.

E.g. ***Next month's*** *meeting . . . The* ***present*** *situation . . .*

4 **Use of the prepositions *on* and *in* to describe time**
[See ON and IN.]

4a We use ***on*** before days:

E.g. ***on*** *Tuesday,* ***on*** *9th July*
They first met ***on*** *Tuesday 9th July, 1985.*

4b But we use ***in*** for other periods, including:

(A) periods of the day: ***in*** *the morning,* ***in*** *the evening,* ***in*** *the night,* ***in*** *the day**
(B) weeks: ***in*** *the third week of November*
(C) months: ***in*** *January,* ***in*** *the month of May*
(D) seasons: ***in*** *(the) spring,* ***in*** *(the) summer*
(E) years: ***in*** *1987,* ***in*** *the following year*
(F) centuries: ***in*** *the 16th century*

* We say ***in the night (time)***, but also ***by night***, ***at night***, and ***during the night***. We say ***in the day (time)***, and also ***by day***, and ***during the day***; we do not say ~~*at day*~~.

NOTE: [On the use of ***at*** for clock-time and other points of time, see AT 2.]

4c Omitting ***on*** or ***in***:
We omit ***on*** or ***in*** before these words [look them up separately for further details]: ***last, this, next, that, every, some***

E.g. We say: *We meet* ***every*** *Sunday.*
Not: *We meet* ~~*on*~~ ***every*** *Sunday.*

NOTE: In <informal English, especially U.S.>, ***on*** and ***in*** can be omitted before the name of a day (singular or plural).
E.g. *I'll phone you (on)* ***Tuesday***.
Let's meet (on) ***Friday*** *evening.*
Tina has to work (on) ***Saturdays*** *and* ***Sundays***.

5 **Use of *last, this,* and *next* to describe time**
Here are some examples of ***last***, ***this***, and ***next***.

E.g. *We arrived* / *The baby was born* } ***last*** { *Saturday.* / *week.* / *March.*

I'm playing football / *There'll be an election* } ***this*** { *evening.* / *month.* / *winter.*

Make sure you're ready / *Our team's going to win* } ***next*** { *Friday.* / *time we meet.* / *year.*

NOTE: Remember to say ***yesterday***, ***today***, and ***tomorrow*** instead of ~~***last day, this day,***~~ and ~~***next day.***~~ Also, say ***yesterday morning***, ***tomorrow afternoon***, etc. instead of ~~***last morning, next afternoon.***~~ [See TODAY, TOMORROW AND YESTERDAY.]

6 Use of *that*, *every*, and *some* to describe time

That March*, *that year, etc refer to a period in the past.

E.g. *When I was five, I went to live on a farm.* ***That year*** *the weather was very hot and dry.*

Every Sunday*, *every year, etc.
Some evenings*, *some weekends, etc. } are phrases of FREQUENCY

E.g. ***Every spring*** *the birds return to their nests.*
Some weekends *we go climbing in the mountains.*

7 Time and the verb phrase

In addition to adverbials, we use the form of the verb phrase (tense) to indicate position in time. [See PAST TIME, PRESENT TIME, FUTURE.]

7a [See AFTER AND BEFORE, SINCE, and WHEN for details of how to use the verb forms in clauses beginning with these words.]

---

telling the **time**

1 Asking the time

E.g. *Can you tell me the time, please?*
What's the time, please?

2 Telling the time

2a The hours.

E.g. *It's* ***one o'clock****.*  *It's* ***ten o'clock****.* 

2b The half hours.

E.g. *It's* ***half-past seven****.* 

2c The quarters.

E.g. *It's* ***(a)**** ***quarter-past four****.*  *It's* ***(a)**** ***quarter to twelve****.* 

* ***a*** is optional.

2d Minutes.

The hour is divided into 60 minutes.

E.g. *It's* ***four minutes*** *past two.*

But if the number of minutes can be divided by five, you don't need to say 'minutes'.

E.g. *It's **five** past two.*

The five-minute divisions are easy.

E.g. *It's **twenty-five past ten**.*
*It's **ten to six**.*

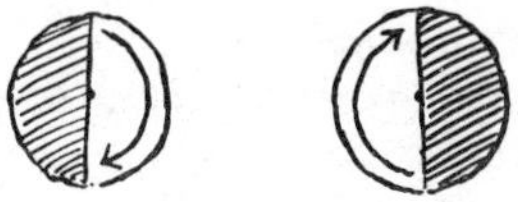

NOTE: If your watch is not correct, say.
E.g. (i) *My watch is (five minutes)* ***fast***.
(ii) *My watch is (ten minutes)* ***slow***.

(i) (ii)

3 The easy way to say the time

hours ——→ | 9. | 15 | ←—— minutes

It's nine fifteen.

E.g. 10.25: say *ten twenty-five* (longer way: *twenty-five past ten*)
11.44: say *eleven forty-four* (longer way: *sixteen minutes to twelve*)
8.30: say *eight thirty* (longer way: *half-past eight*)
8.05: say *eight five* (longer way: *five past eight*)

3a In the easy way of saying the ***time***, we can add **a.m.*** (/eɪˈem/) (= Latin *ante meridiem*) for 'before noon (or midday)', and **p.m.*** (piːˈem/) (= Latin *post meridiem*) for 'after noon (or midday)'.

E.g. *7.30* ***a.m.*** *(= half-past seven in the morning)*
8.00 ***p.m.**** * *(= eight o'clock in the evening)*

* Only use ***a.m.*** and ***p.m.*** when it is useful to distinguish between them.
** We pronounce ***8.00*** simply as ***eight***: ***8.00 a.m.*** = ***eight a.m.***, ***2.00 p.m.*** = ***two p.m.***

NOTE: Airports, railways, etc. use a 'twenty-four hour clock'. You add 12 to hours of p.m. ***time***.
E.g. *10.15 a.m. = 1015 hours ('ten fifteen')*
5.00 p.m. = 1700 hours ('seventeen hundred')
7.30 p.m. = 1930 hours ('nineteen thirty')
11.44 p.m. = 2344 hours ('twenty-three forty-four')

---

titles [See NAMES OF PEOPLE 1]

to /tu:/ (weak forms /tʊ/tə/) (*preposition or infinitive marker*) [see also TO-INFINITIVE]

► ***To*** is a preposition of MOTION (OR MOVEMENT) and direction.
► ***To*** also has other meanings such as TIME [see 2 below] and 'receiver' [see 3 below].

1 ***To*** **(= motion)**
To indicates the place you reach as a result of moving.

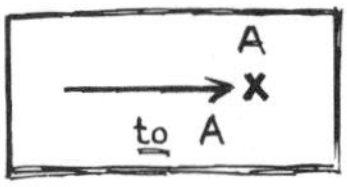

E.g. ***come to,*** ***go to,*** ***bring to,*** ***send to,*** ***walk to***. [See COME AND GO, BRING AND TAKE.]

E.g. *'Are you **coming to the party** this evening?' 'No, I have to **go to a meeting**.'*
*'How are you **getting to the airport** tomorrow?' 'I'm **taking** a taxi **to the town centre**, where I will **catch** a bus **to the airport**.'*

NOTE (i): The ***to***-phrase usually follows the verb (and / or OBJECT) as in the examples above, but it can also follow a noun (as MODIFIER).
E.g. *Is this the **way to the zoo**?*
***The train to Dundee** will leave from Platform 4.*

NOTE (ii): The following are common idioms (= ***to*** + noun) with zero article [see ZERO ARTICLE 4d]:
(go) ***to work*** ***to church*** ***to school*** ***to bed***

1a FROM + NOUN PHRASE + TO + NOUN PHRASE:

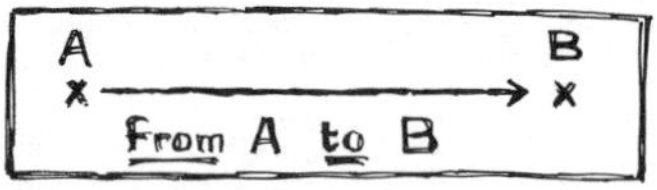

E.g. *The first passenger train ran **from** Liverpool **to** Manchester.*
*I used to cycle all the way **from** home **to** the office and back every day.*

1b ***From . . . to*** can also be used for DISTANCE:

E.g. *How many miles is it **from** here **to** Istanbul?*

Or change of state:

E.g. *The traffic lights changed **from** red **to** green.*

[See FROM.]

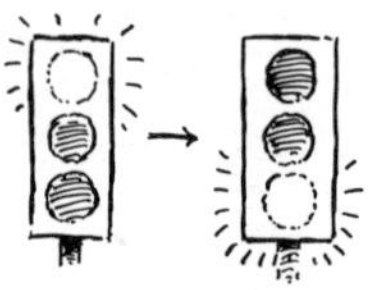

2 ***To* (= time)**
To indicates the end-point of a time period:

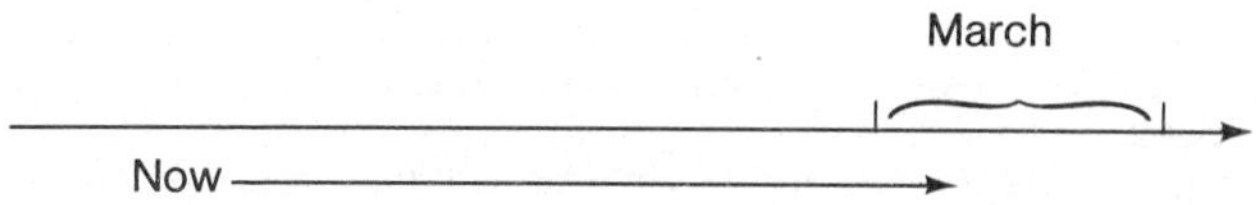

E.g. *It will take* ***from*** *now* ***to*** *next March to repair the bridge.*
The normal working week is ***from*** *Monday* ***to*** *Friday.*

NOTE: ***To*** usually indicates time only in the pattern '***from A to B***.' Otherwise, we use UNTIL or ***up to*** [see UP AND DOWN 5].

E.g. *We are staying here* { ***until*** / ***up to*** / ~~*to*~~ } *Saturday.*

* <U.S.> prefers *Monday* ***through*** *Friday.* ***Through*** indicates that Friday is part of the period you are measuring.

3 ***To* (= 'receiver')**
To is usually followed by a person.

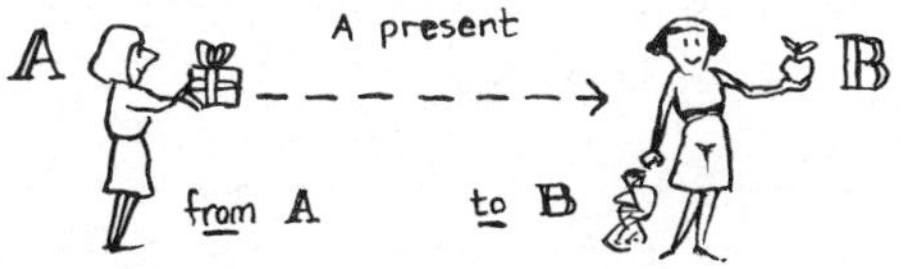

E.g. *Betty gave a present* ***to*** *her best friend Freda.*

In the example above, *Freda* is the 'receiver', i.e. the person who receives something from another person.

3a Many verbs which can be followed by ***to*** (= 'receiver') can also be followed by an INDIRECT OBJECT.

E.g. { *Betty gave a present* ***to*** *her best friend.*
Betty gave her best friend a present. }

Other verbs like ***give*** include ***offer, hand, lend, owe*** [see VERB PATTERN 11].

E.g. *He offered some rare Roman coins* ***to*** *the museum.*
Would you mind handing that gun ***to*** *me? It's dangerous.*

3b ***To*** also applies to the 'receiver' of a message.

E.g. *I've just written a letter* ***to*** *my parents.*
I've got something to say ***to*** *you.*
Marion announced ***to*** *her guests that dinner was ready.*

4 **Idioms**
To is used to form many PREPOSITIONAL VERBS and PHRASAL-PREPOSITIONAL VERBS. Look these up in a dictionary: ***add (. . .) to listen to see to look forward to belong to object to take to get down to***

To also follows some adjectives [see ADJECTIVE PATTERNS 1c].

E.g. ***close to*** ***due to*** ***similar to*** ***used to****

* ***Used to*** (= 'accustomed') is different from the modal auxiliary USED TO, where ***to*** is the infinitive marker.
E.g. *I'm **used to** hard work.* or: *I'm **used to** working hard.*
('accustomed to . . .')
But: *I **used to** work hard.* ('Once I worked hard'.) (***used to*** = MODAL AUXILIARY)

to-infinitive [See also INFINITIVE, INFINITIVE CLAUSE]

► The ***to-infinitive*** form of the verb consists of ***to*** (= infinitive marker) and the basic form of the verb. (***to*** + Verb).

► The ***to-infinitive*** has many different roles in English sentences. [For the details of these, see INFINITIVE CLAUSE.]

1 ***To***-infinitive clauses are NONFINITE CLAUSES. This means they do not stand alone as a sentence, but must be part of a MAIN CLAUSE.

E.g. *I want **to make everyone happy**.*

2 The infinitive phrase can be:

2a Simple: ***to*** + Verb.

E.g. *Mrs. Dale expects **to resign** next week.*

2b Perfect: ***to have*** + Verb-*ed*. [See PERFECT.]

E.g. *I'm sorry **to have kept** you waiting.*
*I'd like **to have stayed** longer – but I had to leave early to catch a bus.*

2c Progressive: ***to be*** + Verb-*ing*. [See PROGRESSIVE.]

E.g. *This time next month I hope **to be climbing** in the Andes.*
*I'm pleased **to be working** again after my illness.*

2d Passive: [See PASSIVE.]

E.g. *Mr Coe hopes **to be elected** president.*
*Everyone likes **to be admired** by their friends.*

2e Perfect Progressive: ***to have been*** + Verb-*ing*. [See VERB PATTERN 17.]

E.g. *The murderer is thought **to have been hiding** in the country.*

2f Perfect Passive: ***to have been*** + Verb-*ed*.

E.g. *The building appears **to have been repainted**. It looks much better now.*

3 When we make an infinitive negative we put ***not*** before the ***to***.

E.g.

*We are sorry **not to** have met your wife at the party.*

I told you not to go skating!
You should be more careful in future.

4 When we link two infinitive clauses with ***and*** or ***or***, we can omit the second ***to***.

E.g. *I want you **to sit** down **and listen** to me.*

We can also omit the whole infinitive clause after ***to***, if it repeats what has been said already.

E.g. *'Would you like to have dinner with us tonight?' **'I'd love to'**.* (= 'I'd love to have dinner . . .')
*'I'm going skating tomorrow.' 'I'd like to come too, but my mother **told me not to.**'* (= '. . . not to go skating.')

5 **Idioms**

5a ***In order to, so as to***: [see PURPOSE 1b].

5b There are many verb idioms containing the ***to***-infinitive. [See (be) ABLE TO, BE (to), (be) GOING TO, HAVE GOT TO, HAVE TO; the modal auxiliaries OUGHT TO and USED TO; also VERB IDIOMS.]

NOTE (i): Some ***to***-infinitive clauses begin with a WH-word [see VERB PATTERNS 6, 16].
E.g. *I don't know **where to go.*** *Please tell me **what to say**.*

NOTE (ii): the 'split infinitive' (social usage note). Some people believe that it is not 'correct' to put any words between ***to*** and the infinitive verb.
E.g. *Your job is **to thoroughly understand** the students' problems.* (= 'to understand thoroughly')
*It was wrong **to even think** of leaving without paying.* (= 'even to think')
<In writing> it is best to avoid doing this if possible. But do not worry about it if there is no other way of saying what you want to say.

---

today /tə'deɪ/, *tomorrow* /tə'mɒrəʊ/, and *yesterday* /'jestəʳdeɪ/ [See TIME]

► These can all be both adverbs and nouns.
► ***Today*** = 'this day'* ***tomorrow*** = 'the day* after today'
yesterday = 'the day* before today'.

1 Examples

1a ***today*** (adverb): *Have you been shopping **today**?*
(noun): ***Today**'s my birthday.*

1b ***tomorrow*** (adverb): *I'm going to speak to her **tomorrow**.*
(noun): ***Tomorrow**'s the day I start my new job.*

1c ***yesterday*** (adverb): ***Yesterday*** I went to the park.
(noun): ***Yesterday** was a busy day.*

* ***Day*** can mean either a period of 24 hours, or the period from the time you wake up until it gets dark.

---

tone [For falling, rising, and fall-rise tones, see INTONATION]

---

too /tu:/ (*adverb*)

- ***Too*** is an adding adverb [see ADVERB 1] meaning 'also', 'in addition'.
- ***Too*** is also an adverb of degree [see DEGREE, also VERY and ENOUGH].

1 *Too* as an adding adverb

E.g. *My friend Mr. Yano is Japanese, and his wife is Japanese, **too**.*
(= 'Both Mr. Yano and his wife are Japanese.')

Usually ***too*** is placed at the end of the clause.

NOTE: ***Too*** usually has heavy stress. It cannot be used in front position.

1a Other examples:

(i) *I like bananas and I like oranges, **too**.*
(ii) *'I'm staying at the Holden Hotel.' 'That's funny, I'm staying there, **too**.'*

1b The negative of ***too*** is ***-n't*** + ***either*** [see EITHER 2].
E.g. compare (i) above with:

*I do**n't** like bananas, and I do**n't** like oranges, **either**.*

2 ***Too* as a degree adverb**

As a degree adverb, ***too*** is the opposite of ENOUGH:

too = more than is needed.
enough = as much as is needed.

E.g.

That dress is too expensive.
I can only afford £50.
That dress is too big.
I take size 12.
£100
SIZE 20

2a Different patterns with ***too***:

TOO + ADJECTIVE (+ FOR + . . .).

E.g. *This suit is **too** big (**for** my husband). He needs a smaller size.*

TOO + ADJECTIVE (+ FOR + . . .) TO + Verb . . .

E.g. *My father is **too** old **to** play football, so he goes walking instead.*
*The house was **too** small **for** us **to** live in, so we moved to a bigger one.*
*It's **too hot to** go out: let's stay at home.*

TOO + QUANTITY WORD (+ NOUN) . . .

(QUANTITY WORD = ***many***, ***much***, ***few***, or ***little***. Look these words up under their separate entries).

E.g. *The party was a failure: they invited **too** {**few** / **many**} guests.*
(***too few*** . . . = not enough)
*There is **too little** water in the stream for us to go swimming.*
(= not enough water)
*I'm feeling ill: I ate **too much** at dinner.*

TOO + ADVERB (+ FOR . . .) (TO + Verb)

E.g. *I got up **too late to** catch the train so I had to go by plane.*
*The chairman was enjoying the party **too much for** anything **to** upset him.*
*William was driving **too fast** (for safety).*

---

topic [See PARAGRAPH, SUBJECT 4]

---

toward /tə'wɔːʳd/ <especially U.S.>, **towards** /tə'wɔːʳdz/ <especially G.B.> (*prepositions*)

► ***Toward*** or ***towards*** means 'in the direction of':

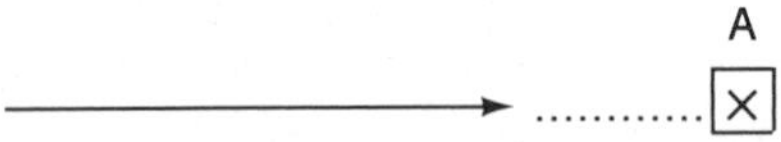

toward(s) A

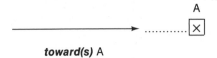

1 MOTION (OR MOVEMENT). E.g. *The train rushed **toward(s)** the tunnel.*

2 PLACE. E.g. *When Muslims pray, they face **toward(s)** Mecca.*

3 TIME. E.g. *This time of year, the weather gets cold **toward(s)** the evening.*

transitive verb [See VERB PATTERNS 1, 11–20, OBJECT]

1 **Transitive verbs** require an OBJECT to complete their meaning.

E.g. (i) *Everyone **admired** Bella's new watch.*
(ii) *I have **cut** the bread.*

We could not say:

(i) *Everyone ~~admired.~~* Or: (ii) *I have ~~cut~~.*

2 Transitive verbs can usually have a PASSIVE form.

E.g. *The police **stopped** the car.*
*The car **was stopped** (by the police).*

3 Transitive verbs include PHRASAL VERBS such as ***run over***.

E.g. *The bus **ran over** the dog.*
*The dog was **run over** (by the bus).*

4 Contrast INTRANSITIVE VERBS, which have no object.

E.g. *The children **laughed**.*

transport, means of [See ZERO ARTICLE 4e]

1 **By** [see BY 2b.]

E.g. *'How did you come to this country?* { *'**By** plane' (**by** air)* / *'**By** car' (**by** land)* / *'**By** train' (**by** rail)* / *'**By** boat' (**by** sea)* / *'**By** bicycle!'* }

2 **On** [see ON 2.]

E.g. *'How did you get home from the party?'* { *'**On** foot.'* / *'**On** a bicycle.'* / *'**On** a motorbike.'* / *'**On** horseback.'* }

There were lots of passengers { ***on** the bus.* / ***on** the plane.* / ***on** the ship.* / ***on** the train.* }

3 **In** [see IN 1.]

E.g. *'How many people were **in** the car?' 'Just the driver.'*
(Not: ***on the car***)

But: *There were only a few vacant seats* { ***in*** / ***on*** } *the* { *bus.* / *train.* }

twice /twaɪs/ (*adverb of frequency*)

Twice = × 2. We never say 'two times'. We always say **twice**.

E.g. *'How many times has she been married?'* ***'Twice**. Once to a businessman and once to an actor.'*

type (of) (*noun*)

Type is a noun of kind [see KIND (OF), SORT (OF), TYPE (OF)].

E.g. *Coal is a **type of** fuel.*
*In this factory we are making a new **type of** washing machine. It's much better than the **type** we used to make.*

uncountable noun (also called 'noncount noun')

- ***Uncountable nouns*** take a SINGULAR verb.
- [For more information, see COUNTABLE AND UNCOUNTABLE NOUNS.]
- UNIT NOUNS (e.g. *piece, lump*) are useful words to use with ***uncountable nouns***.

1 **What are uncountables?**

Uncountables refers to masses which we cannot easily think of as consisting of separate items: i.e. liquids, powders. We can divide many of these masses into subgroups, which are also uncountable:

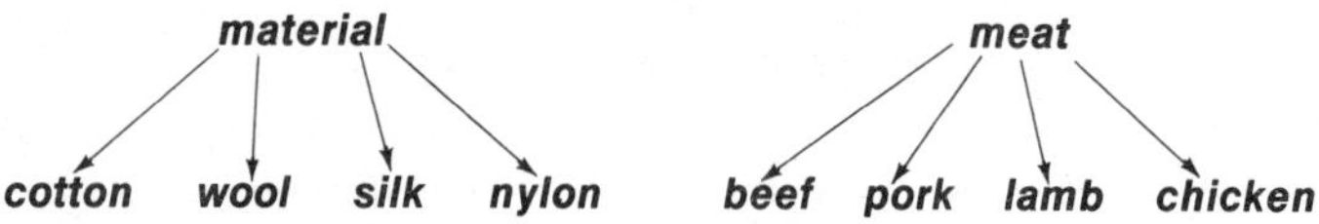

E.g. *Are these socks made of **wool** or of **cotton**?*
*I prefer **lamb** to **chicken**.*

2 **Types of uncountable**

To remember easily, think of substances, liquids, gases, and abstract ideas as uncountable. In the lists of words in 2a–2e, those uncountable nouns which have subgroups of uncountable nouns are marked in ***bold italic*** type.

2a Substances:

wood, *plastic, leather, cement, chalk, plaster, paint, sand, coal, rock, paper*
material: *cloth, cotton, silk, wool, nylon*
metal: *iron, gold, silver, brass, lead*
food: *flour, rice, bread, wheat, rye, sugar, salt, pepper,* ***meat, fish, fruit***, *butter, cheese, jam,*
fur, skin, hair, ice, snow, rain, soil, grass, land, ground

2b Liquids:
water, milk, coffee, tea, oil, petrol <G.B.>, *gasoline* <U.S.>, *juice, alcohol*

2c Gases:
air, smoke, steam, oxygen, hydrogen

2d Others (You might expect some of these to be plural, but they are not!):
furniture, luggage, baggage, money, pay, noise, traffic, music, accommodation

2e Abstract ideas:
information, knowledge, advice, education, fiction, (outer) space, time, power, experience, history

NOTE (i): ***News*** looks like a plural noun, but in fact it is singular uncountable.
E.g. *There's not much **news** on the radio today.*
Note also that ***work***, ***homework***, and ***housework*** are uncountable.

NOTE (ii): Many uncountable nouns can also be countable [see COUNTABLE AND UNCOUNTABLE NOUNS].
E.g. *egg, glass, time*

NOTE (iii): Uncountable nouns can follow QUANTITY WORDS like *some* and *any*, *all* and *much*.
E.g. *Some cloth is made of cotton and some is made of nylon.*

---

under [See OVER AND UNDER]

---

unit noun [see OF 7]

► ***Unit nouns*** are words like ***piece*** which allow us to divide uncountables into countable units. [See COUNTABLE AND UNCOUNTABLE NOUNS.]

1 We use different unit nouns for different uncountable nouns. But we use ***piece*** and ***bit*** more generally.

E.g.

*a **piece** of furniture*	*a **bar** of chocolate*	*a **block** of ice*
*an **item** of news*	*a **lump** of sugar*	*a **lock** of hair*
*a **length** of rope*	*a **stick** of chalk*	*a **slice** of bread*
*a {**sheet** / **pane**} of glass*	*a {**piece** / **bit**} of information*	*a **bit** of fun*

2 We also use unit nouns in the plural.

E.g. *'How many **lumps** of sugar do you like in your tea?' 'Two **lumps**, please.'*

---

unless (*subordinating conjunction*)

► ***Unless*** introduces adverbial clauses of condition. [See CONDITIONAL CLAUSE.]
► ***Unless*** has a negative meaning: it often means the same as *if . . . not . . .* [see IF].

1 ***Unless*** can replace *if . . . not . . .* when it introduces an exception to whatever is stated in the main clause.

E.g. ***Unless*** *you take more care, you'll have an accident.*
(= 'If you don't take more care.')
I want you to keep working ***unless*** *I tell you to stop.*
(= 'if I don't tell you otherwise.')
Unless *there's a strike, the trains will be running normally.*
(= 'If there's not a strike . . .')
Bill never does anything ***unless*** *you tell him what to do.*
(= 'if you don't tell him.')

NOTE: A 'simplified' ***unless***-clause begins with ***unless*** + PAST PARTICIPLE.
E.g. ***Unless told otherwise****, students should answer all questions on the examination paper.*
<rather formal>

2 ***Unless*** cannot replace *if . . . not . . .* in other types of sentence.

2a ***Unless*** cannot replace *if . . . not . . .* in *would (have)* conditions [see IF 1d] (i.e. if the condition has UNREAL MEANING).

E.g. *King would be our best player* ***if*** *he* ***weren't*** *so lazy. (~~unless~~)*
If she hadn't had an alarm clock*, she would have missed the train.*
(~~unless~~)

2b ***Unless*** cannot replace *if . . . not . . .* where ***if*** = *whether* (in INDIRECT QUESTIONS).

E.g. *She promised to let me know* ***if*** *she* ***wasn't*** *coming. (~~unless~~)*

2c **Unless** cannot replace *if . . . not . . .* where the negative condition is in someone's mind.

E.g. *I'll be really surprised* ***if*** *they* ***don't*** *come to the meeting. (~~unless~~)*
What shall we do ***if*** *they* ***don't*** *reply to our letter? (~~unless~~)*

---

unreal meaning (also called 'hypothetical' or 'contrary to fact')

1 **Use of 'unreal' Past Tense for present meaning**
We sometimes use the PAST TENSE to describe something which is supposed to be happening at the present time.

E.g. *It's time you children* ***were*** *in bed.*
(implies 'you are not in bed.')

We call this the unreal use of the Past Tense, because it means that the event or state is not taking place: it is 'imaginary'.

2 Unreal meaning after particular words

2a Unreal present time:
Here are the words and phrases introducing the unreal use of the Past.

if*	***If** I had enough money, I would retire early.*
if only*	***If only** the world was* * * *a better place!*
{ ***as* if***	*He spends money **as if** he were* * * *a millionaire.*
{ ***as* though***	('He's not a millionaire')
{ ***suppose**** *(that)*	*Just **suppose** (that) we were living on a desert*
{ ***imagine** (that)*	*island. ('Luckily, we are not')*
wish* *(that)*	*I **wish** (that) I knew who's taken the radio.*
it's time	***It's time** (that) you changed this car for a new one.*

* [These words have separate entries in this book. Look them up for further details. For ***if***, see especially IF 1c.]
* * ***Were*** can be used instead of ***was*** for unreal meaning. ***Were*** is <more formal> and some people consider it more 'correct' [See WERE 2].

2b Unreal past time:
To describe something in the past which didn't happen, and so is imaginary, use **had** + PAST PARTICIPLE.

E.g.

2c Unreal future:
To describe something which is not likely to happen in the future, use one of these forms:

(A) ***would*** * + Verb
(B) ***were* to*** + Verb
(C) **Past Simple*** (as for unreal present time)

E.g. If you {(A) ***would lend*** / (B) ***were to lend*** / (C) ***lent***} *me your bicycle tomorrow, I would get home quite easily.*

'Suppose I ***were to*** *be offered the post of manager.' 'Whoever did that would be mad!'*

* [These words have separate entries in this book. Look them up for further details.]

3 Unreal meaning in main clauses

3a In all the above examples we have looked at unreal meaning in subordinate clauses. In main clauses, use ***would*** + Verb for unreal present or future time.

E.g. *What* ***would*** *you do if I left?*
'Suppose I were to resign.' 'That ***would*** *be a mistake.'*

(See also the use of ***would*** in examples 2b and 2c above.)

3b Use ***would have*** + past participle for unreal past time.

E.g.

4 Modal auxiliaries with unreal meaning
To express unreal modal meanings in both main clauses and subordinate clauses:

can becomes ***could***, ***may*** becomes ***might*** [see COULD AND MIGHT]
will becomes ***would***, ***shall*** becomes ***should*** [see SHOULD AND OUGHT TO]

E.g. *If only we* ***could*** *meet regularly!*
If we lived in the same town, we ***could*** *meet regularly.*
If you had listened to me, you ***might*** *have succeeded.*

5 Summary of verb phrases expressing unreal meaning

	in subordinate clauses	in main clauses
unreal present time	Past Tense (with modal meanings: ***could would might should***)	***would*** + Verb (with modal meanings: ***could would might should***)
unreal future time	Past Tense, ***were to***, ***would*** (with modal meanings: ***could would might should***)	***would*** + Verb (with modal meanings: ***could would might should***)
unreal past time	***had*** + past participle (with modal meanings: ***could*** / ***would*** / ***might*** / ***should*** + ***have*** + past participle)	***would have*** + past participle (with modal meanings: ***could*** / ***would*** / ***might*** / ***should*** + ***have*** + past participle)

NOTE: Unreal modal meanings (i.e. WISHES, PERMISSION, POSSIBILITY) are important for being <polite> in functions such as REQUESTS, OFFERS, INVITATIONS. [See the modal auxiliaries COULD AND MIGHT, WOULD.]

---

until /ʌnˈtɪl/ (weak form /ənˈtil/) (*preposition or conjunction*)

► ***Until*** means 'up to a particular time.' [See TIME].

1 *Until* as a preposition of time

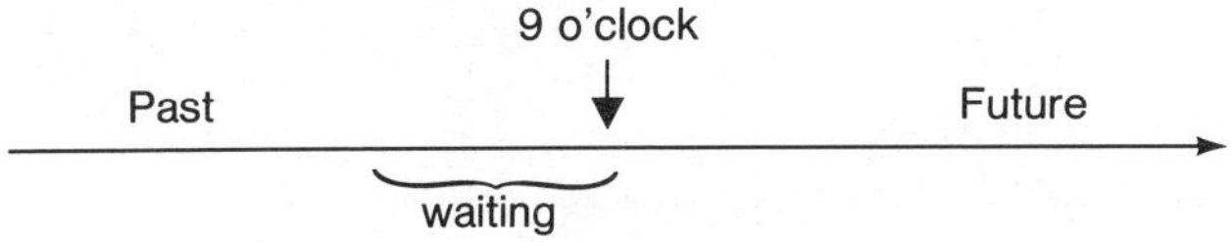

E.g. *I waited* ***until 9 o'clock****, and then I left.*

2 *Until* as a subordinating conjunction of time

2a ***Until*** referring to the present or future:
Use these verb forms:

main clause: { Present Simple / modal / Progressive }

until-clause: { Present Simple / Present Perfect }

E.g. (i) *Everything is quiet* ***until*** *the children* ***get*** *home from school.* ('after that, it's noisy!')

(ii) *We* {***must stay*** / ***are staying***} *here* ***until*** *the weather* {***improves.*** / ***has improved.***}

Sentence (ii) describes the future. Notice that ***will*** cannot be used in the ***until***-clause [see FUTURE 3b].

2b ***Until*** referring to the past:
Use these verb forms:

main clause: Past Simple ***until***-clause: {Past Simple / Past Perfect}

E.g. *He* ***was*** *not allowed to work* ***until*** *he* ***had been*** *in the country six months.*

The villagers ***stayed*** *indoors* ***until*** *the soldiers* {***left.*** / ***had left.***}

NOTE (i): ***Until clauses*** can be 'simplified' by omitting the subject and the verb BE.
E.g. *Leave the pie in the oven* ***until thoroughly cooked***.

NOTE (ii): Usually, we do not say '***from*** . . . ~~*until*~~ . . .': we say '***from*** . . . ***to***'. [See TO 2 for details.]

up and ***down*** /ʌp/, /daʊn/ (*adverbs or prepositions*)

1 Meanings of *up* and *down*

Up and ***down*** are words of opposite meaning, as the picture below shows. Their basic meanings are: ***up*** = 'motion towards the sky' and ***down*** = 'motion towards the centre of the earth'

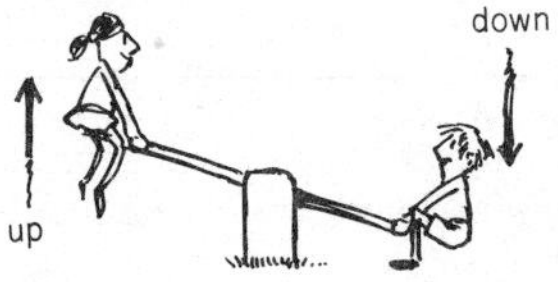

2 Adverbs of motion [See MOTION (OR MOVEMENT)]

E.g. (i) *Come* ***up*** *here! We live at the top of the house.*
(ii) *The road runs* ***down*** *into a valley.*
(iii) *What goes* ***up*** *. . . must come* ***down***. (a saying)

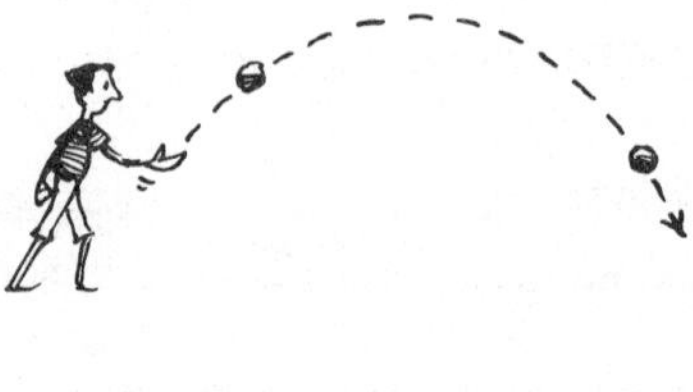

3 **Adverbs of position** [See PLACE]

E.g.

How do you like it living up on the thirtieth floor of this building ?
Fine! I like watching the people and the traffic down there in the streets.

NOTE: In ***get up***, ***be up***, ***stay up***, '***up***' means 'out of bed'.

E.g. *'Is your brother* ***up*** *yet?' 'No, he* ***stayed up*** *late last night to watch TV, so he'll be* ***getting up*** *late today.'*

4 **Prepositions**

(i)

(ii)

E.g. (i) *Every day I have to walk* ***up*** *a hill to reach my house.*
(ii) *If you throw a coin* ***down*** *this well, it brings you good luck.*
(iii) *Climbing* ***up*** *the mountain is quite easy, but climbing* ***down*** *again is difficult.*

5 **Idioms**

Up to is a preposition meaning 'as far as' or 'until'.

E.g. *We can have visitors* ***up to*** *ten o'clock, and then they must leave.*
Up to *what time does this programme last?*

5a ***Up*** and ***down*** are common in PHRASAL VERBS.

E.g. ***keep up***, ***stand up***, ***sit down***, ***wake up***, ***lie down***, ***cut up***, ***turn down***, ***set up***, ***play down***, ***look up***.

Look these ***up*** in a dictionary!

---

us /ʌs/ (weak form /əs/) (1st person plural PERSONAL PRONOUN)

Us is the object pronoun form of WE.

E.g. *Everyone in the neighbourhood knows* ***us***.

NOTE: ***Us*** is contracted to **'s** /s/ only in the special Imperative form ***let's***.

use /ju:s/ (*noun*) and **use** /ju:z/ (*regular verb*)

1 ***Use*** (noun) and ***use*** (verb) are spelled the same, but pronounced differently.

E.g. noun: *This book will be of great* ***use*** /ju:s/.
verb: *Can I* ***use*** /ju:z/ *your pencil?*

2 Note the special pattern of ***no*** / ***any use*** /ju:s/ <informal>:
No use = 'useless, pointless.'

E.g. *It is* ***no use*** *staying here all night.*
'I've just bought this grammar book.' 'Is it ***any use****?' 'No, it's* ***not much use****, but I like the pictures.'*

used to /ju:stu:/ (weak form /ju:stʊ/tə/) (*modal auxiliary*)

► ***Used to*** + Verb refers to a state or habit in the past.
► ***Used to*** is always Past Tense. There is no Present form ~~use(s) to~~.

1 ***Used to*** contrasts a past state of affairs with the present.

E.g. *I* ***used to work*** *in Perth. Now I work in Kuala Lumpur.* (***used to work*** = 'worked in the past')
Do you remember John Snagge? He ***used to be*** *a radio announcer on the B.B.C.* (but he isn't any more)

1a ***Used to*** can describe a habit in the past.

E.g. *When we were children, we* ***used to*** *play in that wood, and you always* ***used to*** *hide from me.*

[Compare WOULD 3b.]

NOTE: ***Used to*** is not common with negatives or in questions. All these forms are possible, but they are rather awkward:

Did(n't) *he* ***use*** / ***Used(n't)**** *he* } **to** { *be a pop singer?* / *run a factory?*

We { ***used not*** / ***usedn't**** / ***didn't use*** } ***to*** *be vegetarians: we gave up eating meat only two years ago.*

* ***Usedn't*** (or ***usen't***) is pronounced /ˈju:sn̩t/.

2 In the pattern BE + USED TO + { NOUN PHRASE / VERB-*ING* (. . .) }

used is an adjective (= 'accustomed') and ***to*** is a preposition.

E.g. *Now I'm in New York, I'm* ***used to*** *noise and pollution.*
Malcolm is unmarried: he's ***used to*** *looking after himself.*

usually /ˈjuːʒəlɪ/ (*adverb of frequency*)

Usually means 'most times', 'on most occasions'.

E.g. *I **usually** spend Christmas with my parents.*

[See FREQUENCY 1.]

verb

► To find out about verbs, look up the words in small capitals in the following summary.

1 Verbs (as a WORD CLASS) are divided into AUXILIARY VERBS and MAIN VERBS

1a Auxiliary verbs go before main verbs in VERB PHRASES. The main verb is followed by its VERB PATTERN (of OBJECT, COMPLEMENT, etc.).

	auxiliary verb	main verb	verb pattern
E.g. *I*	*have*	*asked*	*them to leave.*

1b Main verbs refer to states and actions [see STATE VERBS AND ACTION VERBS].

1c When we choose different verb forms we choose between:
PRESENT or PAST TENSE, PERFECT or PROGRESSIVE aspect,
ACTIVE or PASSIVE voice.

1d Verbs express different types of meaning, including PRESENT, PAST and FUTURE TIME, UNREAL MEANING, POSSIBILITY, and OBLIGATION.

1e Verbs are either REGULAR or IRREGULAR. You can learn the regular verbs by rule, but you have to learn the irregular verbs separately, (see the A–Z list of IRREGULAR VERBS at the back of the book).

1f Verb forms are either FINITE (e.g. ***has***) or NONFINITE VERBS (e.g. ***having***). The nonfinite verbs are INFINITIVES (e.g. ***to have***) and PARTICIPLES (e.g. ***having***, ***had***), which can be used to form NONFINITE VERB PHRASES and NONFINITE CLAUSES.

E.g. *It's fun **having your own car**.*

1g The most common verbs in English are the primary verbs BE, DO, and HAVE.

1h There are two types of auxiliary verb: primary auxiliary (i.e. ***be***, ***have*** and ***do***) and modal auxiliary (e.g. ***will***, ***can*** and ***would***).

2 **Endings used for forming verbs from other words** [see SUFFIXES 3e]:

ise / ***-ize***. E.g. ˈ*public* → ˈ*public**ize*** (= 'make something public')
-ify. E.g. ˈ*simple* → ˈ*simpl**ify*** (= 'make something simpler')
-en. E.g. ˈ*deaf* → ˈ*deaf**en*** (= 'make someone deaf')

2a Also, these prefixes are useful for changing the meaning of verbs [see PREFIXES]:

un-. E.g. ***un***ˈ*tie* ('do the opposite of tie'), ***un****pack*.
out-. E.g. ***out***ˈ*live* ('to live longer than'), ***out****stay*.
over-. E.g. ˌ***over***ˈ*eat* ('eat too much'), ***over****charge*.
under-. E.g. ˌ***under***ˈ*feed* ('feed too little'), ***under****estimate*.

2b Many verbs have no prefixes or suffixes, and have the same form as NOUNS.

E.g. *call, move, place, walk.*

But some verbs have a similar form to nouns but a slightly different pronunciation and spelling, i.e. the verb has a voiced consonant at the end [see CONSONANTS AND VOWELS]:

E.g.

noun		verb
house /haʊs/	~	*house* /haʊz/
advice /ədˈvaɪs/	~	*advise* /ədˈvaɪz/
use /juːs/	~	*use* /juːz/
thief /θiːf/	~	*thieve* /θiːv/
belief /bəˈliːf/	~	*believe* /bəˈliːv/
mouth /maʊθ/	~	*mouth* /maʊð/

2c [Look up STRESS 5 for differences of stress between nouns and verbs.]

verb idioms [See IDIOM]

1 **Verbs in English are divided into AUXILIARY VERBS and MAIN VERBS.**
But there are some verb expressions which behave a little like both. We call them verb idioms.

1a Think of verb idioms as auxiliaries which contain main verbs (for example, ***be going to*** contains the main verb ***go***).

2 The following is a table of verb idioms

kind of meaning	common verb idioms	examples (each idiom is followed by the basic form* of the verb)
future*	***be going* to***	*Next year, we**'re going to** go to the theatre more often.*
	be to	*The administration **is to** introduce a new law on bad driving.*
	be about to	*Margaret **is about to** get married: the wedding is next Saturday.*
obligation* or necessity (definite and strong in meaning)	***have* to***	*Someone will **have to** mend the tent before we go camping.*
	have got* to	*We**'ve got to** work hard if the business is going to succeed.*
	be bound to	*If you hurry too much, you **are bound to** make mistakes.*
	be {certain* / sure*} (to)	*Why don't you go shopping in the market? You**'re** {**certain** / **sure**} to find what you want there.*
obligation* or necessity (less definite and weaker)	***had better****	*You**'d better** listen to me. Otherwise, things might go wrong.*
	be supposed* to	*You**'re supposed to** help me. Why don't you clean the floor?*
	be likely to	*The plane is **likely to** be delayed.*
wish [see WISHES]	***be willing* to***	*I've run out of money. Luckily my bank manager **is willing to** lend me some more.*
	would* rather	*Would you like to watch television, or **would** you **rather** read a book?*
permission*	***be {allowed / permitted}***	*Students **are** not {**allowed** / **permitted**} to borrow more than six library books at one time.*
ability	***be able* to***	*If I practise, I'll **be able to** beat the boxing champion.*

* Look up these words for further information and examples. For ***be supposed to***, look up SUPPOSE. For ***be going to***, look up GOING, etc.

verb patterns

[See also ADJECTIVE PATTERNS]

► The MAIN VERB of a CLAUSE can be followed by various elements which complete its meaning. These elements form ***verb patterns***. [For similar patterns following adjectives, see ADJECTIVE PATTERNS.] For example, ***want*** and ***wish*** have similar meanings, but they fit different patterns:

. . . + noun phrase:	*I*	***want*** / ~~*wish*~~	*a cup of tea.*
. . . + to + Verb . . .:	*I*	***want*** / ***wish***	***to*** *be alone.*
. . . + ***that***-clause:	*I*	~~*want*~~ / ***wish***	***that*** *I was young.*

Below we illustrate the most important verb patterns, and list their most common verbs. (Here N = 'NOUN PHRASE or PRONOUN' and V = VERB PHRASE.] We illustrate each pattern with the statement form [see STATEMENT].

E.g. N + V + N
I ***want*** *a cup of tea.*

You will need to change this if you want to ask a question or make the statement negative.

E.g. *Do you want a cup of tea?* [see YES-NO QUESTION]
What do you want? [see WH- QUESTION]
I don't want a cup of tea. [see NEGATIVE WORDS AND SENTENCES]

NOTE (i): You can always add extra ADVERBIALS to the pattern.
E.g. *I* ***very much want*** *a cup of tea tonight.*

NOTE (ii): Each verb pattern below begins N + V, where N is the subject and V is the verb phrase containing the main verb. For a summary of patterns, see the table below. [Also see IT-PATTERNS and THERE IS, THERE ARE.]

In the table opposite, we list the patterns in the following order:

0	patterns with no element after the Verb
1–10	patterns with one element after the Verb
11–20	patterns with two elements after the Verb

a summary of verb patterns: N = noun phrase or pronoun **V** = main verb phrase	
pattern with no element after the Verb:	
0 N+**V**	*The bus **has arrived**. It doesn't **matter**.*
patterns with one element after the Verb:	
1 N+**V**+N	*Everyone enjoyed **the show**.*
2 N+**V**+N / adjective	*She **is** my friend. She **is** busy.*
3 N+**V**+adverbial	*The children **are** at the zoo.*
4 N+**V**+*that*-clause	*I **admit** (that) I've been foolish.*
5 N+**V**+*wh*-clause	*The police **asked** where we were going.*
6 N+**V**+*wh- to*-clause	*Everyone should **learn** how to swim.*
7 N+**V**+*to*+Verb . . .	*I'd **love** to visit Yugoslavia.*
8 N+**V**+Verb . . .	*You **had better** come early tomorrow.*
9 N+**V**+Verb-*ing* . . .	*I **like** watching football.*
10 N+**V**+past participle	*The thief **got** arrested by the police.*
patterns with two elements after the Verb:	
11 N+**V**+N_1+N_2	*They have **given** her a beautiful present.*
12 N+**V**+N+N / adjective	*The queen **kept** her marriage secret / a secret.*
13 N+**V**+N+adverbial	*I **took** the key out of my pocket.*
14 N+**V**+N+*that*-clause	*John **told** me (that) his father was ill.*
15 N+**V**+N+*wh*-clause	*I didn't **tell** anyone where I had hidden the key.*
16 N+**V**+N+*wh- to*-clause	*The pilot **taught** me how to land safely.*
17 N+**V**+N+*to*+Verb . . .	*I **want** you to feel at home.*
18 N+**V**+N+Verb . . .	*She **lets** the boys play football on the lawn.*
19 N+**V**+N+Verb-*ing* . . .	*They **dislike** the house being left empty.*
20 N+**V**+N+past participle	*The boss **wants** these letters typed.*

0 N + **V**

These verbs do not need anything to follow them, and are called intransitive verbs. [See TRANSITIVE VERB, INTRANSITIVE VERB.]

E.g. *The bus has **arrived**.* *It doesn't **matter**.*
*His son was **working**.* *Someone is **lying**.*

Other examples:

begin, come, drink,* drive,* fall, go, happen, help,* lie, occur, rise, wait, write**

* These verbs also belong to pattern **1** (transitive verbs).
E.g. ***I have been writing*** *(some letters).*

1 N + **V** + N

These verbs need a NOUN PHRASE to follow them, and are called transitive verbs. The N following is an object, and becomes subject in the PASSIVE.

E.g. *Everyone enjoyed **the show**. → **The show** was enjoyed by everyone.*
*Mary was **cleaning** the kitchen.*
*Her husband **laid** the table.*

*No one **knows** the answer.*
*You will **need** some more money.*

Other examples:

believe, bring, carry, cut, do, find, get, hear, hold, keep, lay, like, love, make, raise, remember, say, take, use, want

NOTE: Don't confuse ***raise*** and ***lay*** (pattern **1**) with ***rise*** and ***lie*** (pattern **0**), [see INTRANSITIVE VERB.]

2 N + **V** + N / adjective
These verbs are followed by either a NOUN PHRASE or an ADJECTIVE acting as complement. (The adjective may be expanded into an adjective phrase such as *very busy*, *too busy to help us*, etc.) The most common verb in this pattern is BE.

E.g. *She **is** my friend.* *She **is** busy.*

But other verbs can replace ***be***.

E.g. *She **became** my friend.* *She **became** busy.*

[We discuss these verbs in the separate entry for LINKING VERBS.]

3 N + **V** + adverbial
This pattern, like pattern **2**, is found with linking verbs, especially ***be***.

E.g. *The children **are** at the zoo.*
*The kitchen **is** downstairs.*

Usually the ADVERBIAL is an adverb or prepositional phrase of place in this pattern. But adverbials of time / length of time can also be used.

E.g. *The party **will be** tomorrow.*
*The meeting **lasted** for several hours.*

[For further examples, see TIME, and LINKING VERB, pattern (c).]

4 N + **V** + *that*-clause
Many verbs are followed by a THAT-CLAUSE as object [see THAT 1]. We can omit *that* [see ZERO THAT-CLAUSE]:

verbs of 'speaking',

E.g. *I **admit** (that) I've been foolish.*
*No one **denies** (that) the jewels were stolen.*
*Everyone **agreed** (that) the show was a success.*
*They **say** (that) Sue is getting married.*
*Scientists have **predicted** (that) this forest will die.*

verbs of 'thinking',

E.g. *We **believe** (that) the government is losing.*
*Sam **discovered** (that) the house was on fire.*
*People used to **think** (that) the earth was flat.*

[For other verbs taking *that*-clause, see IT-PATTERNS, SHOULD AND OUGHT TO 6b, SUBJUNCTIVE 1 and UNREAL MEANING.]

5 N + **V** + *wh-* clause

These verbs take a WH- CLAUSE (or INDIRECT QUESTION).

E.g. *The police **asked where** we were going.*
*I **wonder whether** the air tickets are ready.*
*Do you **know who** is chairing the meeting?*
*I couldn't **decide what** present to buy for her.*
*No one **realizes how** hard we work.*

Examples of Pattern **5** verbs:

ask, (not) care, choose*, discuss*, find out*, forget*, know*, (not) mind, point out, prove, see, wonder**

* These verbs can be used in pattern **6** too.

NOTE (i): *Find out, forget, know, point out* and *prove* also belong to pattern **4**.

NOTE (iii): These verbs often take a *wh-* clause after ***can't*** or ***couldn't***:
decide, explain, make out, remember, say, think.

6 N + **V** + *wh- to*-clause

A *wh- to-* clause begins with a *wh-* word and contains a TO-INFINITIVE (***to*** + Verb).

E.g. *Everyone should **learn how to** swim.*
*Have you **chosen what to** wear at the party?*
*I don't **know which** of these watches to buy.*
*They are **discussing where to** go for their {holiday <G.B.>. / vacation <U.S.>.}*

NOTE: The verbs marked '*' in **5** can be used in this pattern too.

7 N + **V** + *to* + Verb . . .

Verbs of many different kinds take this pattern. The verb is followed by a *to*-infinitive clause. [See -ING CLAUSE 6b, 6c for differences of meaning between this pattern and pattern **9**].

E.g. *I'd **love to** visit Yugoslavia.*
*Most people **want to** own their own houses.*
*Did you **remember to** water the flowers?*
*Williams **started to** write novels in 1960.*
*Joan and I have **promised to** take the children to the zoo.*
*They have been **trying to** improve the roads.*
*The building **seems to** be empty.*
*(Please) don't **bother to** cook anything for me.*
*The children are **helping to** paint the walls.*

NOTE: [See separate entries for HAVE TO, HAVE GOT TO, and (BE) GOING TO. Also, see VERB IDIOMS.]

8 N + **V** + Verb . . . [see BASIC FORM]
Only a few verbs take this pattern:
(a) The modal auxiliaries [see MODAL AUXILIARY]
(b) The verb idioms ***had better*** and ***would rather***
(c) The main verb ***help***, which can also take ***to*** + Verb (see pattern **7**).

E.g. *You **had better come** early tomorrow.*
This liquid will { ***help*** <esp. U.S.> / ***help to*** <esp. G.B.> } ***cure*** *your cold.*

9 N + **V** + Verb-*ing* . . . [see -ING FORM*]
Like pattern **7**, this pattern includes many different kinds of verbs. [See -ING CLAUSE 6b, 6c for differences of meaning between this pattern and pattern **7**].

E.g. *I **like watching** football.*
*Some people can't **bear listening** to jazz.*
*Anthony has **started working** at the factory.*
*(Please) **stop annoying** the cat.*
*The prisoner **denied stealing** anything.*
*(But) he **admitted breaking** into the house.*
*A mother **can't help feeling** proud of her child.*
*We must **avoid making** too much noise.*
*She **goes running** every morning.*

* The *-ing* form here is often called a 'gerund'.

10 N + **V** + past participle (. . .)
The only verb in this pattern (apart from the auxiliary ***be*** in the PASSIVE) is GET.

E.g. *The thief **got arrested** by the police.*
*Our team **got beaten** several times.*

The meaning is similar to the passive.

E.g. *He **got** arrested.* ↔ *He **was** arrested.*

11 N + **V** + N_1 + N_2
(In this pattern, the N_1 is the INDIRECT OBJECT, and the N_2 is the direct object.)

E.g. *They have **given** her a beautiful present.*
*Could you **lend** me some clothes?*
*John **owes** his sister $10,000.*
*Let me **make** (you) a cup of tea.*
*I'll **reserve** (us both) some tickets for the theatre.*
*We **wish** all our friends a happy New Year.*
*She **asked** them a favour.*

[For more details of this pattern, see INDIRECT OBJECT].

11a In pattern **11** we can also include verbs which take a preposition between N_1 and N_2, i.e. PREPOSITIONAL VERBS:

N + **V** + N_1 + preposition + N_2

E.g. *Everyone* ***thanked*** *Polly* ***for*** *the party.*
His enemies ***accused*** *him* ***of*** *laziness.*
Let me ***introduce*** *you* ***to*** *my neighbours.*

Other examples:

compare . . . with	*prevent . . . from*	*sentence . . . to*
congratulate . . . on	*protect . . . from*	*suspect . . . of*
convict . . . of	*remind . . . of*	*treat . . . of*
deprive . . . of	*rob . . . of*	*warn . . . of*

12 N + **V** + N + N / adjective

E.g. *The queen* ***kept*** *her marriage a secret / secret.*
The army ***left*** *the building a ruin / empty.*
Jim and I are ***getting*** *the house straight.*
The noise was ***driving*** *them all mad.*
The chairman has ***declared*** *the meeting official.*
Newspapers ***reported*** *Miss Brown dead.*
We all ***thought*** *him an excellent boss.*
Do you ***prefer*** *your coffee black?*

(In this Pattern, the N / adjective is called an OBJECT COMPLEMENT.)

Other examples:

call, elect, hold, make, send, turn

NOTE (i): Some verbs, like ***declare***, ***report*** and ***think***, can take a *that*-clause [see THAT 1], (see pattern **4**).
E.g. *We all* ***thought that*** *he was an excellent boss.*
These verbs can also take an object + *to* + infinitive (see pattern **17**).
E.g. *We all* ***thought him to be*** *an excellent boss.*
In general, pattern **12** and pattern **17** are <more formal> and <less common> than pattern **4**. But they are quite common in the PASSIVE.
E.g. *He* ***was thought*** *(to be) an excellent boss.*

NOTE (ii): There is also a PREPOSITIONAL VERB pattern with ***as*** [see AS]:
N + **V** + N + **as** N / adjective
E.g. *He* ***treated*** *her* ***as*** *his servant.*
The news broadcast ***described*** *the situation* ***as*** *very dangerous.*

13 N + **V** + N + adverbial
Most of the adverbials in this pattern are adverbials of MOTION (or movement) or PLACE.

E.g. *(First)* ***I took*** *the key out of my pocket.*
(Then) ***I put*** *it into the lock.*
They are ***sending*** *their son home.*
(Always) ***keep*** *your eyes on the road.*

Other verbs are:

bring, get, lead, place, show, stand, drive, lay, leave, see, sit

NOTE: The verb ***treat*** takes an adverbial of MANNER in this pattern.

E.g. *Her parents* ***treated*** *her* { ***well***. / ***badly***. }

14 N + **V** + N + *that*-clause

E.g. *John* ***told*** *me (that) his father was ill.*
They ***informed*** *her (that) her bag had been found.*
I ***bet*** *(you) (that) our team will win.*
We ***assure*** *you (that) we are doing our best.*
No one could ***convince*** *Linda (that) she was wrong.*

These verbs are mainly 'speaking' verbs introducing INDIRECT STATEMENTS. Other examples:

advise, persuade, promise, remind, satisfy, teach

15 N + **V** + N + *wh-* clause

E.g. *Jim* ***asked*** *us* { ***how long*** *we had been waiting.* / ***when*** *the meeting would end.* / ***whether*** *the train had gone.* }

Apart from **ask**, this pattern can be used with verbs in pattern **14**, especially in QUESTIONS and after NEGATIVES.

E.g. *I didn't* ***tell*** *anyone* ***where*** *I had hidden the key.*
Have you ***reminded*** *the audience* ***what*** *you are going to sing?*

16 N + **V** + N + *wh- to*-clause
The *wh-* clause in this case is a TO- INFINITIVE clause (compare patterns **6** and **15**):

E.g. *The pilot* ***taught*** *me* ***how to*** *land safely.*
Could you ***tell*** *us* ***which*** *museums* ***to*** *visit?*
(Please) ***remind*** *them (of)* ***what to*** *wear.*

Other verbs include:

advise, ask, instruct, show, warn

17 N + **V** + N + *to* + Verb . . .
In pattern **17**, the object is followed by a TO-INFINITIVE clause. Many different kinds of verbs take this pattern.

E.g. *I* ***want*** *you* ***to*** *feel at home.*
They don't ***like*** *us* ***to*** *arrive late.*
They ***reported*** *the car* ***to*** *be missing.*
We ***believed*** *it* ***to*** *have been stolen.*
He ***expected*** *the guests* ***to*** *arrive late.*
She ***asked*** *the doctor* ***to*** *give her advice.*
He ***advised*** *her* ***to*** *take a long rest.*

*They are **forcing** him **to** change his mind.*
*You must **get** them **to** clean their rooms.*
*She won't **allow** the class **to** borrow her books.*
*This **compels** them **to** buy new copies.*
*I am **helping** Mimi **to** finish her homework.*

18 N + **V** + N + Verb . . .

In pattern **18**, the BASIC FORM of the verb follows the object.

E.g. *She **lets** the boys **play** football on the lawn.*
*She should **make** them **behave** themselves.*
*Did you **see** anyone **leave** the building?*
*No, but I **heard** someone **bang** the door.*
*The judge **had** the witness **repeat** this statement.*
*Let me **help** you **tidy** these papers.*
*I've **known** him **eat** a pound of snails.*

Other verbs in this pattern:

feel, notice, watch, observe

NOTE: ***Have, let*** and ***watch*** here have no passive. The other verbs of pattern **18** form their passive with a TO- INFINITIVE.

E.g. *The thief was* $\left\{\begin{array}{l}\textbf{seen}\\ \textbf{observed}\end{array}\right\}$ ***to escape*** *by the back door.*

19 N + **V** + N + Verb-*ing* . . . [see -ING CLAUSE].

E.g. *They **dislike** the house **being** left empty.*
*Martine can't **bear** anyone **interfering** with her work.*
*Do you **mind** him / his * **borrowing** your bicycle?*
*I can **hear** someone **knocking** on the windows.*
*We **watched** the crowd **gathering** in the street.*
*We **found** the children **playing** tennis on the beach.*
*The driver **stopped** his bus **crashing** into the wall.*

Other examples:

feel, hate, like, love, notice, see, smell

[See PERCEPTION VERBS.]

* On the use of *his* instead of *him*, see -ING CLAUSE 1.

20 N + **V** + N + past participle (. . .)

E.g. *Can you* $\left\{\begin{array}{l}\textbf{get}\\ \textbf{have}\end{array}\right\}$ *this watch **repaired**, please?*
*The boss **wants** these letters **typed** before tomorrow.*
***I'd like** my room **cleaned** now, please.*
*They **saw** the home team **beaten**.*

verb phrase

► The 'Verb' part of an English sentence is called a ***verb phrase*** [see CLAUSE 1].

► The ***verb phrase*** can contain one verb, e.g. *Guy* ***came*** *yesterday*. (simple), or more than one verb, e.g. *Guy* ***is coming*** *today.* (complex).

► English has a small number of AUXILIARY VERBS which help the MAIN VERB to make up ***verb phrases***. They are: *be, have, do,* and the modal auxiliaries: *will, would, can, could, may, might, shall, should, must, ought to, used to* (note that *be, have,* and *do* also act as main verbs). [All these words have separate entries in this book. Look them up for further details.]

1 The auxiliary verbs combine with other verbs in four patterns

A modal* pattern: MODAL + VERB	*The shop(s)* {***will*** / ***may*** / ***could***} ***open***.
B perfect* pattern: HAVE + PAST PARTICIPLE	*The* {*shop* ***has*** / *shops* ***have***} ***opened***.
C progressive* pattern: BE + VERB-ING	*The* {*shop* ***was*** / *shops* ***were***} ***opening***.
D passive* pattern: BE + PAST PARTICIPLE	*The* {*shop* ***was*** / *shops* ***were***} ***opened***.

* Look these up under their separate entries for further details. For modals look up MODAL AUXILIARY.

The patterns can combine with each other, but they must keep the order: 'A before B before C before D'. (See Table I below for examples.)

2 In Table I is the complete set of verb phrases for one main verb (*play*).

NOTE: We use only Present Tense forms, and we use ***should*** to represent modal auxiliaries.

Table I

The child ***plays*** *(the piano).*	simple
The child ***should play*** *(the piano).*	modal
The child ***has played*** *(the piano).*	perfect
The child ***is playing*** *(the piano).*	progressive
The piano ***is played*** *(by the child).*	passive
The child ***should have played*** *(the piano).*	modal perfect
The child ***should be playing*** *(the piano).*	modal progressive
The piano ***should be played****.*	modal passive
The child ***has been playing*** *(the piano).*	perfect progressive
The piano ***has been played****.*	perfect passive
The piano ***is being played****.*	progressive passive
The child ***should have been playing*** *(the piano).*	modal perfect progressive
The piano ***should have been played****.*	modal perfect passive
The piano ***should be being played**** *.	modal progressive passive
The piano ***has been being played**** *.	perfect progressive passive
The piano ***should have been being played**** *.	modal perfect progressive passive

* These patterns are <very rare>.

3 There are three useful terms for words in the verb phrase

You can learn them from Table I:

(i) 'Main verb' (i.e. ***plays*** etc.) is the last word in each verb phrase (i.e. the last word in ***bold type***).

(ii) 'Finite verb' is the first word in each verb phrase (i.e. the first word in ***bold type***). It normally changes for Present / Past Tense.

(iii) 'Operator' (i.e. *must* etc.) is the first (i.e. 'finite') auxiliary in Table I: it is useful for forming QUESTIONS, NEGATIVE WORDS AND SENTENCES, SHORTENED SENTENCES, etc. [see OPERATOR]

4 Table II shows the different verb phrase structures and how they are used for expressing PRESENT TIME, PAST TIME, and FUTURE (with WILL). [For further details of structure and meaning in the verb phrase, see PRESENT TENSE and PAST TENSE, PERFECT and PROGRESSIVE aspects, and PASSIVE voice.]

This table does not show short forms or negative forms such as ***'s, 're***. [For these forms, see CONTRACTIONS OF VERBS AND NEGATIVES.]

Table II

		(not Progressive)	
		active voice	passive voice
Simple (not Perfect)	Present	basic form: *play* -s form: *plays*	*am* * *is* * *are* * } *played*
	Past	*played*	*was* *were* } *played*
	Future	*will play*	*will be played*
Perfect	Present	*has* *have* } *played*	*has* *have* } *been played*
	Past	*had played*	*had been played*
	Future	*will have played*	*will have been played* * *

		Progressive	
		active voice	passive voice
Simple (not Perfect)	Present	*am* * *is* * *are* * } *playing*	*am* * *is* * *are* * } *being played*
	Past	*was* *were* } *playing*	*was* *were* } *being played*
	Future	*will be playing*	*will be being played*
Perfect	Present	*has* *have* } *been playing*	*has* *have* } *been being played* * *
	Past	*had been playing*	*had been being played* * *
	Future	*will have been playing*	*will have been being played* * *

5 **Finite and nonfinite *verb phrases***
Most ***verb phrases*** are finite ***verb phrases***. This means they begin with a finite verb. All the ***verb phrases*** in tables I and II above are finite ***verb phrases***.
Nonfinite ***verb phrase*** begin with a nonfinite verb, these can be of three kinds:

INFINITIVE (usually with ***to***)

E.g. ***to** want*

-ing participle (or -ING FORM)

E.g. *want**ing***

PAST PARTICIPLE (usually an -ED FORM)

E.g. *want**ed***

Nonfinite ***verb phrases*** are usually used only in subordinate clauses [see NONFINITE CLAUSE].

6 In table III we show the structures of infinitive and -ing participle ***verb phrases***. Table III is simpler than table I because nonfinite ***verb phrases*** have no modal pattern. Also, -ing participle phrases have no progressive pattern, and past participle phrases have no complex patterns at all. [For examples of nonfinite clauses and their use, see INFINITIVE CLAUSE, -ING CLAUSE, PAST PARTICIPLE CLAUSE.]

Table III

infinitive phrases	participle phrases	form of verb phrase
to play	*playing*	simple
to have played	*having played*	perfect
to be playing	*playing* *	progressive
to be played	*played* * *	passive
to have been playing	*having been playing*	perfect progressive
to have been played	*having been played*	perfect passive
to be being played	*being played*	progressive passive

* The -ing participle can have a progressive meaning (referring to a temporary action in progress).
E.g. *We saw her **swimming** across the lake.* (This contrasts with: *We saw her **swim** across the lake.*)
[See VERB PATTERNS 18, 19.]
* * The past participle has a passive meaning.

verbless clause

1 **A verbless clause is a CLAUSE with no verb.**
Why do we call it a clause?
(a) Because it has the meaning of a clause, and
(b) Because it can have elements like SUBJECT, COMPLEMENT, OBJECT, and ADVERBIAL, like other clauses.

2 **Some examples of verbless main clauses**
(Use these in <informal speech>).

E.g. *How about a walk?* / *What about a cup of tea?* } suggestions*
Why all the noise? a question*
Everybody out! / *Off with your coat!* } commands [compare IMPERATIVES.]
('She left him.') 'A good thing, too.' a reply
Sorry about the mistake. an apology*
'Another piece of toast?' ('Yes, thanks.') an offer*
What lovely weather! an exclamation*

* These words have separate entries. Look them up for more details.

3 **Some examples of verbless subordinate clauses**
(Use these mainly in <formal writing>).

E.g. ***If in doubt**, contact your local safety officer.*
***Whenever possible**, the public should be informed about dangerous conditions on the roads.*
***Once inside the building**, the police lost no time in arresting the thieves.*
***With their best player in hospital**, Benfica will find it difficult to win the game.*
*Maureen was talking happily, **with a sandwich in one hand and a glass of milk in the other**.*
*They have two children: **one a girl of 15 and the other a boy of 10**.*
***Tired and hungry after their long journey**, the climbers decided to take a rest.*

very /ˈverɪ/ (*adverb of degree or adjective*)

1 ***Very*** (adverb) means 'to a high degree', and it comes before the word it applies to.

E.g. ***very*** + ADJECTIVE: *The coat's **very** expensive.*
very + ADVERB: *I saw her **very** recently.*
very + QUANTITY WORD: *He earns **very** little.*

2 Don't confuse ***very*** with TOO (= 'more than is needed') or ENOUGH (= 'as much as is needed'). You can see the difference in these examples.

E.g. ***very:*** *These trousers are **very** big.*
too: *These trousers are **too** big: they don't fit me.*
enough: *These trousers are big **enough**: they fit me well.*

NOTE: As an adjective, ***very*** comes after ***the*** (or some other definite determiner) and normally comes before a noun; it means 'exactly' or adds emphasis.
E.g. *Mary and I are twins: we were born on **the very same day**.* (= 'precisely the same')
*We climbed to **the very top of the mountain**.* (= 'the highest point')

viz. (*linking adverb*) [Compare E.G., I.E.]

We use ***viz.*** in <formal writing>. It means 'namely', and often links phrases in APPOSITION.

E.g. *We are making a study of the largest land animal in the world, **viz.** the African bush elephant.*

NOTE: ***Viz.*** is from the Latin ***videlicet***. We rarely pronounce ***viz.***, but if we do, we call it /vɪz/, or ***namely*** /ˈneɪmlɪ/.

vocative [See NAMES OF PEOPLE]

Vocatives are the words we use to name or to refer to people when talking to them.

E.g. *Mrs. Lake, Suzy, Madam*

Very often we do not use a vocative at all when talking to someone in English. This is usually not <impolite>.

voice [See ACTIVE and PASSIVE]

Voice is a grammatical term. Verbs have an active voice and a passive voice.

E.g. Active voice: *The dog **bit** the visitor.*
Passive voice: *The visitor **was bitten by** the dog.*

vowels

The basic vowel letters of the alphabet are ***a***, ***e***, ***i***, ***o*** and ***u***. But there are many more vowel sounds in English. [See CONSONANTS AND VOWELS.]

-ward, -wards -/wəʳd/, -/wəʳdz/ [See also TOWARD / TOWARDS]

1 ***-Ward(s)*** is a SUFFIX added to other words to form an ADVERB, meaning 'in the direction of . . .'.

E.g. ***upward(s), forward(s)*, homeward(s), downward(s), backward(s), eastward(s)***

NOTE: ***-ward*** is more common in <U.S.>, and ***-wards*** is usually more common in <G.B.>

* ***Forward*** is the usual form. ***Forwards*** is <rare> even in <G.B.>

2 E.g.

NOTE: Words ending ***-ward*** (but not -~~wards~~) can be used as ADJECTIVES.
E.g. *We've finished our visit to Africa. We start our **homeward** journey tomorrow morning.*

warnings

1

These warnings are for something sudden.

* <G.B.> only.

2 ***If*** or ***unless*** + Present Simple is often used to give a warning about the future.

E.g. ***If** you're so rude, you'll soon have no friends.*
*You'll find yourself in prison **unless** you learn to drive more carefully.*

3 Other examples:

---

was /wɒz/ (weak form /wəz/) singular Past Tense form of the verb ***be*** [See BE, WERE.]

E.g. *My teacher **was** ill, but she's better now.*

---

watch /wɒtʃ/ (*regular verb or noun*) [For the difference between LOOK (AT), SEE, and WATCH, see LOOK 3]

---

we /wi:/ (weak form /wɪ/), ***us, our, ours, ourselves,*** (*1st person plural personal pronoun*) [See PERSONAL PRONOUN]

► ***We*** refers to the speaker or writer and other people.

1 **The meaning of *we***
We may or may not include the hearer: 'you'.
We does not include 'you' in,

E.g. ***We**'ll lend you our* {*apartment* <U.S.> / *flat* <G.B.>} *in Rome.*

We does include 'you' in,

E.g. *'When shall **we** meet again?' 'Let's meet on Friday, shall **we**?'*

2 **Special uses of *we***

2a ***We*** is used for general remarks about the human race. [To compare the general uses of ***they*** and ***you***, see THEY 3 and YOU 2].

E.g. ***We** live in a period of great change.*
*Science tells **us** that the earth is getting cooler.*

2b ***We*** is often used in books, in referring to writer and reader together.

E.g. *In this chapter,* ***we*** *will briefly look at the history of art since Picasso.*

weak forms [See STRESS 4]

well /wel/ (*adverb or adjective*)

1 *Well* as an adverb of manner
Well is the (irregular) adverb of the adjective ***good***.

E.g. *She is a* **good** *tennis-player = She plays tennis* **well**.

1a ***Well***, like *good*, has COMPARATIVE and SUPERLATIVE forms ***better*** and ***best***. The opposite of ***well*** is ***badly***.

E.g. *My father speaks Chinese* **well** *because he has lived in China. But I speak it very* **badly**. *He knows China much* **better** *than I do.*

2 *Well* as a linking adverb
Well is a very useful word for beginning something new that you have to say.

E.g. ***Well,*** *what shall we do today?*

2a ***Well*** (adverb) is used to begin an answer when you need time to think.

E.g. *'What's your opinion?'* *'**Well,** I don't really know.'*

2b ***Well*** is often our first word when we can't give the answer the other person wants or expects.

E.g. *'I think Scotland is beautiful!'* *'**Well,** yes, but* * *the weather can be terrible!'*

* [See BUT 1c]

3 *Well* as an adjective
Well (adjective) means 'in good health', and generally follows the verb ***be*** or ***feel***. The opposite of ***well*** is ***ill***. Both words answer the question 'How?'

E.g. *'How are you (feeling) today? I heard you were* **ill.**' *'I'm getting* **better**, *thank you. In fact, I'm feeling quite* **well** *again.'*

Notice that ***better*** is the comparative: '*I am* **better**' means '*I am* **well** *again*'. (There is no superlative of the adjective ***well***.)

NOTE: ***Well*** and ***ill*** (adjectives) do not normally come before a noun: we do not say ~~*well*~~ *people* or *an* ~~*ill*~~ *child*. (Instead, we can say ***healthy people*** or ***a sick child***.)

4 **Idioms**

As well forms a single adverb, meaning '*also*', '*in addition*', '*too*'.
As well as forms a single preposition or conjunction meaning '*in addition to*', '*and also*'. Notice the difference between:

(i) ***well*** = adverb

E.g. *She speaks Spanish as **well** as (she speaks) Turkish.* ('She speaks Spanish and Turkish equally well.')

(ii) ***as well as*** = preposition

E.g. *She speaks Spanish, **as well as** Turkish.* ('She speaks Spanish, and also Turkish.')

---

were /wɜːʳ/ (weak form /wəʳ/) is the plural Past Tense form of ***be***

► *we / you / they **were***. [See BE.]

E.g. *We **were** beaten by Spain last night. Their players **were** much better than ours.*

1 ***Was / were* in the Past Tense**

When the SUBJECT of the verb is 1st or 3rd person singular, we generally use ***was***, not ~~*were*~~.

E.g. ***I was** watching the game. **It was** played in Madrid.*

2 ***Were* in the unreal use of the Past Tense**

But if the Past Tense has UNREAL MEANING (i.e. in ***would*** conditionals [see IF 1c]), we can use ***were***, instead of ***was*** with all subjects, including 3rd person singular subjects. For unreal meaning, ***were*** is more <formal> and 'correct' than ***was***.

E.g. *I wouldn't lend that man the money, even **if he were** my own brother.*
***If I were** living here in London, we could meet more often.*

NOTE (i): [See UNREAL MEANING on the use of ***were to***.]

NOTE (ii): In the idiom ***if I were you*** we use ***were*** rather than ***was***, even in <informal speech>. [See ADVISING / ADVICE.]

wh- clause

- ► A ***wh-* clause** is a SUBORDINATE CLAUSE which begins with a WH- WORD. *
- ► The basic word order of a ***wh-* clause** is simple: it is just like a main clause (statement) except that the ***wh-***word or ***wh-*** element goes in front [see MAIN CLAUSE].

* Except that in <formal writing>, a preposition can go before the wh- word.
E.g. *No one told him **of what** crime he was accused.*

1 Notice the way the word order changes in these ***wh-*** clauses [see WORD ORDER, CLAUSE 1a]. We shall call the following examples: *The Diary of a Forgetful Person*.

S = SUBJECT, V = VERB PHRASE, O = OBJECT, C = COMPLEMENT,
A = ADVERBIAL

I	*got up*	*early,*	*but I don't remember*	***what time***	*I*	***got up.***
S	V	**A**		**A**	S	V

I	*ate*	*a good breakfast,*	*but I don't remember*	***what***	*I*	*ate.*
S	V	**O**		**O**	S	V

I	*met*	*someone*	*at the bus stop,*	*but I don't remember*	***who*** / ***whom****	*I*	*met.*
S	V	**O**			**O**	S	V

Something	*happened*	*at the office,*	*but I don't remember*	***what***	*happened.*
S	V			**S****	V

I	*went*	*to the theatre,*	*but I don't remember*	***which theatre***	*I*	*went*	*to.*
S	V	**A**		**A*****	S	V	

The play	*was*	*very long,*	*but I don't remember*	***how** long*	*it*	*was.*
S	V	**C**		**C**	S	V

NOTE: The elements (i.e. S, V, O, C or A) in ***bold*** go in front in the ***wh-*** clause.

* ***Whom*** is more <formal> and 'correct'. [See WHO / WHOM / WHOSE].
** Notice that there is no change of normal word order if the ***wh-*** word is (in) the subject.
*** Notice that we usually leave the preposition at the end. But in <formal style> we can use: '***to which** theatre I went*'.

2 Different kinds of *wh-* clause

2a Indirect questions are NOUN CLAUSES. For example, they can be SUBJECT or OBJECT of a sentence.

E.g. ***What he does with his money*** *doesn't interest me.*
I wonder ***what he does with his money.***

Indirect questions are 'questions in the mind', as well as questions spoken aloud. All the examples in the right-hand boxes in 1 above are indirect questions. [See the separate entry for INDIRECT QUESTIONS.]

2b Relative clauses generally follow nouns. ***Wh-*** clauses which are relative clauses begin with ***who*** / ***(whom*** / ***whose)*** or ***which*** as relative pronouns, or ***when*** or ***where*** as relative adverbs.

E.g. *People* ***who work in offices*** *should take plenty of exercise.*
The dining room, ***which we have recently repainted,*** *is the nicest room in the house.*

[Look up RELATIVE CLAUSE for more details].

2c 'Referring clauses'.

E.g. { ***Whoever*** / *The person who* } ***wrote this novel*** *is a genius.*

{ ***What*** / *The thing that* } ***we need*** *is a new typewriter.*

You can buy { ***what food*** / *the food that* } ***you like***.

I'm going back to { ***where*** / *the place where* } ***I was born***.

We call these 'referring clauses' because they refer to people, or things or places. They replace a whole NOUN PHRASE. In meaning, they are similar to RELATIVE CLAUSES.

NOTE: A referring clause cannot begin with a preposition.

2d Indirect exclamations begin with . . . ***what a*** or . . . ***how*** [see EXCLAMATIONS 5, 6].

E.g. *Do you remember* ***what a wonderful time we had****?*
(Compare: ***What*** *a wonderful time we had!*)
It's surprising ***how young she looks***.
(Compare: ***How*** *young she looks!*)

3 [See also WH- EVER WORDS for clauses beginning with WHATEVER, WHOEVER, etc.]

wh-ever words [See WH- WORDS, WH- CLAUSE]

► ***Wh-ever*** words are ***wh-*** words with the ending ***-ever*** added.

► They are:

pronouns / determiners:	***whatever whichever whoever***
adverbs:	***however whenever wherever***

► ***Wh-ever*** words generally go at the beginning of SUBORDINATE CLAUSES.
► The word order of ***wh-ever*** clauses is the same as the word order of ***wh-*** clauses. [See WH- CLAUSE 1.]

1 How *wh-ever* words behave in sentences

1a ***Wh-ever*** words begin 'referring clauses' [see WH- CLAUSE 2c.]
The meaning is: 'any X that . . .' or 'the X that . . .'

E.g. *'**What** shall we do?' 'We can do **whatever** you like.'* (= 'anything that you like.')
*'**Who** are you inviting to the party?' 'I'll invite **whoever** you suggest.'* (= 'anyone that you suggest.')
*'**When** does the restaurant close?' 'The restaurant closes **whenever** the last customer leaves.'* (= 'the time when the last customer leaves.')

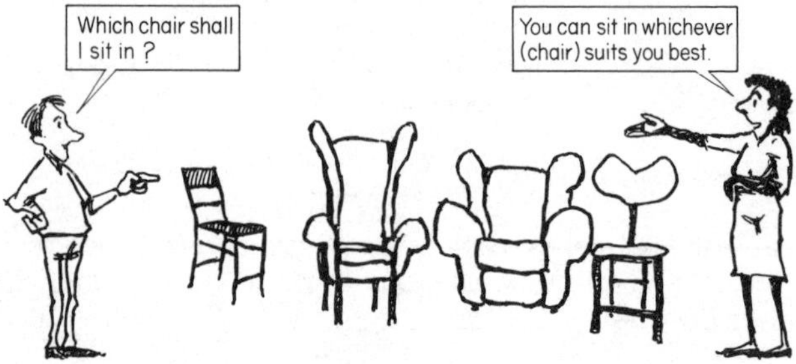

1b ***Wh-ever*** words begin 'any condition' clauses:
These are adverbial (conditional) clauses which mean that the main clause applies to any condition mentioned in the ***wh-ever*** clause.

E.g. ***Whatever else you do,*** *don't argue with Brian about politics!* ('It doesn't matter what else you do . . .')
Come in and sit down, ***whoever you are!*** ('It doesn't matter who you are . . .')
However hard I try, *I'll never beat Sue at tennis.* ('It doesn't matter how hard I try, . . ')

NOTE: We sometimes omit the verb ***be*** in 'any condition' clauses.
E.g. ***Whatever your problems*** *(are), we can give you advice.*

2 Adding *ever* for emphasis
We can add ***ever*** after a ***wh-*** word [see WH- WORD 2 NOTE], for emphasis, in DIRECT or INDIRECT QUESTIONS.

E.g. ***Who ever*** *can that be at the door?*

This is not a ***wh-ever*** word, but two words *wh-* + *ever*. But quite often people spell them as one word.

E.g. { ***What ever*** / *(Whatever*)* } *are you doing in my house?*

* ***Whatever*** is not 'correct', but it is < quite common >.

3 ***Wh-ever*** **words have other uses**. For example, ***however*** is a LINKING ADVERB.
[Look up each ***wh-ever*** word under its separate entry for further details and examples.]

wh- question

- WH- WORDS introduce WH- QUESTIONS.
- ***Wh-*** words can be used alone or in a sentence.
- They expect information in the REPLY (or answer): not just *yes* or *no*, but something you didn't know before.

► ***Wh-* questions** are usually spoken with a falling intonation [see INTONATION 1, 3b].

► Here are examples of questions with different ***wh-*** words which have separate entries in this book:

1 ***Who?*** (pronoun) i.e. you want to know about a person or some people.

E.g. *'**Who**'s that?'* *'It's **my father**.'*

NOTE: ***Whom*** is the OBJECT PRONOUN form of ***who***, but it is <formal> and <rather rare>. [See WHO / WHOM / WHOSE].
E.g. *'**To whom** did you give the ticket?'* *'To Zoe.'* <formal>

2 ***Whose?*** (possessive determiner or pronoun) i.e. you want to know who something belongs to.

E.g. *'**Whose** is this bucket?'* *'It's **mine**.'*
*'**Whose** baby is this?'* { *'It belongs **to Mary**.'* / *'It's **my sister's**.'* }

3 ***What?*** (pronoun) i.e. you want to know about something (not a person).

E.g. *'**What** are you reading?'* ***'A book on sport.'***

3a **What?** (determiner) i.e. you want to know more about somebody or something.

E.g. *'**What** magazine are you reading?'* ***'The T.V. Times.'***

4 ***Which?*** (pronoun) – use this instead of ***who*** (for people) or instead of ***what*** (for things) when there is a limited set of possibilities to choose from.

E.g. *'**Which** of Shakespeare's plays have you seen?'* ***'Hamlet and Othello.'***

4a ***Which?*** (determiner) – use this instead of ***what*** when there is a limited set of possibilities to choose from.

E.g. *'**Which** coat do you like best? The green, the red, or the blue?'* *'I like **the blue one** best.'*

4b [For more details about when to use ***which*** instead of ***what*** or ***who***, look up WHICH 1.]

NOTE: There is sometimes little difference between ***which*** and ***who***, or ***which*** and ***what***.
E.g. ***Which** / **who** is your favourite actress?*
***Which** / **what** magazines do you read?*

5 ***When?*** (adverb) i.e. you want to know the time at which something happens.

E.g. *'**When** did you go to Russia?'* ***'Two years ago.'***

6 ***Where?*** (adverb) i.e. you want to know what place.

E.g. ***'Where** are you staying?'* ***'At the camp site.'***

NOTE: We also use ***where*** in asking about motion to or from a place [see MOTION (OR MOVEMENT)].
E.g. ***'Where** have you been **(to)**?'* *'I've been **to the races**.'*
***'Where** do they come **from**?'* ***'From Poland**.'*

7 ***How?*** (adverb) i.e. you want to know the way or manner in which something happens or is done [see MANNER].

E.g. ***'How** did the accident happen?'* ***'The driver of the truck didn't notice the traffic lights.'***

NOTE: In asking about the instrument, we can say ***what (. . .) with?***, as well as ***how . . .?***, [see INSTRUMENT].
E.g. ***'What** shall I write **with**?'* *'You can use **this pen**.'*

7a ***How long?*** i.e. you want to ask about length of time.

E.g. ***'How long** are you staying here at the hotel?'* ***'Until next Sunday**.'*

7b ***How often?*** i.e. you want to ask about frequency.

E.g. ***'How often** do they clean the windows?'* ***'Every month**.'*

7c **How?** (adverb) + adjective i.e. you want to ask about degree or extent.

E.g. ***'How old** is your daughter?'* *'She's **nearly 18**.'*

NOTE: ***How?*** + adverb also asks about degree.
E.g. ***'How well** does she speak German?'* ***'Very well** – just like a native, in fact.'*

7d ***How?*** (adverb) + ***many*** or ***much*** asks about amount or quantity.

E.g. ***'How many** people are coming to the party?'* ***'About 20.'***
'How much** do I owe you?'* ***'Exactly £50.'

8 ***Why?*** (adverb) i.e. you want to know a REASON or CAUSE. Answer: *'Because . . .'*

E.g. ***'Why** did the plants die?'* ***'Because** they didn't get enough water.'*

NOTE: ***Why?*** can also ask about PURPOSE (i.e. the REASON for an ACTION.) In this use we can replace ***why?*** by ***what . . . for?***
E.g. ***'What** are you singing **for?'*** ***'I'm feeling happy**.'*

Notice that all these QUESTIONS expect ANSWERS with information, it is not enough to say just '*Yes*' or '*No*'!

9 **How to form *wh-* questions**

(i) Put the ***wh-*** word at the front of the sentence, together with any words in the same phrase.

E.g. ***Why*** *. . .?* ***Who*** *. . .?* ***Which*** *hat . . .?* ***What*** *size . . .?* ***How*** *fast . . .?*

(ii) If the ***wh-*** word is (part of) the SUBJECT, you don't have to make any change to the usual WORD ORDER of a statement.

	subject			
E.g.	***Who***	*lives here?*	→	***Rita*** *lives here.*
	Which hat	*is yours?*	→	***This*** *hat is mine.*

(iii) But if the ***wh-*** word is not (part of) the subject, you place the AUXILIARY VERB or *be* in front of the subject. This is inversion [see INVERSION 2, 3].

E.g. ***How fast can they*** *run?* → *They can run* ***fast****.*

Where is Ada*?* → *Ada is* ***at home****.*

(iv) If you cannot do (iii) because there is no auxiliary verb, use the 'empty' auxiliary **do** [see DO 2].

E.g. ***How fast did*** *they run?* → *They ran* ***fast****.*

Where does *Ada live?* → *Ada lives* ***in Paris****.*

How do *you like it?* → *I like it* ***very much****.*

9a Compare ***wh-*** words as subjects and as non-subjects:

	subject	verb	object	adverbial
statement:	*Diana*	*drinks*	*tea*	*regularly*
question:	***Who***	*drinks*	*tea*	*regularly?*

	object	auxiliary	subject	verb	(adverbial)
question:	***What***	*does*	*Diana*	*drink*	*(usually)?*

	adverbial	auxiliary	subject	verb	object
question:	***How often***	*does*	*Diana*	*drink*	*tea?*

Now compare: subject + verb . . .

E.g. ***How many accidents*** *happen because of bad roads?*
How much money *was stolen?* (PASSIVE)

with: object + auxiliary + subject + verb

E.g. ***How many accidents*** *have you had?*
How much money *do you have?*

NOTE (i): Now compare direct ***wh-*** questions with INDIRECT QUESTIONS.
E.g. *'**What** do you want?' → Tell me **what** you want.*
*'**Who** are you looking for?' → She wants to know **who** you are looking for.*
The indirect question has no inversion of subject and AUXILIARY or ***be***.

NOTE (ii): When the ***wh-*** word is part of a prepositional phrase, we have a choice in <formal> English between putting the preposition at the end of the question, or moving the whole prepositional phrase to the front [see PREPOSITIONAL PHRASE].
E.g. *'I'm staying at a hotel in Brighton.'*
'Oh. { ***Which hotel** are you staying **at**?'*
{ ***At which hotel** are you staying?'* <formal>

10 Special kinds of *wh-* question

10a Short ***wh-*** questions:
If you need to, you can ask a very short question containing the ***wh-*** word.

E.g. *'It's time you were in bed, Tom.' '**Why**?'*
*'I'd like to have a talk with you.' 'O.K. **When**?'*
*'We mustn't stay any longer.' '**Why** not?'*

10b Some short questions end in a preposition:

E.g.

NOTE (i): Questions with more than one ***wh-*** word.
E.g. *'**Who** does **what**?' 'I'll do the shopping, and you can cook the dinner.'*

NOTE (ii): Questions which ask about things / people in subordinate clauses.
E.g. *'**Who** did they want her **to marry** □ ?'*
'(They wanted her to marry) an army officer.'
*'**How much** money do you think **he earns** □ ?'*
The box □ shows where the ***wh-*** word 'belongs' in the subordinate clause.

NOTE (iii): Questions which ask the other person to repeat words that you didn't hear (or the words that you didn't believe!).
E.g. *'His grandmother is 95 years old.' '**How old** is she?'*
*'It cost $100.' '**How much** did it cost?'*

These are called 'echo questions'. They are spoken with a rising intonation, and with the main stress on the ***wh-*** word. Echo questions are sometimes <impolite>, so it may be best to begin with an apology [see APOLOGIES].
E.g. *I'm sorry;* ***how old*** *is she?*
Sometimes an echo question has the same word order as a statement, and the ***wh-*** word is in a later position in the sentence.
E.g. *She is* ***hów*** *old? It cost* ***hów*** *much?*

NOTE (iv): [On ***should*** in ***wh-*** questions, see SHOULD AND OUGHT TO 7.]

wh- words

1 ***wh-*** words is the name we give to the following 10 words which you can look up in separate entries [WHO / WHOM / WHOSE are in one entry]:

who, whom		pronouns
what, which	determiners	pronouns
whose	determiners	pronouns
how*, why	adverbs	
where, when	adverbs	subordinating conjunctions
whether		subordinating conjunctions

* We call ***how*** a ***wh-*** word even though it is not spelled with ***wh-***.

NOTE: There are also ***wh-*** words which end in ***-ever***, like ***whatever***. [See WH-EVER WORDS.]

2 **The use of *wh-* words**

2a All the ***wh-*** words except ***whether*** can introduce WH- QUESTIONS.

E.g. ***What's*** *the time?*

2b All the ***wh-*** words (including ***whether***) can introduce INDIRECT QUESTIONS.

E.g. *He asked me* ***what the time was.***
'Can you tell me ***what the time is****, please?'*

[For details of ***wh-*** words introducing subordinate clauses, see WH- CLAUSE.]

NOTE: To express strong feeling about a question, e.g. *surprise*, you can add ***ever*** or ***on earth*** to the ***wh-*** word. [See WH-EVER WORDS]
E.g.
How on earth *did you win so many prizes?*

Whoever can be phoning at this time ? It's 2a.m.
Brrrrr
Brrrrr

what /wɒt/ (*pronoun or determiner*)

- ***What*** is a WH- WORD used to refer to 'things'.
- ***What*** is used to form *wh-* questions [see WH- QUESTIONS 3], WH- CLAUSES, and exclamations [see EXCLAMATIONS 5, 6].
- ***What*** does not change its form.
- [On the difference between ***what*** and ***which***, see WHICH 1.]

1 *What* refers to things

What asks about something:

E.g. *'**What** are you looking for?' 'I'm looking for **a pen**.'*

Who asks about someone:

E.g. *'**Who** are you looking for?' 'I'm looking for **the manager**.'*

NOTE: You can ask ***what*** about a person's job.
E.g. *'**What** was her first husband? 'He was **a lawyer**.'*
But its meaning is different from:
*'**Who** was her first husband?' 'He was **John Forbes, the son of a famous writer**.'*
What asks about a person's job. ***Who*** asks about the person as a person.

2 *What* introducing *wh-* questions

2a ***What*** as a pronoun can be SUBJECT, OBJECT, or COMPLEMENT.

Subject: E.g. ***What*** *happened?*
Object: E.g. ***What*** *are you doing?*
Complement: E.g. ***What*** *is your name?*

Other examples:

*'**What** would you like to drink?' '**An orange juice**, please.'*
*'**What** is her job?' 'She's **a nurse**.'*

NOTE (i): [See WH- QUESTION 10 about short questions such as ***'What for?'***.]

NOTE (ii): The simple question ***'What?'*** is a <rather impolite> request for repetition.

2b ***What*** as a determiner goes before a noun: ***what*** + noun.

E.g. *'**What time** is it?' 'It's **ten past five**.'*
*'**What colour** is her hair?' 'It's **black**.'*
*'**What job** does he do?' 'He's **an electrician**.'*
*'**What year** were you born (in)?' 'In **1956**.'*

NOTE: When it is a DETERMINER, ***what*** can ask about people as well as things. It often means '***what kind of***'.
E.g. ***What (kind of) painters*** *do you admire most?*
What (kind of) people *visit this restaurant?*

3 ***What* introducing *wh-* clauses (= subordinate clauses)**

3a ***What*** as a pronoun.

E.g. { *We asked her **what** she wanted.* / *I don't know **what** you mean.* } INDIRECT QUESTIONS

(Talking about a holiday):

*'**What** I enjoyed most was swimming.'*
*'Did you? Well, the food was **what I** enjoyed most.'*
} 'referring clauses' [see WH- CLAUSE 2c]

3b ***What*** as a determiner: ***what*** + noun

E.g. *Can you tell me **what size** * this dress is?*
*I don't care **what difficulties** we face.*
} indirect questions
*They stole **what** (little) **money** we had.*
***What** (few) **supporters** he had soon left him.*
} 'referring clauses'

(***What money*** and ***what supporters*** here imply that the amount or quantity is small.)

* ***What size*** + noun is useful when you are talking about clothes.
E.g. *'**What size** { shoes / dress } do you take?'* *'**Size 10**.'*

4 ***What (a / an)* introducing exclamations** [see EXCLAMATIONS 5, 6]

4a ***What*** + ***a*** / ***an*** + (. . .) singular countable noun [see COUNTABLE AND UNCOUNTABLE NOUNS].

E.g. ***What a*** *lovely dress!* ***What a*** *beautiful day!*
What a *time we had!* (= 'we had a very good time')

4b ***What*** + (. . .) plural or uncountable noun.

E.g. ***What strange neighbours*** *you have!*
What luck! (= good luck or bad luck).

whatever /wɒˈtevəʳ/ (*pronoun or determiner*)

► ***Whatever*** is the WH-EVER WORD that belongs with ***what***. It means 'any(thing) that . . .'

E.g. *I'll eat **whatever (food)** you have to offer.*

Whatever also emphasises a negative word or an *any*- word (= 'at all').

E.g. *The crash had **nothing whatever** to do with me.*
*We haven't mentioned the matter to **anyone whatever**.*

when /wen/ (*adverb or conjunction*)

► ***When*** is a WH- WORD introducing questions about TIME.
► ***When*** is also a subordinating CONJUNCTION: it introduces ADVERBIAL CLAUSES of TIME.

1 **When (adverb) in questions means '(at) what time?'**

E.g. *'**When** did you leave?'* *'On the third of July.'*

In indirect questions:

E.g. *'Do you know **when** they're coming?'* *'Yes. Tomorrow.'*

In other *wh-* clauses:

E.g. *Summer is the season **when** the farmers are busiest.*

[See RELATIVE CLAUSE 8.]

*Next Monday is **when** we return to school.*

[See 'referring clause', WH- CLAUSE 2c.]

2 ***When*** **(conjunction) means 'at the time at which'**

E.g. *We were all very pleased **when** she passed her exam.*

2a In the ***when***- clause, use a Present Simple verb to refer to the future [see FUTURE 3b].

E.g. *Phone me **when** you **get back**.*
***When** the T.V. star **arrives**, there will be a big crowd.*

2b Use a Present Perfect verb in the ***when***- clause
(i) to describe something past from the point of view of the future.

E.g. *I will feel much happier **when I have finished**.*

(ii) to describe something past when the main clause contains a Present Simple verb for describing habit.

E.g. *They cut the corn **when** it **has ripened**.*

2c In statements of habit, ***when*** = IF or WHENEVER.

E.g. *People don't like making speeches* **when** (=if) *they've never spoken in public before.*
When (=whenever) *water boils, it changes into steam.*

2d With a Progressive form, ***when*** = WHILE or AS.

E.g. *We saw a strange animal when* (=while) *we were driving through the forest.*

3 **Idiom**
Since when (conjunction):

She moved to Egypt in 1943, **since when** *she has rarely left that country.*

---

whenever /weˈnevəʳ/ (*adverb or conjunction*)

► ***Whenever*** is the WH- EVER WORD which belongs with ***when***.

1 ***Whenever*** (adverb of time) means 'at any time that'.

E.g. ***Whenever*** *you arrive, you'll be welcome.*
('At whatever time you arrive . . .')
'When would you like to meet?' *'**Whenever** you like.'*

2 ***Whenever*** (conjunction of time) means 'every time that'.

E.g. ***Whenever*** *there's a rail strike, the passengers have to travel by road.*
I visit my sister ***whenever*** *I go to London.*

---

where /weəʳ/ (*adverb or conjunction*)

► ***Where*** is a WH- WORD introducing questions about PLACE.
► ***Where*** is also a subordinating CONJUNCTION: it introduces ADVERBIAL CLAUSES of PLACE or MOTION (OR MOVEMENT)

1 ***Where* (adverb)**
Where in *wh-* questions means '(in) what place?'

E.g. '***Where***'s *my raincoat? I can't find it.*'
'***Where*** *are you going (to)?*'
'***Where*** *do you come from?*'

In *wh-* clauses:

E.g. '*I don't know* ***where*** *she lives.*' (INDIRECT QUESTION)
This is the place ***where*** *I first met my wife.*
(***where*** = 'at which') (RELATIVE CLAUSE)
You have to go back **to where** *you started.*
(***where*** = 'the place at which') ('referring clause')

NOTE: There are short questions ***Where to?*** and ***Where from?*** [see WH-QUESTION 10b].
E.g. *'The plane has just arrived.'* *'Where from?'* *'From Nairobi.'*

Taxidriver: *'Where to?'*
Passenger: *'To Victoria Station, please.'*

2 ***Where*** **(conjunction)**

Where in the following examples means '{in / to} the place (in) which . . .'

E.g. *Young people have to go* ***where*** *they can find jobs.*
Where *I come from, the summer is very dry and hot.*

---

whereas /weəˈræz/ (*conjunction*) [see CONTRAST 2a]

---

wherever /weəˈrevəʳ/ (*adverb or conjunction*)

► ***Wherever*** is the WH-EVER WORD which belongs with ***where***.

1 **Adverb** (= 'it doesn't matter where')

E.g. *Come here, Janet,* ***wherever*** *you are.*

2 **Conjunction** (= 'in / to every place')

E.g. *His dog follows after him* ***wherever*** *he goes.*
I try to save money ***wherever*** *and whenever I can.*

---

whether /ˈweðəʳ/ (*subordinating conjunction*)

► ***Whether*** always begins a subordinate clause.
► Also, ***whether*** always introduces a choice between alternatives.

1 ***Whether*** **introduces indirect** YES-NO **questions**
[See INDIRECT QUESTION 1: NOTE (i).]

E.g. *'Are you hungry?'* (Yes or No?) → *She asked me* ***whether I was hungry***.
'Have you seen my sister?' (Yes or No?) → *He asked* ***whether I had seen his sister***.

1a The question may not be asked; it may just be a question in the mind.

E.g. *'Shall we go for a picnic tomorrow?'*
'That depends on ***whether it's* a fine day****.'*
I wonder { ***whether*** / ***if***** } *the journey will last a long time.*

* We generally use the Present Tense to refer to the future after ***whether***.
** ***If*** can usually replace ***whether*** in front of an indirect question [see INDIRECT QUESTION 1].

2 ***Whether*** **X or Y**
This idiom introduces two matching alternatives, 'X' or 'Y':

2a Alternative indirect questions:

E.g. *They have a baby, but I can't remember* ***whether*** *it's a boy* ***or*** *a girl.* (X = 'It's a boy'; Y = 'It's a girl')
I don't know ***whether*** *she agrees* ***or*** *disagrees with us.*
(X = 'She agrees with us'; Y = 'She disagrees with us')

2b Alternative conditions:
The examples above are indirect questions. ***Whether . . . or*** is also used in CONDITIONAL CLAUSES expressing alternative conditions.

E.g. ***Whether*** *you're young* ***or*** *old, you can still enjoy sport.*
(X = 'If you're young'; Y = 'Even if you're old')
The races will take place ***whether*** *it's raining* ***or*** *it's sunny.*

3 ***Whether or not***
A simple way to form a clause with two alternatives is to add ***or not***. You can add ***or not*** to all the examples of ***whether*** in 1 and 1a above. It makes them rather more insistent.

E.g. *She asked me* ***whether*** *I was hungry* ***or not****.*
That depends on ***whether*** *it's a fine day* ***or not****.*
You have to pay taxes ***whether*** *you want to* ***or not****.*

3a Another way of saying the same thing is to add ***or not*** just after ***whether***.

E.g. *She asked me* ***whether or not*** *I was hungry.*
That depends on ***whether or not*** *it's a fine day.*

which /wɪtʃ/ (*pronoun or determiner*)

► ***Which*** is a WH- WORD
► ***Which*** is used to form *wh-* questions [see WH-QUESTION 4] or WH- CLAUSES.
► ***Which*** is also a relative pronoun referring to something (i.e., not a person) [see RELATIVE CLAUSE].

1 When to use *which* instead of *what* or *who*

Which as a question pronoun can refer to both people and things. It is different from ***who*** and ***what*** because it asks for a choice from a definite, limited set of possibilities.

E.g. { ***What***: ***What*** *are you buying?* (I can't see what it is)
{ ***Which***: ***Which*** *are you buying?* (I can see five dresses. I don't know which one you are buying.)
{ ***Who***: ***Who*** *do want to speak to?* (It could be anyone)
{ ***Which***: *I have two daughters.* ***Which*** *do you want to speak to?*

2 *Which* introducing *wh-* questions

2a ***Which*** as a question pronoun can be SUBJECT or OBJECT.
It is often followed by an ***of***-phrase:

which + ***of*** + plural noun phrase or pronoun

E.g. ***Which of these chocolates*** *would you like?*

Which asks you to make a choice from a limited set of possibilities. The ***of***-phrase describes this set. But you can omit the ***of***-phrase if the set of possibilities is clear from the situation:

Which of these chocolates would you like ?
CHO LATES

2b ***Which*** as a question determiner:

Which (determiner) goes before a noun: ***which*** + noun

Again the choice is from a definite, limited set.

E.g. '***Which*** *party do you support? The Democrats or the Republicans?*'
'***Which*** *children have won prizes?*' '*Mary, Raymond, and Wendy.*'

* ***What*** can also be used here. It means *'what kind of . . .?'*
E.g. ***What*** *bus are you waiting for?*

Many people say ***what*** meaning ***which*** in <informal> English.

3 *Which* introducing *wh-* clauses

3a ***Which*** as a pronoun or determiner introducing indirect questions:

E.g. *There are so many beautiful clothes. I don't know* ***which (of them)*** *to buy.*
I asked Judy ***which programme*** *she wanted to watch. She answered that she didn't mind* ***which***.

3b ***Which*** (= 'whichever') as a pronoun or determiner in 'referring clauses' [see WHICHEVER].

3c ***Which*** (= 'that') as a relative pronoun has a different meaning from ***which*** in other uses. [See RELATIVE CLAUSE for further details.]

---

whichever

/wɪˈtʃevə^{r}/ (*pronoun or determiner*) [See WHICH 3b and WH-EVER WORDS]

E.g. *I have several umbrellas. You can borrow* $\left\{ \begin{array}{l} \textbf{which} \\ \textbf{whichever} \end{array} \right\}$ *(one) you like.*

---

while

/waɪl/ (*subordinating conjunction or noun*)

- ► ***While*** introduces an ADVERBIAL CLAUSE of TIME.
- ► ***While*** means 'during the time when X' (X is an action or state lasting for a period of time.) The period of time may be long or short.
- ► ***While*** is often followed by the Progressive form of the Verb.

1 The *while*-clause can go before or after the main clause

E.g.

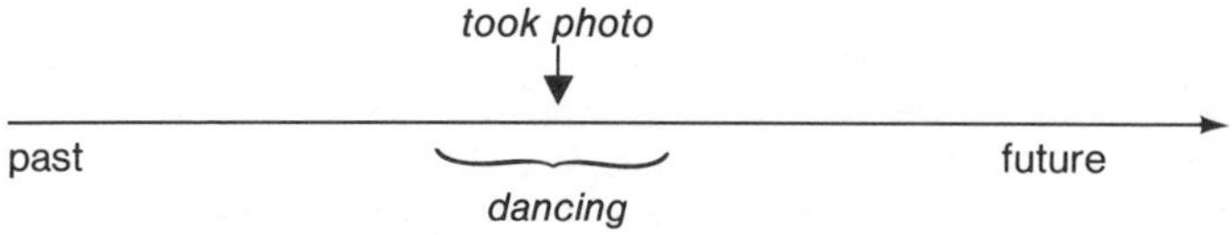

While they were dancing, *someone took a photograph.*
We arrived ***while Pete was (talking) on the phone.***
While you're* cutting the grass, *I'll make a cup of tea.*

* [For the use of the Present Tense for future time, look up FUTURE 3b.]

1a Both clauses can have the Progressive form of the verb:

E.g. *While he was making a speech, the TV camera crew were filming.*

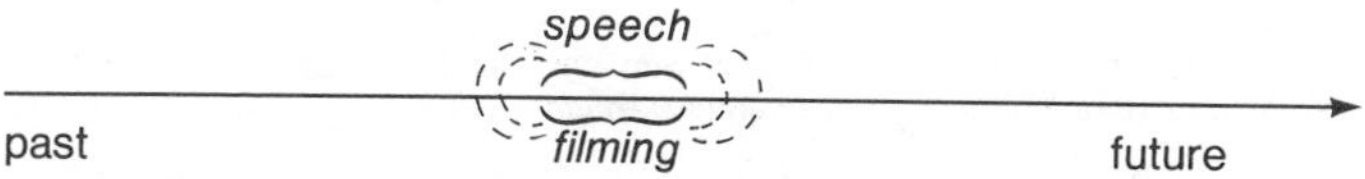

NOTE (i): Short Clauses with ***while*** omit the subject and the verb *be*:
while + Verb-*ing* . . .
E.g. *Marion wrote her first novel* ***while*** *(she was)* ***working*** *for a newspaper.*
While + complement or adverbial.
E.g. ***While*** *(he was) a student, Sam had to borrow money.*
While *(she was) in the hospital she was visited every day by her family.*

NOTE (ii): As a noun, ***while*** means 'a (short) time'.
E.g. *'I'm going out for a while.'*
'Well, don't be too long. Dinner will be ready in a while.' (= 'soon')

2 ***While*** (subordinating conjunction) does not always refer to time. It is also used to link two ideas which contrast with each other [see CONTRAST 2].

E.g. ***'While*** *I like mussels, I hate oysters.'*

---

whilst /waɪlst/ (*conjunction*) is a <rarer> form of ***while***

who / whom / whose /hu:/, /hu:m/, /hu:z/ (*pronouns*)

- ***Who*** is a *wh-* word, used to refer to people.
- ***Who*** is used to form WH-QUESTIONS and WH-CLAUSES.
- ***Who*** is also a relative pronoun [see RELATIVE CLAUSE].
- ***Whom*** is the OBJECT PRONOUN form of ***who***. It is rather <rare>.
- ***Whose*** is the possessive form of ***who***. [See POSSESSIVE DETERMINER AND POSSESSIVE PRONOUN.]

1 The uses of *who* in questions

(A) SUBJECT.

E.g. '***Who*** *lives in that house?*' ***'A farmer, Mr Gray.'***

(B) OBJECT.

E.g. '***Who*** *do you teach?*' <informal> * *'I teach* ***medical students****.'*

(C) COMPLEMENT.

E.g. '***Who*** *are her parents?*' *'They are* ***Mr and Mrs Walker****.'*

(D) With a PREPOSITION at the end.

E.g. '***Who*** *were you speaking* ***to****?*' <informal> * *'****To*** *a friend of my sister's.'*

* ***Whom*** is <rare> compared with ***who***. It is <formal> and it is considered more correct than ***who***. But in <speech> we rarely hear ***whom***.

1a ***Whom*** can be used in these positions:

(B) Object.

E.g. '***Whom*** *do you teach?*' <formal>

(E) After a preposition (compare (D) above).

E.g. '***To whom*** *were you speaking?*' <formal>

2 Comparing *who, whom* and *whose*

	subject pronoun	object pronoun	possessive	
			determiner	pronoun
<informal>	***who***	***who***	***whose***	
<formal>		***whom***		

2a To illustrate ***who***, ***whom***, and ***whose*** here is:

A Report on a Bicycle Accident	
Who *was riding the bicycle?*	*Tom Hall.*
Who(m) *did he hit?*	*Barry Mann.*
Whose *shopping basket was upset?*	*Mrs Mann's.*
Whose *was the bicycle?*	*Paula Hall's.*
{ ***To whom*** *was the accident reported?* { ***Who*** *was the accident reported* ***to****?*	*To Police Constable Woods.*

3 ***Who, whom, and whose in wh-clauses***
In *wh-* clauses, ***who***, ***whom*** and ***whose*** behave as they do in direct *wh-* questions (see 1–2 above).

3a ***Who, whom***, and ***whose*** in INDIRECT QUESTIONS:

E.g. *The policewoman asked* ***who was riding the bicycle.***
I don't remember ***who(m) we met at the party.***
I recognize the bicycle, but I don't know ***whose it is.***
She didn't say ***whose house*** *she was visiting.*
Can you tell us { ***to whom*** *you wish to speak?* <formal>
{ ***who*** *you want to speak* ***to****?* <informal>

3b ***Who, whom***, and ***whose*** in relative clauses:
Who, whom and ***whose*** (determiner) are used in both defining and nondefining relative clauses [see RELATIVE CLAUSE 4].

E.g. *Everyone* ***who lives here*** *has to share in the housework.*
Our daughter Cora, ***who(m) you met last year****, is getting married on 5th October.*
These papers belong to Bernard,
{ ***with whom*** *I am sharing a room.* <formal>
{ ***who*** *I'm sharing a room* ***with****.* <informal>

NOTE (i): With singular GROUP NOUNS like *committee*, *family*, and *club*, we can use either of these patterns:
Group Noun + ***who*** + Plural Verb
Group Noun + ***which*** + Singular Verb
E.g. *The castle belongs to the Clifford **family**, {**who have** / **which has**} lived here ever since the fourteenth Century.*

---

whoever /hu:ˈevəʳ/ (*pronoun*) is the WH-EVER WORD which belongs with ***who***.

E.g. *Jason is very hardworking. **Whoever** offers him a job will never regret it.*

---

whole /həʊl/ (*adjective or noun*)

► ***Whole*** is a QUANTITY WORD meaning 'all, not part' of something. [Compare ALL.]

1 Adjective

E.g. *He owns the **whole** building, and not just part of it.*
*They spend the **whole** day learning English.*

2 Noun

E.g. *The **whole** of the country is covered with snow.* (= ***all*** the country)

3 It is best to use ***whole***, not ~~*all*~~, before a singular countable noun [see COUNTABLE AND UNCOUNTABLE NOUNS]:

*a **whole** melon*

part of the melon

a piece of melon

4 Idiom
On the whole (adverb) = 'generally, in general'

E.g. *I don't like John's views **on the whole**, but I agree with what he says on education.*

---

whom /hu:m/ (*pronoun*) [See WHO / WHOM / WHOSE]

Whom is the OBJECT PRONOUN form of ***who***.
It is quite rare in <speech>, but is still used in <writing>.

whose /hu:z/ (*possessive determiner and pronoun*) [see WHO / WHOM / WHOSE]

1 ***Whose*** is a *wh-* word. It is the possessive form of ***who***. ***Whose*** is used in direct and indirect WH- QUESTIONS.

E.g. ***Whose*** *book is this?* (determiner)
I've found a book. I wonder ***whose*** *it is.* (pronoun)

2 ***Whose*** (determiner) introduces RELATIVE CLAUSES.

E.g. *I know* ***Mrs Short, whose daughter*** *lives near you.*

This means the same as:

I know ***Mrs Short. Her daughter*** *lives near you.*

why /waɪ/ (*wh- adverb*)

- ***Why*** always asks a question.
- ***Why*** always means 'For what reason?'
- You can answer the question ***why***? with '***because***' (giving a reason).
- ***Why*** goes at the beginning of a main clause [see WH- QUESTION 8], or a subordinate clause [see INDIRECT QUESTION].
- ***Why*** can also be a one-word question standing alone.

1 E.g.

2 Special questions with *why*

2a ***Why don't you* / *we*** begins a SUGGESTION or piece of advice [see ADVISING / ADVICE].

E.g. ***Why don't you*** *sell your car by advertising it in the paper?*
*'**Why don't we** have a drink?'* *'Good idea!'*

2b ***Why*** + Verb . . . and ***why + not*** + Verb are special question patterns without a SUBJECT, for giving advice or making a suggestion.

E.g. ***Why*** *cause difficulties for yourself?*
'I don't know what to say to them.' *'**Why not** tell the truth?'*

NOTE: You can sometimes use **why** in NOUN CLAUSES and RELATIVE CLAUSES.
E.g. *That's not **why** I did it: the reason **(why)*** I did it was to help our friends.*

* Some people consider that ***the reason why*** is bad English. You can omit **why** here if you like.

---

will /wɪl/ (contraction: '***ll***/l̩/, /əl/, negative form ***won't*** /wəʊnt/ (*modal auxiliary*)

- ***Will*** is followed by the BASIC FORM of the verb: ***will*** + Verb. (E.g. ***will*** *go*).
- ***Will*** + Verb is the most common way of indicating future time in English.
- [You will find more about ***will*** if you look up FUTURE 1, 5a.]
- The Past Tense form of ***will*** is WOULD.

1 Forms

1a simple form:

I *You* *We* *They* *He / She / It* noun phrase	***will*** ***'ll***	*be . . .* *have . . .* *go soon.* *take . . .* *see . . .* etc.

negative:

I *You* *We* *They* *He / She* etc.	***won't*** ***will not***	*be . . .* *have . . .* *go yet.* *take . . .* *see . . .* etc.

question:

Will	*you* *we* *they* noun phrase etc.	*be . . .* *have . . .* *go soon* *take . . .* *see . . .* etc.	?

negative question:

Won't*	*you* *we* etc.		*be . . .* *have . . .* *go soon* *take . . .* *see . . .* etc.	?
Will	*you* *we* etc.	***not**** *		

* ***Won't*** is the usual form in <speech>.
** ***Will . . . not*** is <formal and rare>.

1b ***Will*** with other forms in the verb phrase:

Perfect: [see FUTURE 1]	E.g. *The exams **will have** finished by Friday.*
Progressive: [see FUTURE 5a]	*Next week **I'll be giving** a lecture on business and the law.*
Passive:	*The rules **will be changed**.*
Perfect Passive:	*That car **will have been sold** by now.*
etc. [see VERB PHRASE]	

2 Uses of *will*: prediction

2a ***Will*** = future (prediction): [see FUTURE 1].

E.g. *Susan **will be** here in half an hour.*

Will is used especially in a main clause with conditional clauses [see IF 1].

E.g. *If you sit by the fire, you **will feel** warmer.*

2b ***Will*** = 'present prediction' (i.e. your observation tells you that something is likely to be happening now):

E.g. *'It's eleven o'clock. Norma **will be** in bed by now.'* (She normally goes to bed at ten.)

*'Ah, that'**ll be** my husband. He said he would phone at this time.'*

2c ***Will*** = 'present habit' (predictable behaviour):

E.g. *A lion **will** never **attack** an elephant.*

She's a good little girl.
She'll play quietly for hours.

NOTE: ***Will*** sometimes means the same as ***can***.
E.g. *This theatre **will hold** a thousand people.*
('***will hold***' = 'can hold')
*This window **won't open**.* (= 'I can't open it')
*That's a nice car. How fast **will** it go?*

2d ***Will*** = 'making a decision now about the future' [see FUTURE 2c]:

E.g. *'Which shirt do you want?'*
*'**I'll** take the blue one, please.'*

3 **Uses of *will*: wishing**
Will often has a meaning of wishing (with future meaning).

3a ***Will*** = 'intention' + future:

E.g. ***I'll write** to you as soon as I can.* [See PROMISES.]
*We **won't stay** longer than two hours.*
*John says he'**ll phone** us after lunch.*

3b ***Will*** = 'be willing' (with future meaning).

E.g. *'**Will** you **help** me to answer these letters?'*
*'Yes, I'**ll** do it, if you like.'* [See REQUEST.]

The negative does not always refer to the future.

E.g. *Stephen is very annoying. He **won't** do anything I say.* (***won't*** = 'is unwilling', i.e. 'refuses').

3c ***Will*** = 'insist on' + Verb-***ing***' (mainly <G.B.>):
Will is stressed in this use. We cannot use the contraction ***'ll***.

James will go out without his coat.
He'll catch a cold one of these days.

(be) ***willing to*** /bɪ ˈwɪlɪŋ tʊ/tə/ *(verb idiom)*

1 The idiom ***be* + *willing* + *to* + Verb** is useful for expressing a wish to help somebody [see WISHES].

E.g. *'**Are** you **willing to** arrange a meeting for next week?'*
*'Yes, **I'm willing to** do anything you like.'*

2 Sometimes ***willing*** follows another LINKING VERB, apart from ***be***, such as ***seem, look, sound***.

E.g. *'What did he say?'* *'Well, he **seems willing** to help us.'*

NOTE: The negative adjective is ***unwilling***. The adverb is ***willingly***.

wishes and how to express them

► To ***wish*** = to want { what is not happening, or / what did not happen }

1 **Wishing about the past**
You cannot change the past, so you can only wish (with regret) about things which did not happen [see UNREAL MEANING]:

noun phrase or pronoun	+	***wish***	+	*that*-clause [see THAT 1] containing ***had*** + past participle

E.g. *I **wish** I **had gone** to that party last night. I stayed at home – I was so bored!*

*Do you ever **wish** you'**d remained** single instead of marrying?*

NOTE (i) To express a wish in the past about something which happened further in the past use: ***wished*** + . . . Past Perfect.

E.g. *When she looked at the photograph, she often **wished** she **hadn't lost** her beautiful black hair and her good looks.*

NOTE (ii): We can also use IF ONLY to express a present wish about the past.

2 **Wishing about the present or future**

You can use the Past Tense to express a wish about something which is not true of the present.

E.g. ***I wish I were*** a millionaire. [See WERE 2.]
*Mike **wishes** he **had** a job: at the moment he's unemployed.*

NOTE: To express a wish in the past about something which was not true at that time use: ***wished*** + . . . Past Simple.
E.g. *Aunt Martha **wished** that she **didn't have** so many friends and relatives. At Christmas time, there were so many cards and presents to buy!*

2a When the verb after ***wish*** is an action verb, the wish refers to the future, and we use ***would(n't)*** or ***could*** instead of the Past Simple. [See STATE VERBS and ACTION VERBS.]

Compare:

*I **wish** the weather **was** warmer.* (state)

but:

*I **wish** the weather **would get** warmer.* (action)

Other examples:

E.g. *I **wish** we **could meet** more often.*
*The princess **wishes** that the press photographers **would leave** her alone.*

NOTE: A wish in the past of this kind also contains ***would(n't)*** or ***could***.
E.g. *She often **wished** Mark **would give** more thought to his appearance, but she didn't say anything.*

3 **Wishing about the future**

3a We use other verbs, as well as ***wish***. And the wish may come true!

E.g. *We **wish** you a happy New Year.* [See VERB PATTERNS 11.]
*The manager **wants** to talk to the work force.* [See VERB PATTERNS 7.]
*He **wants** everyone to work harder.* [See VERB PATTERNS 17.]
I hope { *to see you soon.* [See VERB PATTERNS 7.]
{ *you will be very happy.* [See VERB PATTERNS 4.]

3b The verb ***wish*** itself goes before a TO-INFINITIVE, but only in <formal> English.

E.g. *Miss Garbo* ***wishes to be*** *alone.*

3c To express a rather <tentative> and <polite> **wish** about the future, use ***would like to**** (or ***should like to***).

E.g. ***Would*** *you* ***like to*** *use the telephone?*
*We****'d like*** *the meeting* ***to*** *take place as soon as possible.*

* ***Would prefer to*** or ***would love to*** can also be used.

---

with /wɪð/ and ***without*** /wɪðˈaʊt/ (*prepositions*)

► ***With*** is a common preposition: it comes before a noun phrase or a pronoun.
► ***Without*** is usually the opposite of ***with*** (= 'not with') – see meanings 1, 2, 3, 4 below.

1 ***With*** **= 'together with' or 'in company with' someone.**

E.g. *'Sheila was at the race.' 'Who was she* ***with****?' 'She was* ***with her friends****.'*
'We're going out for a meal. Are you coming ***with us****?'*

1a ***Without*** here is the negative of ***with***.

E.g. *'The President attended the meeting* ***without*** *his wife.'*

2 ***With*** **= 'by means of' comes before an INSTRUMENT.**

E.g. *'****How*** *did you open the door?' 'I did it* ***with this key****.'*
'He hit the thief.' 'What ***with****?' 'He hit him* ***with a stick****.'*

2a ***Without*** is the negative of ***with*** = instrument.

E.g. *In the old days, we had to cook* ***without gas or electricity****.*

3 ***With*** **= 'having': . . . noun +** ***with*** **+ noun phrase.**

E.g. *a girl* ***with*** *a diamond ring* — *that house* ***with*** *the new roof*
the man ***with*** *grey hair* — *a woman* ***with*** *a large family*

3a ***Without*** (= 'not having') is the negative of ***with***.

E.g. *a house* ***without*** *a garden* — *a life* ***without*** *any * fun or excitement*

* After ***without***, we can use *any* or *any*-words. [See SOME- AND ANY-WORDS.]

3b ***With*** and ***without*** (= '(not) having') can begin a NON-FINITE CLAUSE or VERBLESS CLAUSE similar to patterns which can follow ***have*** [see HAVE]:

with / ***without***	+	noun phrase	+	*to* + Verb . . . / Verb-*ing* . . . / preposition + noun phrase / etc.

E.g. ***With** a large family to feed, they had to work very hard.*
(= '**Having** *a large family . . .*')
*a factory **with** all its labour force* {*working* / *on strike*}
(= '*a factory* **which has** . . .')
a young man {**with** *plenty of money* / **without** *a penny*} *in his pocket.*

NOTE: More generally ***with*** and ***without*** can link a PHRASE or -ING CLAUSE loosely to the main clause.
E.g. ***With** such a large family, Meg has no time to visit her friends.* ('having such a large family, . . .')
*The police searched the building **without** finding anything suspicious.* ('and did not find anything suspicious.')
*Please leave the room **without** making a noise – other students are still doing their exams.*

4 ***With*** **+ abstract noun = MANNER.**
Here the ***with***-phrase is an adverbial, and is <rather formal>.

E.g. *'**How** did she sing?'*
*'She sang **with great skill**.'* (= 'very skilfully')
*The soldiers moved the bomb carefully, quietly, and **without haste**.*
(= 'not hastily')

5 ***With*** **and** ***without*** **are not always opposites.**

5a Here, ***with*** is the opposite of ***against***.

E.g. *If you are not **with** us,* (= 'on our side') *you must be against us.*
(= 'on the other side')

5b In the idioms ***fight with*** and ***argue with***, ***with*** means the same as ***against***.

E.g. *Don't **argue with me**: you make me angry.*

Other idioms: ***bother with, do without*** [see PREPOSITIONAL VERB], ***angry with*** [see ADJECTIVE PATTERNS 1b].

---

within /wɪˈðɪn/ (*preposition*)

► ***Within*** means 'inside the limits' of something.
► ***Within*** mainly refers to (i) LENGTH OF TIME and (ii) DISTANCE or PLACE.

1 ***Within* (length of time)**
Here ***within*** has the same meaning as ***in*** [see IN] (= 'before the end of').

E.g. ***Within an hour,*** *the fire service had put out the fire, and the injured had been taken to hospital.*

2 ***Within* (distance or place)**

E.g. *I live* ***within two miles*** *of the city centre.*

---

without [See WITH AND WITHOUT]

---

woman /ˈwʊmən/ (*noun*) has the irregular plural **women** /ˈwɪmɪn/

E.g. ***That woman*** *works in the office.*
Those women *work in the factory.* [See SEX.]

---

wonder /ˈwʌndəʳ/ (*regular verb or noun*)

1 ***Wonder*** (verb) introduces an INDIRECT QUESTION:

SUBJECT + ***wonder*** + { *if* / *whether . . .* / *what* / etc. }

E.g. *'****I wonder if*** *Peter phoned while I was out?' 'Yes, he did. He* ***wondered whether*** *you could see him tonight.'*

2 ***I*** + ***wonder*** + ***if*** introduces a <polite> REQUEST.

E.g. ***I wonder if*** *you'****d**** mind mending this tape.*
I { ***wondered*** * * / ***was wondering*** * * } ***if*** *you were free tonight.*

* The contraction ***'d*** stands for ***would***. The verb in the *if*-clause uses the unreal Past Tense.
* * The Past or Progressive with ***wonder*** helps to make the request less direct and <more polite>.

---

won't /wəʊnt/ = ***will not*** [See WILL, CONTRACTION OF VERBS AND NEGATIVES 3]

word classes (sometimes called 'parts of speech')

► The different kinds of word, such as noun, verb, and preposition, are called ***word classes***.

1 Look up the following word classes in this book:

NOUN VERB ADJECTIVE ADVERB DETERMINER PRONOUN PREPOSITION CONJUNCTION NUMBER INTERJECTION

2 Each class can be divided into smaller classes. For example, verbs can be divided in AUXILIARY VERBS and MAIN VERBS.

word order

► When we talk of ***word order*** we usually mean the order of the elements in a SENTENCE or CLAUSE: SUBJECT, VERB, OBJECT, etc.

► English word order is rather fixed, because the order tells us which element is the subject or object.

1 **Normal order**

In English, the normal order in STATEMENTS is this (the brackets mean you can omit these elements):

	subject	verb	(object)	(complement)	(adverbial*)
E.g.	*She*	*has left*	*the letters*	*unopened*	*on the table.*

* But you can add adverbials in front, middle, or end positions [see ADVERB 3, ADVERBIAL 4].

[See VERB PATTERNS 0–20 for many other examples of normal word order.]

1a We generally use special word order in sentences or clauses which are not statements. [See: YES-NO QUESTION 1, WH- CLAUSE 1, WH- QUESTION 9, EXCLAMATIONS 6b, and RELATIVE CLAUSE 2.]

► One kind of special word order is inversion: i.e. we place the (first word of the) verb phrase in front of the subject. Most questions are formed by inversion.

E.g.	*Has*	*she*	*left*	*the letters*	*unopened*	*on the table?*

[For further details, look up INVERSION.]

2 Emphasis

In general, the most important part of a sentence or clause is the end. So to give elements emphasis, we put them at the end. One way of doing this is to use PASSIVE word order:

Active:

(i) *The computer can easily solve most of our problems.*

Passive (places emphasis on 'the computer'):

(ii) *Most of our problems can be easily solved* ***by the computer***.

Emphatic word order:

(iii) ***Most of our problems*** *the computer can solve easily.*

In (iii) the first element is the object, so this element is 'fronted' (i.e. placed at the front, not in its normal position) to get the right emphasis. We call this 'emphatic word order'. It is not <common> in English.

2a Negative emphasis

[For inversion after negative words and phrases, see NEGATIVE WORDS and SENTENCES 6a.]

3 [For special word order with ***so***, look up SO 4.]

---

worse, (the) worst /wɜːʳs/, /wɜːʳst/ (*adjectives and adverbs*)

These are the comparative and superlative forms of BAD / BADLY.

E.g. *'Alec is the* ***worst*** ** speller in the class. I don't know anyone who spells* ***worse*** ** * than he does.'*
'Well, Patricia is ***worse*** ** than he is. She can't even spell her own name!'*

* = adjective; * * = adverb.

---

would /wʊd/ (weak form /wəd/) (contraction: ***'d*** /d/, negative form ***wouldn't*** /ˈwʊdn̩t/) (*modal auxiliary*)

► ***Would*** is a very common modal auxiliary. It is followed by the BASIC FORM of the verb.
► ***Would*** is often shortened to ***'d*** [see CONTRACTION OF VERBS AND NEGATIVES 2].
► ***Would*** indicates UNREAL MEANING in main clauses (e.g. following conditional clauses). This has no connection with ***will***. (See 1 below.)
► ***Would*** is also the Past Tense form of ***will***. This means that it has the same meanings as ***will***, except that ***would*** indicates UNREAL MEANING (2 below) or PAST TIME (3 below).

1 *Would* with unreal meaning

1a ***Would*** + basic form of verb:

This indicates something we do not think is true (in the present) or probable (in the future). This is common with *if*-clauses [See IF 1c].

E.g. ***If** I were rich* (subordinate clause) *I* {***would*** / ***'d***} {*live in a large house.* * / *travel around the world.* * *}

* = untrue at present.
* * = improbable in the future.

If** Irene were younger, she* {would*** / ***'d***} *be able to take part in the competition.*

1b ***Would have*** + past participle:

This indicates something unreal in the past – i.e. something that did not happen and could not have happened ('imaginary past').

E.g. ***If** you* {***had*** / ***'d****} *lived in the 19th century,* (subordinate clause)

{*you **wouldn't have** driven a car,* (i) / *you* {***would*** / ***'d*** *} ***have** travelled by horse and carriage.* (ii)}

(i) = '*Now you do drive a car*'
(ii) = '*Now you don't travel by horse and carriage*'

If** Max **had** studied medicine, he* {would*** / ***'d****} ***have** become a doctor by now.*

* Note that ***'d*** is the contraction for both ***would*** and ***had***.

NOTE: The unreal use of ***would*** can make a REQUEST or OFFER more tentative, and so more <polite>.
E.g. ***Would** you mind helping me?* <very polite> request
(Compare: *Do you mind helping me?* <polite> request)

2 ***Would* as the unreal form of *will***
As the Past Tense of ***will***, ***would*** has unreal meanings of intention, etc. [See WILL]:

2a Intention.

E.g. *I **would stay** and help you if I **could**.* ('*but I can't*')
(Compare: *I **will stay** and help you if I **can**.*) ('*I may be able to*')

2b Willingness (especially in REQUESTS).

E.g. ***Would** you please **unlock** this door?* <polite>
(Compare: ***Will** you please **unlock** this door?*) <less polite>

2c Refusal (with the negative).

E.g. *Jack **wouldn't help** you, even if you begged him.*
(Compare: *Jack **won't help** you, even if you beg him.*)

3 ***Would* as the past time form of *will***
As the Past Tense of ***will***, ***would*** has the same meanings as ***will*** except that they apply to past time.

3a Future in the past [see PAST TIME 4 (III)]:
This is used mainly in reporting the past words or thoughts of someone in a story. [See INDIRECT SPEECH AND THOUGHT 1c].

E.g. *He warned us that the journey **would be** dangerous.*
(Direct speech: '*The journey **will be** dangerous.*')
*At that time I thought **I'd** never **see** my parents again.*
(Direct thought: '***I'll** never **see** my parents again.*')
*The crowd was excited. Everyone was wondering who **would win**. Who **would be** this year's tennis champion?*

3b Past habit [compare WILL 2c]:
In telling stories, we use ***would*** to describe a habit (or predictable behaviour) in the past.

E.g. *Before they got married, Simon* ***would wait*** *for Benita every evening after work. Then they* ***would walk*** *home across the park, and Benita* ***would feed*** *the ducks on the lake.*

(***Used to*** [See USED TO 1a] could replace ***would*** here.)

3c Past intention or willingness.
Again, these uses are mainly found in INDIRECT SPEECH AND THOUGHT:
(i) intention [see WILL 3a].

E.g. *I promised that I* ***would repay*** *the money they had lent me.* ('intended to repay')

(ii) willingness [see WILL 3b].

E.g. *I asked if they* ***would mend*** *the watch as soon as possible.* ('were willing to mend')

3d Past insistence or refusal [see WILL 3c].

E.g. *I tried to explain the problem to Charles, but he* ***'would keep*** *interrupting me.* ('insisted on interrupting')

This ***would*** is always stressed, and cannot be contracted to ***'d***. The negative meaning is one of refusal.

E.g. *I tried to explain the problem to Marcia, but she* ***wouldn't listen***. ('refused to listen')
When I asked them to help, they ***wouldn't lift a finger***. ('refused to lift a finger' to help)

---

yes /jes/ is a word for giving a positive answer to questions, etc. [See YES-NO QUESTION, and compare NO 1]

E.g. '*Did you enjoy the meal?*'
'***Yes,*** *it was delicious*'.

---

yes-no question

► The two most common kinds of question are ***yes-no questions*** and WH-QUESTIONS.

► ***Yes-no questions*** ask for an answer ***yes*** (positive) or ***no*** (negative).

1 How to form normal yes-no questions

[subject] + [auxiliary / ***be*** / . . .] . . . ⟶ [auxiliary / ***be*** / ***do***] + [subject] . . . ?

E.g. *You are cold.* → *Are you cold?* (Yes or No)
He speaks English. → *Does he speak English?* (Yes or No)

(a) Start with the sentence in statement WORD ORDER.
(b) Put the first verb of the verb phrase (if it is an AUXILIARY or a main verb *be*) in front of the subject [see INVERSION 3].
(c) If the statement has no auxiliary or form of *be*, add the correct form of *do* [see DO 2] (the 'empty' auxiliary) before the subject.
(d) Change the falling tone at the end of the statement into a rising tone at the end of the question [see INTONATION].

1a Forming yes-no questions with an auxiliary or *be*:

	(a) statement	(b) yes-no question
E.g.	*Joan is eating her lunch.*	*Is Joan eating her lunch?*
	The ship has arrived.	*Has the ship arrived?**
	The children were sent home.	*Were the children sent home?*
	We should have complained.	*Should we have complained?*
	He'll be waiting for us.	*Will he be waiting for us?*
	They're from Austria.	*Are they from Austria?*

* <U.S.>: ***Did** the ship arrive?* (See 1b below.)

NOTE: In <spoken English>, rising intonation is enough to turn a statement into a question (see 4 below).

1b Forming yes-no questions with *do*:

	statement	(c) yes-no question with **do**
E.g.	*Rabbits eat grass.*	*Do rabbits eat grass?*
	Mary enjoys swimming.	*Does Mary enjoy swimming?*
	The train arrived late.	*Did the train arrive late?*

NOTE: The 'empty' auxiliary *do* has no meaning in itself. It takes the form matching the main verb of the statement:

Verb	***Do*** + Verb
Verb **-s**	***Does*** + Verb
Verb ***-ed***	***Did*** + Verb

2 **Negative yes-no questions** [see NEGATIVE WORDS AND SENTENCES]
To form negative yes-no questions, simply place the negative auxiliary (or negative *be* form) in front of the subject:

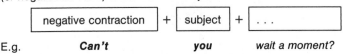

	negative contraction	+	subject	+	. . .
E.g.	***Can't***		***you***		*wait a moment?*

Use a negative question when you thought the answer would be 'Yes', but now realise it will be 'No':

E.g. *Don't you like ice-cream?* ('I thought you did.')
Didn't you want me to help you? ('I thought you did.')
Haven't you two met before? ('I thought you had.')
Aren't you going to church tonight? ('I thought you were.')

NOTE: A negative question with a falling tone is an exclamation [see EXCLAMATION 7].
E.g. *'Wasn't it a wonderful game?' 'Yes, wasn't it!'*
'This is my daughter Mary.'
'Hasn't she grown?' (= 'She's grown such a lot!')

3 How to choose between *some*, *someone*, etc. and *any*, *anyone*, etc.

3a Normal yes-no questions do not contain words like ***some***. Instead, they contain words like ***any***, ***anyone***, and ***anything***. [See SOME and ANY, SOME-WORDS and ANY-WORDS.]

E.g.

statement	yes-no question
Someone *phoned this evening.*	*Did* ***anyone*** *phone this evening?*
I need ***some*** *money.*	*Do you need* ***any*** *money?*
They have ***somewhere*** *to live.*	*Do they have* ***anywhere*** *to live?*
We've learned to ski ***already***.	*Have you learned to ski* ***yet***? <G.B.> *Did you learn to ski* ***yet***? <U.S.>

3b But some yes-no questions contain ***some***-words.

E.g. *Did* ***someone*** *phone this evening?* ('I was expecting a call.')
Do you need ***some*** *money?* ('It looks as if you have none.')
Have you learned to ski ***already***? ('It looks as if you can ski.')

We can call these questions 'yes-no-yes questions', because they expect the answer 'Yes'.

3c Loaded questions:

(i)

(ii)

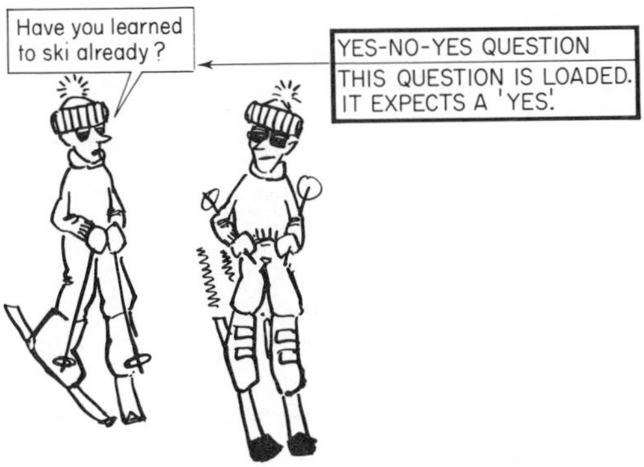

(iii)

(iv) A negative question with ***some***-words (instead of ***any***-words) is a strongly loaded question expecting 'Yes'.

E.g. ***Haven't*** *I met you* ***somewhere*** *before?* ('I recognize your face.')

4 **Questions that look like statements**

These questions are just like statements, except that they have a rising tone.

E.g. *You want to go home alréady?* *You haven't had téa yet?*

This is another kind of loaded question. These questions often express surprise. The speaker asks the hearer to confirm that the statement is true. [Compare TAG QUESTIONS.]

yesterday [See TODAY, TOMORROW, and YESTERDAY]

yet /jet/ (*adverb or conjunction*)

► In middle or end position, ***yet*** is an adverb of TIME.
► In front position, ***yet*** is a linking adverb or conjunction.

1 ***Yet*** is an adverb of time meaning 'up to now' especially used after negatives and in questions:

[See ALREADY, STILL, AND YET for further details.]

2 ***Yet*** is also a linking adverb [see LINKING ADVERBS AND CONJUNCTIONS], which comes at the beginning of a clause or sentence, and has a similar meaning to ***but*** [see CONTRAST 1b(III)].

E.g. *The climbers were very tired and hungry, (and)* ***yet*** *they refused to give up their attempt to climb the mountain.*

(***Yet*** has a slightly stronger effect than ***but***.) You can place ***and*** in front of ***yet*** when ***yet*** comes at the beginning of a clause.

2a Like ***but***, ***yet*** can also sometimes go in the middle of a phrase, for example, in linking two adjectives.

E.g. *Being a miner is an* ***unpleasant, yet important*** *job.*
This chair is ***old, yet very comfortable***.

Here ***yet*** behaves like a conjunction.

you /ju:/ (weak form: /jʊ/) ***your, yours, yourself***

► ***You*** is the 2nd person personal pronoun [see PERSONAL PRONOUN].
► ***You*** refers to the hearer or hearers.

1 Use the same form ***you*** for (a) singular and plural
(b) subject and object pronouns:

<table>
<tr><th rowspan="2"></th><th rowspan="2">subject pronoun</th><th rowspan="2">object pronoun</th><th colspan="2">possessive</th><th rowspan="2">reflexive pronoun</th></tr>
<tr><th>determiner</th><th>pronoun</th></tr>
<tr><td>singular</td><td colspan="2" rowspan="2">you</td><td rowspan="2">your</td><td rowspan="2">yours</td><td>yourself</td></tr>
<tr><td>plural</td><td>yourselves</td></tr>
</table>

(The situation will make clear whether ***you*** refers to one, or more than one person.)

E.g. ***You*** *look well.*
Can I help ***you****?*
This letter is for ***you****.*
How are ***your*** *children?*
This cup must be ***yours****.*
Please help ***yourself****.* / ***yourselves****.*

2 **The general use of *you* = 'one' <informal>**
We can use ***you*** to mean 'people in general, including the hearer and the speaker'.

E.g. *Marilyn is a truthful girl.* ***You*** *can always believe what she says.*
All this exercise makes ***you*** *hungry, doesn't it?*
These days, ***you*** *have to be careful with* ***your*** *money.*

We can replace ***you*** by ***one*** [see ONE 3], but ***you*** is more <informal> and more common. [Compare the general uses of THEY 3a and WE 2a.]

NOTE: Sometimes we add words (especially nouns) after ***you***. For example, a schoolteacher may say.
E.g. *'I want* ***you children*** / ***you two boys*** *to help me.'*

zero

Zero = '0'.
We use the term ***zero*** in grammar where some element in a pattern is omitted. [See ZERO ARTICLE, ZERO PLURAL, ZERO RELATIVE PRONOUN, ZERO THAT-CLAUSE.]

E.g. '**zero** past tense':

For most verbs, we add the ending ***-ed*** to show Past Tense.
But with some verbs, like ***cut*** and ***set***, no ending is added.

E.g. *need* → *need-**ed***
but: ***cut*** → ***cut***
We can say that ***cut*** has a **zero** Past Tense form.

zero article [See ARTICLES, A / AN, THE]

- Most nouns have an article (***a*** / ***an*** or ***the***), or another DETERMINER in front of them.
- When there is no determiner in front of a noun or noun phrase, we say that it has a ***zero article***.

1 Main uses of the zero article

English has no article like ***a*** / ***an*** to place before plural or uncountable nouns for indefinite meaning. * We use the zero article instead:

1a Zero article before plural nouns:

	a / ***an*** + singular noun	zero + plural noun
E.g.	*We're expecting **a visitor**.*	*We're expecting **visitors**.*

* However, see 2 below on the use of *some* as 'article'.

1b Zero article before uncountable nouns:

	a / ***an*** + countable noun	zero + uncountable noun
E.g.	*He picked up **a stone**.*	*The wall's made of **stone**.*

1c Zero article before names:

	a / ***an*** + common noun	zero + name
E.g.	*He gave her **a rose**.*	*My sister's name is **Rose**.*

[See NAMES 2, GEOGRAPHICAL NAMES 2–4 for exceptions to this.]

NOTE: With names we include titles like ***doctor*** in front of names (***Doctor** Mills*), and family nouns like ***Mum***, ***Dad***, ***Uncle***.
E.g. ***Dad** is looking after the children today.*

2 Choosing between zero article and *some* /səm/

Before plural and uncountable nouns, we can either use the zero article or unstressed ***some***, pronounced /səm/ [see SOME AND ANY 2].

E.g. *We're expecting* { *visitors.* (i) zero / ***some** visitors.* (ii) /səm/ }

Would you like { *black coffee?* (i) zero / ***some** black coffee?* (ii) /səm/ }

There is a small difference between (i) and (ii) above:
(i) 'zero article' means that the noun represents a general type of 'thing, person, material, abstraction'.

E.g. *black coffee* = 'black, not white coffee'.

(ii) ***some*** /sәm/ means 'a quantity of', where the exact quantity is not known or is not important.

2a Sometimes, only zero article is possible, especially after *be*:

E.g. *His father and grandfather were* { ***fishermen***. / ~~*some fishermen*~~. }

(This tells us what 'type' of people they were.)

2b In other examples, only ***some*** /sәm/ is usual:

E.g. *Could you lend me* { ~~*sugar?*~~ / ***some sugar****?* }

(This refers to a 'quantity' of sugar.)

NOTE: In negative sentences or questions, ***any*** usually replaces ***some*** [see SOME AND ANY 1a].
E.g. *Have you bought **any** sugar?*

3 **The zero article to refer to people and things in general**

3a Zero article + plural noun:

E.g. *I like **dogs** better than **cats**.* ***Children*** *enjoy **games**.*

3b Zero article + uncountable noun:
We use uncountable nouns for 'substances, liquids, gases, materials'.

E.g. ***Water*** *contains **oxygen**.* ***Steel*** *is much stronger than **copper**.*

And for abstractions:

E.g. *Which do you like best, **history** or **music**?*
*All **nations** should work for **peace**.*

4 **Special uses of the zero article with singular countable nouns** [see COUNTABLE AND UNCOUNTABLE NOUNS]

4a Zero can replace ***the*** before a noun describing a person's 'role' or 'function', when that person is the only one.

E.g. *Margaret is **(the) captain** of the tennis team.*
*As **(the) Secretary** of the club, I welcome new members.*
*John F. Kennedy was elected **(the) President** of the U.S.A. in 1961.*
*Elizabeth II became **(the) Queen** of England in 1952.*

NOTE: We cannot use the zero article after *be* where more than one person has the same role or function, for example, in naming someone's job.

E.g. *'What's **your job**?' 'I'm* { ~~*doctor.*~~ / ***a doctor****.'* }

(There is more than one person who is ***a doctor***, so we have to use ***a*** here.)

4b The zero article before nouns of time and season:

*at **night***	*at* } **noon**	***Morning** came.*
*by **day** / **night***	*before* } **midday**	***Night** fell.*
before } **sunrise**	*after* } **midnight**	*It's **spring**.**
after } **sunset**		

But other phrases have ***the***:

*in **the** morning* *during **the** night* ***the** next day*

* It is often possible to use ***the*** before nouns of season.
E.g. ***In (the) summer*** the weather is very hot in this country.

4c The zero article for meals:

E.g. *What did you have **for*** { ***breakfast**?* / ***lunch**?* }

I've invited the Johnsons { ***to*** / ***for*** } { ***dinner**.* / ***supper**.* }

But also.

E.g. *We had **a** very good **dinner**.*
***(The) breakfast** was late this morning.*

4d The zero article for some prepositional phrases of place:

*He is **in*** / *She went **to*** } { ***bed.*** / ***class.*** / ***hospital.*** <G.B.>* / ***prison.*** }	*She is **at*** / *He went **to*** } { ***church.*** / ***college.*** / ***school.*** / ***university.*** <G.B.>* / ***sea.*** / ***work.*** }

* <U.S.>: ***at** / **to the** hospital / university.*

These are idioms referring generally to places where we go for a special reason. We use ***a*** or ***the*** when we have a particular *hospital*, *prison*, etc. in mind.

E.g. *She's working in **a hospital** in Montreal.*
*I'm attending classes at **the University of Texas**.*

4e The zero article for **by**-phrases describing means of transport and means of communication:

E.g. *I came home **by*** { ***car**.* / ***bus**.* / ***train**.* }

[See TRANSPORT.]

4f The zero article in prepositional phrase idioms:

E.g. *at speed* *in front (of)* *in line (with)* *in turn*
on foot *on top (of)* *off colour* *out of step*

(Look these up in a dictionary.)

E.g. *I'm feeling a bit* ***off colour***. (= 'not very well')

4g The zero article in noun + preposition + noun idioms:

E.g. *day by day* *arm in arm* *hand in hand* *eye to eye*
face to face *side by side*

(Look these up in a dictionary.)

E.g. *James and his son never see* ***eye to eye***. (= 'never have the same views or opinions.')

zero plural

Some nouns have a zero plural, i.e. their plural form is exactly the same as the singular.

E.g. *a sheep ~ several sheep* *one fish ~ two fish*

[For more examples, look up IRREGULAR PLURAL 4.]

zero relative pronoun [See RELATIVE CLAUSE 2b]

Often we omit the relative pronoun ***that*** at the beginning of a relative clause.

E.g. *The people (that)* ***we've invited to dinner*** *are your neighbours.*

In '*The people we've invited to dinner*', the clause '***we've invited to dinner***' is a 'zero relative clause'. It has a zero relative pronoun.

zero *that*-clause

Normally a subordinate clause begins with a SUBORDINATING CONJUNCTION or some other introductory word.

E.g. *It's strange* ***that*** *no one has complained.*

A zero ***that***-clause is a ***that***-clause (i.e. a NOUN CLAUSE) from which the conjunction ***that*** has been omitted.

E.g. *It is strange* □ *no one has complained.*

[For further details, see THAT 1.]

a–z list of irregular verbs

NOTES: [1] [2] [3] and [4] are explained at the end of the list. The most common verbs are written in **bold**. The less common verbs are printed in ordinary letters (not bold). On the phonetic symbols, see CONSONANTS AND VOWELS.

Basic Form	Past Tense Form	Past Participle Form
arise	arose	arisen [see *rise*]
awake	awoke[1]	awoke[1] [see *wake*]
be[4] /biː/	**was, were** /wɒz/, /wɜːʳ/	**been** /biːn/
bear /beəʳ/	bore /bɔːʳ/	borne /bɔːʳn/
beat /biːt/	beat	beaten /ˈbiːtn̩/
become[4] -/ˈkʌm/	**became** -/ˈkeɪm/	**become**
begin -/ˈgɪn/	**began** -/ˈgæn/	**begun** -/ˈgʌn/
bend /bend/	bent /bent/	bent
bet /bet/	bet[1]	bet
bid /bɪd/	bade, bid /beɪd/, /bæd/, /bɪd/	bid(den) /ˈbɪd(n̩)/
bind /baɪnd/	bound /baʊnd/	bound
bite /baɪt/	bit /bɪt/	bitten /ˈbɪtn̩/
bleed /bliːd/	bled /bled/	bled
blow /bləʊ/	blew /bluː/	blown /bləʊn/
break /breɪk/	**broke** /brəʊk/	**broken** /ˈbrəʊkən/
breed /briːd/	bred /bred/	bred
bring[4] /brɪŋ/	**brought** /brɔːt/	**brought**
broadcast	broadcast	broadcast [see *cast*]
build /bɪld/	built /bɪlt/	built
burn /bɜːʳn/	burnt[2] /bɜːʳnt/	burnt[2]
burst /bɜːʳst/	burst	burst
buy /baɪ/	**bought** /bɔːt/	**bought**
cast /kɑːst ‖ kæːst/	cast	cast
catch /kætʃ/	**caught** /kɔːt/	**caught**
choose /tʃuːz/	**chose** /tʃəʊz/	**chosen** /ˈtʃəʊzən/
cling /klɪŋ/	clung /klʌŋ/	clung
come[4] /kʌm/	**came** /keɪm/	**come**
cost /kɒst/	cost	cost
creep /kriːp/	crept /krept/	crept
cut /kʌt/	cut	cut

Basic Form	Past Tense Form	Past Participle Form
deal /di:l/	dealt /delt/	dealt
dig /dɪg/	dug /dʌg/	dug
do[4] /du:/	**did** /dɪd/	**done** /dʌn/
draw /drɔ:/	drew /dru:/	drawn /drɔ:n/
dream /dri:m/	dreamed, dreamt /dremt/[2]	dreamed, dreamt[2]
drink /drɪŋk/	drank /dræŋk/	drunk /drʌŋk/
drive /draɪv/	**drove** /drəʊv/	**driven** /ˈdrɪvən/
dwell /dwel/	dwelt[2] /dwelt/	dwelt[2]
eat /i:t/	**ate** /et‖eɪt/	**eaten** /i:tn̩/
fall /fɔ:l/	**fell** /fel/	**fallen** /ˈfɔ:lən/
feed /fi:d/	fed /fed/	fed
feel[4] /fi:l/	**felt** /felt/	**felt**
fight /faɪt/	fought /fɔ:t/	fought
find /faɪnd/	**found** /faʊnd/	**found**
flee /fli:/	fled /fled/	fled
fling /flɪŋ/	flung /flʌŋ/	flung
fly /flaɪ/	flew /flu:/	flown /fləʊn/
forbid	forbad(e)	forbidden [see *bid*]
forecast /ˈfɔ:^{r}kɑ:st‖-kæst/	forecast	forecast [see *cast*]
foresee	foresaw	foreseen [see *see*]
foretell	foretold	foretold [see *tell*]
forget -/get/	forgot -/gɒt/	forgotten -/ˈgɒtn̩/
forgive	forgave	forgiven [see *give*]
freeze /fri:z/	froze /frəʊz/	frozen /ˈfrəʊzən/
get[4] /get/	**got** /gɒt/	**got** <G.B.>, **gotten** <U.S.>
give /gɪv/	**gave** /geɪv/	**given** /ˈgɪvən/
go[4] /gəʊ/	**went** /went/	**gone**, **been** /gɒn/, /bi:n/
grind /graɪnd/	ground /graʊnd/	ground
grow /grəʊ/	**grew** /gru:/	**grown** /grəʊn/
hang /hæŋ/	hung[1] /hʌŋ/	hung[1]
have /hæv/	**had** /hæd/	**had**
hear[4] /hɪə^{r}/	**heard** /hɜ:^{r}d/	**heard**
hide /haɪd/	hid /hɪd/	hidden /ˈhɪdn̩/
hit /hɪt/	hit	hit
hold /həʊld/	**held** /held/	**held**
hurt /hɜ:^{r}t/	hurt	hurt

Basic Form	Past Tense Form	Past Participle Form
keep /ki:p/	**kept** /kept/	**kept**
kneel /ni:l/	knelt[2] /nelt/	knelt[2]
knit /nɪt/	knit[1]	knit[1]
know /nəʊ/	**knew** /nju:/	**known** /nəʊn/
lay /leɪ/	laid[3] /leɪd/	laid[3]
lead /li:d/	led /led/	led
lean /li:n/	leant[2] /lent/	leant[2]
leap /li:p/	leapt[2] /lept/	leapt[2]
learn /lɜ:ʳn/	learnt[2] /lɜ:ʳnt/	learnt[2]
leave /li:v/	**left** /left/	**left**
lend /lend/	lent /lent/	lent
let[4] /let/	**let**	**let**
lie /laɪ/	**lay** /leɪ/	**lain** /leɪn/*
light /laɪt/	lit[1] /lɪt/	lit[1]
lose /lu:z/	lost /lɒst/	lost
make[4] /meɪk/	**made** /meɪd/	**made**
mean /mi:n/	meant /ment/	meant
meet /mi:t/	met /met/	met
mislead /mɪsˈlɪ:d/	misled /mɪsˈled/	misled [see *lead*]
mistake	mistook	mistaken [see *take*]
misunderstand	misunderstood	misunderstood [see *understand*, *stand*]
mow /məʊ/	mowed /məʊd/	mown[1] /məʊn/
overcome	overcame	overcome [see *came*]
overdo	overdid	overdone [see *do*]
override	overrode	overridden [see *ride*]
overrun	overran	overrun [see *run*]
oversee	oversaw	overseen [see *see*]
overtake	overtook	overtaken [see *take*]
overthrow	overthrew	overthrown [see *throw*]
partake	partook	partaken [see *take*]
pay /peɪ/	paid[3] /peɪd/	paid[3]
prove /pru:v/	proved /pru:vd/	proven[1] /ˈpru:vən/
put /pʊt/	**put**	**put**
quit /kwɪt/	quit[1]	quit[1]
read /ri:d/	**read** /red/	**read** /red/
rid /rɪd/	rid[1]	rid[1]

**lie* meaning *not telling the truth* is regular

Basic Form	Past Tense Form	Past Participle Form
ride /raɪd/	rode /rəʊd/	ridden /ˈridn̩/
ring /rɪŋ/	rang /ræŋ/	rung /rʌŋ/
rise /raɪz/	rose /rəʊz/	risen /ˈrɪzən/
run /rʌn/	**ran** /ræn/	**run**
saw /sɔ:/	sawed /sɔ:d/	sawn[1] /sɔ:n/
say /seɪ/	**said** /sed/	**said**
see /si:/	**saw** /sɔ:/	**seen** /si:n/
seek /si:k/	sought /sɔ:t/	sought
sell /sel/	sold /səʊld/	sold
send /send/	**sent** /sent/	**sent**
set /set/	**set**	**set**
sew /səʊ/	sewed /səʊd/	sewn[1] /səʊn/
shake /ʃeɪk/	shook /ʃʊk/	shaken /ˈʃeɪkən/
shed /ʃed/	shed	shed
shine /ʃaɪn/	shone[1] /ʃɒn ‖ ʃəʊn/	shone[1]
shoe /ʃu:/	shod[1] /ʃɒd/	shod[1]
shoot /ʃu:t/	shot /ʃɒt/	shot
show /ʃəʊ/	showed /ʃəʊd/	shown[1] /ʃəʊn/
shrink /ʃrɪŋk/	shrank /ʃræŋk/	shrunk /ʃrʌŋk/
shut /ʃʌt/	shut	shut
sing /sɪŋ/	sang /sæŋ/	sung /sʌŋ/
sink /sɪŋk/	sank /sæŋk/	sunk /sʌŋk/
sit /sɪt/	**sat**	**sat**
sleep /sli:p/	slept /slept/	slept
slide /slaɪd/	slid /slɪd/	slid
sling /slɪŋ/	slung /slʌŋ/	slung
slink /slɪŋk/	slunk /slʌŋk/	slunk
slit /slɪt/	slit	slit
smell /smel/	smelt[2] /smelt/	smelt[2]
sow /səʊ/	sowed /səʊd/	sown[1] /səʊn/
speak /spi:k/	spoke /spəʊk/	spoken /ˈspəʊkən/
speed /spi:d/	sped[1] /sped/	sped[1]
spell /spel/	spelt[2] /spelt/	spelt[2]
spend /spend/	spent /spent/	spent
spill /spɪl/	spilt[2] /spɪlt/	spilt[2]
spin /spɪn/	span, spun /spæn/, /spʌn/	spun
spit /spɪt/	spat, spit /spæt/, /spɪt/	spat, spit
split /splɪt/	split	split

Basic Form	Past Tense Form	Past Participle Form
spoil /spɔɪl/	spoilt[2] /spɔɪlt/	spoilt[2]
spread /spred/	spread	spread
spring /sprɪŋ/	sprang /spræŋ/	sprung /sprʌŋ/
stand /stænd/	**stood**	**stood**
steal /stiːl/	stole /stəʊl/	stolen /ˈstəʊlən/
stick /stɪk/	stuck /stʌk/	stuck
sting /stɪŋ/	stung /stʌŋ/	stung
stink /stɪŋk/	stank /stæŋk/	stunk /stʌŋk/
stride /straɪd/	strode /strəʊd/	stridden /ˈstrɪdn̩/, strode
strike /straɪk/	struck /strʌk/	struck
string /strɪŋ/	strung /strʌŋ/	strung
strive /straɪv/	strove[1] /strəʊv/	striven[1] /ˈstrɪvən/
swear /sweəʳ/	swore /swɔːʳ/	sworn /swɔːʳn/
sweep /swiːp/	swept /swept/	swept
swell /swel/	swelled /sweld/	swollen[1] /ˈswəʊlən/
swim /swɪm/	swam /swæm/	swum /swʌm/
swing /swɪŋ/	swung /swʌŋ/	swung
take[4] /teɪk/	took /tʊk/	taken /ˈteɪkən/
teach /tiːtʃ/	taught /tɔːt/	taught
tear /teəʳ/	tore /tɔːʳ/	torn /tɔːʳn/
tell /tel/	**told** /təʊld/	**told**
think /θɪŋk/	**thought** /θɔːt/	**thought**
throw /θrəʊ/	threw /θruː/	thrown /θrəʊn/
thrust /θrʌst/	thrust	thrust
tread /tred/	trod /trɒd/	trod
undergo	underwent	undergone [see *go*]
understand	understood	understood [see *stand*]
undertake	undertook	undertaken [see *take*]
undo	undid	undone [see *do*]
uphold	upheld	upheld [see *hold*]
upset	upset	upset [see *set*]
wake /weɪk/	woke[1] /wəʊk/	woken[1] /ˈwəʊkən/
wear /weəʳ/	wore /wɔːʳ/	worn /wɔːʳn/
weave /wiːv/	wove /wəʊv/	woven /ˈwəʊvən/
wed /wed/	wed[1]	wed[1]
weep /wiːp/	wept /wept/	wept
win /wɪn/	won /wʌn/	won
wind /waɪnd/	wound /waʊnd/	wound

Basic Form	Past Tense Form	Past Participle Form
withdraw	withdrew	withdrawn [see *draw*]
withhold	withheld	withheld [see *hold*]
withstand	withstood	withstood [see *stand*]
wring /rɪŋ/	wrung /rʌŋ/	wrung
write /raɪt/	wrote /rəʊt/	written /ˈrɪtn̩/

Key:

1 means that regular forms are also used.

2 means that both regular forms and irregular forms exist. The regular spellings are particularly common in U.S., e.g. *leaped*.

3 *lay* and *pay* are regular verbs in pronunciation, but the spellings *laid* and *paid* are irregular. (Compare *stayed*.)

4 these verbs have special entries in the book. Look them up for further information.

Complete list of entries in this book

Note: The items in brackets are cross-references only